THE CENTRAL SCHOOL OF SPEECH AND DRAMA

UNIVERSITY OF LONDON

Please return or renew this item by the last date shown.

The Streets of London
a dictionary of the names and their origins

S. Fairfield

Macmillan London

First published 1983 by
PAPERMAC
a division of Macmillan Publishers Limited
4 Little Essex Street, London WC2R 3LF
and Basingstoke

Associated companies in Auckland, Dallas,
Delhi, Dublin, Hong Kong, Johannesburg,
Lagos, Manzini, Melbourne, Nairobi,
New York, Singapore, Tokyo, Washington
and Zaria

ISBN 0 333 28649 9

Illustrations by Bryan Reading

Typeset by Leaper & Gard,
108 Church Road, Redfield, Bristol, England

Printed in Hong Kong

To
John, Joan,
Nicholas and Jonathy

Contents

List of Illustrations

Foreword

Investigating all the street names of the County of Greater London is a task that could occupy one person for a lifetime. This book cannot be a comprehensive survey; it represents what I have been able to do in the time available to me, and I hope it contributes something new to a study which has attracted increasing interest in the last ten years.

In addition to the printed sources listed in the Bibliography, I have used the Greater London Council (and formerly London County Council) *Survey of London*; Kent's, Robson's, Holden's and other commercial directories; the Post Office Directory; the *Argus Guide to Municipal London* and the *Municipal Year Book*; the 25-inch Ordnance Survey maps surveyed in 1870 and 1895, and the Ground Plan of London which was based on them; John Rocque's maps of London of 1746 and 1769, and Horwood's map of 1799. I also used the many historical and topographical works (not listed separately in the Bibliography) of Sir Walter Besant.

My thanks are due particularly to the staff of the Greater London Council History Library and of the Council's Record Office and Maps and Prints Room.

Introduction

The method of compiling this dictionary was to begin in the middle of London and to see how far I could get in two years, concentrating on those streets which reveal something of local history. As a general rule when working north of the Thames I did not go east of the Lea or west of Hammersmith; south of the Thames I did not go east of the Ravensbourne or west of the Wandle. However, if something of interest from beyond those limits came to me by happy accident, I included it.

I have not attempted to cover every street in my area because many have names of no known history. At times of rapid expansion, particularly in south and north-west London, streets rolled out like matting in all directions, and dozens of names were needed all at once. Anything would do that sounded pleasant: lists of English towns, Scottish lochs, holiday resorts, great rivers and famous peaks were all pressed into service from 1850 onwards. They had no local relevance at all; they were a kind of topographical formica. Names with a rural flavour were very popular: the beauty of north Surrey was obliterated by streets with names recalling fields and woodland. 19th-century rural names are often more robust than their successors of the same type; perhaps the Victorian property-buying householder, usually male, had no strong aversion to being identified with nature provided it took the form of beech trees and not daffodils.

There was extensive renaming in central London after 1856, when the Metropolitan Board of Works began to operate. To avoid confusion, dozens of 'New Streets', 'Union Streets' and 'King Streets' had to go. This explains why English and Scottish place names, holiday resorts and the like appear in the centre as well as in the suburbs. There were protests from local historians over the 'six English rivers' approach, and in the late 19th century a number of authorities changed their policy. Old local field names and personal names were revived for new streets, and I have tried to include as many of these as possible.

Areas developed before 1800 produce another large group of 'unknowns'. In many cases there is no accessible documentary evidence that sheds light on their origin. The commonest derivation for a 17th or 18th-century street name is from builder or landowner, but the names of his relations, his birthplace or the home town of his married daughter are all equally good candidates. I did not have time to investigate in depth to that extent.

Certain terms recurring frequently require brief explanation.

Old English endings to place names may indicate the status of the place in Saxon society. 'Worth' is usually a farm, and so is 'wick'; 'ham' is a small village centred on a farm, and immediately dependent on one man whose 'ham' or home it is; 'ton' is a small town. One ending which recurs frequently in London is 'bury', from Old English *burgh*. Some burghs went on to great things, achieving a status recognizable as a borough. Some did not, and remained as they were founded: stockaded, self-sufficient combinations of settlement and garrison, bases for the defence of the surrounding country. All these communities were palisaded and their land fenced; anything from a ham to a burgh was a clearly defined unit easily assimilated into the Norman manorial system.

Signs of inns and shops are a study in themselves. I have given the dates of an inn, for example the *Black Lion*, where I could, but I have not attempted to go into the significance or history of the black lion as an emblem.

Victorian church-building is also a study on its own. I have indicated the circumstances wherever I could, since a new church was sometimes part of a necessary parish mission and sometimes a developer's gesture to respectability. The difference is relevant to the names: St Phillip's in Queenstown Road, for instance, was financed by Philip Flower who built the surrounding estate. Flower was a genuinely pious man, but many who were not did exactly the same thing. Names taken from mission churches indicate the opposite process, rapid development and large, churchless areas. A new population swarmed across the empty spaces and a clerical armoured division set off after it, armed with small harmoniums, cheerful hymnbooks and the famous iron churches: prefabricated, Gothic garden-sheds which were said to be icy in winter, furnace-like in summer, and deafening when it rained.

Lastly, there is the influence of the dissolution of the monasteries, which took place c1535–40 as part of the conflict between Henry VIII and Rome. The enormous religious significance of the dissolution is not within the scope of this book, but its secular aspects are important, because in addition to its political impact, it was the biggest land-grab since the Norman Conquest. Some small monasteries were suppressed in 1533 by order of Cardinal Wolsey. The suppression was carried through by Thomas Cromwell, who on attaining power, ordered a Royal Commission into the conduct of all religious houses. The Commission reported to Parliament in 1536; its conclusions were that the great abbeys were well-conducted and that many of the small houses were not. After long debate, all monasteries with an income of under £200 a year were ordered to be suppressed, and their revenues made over to the Crown. In 1539 Cromwell brought about the suppression of the great abbeys also, and the confiscation of their property, which passed to the king. It is estimated that about one-fifth of English land changed hands as Henry redistributed the Church estates to his nobles, courtiers and servants. Many street names denoting landownership reflect this change, and do not otherwise make sense.

The following designations appear throughout the dictionary:

Avenue — Originally a tree-lined way of approach to a great house or an important landscape feature.

Buildings — Literal and self-explanatory, as are **Gate**, **Passage**, **Path**, **Row** (of buildings), **Villas** and **Walk**.

Circus — From the Latin, meaning circular.

Close — A closed road or cul-de-sac, or else built on a close in the sense of a small, enclosed field.

Court — Buildings surrounding a courtyard, usually a means of building back from the line of the street.

Crescent — Self-explanatory, from the form of the street, as are **Square** and **Terrace**.

Drive — Originally a carriage-drive, a specially made broad and even way designed for smooth passage of driver and vehicle.

Gardens — A residential street with a communal garden, or else built on former garden land; later the term was more widely used, as were **Grove** and **Park**, to indicate a spacious, well-planted street.

Lane — Usually a survival indicating an old, narrow, city or country side road.

Mansions — A group of large buildings normally designed for apartments or offices.

Mews — Originally a place for keeping hawks; with urbanization a mews became a place for keeping carriages.

Road — A route to a certain destination. The immense importance of roads from earliest times, and the amount of effort involved in their upkeep, is still reflected in speech. In 'Harley Street' the accent is on 'Harley'; in 'Edgware Road' the honours are even.

Street — A paved way or, more commonly, a paved way lined with buildings. Paved Roman roads were called streets, but in later use the urban street did not lead to a destination; it existed to serve its buildings.

Way — Currently favoured as embracing all meanings and conveying none.

The Streets of London

A

Abbey Orchard Street SW1 (Cit. West.). Site of the mediaeval orchard which belonged to the monks of St Peter's Abbey, Westminster.

Abbey Road NW6, NW8 (Kilburn, Camden/Cit. West.). Runs E of the grounds of the former abbey called **Kilburn Priory**. **Abbots Place** adjoins.

Abbey Road E15 (Lea Valley, Newham). The Cistercian abbey of Stratford Langthorne was founded here by Walter de Montfichet in c1135. The monks had special responsibility for the mediaeval bridge over the River Lea (*see* **Bow Road**). Sir Hubert Llewellyn in his history of E London suggests that the nursery rhyme *London Bridge is Falling Down* applies to this bridge and not that over the Thames. The verses about building it up with loaves of bread, iron bars, gold and silver etc describe the monks' various devices for maintaining it.

Abbey Street SE1 (Bermondsey, Southwark). Crosses the site of the Cluniac abbey of St Saviour, Bermondsey, which was founded in 1081 and dissolved in 1539. The church of St Mary Magdalene is on the site, having been built by the monks next to their own chapel as a church for the people. It became the parish church after the dissolution.

Abbotsbury Road W14 (Holland Park, Ken. Chel.). Built on land belonging to Edward Fox-Strangways, Fifth Earl of Ilchester, who acquired Holland House and its estate in 1874. He also owned property at Abbotsbury in Dorset. **Abbotsbury Close** adjoins.

Abbots Lane SE1 (Tooley Street, Southwark). Refers to the Abbot of Battle, near Hastings (*see* **Battle Bridge Lane**).

Abbots Place NW6 (Kilburn, Camden). *See* **Abbey Road** (Kilburn).

Abchurch Lane EC4 (Cit. Lond.). The church of St Mary Abchurch here was dedicated to the Virgin Mary and was also given the name of an early patron or priest called Abba. Early City churches, particularly those dating from the Danish settlement, were commonly known by a patron's name. St Mary Woolnoth (i.e. the church dedicated to St Mary and built by Wulfnoth) is an example.

Abercorn Place NW8 (St John's Wood, Cit. West.). One of a group of streets built on land belonging to Harrow School. Harrow's founder endowed the school with this property, and the streets commemorate school governors. The Marquis of Abercorn was elected a governor in 1810 (*see* **Lyons Place**).

Aberdeen Park N5 (Highbury, Islington). Commemorates George Hamilton Gordon, Earl of Aberdeen (1784–1860). He served as Foreign Secretary 1828–30 and 1841–6, and became Prime Minister in 1852. His indecisiveness over the Crimean War brought about his downfall in 1855.

Aberdeen Place NW8 (St John's Wood, Cit. West.). The Earl of Aberdeen (*see* **Aberdeen Park**) became a governor of Harrow School in 1823; this is one of the streets on the school's land (*see* **Lyons Place**).

1

Aberfeldy Street E14 (Poplar, T. Ham.). *See* **Leven Road**.

Abingdon Road W8 (Kensington, Ken. Chel.). Crosses part of the land given to the abbots of Abingdon by the lord of the manor of Kensington *c*1100. **Abingdon Villas** adjoins (*see* **St Mary Abbot's Place**).

Abingdon Street SW1 (Cit. West.). James Bertie, First Earl of Abingdon, had a house in **Dean's Yard** W of this street, where he died in 1699.

Achilles Road NW6 (W Hampstead, Camden). One of a group named in 1886 and inspired by Homer's account of the war between the Greeks and the Trojans. The Greek heroes of the war were: Achilles, son of Peleus of Thessaly; Agamemnon, king of Mycenae; Ajax, son of Telamon of Salamis; and Odysseus, king of Ithaca, who appears in his Latin form as Ulysses. **Agamemnon**, **Ajax** and **Ulysses** Roads adjoin.

Acol Road NW6 (Kilburn, Camden). Kentish place name; built by the Powell-Cotton family of Quex Park, Birchington, Kent (*see* **Quex Road**).

Acorn Walk SE16 (Rotherhithe, Southwark). That part of the Surrey Commercial Dock system called the Acorn Pond ran S from a point nearby. Together with its cargo-handling area – Acorn Yard – it extended to a point level with Odessa Street. A small row of houses called Acorn Place lay across the N side of Trinity Churchyard (*see* **Rotherhithe Street**).

Acton Street WC1 (Gray's Inn Road, Islington). Built from 1773 on open land called Acton Meadow which was probably named from a former proprietor.

Adam and Eve Court W1 (Oxford Street, Cit. West.). From the sign of a tavern here, now demolished.

Adams' Row W1 (Mayfair, Cit. West.). Probably developed by John Adams, who was active in this area as a land agent in the 1720s and 1730s.

Adam Street WC2 (Strand, Cit. West.). Built by the brothers John and Robert Adam as part of the Adelphi development *c*1768 (*see* **Adelphi Terrace**).

Ada Street E8 (Hackney). *See* **Pritchard's Road**.

Addington Square SE5 (Peckham, Southwark). Probably commemorates Henry Addington, an undistinguished Prime Minister (1801–4) who was created Viscount Sidmouth after his term of office. Said his critics: 'Pitt is to Addington as London is to Paddington'.

Addison Road W14 (Holland Park, Ken. Chel.). Charlotte, widow of the sixth Earl of Warwick of Holland House (*see* **Warwick Gardens**), married the writer Joseph Addison in 1716. Addison is best remembered for his essays in *The Spectactor*. **Addison Crescent** adjoins, and **Addison Avenue** and **Addison Place** are nearby.

Addle Hill EC4 (Cit. Lond.). Derived from an OE word meaning a prince; presumably the site of a house belonging to a member of one of the Saxon royal houses.

Addle Street EC2 (Cit. Lond.). Derived from an OE word meaning filth: a filthy or dung-strewn street.

Adelaide Grove W12 (Shepherd's Bush, Hammersmith). From a public house here named after Queen Adelaide. After the death of George IV's only child in 1817, there was a hasty marrying-off of royal dukes.

The Duke of Clarence, who became William IV, married Princess Adelaide of Saxe-Meiningen in 1818.

Adelaide Road NW3 (Chalk Farm, Camden). As **Adelaide Grove**.

Adelaide Street WC2 (Strand, Cit. West.). Part of the Charing Cross improvement scheme designed by John Nash, the street was built in 1831 and named from the Queen consort (*see* **Adelaide Grove**).

Adeline Place WC1 (Bloomsbury, Camden). Built on the Bedford estate. The tenth Duke of Bedford (1852–93) married Adeline, daughter of Lord Somers.

Adelphi Terrace WC2 (Strand, Cit. West.). The brothers John and Robert Adam built the Adelphi complex from 1768, clearing away the slum streets built there by the Earl of Pembroke at the Restoration (*see* **Durham House Street**). The Adams named their scheme from the Greek *adelphos*, meaning brother. The terrace and surrounding streets were raised up from the river bank on arches; the place was elegant and became very fashionable. The original Adelphi was demolished in 1936.

Adler Street E1 (Whitechapel, T. Ham.). Commemorates Dr Hermann Adler (1839–1911), Chief Rabbi. The street contained the Jewish ecclesiastical courts. Dr Adler came to England from Germany in 1845 when his father, Nathan Adler, became Chief Rabbi in England. He was a pioneer of religious classes for Jewish children in London schools, and was famous for his work for international Jewry. He became Chief Rabbi on the death of his father in 1891.

Admiral Street SE8 (Deptford, Lewisham). *See* **Vanguard Street**.

Adolf Street SE6 (Bellingham, Lewisham). *See* **King Alfred Avenue**.

Adpar Street W2 (Paddington, Cit. West.). *See* **Hall Place**.

Ady's Road SE15 (E Dulwich, Southwark). By association with the manor of Dulwich (*see* **Alleyn Park**). John Ady or Adey was legal adviser to Edward Alleyn.

Afghan Road SW11 (Battersea, Wandsworth). *See* **Cabul Road**.

Agamemnon Road (W Hampstead, Camden). *See* **Achilles Road**.

Agar Grove (St Pancras, Camden). William Agar (1767–1838), lawyer of Lincoln's Inn, obtained the lease of the prebendal manor of St Pancras from St Paul's Cathedral in 1816. His house, Elm Lodge, stood at the junction with St Pancras Way. The surrounding streets, which he developed, were known as Agar Town. The houses were of poor quality and quickly declined into slums. They were cleared to make way for the railway yards N of King's Cross and St Pancras stations. **Agar Place** adjoins.

Agar Street WC2 (Strand, Cit. West.). Built following the Strand Improvement Act of 1829. The government commissioners in charge of redevelopment were George Agar Ellis and his successor John Ponsonby, Earl of Bessborough, who was created Baron Duncannon of Bessborough in 1834. **Duncannon Street** is nearby.

Agdon Street EC1 (Clerkenwell, Islington). Part of the estate of the Compton family, marquises of Northampton, who have seats at Compton Wynyates and Castle Ashby. Agdon is a property near Compton Wynyates (*see* **Compton Road**).

Agincourt Road NW3 (Hampstead, Camden). Commemorates the battle of Agincourt (1415) in which English forces led by Henry V defeated the French. Adjacent **Cressy Road** commemorates the earlier English victory, under Edward III, at the battle of Cressy or Crecy (1346). Both battles took place during the continuing hostilities which lasted from 1337 until 1453 and are known as the Hundred Years' War, caused by English claims to the French crown.

Ailsa Street E14 (Poplar, T. Ham.). *See* **Leven Road**.

Ainsty Street SE16 (Rotherhithe, Southwark). Formerly York Street. One of a group of Rotherhithe streets, built in the early 19th century, ——which complimented members of the royal family. York Street was named from the Duke of York who was George III's second son. It was renamed Ainsty Street in 1873.

Ainsworth Road E9 (Hackney). Dr Robert Ainsworth (1660–1743), nonconformist schoolmaster, antiquarian and lexicographer, lived in St Thomas's Square nearby. As well as his *Compendium Dictionary of the Latin Tongue* (1734) he wrote much on coins and other antiquities, and an enlightened pamphlet on education.

Ainsworth Way NW8 (Hampstead, Camden). The popular Victorian historical novelist Harrison Ainsworth (1805–82) lived in Kilburn at the time of writing his first successful novel *Rookwood*. His best-known books are *The Tower of London* and *Old Saint Paul's*. He later moved to Kensal manor house.

Air Street W1 (Piccadilly Circus, Cit. West.). Uncertain, possibly a corruption of Ayres. One Thomas Ayres, brewer, held property here in the mid-17th century. He may have developed the street; he almost certainly owned its most important business.

Aisgill Avenue SW5 (W Kensington, Hammersmith). One of a group of streets built on a former goods yard of the London, Midland and Scottish Railway. Ais Gill is the highest point on the line between Settle and Carlisle (*see* **Franklin Square**, **Ivatt Place** and **Stanier Close**).

Ajax Road NW6 (W Hampstead, Camden). *See* **Achilles Road**.

Akerman Road SW9 (Brixton, Lambeth). Formerly Loughborough Road North, its name was changed in 1873 to a local family surname. P.B. Akerman was a member of the Lambeth vestry.

Albany W1 (Piccadilly, Cit. West.). Melbourne House, rebuilt here for Sir Penistone Lamb (later Lord Melbourne) in 1771–5, was acquired in 1791 by Frederick, Duke of York and Albany. In 1802 it was sold and converted into apartments named from his second title (*see* **Albany Street**).

Albany Road SE5 (Peckham, Southwark). The road appears on a map of 1832 as built up with large houses, well spaced. 'Albany' ensured a respectable address; the royal duke had no connection with the area (*see* **Albany Street**).

Albany Street NW1 (Regent's Park, Camden). Built as part of John Nash's Regent's Park scheme (*see* **Regent Street**) and named from the Regent's brother Frederick, Duke of York and Albany (*d* 1827). **Little Albany Street** runs parallel.

Albemarle Street W1 (Mayfair, Cit. West.). Built from 1684 on the site of

Clarendon House which the Duke of Albemarle bought from Edward Hyde, Earl of Clarendon, in 1675. He sold it again to Sir Thomas Bond (*see* **Old Bond Street**) who laid out the street.

Albemarle Way EC1 (Clerkenwell, Islington). Newcastle House nearby (*see* **Newcastle Row**) was the home of Elizabeth, Dowager Duchess of Albemarle and Montague, where she lived after the death of her second husband in 1704. The Duke of Newcastle was her father. Her first husband, the Duke of Albemarle, left her extremely rich. Her second husband, the Earl of Montague, married her for her fortune in spite of her undoubted lunacy. Believing herself to be of royal rank, she refused all commoners; the earl succeeded by presenting himself as the Emperor of China.

Albert Bridge Road SW11 (Battersea, Wandsworth). Approaches the Thames bridge which was opened in 1873 and named in memory of Albert of Saxe-Coburg and Gotha, Prince Consort to Queen Victoria. He died of typhoid fever in 1861, aged 42. Royal names surround Battersea Park (*see* **Queenstown Road**).

Albert Court SW7 (Kensington, Cit. West.). Approaches the Royal Albert Hall (*see* **Albert Bridge Road**).

Albert Embankment SE1, SE11 (Lambeth). Built in 1866–70 to improve the marshy shore of the Thames. The scheme was named in memory of the late Prince Albert (*see* **Albert Bridge Road**).

Albert Place W8 (Kensington, Ken. Chel.). *See* **Prince of Wales Terrace**.

Albion Avenue SW8 (Vauxhall, Lambeth). One of the ancient names for Britain, considered heroic and

stirring to patriotic feeling, and very popular in the 18th and early 19th centuries. There are 17 'Albion' streets in the London postal districts. The name was first revived by classical poets, who also favoured 'Britannia' (*see* **Britannia Walk**).

Albion Gardens W6 (Hammersmith). Off Dalling Road, which was originally called Albion Road (*see* **Albion Avenue**).

Albion Place EC1 (Cit. Lond.). The Albion Chapel was built here for a sect of the nonconformist church in *c*1820. The site of the chapel was provided by the removal of the Bethlehem Hospital for the insane ('Bedlam') to St George's Fields.

Albrighton Road SE22 (Camberwell). *See* **Belvoir Road**.

Albury Street SE8 (Deptford, Lewisham). On the Evelyn estate; named from a house near Wotton, Surrey, which John Evelyn wanted to buy (*see* **Evelyn Street**).

Aldenham Street NW1 (St Pancras, Camden). Built on land given for the endowment of Aldenham School in Hertfordshire by Richard Platt, brewer, in the 16th century (*see* **Platt Street**).

Aldermanbury EC2 (Cit. Lond.). The site of a Saxon 'burgh' or enclosed settlement belonging to an alderman.

Alderman's Walk EC2 (Cit. Lond.). A path which presumably led to the house of a city alderman.

Alderney. Street SW1 (Pimlico, Cit. West.). Originally called Stanley Street, from the landowner. In 1719 George Stanley of Paulton, Hampshire, married Hans Sloane's daughter Sarah. Stanley owned the manor of Neate, of which this land is part. There being many 'Stanley' streets, the name was changed to Alderley Street in 1879; this was by association with the noble family of Stanley of Alderley. They, however, did not see it as a compliment, and it was changed again to Alderney.

Aldersgate Street EC1 (Cit. Lond.). Leading through a gate in the city wall which is recorded in Saxon times as Ealdred's Gate. The name was later corrupted to Alder's Gate.

Aldford Street W1 (Mayfair, Cit. West.). On the Grosvenor family's estate, and named in 1886 from a property on their land in Cheshire. It was formerly Chapel Street, as approaching the Grosvenor Chapel.

Aldgate High Street EC3 (Cit. Lond.). High or principal street of the area around the Aldgate, one of the oldest in the city wall. The name is a corruption of Eald (OE 'old') or Ealh, a personal name; alternatively it may mean 'ale-gate' in reference to a travellers' dole. The gate was maintained by the monks of nearby Holy Trinity and was known as a free gate (without toll). It was demolished in 1761.

Aldrich Terrace SW18 (Wandsworth). Said to commemorate Dr Henry Aldrich (1647–1710) who was a clergyman and Oxford don. In 1691 he wrote *Artis Logicae Compendium* which remained a standard textbook on logic for nearly 200 years.

Aldridge Road Villas W11 (Westbourne Park, Cit. West.). Built on land which is recorded as belonging to a family called Aldridge in 1743 (*see* **Queensborough Terrace**).

Aldwych WC2 (Strand, Cit. West.). Derived from the OE 'ald wic', or old village, referring to the local settlement of Danes established here

in the 9th century. The church at the E end is St Clement Danes.

Alexander Square SW7 (Kensington, Ken. Chel.). John Alexander inherited land here from his godfather Harris Thurloe Brace in 1799. He laid out the square and surrounding streets after 1822. **Alexander Place** adjoins (*see* **Thurloe Square**).

Alexander Street W2 (Paddington, Cit. West.). Built on land belonging to Alexander Hall, quarry owner, in 1853.

Alexandra Avenue SW11 (Battersea, Wandsworth). *See* **Prince of Wales Drive**.

Alexandra Park Road N10, N22 (Haringey). Approaches the park opened to the public in 1873 and named from Alexandra, Princess of Wales. Alexandra Palace there, a combined concert and exhibition hall, was intended as N London's answer to the Crystal Palace, which had recently opened at Sydenham. It was burnt out after two weeks and rebuilt in 1873–5. It was burnt out again in 1980, and an ambitious replacement was planned.

Alexandra Street SE14 (Deptford, Lewisham). *See* **Edward Street**.

Alford Place N1 (Shepherdess Walk, Hackney). The Rev. Bradley Huntley Alford was curate in charge of Holy Trinity church here in the 1870s.

Alfred Place WC1 (Tottenham Court Road, Camden). Built in 1806 by John Waddilove of St Marylebone, who called it after his son Alfred Waddilove.

Alfred Road W2 (Westbourne Green, Cit. West.). From the *Royal Saxon* public house which

Aldford Street and the Grosvernor Chapel

commemorated the Saxon king Alfred the Great (871–99).

Alie Street E1 (Whitechapel, T. Ham.). The Alies were a local landowning family united by marriage with the Lemans (*see* **Leman Street**). Richard Alie was landlord of property acquired by the London Hospital when it opened as the London infirmary in Prescot Street in 1744. He was the son-in-law of Sir William Leman.

Allcroft Road NW5 (Kentish Town, Camden). J.D. Allcroft (1821–93) founded St Martin's church in nearby Vicar's Road as a memorial to his late wife. The church was consecrated in 1865.

Allen Edwards Drive SW8 (S Lambeth, Lambeth). The Rev. T. Allen Edwards was vicar of St Philip's church in Kennington in the 1860s and 1870s.

Allen Road N16 (Stoke Newington, Hackney). Commemorates a local nonconformist family. John Allen (1771–1839) was born in Truro, moved to Hackney and kept the Madras House Grammar School there. He published *Modern Judaism* in 1816. His son Alexander Allen (1814–42) carried on the school and published textbooks on the teaching of Latin and Greek.

Alleyn Park SE21 (Dulwich, Southwark). The Elizabethan actor-manager Edward Alleyn (*d* 1626) bought the manor of Dulwich in 1605. He built Dulwich College and endowed it with the manor and its income. Alleyn's School, Towneley Road, was built to accommodate the Lower School of the college in 1883. James Allen's Girls' School in E Dulwich Grove was built in 1882 through a foundation set up by Alleyn's descendant James Allen or Alleyn in 1741. **Alleyn Road** adjoins.

Allfarthing Lane SW18 (Wandsworth). Crosses the mediaeval manor called Allfarthing, meaning half a 'fourthing' or quarter – that is, an eighth of the original estate. John and Gilbert of Allfarthing are recorded as holding land here in the 13th century. They were tenants of the Abbot of Westminster, who held Battersea Manor.

Allgood Street E2 (Bethnal Green, T. Ham.). Commemorates a local antiquarian who published a history of Bethnal Green in 1894. Formerly Henrietta Street, from Henrietta Wentworth (*see* **Wentworth Mews**). She died in 1686, allegedly of a broken heart following the fall and execution of her lover the Duke of Monmouth.

Allhallows Lane EC4 (Cit. Lond.). The mediaeval churches of All Hallows the Great and All Hallows the Less stood here until destroyed in the Great Fire of 1666. All Hallows the Less was not rebuilt. All Hallows the Great was rebuilt by Sir Christopher Wren and demolished in 1894.

Allingham Street N1 (Islington). John Till Allingham, dramatist, lived in Colebrooke Terrace (which lay opposite Colebrooke Row). He produced a number of popular comedies between 1799 and 1810.

Allitsen Road NW8 (St John's Wood, Cit. West.). A popular Victorian and Edwardian songwriter called Frances Allitsen lived for a time in nearby Queen's Grove.

Allnutt Way SW4 (Clapham, Lambeth). John Allnutt, art collector, lived in a house on the corner of Elms Road and Clapham Common South Side. His collection of paintings was locally famous. He died in 1863.

All Saints Street N1 (King's Cross, Islington). The district church of All Saints stood here. Designed by William Tress, it was consecrated in 1838. Its district was considered the poorest in the parish of Islington.

Allsop Place NW1 (Regent's Park, Cit. West.). Built c1800 on the former Allsop's or Alsop's farm. The site of the present Baker Street station remained a cow-yard and dairy until the middle of the 19th century.

Alma Grove SE1 (Bermondsey, Southwark). One of many streets commemorating the battle of the River Alma, 20 September 1854, during the Crimean War. The war was fought by allied French, British and Turkish forces attempting to frustrate Russian ambitions regarding the Turkish empire. A feature of this battle was the conquest of strong Russian gun emplacements above the river. The action appealed to the public because of the courage and steadiness of British infantry under heavy fire, moving in the formation which came to be called 'The Thin Red Line'.

Almond Road SE16 (Bermondsey, Southwark). From a family of builders of whom one, R. Almond, served on the Bermondsey parish vestry in the 1890s.

Alpha Place SW3 (Chelsea, Ken. Chel.). From the Greek *alpha*, first letter of the alphabet. A fashionable late 18th-century and early 19th-century name for the first street (either in timing or position) in a new development. This was the first street to be added to an existing road. There is also an **Alpha Place** in Kilburn and an **Alpha Close** in Regent's Park.

Alsace Road SE17 (Walworth, Southwark). *See* **Sedan Way**.

Alvanley Gardens NW6 (Hampstead, Camden). Richard Pepper Arden, Chief Justice Lord Alvanley (1745–1804), lived at nearby Frognal Hall. He took silk in 1780 and first entered parliament as MP for Newtown in the Isle of Wight (1783). He served as Solicitor General in Pitt's government, and became Lord Chief Justice in 1801.

Alwyne Road N1 (Islington). Built on land belonging to Spencer Joshua Alwyne Compton, Second Marquis of Northampton. **Alwyne Park** and **Alwyne Villas** adjoin (*see* **Compton Road**).

Amberley Road W9 (Paddington, Cit. West.). The *Lord Amberley* public house here commemorates the politician Lord John Russell, who was created Viscount Amberley in 1861.

Ambrose Street SE16 (Bermondsey, Southwark). Referred to in 1865 as replacing Manor Street (*see* **Galley Wall Road**). The inspiration for 'Ambrose' is unknown.

Amelia Street SE17 (Kennington, Southwark). Built in the 1780s. Amelia was a Christian name made fashionable by the reigning house of Hanover.

Amen Corner EC4 (Cit. Lond.). Leads to **Amen Court** near St Paul's cathedral. It was possibly named in association with nearby **Paternoster Row** which may have been thought to refer to the Lord's Prayer. **Ave Maria Lane** and **Creed Lane** would be similar. Alternatively they may have been processional points, or the abodes of craftsmen who wrote and sold texts and prayers. Creed Lane was originally Spurrier (spur-maker) Row.

America Square EC3 (Cit. Lond.). Laid out in 1767–70 as part of a development by the architect George Dance the Younger; named to compliment the American colonies. It has largely been destroyed by Fenchurch Street station and its approaches, and is therefore no longer a square.

Amersham Road SE14 (Brockley, Lewisham). *See* **Shardeloes Road**.

Amhurst Road E8, N16 (Hackney). The Amhurst or Amherst family, later Tyssen Amherst, were lords of the manor of Hackney, which they acquired through marriage to a descendant of William Daniel and Amelia Tyssen (*see* **Tyssen Street**). They became barons of Hackney in 1892.

Amiel Street E1 (Stepney, T. Ham.). One of ten streets commemorating Stepney residents killed in the air-raids of World War II. The names were chosen by lot. The others are: **Colebert Avenue, Fox Close, Gibson Close, Ibbott Street, Lang Street, Mantus Close, Pemell Close, Rickman Street** and **Stothard Street**.

Amor Road W6 (Hammersmith). From a local builder of the mid-19th century, William Amor.

Amott Road SE15 (E Dulwich, Southwark). By association with Dulwich College. John Amott or Amyott was a friend of the Master of the college in the 1830s.

Amoy Place E14 (Limehouse, T. Ham.). *See* **Oriental Street**.

Ampton Street WC1 (Islington). *See* **Pakenham Street**.

Amwell Street EC1 (Islington). The nearby New River Head (now a water authority headquarters) is the original head of the man-made New River which was cut to bring fresh water to London from springs at Amwell, Hertfordshire, in 1609–13 (*see* **Myddelton Square**).

Amyruth Road SE4 (Lewisham). One of a group combining the Christian names (or parts thereof) of the landowner's relations. The others are: **Arthurdon, Elsiemaud, Francemary** and **Phoebeth** Roads.

Anchor Street SE16 (Rotherhithe, Southwark). Runs S from the former Blue Anchor Road (now called Southwark Park Road), which was named from an inn.

Anderson Street SW3 (Chelsea, Ken. Chel.). *See* **Coulson Street**.

Anderton Close SE5 (Denmark Hill, Southwark). Alfred Anderton was mayor of Camberwell in 1921.

Andover Place NW6 (Maida Vale, Cit. West.). Named by association with other Hampshire place names used for neighbouring streets (*see* **Southwick Street**).

André Street E8 (Hackney). Commemorates Major John André, who was born in Hackney in 1751 and executed by the Americans during the War of Independence on a charge of spying.

Angela Gardens E2 (Bethnal Green, T. Ham.). Christian name of the Baroness Burdett-Coutts (*see* **Baroness Road**). This street and **Georgina Gardens** ran on either side of the Columbia Market.

Angel Court EC2 (Cit. Lond.). Probably named from an inn, *The Angel*, long since demolished.

Angell Road SW9 (Stockwell, Lambeth). The Angell family acquired land in Lambeth and Stockwell manors in the late 17th century. John Angell (*d*1750) built Stockwell Park House at the W end of the present Stockwell Park Walk; it was demolished c1882. The family were copyholders of land on which this road was built in the 1850s; it was part of a development called Angell Town.

Angel Mews N1 (Islington). The *Angel Inn* is first recorded here in the 17th century, immediately E of this mews. It was a coaching inn and overnight stopping-place for travellers between the City of London and the north.

Angel Place SE1 (Borough, Southwark). Named from the sign of an inn, now demolished, which stood to the N of this court.

Angel Street EC1 (Cit. Lond.). Formerly Angel Alley, and named from the sign of an inn, now demolished.

Angel Walk W6 (Hammersmith). The *Angel* public house, in **King Street**, is recorded in the late 18th century.

Anglers Lane NW5 (Kentish Town, Camden). An inn called *The Jolly Anglers* stood S of the junction with Kentish Town Road. It was burnt down in the 1820s.

Annis Road E9 (Victoria Park, Hackney). *See* **Cassland Road**. John Annis was treasurer of the Sir John Cass Foundation in 1834.

Ansdell Street W8 (Kensington, Ken. Chel.). The artist Richard Ansdell (1815–85) who lived nearby specialised in animal subjects. He is also commemorated in **Ansdell Road**, Peckham.

Ansell Road SW17 (Tooting, Wandsworth). The Ansell family were prominent in the parish affairs of Tooting in the 17th and 18th centuries.

Antcliff Street E1 (Stepney, T. Ham.). Probably by William Antcliff, builder, of Newham Street, who was active in E London when the street was built in 1859.

Antill Road E3 (Bow, T. Ham.). As **Antill Terrace**, Stepney, probably laid out by Antills, builders active in E London in the 1860s and 1870s.

Apothecary Street EC4 (Cit. Lond.). The Apothecaries' Company was founded in 1617 and their first hall was built here in 1633. Destroyed in the Great Fire of 1666, it was rebuilt in 1786.

Apsley Way W1 (Hyde Park Corner, Cit. West.). Former approach to Apsley House, built in the late 18th century for Lord Apsley, bought by the Marquis of Wellesley in 1805 and sold to his younger brother Arthur Wellesley, Duke of Wellington, in 1817.

Arbour Square E1 (Stepney, T. Ham.). Built on open land recorded in the 18th century as the Arbour Field, an arbour being a leafy shelter. **East Arbour Street** and **West Arbour Street** approach. The square was rebuilt after World War II.

Archer Street W1 (Soho, Cit. West.). Recorded as Arch Street in 1675, it had become Archer Street by 1745. The position of the original arch is not known.

Archery Close W2 (Bayswater, Cit. West.). Site of a practice field belonging to an archery society in the early 19th century. The field was built upon from c1835.

Ardwell Road SW2 (Streatham Hill, Lambeth). Built on land belonging to Sir Edward Stewart of Southwick and Blairderry who lived at Ardwell in Wigtownshire. **Blairderry Road** adjoins.

Ardwick Road NW2 (W Hampstead, Camden). *See* **Burgess Hill**.

Argyll Road W8 (Holland Park, Ken. Chel.). A house on the site of the present Holland Park School was owned by the Duke of Argyll, having previously belonged to the Duke of Bedford in the early 19th century (*see* **Duchess of Bedford's Walk**).

Argyll Street W1 (Oxford Circus, Cit. West.). Built in 1736–7 on land belonging to John Campbell, Second Duke of Argyll. **Little Argyll Street** adjoins.

Aristotle Road SW4 (Clapham, Lambeth). Built on land belonging to a Mr Foster, who expressed his admiration of the classics, and Greek philosophy in particular, in naming this road (1893) and his other development off Acre Lane, **Plato Road** (1878).

Arklow Road SE14 (Deptford, Lewisham). On the Evelyn estate (*see* **Evelyn Street**). A member of the family, William Evelyn, was born at Arklow in Ireland and became Dean of Emly; he died in 1776. Neighbouring **Kerry Road** and **Trim Street** are from Irish place names.

Arlington Street SW1 (Piccadilly, Cit. West.). The first Earl of Arlington bought 35 acres of the Grosvenor estate, including parts of the present Green Park, in 1681, and built a number of houses. His title is from Arlington in Middlesex, now more commonly called Harlington.

Armada Street SE8 (Deptford, Greenwich). Lord Howard of Effingham, Lord High Admiral in command of the fleet against the Spanish *Armada* of 1588, lived at Deptford Green for a time. Many English ships which fought the *Armada* or battle fleet of Spain were fitted out in the royal dockyards at Deptford. The history of this street is confusing. It was (like many others) at first called New Street. This was changed to Trevithick Street. In 1889 the name Trevithick was transferred to another street and the name of that street – Armada – transferred to this one.

Armoury Way SW18 (Wandsworth). A building here (demolished) was traditionally held to have been the home of Jane Shore, mistress to Edward IV (1461–83). The house was later used as an armoury by a local band of militia, the Loyal Wandsworth Volunteers.

Arne Street WC2 (Covent Garden, Cit. West.). Dr Thomas Arne, composer and teacher, lived in the parish and is buried at St Paul's, Covent Garden. His father was an upholsterer in King Street, where the composer was born. His best-known works are the opera *Artaxerxes* (1762) and the masque *Alfred* (1740). It was for the latter that he wrote 'Rule, Britannia'. He died in 1778.

Arneway Street SW1 (Cit. West.). Commemorates a past benefactor to the parish of St Margaret's, Westminster.

Arnold Circus E2 (Bethnal Green, T. Ham.). Commemorates Sir Arthur Arnold, London County Councillor 1889–1902. He was made assistant commissioner of public works in 1863 and subsequently became an inspector. A radical in politics, he was MP for Salford 1880–5, and was influential in electoral reform. He was chairman of the London County Council in 1895 and 1896. His name was chosen for this development which was among the first LCC slum clearance programmes. He published *Social Politics* in 1878.

Arnould Avenue SE5 (Denmark Hill, Southwark). Sir Joseph Arnould, judge, was born in Camberwell in 1814. He came of a Berkshire family. As judge of the high court in Bombay he became an expert on Hindu and Mohammedan law. He died in 1886.

Arnulf Street SE6 (Bellingham, Lewisham). *See* **King Alfred Avenue**.

Artesian Road W2 (Paddington, Cit. West.). An artesian well here (sunk by boring to a natural fount) supplied water during the first half of the 19th century.

Arthurdon Road SE4 (Lewisham). *See* **Amyruth Road**.

Arthur Street EC4 (Cit. Lond.). Built in 1835 as part of the improved approaches to the new (1831) London Bridge. The reason for the name is not known.

Artillery Lane E1 (Spitalfields, T. Ham.). Originally led to the Tasel Close Artillery Yard, recorded in the 16th century (*see* **Gun Street**). **Artillery Passage** adjoins. The Tasel Close was originally Teasle Close, leased from the priory of St Mary Spital by clothworkers growing teasles with which to raise the nap on woollen cloth. After the dissolution of the priory (c1539) the land was used by officers of the Tower of London for artillery practice. Their use was disputed by the Honourable Artillery Company, who also practised there. Archery and gunnery continued until the yards were sold for building in 1682.

Artillery Row SW1 (Victoria Street, Cit. West.). Approaches **Artillery Place**, site of an artillery practice ground in use until the 19th century.

Arundel Street WC2 (Strand, Cit. West.). Laid out in the 17th century on the site of Arundel House, which was originally built for the bishops of Bath. After the dissolution of the monasteries c1539 the house was acquired by Thomas Seymour, Lord High Admiral. After his execution it passed to the Earl of Arundel.

Ascalon Street SW8 (Battersea, Wandsworth). Named from the town in Israel that is now called Ashquelon. In the Old Testament it is Ascalon, a city of the Philistines, where Samson killed 30 of their number.

Ascham Street NW5 (Kentish Town, Camden). On the estate of St John's College, Cambridge, of which the Elizabethan educationist Roger Ascham became a fellow in 1533. Ascham, a famous scholar of classical Greek, was also an enthusiastic archer; he published a book on archery, *Toxophilus*, in 1545. From 1563 he wrote *The Scholemaster*, a practical guide to teaching which contains much autobiography. He was a pioneer in the use of English (rather than Latin) in scholarly work. Nearby **Falkland Road** commemorates another scholar of the college, Lucius Carey, Second Viscount Falkland, killed at the battle of Newbury in 1643 (*see* **College Lane**).

Ashbourne Grove SE22 (E Dulwich, Southwark). *See* **Melbourne Grove**.

Ashbridge Street NW8 (Marylebone, Cit. West.). Commemorates Arthur Ashbridge, Marylebone District Surveyor 1884–1918, who left his personal collection of local records to the borough.

Ashburnham Road SW10 (Chelsea, Ken. Chel.). Ashburnham House which stood here was incorporated in Cremorne pleasure gardens in 1850 (*see* **Cremorne Road**). It had been at one time occupied by the second Earl of Ashburnham. The road is on the line of an old path called Hob Lane or Goblin Lane.

Ashby Road SE4 (Lewisham). Probably from J. Ashby, Lewisham borough councillor c1903.

Ashby Street EC1 (Clerkenwell, Islington). Built on land belonging to the Marquis of Northampton, one of whose seats was at Castle Ashby, Derbyshire (see **Compton Road**).

Ashmill Street NW1 (Lisson Grove, Cit. West.). On the Portman estate, and originally called Devonshire Street, the family holding land in Devon. Renamed after a Devon village, near South Molton, in 1912, in order to avoid confusion with other 'Devonshire' names.

Ashmole Street SW8 (Kennington, Lambeth). Elias Ashmole, antiquary, lived in a house next door to John Tradescant (see **Tradescant Road**) from 1674. It was through Ashmole that the Tradescant collection of specimens passed to the Ashmolean Museum in Oxford.

Aske Street N1 (Hoxton, Hackney). Robert Aske, of the Haberdashers' Company, founded a school and almshouses nearby; the first buildings were completed in 1695. In 1873 the almshouses were demolished and the school enlarged. In 1898 the school was moved: the boys went to W Hampstead and the girls to Acton. The building became a technical institute.

Askew Road W12 (Hammersmith). From a local landowner of the 18th century, Anthony Askew.

Asmara Road NW2 (W Hampstead, Camden). Built by the Powell-Cotton family of Birchington, Kent. Travellers and big-game hunters, they gave their streets East African names: Asmara Road, **Gondar Gardens**, **Menelik Road**, **Somali Road**.

Aspinall Road SE4 (Brockley, Lewisham). Named in 1898 and said to commemorate James Aspinall, a local man active in adult education.

Aspland Grove E8 (Hackney). The Rev. Robert Aspland (1782–1845) was Unitarian minister of the Gravel Pit Meeting House from 1805. He set up the Hackney Academy for training Unitarian ministers, and was generally a leading figure of the sect.

Astell Street SW3 (Chelsea, Ken. Chel.). Mary Astell (1668–1731), author and religious controversialist, lived in Chelsea. She was a highly articulate and intelligent writer on religious doctrines, and widely respected as such. She is best known for her proposal to set up a community for women, where they might apply themselves to worship, learning and self-discipline – not as a vocation but as training for a useful life. This aroused the scorn of society and the horror of Protestants, who saw it as a step back to the nunnery.

Astle Street SW11 (Battersea, Wandsworth). Thomas Astle, antiquary (1735–1803), lived in Battersea and was buried in St Mary's churchyard. He was keeper of His Majesty's Records in the Tower of London, and a trustee of the British Museum.

Astwood Mews SW7 (Kensington, Ken. Chel.). John Thurloe Brace of Astwood, Buckinghamshire, held land here by 1713; building began under his descendants in 1826.

Asylum Road SE15 (Peckham, Southwark). The Licensed Victuallers Asylum for distressed members of the trade, or their widows, was opened here in 1827.

Athelney Street SE6 (Bellingham, Lewisham). See **King Alfred Avenue**.

Athlone Street NW5 (Kentish Town, Camden). A block of flats here was opened by Princess Alice, Countess of Athlone, in 1933.

Athol Street E14 (Poplar, T. Ham.). *See* **Leven Road**.

Atkins Road SW12 (Clapham, Lambeth). Built from the Brixton end by James Atkins from 1830, it was completed later by others; Atkins went bankrupt in 1843.

Atterbury Street SW1 (Cit. West.). Commemorates Francis Atterbury (1662–1732), Dean of Westminster in 1713. He wrote a famous vindication of the Church of England, *An Answer to some Considerations on the Spirit of Martin Luther, and the Original of the Reformation* (1687), and was known as a controversial writer and outstanding preacher. He was a royal chaplain from *c*1692, but he had Jacobite sympathies, was convicted of Jacobite activities and was exiled in 1723.

Attneave Street WC1 (Islington). Named in 1895, probably laid out by a builder called Attneave, active in N London in the 1880s and 1890s.

Atwood Road W6 (Hammersmith). The Rev. T.S. Atwood was incumbent of St Paul's, Hammersmith from 1788 and was succeeded by his son Francis Atwood, who became the first vicar when St Paul's was promoted from district church to parish church in 1834. Atwood was a local name. A farm on the Pallingswick estate (*see* **Paddenswick Road**) was leased to a John Atwood in 1750 and was known thereafter as Atwood's Farm. Atwoods also flourished as market-gardeners at North End in the mid-19th century.

Aubert Park N5 (Highbury, Islington). Alexander Aubert, astronomer, set up an observatory in Highbury House in *c*1790. The house, built about ten years earlier on the site of a mediaeval manor house, stood between this road and Hamilton Park (a later Highbury House was built in Leigh Road). Mr Aubert also commanded the Loyal Islington Volunteers, 1797–1801.

Aubrey Walk W8 (Kensington, Ken. Chel.). Before 1893 this was Notting Hill Grove, leading to Notting Hill House which is now called 'Aubrey House'. It was built as a private house in the 18th century on the site of an earlier 'Wells House' – a spa with mineral springs. **Aubrey Road** approaches.

Augustus Street NW1 (Regent's Park, Camden). Named from Ernest Augustus, Duke of Cumberland (*see* **Cumberland Terrace**).

Auriol Road W14 (Hammersmith). The Rev. Edward Auriol was formerly rector of the church of St Dunstan's-in-the-West, which owned this land.

Austin Friars EC2 (Cit. Lond.). The Austin or Augustinian friars were given land here in 1253 on which to build a monastery. Their church (now replaced) became a Dutch Protestant church in 1550.

Austin Street E2 (Bethnal Green, T. Ham/Hackney). Recorded in 1703, at a time when a local Austin family was living nearby, but the connection is not proved.

Australia Road W12 (Shepherd's Bush, Hammersmith). Part of a 1930s development inspired by the then British Empire. The Commonwealth of Australia, a federation of former British colonies, came into being in January 1901. **Commonwealth Avenue** adjoins, and links this road to **India Way** and **Canada Way**. India had been under

British rule since the powers of the East India Company were transferred to the crown in 1858. The Dominion of Canada had been created in 1867.

Avalon Road W13 (Sand's End, Hammersmith). John Mordaunt, Viscount Mordaunt of Avalon, was the second son of the Earl of Peterborough. In c1656 he married Elizabeth Carey, who brought him an estate at Parson's Green which had belonged to her maternal grandfather Thomas Smith. The viscount died at Parson's Green in 1675 (*see* **Peterborough Road**).

Avarn Road SW17 (Tooting Graveney, Wandsworth). John Avarn, benefactor of Tooting Graveney, left £500 for a parish school and £300 to provide bread for the poor. His charity dates from 1809.

Ave Maria Lane EC4 (Cit. Lond.). *See* **Amen Corner**.

Avenue Road NW8, NW3 (St John's Wood, Camden/Cit. West.). Originally a broad, well-planted avenue running S to approach Regent's Park.

Avery Farm Row SW1 (Victoria, Cit. West.). On part of the former Avery Farm which was part of the Ebury manor estate. Avery is a corruption of Ebury (*see* **Ebury Street**).

Avery Row W1 (Mayfair, Cit. West.). Built over the course of the Tyburn Brook. The stream was arched over with brick and the roadway made by Henry Avery, bricklayer, in the 1720s.

Avondale Park Road W11 (N Kensington, Ken. Chel.). Approaches Avondale Park, named in honour of Prince Albert Victor Christian Edward, eldest son of Edward, Prince of Wales. He was created Duke of Clarence and Avondale in 1890 and died suddenly in 1892, aged 28. His fiancée, Princess May of Teck, subsequently married his brother, the future king George V.

Avondale Rise SE15 (Peckham, Southwark). Uncertain. Named in 1873, which is too early for the royal association of Avondale Park (*see* **Avondale Park Road**). **Avondale Square** near the Old Kent Road is also too early.

Axe Court E2 (Hackney Road, Hackney). The *Axe* tavern, sometimes called the *Old Axe*, is recorded here in 1840–5.

Aybrook Street W1 (Marylebone, Cit. West.). Runs S to the course of the Aye Brook or Eye Brook, otherwise called Tyburn, which ran roughly down the line of Marylebone Lane (*see* **Marylebone High Street**).

Aylesbury Street EC1 (Clerkenwell, Islington). The Earl of Aylesbury's house stood here. It was formerly part of the priory of St John's, Clerkenwell. The earl acquired it by marriage in 1641 and the family held it until 1706 (*see* **Seymour Close**).

Aylmer Road N2 (Haringey). Built across part of Hornsey Great Park which belonged to the bishops of London (*see* **Bishop's Avenue, The**). Bishop Aylmer held office in 1576–94. There is also an **Aylmer Road** in Hammersmith, which manor the bishops also held.

Aylwin Estate SE1 (Bermondsey). Aylwin Child, citizen of London, founded Bermondsey Abbey in 1089 for monks of La Charité sur la Loire; he had already founded a church on the site in 1081.

Aynhoe Road W14 (Brook Green, Hammersmith). *See* **Masbro Road**.

Ayres Street SE1 (Southwark). Alice Ayres lived at a house on the corner of the then Gravel Lane (Great Suffolk Street) and Union Street. In 1885 the house, which was also an oil shop, caught fire. Alice Ayres saved three children at the cost of her own life.

Aysgarth Road SE21 (Dulwich, Southwark). An estate belonging to Edward Alleyn, founder of nearby Dulwich College (*see* **Alleyn Park**). Alleyn bought Simondstone in Aysgarth, Yorkshire, shortly before his death in 1626.

B

Babmaes Street SW1 (St James's, Cit. West.). Originally Babmay's Mews. It was named after Baptist Mays or May, trustee for Henry Jermyn, Earl of St Albans (*d* 1684), who was the developer of the surrounding estate.

Back Church Lane E1 (Whitechapel, T. Ham.). Ran originally S from the back of St Mary's church (*see* **Whitechapel Road**). It was gradually separated from the church by the occupation of land S of the churchyard and by the building of Commercial Road, S of which it now begins.

Bacon Grove SE1 (Bermondsey, Southwark). Josiah Bacon, by his will of 1709, founded Bacon's School nearby and endowed it with £150 a year.

Bacon's Lane N6 (Highgate, Camden). Francis Bacon, scholar, scientist and essayist, died in the Earl of Arundel's house here in 1626. He had been experimenting with refrigeration – stuffing a dead hen with snow to see if it would keep – caught a chill and developed pneumonia.

Bagford Street N1 (Shepperton Road, Islington). Commemorates John Bagford (1675–1716), antiquary and collector, who lived in Islington.

Bagley's Lane SW6 (Fulham, Hammersmith). Robert Bagley bought Grove Farm at the S end of this lane as a market garden in 1812. The place became famous for fruit and the family worked it until 1868; it was sold for development (38 acres) in 1881, and brought £32,500.

Bainbridge Street WC1 (New Oxford Street, Camden). Records a 17th-century resident, Henry Bainbridge, who is mentioned in a survey of 1649.

Baird Gardens SE19 (Dulwich, Southwark). John Logie Baird, inventor of television, lived in Crescent Wood Road nearby. He made his first transmission (of shapes seen in outline only) in 1924.

Bakers' Hall Court EC3 (Cit. Lond.). Approach to the guildhall of the Bakers' Company. The hall was built in the early 16th century and destroyed in the Great Fire of 1666; it has subsequently been rebuilt three times.

Baker's Hill E5 (Clapton, Hackney). Formerly led to a works owned by George Baker, 19th-century calico printer and dyer. The works stood on the banks of the River Lea.

Baker's Row EC1 (Clerkenwell, Islington). Built by one Richard Baker, carpenter, *c*1724.

Baker Street NW1, W1 (Marylebone, Cit. West.). Built on the estate of the Portman family (*see* **Portman Square**) and named from Henry William Portman's friend Sir Edward Baker, of Ranston. The Bakers had been agents for and business associates of the Portmans for several generations.

Balaclava Road SE1 (Bermondsey, Southwark). Commemorates the battle of Balaclava, fought on 25 October 1854 during the Crimean War and notable for the destruction of the 17th Lancers in the charge of

18

the Light Brigade (*see* **Alma Grove**).

Balchier Road SE22 (Dulwich, Southwark). Properly Belchier; Mrs Belchier owned the land at the time of development.

Baldwin Crescent SE5 (Camberwell, Southwark). Charles Baldwin, JP, was a 19th-century resident of Grove Hill (*see* **Grove Hill Road**).

Baldwin's Gardens EC1 (Holborn, Camden). Richard Baldwin or Baldwyn, keeper of gardens to Elizabeth I and treasurer of the Middle Temple, held property here in 1590. His descendants sold it in 1689 to one Leigh. **Leigh's Place** adjoins.

Baldwin Street EC1 (Finsbury, Islington). Built *c*1811 on land belonging to St Bartholomew's Hospital. Richard Baldwin or Baldwyn was treasurer of the hospital in 1791–1812. Originally the street ran W to Bath Street, parallel with Peerless Street; most of it was demolished and the land taken by the adjacent Bank of England printing works in the 1920s.

Balfe Street N1 (Caledonian Road, Islington). Commemorates Michael Balfe (1808–70), theatre manager, composer and producer of operas, of which *The Bohemian Girl* (1843) is the best known.

Balfour Place W1 (Mayfair, Cit. West.). Built on the Grosvenor estate, and named in honour of Eustace Balfour, surveyor to the estate 1890–1910. He was brother to the future Prime Minister Arthur Balfour. **Balfour Mews** adjoins.

Balham High Road SW12, SW17 (Balham, Wandsworth). High or principal road through Balham; the name is from OE 'bealgaham', the 'ham' or homestead of a Saxon called

Bealga. **Balham Grove**, **Hill**, **New Road**, **Park Road** and **Road** are all nearby.

Balls Pond Road N1 (Islington). John Ball kept a tavern and a duck pond here in the 17th century. The pond provided sportsmen with duck-shooting.

Balmes Road N1 (De Beauvoir Town, Hackney). Site of the mediaeval manor house and farm of Balmes or Bammes. Disputes between the parishes of Hackney and Shoreditch meant that parts of the manor lands were claimed by one or the other until 1697, when the boundary was finally settled S of this road.

Baltic Street EC1 (Finsbury, Islington). *See* **Timber Street**.

Banbury Road E9 (Hackney). One John de Banbury is recorded as owning land in Hackney in the 14th century. He held the property later called Shoreditch Place.

Bancroft Road E1 (Mile End, T. Ham.). Francis Bancroft, officer to the Lord Mayor of London, left £28,000 to endow almshouses which were built N of the Mile End Road in 1735. They were demolished and their associated school was moved into Essex *c*1885. The site was used for the People's Palace, part of which became the nucleus of Queen Mary College in 1934 (*see* **Beaumont Square**).

Bank End SE1 (Southwark). *See* **Bankside**.

Bankhurst Road SE6 (Catford, Lewisham). Probably an adaptation of Bankers or Banquers, to match the surrounding 'hurst' street names. The Banquer family bought a sub-manor of Lewisham *c*1260. The land lay between the present Loampit Hill and Stanstead Road, bounded E by the River Ravensbourne and W by the parish boundary. It became known as Bankers Manor. The family later became lords of the manor of Lee and of Shrafholt or Shroffolds.

Bankside SE1 (Southwark). The road beside the mediaeval earth embankment built along the Thames to protect the hinterland, which was below high-water level. **Bank End** adjoins. Efforts at embankment to protect land S of the Thames appear to have been made since the Roman occupation.

Banner Street EC1 (Finsbury, Islington). The Banner family held property here, or in the vicinity, in the late 18th century. There is no direct evidence that they had a share in building the street, but it is probable; building began in 1789.

Barbauld Road N16 (Stoke Newington, Hackney). The poet Anna Letitia Barbauld (*d* 1824) lived in Stoke Newington; among her most popular works were a number of children's hymns.

Barbon Close WC1 (Holborn, Camden). The 17th-century property developer Nicholas Barbon was responsible for much of the speculative building of his time. His projects near this street were Red Lion Square (1684) and parts of nearby Bedford Row; the latter brought about his bankruptcy.

Barchard Street SW18 (Wandsworth). Local family name. Elizabeth Barchard, who left £200 to be invested for charity, died in 1827. Robert Barchard, Deputy Lieutenant of Surrey (in which county Wandsworth then was), died in 1848.

Barge House Street SE1 (South-

wark). Leads to **Old Barge House Alley**, the site of the royal barge-houses. The royal barge of Elizabeth I (1558–1603) was kept there, and the yard was probably in royal use before that. It was abandoned in the 17th century.

Bark Place W2 (Bayswater, Cit. West.). Built on land held from 1822 by John Bark.

Barkston Gardens SW5 (Kensington, Ken. Chel.). Built on land owned by the Gunter family. Sir Robert Gunter (1831–1905) of Wetherby, Yorkshire, was MP for Barkston Ash in Yorkshire. **Wetherby Gardens** and **Place** are nearby.

Barlow Place W1 (Mayfair, Cit. West.). Built on the Grosvenor estate and named in honour of Thomas Barlow (*d* 1730), builder and surveyor to the estate from 1720.

Barlow Street SE17 (Newington, Southwark). The scholar Henry Clark Barlow (1806–76) lived in Newington. He published his first paper on the poet Dante in 1850, and devoted the rest of his life to the study of the poet's work (*see* **Dante Road**).

Barnabas Road E9 (Homerton, Hackney). Approaches the Anglican church of St Barnabas, Homerton, consecrated in 1847. **St Barnabas Terrace** runs to the N (*see* **St Barnabas Street**).

Barnardo Street E1 (Stepney, T. Ham.). The philanthropist Dr Thomas Barnardo (1845–1905) opened his first home for destitute children at 18 Stepney Causeway (adjoining) in 1870. Barnardo was brought up in Dublin and his family was of Spanish origin. A Protestant, he worked as an evangelist in Dublin and came to London intending to train as a missionary to China. He stayed to work for children in E

London, and opened his home under the patronage of Lord Shaftesbury.

Barnard Road SW11 (Clapham, Wandsworth). Sir John Barnard (1685–1764), city wine merchant and Lord Mayor in 1737, lived in Clapham. He was MP for the City of London 1722–61, and was known for his interest in public finance, especially for his personal intervention to prevent a 'run' on the Bank of England, and to restore confidence in it, in 1745.

Barnard's Inn EC1 (Cit. Lond.). A town house here was called 'Mackworth's Inn' when the executors to John Mackworth, Dean of Lincoln, acquired it in the 15th century. During the next century it became known as 'Barnard's Inn' from a later occupier, and was leased to lawyers of Chancery. An 'inn' was a large town house.

Barnby Street NW1 (St Pancras, Camden). Sir Joseph Barnby (1838–96) was a composer, conductor and organist, but was best known as a conductor of choral music. He was principal of the Guildhall School of Music, having previously been director of music at Eton College.

Barnes High Street SW13 (R. upon T.). High or principal street of Barnes. The name is from OE 'berne', meaning a barn.

Barnes Street E14 (Stepney, T. Ham.). *See* **Senrab Street**.

Barnet Grove E2 (Bethnal Green, T. Ham.). Commemorates the Rev. Canon Samuel Augustus Barnett and his wife Henrietta. The canon was incumbent of St Jude's, Whitechapel, from 1886. Both were reformers. The canon was instrumental in setting up Toynbee Hall (*see* **Toynbee Street**).

Barnsbury Road N1 (Islington).

Corruption of Bernersburgh, the Saxon 'burgh' or enclosed settlement which, after the Norman Conquest, was given to the Norman Hugh de Berneres or Berners. His descendants held it until 1502 as the manor of Barnsbury.

Barn Street N16 (Stoke Newington, Hackney). Built on the site of the barns and outhouses attached to Stoke Newington manor (*see* **Lordship Road**).

Baroness Road E2 (Bethnal Green, T. Ham.). Baroness Burdett-Coutts (1814–1906) built nearby Columbia Square dwellings, which were opened in 1862, and the Columbia Market (1869). The dwellings were designed to provide clean and cheap accommodation for workmen and their families. The market was to provide sound foodstuff at fair prices; it did not succeed, and was converted into workshops c1874. Not all the baroness's philanthropic schemes were successful, but the improvements she brought about were significant, and the size of her fortune was matched only by the strength of her religious conviction as to how she should spend it.

Baron's Court Road W14 (Hammersmith). By association with the mediaeval courts baron held regularly by the lord of the manor.

Baron's Place SE1 (Southwark). Built on land belonging to the Baron family, who held it in the late 18th century (*see* **West Square**).

Barrett Street W1 (Marylebone, Cit. West.). Built on land held by Thomas Barrett in the early 18th century.

Barringer Square SW17 (Tooting, Wandsworth). James Barringer was active in local public life for some 50 years. He was a member of the first elected vestry in 1855, and held nearly every parish office in succession. He was the vestry's representative to the District Board of Works, 1859–71.*

Barrow Hill Road NW8 (St John's Wood, Cit. West.). Intended to lead to Barrow Hill, which lies NE. No barrow (burial mound) has been found there. The *Oxford Dictionary of English Place Names* gives 'barrow' as most commonly deriving from OE 'bearuwe', a grove.

Barter Street WC1 (Bloomsbury, Camden). Records the nature of Bloomsbury Market, founded here by the Earl of Southampton in the 1660s. His successors, the dukes of Bedford, allowed it to decline and it was demolished in 1847.

Bartholomew Close EC1 (Cit. Lond.). Close or precinct of the former priory of St Bartholomew, founded here in 1123 by Rahere, jester to Henry I. The priory established its own hospital, which survived the dissolution and was re-established in 1544. The priory church nearby, St Bartholomew-the-Less, within the hospital precincts, became a parish church in 1547, as did St Bartholomew-the-Great which stands NW of the close.

Bartholomew Lane EC2 (Cit. Lond.). The mediaeval church of St Bartholomew-by-the-Exchange stood on the SE corner. It was rebuilt in the 15th century and demolished in 1840.

Bartholomew Road NW5 (Kentish Town, Camden). The S and earliest section ran through a small estate bequeathed to St Bartholomew's Hospital in 1667. **Bartholomew Villas** adjoins.

Bartholomew Square EC1 (Finsbury, Islington). Built in 1811 on land belonging to the hospital of St Bartholomew, Smithfield (*see* **Baldwin Street**).

Bartholomew Street SE1 (Newington, Southwark). The Lock or Leper Hospital which stood at the junction of the present Tabard and Great Dover Streets was run by the governors of St Bartholomew's Hospital in the City. When the Lock closed in 1760, the governors laid out this street on part of their land.

Bartlett Court (Cit. Lond.). *See* **Plough Place** for this and **Bartlett's Passage**.

Barton Street SW1 (Cit. West.). Built by Barton Booth, actor (1681–1733), who was brought up in Westminster and attended Westminster School. He first appeared on the London stage in Betterton's company in 1700, and became a successful tragedian, with Addison's *Cato* as the summit of his career (1713). He held property here and at Cowley, near Uxbridge. **Cowley Street** adjoins.

Basinghall Street EC2 (Cit. Lond.). Corruption of Basinghaga, the Saxon 'haga' belonging to the men of Basing in Hampshire. Mediaeval London had a number of these small areas which were outposts of manors in the country. Some had special liberties and privileges.

Basing Street W11 (Westbourne Park, Ken. Chel.). William Paulet was created Baron St John of Basing, Hampshire, in 1539 and acquired the surrounding manor of Notting Hill in 1549. In 1551 he became first Marquis of Winchester (*see* **Great Winchester Street**).

Basire Street N1 (New North Road, Islington). Isaac and James Basire, father and son, lived and worked in Islington. Isaac (1704–68) was an engraver and printer. James (1730–1802) was engraver to the Royal Society.

Bassano Street SE22 (E Dulwich, Southwark). On the Dulwich College estate, and probably inspired by the proximity of the College art gallery. The north-Italian family of Da Ponte Bassano specialised in painting pastoral and biblical scenes. Jacopo (c1518–92) and his sons Francesco and Leandro were the most famous.

Bassett Street NW5 (Kentish Town, Camden). Built on the Southampton estate (*see* **Fitzroy Road**). George Bassett was agent to the estate in the 1840s.

Basuto Road SW6 (Parson's Green, Hammersmith). Named in 1884, when the territory of Basutoland became a crown colony.

Bateman's Buildings W1 (Soho, Cit. West.). In 1717 Sir James Bateman bought a house here which had been built for the Duke of Monmouth, natural son of Charles II. The house was demolished in 1773 and replaced by two houses with this narrow lane of small dwellings in between. **Bateman Street** runs S of it.

Bateman's Row EC2 (Shoreditch, Hackney). James Bateman bought part of the former precinct of Holywell Priory (*see* **Holywell Lane**) in 1692. The Batemans held it until the death of the second Viscount Bateman in 1802. This street marked their N boundary.

Bath Place EC2 (Shoreditch, Hackney). A well or cistern of spring water here, recorded in the 16th century as the well of 'Dame Annis the Cleare' (*see* **Clere Street**), was used by local brewers in the 17th century and became a medicinal bath and spa in the early 18th century.

Bath Street EC1 (Finsbury, Islington). The Peerless Pool (*see* **Peerless Street**) was turned into an outdoor bath and pleasure garden c1750; the bath itself survived into the 19th century. The street was formerly Pest House Row, from a plague hospital opened c1595 which stood W of the street, between the present Radnor and Lever Streets. The surrounding land was called Pest House Fields. The building was demolished as a ruin in 1736.

Bathurst Street W2 (Bayswater, Cit. West.). On the Frederick estate (*see* **Frederick Close**). Elizabeth Bathurst of Clarendon Park married into the Frederick family in the 18th century. **Clarendon Close, Mews** and **Place** are nearby.

Battersea Bridge Road SW11 (Wandsworth). Built as an approach to Battersea Bridge which was built in 1890 in place of a wooden structure. The wooden bridge had superseded the ferry by which the river was originally crossed at this point (*see* **Battersea High Street**).

Battersea Church Road SW11 (Battersea, Wandsworth). The church is the parish church of St Mary, first recorded in 1162 when it belonged to the Abbey of Westminster; the present building dates from 1777 (*see* **Battersea High Street**).

Battersea High Street SW11 (Battersea, Wandsworth). High or principal street of Battersea. The first part of the name appears in OE charters as Badric, Batric or Badoric; a later copy of a 7th-century document calls the place 'Badrices ege', meaning Badric's island. As in Bermondsey, the 'island' may have been formed by streams running into the Thames and surrounding a small area of firm ground with marshes.

Battersea Park Road SW8, SW11 (Battersea, Wandsworth). Battersea Park was opened to the public in 1855; it was laid out on the site of Battersea Fields, an area of grazing land which had been used for disorderly Sunday fairs, and also for duelling.

Battersea Rise SW11 (Battersea, Wandsworth). A field here is recorded as The Rise in 1605, probably from the land steeply sloping up from the river bank.

Battle Bridge Lane SE1 (Tooley Street, Southwark). A stream flowing into the Thames here was bridged in the middle ages by the abbots of Battle, who owned the land. They also had a London house here until the dissolution of the monasteries c1539 (*see* **Great Maze Pond**).

Battle Bridge Road NW1 (King's Cross, Camden). Nearby King's Cross is traditionally (but not historically) the site of an important battle between British and Roman armies (*see* **Boadicea Street**). The bridge was that crossing the River Fleet N of St Chad's Place. The whole area between the present Gray's Inn, Pentonville and King's Cross Roads, N of Swinton Street, was called Battlebridge until the 1830s when the name King's Cross was adopted (*see* **King's Cross Road**).

Bavent Road SE5 (Camberwell, Lambeth). Commemorates a family who held land in this part of S London in the middle ages. Roger de Bavant or Bavent held land under obligation to Baron Wakelin de Maminot (lord of the manor of Deptford) in 1262. His son Adam de Bavent held the right of free warren (taking wild animals for food) in Hatcham in 1285; the Bavents held part of Hatcham manor until Roger

de Bavent gave it to Edward III (1327–77).

Bayham Street NW1 (Camden Town, Camden). Charles Pratt, Viscount Bayham and later Earl Camden, developed Camden Town from 1790. **Bayham Place** adjoins (*see* **Camden High Street**).

Bayley Street WC1 (Bloomsbury, Camden). Sir John Bayley (1763–1841), judge, lived in adjacent Bedford Square. He became a judge in 1808. In 1819 he judged the famous case of libel brought by the Attorney General against Richard Carlile for republishing Thomas Paine's pamphlet *Age of Reason*.

Baylis Road SE1 (Lambeth). The Royal Victoria Coffee Music Hall nearby (the 'Old Vic') became a theatre staging classical drama, particularly Shakespeare, under the management of Lilian Baylis, niece of Emma Cons (*see* **Cons Street**). Miss Baylis became manager in 1898; her first season of Shakespeare was in 1914.

Baynes Court EC1 (Clerkenwell, Islington). Built on land owned by Walter Baynes. It was he who discovered that a spring of water on the land had medicinal properties (*see* **Cold Bath Square**).

Bayswater Road W2 (Cit. West.). Road through Bayswater, or Bayardswater, which may have been a watering place for horses or a stretch of water belonging to a family of French descent called Bayard. The name is first used in the 14th century: 'Bayard' was a common mediaeval nickname (like 'Dobbin' in the 19th century) for any horse.

Baytree Road SW2 (Brixton, Lambeth). Built on the site of a large house called 'Baytrees' which stood on Brixton Hill.

Bazeley Street E14 (Poplar, T. Ham.). The Rev. Thomas Bazeley was vicar of All Saints, in the East India Dock Road, in the 1850s.

Beak Street W1 (Regent Street, Cit. West.). Thomas Beak or Beake acquired ground between the present Regent Street and Kingly Street between 1673 and 1685, and the original Beak Street was built on it. The part E of Kingly Street was called Silver Street (possibly by association with Golden Square) until 1883.

Bear Alley EC4 (Cit. Lond.). Probably named from an inn sign, now vanished. This alley is mentioned in 1666. Before Holborn Viaduct Station was built it ran through to Seacoal Lane.

Bear Gardens SE1 (Southwark). Site of a 17th-century bear-baiting ring (S end) and of the Elizabethan bear-garden which lay slightly further N near the river. The entertainment was such that the term 'bear garden' still describes a rough, noisy gathering which has got completely out of hand

Bear Lane SE1 (Southwark). By association with the nearby **Bear Gardens**).

Bear Street WC2 (Cit. West.). Uncertain, a 17th-century street probably named from an inn called *The Bear* which has now vanished.

Beatson Street SE16 (Rotherhithe, Southwark). The Beatson family were noted local ship-breakers. David Beatson came from Scotland in 1790 to join a family firm at Surrey Canal Wharf; his son John Beatson succeeded him in Rotherhithe Street. Among famous warships broken up by them were the *Bellérophon* and the *Téméraire* (*see* **Téméraire Street**).

Beatty Street NW1 (Camden Town, Camden). Originally Nelson Street, it was renamed in 1937 to commemorate a more recent naval commander, Admiral Lord Beatty, Commander-in-Chief of the fleet during World War I. He died in 1936.

Beauchamp Street EC1 (Holborn, Camden). Named from Beauchamp Court, the Warwickshire seat of Fulke Greville, Lord Brooke (1554–1628), courtier and scholar, who had a town house on the site of Brooke Street adjoining.

Beaufort Street SW3 (Chelsea, Ken. Chel.). Sir Thomas More (*d* 1535) owned a house here which was confiscated after his execution and finally sold to the Marquis of Worcester in 1682. The marquis became Duke of Beaufort and the house became known as 'Beaufort House'; it has since been demolished.

Beaufoy Road SW11 (Battersea, Wandsworth). Beginning of an estate built by the Beaufoy family of Lambeth, vinegar distillers. The site formerly held one of their factories (*see* **Beaufoy Walk**).

Beaufoy Walk SE11 (Lambeth). The Beaufoys, distillers of vinegar, are recorded in business in Lambeth in the late 18th century, and remained prominent in local business and civic affairs. Henry Beaufoy founded the Ragged Schools nearby in Newport Street in 1851.

Beaumont Place W1 (Euston, Camden). Built by one Joseph Beaumont from 1791.

Beaumont Square E1 (Stepney, T. Ham.). Built on the estate of Joseph Barber, who was born in St Marylebone in 1774 and took the name of Beaumont in 1812. A pioneer of insurance and self-help, he founded the County Fire Office in

1807. In 1840 he built and endowed the Beaumont New Philosophical Institute in the Mile End Road. He died in 1841. His trustees, in association with the Drapers' Company, began to develop the institute's technical school which later became the nucleus of Queen Mary College. The institute itself was the forerunner of the People's Palace.

Beaumont Street W1 (Marylebone, Cit. West.). Built from 1777 by Sir Beaumont Hotham, who acquired a building lease from the Duke of Portland, the landowner. **Beaumont Mews** runs parallel.

Beavor Lane W6 (Chiswick, Hammersmith). Samuel Beavor or Bever (*d* 1762) owned a house here called 'Beavor Lodge'.

Becket Street SE1 (Southwark). Associated with nearby **Pilgrimage Street**. Mediaeval pilgrims travelled to the Canterbury shrine of St Thomas Becket, London-born Archbishop of Canterbury. Becket was murdered in 1170 by knights who believed they were carrying out the wishes of Henry II, with whom Becket was in dispute over the respective powers of church and state.

Beck Road E8 (Hackney). Commemorates Joseph Beck (1829–91), London County Councillor for North Hackney from 1889.

Beclands Road SW17 (Tooting, Wandsworth). *See* **Tooting Bec Road**.

Becmead Avenue SW16 (Tooting, Wandsworth). *See* **Tooting Bec Road**.

Bedford Gardens W8 (Holland Park, Ken. Chel.). *See* **Duchess of Bedford's Walk**.

Bedford Hill SW12, SW16 (Streatham, Lambeth/Wandsworth). Crosses the manor of Tooting Bec which was held by the Russells, dukes of Bedford. The second duke's marriage to the manorial heiress Elizabeth Howland took place in 1695. The Russells sold the manor (except the living of the church) in 1816.

Bedford Road SW4 (Clapham, Lambeth). Runs S from Clapham near the *Bedford Arms* public house in Clapham Road, towards the Duke of Bedford's property in Streatham (*see* **Bedford Hill**).

Bedford Row WC1 (Holborn, Camden). Laid out in the early 18th century on land belonging to Peter Harpur of Bedford, after an abortive start to development by Nicholas Barbon (*see* **Barbon Close**). Harpur was able to endow a school in Bedford with the income from his London properties.

Bedford Square WC1 (Bloomsbury, Camden). Part of the estates of the Russell family, earls (later dukes) of Bedford. Their main 18th-century London house was here. **Bedford Avenue, Place** and **Way** are nearby.

Bedford Street WC2 (Covent Garden, Cit. West.). Laid out for the fourth Earl of Bedford in 1631 as part of his Covent Garden development, which was designed for him by Inigo Jones.

Beech Street EC2 (Cit. Lond.). Called Bechestrete in the 13th century and later Bechelane or Beech Lane. Named from beech trees, either because there was a natural grove, or because beech hedging had been used as a windbreak by a householder on the flat, exposed ground N of the City.

Beeston Place SW1 (Belgravia, Cit. West.). *See* Kinnerton Street.

Belgrave Square SW1 (Belgravia, Cit. West.). The Grosvenor family who own the square and surrounding streets named it after their Leicestershire estate, Belgrave. Development by the builder Thomas Cubitt started in 1825. **Belgrave Place** and **Street** approach the square.

Belitha Villas N1 (Barnsbury, Islington). From a mid-Victorian landlord of the *Angel Inn*, Islington.

Bellamy Street SW12 (Balham, Wandsworth). The Rev. Richard Bellamy was the first vicar of St Mary's church, Balham, from 1855 until 1879.

Bellenden Road SE15 (Peckham, Southwark). Uncertain, thought to have been inspired by a character in a novel by Sir Walter Scott (*see* **Ivanhoe Road**). The name was extended N along the present road, which originally consisted of numerous individually-named groups and terraces, two of which were called Bellenden. The N section, off Peckham High Street, was formerly Basing Road, and the manor house of Basing lay E of it. In the 16th century Basing manor was acquired by the Gardyner family, of whom one member, Thomas, used to send presents of home-grown melons to Charles I. George Gardyner sold the manor in 1651.

Bell Green SE26 (Sydenham, Lewisham). Traditionally the site of a bell-tower attached to the manor house of Sydenham, Place House, which stood E of Perry Hill. **Bell Green Lane** approaches. 'Bell' names are usually from inn signs or, in open country, bell-founders' pits.

Bell Lane E1 (Spitalfields, T. Ham.). A *Bell Inn* is recorded in Crispin Street in 1761, and this lane would have approached it.

Bell's Garden Road SE15 (Peckham, Southwark). Built on the site of a nursery-garden belonging to a Mr Bell. S and W London at first profited from the expansion of the City by growing its food on the excellent land fertilised by the City's night-soil. In the explosive expansion of the later 19th century all this thriving horticulture vanished under bricks and mortar, so great was the profit from the sale of land for building.

Bell Street NW1 (Lisson Green, Cit. West.). Formerly Bell Lane, running through a field called the Bell Field.

Bell Wharf Lane EC4 (Cit. Lond.). Originally led to a wharf which is recorded in 1755 and was probably named from an inn sign.

Bell Yard (Cit. Lond.). Named from the *Bell Inn* (demolished) which stood here in the 16th century. A letter to William Shakespeare from Richard Quiney was written from the inn.

Bell Yard WC2 (Cit. Lond./Cit. West.). Named from the sign of an inn. The inn has gone, the bell sign remains.

Belmont Hill SE13 (Lewisham). From a house called 'Belmont' built here *c*1830 for the surveyor of the Deptford Dockyards.

Belsham Street E9 (Hackney). Thomas Belsham (1750–1829) was a Unitarian preacher at the Old Gravel Pit Meeting House, Hackney, from 1794 until 1805. He was also resident tutor in divinity at Hackney College.

Belsize Lane NW3 (Hampstead, Camden). An old road through part of the mediaeval manor of Belsize, Belassis or Belses. The name is from the French, meaning well placed. The manor house stood in the present

Belsize Square. **Belsize Avenue, Court, Crescent, Place** and **Terrace** adjoin. **Belsize Road** is nearby.

Belsize Park NW3 (Hampstead, Camden). *See* **Belsize Lane**. The parkland attached to Belsize manor house ran SE from Belsize Avenue. **Belsize Gardens** and **Belsize Park Gardens** were laid out on part of it when the house was demolished in 1841.

Belvedere Road SE1 (Lambeth). Made in 1824–9 by the widening and general improvement of an old rampart called Narrow Wall, the N end of which became **Upper Ground**. This street was named from Belvedere House and pleasure gardens which opened in 1718 on the site of the present Royal Festival Hall. 'Belvedere' was a fashionable name, bringing to mind grand Italian gardens and views across delightful country.

Belvoir Road SE22 (Dulwich, Southwark). By association with local traditions of hunting in Dulwich woods and elsewhere (*see* **Denmark Hill**). This is one of a group of place names connected with famous hunts or packs of hounds. The other roads are **Albrighton, Pytchley** and **Quorn** Roads.

Benbow Street SE8 (Deptford, Greenwich). Commemorates Admiral Benbow (1653–1702) who lived in Deptford, where he rented Sayes Court 1696–9. He was Master of Deptford dockyards 1690–6, a period interrupted by commands at sea. He was mortally wounded in a controversial action against the French in the West Indies.

Bendall Mews NW1 (Lisson Grove, Cit. West.). *See* **Shroton Street**.

Benhill Road SE5 (Camberwell, Southwark). Built on land belonging to a market-gardener of that name.

Ben Johnson Road E1 (Stepney, T. Ham.). 'Ben Johnson's Head' became a popular inn sign during the 17th century. The satiric dramatist Johnson or Jonson died in 1637.

Bennet Street SW1 (St James's, Cit. West.). Built by Henry Bennet, created Baron Arlington in 1663 and Earl of Arlington in 1672 (*see* **Arlington Street**). He was a member of Charles II's cabal ministry, and was impeached in the Commons in 1674 as the main instrument of the king's unpopular measures, although further proceedings were dropped.

Bentinck Street W1 (Marylebone, Cit. West.). William Bentinck, Duke of Portland, inherited the surrounding estate through his wife, the former Lady Margaret Cavendish Harley (*see* **Cavendish Square**), daughter of the Earl of Oxford and Mortimer (*see* **Mortimer Street**).

Bentworth Road W12 (Wormwood Scrubs, Hammersmith). Richard de Bentworth or Wentworth was Bishop of London in 1338–9 and, as such, held the manor of Hammersmith.

Benyon Road N1 (De Beauvoir Town, Hackney). Richard Benyon inherited the De Beauvoir estate in 1822 (*see* **De Beauvoir Road**).

Beresford Road N5 (Newington Green, Islington). Built on the site of a large house called 'Beresford Lodge', which in turn occupied the site of Dells Farm.

Bere Street E1 (Ratcliff, T. Ham.). Commemorates Peter Bere, famous for his presence of mind and resourcefulness in the great fire of Ratcliff in 1794. The outbreak, at St George's Stairs near Cock Hill, ignited a cargo of saltpetre which blew up and spead the fire to the saltpetre warehouses of the East India Company. Peter Bere saved his own house, but nearly 600 were lost.

Berger Road E9 (Hackney). Compliments the local Hackney company of Lewis Berger and Sons, paint and colour manufacturers. The Berger family lived in nearby Shepherd's Lane in the 1840s.

Berkeley Gardens W8 (Kensington, Ken. Chel.). Lady Jane Berkeley bought the house later known as 'Sheffield House' from Sir George Coppin between 1603 and 1613. She held the house and three and a half acres adjoining (*see* **Sheffield Terrace**).

Berkeley Square W1 (Mayfair, Cit. West.). The original estate of Lord Berkeley of Stratton (*see* **Berkeley Street**) had lost its mansion and adjacent land by 1700, leaving a remnant of fields. This last piece of land was leased out for building as a square in 1737.

Berkeley Street W1 (Mayfair, Cit. West.). Berkeley House was built nearby for Lord Berkeley of Stratton after the Restoration of 1660. His widow sold some of her land for building in 1684 and this street was built to the E of the house. The mansion itself was sold to the Duke of Devonshire in 1698.

Bermondsey Street E1 (Bermondsey, Southwark). Leads through Bermondsey; the name is OE and means 'Beormund's island'. The island in this case would have been a piece of firm ground surrounded by marshes and channels of slow-moving water. The nature of the place proved extremely unhealthy for the rapidly-growing population of the 19th century. **Bermondsey Square** adjoins.

Bermondsey Wall SE16 (Bermondsey, Southwark). The wall was an embankment of the Thames, most of Bermondsey and Rotherhithe being below high-water level (*see* **Bermondsey Street**).

Bernard Street WC1 (Bloomsbury, Camden). Laid out from 1799 to 1820 on land belonging to the Foundling Hospital (*see* **Coram Street**). Sir Thomas Bernard was governor of the hospital in 1787, treasurer 1795–1806 and vice-president 1806–10.

Bernays Grove SW9 (Brixton, Lambeth). Albert Bernays, professor of chemistry, lived in Brixton. He served as public analyst to Camberwell vestry, among others, and died in 1892.

Berners Road N1 (Islington). Commemorates the Norman lord of the manor, Hugh de Berners (*see* **Barnsbury Road**).

Berners Street W1 (Oxford Street, Cit. West.). Built *c*1720 on land acquired by the Berners family in 1654. **Berners Mews** and **Place** adjoin.

Berry Street EC1 (Clerkenwell, Islington). Built on land belonging to Thomas Berry, some time before 1803.

Berwick Street W1 (Soho, Cit. West.). Built from 1687 on land held on lease by James Pollett, a Roman Catholic. Pollett probably named it in honour of the Catholic royal house of Stuart; the Duke of Berwick was the younger son of James II.

Bessborough Gardens SW1 (Pimlico, Cit. West.). Commemorates John Ponsonby, Baron Duncannon of Bessborough. **Bessborough Street** approaches; **Bessborough Place**,

Ponsonby Place and **Ponsonby Terrace** are nearby (*see* **Agar Street**).

Bessborough Road SW15 (Putney, Wandsworth). William, Second Earl of Bessborough, lived at Parkstead House, Roehampton, after 1750. The house later became Manresa House Jesuit College.

Bessemer Road SE5 (Denmark Hill, Southwark). Sir Henry Bessemer, engineer and inventor, developed a new process for making cheap steel in 1855. He lived on Denmark Hill in his later years and died in 1898.

Bethnal Green Road E1, E2 (T. Ham.). Road to the green at Bethnal, called Blithenhale and Blithehale in the 14th century. 'Hale' comes from OE 'healh' or' halh', meaning a sheltered or hidden place. 'Blithe' may have been a local landowner or a feature such as a stream.

Betterton Street WC2 (Covent Garden, Camden). The actor Thomas Betterton made his début at the Cock Pit Theatre in nearby Drury Lane, in 1659.

Betton Place E2 (Shoreditch, Hackney). Thomas Betton, benefactor of the Ironmongers' Company, was buried at the company's Geffrye almshouses in Kingsland Road. He died in 1724.

Beverley Road SW13 (Barnes, R. upon T.). Runs beside the Beverley Brook which flows across Barnes Elms into the Thames. Called Beferithi and Baeverithe in the 7th and 10th centuries respectively. Both names mean 'a stream with beavers'.

Beverstone Road SW2 (Brixton, Lambeth). Built on the site of a large house called 'Beverstone'.

Bevill Allen Close SW17 (Tooting, Wandsworth). The Rev. Bevill Allen (*d* 1929) was minister of Tooting Congregational Church for 36 years. He was active in local life and politics. He was a Progressive member of the London County Council, representing Balham and Tooting, 1919–22.

Bevington Street SE16 (Bermondsey, Southwark). Named from a prominent local family. The Neckinger Mills leather factory was opened *c*1800 by Samuel, Henry and Timothy Bevington. By the 1870s Colonel Samuel Bevington was organising the local volunteer militia, for whom he built Bermondsey Drill Hall (opposite Christ Church) in 1876. He later became the first mayor of the borough of Bermondsey.

Bevin Way WC1 (Islington). Approaches an estate named after Sir Ernest Bevin, labour politician (1881–1951). He was a pioneer of trade-union negotiation and one of the builders of the Transport and General Workers' Union. He became Minister of Labour and National Service in 1940, and the 'Bevin boys' were those directed to essential productive work. He was Foreign Secretary 1945–51.

Bevis Marks EC3 (Cit. Lond.). Corruption of Bury's Marks. A large house on the site was given to the abbey of Bury or St Edmundsbury some time before 1160; a deed records a London citizen, David the Dane, as donor. 'Marks' probably refers to boundary markers (*see* **Heneage Lane**).

Bewick Street SW8 (Battersea, Wandsworth). Commemorates the 18th-century engraver Thomas Bewick whose work, long neglected, had appeared in a new edition shortly before the street was named in 1877.

Bickenhall Street W1 (Marylebone, Cit. West.). Built on the Portman estate. The family also owned property at Bickenhall in Somerset and at two other Somerset villages: Capland and Huntsworth. **Capland Street** and **Huntsworth Mews** are nearby.

Bickley Street SW17 (Tooting, Wandsworth). Commemorates the Rev. Richard Bickley who was rector of Tooting from 1663 and left a bequest to the parish poor when he died.

Bidborough Street WC1 (Blooms-bury, Camden). *See* **Leigh Street**.

Biddestone Road N7 (Islington). Built on land belonging to Lord Islington; his principal home was in Wiltshire, where he held property at Biddestone. Sir John Poynder Dickson-Poynder, created First Baron Islington in 1910, was London County Council member for Finsbury from 1898. He was MP for Chippenham, Wiltshire, 1892–1910, and Honorary Colonel of the Wiltshire Yeomanry. Other names on this land are from Wiltshire and neighbouring Dorset: **Sturmer Way, Stock Orchard Crescent** and **Street, Quemerford Road** and **Widdenham Road**.

Billiter Street EC3 (Cit. Lond.). Corruption of 'belzeter' (or bell-founder). Mediaeval bell-founders often set up temporary foundries near their customer church, abandoning them as soon as the bells had been cast and hung. In a city this would have been impractical and – given the large number of churches in a small area – unnecessary. This foundry is more likely to have been permanent.

Bingham Place W1 (Marylebone, Cit. West.). *See* **Nottingham Street**.

Binney Street W1 (Mayfair, Cit. West.). Commemorates Dr Thomas

Binney (1798–1874), famous dissenting minister of the Weigh House Chapel, before its establishment on this site (*see* **Weighhouse Street**).

Birchington Road NW6 (Kilburn, Camden). Kentish place name. Built by the Powell-Cotton family of Quex Park, Birchington, Kent.

Birchin Lane EC3 (Cit. Lond.). Called Berchervere Lane in the 12th century, Berchervereslane and Bercherverelane in the 13th, it is Berchenes Lane and Birchenlane in the 14th century. Eilert Ekwall (*Street Names of the City of London*, 1954) interprets it as 'barbers' lane'. He supposes an unrecorded OE word, 'beardceorfere', meaning literally beard-carver, as the original.

Birdcage Walk SW1 (Cit. West.). Probably named from an aviary. Charles II had St James's Park laid out after 1660 as a pleasure garden; it was stocked with unusual waterfowl and other birds.

Bird in Bush Road SE15 (Peckham, Southwark). Revival of an early field name, of which the derivation is unknown.

Bird Street W1 (Marylebone, Cit. West.). Built by Thomas Bird, bricklayer, from 1763.

Birkbeck Road E8 (Kingsland, Hackney). From the Birkbeck school opened in Kingsland. George Birkbeck (1776–1841) was a doctor with a strong interest in education. He started the mechanics' institutes and was one of the founders of University College London.

Bisham Gardens N6 (Highgate, Camden). Site of Bisham House, demolished in 1884.

Bishop King's Road W14 (Hammersmith). Commemorates John King, Bishop of London 1611–21, holder of the manors of Hammersmith and Fulham (*see* **Fulham Palace Road**). He left four acres of land here for the benefit of the poor of the parish in 1620.

Bishop's Avenue, The N2 (Hampstead Garden Suburb, Barnet). Part of the manor of Hornsey which belonged to the bishops of London from the Saxon period until the Reformation.

Bishop's Bridge Road W2 (Paddington, Cit. West.). An old track which crossed the Westbourne by a bridge, and lay on the land of the Bishop of London who held the manor (*see* **Porteus Road**).

Bishop's Court WC2 (Chancery Lane, Camden). Formerly led to the London palace of the bishops of Chichester, built in the reign of Henry III (1216–72). The palace was later acquired by the earls of Lincoln (*see* **Lincoln's Inn Fields**).

Bishop's Court EC4 (Cit. Lond.). A 17th-century court off Old Bailey, this was originally called Bishopshead Court, from the sign of an inn, now demolished.

Bishopsgate EC2 (Cit. Lond.). Street through the Bishop's Gate in the NE wall of the City. A gate existed here in Roman times. The name is thought to commemorate St Erkenwald who was Bishop of London in the 7th century. The nearby church of St Ethelburga is dedicated to his sister. The gate would have been the natural entrance to the City for all the bishops of London approaching from their manor house at Bethnal Green (*see* **Bishop's Way**).

Bishop's Road SW6 (Fulham, Hammersmith). Part of the original

approach to the Bishop of London's Palace from London, through Walmer Green (*see* **Fulham Palace Road**).

Bishop Street N1 (Islington). *See* **Prebend Street**.

Bishop's Way E2 (Bethnal Green, T. Ham.). The bishops of London, as lords of the manor of Stepney since before the Norman Conquest, had a manor house here, originally called 'The Bishops' Hall'. The manor was surrendered to Edward VI by Bishop Nicholas Ridley in 1551 (*see* **Bonner Road**).

Bishopswood Road N6 (Hornsey, Haringey). Originally a stretch of woodland forming part of the extensive Hornsey Woods and belonging to the manor of Hornsey (*see* **Bishop's Avenue, The** and **Southwood Lane**).

Blackall Street EC2 (Shoreditch, Hackney). Offspring Blackall or Blackhall was born in Kingsland Road in 1654. He became chaplain to William III, although his private sympathies lay with the deposed house of Stuart. An outstanding and controversial preacher, he was made Bishop of Exeter (where he founded a school) in 1708. His father, and other members of his family, is buried in Hackney parish church.

Blackburne's Mews W1 (Mayfair, Cit. West.). William Blackburne lived in Upper Brook Street in the 1720s. The mews, to serve **Grosvenor Square**, was cut after 1731 and probably passed through some of his property.

Blackfriars Lane EC4 (Cit. Lond.). The Dominicans or Black Friars (so called from their black robes) established a monastery here in 1276–8; it closed at the dissolution in

1538 (*see* **Playhouse Yard**).

Blackfriars Road SE1 (Southwark). This was built in 1769–70 as an approach to Blackfriars Bridge, newly complete. The road was originally called Great Surrey Street, since the county of Surrey then extended this far, and it was renamed from the bridge in 1810. The bridge was named from the monastic site at its N head (*see* **Blackfriars Lane**).

Black Horse Court SE1 (Great Dover Street, Southwark). The *Black Horse* tavern here is first recorded in 1799.

Blackhorse Road SE8 (Deptford, Lewisham). Built on open land called Blackhorse Fields, by association with the nearby *Blackhorse Inn*, which was built by the canal bridge in Evelyn Street.

Blacklands Terrace SW3 (Chelsea, Ken. Chel.). Blacklands Farm stood on the site of the present Duke of York's Headquarters; its land extended N to Knightsbridge and formed part of the estate of Sir Hans Sloane. The derivation of its name is not known.

Black Lion Lane W6 (Chiswick, Hammersmith). The *Black Lion* public house is recorded here in the late 18th century, but is probably older.

Black Lion Yard E1 (Whitechapel, T. Ham.). The *Black Lion* inn is recorded here in 1668.

Black Prince Road SE1, SE11 (Kennington, Lambeth). Runs through the manor of Kennington, which was given to Edward, Earl of Chester and Duke of Cornwall, known as the Black Prince, by his father Edward III in 1337. The manor house stood near the junction of this street with Kennington Road. The manor is still held by the Duchy of

Cornwall. The street was built on the line of an old lane called Lambeth Butts, butts being targets for archery.

Black Swan Yard SE1 (Bermondsey Street, Southwark). From the *Black Swan* tavern, recorded here in 1826.

Blackthorn Street E3 (Bow Common, T. Ham.). One of a group of tree and plant names recalling the once rural nature of the common. The others are: **Fern, Furze** and **Whitethorn** Streets – named at a time when the district was full of gas works, chemical plants and assorted industrial stenches.

Blackwall Way E14 (Poplar, T. Ham.). The ancient 'black wall' along this reach of the Thames was probably an embankment of earth.

Blackwater Street SE22 (Lordship Lane, Southwark). Built on the site of a house called 'Blackwater Cottage'.

Blackwood Street SE17 (Walworth, Southwark). Captain Blackwood, already noted for outstanding seamanship, commanded the frigate *Euryalus* at the battle of Trafalgar (*see* **Trafalgar Square**).

Blairderry Road SW2 (Streatham Hill, Lambeth). *See* **Ardwell Road**.
Blair Street E14 (Poplar, T. Ham.). *See* **Leven Road**.

Blake Street SE8 (Deptford, Lewisham). Named at the same time as **Benbow Street**. Commemorates Admiral Blake, Commander of the English fleet under Cromwell. He came to prominence in a war against the Dutch in 1652–3. After three major engagements in which he and the Dutch commander Van Tromp seemed evenly matched, he was ultimately the victor. His other notable actions were the destruction of a pirate fleet in Algiers and the storing of Santa Cruz harbour to destroy a Spanish treasure fleet in 1657.

Blandford Street W1 (Marylebone, Cit. West.). Built on the Portman estate. The Portman family had a Dorset seat at Bryanston near Blandford Forum. (*See* **Portman Square**.)

Bleeding Heart Yard EC1 (Holborn, Camden). Probably named from a sign. The bleeding heart would have been a Christian symbol used at first by a religious body and later adopted by an inn or trade.

Blenheim Road NW8 (Maida Vale, Cit. West.). Commemorates a victory over the French by English and allied forces under Marlborough at Blenheim in Bavaria, 1704. **Blenheim Place** and **Terrace** adjoin (*see* **Marlborough Place**).

Blenheim Street W1 (Oxford Street, Cit. West.). *See* **Blenheim Road**.

Bloemfontein Road W12 (Shepherd's Bush, Hammersmith). Formerly a short street off Uxbridge Road, it was named in 1881 after the capital of the Orange Free State, South Africa. In 1927 it was extended N. In the 1930s, when the Union of South Africa was still part of the British Empire, the road became the basis of a new estate inspired by the Empire (*see* **Australia Road**).

Blomfield Road W9 (Paddington, Cit. West.). *See* **Porteus Road** and **Blomfield Street**.

Blomfield Street EC2 (Cit. Lond.). Dr Blomfield was installed as Bishop of London in 1829. He was noted for his work in increasing the number of London churches and clergy, to serve a rapidly-growing population. He was incumbent of nearby St Botolph, Bishopsgate, 1815–22.

Bloomfield Road N6 (Highgate, Haringey). *See* **Park, The**.

Bloomfield Terrace SW1 (Victoria, Cit. West.). Properly Blomfield (*see* **Blomfield Street**). St John's School, mainly for the daughters of clergymen, was founded here in 1859 by the Anglican sisterhood of St John.

Bloomsbury Street WC1 (Bloomsbury, Camden). Street through Bloomsbury, called Blemondisbery in the 13th century, and named from the Blemunds or Blemunts, a Norman family, who then owned this manor (or former Saxon 'burgh').

Blossom Street E1 (Spitalfields, T. Ham.). Built by the Tillard family who acquired the estate in 1716. They built three streets and gave them all flower names, the others being **Elder Street** and **Fleur de Lis Street**. The Tillards were a Huguenot family who had settled in Totnes, Devon, in the 16th century.

Blucher Road SE5 (Camberwell, Southwark). Survivor of a set of names which commemorated the battle of Waterloo in 1815. Prince Blücher commanded the Prussian army which, together with Wellington's British force, defeated Napoleon. The S end of Elmington Road was Waterloo Street. N of it lay Waterloo Square, and the present Lomond Road was patriotically named George Street.

Blue Anchor Lane SE16 (Rotherhithe, Southwark). Named from the sign of an inn which stood at the junction with Southwark Park Road; the latter was formerly called Blue Anchor Road.

Blue Anchor Yard E1 (Whitechapel, T. Ham.). A *Blue Anchor* tavern is recorded in Upper East Smithfield in the 1790s, and was probably older. A *Blue Anchor* tavern in Rosemary

Lane (now Cable Street) is recorded in 1746.

Bluebell Close SE26 (Upper Sydenham, Lewisham). *See* **Low Cross Wood Lane**.

Blythe Road W14 (Hammersmith). A house called 'Blythe House' (now demolished) stood at the junction of this lane and the present Augustine Road. It is not clear whether the lane was named from the house, or whether Blythe is a corruption of 'Blinde'. Blinde Lane and Blinde Lane House are referred to in the 17th century. 'Blinde' could mean either a blind turning or a cul-de-sac.

Boadicea Street N1 (King's Cross, Islington). There is a tradition (without much foundation) that at King's Cross nearby there was a battle between Roman and British forces which proved to be the last stand of Queen Boadicea of the Iceni, during the British rebellion of 61 AD. A battle of some kind must have taken place there, in order to account for the persistent tradition which named the whole area 'Battlebridge'. There is evidence, however, that Boadicea's final battle was fought in the Midlands.

Boathouse Walk SE15 (Peckham, Southwark). This path originally approached sheds for craft using the Surrey Canal, which has now been filled in (*see* **Canal Head**).

Bohemia Place E8 (Hackney). Site of a house called 'Bohemia Palace', 1578–1796, built by a London merchant. It is said to have been occupied by Frederick, Elector Palatine and son-in-law to James I, who became King of Bohemia in 1619. There is no documentary evidence, but the house contained the coats of arms of both kings (*see* **Vyner Street**).

Boleyn Road N16 (Newington Green, Hackney). Formerly called The Back Road, and renamed in association with a royal hunting lodge at Newington Green which was visited by Henry VIII (1509–47) and possibly by his second queen, Anne Boleyn (*see* **King Henry's Walk**).

Bolingbroke Grove SW11 (Wandsworth). Runs beside Wandsworth Common, which was originally called West Heath and formed part of the manor of Battersea (*see* **Bolingbroke Walk**). Bolingbroke House stood at the junction with Belleville Road.

Bolingbroke Walk SW11 (Battersea, Wandsworth). Henry St John, Viscount Bolingbroke (*d* 1751), was lord of the manor of Battersea. The manor house, which stood near the N end of this land, was demolished in 1778.

Bolsover Street W1 (Marylebone, Cit. West.). Built on land belonging to the dukes of Portland, who also have the title of Baron Bolsover.

Bolt Court EC4 (Cit. Lond.). Uncertain, possibly associated with the *Bolt-in-Tun* tavern which stood nearby.

Bolton Crescent SE5 (Kennington Park, Lambeth). *See* **Farmer's Road**. James Bolton, city businessman, was a great-uncle of Thomas Farmer.

Bolton Road NW8 (Kilburn, Camden). Built from 1825 by Henry Bolton on a lease obtained from the Eyre family, the ground landlords.

Boltons, The SW10 (Kensington, Ken. Chel.). William Bolton is recorded as holding land here in 1538; it remained in the family until sold for building in the 1860s. **Bolton Gardens, The Little Boltons, Bolton Gardens Mews** and **South Bolton**

Gardens adjoin.

Bolton Street W1 (Mayfair, Cit. West.). Laid out on land belonging to Charles Powlett, Marquis of Winchester, who was created Duke of Bolton in 1689. He died at about the time the street was built (1699).

Bond Court EC4 (Cit. Lond.). Named from a 17th-century property owner, and formerly called Bond's Court.

Bondway SW8 (Vauxhall, Lambeth). Built by John and Sarah Bond who bought the land in 1766 and began building in 1778.

Bonhill Street EC2 (Finsbury, Islington). An early form of Bunhill (*see* **Bunhill Row**).

Bonner Road E2 (Bethnal Green, T. Ham.). Built on the former Bonner's Fields, site of an old house owned by the bishops of London and known by the name of one particular bishop. Edmund Bonner (*d* 1569) appears to have persecuted Catholics on behalf of Henry VIII and Protestants on behalf of Mary I. **Bonner Street** lies opposite.

Bonny Street NW1 (Camden Town, Camden). Built in the 1870s when two local businessmen – James Bonny, architect, and George Bonny, restaurant owner – had premises here.

Booth's Place W1 (Marylebone, Cit. West.). Joseph Booth of Wells Street held this land on lease in the 1760s.

Borland Road SE15 (Nunhead, Southwark). John Borland served on Camberwell vestry in 1870.

Borough High Street SE1 (Southwark). The 'borough' is the Borough of Southwark, of which this is the principal street. **Borough Road** approaches.

Boscastle Road NW5 (Highgate, Camden). From the name of the first house built here.

Boscobel Street (Lisson Grove, Cit. West.). By association with a public house (now demolished) called *The Royal Oak*, in commemoration of Charles II's escape from Parliamentarian forces in Boscobel woods. The king is said to have hidden in an oak tree during his flight after the battle of Worcester (1651). There is a **Boscobel Place** in Belgravia.

Boston Place NW1 (Marylebone, Cit. West.). Built on former wasteland called Boston Field, probably from a former occupier.

Boswell Street WC1 (Bloomsbury, Camden). Built *c*1710 by Edward Boswell, bricklayer, of St Giles-in-the-Fields parish. **Boswell Court** adjoins.

Botolph Lane EC3 (Cit. Lond.). The mediaeval church of St Botolph (now demolished) stood on Thames Street at this point. St Botolph was the patron of travellers; churches were dedicated to him near city gates and (as in this case) quaysides.

Boulcott Street E1 (Ratcliff, T. Ham.). John Boulcott raised a troop of militia, called the Ratcliff Volunteers, at the time of a threatened invasion by Napoleon.

Boundary Lane SE17 (Walworth, Southwark). Remnant, in two parts, of a lane which formerly extended from Camberwell Road to the present Albany Road Garden; it ran along the boundary between the parishes of Camberwell and Newington.

Boundary Road NW8 (St John's Wood, Camden/Cit. West.). Part of the N boundary of the mediaeval manors of Lilestone and Tyburn. The road is now part of the boundary between the modern districts of Camden and the City of Westminster.

Boundary Street E2 (Shoreditch, Hackney/T. Ham.). E boundary of the parish of St Leonard, Shoreditch, which runs along the course of the upper Walbrook. The street is also part of a modern district boundary. **Boundary Passage** adjoins. The old name was Cock Lane, possibly from cock-fighting. There was a *Cock-in-the-Hoop Inn* on Shoreditch High Street, backing on to this lane, in the 16th century.

Bourchier Street W1 (Soho, Cit. West.). Appears as Hedge Lane in 1664 and, after building, as Milk Alley in 1692, when presumably there was a dairy there. The street became Little Dean Street in 1838 and was renamed in 1937 in memory of the Rev. Basil Bourchier, rector of St Anne's, Soho, 1930–3.

Bourdon Street W1 (Mayfair, Cit. West.). The Bourdon or Burden family lived in Bourdon House here, on the corner with Davies Street, from *c* 1725.

Bourne Street SW1 (Belgravia, Cit. West./Ken. Chel.). Runs along the course of the River Westbourne which here runs S from Hyde Park to the Thames.

Bourne Terrace W2 (Paddington, Cit. West.). *See* **Westbourne Terrace**, of which this is a continuation.

Boutflower Road SW11 (Battersea, Wandsworth). The Rev. Henry Boutflower Verdon was appointed to the newly-developed Chatham Road District in the parish of St Mary's, Battersea. An iron church was built on Chatham Road in 1872, and dedicated to St Michael. Mr Boutflower Verdon was to have been the first vicar of a new parish church, St Mark's, Battersea Rise. In 1879 he died, at 33, before he could be inducted.

Bouverie Place W2 (Paddington, Cit. West.). Commemorates Lady Catherine Pleydell-Bouverie, who died in childbirth at Paddington in 1804. Her husband was heir to the earldom of Radnor, and **Radnor Place** is nearby. She was the object of much contemporary sympathy, and her husband was widely held to have contributed to her weak state by ill-treatment.

Bouverie Street EC4 (Fleet Street, Cit. Lond.). Built in the late 18th century and probably named after William Bouverie, Second Viscount Folkestone, who was created Earl of Radnor in 1765 (*see* **Pleydell Street**).

Bow Common Lane E3 (Bow Common, T. Ham.). An old lane running along the S and W border of the former Bow Common, which was completely built over from 1862.

Bowden Street SE11 (Kennington, Lambeth). Built on the former Cleaver estate (*see* **Cleaver Street**) which was bought by John Bowden in 1815 and held by the Bowden family until 1907.

Bowen Drive SE21 (Dulwich, Southwark). Named in 1872 after C.S.C. Bowen, a governor of Dulwich College.

Bow Lane EC4 (Cit. Lond.). The first recorded name (13th century) is Cordewanere Street, meaning street of leather-workers; under this name the lane extended down the present Garlick Hill. From the late 14th century that part which is now Bow

Lane was called Hosier Lane, meaning lane of stocking-makers. During the 16th century the name of Bow Lane came into use, after the church of St Mary-le-Bow at the N end; the 'bows' are the Norman arches supporting the building.

Bowles Road SE1 (Old Kent Road, Southwark). Built by the trustees of a local charity called Bowles's Charity, on land called Bowles's Five Acres.

Bowling Green Close SW15 (Putney, Wandsworth). Site of Bowling Green House, which was demolished in 1933. It was the last home of William Pitt, Prime Minister 1783–1801 and 1804–6. The house was built on a bowling green which had been famous since the early 18th century.

Bowling Green Lane EC1 (Clerkenwell, Islington). Site of one of several bowling greens in Clerkenwell. The district was a favourite place of recreation for London citizens from the early middle ages until the 19th century.

Bowling Green Place SE1 (Borough, Southwark). An enclosed area to the rear of Borough High Street and bounded S by Long Lane was laid out as a bowling green in the late 17th century; building on it began before 1750.

Bowling Green Street SE11 (Kennington, Lambeth). In the late 18th century this land was leased from the owner of the *Horns Tavern* (across Kennington Park Road) for use as a garden and bowling green; it became a tea-garden in 1820 and was built upon shortly afterwards.

Bowling Green Walk N1 (Hoxton, Hackney). This path originally approached a bowling green which is marked on a map of 1769.

Bow Road E3 (T. Ham.). Road

leading to the 'Bow' bridge, i.e. the bridge on stone arches, built in the reign of Henry I (1100–35) over the River Lea. Henry's queen, Matilda, ordered the bridge to be built, traditionally after an accident while fording the river.

Bow Street WC2 (Covent Garden, Cit. West.). Named from its curving shape, which was thought to resemble that of a bow.

Bowyer Place SE5 (Camberwell, Southwark). Commemorates the Bowyer family and their 17th-century mansion Bowyer House, which stood W of Camberwell Road. Sir Edmund Bowyer bought part of the manor of Camberwell Friern in 1581. His descendants the Bowyer-Smijths still held land in Camberwell in the late 19th century. Bowyer House was bought and demolished by the Chatham and Dover Railway Company in 1861.

Boxall Road SE21 (Dulwich, Southwark). Named in 1876, replacing a number of groups of cottages including Boxall Row. The Row might have been built by the local Boxalls who kept the *Greyhound Inn* in the 1870s.

Boyfield Street SE1 (Southwark). Built on land formerly a tenter ground belonging to one Josiah Boyfield, clothworker (*see* **Tenter Ground**).

Boyle Street W1 (Mayfair, Cit. West.). Part of the Burlington Estate. Richard Boyle, Third Earl of Burlington (*d* 1753), was the main English enthusiast for the work of the Italian architect Andrea Palladio. English Palladianism grew from his example. He rebuilt his own Burlington House N of Piccadilly in Palladian style. Chiswick House was also built for him in 1725, on land where his family already owned a

Jacobean mansion.

Boyson Road SE17 (Walworth, Southwark). A Victorian street named after Ambrose Boyson who represented the parish of St Mary, Newington, on the Metropolitan Board of Works when the Board was set up in 1855.

Brabant Court EC3 (Cit. Lond.). Called Brovens Court in the 17th century and Braben Court in the 18th. The name is probably a personal name which was corrupted to something more topical in the mercantile, Dutch-minded 1720s.

Brabazon Street E14 (Poplar, T. Ham.). Reginald Brabazon, Lord Brabazon and Twelfth Earl of Meath, founded the Metropolitan Gardens Association in 1882. This society aimed at converting the disused churchyards, burial-grounds and waste lots in central London into gardens and playgrounds. Lord Brabazon was an alderman of the London County Council in 1889–92 and 1898–1901. He was the first chairman of the London County Council Parks Committee.

Brabourn Grove SE15 (Peckham, Southwark). *See* **Bowyer Place**. Henry Brabourn or Brabourne, a 15th-century gentleman who was keeper of hawks to Edward IV, was connected to the Bowyers by marriage.

Bracken Avenue SW12 (Balham, Wandsworth). Built on the site of a large house called 'The Brackens'.

Brackley Street EC1 (Cit. Lond.). First recorded, N of the present line, on the former gardens of the Earl of Bridgewater's house; the earl was also Viscount Brackley (*see* **Bridgewater Square** and **Viscount Street**).

Bracknell Gardens NW3 (Hampstead, Camden). *See* **Canfield Gardens**. The Maryon-Wilson family owned property at Bracknell in Berkshire.

Bradbourne Street SW6 (Fulham, Hammersmith). One of a group of Kentish place names to commemorate an early settlement in Fulham of workers from Kent. The others are: **Chiddingstone** and **Chipstead** Streets and **Epple** and **Harbledown** Roads.

Braden Street W9 (Westbourne Green, Cit. West.). *See* **Grittleton Road**.

Bradmore Park Road W6 (Hammersmith). Built on open land formerly called Bradmore Fields which, in the 18th century, extended N from King Street to the present Goldhawk Road.

Brady Street E1 (Whitechapel, T. Ham.). George F. Brady was a member of Whitechapel District Board of Works in the 1890s. He became a Stepney borough councillor on the formation of the borough.

Braham Street E1 (Whitechapel, T. Ham.). The singer and composer John Braham (c1774–1856) made his début at the Royalty Theatre in Wellclose Square in 1787. Braham's talent was encouraged by Leoni, a musician of the Duke's Place synagogue. He sang at Drury Lane in 1796–7, and remained a popular operatic tenor for 40 years.

Braidwood Street SE1 (Tooley Street, Southwark). Captain James Braidwood was superintendent of the London insurance companies' small fire brigade. He was killed fighting a fire in Tooley Street, in 1861, when three acres of food and textile warehouses were burnt. The city went into mourning on the day he was buried, and his funeral procession was one-and-a-half miles long. Public reaction to the disaster, and the enormous losses of the fire, finally forced the government to provide an adequate, state-financed fire-brigade.

Braintree Street E2 (Stepney, T. Ham.). *See* **Hadleigh Street**.

Bramham Gardens SW5 (Kensington, Ken. Chel.). *See* **Knaresborough Place**.

Bramley Road W5 (N Kensington, Ken. Chel.). Developed by James Whitchurch of Southampton, who used Hampshire place names for his streets. Bramley is a village NE of Basingstoke.

Branch Place N1 (Hoxton, Shoreditch). *See* **Rosemary Street**.

Brandon Street SE16 (Rotherhithe, Southwark). Site of a market garden owned by Richard Brandon in 1805.

Brandon Street SE17 (Walworth, Southwark). The Brandon family and their heirs held parts of the manor of Walworth from 1789 until 1941, when their interest reverted to the Church Commissioners (*see* **Manor Place**).

Brantwood Road SE24 (Denmark Hill, Lambeth). The Victorian scholar John Ruskin, who lived nearby, also had a house called 'Brantwood' at Coniston, where he died in 1900. **Ruskin Walk** is nearby.

Brassey Square SW11 (Battersea, Wandsworth). Sir Thomas Brassey (1805–70) was an eminent engineer and railway contractor.

Braxted Park SW16 (Streatham Common, Lambeth). Built on land belonging to C.H. Copley Du Cane, who lived at Braxted Park, Witham, Essex. **Copley Park** runs parallel.

Brayards Road SE15 (Peckham, Southwark). A 19th-century street named after the builder.

Braybrook Street W12 (Wormwood Scrubs, Hammersmith). Robert Braybrook or Breybrook was Bishop of London 1382–*c*1404 and, as such, held the manor of Hammersmith.

Bray Place SW3 (Chelsea, Ken. Chel.). Sir Reginald Bray was lord of the manor of Chelsea in the time of Henry VII (1485–1509).

Bread Street EC4 (Cit. Lond.). Originally this street led to that part of the mediaeval **Cheapside** food market where the bakers sold their bread. As trade expanded, bakeries spread S along the line of the street.

Breakspears Road SE4 (Brockley, Lewisham). Built on the Tyrwhitt-Drake estate and preserving the name of a family property (*see* **Drake Road**).

Bream's Buildings EC4 (Cit. Lond./ Cit. West.). Originally a cul-de-sac which led E from Chancery Lane, the street was extended to Fetter Lane in 1877. The identity of Bream or Breem, whether he was the builder or property owner, is not known.

Brecknock Road N19, N7 (Camden Town, Camden/Islington). The road runs N from the *Brecknock Arms* public house, Camden Town. The Marquis of Camden was also (from 1812) Earl of Brecknock; Breconshire was the home of his mother's family (*see* **Camden High Street**).

Brenchley Gardens SE23 (Honor Oak, Southwark). William Brenchley was active in Camberwell local government. He was a vestryman in the 1890s and later served for many years on the borough council.

Brett Road E8 (Hackney). Named in 1874, probably in honour of Robert Brett, doctor and churchman, who died in that year. He was active in the creation of new parishes for the expanding population of N London in the 1840s and later.

Brewer Street W1 (Soho, Cit. West.). Named from 17th-century breweries (now demolished) established on the N side near Lexington Street by Thomas Ayres and Henry Davies. The E end was called Little Pulteney Street until 1937, by association with Great Pulteney Street nearby.

Brewery Road N7 (Caledonian Road, Islington). In 1869 Gerrish, Brown and Pragnell, brewers of vinegar, established themselves here. Crosse and Blackwell, also vinegar brewers, moved in later and built themselves a large new factory in 1881.

Brewhouse Lane E1 (Wapping, T. Ham.). Noted for breweries since the 18th century, as was the adjoining part of Wapping High Street.

Brewster Gardens W10 (Wormwood Scrubs, Hammersmith/Ken. Chel.). Sir David Brewster, Scottish physicist (*d*1868), was noted mainly for his work on the properties of light.

Brickfield Road E3 (Bromley, T. Ham.). The former brick-field in Devon's Road was advertised for sale in 1863 and described then as a working plant.

Brick Lane E1, E2 (Spitalfields, T. Ham.). First recorded in 1550 as passing a place where earth was dug to make bricks or tiles. Building

began in the 17th century.

Brick Street W1 (Mayfair, Cit. West.). Crosses the site formerly called Brick Close, a series of small fields dug for brick earth.

Bridewell Place EC4 (Cit. Lond.). Site of the Bridewell. The church of St Bride or Bridget was probably dedicated in the 11th century. The well beside it must have been much older; it was also associated with the saint, an abbess of Kildare who died *c*525 and inspired a cult almost as strong as that of St Patrick. Bridewell Palace near the church was built for Henry VIII in 1522 and abandoned in *c*1530. In 1552 Edward VI ordered that it be reopened as a house of correction and training for the able-bodied unemployed. It degenerated into a prison and was demolished in 1864.

Bridford Mews W1 (Marylebone, Cit. West.). Runs S from Devonshire Street, and is named after a Devonshire village.

Bridge Court SW11 (Wandsworth). A mediaeval hamlet called Bridge lay around a bridge across the Falcon Brook. It gave its name to a house and estate called Bridge Court, which belonged to the archbishops of York. This house, now demolished, was leased by the archbishops to the Battersea Enamel Works *c*1750 (*see* **York Place**).

Bridgeman Road N1 (Barnsbury, Islington). Properly Bridgman; the Rev. Arthur J. Bridgman was vicar of St Andrew's, Thornhill Square, in the 1870s and 1880s.

Bridgeman Street NW8 (St John's Wood, Cit. West.). William Bridgeman, First Viscount Bridgeman (*d* 1935), was London County Council member for Marylebone from 1904. He was Home Secretary

1922–4 and First Lord of the Admiralty 1924–9. He was president of the Marylebone Cricket Club at Lord's cricket ground, nearby, in 1931.

Bridgewater Square EC2 (Cit. Lond.). Site of the town house of the earls (later dukes) of Bridgewater. John Egerton, Fourth Earl of Bridgewater and Viscount Brackley, married here in 1664. The first Duke of Bridgewater was baptised at St Giles's, Cripplegate, in 1681. The house was burnt down in 1687. **Bridgewater Street** approaches.

Bridle Lane W1 (Soho, Cit. West.). Probably named from Abraham Bridle, who leased land here in the 1680s.

Bridstow Place W2 (Westbourne Grove, Cit. West.). Built by W.K. Jenkins, who also held property in Herefordshire, and named his streets accordingly. Bridstow is a village near Ross-on-Wye.

Brighton Grove SE14 (New Cross, Lewisham). Next to New Cross Gate Station, which was opened by the London and Croydon Railway in 1839 and later used by the London, Brighton and South Coast Railway.

Bright Street E14 (Poplar, T. Ham.). With **Cobden Street**, commemorates John Bright (1811–89) and Richard Cobden (1804–65), radical political and economic reformers who founded the Anti-Corn-Law League. The league achieved the repeal of the protectionist corn laws in 1846. Bright continued to be active for electoral reform. Cobden's main concerns were free trade and international arbitration.

Briset Street EC1 (Clerkenwell, Islington). In c1110 Jordan de Briset gave land here for the English headquarters of the Order of Knights of St John of Jerusalem (*see* **St John Street**). Briset also founded the local convent of St Mary. The street was formerly called Berkeley Street, from the residence there of the 16th-century courtier Sir Maurice Berkeley, his son and grandson.

Bristol Gardens W9 (Paddington, Cit. West.). *See* **Clifton Gardens**.

Bristol Gardens SW15 (Putney, R. upon T.). The Marquis of Bristol had a house here in the early 19th century. It passed into other hands and was demolished c1900.

Britannia Road SW6 (Fulham, Hammersmith). From a tavern here, first recorded c1770.

Britannia Street WC1 (Gray's Inn Road, Camden). Built from 1767 and given a patriotic name, the street was originally flanked by the equally patriotic George Street and Charlotte Street, from the reigning king and his consort.

Britannia Walk N1 (City Road, Shoreditch). The *Britannia* tavern on City Road is recorded in 1826. A female figure with a Roman name became popular as the symbol of Britain in the 17th century. Poets of the classical school preferred 'Britannia' to 'Britain'. The figure, complete with antique helmet, shield and trident (as ruling the sea), first appeared on coins in the reign of Charles II.

Britten Street SW3 (Chelsea, Ken. Chel.). *See* **St Luke's Street**.

Britton Street EC1 (Clerkenwell, Islington). Formerly Red Lion Street, from an inn sign, the street now commemorates Thomas Britton (*d* 1714), described as a seller of small coal, who became famous for staging and playing in concerts at his house, which stood on the corner of

Jerusalem Passage and Aylesbury Street nearby.

Brixton Hill SW2 (Brixton, Lambeth). Brixton is called Brixes stān in 1062 and Brissistan in 1230. The 'stān' would have been a stone marking the territory of a man called Brix or Briss, and the name is thought to have been a corruption of an OE name such as Beorhtsige.

Brixton Station Road SW9 (Brixton, Lambeth). Brixton Station at the W end of this road was opened by the London, Chatham and Dover Railway in 1862. In 1866 the company joined forces with the London, Brighton and South Coast Railway to operate a line from London Bridge through S London to Victoria. East Brixton Station at the E end of this road was opened to serve the new line.

Brixton Water Lane SW2 (Brixton, Lambeth). Formerly Watery Lane, indicating that the whole area was marshy. The surrounding land was called Rush Common (*see* **Rushcroft Road**) and this end of Brixton Hill was originally called Brixton Causeway. A tributary to the Effra also ran from Tulse Hill along the E part of the road.

Broadbent Street W1 (Mayfair, Cit. West.). Commemorates Sir William Broadbent (1835–1907), royal physician, who lived in Brook Street nearby.

Broadhurst Gardens NW6 (Hampstead, Camden). *See* **Canfield Gardens**. The Maryon-Wilson family owned property at Broadhurst in Sussex.

Broadley Street NW8 (Lisson Grove, Cit. West.) On the Portman estate. The family held property at Broadley Wood in Dorset (*see* **Portman Square**).

Broadmead SE6 (Catford, Lewisham). Built on part of the mediaeval manorial field called Broadmead, the broad river meadow.

Broad Sanctuary SW1 (Cit. West.). The right of sanctuary (freedom from arrest by secular authority) was attached to certain monastic or church precincts. At the Abbey of St Peter, Westminster, there was a stone-built refuge called St Peter's Sanctuary on the site of the present Guildhall. This broad street and another narrower way called **Little Sanctuary** approached it.

Broadstone Place W1 (Marylebone, Cit. West.). A Dorset place name, this was chosen by association with surrounding streets built on the Portman estate and named from Portman properties in Dorset: **Melbury Terrace, Rossmore Road, Melcombe Street** and **Stourcliffe Street**.

Broadwall SE1 (Lambeth/Southwark). Short surviving relic of a street which ran S to Boundary Row and formed the W boundary of the mediaeval manor of Paris Garden and the parish of Christchurch. The 'broad wall' was an earth dyke flanking a boundary ditch.

Broadway SW1 (Cit. West.). Formerly Broad Place, and self-explanatory.

Broadwick Street W1 (Soho, Cit. West.). Originally called Broad Street as far E as Berwick Street, the E end being called Edward Street after Edward Wardour (*see* **Wardour Street**). The whole street was renamed Broadwick in 1936, probably to avoid confusion with other 'Broad' streets.

Brockill Crescent SE4 (Brockley, Lewisham). Recorded in the 16th century as an alternative form of the name Brockley (*see* **Brockley Road**).

Brockley Hall Road SE4 (Lewisham).
Brockley Hall (the manor house)
stood at the junction of Brockley
Grove and **Brockley Road**.

Brockley Road SE4 (Lewisham).
Runs S through the mediaeval manor
of Brockley, called Brocele in the
12th century and sometimes Brockill.
The name probably derives from OE,
meaning Broca's wood.

Brockwell Park Gardens SE24 (Tulse
Hill, Lambeth). Runs beside
Brockwell Park, opened to the public
in 1892 and formed from the estate of
Brockwell Hall.

Brodrick Road SW17 (Wandsworth).
The Brodrick family acquired the
manor of Dunsford, S Wandsworth,
in 1664; it included the hamlet of
Garratt. Sir Alan Brodrick bought
the manor, which passed to the
descendants of his brother Thomas
Brodrick, Viscount Midleton.

Broken Wharf EC4 (Cit. Lond.).
Described as 'broken' or in bad
repair in the 14th century. Two users
of the wharf disputed whose duty it
should be to maintain it, with the
inevitable result.

Bromells Road SW4 (Clapham,
Lambeth). Preserves the name of a
point on the parish boundary
between Clapham and Battersea.
Bromells or Browmells Corner was at
the SE end of Wix's Lane. The
boundary continued as a ditch across
the common, the scene of frequent
parish disputes.

Bromley Hall Road E14 (Poplar,
T. Ham.). Bromley Hall here was
the manor house of Bromley
lower manor which belonged to
Christchurch Priory before the
Reformation. It then passed to

various owners before it came to
Joseph Foster, calico printer, in 1799.
He sold it in 1823 to Hugh MacIntosh
(*see* **Leven Road**).

Brompton   Road   SW1,   SW3
(Kensington, Ken. Chel.). Road
leading SW to Brompton, called
Bromton in the 14th century,
meaning the village where broom
grows. **Brompton Place** and **Square**
are nearby. **Old Brompton Road**
leads NE to Brompton.

Bromwich Avenue N6 (Highgate,
Camden). Formerly a footpath called
Bromwich Walk; Thomas Bromwich
bought an estate here, including
Holly Lodge, in 1770. A descendant
of his nephew, who inherited it, was
Anna Maria Chester. **Chester Road**
adjoins.

Bronti   Close   SE17   (Walworth,
Southwark).   Properly   Brontë;
Admiral Lord Nelson, hero of the
battle of Trafalgar (*see* **Trafalgar
Square**), was also Duke of Brontë,
Sicily.

Brookdale Road SE6 (Lewisham).
Part of a Victorian development in
the grounds of a house called
'Springfield'. The spring which had
named it was still there; it fed a brook
which flowed down Lewisham High
Street to join the Ravensbourne at
Lewisham Bridge. The brook was
covered over in 1855.

Brook   Drive   SE11   (Kennington,
Lambeth/Southwark). Runs along
the line of a brook which marked the
parish boundary between St Mary,
Lambeth, and St George the Martyr,
Southwark.

Brookehowse   Road   SE6   (Bell-
ingham, Lewisham). All the names
of the Bellingham estate are from
local history. This one appears on an
18th-century rent roll, where a James

Brookehowse is listed.

Brooke Road N16, E5 (Clapton, Hackney). Site of Brooke House, home of Henry Percy, Duke of Northumberland, (*d* 1537) and granted to Fulke Greville, Lord Brooke, in 1596. It was demolished in 1954. S lies the Hunsden estate. Henry Carey, Lord Hunsden, lived at Brooke House from 1578 and installed a magnificent plaster ceiling. He was Anne Boleyn's nephew and therefore first cousin to Elizabeth I. He sold Brooke House to Sir Rowland Hayward in 1583.

Brooke Street WC1 (Holborn, Camden). Led to the house purchased in 1619 by Fulke Greville, Lord Brooke. **Brooke's Court** is nearby.

Brookfield Park NW5 (Highgate, Camden). Built on a field of that name. The brook was the River Fleet, now underground. In **Brookfield Road**, Hackney, another brook ran into the River Lea.

Brook Green W6 (Hammersmith). Named from a brook which ran from Shepherd's Bush to Hammersmith Road as the Black Bull Ditch and then further S as the Parr Ditch.

Brook Mews North W2 (Bayswater, Cit. West.). The Bayswater or Westbourne Brook runs S into Hyde Park down the line of this street. **Smallbrook Mews** and **Upbrook Mews** are nearby.

Brookmill Road SE8 (Deptford, Lewisham). A replacement and extension of the former Mill Lane, from a watermill on Deptford Creek.

Brooksbank Street E9 (Hackney). Commemorates Stamp Brooksbank, a local landowner who built Hackney House in *c*1725. The house stood near the SE end of the present Lower Clapton Road; it was demolished in 1880.

Brooksby's Walk E9 (Homerton, Hackney). A large house called 'Brooksby Villa' stood N of the junction with Homerton Grove. The Brooksby family are recorded as landowners in Hackney in 1745.

Brook Street W2 (Bayswater, Cit. West.). Near the entry of the Westbourne Brook into Hyde Park (*see* **Westbourne Terrace**).

Brook Street W1 (Mayfair, Cit. West.). The Tyburn Brook flowed SE across the line of this street, approximately down the line of South Molton Street.

Broomfield Street E14 (Poplar, T. Ham.). Built on a former field of that name.

Broomhouse Lane SW6 (Fulham, Hammersmith). A group of cottages called 'Broomhouses' stood at the S end in the 18th century, named from broom bushes that grew nearby. Broomhouse Road approaches. There was also a large house, Broom House (*see* **Sulivan Road**).

Broomwood Road SW11 (Clapham, Wandsworth). Runs across the site of Broomfield Lodge (later called 'Broomwood House'), the home of William Wilberforce, campaigner for the abolition of the slave trade. The house stood at the junction with Wroughton Road.

Broughton Street SW8 (Battersea, Wandsworth). On Philip Flower's Park Town estate (*see* **St Philip's Street**). Flower had extensive Australian business interests; this name may compliment the first Bishop of Australia, W.G. Broughton, who preached his first sermon in Australia at St Philip's church, Sydney.

Brown Hart Gardens W1 (Mayfair, Cit. West.). Originally two streets: Brown Street built by John Brown, bricklayer, in 1738, and its contemporary Hart Street, named either from a personal name or from an inn sign. The two were joined in 1936.

Browning Close W9 (Paddington, Cit. West.). Near that part of the Regent's Canal called Little Venice. The poet Robert Browning lived near Little Venice after the death of his wife Elizabeth in 1861. **Robert Close** and **Elizabeth Close** run parallel. The former Elizabeth Barrett had lived as a semi-invalid at 50 Wimpole Street, whence she eloped with the poet in 1846. **Browning Mews** runs behind Wimpole Street. Browning himself was born in South London in 1812 and baptised in the Congregational Chapel in the present **Browning Street** in Walworth. The chapel was later called Browning Hall and was known as a centre for relief work.

Brownlow Street WC1 (Holborn, Camden). Built by William Brownlow (*d* 1675) on land originally held by his great-grandfather John Brownlow in the 16th century. **Brownlow Mews** is further N, on land held by the Doughty family, into which William's daughter Elizabeth married. Their descendants built **Doughty Street**.

Brown Street W1 (Marylebone, Cit. West.). An early 19th-century street on the Portman estate, named after the builder.

Broxash Road SW11 (Clapham Common, Wandsworth). On the site of a large house, said to have been in the Chinese style, called 'Broxash'; it was demolished *c*1910.

Bruce Grove N17 (Tottenham, Haringey). Tottenham Castle nearby is now called 'Bruce Castle'. The manor of Tottenham passed to the

Scottish lord Robert de Bruis in 1254. It was confiscated by Edward I in 1306 when de Bruis's descendant Robert Bruce claimed the Scottish throne.

Brudenell Road SW17 (Tooting, Wandsworth). The widow of Lord Charles William Brudenell-Bruce left money to build All Saints' church (on the corner with Franciscan Road) in 1901.

Brunel Road SE16 (Rotherhithe, Southwark). Runs beside the S end of the Thames Tunnel from Wapping to Rotherhithe, which was designed by Sir Marc Brunel (*d* 1849). It was intended as a carriage-way but was used only by pedestrians until it became part of the London underground railway system in 1865. Work began in 1825 and was finished, after several disasters, only in 1843. The engineer's son, Isambard Kingdom Brunel, worked on the tunnel 1825–8.

Brunel Street E16 (Lea Valley, Newham). Commemorates the engineer Isambard Kingdom Brunel (*d* 1859), who was associated with this part of the Thames, if not specifically with Canning Town, through three of his ships. The paddle and steam ship *Great Eastern* was built at Millwall; the paddle steamer *Great Western* and steam ship *Great Britain*, built in Bristol, were fitted out at Blackwall.

Brune Street E1 (Spitalfields, T. Ham.). Walter Brune and his wife founded the nearby hospital of St Mary in *c*1200 (*see* **Spital Square**).

Brunswick Road E14 (Poplar, T. Ham.). Originally approached the Brunswick Dock, built by a ship-owner named Perry in 1789 and named as a compliment to the reigning royal house (*see* **Brunswick Square**). This small dock was later enlarged and incorporated into the East India Dock system.

Brunswick Square WC1 (Bloomsbury, Camden). Laid out in the late 18th century on land belonging to the Thomas Coram Foundation in order to raise money for their hospital (*see* **Coram Street**). Named as a compliment to the reigning royal house of Hanover, as Brunswick in Hanover was their second capital city.

Brushfield Street E1 (Spitalfields, T. Ham.). The E end was built c1672–3 and called Paternoster Row. The W extension to Bishopsgate (1784–6) was called Union Street. In 1870 the whole was renamed after Thomas Brushfield, local representative on the Metropolitan Board of Works 1865–75.

Bruton Lane W1 (Mayfair, Cit. West.). Built c1727 on land belonging to Lord Berkeley of Stratton (*see* **Berkeley Square**) and named from his Dorset estate. **Bruton Place** and **Street** adjoin.

Bryanston Square W1 (Marylebone, Cit. West.). Built c1810 on the Portman estate (*see* **Portman Square**). The family owned property at Bryanston, Dorset. **Bryanston Place** and **Mews** approach. **Bryanston Street** is nearby.

Buckingham Palace Road SW1 (Cit. West.). Leads to Buckingham Palace, built for George IV (1819–30) by John Nash on the site of a house originally built for Lord Goring in 1640 and later sold to the Duke of Buckingham. George III bought it as Buckingham House in 1762, and Londoners still call it 'Buck House'. **Buckingham Gate, Buckingham Place** and **Palace Street** adjoin.

Buckingham Street WC2 (Strand,

Cit. West.). The Duke of Buckingham sold his house on this site for development in the 1670s. He made it a condition that the streets built on the land should commemorate his name and titles. The others are **George** (Court), **Villiers** (Street), Duke (Street, now gone) and the former Of Alley, which is now **York Place**.

Bucklersbury EC4 (Cit. Lond.). Called Bokerelesbury in the 13th century, meaning the 'burgh' or small settlement of the Bukerel or Bucherel family who held property in London from c1100.

Buckmaster Road SW11 (Battersea, Wandsworth). Commemorates a local citizen, J.C. Buckmaster, who defended local footpaths and common land in the 1860s. It is estimated that Battersea, Clapham and Wandsworth lost over 500 acres of common land in the late 19th century, most of it to builders and railway companies. What remains was preserved only by strenuous local effort.

Bucknall Street WC2 (St Giles's, Camden). Built on land belonging to Sir John Hanmer, later Lord Hanmer (1809–81). His mother was the former Miss Arabella Bucknall or Bucknell.

Buckner Road SW2 (Brixton, Lambeth). Dr Buckner was Bishop of Chichester 1798–1824. He was the main promoter of the national thanksgiving after the allied victory at Waterloo in 1815; this took the form of building the 'Waterloo' churches, of which nearby St Matthew's, Brixton, is one.

Buck Street NW1 (Camden Town, Camden). *See* **Hawley Road**.

Budge Row EC4 (Cit. Lond.). Lane off **Cannon Street** which was the centre of the drapers' trade in the late middle ages. 'Budge' was a particular type of lambswool.

Buer Road SW6 (Fulham, Hammersmith). Built on land belonging to William Beaumont Buer of Rivercourt Road.

Bulinga Street SW1 (Cit. West.). Built in the area S of Thorney Island which was covered by the Bulinga Fen or marsh in Saxon times (*see* **Thorney Street**).

Bull Alley SE1 (Upper Ground, Southwark). From an old inn called *The Bull in the Pound*.

Buller Square SE15 (Peckham, Southwark). Probably commemorates General Sir Redvers Buller (1839–1908). His most famous, if controversial, command was in Natal during the Boer War of 1899–1900.

Bull Inn Court WC2 (Strand, Cit. West.). Originally led to the *Bull Inn*, now demolished, which stood on the Strand.

Bullivant Street E14 (Poplar, T. Ham.). W.P. Bullivant was London County Council member for Poplar from 1889.

Bull's Gardens SW3 (Chelsea, Ken. Chel.). *See* **Hasker Street**.

Bull's Head Passage EC3 (Cit. Lond.). Uncertain, probably named from the sign of a bull's head, but whether this denoted an inn or a shop is unknown.

Bull Wharf Lane EC4 (Cit. Lond.). Originally led to Bull Wharf, recorded here on the Thames in 1666 and probably named from an inn sign.

Bulstrode Street W1 (Marylebone, Cit. West.). *See* **Bentinck Street**. The

Bentinck family also held Bulstrode Park, Buckinghamshire, where Hans Willem Bentinck, First Duke of Portland and favourite of William III, died in 1709. **Bulstrode Place** runs parallel.

Bulwer Street W12 (Shepherd's Bush, Hammersmith). Edward George Lytton Bulwer, novelist, lived at Craven Cottage in Fulham, 1840–6; he died in 1873. His brother Henry Lytton Bulwer, a diplomat who was created Lord Dalling, died in 1872 and is commemorated in **Dalling Road**.

Bunhill Row EC1 (Finsbury, Islington). Runs beside Bunhill Fields – a corruption of Bonehill Fields – where, in 1549, waggonloads of bones from the charnel house at St Paul's Cathedral were deposited. The Fields became a burial-ground for dissenters in the late 17th century.

Bunhouse Place SW1 (Pimlico, Cit. West.). Site of the old Bun House which sold Chelsea buns; it was established in the early 18th century and demolished in 1839.

Burbage Close SE1 (Great Dover Street, Southwark). The actor-manager Richard Burbage and his brother Cuthbert built the Globe Theatre on nearby Bankside in 1599. Shakespeare was closely associated with the Globe, which was demolished in 1644. Richard Burbage joined the Earl of Leicester's players (later called the Lord Chamberlain's Company) in 1588. He enjoyed great popular success as a Shakespearian tragic lead, and also played Jonson, Webster and Beaumont and Fletcher.

Burbage Road SE21, SE24 (Dulwich, Southwark). *See* **Burbage Close**. Burbage was the main rival to Edward Alleyn (*see* **Alleyn Park**).

This road is on Alleyn's Dulwich manor estate.

Burchell Road SE15 (Peckham, Southwark). Named in 1868 and probably laid out by Burchells, builders active in this area at the time.

Burder Road N1 (Kingsland, Islington). Probably commemorates the Rev. George Burder (1752–1832), an active and highly-regarded clergyman. He was secretary to the London Missionary Society 1803–27. He lived in Colebrooke Row, Islington.

Burdett Road E3, E14 (Limehouse, T. Ham.). Named in honour of Baroness Burdett-Coutts, Victorian millionairess and philanthropist, and her work for the London poor (*see* **Baroness Road**).

Burford Road SE6 (Perry Hill, Lewisham). Frances Burford was a benefactor to the parish of Lewisham. In 1871 she left £200 to be invested, the income to be given to six poor men and six poor women each Christmas Eve.

Burgess Hill NW2 (W Hampstead, Camden). Laid out in 1903 by the landowner, Major Ardwick Burgess, whose father Henry Weech Burgess had built **Weech Road** in 1880. **Ardwick Road** adjoins.

Burghley Road NW5 (Kentish Town, Camden). *See* **Lady Margaret Road**.

Burgh Street N1 (Islington). James Burgh, writer and schoolmaster, kept an academy at Stoke Newington and later at Newington Green. He published a famous 'no popery' tract, *Britain's Remembrancer*, in 1746 and died in Islington in 1775.

Burgon Street EC4 (Cit. Lond.).

Formerly New Street, and renamed in 1885 in honour of Dean Burgon of St Paul's Cathedral.

Burgundy Street SE1 (Old Kent Road, Southwark). Possibly by association with adjoining **Humphrey Street**. The relations of Henry V with the dukedom of Burgundy were crucial to his fortunes in the French war.

Burleigh Street WC2 (Strand, Cit. West.). Site of a house built by William Cecil, Lord Burleigh, Secretary of State to Elizabeth I (*see* **Exeter Street**).

Burlington Arcade W1 (Piccadilly, Cit. West.). Runs beside Burlington House, built for the first Earl of Burlington in 1668. The arcade was added by Lord George Cavendish who bought the house in 1815. Charlotte, only daughter and heiress of the last Lord Burlington, had married a Cavendish.

Burlington Gardens W1 (Mayfair, Cit. West.). *See* **Old Burlington Street**.

Burlington Lane W4 (Chiswick, Hounslow). The first Lord Burlington bought Chiswick House, N of this lane, in 1628. The building now known as Chiswick House was built as a connoisseur's piece for the third earl in 1725; it was designed as a pavilion, not as a dwelling house. The old Chiswick House and estate belonged to the earls of Burlington until 1753 when it passed to a daughter who had become Duchess of Devonshire (*see* **Duke Road**).

Burlington Road SW6 (Fulham, Hammersmith). Formerly Back Lane, as running behind Fulham High Street. Mr Roy of Old Burlington Street ran a school here, which he called Burlington House, in the middle of the 18th century.

Burnsall Street SW3 (Chelsea, Ken. Chel.). Commemorates Martha Burnsall, a parish benefactor who died in 1805.

Burns Road SW11 (Battersea, Wandsworth). John Burns (1858–1943), radical politician, was MP for Battersea 1892–1918. He began work at Price's Candle Factory in Battersea when he was ten years old, was educated in Battersea and later lived on the North Side, Clapham Common.

Burntwood Lane SW17 (Earlsfield, Wandsworth). Runs NE to the site of Burntwood Grange, an 18th-century house famous for its gardens. **Burntwood Close** and **Burntwood Grange Road** mark the site.

Burrows Mews SE1 (Blackfriars Road, Southwark). Originally ran behind a group of houses called Burrows Buildings, built c1770. The builder may have been related to the Rev. John Burrows, rector of Christ Church in 1770–87.

Bursar Street SE1 (Bermondsey, Southwark). *See* **Magdalen Street**.

Burton Street WC1 (Bloomsbury, Camden). Commemorates the architect James Burton who worked on the Foundling Hospital estate and on the Bedford estate at the end of the 18th century. **Burton Place** adjoins.

Burwood Place W2 (Bayswater, Cit. West.). *See* **Frederick Close**.

Bury Place WC1 (Bloomsbury, Camden). A shortened version of Bloomsbury (*see* **Bloomsbury Street**).

Bury Street EC3 (Cit. Lond.). Built on land which belonged to the Abbot of Bury or St Edmundsbury before the Reformation (*see* **Bevis Marks**).

Bury Street SW1 (St James's, Cit. West.). Built on the estate of Henry Jermyn, Earl of St Albans and Baron Jermyn of St Edmundsbury (now called Bury St Edmunds; *see* **Jermyn Street**).

Busby Place NW5 (Kentish Town, Camden). On the estate of Christchurch Cathedral, Oxford. Dr Richard Busby (1606–95) was a student of Christchurch College and a benefactor to the cathedral. As headmaster of Westminster School he boasted at one time that he had educated 16 of the current bishops. He had a reputation for severity as a schoolmaster.

Bushey Hill Road SE5 (Peckham, Southwark). Properly Bushy; site of Bushy Hill House, demolished in 1877.

Bush Lane EC4 (Cit. Lond.). Recorded in the 15th century as Le Busshlane, or the lane passing the tavern with a bush sign. The bush was a common inn sign and derived from the ancient practice of hanging up green branches outside to advertise that a fresh brew was ready.

Butcher Row E14 (Ratcliff, T. Ham.). An old name, from resident butchers. Skilled tradesmen from the provinces were unable to gain admission to the City guilds or to practise their trade within the walls. They were often drawn to the port of London as the next most profitable place.

Bute Gardens W6 (Brook Green, Hammersmith). Site of a house called 'Bute House'.

Bute Street SW7 (S Kensington, Ken.

Burlington Arcade

Chel.). Site of a house called 'Bute House' which is recorded here in the 1840s.

Butler Place SW1 (Cit. West.). Nicholas Butler founded almshouses here in 1675. The buildings were demolished and the charity incorporated into the Westminster United Almshouses in 1881.

Butterwick W6 (Hammersmith). Butterwick House stood opposite the parish church, and it was originally the manor house of an estate called Butterwick Manor. A 14th-century Fulham landowner is recorded as 'John Doget de Boterwyk'. Most of the house was demolished in 1836; an 18th-century addition called 'Bradmore House' was demolished in 1913, except for its façade which was incorporated into the garages of the London General Omnibus Company. It is still standing as part of London Transport's Hammersmith Garage.

Buxton Street E1 (Spitalfields, T. Ham.). *See* **Hanbury Street**. Sir Thomas Buxton joined Truman, Hanbury, Buxton and Company *c*1800.

Byng Place WC1 (Bloomsbury, Camden). Part of the Bedford estate. George Byng, Viscount Torrington, was father-in-law to the sixth Duke of Bedford.

Byng Street E14 (Isle of Dogs, T. Ham.). John Byng, created Baron Strafford in 1835 and Earl of Strafford in 1847, owned land here. **Strafford Street** runs parallel. The Byngs were connected to a branch of the Wentworth family who owned Stepney manor in the 17th century.

Byward Street EC3 (Cit. Lond.). Named from the nearby Byward Tower, which is part of the Tower of London.

Bywater Street SW3 (Chelsea, Ken. Chel.). Uncertain, although a Thomas Bywater did hold property in Chelsea in the mid-19th century.

C

Cabbell Street NW1 (Marylebone, Cit. West.). George Cabbell bought this part of the manor of Lilestone in 1792; the street was built by his family at a later date (*see* **Lilestone Street**).

Cable Street E1 (Whitechapel, T. Ham.). On a map of 1703 the Ratcliff end of this street appears, unnamed, with 'A Rope Walk' indicated parallel with its N side. By *c*1750 Cable Street appears on the section between Back Church Lane and Golding Street, with 'A Rope Walk' indicated running N. In Rocque's map of 1769 the other sections are called Rosemary Lane (W to the Minories), Knockfergus (E to Cannon Street Road) and, further E, Bluegates Fields, Sun Tavern Fields and Brook Street. The name of the central section which was later applied to the whole street is probably derived from the manufacture of ships' cables on the rope walks.

Cabul Road SW11 (Battersea, Wandsworth). Properly Kabul, capital of Afghanistan. Neighbouring **Candahar Road** is properly Kandahar. The British, nervous of Russian infiltration along the NW frontier of India, fought the Afghans (whose ruler favoured Russia) in 1878–9. This war was followed by a further expedition and Sir Frederick Roberts's 23-day march, with 10,000 men, from Kabul to Kandahar. **Afghan Road** and **Khyber Road** (from Afghanistan's Khyber Pass) adjoin.

Cadiz Street SE17 (Walworth, Southwark). The combined French and Spanish fleets defeated by Nelson at Trafalgar were gathered before the battle in the harbour of

Cadiz (*see* **Trafalgar Square**).

Cadogan Square SW1 (Chelsea, Ken. Chel.). Laid out by the architect Henry Holland on land which he leased from Lord Cadogan after 1753. **Cadogan Gardens, Gate, Lane, Place** and **Street** adjoin (*see* **Sloane Street**).

Cahir Street E14 (Isle of Dogs, T. Ham.). *See* **Glengall Grove**.

Calais Street SE5 (Camberwell, Lambeth). The Minet family who owned the land came originally from Calais.

Caledonian Road N7, N1 (Islington). The Caledonian Asylum, a home for the children of Scottish servicemen who had been killed or disabled, was established here in 1815, at the close of the Napoleonic Wars.

Cale Street SW3 (Chelsea, Ken. Chel.). Commemorates Judith Cale, past benefactor to the parish of St Luke's, Chelsea.

Callow Street SW3 (Chelsea, Ken. Chel.). The Callows were a family of builders active on the Chelsea manor estate from *c*1840, when John Callow opened a builder's yard in Royal Hospital Road.

Calthorpe Street WC1 (Gray's Inn Road, Camden). Built in two sections, 1821–6 and 1842–9, on the Calthorpe estate. This land, which is thought to have been part of the manor of Portpool, passed through various hands until it came to Sir Henry Gough-Calthorpe, son of Sir Henry Gough of Edgbaston and Barbara Calthorpe of Elvetham; he added his mother's family name to his own in 1788. He was made Baron Calthorpe in 1796. The land was largely developed by his son George, Third Baron Calthorpe (1787–1851) (*see* **Gough Square**).

Calton Avenue SE21 (Dulwich, Southwark). *See* **Court Lane**.

Calvert Avenue E2 (Bethnal Green, T. Ham.). *See* **Camlet Street**.

Calvert's Buildings SE1 (Southwark). Felix Calvert, local brewer, is recorded as operating here in the late 18th century.

Calvin Street E1 (Spitalfields, T. Ham.). John Calvin was the founder of the religious sect to which many of the French Protestant community of Spitalfields belonged. Calvin, unlike Luther, believed that some were predestined for salvation and some for damnation. He also believed that the Church should govern the state and, in company with other Protestant reformers, he ruled the city of Geneva as a Protestant community, controlled by the disciplines of the Church, from 1541 until his death in 1564.

Camberwell Glebe SE5 (Camberwell, Southwark). A glebe is land allotted to the parish church for the use of its clergy and forming part of their benefice. In the early middle ages the priest literally lived on the glebe by cultivating it. By a private act of parliament of 1813 the vicar of Camberwell received the right to build on parts of his glebeland, and this area N of Camberwell Church Street was gradually developed (*see* **Camberwell Road**).

Camberwell New Road SE5 (Lambeth). Built in 1818 and so-called to distinguish it from the old **Camberwell Road**.

Camberwell Road SE5 (Camberwell, Southwark). Runs S to Camberwell from the City of London. The name is given as Cambrewelle in the *Domesday Book*. 'Welle' is a mere, but the first part of the word is obscure; it could be from an OE word for wildfowl. **Camberwell Green** and **Grove** adjoin.

Camberwell Station Road SE5 (Camberwell, Southwark). Site of Camberwell New Road Station, one of the first opened by the London, Chatham and Dover Railway Company on their line from Herne Hill to the Elephant and Castle in 1862. In 1864 the line was extended to run from Blackfriars Station through W Dulwich to Sydenham.

Cambridge Circus WC2 (Charing Cross Road, Cit. West.). In 1887 the new **Charing Cross Road**, running S through this junction, was opened by George, Duke of Cambridge, cousin to Queen Victoria.

Cambridge Heath Road E1, E2 (Bethnal Green, T. Ham.). Recorded in 1275 as crossing the grazing land called Camprichthesheth, which was called Cambridge Heath by the end of the 16th century. Camprichthe is thought more likely to have been a personal name or nickname than an adjective describing the heath. Cambridge is a later corruption of it.

Cambridge Place W8 (Kensington, Ken. Chel.). Commemorates Adolphus Frederick, Duke of Cambridge, who died in 1850 (*see* **Cambridge Terrace**).

Cambridge Square W2 (Bayswater, Cit. West.). Built on land left to the University of Cambridge by Lady Stanley, Countess of Richmond, mother of Henry VII. She held Paddington manor, and was benefactor to both Oxford and Cambridge universities. **Oxford Square** is nearby.

Cambridge Terrace NW1 (Regent's Park, Camden). Part of John Nash's Regent's Park scheme (*see* **Regent Street**). This street is named from the Prince Regent's younger brother Adolphus Frederick, Duke of Cambridge (*d* 1850). **Cambridge Gate** and **Cambridge Gate Mews** are nearby.

Camden High Street NW1 (Camden Town, Camden). High or principal street of the district laid out as a residential development by Lord Camden, between *c*1790 and 1840. The English historian William Camden, who died in 1623, had a house in N Surrey which was later bought by the Pratt family. Charles Pratt received an earldom, and took his title from the house. His son was created Marquis Camden in 1812. **Camden Passage** and **Camden Walk** in Islington were named in compliment to the family, but neither are on their land. **Camden Lane, Mews, Park Road, Road, Square** and **Street** are all on the marquis's estate.

Camera Place SW10 (Chelsea, Ken. Chel.). Recorded in 1830 as Camera Square, and derived from the Latin word *camera*, meaning a room or chamber. The reason for the name is unknown: the special, optical meaning of *camera* is possible, since the word was in use in the early 17th century to describe the projecting apparatus called *camera obscura*, a device which had become very popular by the 18th century.

Camlet Street E2 (Bethnal Green, T. Ham.). A textile name, and one of a group chosen by association with the Huguenot textile industry in this area (*see* **Nantes Passage**). Nearby **Calvert** (Avenue), **Montclare** (Street) and

Turville (Street) are Huguenot names.

Camomile Street EC3 (Cit. Lond.). An old name which, taken with **Wormwood Street** opposite, would suggest that the land immediately inside the City walls produced a profusion of wild plants in the middle ages. Both camomile and wormwood are medicinally useful, so those places where they grew would have been of interest.

Campbell Street W2 (Paddington, Cit. West.). Captain Alexander Campbell of the East India Company lived on the N side of Paddington Green in the mid-18th century.

Campden Hill W8 (Kensington, Ken. Chel.). Sir Baptist Hicks, merchant, built a house here in 1612. This became known as 'Campden House' when he was created Lord Campden of Chipping Campden in 1628. The house is now demolished. Campden House Court is on the site. **Campden Hill Place** and **Square**, and **Campden Street** are nearby.

Camperdown Street E1 (Whitechapel, T. Ham.). Replaced Duncan Street, and commemorates Adam Duncan, Viscount Duncan of Camperdown (1731–1804). A naval officer, he distinguished himself in a victory over the Napoleonic Dutch fleet off Camperdown in 1797; the Dutch lost nine ships, the English none.

Campsbourne, The N8 (Hornsey, Haringey). A stream called the Campsbourne (c.f. Westbourne and Tyburn) ran through this land from Muswell Hill into Tottenham. The land, when open ground, was therefore called Campsbourne Fields in the 17th century. A large house was later built here and called 'Campsbourne Lodge'. It was demolished when this road was laid out. **Campsbourne Road** is nearby.

Campshill Road SE13 (Lewisham). Runs next to the grounds of Campshill House, now demolished. The house was built on land referred to as Kemphill in the 16th century.

Canada Way W12 (Shepherd's Bush, Hammersmith). *See* **Australia Road**.

Canadian Avenue SE6 (Catford, Lewisham). Commemorates Canadian soldiers camped nearby during World War I.

Canal Grove SE15 (Peckham, Southwark). The Surrey Canal ran parallel with the NW side of this street. 'Grove' is a Victorian builder's euphemism (*see* **Canal Head**).

Canal Head SE15 (Peckham, Southwark). An arm of the Surrey Canal terminated here; it was built *c*1810 and is now closed. This branch ran NNW to join the main canal E of Trafalgar Avenue (*see* **Canal Street**).

Canal Street SE5 (Peckham, Southwark). This street led to the head of the Surrey Canal (*see* **Canal Head**), which was built to link the Surrey Commercial Docks in Rotherhithe with an inland waterway system in Surrey. It never ran further than this point, but its wharfs did provide a stimulus to small business all along its route.

Candahar Road SW11 (Battersea, Wandsworth). *See* **Cabul Road**.

Candover Street W1 (Marylebone, Cit. West.). Surrounding streets on the Duke of Portland's estate are named from his properties in Hampshire. This is a Hampshire village name, and was chosen by association.

Canfield Gardens NW6 (Hampstead, Camden). Built on land owned by the Maryon-Wilson family, who inherited the lordship of the manor of Hampstead in 1821. Streets on their estate were named from places or properties in Essex, Berkshire and Sussex, with which the family was connected. Canfield is in Essex.

Canning Place W8 (Kensington, Ken. Chel.). George Canning, Foreign Secretary 1822–7 and Prime Minister in 1827, lived at Gloucester Lodge nearby, which he bought from the Duchess of Gloucester's heiress.

Cannon Hill NW6 (W Hampstead, Camden). Charles Cannon, a 19th-century India merchant, built Kidderpore Hall nearby and named it from trade associations with Calcutta. The house is now Westfield College, approached by **Kidderpore Avenue** and **Gardens**.

Cannon Place NW3 (Hampstead, Camden). From Cannon Hall, a Georgian house with cannon fixed outside the gates as bollards. **Cannon Lane** approaches.

Cannon Row SW1 (Cit. West.). Former lodgings of the canons of St Stephen's, the chapel within the royal palace of Westminster. The chapel was founded in the late 12th century and rebuilt in 1347. Its college of clergy was suppressed under Edward VI (1547–53) and it became a meeting place for parliament.

Cannon Street EC4 (Cit. Lond.). Contraction of the 14th-century name Candlewick Street, which in turn was a corruption of Candelewrithstrete, meaning the street of candle-makers. There has never been any connection with gunfounders, nor any recorded use of ground here for artillery practice. The mediaeval street only extended

E from Walbrook; the present section from Walbrook to St Paul's is 19th-century.

Cannon Street Road E1 (Whitechapel, T. Ham.). The S end was called Cannon Street in the 18th century, from fortifications built along its line during the Civil War of 1642–9. The **New Road** was built S from Whitechapel Road in the mid-18th century, and the linking section between was called the Cannon Street Road (i.e., road adjoining Cannon Street). This type of name has died out elsewhere in London, where similar street extensions and approaches were once known as the Goswell Street Road, Old Street Road, St John's Street Road etc.

Canonbury Road N1 (Islington). Road to Canonbury, the manor or former Saxon 'burgh' belonging to the canons of St Bartholomew's Priory, Smithfield. Canonbury Tower was built for the prior in the early 16th century. The manor was given to the canons by Ralph de Berners (*d* 1297). **Canonbury Avenue, Grove, Park, Place, Square** and **Street** are nearby.

Canon Street N1 (Islington). *See* **Prebend Street**.

Cantelowes Road NW1 (Kentish Town, Camden). Commemorates the Norman family of Cantelowe or Cantlowe, originally called Canteloup. who gained the surrounding manor under William I (1066–85). The family held it until 1517. The manor extended S from Highgate Village to the present St Pancras Goods Yard, whence the boundary ran S again to Crowndale Road; the manor house, now demolished, stood SE of the junction of the present Camden Road and College Street.

Canterbury Grove SE27 (W Norwood, Lambeth). Laid out from 1810 on land which was formerly part of Lambeth manor and, as such, the property of the archbishops of Canterbury.

Canton Street E14 (Limehouse, T. Ham.). *See* **Oriental Street**.

Capel Court EC2 (Cit. Lond.). Commemorates a City merchant, Sir William Capel, draper and Lord Mayor. He died in 1515 and was buried in St Bartholomew-by-the-Exchange, which used to stand nearby (*see* **Bartholomew Lane**).

Capener's Close SW1 (Belgravia, Cit. West.). John Capener is recorded as the builder of the original yard, *c*1825; he used it for his business as carpenter and undertaker.

Capland Street NW8 (Lisson Grove, Cit. West.). *See* **Bickenhall Street**.

Capper Street WC1 (Bloomsbury, Camden). Site of part of a farm which was held by the Capper family as tenants of the Duke of Bedford. A Christopher Capper is mentioned as farming it in 1693. A house built in 1776 survived behind Heal's shop into the 20th century; Heal's bought it in 1840 and demolished it *c*1914. The land extended N to the present Euston Road and E to Woburn Square.

Capstan Square E14 (Isle of Dogs, T. Ham.). One of a group inspired by shipping: the others are **Tiller Road, Starboard Way, Crew Street** and **Launch Street**. Across the river from Crew Street there is a similar group in Deptford: **Leeway, Longshore, Foreshore** and **Windlass Place**. On a sailing ship the capstan was pushed round by muscle-power to haul in the heavy cables; it became almost a symbol of the seaman's life.

Carburton Street W1 (Marylebone, Cit. West.). Built on land belonging to the dukes of Portland, who had also inherited property at Carburton and Clipstone, both in Nottinghamshire. **Clipstone Street** runs parallel.

Cardinal Bourne Street SE1 (Newington, Southwark). Francis Alphonsus Bourne was Roman Catholic Bishop of Southwark 1897– 1903, Archbishop of Westminster from 1903 and a Cardinal from 1911. He died in 1935.

Cardinal Cap Alley SE1 (Southwark). The 'Cardinal Cap' or 'Cardinal's Hat' inn is first recorded here in 1588; which cardinal is honoured is not known, but there was extensive church property in Southwark before the Reformation, and the name may date from that time.

Cardington Street NW1 (St Pancras, Camden). Built on land belonging to the dukes of Bedford, who also held property at Cardington, Bedfordshire.

Cardwell Road N7 (Holloway, Islington). Named in 1869 when Edward Cardwell was Secretary for War. He introduced sweeping and effective reforms into the army.

Carey Lane EC2 (Cit. Lond.). Called Kyrunelane and Kyroneslane in the 13th century, which possibly derives from a personal name, but it is not certain.

Carey Place SW1 (Cit. West.). William Carey (1769–1846), Bishop of Exeter and of St Asaph, was a King's Scholar of nearby Westminster School . He was also headmaster there 1803–14.

Carey Street WC2 (Lincoln's Inn, Cit. West./Camden). One Nicholas Carey had a house here in the early 17th century, but it is not certain that the whole street was built on his land.

Carlisle Lane SE1 (Lambeth). The bishops of Carlisle had a London house here from 1540 until 1647; the building was then used for various purposes until it was demolished in 1827 (*see* **Rochester Walk**, Southwark).

Carlisle Mews NW8 (Lisson Grove, Cit. West.). *See* **Salisbury Street**.

Carlisle Place SW1 (Victoria, Cit. West.). With adjoining **Howard Place** and parallel **Morpeth Terrace**, this name probably commemorates the chief commissioner responsible for development at the time when they were built, *c*1850. George Howard, Viscount Morpeth and Earl of Carlisle, was the leader of the board of Commissioners for Improving the Metropolis.

Carlisle Street W1 (Soho, Cit. West.). Carlisle House was owned by the earls of Carlisle 1685–1753; it stood on the opposite side of Soho Square on the site of the present St Patrick's church, and was demolished in 1791.

Carlos Place W1 (Mayfair, Cit. West.). Formerly Charles Street, this was renamed in 1886 in honour of Carlos I, king of Portugal.

Carlow Street NW1 (Camden Town, Camden). Originally called Caroline Street, from Queen Caroline (*d* 1821), the estranged wife of George IV. In 1865 it was changed to avoid confusion with other 'Caroline' streets (*see* **Caroline Place**).

Carlton House Terrace SW1 (St James's Park, Cit. West.). Carlton House was built here in 1709 for Lord

Carleton and bought by Frederick, Prince of Wales, in 1732. It was rebuilt in great splendour for George, Prince of Wales, from 1772. This second mansion was demolished c1820 and replaced by the present terrace, designed by John Nash. **Carlton Gardens** leads to it.

Carlyle Square SW3 (Chelsea, Ken. Chel.). The author and philosopher Thomas Carlyle moved to Cheyne Row in 1834 and lived there until his death in 1881.

Carmel Court W8 (Kensington, Ken. Chel.). Approaches the priory of Our Lady of Mount Carmel and St Simon Stock. The priory was founded by a German priest in 1863, in a building on the corner of Kensington Church Street and Duke's Lane.

Carmelite Street EC4 (Cit. Lond.). Land here was granted to Carmelite or White Friars by Edward I (1272–1307). (See **Whitefriars Street**.) Their right of sanctuary – that is, freedom from arrest by secular authority – survived their dissolution in the 16th century, and the area became a thieves' hide-out known as 'Alsatia'.

Carnaby Street W1 (Regent Street, Cit. West.). Richard Tyler, a 17th-century property developer, had a house here called 'Karnaby House', of which the derivation is unknown. The street was laid out in the 1680s.

Carnoustie Drive N1 (Caledonian Road, Islington). Place name from Tayside, Scotland, to go with 'Caledonian'. Neighbouring streets with Scottish names are: **Tapfort Close, Stranraer Way, Earlsferry Way**.

Carnwath Road SW6 (Fulham, Hammersmith). Carnwath House stood at the junction of this road and Broomhouse Road. It was the London home of Robert Harris Dalzell, Eleventh Earl of Carnwath (1847–1910).

Caroline Place W2 (Bayswater, Cit. West.). From Princess Caroline of Brunswick, estranged wife of the Prince Regent, who became Queen Caroline on his accession as George IV. The king refused to admit her to Westminster Abbey for her coronation, and their relations were the subject of bitter public disputes. She died in 1821. **Caroline Close** is nearby.

Caron Place SW8 (Vauxhall, Lambeth). Approached the S boundary of an estate belonging to Noel de Caron, Netherlands envoy to the court of Elizabeth I from 1588. The house stood on the site of the present Vauxhall Park. A later house on the estate was called 'Carroun House'. In 1810 John Hanbury Beaufoy bought land here from the owner; he built a vinegar distillery and a house which he called 'Caron Place' (see **Carroun Road**).

Carrington Street W1 (Mayfair, Cit. West.). Built on land held by Nathan Carrington c1750.

Carroun Road SW8 (Vauxhall, Lambeth). Built on the estate attached to 'Carroun House'; the house was built in the early 19th century to replace a former 'Caron House'.

Carr Street E14 (Limehouse, T. Ham.). Named in 1869, possibly from the Rev. Charles Carr of St John's Church of England, Vincent Street, Limehouse.

Carteret Street SW1 (Cit. West.). Built on land held by Sir Edward de Carteret from 1680. He was the uncle of John de Carteret, First Earl Granville, diplomat and politician.

Carter Lane EC4 (Cit. Lond.). An

old name denoting the street where carters lived; in the 13th century it was called Carterestrate.

Carthusian Street EC1 (Cit. Lond.). The Carthusian Order of Friars founded nearby Charterhouse as a monastery in 1371. Their name derives from the Latin place name Carthusia, which is Chartreuse, near Grenôble. The order was founded there by St Bruno in 1086 (*see* **Charterhouse Street**).

Cartwright Gardens WC1 (Bloomsbury, Camden). Originally Burton Crescent (*see* **Burton Street**), this street was renamed in honour of Major John Cartwright (1740–1824), political reformer, who lived at no. 37 for the last four years of his life. Cartwright worked for universal suffrage and for other aims later adopted by the Chartist movement.

Carver Road SE24 (Dulwich, Southwark). Canon Carver became the first Master of nearby Dulwich College after the Dulwich College Act of 1857 gave the school a new organisation. He was largely responsible for its successful re-establishment.

Casino Avenue SE24 (Herne Hill, Southwark). Built on the site of a large house and grounds called 'Casino'; it was a private house, presumably named from the Italian ('country house'), and not a gaming house.

Cassland Road E9 (Hackney). Built on land belonging to Sir John Cass's charity. Sir John, who died in 1718, was Lord Mayor of London and founder of two Hackney schools.

Casslee Road SE6 (Catford, Lewisham). Marks the meeting point of two estates, one owned by Sir John Cass's charity (*see* **Cassland Road**) and one by a Mr Lee.

Castelnau SW13 (Barnes, R. upon T.). Built across land belonging to and named by a French family who came to Barnes as refugees from religious persecution.

Castlands Road SE6 (Perry Hill, Lewisham). Shortened form of Castle-Lands; this is an old right of way leading across the River Ravensbourne to the manorial great field of Broadmead, of which part was called Castle-lands.

Castle Baynard Street EC4 (Cit. Lond.). Baynards Castle which stood on the river bank nearby was one of London's most important buildings. It was built for the Norman Bainiardus; it belonged to the Fitzwater or Fitzwalter family *c*1200–*c*1400, was rebuilt by Humfrey, Duke of Gloucester, in 1428 and passed to Henry VI in 1446. It remained a royal lodging until the mid-16th century, when it became once more a private town house. It was burnt down in 1666, and not rebuilt.

Castle Court EC3 (Cit. Lond.). Named from the sign of an inn, now demolished.

Castlehaven Road NW1 (Kentish Town, Camden). In St Pancras parish; Elizabeth, Countess of Castlehaven, was buried in St Pancras churchyard in 1743. Castlehaven was an Irish title; it became extinct on the death of her son in 1777.

Castle Lane SW1 (Victoria, Cit. West.). Named from an inn (now demolished) which stood at the SW end.

Castlereagh Street W1 (Marylebone, Cit. West.). Robert Stewart, Viscount Castlereagh (1769–1822), was an unpopular Tory politician who was to have been the principal victim of the frustrated Cato Street conspiracy (*see* **Harrowby Street**). Chief Secretary of Ireland from 1798, Castlereagh was active in bringing about the union of the English and Irish parliaments in 1800. Coming to London to sit in the new united parliament he served successfully as president of the East India Board and as Secretary for War and the Colonial Department. Some of his decisions during the Napoleonic Wars were unpopular, and political intrigue led him to a duel with George Canning (*see* **Canning Place**) in 1809. Success as Foreign Secretary restored his popularity but in 1815 he became chief Commons spokesman on home affairs (the Home Secretary being a member of the House of Lords) and was identified with unpopular domestic policies. He killed himself in 1822.

Castle Road NW1 (Kentish Town, Camden). The *Castle Inn* stood on Kentish Town Road S of this street. The inn is first recorded in the mid-18th century; it was later replaced by a gin palace.

Castle Yard SE1 (Bankside, Southwark). The *Castle Inn* at Bank End is recorded *c*1650–70.

Catford Road SE6 (Lewisham). Road to Catford, or 'the ford where wild cats are found'.

Cathcart Road SW10 (Earl's Court, Ken. Chel.). Probably commemorates General Sir George Cathcart (1794–1854). In 1813 he became ADC to his father, who was ambassador to Russia. He was ADC to Wellington at Waterloo in 1815. In 1850 he published *Commentaries on the War in Russia and Germany in 1812 and 1813*. He led successful campaigns in Africa in 1852, went to the Crimea in 1854 and was killed at Inkerman.

Cathcart Street NW5 (Kentish Town,

Camden). One of a group from the Crimean War (*see* **Cathcart Road**).

Cathedral Street SE1 (Southwark). The priory church of St Mary Overy (or St Mary-by-the-River) became the parish church when the priory was dissolved in 1539. It was renamed as St Saviour's. In 1905 it became the cathedral church of the newly-formed diocese of Southwark.

Catherall Road N5 (Highbury, Islington). Commemorates the Rev. Robert Catherall, former vicar of St Augustine's, Highbury New Park.

Catherine Street WC2 (Aldwych, Cit. West.). Built in 1673 and named after the queen, Catherine of Braganza, consort of Charles II.

Catherine Wheel Alley E1 (Cit. Lond.). From the sign of a galleried inn which was gutted by fire in 1895 and later demolished. The sign is said to derive from the arms of the Turners' Company, which include a Catherine-wheel between two columns (*see* **St Katharine's Way**).

Cato Street W1 (Marylebone, Cit. West.). One of a series commemorating writers of classical Greece and Rome: **Homer Street** is nearby. Cato Street became synonymous with the radical conspiracy of 1820 (*see* **Harrowby Street**) and the name was accordingly changed to commemorate the poet Horace; it has since reverted.

Catton Street WC1 (Holborn, Camden). Commemorates Charles Catton, painter (1728–98). One of 15 children, he trained as a coach-painter and specialised in heraldic insignia. He lived in Gate Street, S of Holborn.

Causeway, The SW18 (Wandsworth). Originally this was a path on a raised bank across the marshy Wandle estuary.

Cavaye Place SW10 (Kensington, Ken. Chel.). Major General William Cavaye was mayor of Kensington 1907–9.

Cavendish Avenue NW8 (St John's Wood, Cit. West.). Built on land belonging to the Cavendish-Bentinck family, dukes of Portland. **Cavendish Close** adjoins.

Cavendish Court EC3 (Cit. Lond.). The Cavendish family, dukes of Devonshire, had a town house at the end of this court until 1670 (*see* **Devonshire Row**).

Cavendish Road W4 (Chiswick, Hounslow). Family name of the dukes of Devonshire (*see* **Duke Road**).

Cavendish Road SW12 (Clapham, Lambeth). The scientist Henry Cavendish (1731–1810) lived at the N end of this road. It was Cavendish who isolated hydrogen, determined the chemical composition of air and water, and also estimated the density of the earth. The Cavendish Laboratory is named after him.

Cavendish Square W1 (Marylebone, Cit. West.). Built from 1717 for Edward Harley, Earl of Oxford and Mortimer, and named from his wife, the former Lady Henrietta Cavendish Holles, through whom he inherited the estate. Cavendish Place and Cavendish Street approached the square, the latter changing to **Old Cavendish Street** when **New Cavendish Street** was built further N.

Caversham Road NW5 (Kentish Town, Camden). The Rev. Dr Robert South of Caversham near Reading owned this land when he died in 1716. He left the estate ultimately to Christchurch Cathe-dral, Oxford, and it was developed after his death.

Caversham Street SW3 (Chelsea, Ken. Chel.). Built on land belonging to the Earl of Cadogan who was also Baron Oakley of Caversham. The earl also held property at Culford, near Ixworth in Suffolk, and at Rosemoor in Devon; **Culford Gardens** and **Rosemoor Street** are nearby.

Cave Street N1 (Pentonville, Islington). The Rev. Dr William Cave was vicar of St Mary's parish church, Islington, from 1662 until his death in 1713. He was a learned writer on the early Church.

Caxton Street SW1 (Cit. West.). Commemorates William Caxton, who established the first printing press in England at Westminster in 1476.

Cazenove Road N16 (Clapton, Hackney). Cazenove House stood here, from a local family name. James and Philip Cazenove are listed as trustees of the parish of Hackney (which then included Clapton) in 1790.

Cecil Court WC2 (Cit. West.). Built on land belonging to the Cecils, earls of Salisbury. Robert Cecil, the first earl, bought the estate in 1609–10 (*see* **Cranbourn Street**).

Cecilia Road E8 (Shacklewell, Hackney). Commemorates Cecilia Heron, daughter of Sir Thomas More (*d* 1535), who lived in Shacklewell at a house later called the 'Manor House'.

Cedars Road SW4 (Clapham, Lambeth). Site of an 18th-century house of that name, fronting Clapham Common; the grounds extended to Wandsworth Road. The house was demolished in 1864.

Centaur Street SE1 (Lambeth). By association with adjoining **Hercules Road**. The Centaurs were creatures of Greek mythology, being half horse and half man, and living in the mountains of Thessaly.

Central Street EC1 (St Luke's, Islington). Improved section of an old lane from the City to Islington; so named in 1861, probably because it was centrally placed in St Luke's parish.

Cephas Avenue E1 (Bethnal Green, T. Ham.). Formerly St Peter's Road, from the church of St Peter. There being a number of 'St Peter' street names, this one was altered to the Aramaic form of the saint's name. **Cephas Road** adjoins.

Cerise Road SE15 (Peckham, Southwark). Named in 1878, on the Crespigny estate (*see* **De Crespigny Park**). Cerise and Cicely were the daughters of Stephen Champion de Crespigny, Fourth Baronet. **Cicely Road** is nearby.

Chadbourn Street E14 (Poplar, T. Ham.). Properly Chadburn: named in 1876 after the Rev. James Chadburn, minister of Trinity Congregational Church in the East India Dock Road.

Chadwell Street EC1 (Islington). Built from *c*1823 on land belonging to the New River Company and named from Chadwell Spring, near Amwell in Hertfordshire, source of the New River (*see* **Myddelton Square**).

Chadwick Road SE15 (Peckham, Southwark). William Chadwick, railway engineer, is recorded as owning this land *c*1830.

Chadwick Street SW1 (Cit. West.). Commemorates a parish benefactor.

Mrs Hannah Chadwick left the nearby charity schools £500 at her death in 1889.

Chagford Street NW1 (Marylebone, Cit. West.). Built on land belonging to the Portman family (*see* **Portman Square**). Baron Portman (created 1837) was Lord Warden of the Stannaries, 1865–88. Chagford on Dartmoor is a Stannary town (*see* **Stannary Street**).

Chalcot Gardens NW3 (Chalk Farm, Camden). This street was built on the site of the original Chalcot Farm (*see* **Chalk Farm Road**). **Chalcot Road** and **Square** are nearby.

Chaldon Road SW6 (Fulham, Hammersmith). Site of a house called 'Chaldon House'.

Chalgrove Road E9 (Hackney). Sir Henry Rowe of Shacklewell, mercer, died in the 17th century and left income from his estate at Chalgrove in Bedfordshire for the poor of Hackney. The sum of £2.16s.0d. annually was to be spent on bread and coal.

Chalk Farm Road NW1 (Chalk Farm, Camden). Corruption of Chalcot Farm, which this road approached. The farm house stood S of England's Lane and became a tea garden during the 18th century (*see* **Chalcot Gardens**).

Chalkhill Road W6 (Hammersmith). Commemorates William Chalkhill, former owner of nearby Butterwick Manor; Chalkhill bought the manor in 1633 and sold it later in the same year.

Chambord Street E2 (Bethnal Green, T. Ham.). Named from a château in the Loire Valley, begun by Francis I of France in 1519. The street was named by association with French settlement in this area (*see*

Nantes Passage).

Champion Hill SE5 (Camberwell, Southwark). From Sir Claude Champion de Crespigny who developed much of the Crespigny Estate in Camberwell from the 1860s. An earlier Sir Claude had held the land in 1783. **Champion Grove** and **Park** are nearby (*see* **De Crespigny Park**).

Chancellors Road W6 (Fulham, Hammersmith). The Chancellor of St Paul's Cathedral, as head of the cathedral grammar school, was endowed with the rent from a meadow and other properties in Fulham in the 12th century. There was still a property called 'The Chancellor's House', with five acres, in Fulham in the 19th century.

Chancery Lane WC2 (Camden/Cit. Lond./Cit. West.). Formerly New Street, this was called Chancery Lane after the reign of Edward III (1327–77). The office of Edward's Master of the Rolls of Chancery was housed there in a building which was formerly a religious house.

Chandos Place WC2 (Covent Garden, Cit. West.). Built from 1636 as part of the fourth Earl of Bedford's Covent Garden scheme, and named from his father-in-law Lord Chandos.

Chandos Street W1 (Marylebone, Cit. West.). The Duke of Chandos built the first mansion in **Cavendish Square** *c*1717, occupying the whole of the north side. The E wing of the house formed the corner of this street. The two central, pillared sections of the house are still standing.

Change Alley EC3 (Cit. Lond.). Properly Exchange Alley, from its proximity to the Royal Exchange. Many of the coffee houses in the alley became unofficial exchanges in

themselves during the 18th century; the best known was *Jonathon's*.

Chapel House Street E14 (Isle of Dogs, T. Ham.). The Chapel House Farm was demolished during the excavation of Millwall Dock. It was built on the site of St Mary's chapel and incorporated parts of its structure. The chapel is first recorded in the 15th century and was possibly connected with the monastery called St Mary of Graces (*see* **Eastminster**).

Chapel Place W1 (Marylebone, Cit. West.). A chapel of ease for the new residential area of Cavendish Square was built here in 1724; it is now the church of St Peter, Vere Street.

Chapel Street SW1 (Belgravia, Cit. West.). Originally the approach to a chapel which was attached to an 18th-century hospital in Grosvenor Place. The buildings were demolished *c*1845.

Chapel Street NW1 (N Marylebone, Cit. West.). A chapel built in 1772 stood on the SW corner of the junction with **Transept Street**, named by association with it. The chapel closed *c*1850.

Chapter Road SE17 (Walworth, Southwark). The Dean and Chapter of Canterbury Cathedral obtained the manor of Walworth in 1052 (*see* **Manor Place**). The Dean and Chapter gave the land on which neighbouring St Paul's church, Lorrimore Square, was built in 1856.

Chapter Street SW1 (Victoria, Cit. West.). Built on land belonging to the Dean and Chapter of Westminster Abbey, who held an estate covering the former Tothill Fields. (The chapter is an assembly of cathedral canons, *see* **Dean Bradley Street**).

Charing Cross Road WC2 (Cit.

West.). Road leading to the cross at Charing. The name is from OE 'cierring', meaning a bend or turning, and probably referring to the marked bend in the Thames at this point. The cross was one of a series marking the overnight resting-places of the body of Queen Eleanor of Castile, consort of Edward I. She died near Lincoln in 1290 and her body was brought to Westminster for burial. The cross stood at the junction of the present Strand and Northumberland Avenue, and it was destroyed in 1647. The Eleanor Cross in front of Charing Cross Station is Victorian. The road was made in 1887 on the line of the former Crown Street and Castle Street.

Charlbert Street NW8 (St John's Wood, Cit. West.). A hybrid of Charles and Albert, connecting as it does Charles Lane and Prince Albert Road. The Charles of **Charles Lane** is unidentified.

Charles Lane NW8 (St John's Wood, Cit. West.). *See* **Charlbert Street**.

Charles II Street SW1 (St James's, Cit. West.). Built as part of a scheme of streets leading to **St James's Square** and named in honour of Charles II.

Charles Square N1 (Hoxton, Hackney). Built in the early 18th century and named in compliment to the House of Stuart, recently defunct. (Nearby Rufus Street was then called King Street, and Boot Street was James Street.)

Charles Street W1 (Mayfair, Cit. West.). Built in the early 18th century on land belonging to Lord Berkeley of Stratton, and named from a family Christian name.

Charlotte Row SW4 (Clapham, Lambeth). Charlotte Elliott, poet and hymn-writer, lived at Grove House, near Scout Lane, until 1827.

Charlotte Street W1 (Camden). Built in the late 18th century and named after George III's queen, Charlotte of Mecklenburg-Strelitz (*d* 1818).

Charlton Kings Road NW5 (Kentish Town, Camden). Joseph Torriano left property at Charlton Kings, Gloucestershire, to Isabella Leighton (*see* **Leighton Road**).

Charlwood Street SW1 (Pimlico, Cit. West.). *See* **Tachbrook Street**.

Charrington Street NW1 (St Pancras, Camden). Built 1842–50 on land belonging to a city livery company – the Brewers' Company – and named after the brewers, Charringtons.

Charterhouse Street EC1 (Cit. Lond./Islington). An Anglicisation of Chartreuse: the nearby Charterhouse was founded as an abbey in 1371 by monks from Chartreuse (*see* **Carthusian Street**). The abbey was dissolved in 1539 and became a private estate in 1545. In 1611 it became a school; the school moved to Godalming in 1872 and the buildings are now mainly used by a medical college (*see* **Great Sutton Street**).

Chase, The SW4 (Clapham, Lambeth). Site of a large house and grounds called 'The Chase'. The house was built after 1760, facing the N side of Clapham Common. It was later occupied by Sir Charles Barry (designer of the Houses of Parliament) and ultimately became a hostel.

Chaston Street NW5 (Kentish Town, Camden). Built in the 1870s by Edward Chaston.

Chatham Street SE17 (Walworth, Southwark). Leads off the NE section of adjoining Darwin Street, which formerly extended to the Old Kent Road and was called Pitt Street. William Street ran N from it. This commemorative street was named in 1875. William Pitt the Elder, First Earl of Chatham, was a statesman of exceptional qualities who dominated English politics from *c*1757 until 1767, when illness persuaded him to accept an earldom and withdraw from the front line of political life. His insight into the realities of the American War of Independence was rejected by king and ministers alike until it was too late. He died in 1778. Pittsburgh, Pennsylvania, USA, is named after him.

Chaucer Road SE24 (Brixton, Lambeth). *See* **Shakespeare Road**.

Cheapside EC2 (Cit. Lond.). The street along the side of the 'cheap', from OE 'chepe' which means market. This area was the centre of the Saxon and mediaeval City's principal food market.

Chelsea Embankment SW3 (Ken. Chel.). Made in 1871 to embank and strengthen the shore of the Thames at Chelsea, called Cealchythe in the 8th century. Scholars disagree on the meaning of the name. 'Hythe' is OE wharf or landing place; the meaning of the first element is uncertain, but it may mean chalk or limestone, as the principal cargo of the wharf. There are, however, other early forms of the name which do not give either 'chalk' or 'hythe'.

Chelsea Manor Street SW3 (Ken. Chel.). Led to the Tudor manor house built in 1536–7 for Henry VIII, who acquired the manor of Chelsea from Lord Sandys. The house stood on what is now Cheyne Walk. The site of the previous manor house is uncertain; it may have been near Lordship Place.

Cheltenham Road SE15 (Nunhead,

Southwark). Formerly Hall Road; a hall here (now demolished) belonged to a church group called the Cheltenham Mission.

Cheltenham Terrace SW3 (Chelsea, Ken. Chel.). *See* **St Leonard's Terrace**.

Cheney Road NW1 (King's Cross, Camden). Built in the early 19th century by William Cheney, local builder.

Chenies Place WC1 (Bloomsbury, Camden). Built on land belonging to the dukes of Bedford (*see* **Chenies Street**).

Chenies Street WC1 (Bloomsbury, Camden). Part of the Duke of Bedford's estate; the duke is also Baron Russell of Cheneys or Chenies in Buckinghamshire. **Chenies Mews** is nearby.

Cheniston Gardens W8 (Kensington, Ken. Chel.). Based on the name of Kensington in the form in which it appears in the *Domesday Book*: Chenesitun.

Chepstow Road W2 (Westbourne Grove, Cit. West.). Laid out by W.K. Jenkins after 1838. Jenkins was a property developer of Welsh origin who frequently used place names from Wales or the Welsh borders. Chepstow is in Monmouthshire. **Chepstow Place, Crescent** and **Villas** are nearby.

Chequer Street EC1 (Shoreditch, Hackney). The *Chequers* tavern is recorded here in Whitecross Street in 1665, with a chequerboard sign outside. In the middle ages this emblem signified a money-changer; it also appeared in the arms of the Earl Warenne who, with his successors the earls of Arundel, had the right to grant beer-selling licences.

Cherry Garden Street SE16 (Rotherhithe, Southwark). The site of a 17th-century public pleasure ground called Cherry Gardens, which had its own landing place at Cherry Garden Pier, or Cherry Garden Stairs.

Chertsey Street SW17 (Tooting, Wandsworth). Commemorates the abbey of Chertsey in Surrey, to which the surrounding manor of Tooting Graveney (*see* **Graveney Road**) belonged. The grant of the manor to the abbey was confirmed by King Aethelstan in 933; the date of the original grant is not known. The manor is recorded as being held of the king in 1500.

Chesham Place SW1 (Belgravia, Cit. West.). Adjoins Lowndes Street, and begins on land belonging to the Lowndes family of Chesham in Buckinghamshire. **Chesham Street** approaches. Chesham Place extends into the Grosvenor estate where the name turned out to be equally appropriate. Katherine Cavendish, daughter of the second Baron Chesham, married the first Duke of Westminster (as his second wife) in 1882.

Chesterfield Grove SE22 (E Dulwich, Southwark). *See* **Melbourne Grove**.

Chesterfield Hill W1 (Mayfair, Cit. West.). By association with nearby Chesterfield Gardens and **Chesterfield Street**.

Chesterfield Street W1 (Mayfair, Cit. West.). Philip Dormer Stanhope, Fourth Earl of Chesterfield, leased land here from Sir Nathaniel Curzon on which he built Chesterfield House in 1749. **Chesterfield Gardens** is built on the same plot. The earl had royal connections: his countess was an illegitimate daughter of George I and Ermengarde de Schulenberg.

Chesterford Gardens NW3 (Hampstead, Camden). *See* **Canfield Gardens**. The Maryon-Wilsons owned property at Chesterford in Essex.

Chester Road N19 (Highgate, Camden). *See* **Bromwich Avenue**.

Chester Square SW1 (Belgravia, Cit. West.). Part of the Grosvenor estate. The family held property in Chester and successive Grosvenors represented the city in parliament. **Chester Close, Mews** and **Street** and **Little Chester Street** are nearby.

Chester Terrace NW1 (Regent's Park, Camden). Built as part of John Nash's Regent's Park scheme. The Prince Regent was Prince of Wales, Duke of Cornwall and Earl of Chester. **Chester Close, Court, Gate** and **Place** adjoin. **Chester Road** approaches.

Chester Way SE11 (Kennington, Lambeth). Part of the manor of Kennington which is owned by the Duchy of Cornwall. The Prince of Wales, who is Duke of Cornwall, is also Earl of Chester (*see* **Black Prince Road**).

Chetwynd Road NW5 (Kentish Town, Camden). *See* **Dartmouth Park Hill**. The fourth Earl of Dartmouth married Frances Chetwynd, daughter of Charles Chetwynd, Lord Talbot, in 1821, when she was 20; she died in 1823, two months after the birth of their son. Her nephew Charles Chetwynd, Lord Ingestre, took the neighbouring land for building in 1857. His partner in the venture was Lord Alfred Spencer Churchill. They built this street, **Ingestre Road, Churchill Road** and **Spencer Rise**.

Chevall Street E14 (Isle of Dogs, T. Ham.). Built on land bought some time after 1660 by John Chevall, citizen and draper. His grand-daughter married Thomas Tooke in 1703 and the Tooke family held the land when the streets were built in the 19th century. This street originally ran N to Strafford Street, and there was also a Tooke Street, which crossed it.

Cheval Place SW7 (Brompton, Ken. Chel.). Originally a row of stables and named from the French *cheval*, a horse. Street names in Brompton indicate a French settlement or a strong French influence in the 1830s.

Cheyne Walk SW3, SW10 (Chelsea, Ken. Chel.). Charles Cheyne, later Lord Cheyne and First Viscount Newhaven, bought the manor of Chelsea in 1657. William Cheyne, Second Viscount, laid out Cheyne Walk and **Cheyne Row** between 1708 and 1720.

Chicheley Street SE1 (Lambeth). Built in 1824 on land belonging to the archbishops of Canterbury (*see* **Lambeth Palace Road**). Named after Archbishop Chicheley or Chichele, 1414–43. He is noted for encouraging Henry V's policy of war with France.

Chichester Rents WC2 (Chancery Lane, Cit. West.). Formerly led to the London palace of the Bishop of Chichester, Ralph Neville (*d* 1244). This street was built up with properties for rent (*see* **Bishop's Court**).

Chichester Road W2 (Paddington, Cit. West.). Built on the Paddington estate of the Frederick family (*see* **Frederick Close**). Lady Caroline Chichester was a 19th-century descendant of Sir John Frederick, who acquired the estate.

Chicksand Street E1 (Spitalfields, T. Ham.). Built on land belonging to the Osborn family of Chicksands Priory, Bedfordshire (*see* **Osborn Street**).

Chiddingstone Street SW6 (Fulham, Hammersmith). *See* **Bradbourne Street**.

Childeric Road SE14 (Deptford, Lewisham). Recorded as a field-name in the 19th century before development.

Child Street SW5 (Earl's Court, Ken. Chel.). Local family name, mentioned in manorial records of the 16th and 17th centuries, and as owners of property in **Child Place** in 1870.

Chilworth Street W2 (Paddington, Cit. West.). By association with neighbouring streets which have Hampshire place names. **Chilworth Mews** adjoins.

Chippenham Road W9 (Paddington, Cit. West.). *See* **Rundell Road**.

Chipstead Street SW6 (Fulham, Hammersmith). *See* **Bradbourne Street**.

Chiswell Street EC1 (Finsbury, Islington). Street running through Chiswell, a place name meaning stony or gravelly earth.

Chiswick High Road W4 (Chiswick, Hounslow). The high or principal road through Chiswick; the name means a farm producing cheese.

Chitty Place W1 (Tottenham Court Road, Camden). Joseph Chitty, writer on law, lived in nearby Conway Street where he died in 1841. His three sons were also distinguished in the same field and the best known, Thomas (*d* 1878), lived in Gower Street.

Cholmeley Park N6 (Highgate, Haringey). Sir Roger Cholmeley (*d* 1565) founded the Highgate Free Grammar School nearby, now Highgate School. He held the manor of Hampstead and served as Lord

Chester Terrace

Chief Justice under Mary I (1553–8). The school was demolished and rebuilt in 1866.

Choumert Road SE15 (Peckham, Lambeth). This land was owned by George Choumert; by 1831 it was being managed by his trustees, and the actual development was done later by the British Land Company.

Chrisp Street E14 (Poplar, T. Ham.). Sir Nicholas Chrisp or Crisp lived at nearby Bromley Hall manor house between 1650 and 1680 (*see* **Crisp Road**).

Christchurch Close E9 (S Hackney, Hackney). Christchurch, an Anglican church which stood here, was consecrated in July 1871. **Vicar's Close** adjoins.

Christchurch Hill NW3 (Hampstead, Camden). Approaches Christchurch Anglican church, consecrated in 1852.

Christian Street E1 (Whitechapel, T. Ham.). Said to compliment Prince Christian of Schleswig-Holstein-Sonderburg-Glücksburg, the father of Queen Alexandra, who became king of Denmark as Christian IX in 1863. A Danish presence in the area had been established with the founding of a Danish church in Well Close Square in 1696. A former king, Christian V, was a benefactor to this church.

Christie Road E9 (Hackney). Built on land belonging to a Mr Christie, 19th-century occupier of this and nearby fields, and possibly the Thomas Christie of Eagle House, Homerton, who was Secretary of Homerton College in 1842.

Chudleigh Street E1 (Stepney, T. Ham.). The Rev. F.W. Chudleigh served on Stepney Borough Council from 1909.

Church Crescent E9 (S Hackney, Hackney). The church of St John of Jerusalem was built here as a chapel of ease for Hackney Parish in 1806, and became a full parish church in 1825. The church was rebuilt in 1842.

Church Entry EC4 (Cit. Lond.). Led to the church of St Anne, of which a small churchyard remains; it was built on the site of the Blackfriars monastery to serve as a parish church after the monastery had been dissolved in 1538. The church was burnt down in 1666.

Churchill Gardens Road SW1 (Pimlico, Cit. West.). The surrounding estate was laid out by Westminster City Council in 1947 and named after Sir Winston Churchill, Prime Minister of the wartime coalition government, 1940–5.

Churchill Road NW5 (Kentish Town, Camden). *See* **Chetwynd Road**.

Church Lane SW17 (Tooting, Wandsworth). *See* **Nicholas Glebe**.

Church Rise SE23 (Forest Hill, Lewisham). Christ Church here was consecrated in 1854 as the first church for Forest Hill.

Church Road SW13 (Barnes, R. upon T.). Passes Barnes parish church: **Church Walk** adjoins, as does **Glebe Road** (*see* **Camberwell Glebe**). **Rectory Road** adjoins **Meredyth Road**, with **Kitson Road** nearby. The Rev. Benjamin Meredyth-Kitson became rector of Barnes in 1892.

Church Road NW3 (Hampstead, Camden). The parish church of St John was built here in 1745 to replace the mediaeval church of St Mary.

Church Street NW8, W2 (Lisson Grove, Cit. West.). Originally the name of that part of the street which lay W of Edgware Road, approaching the church of St Mary, Paddington Green.

Church Walk N16 (Newington Green, Hackney). Originally led from the hamlet of Newington Green to the parish church in Stoke Newington Church Street.

Churchway NW1 (Hackney). A mineral spring with healing properties used to feed a well here beside the church of St John.

Churchwell Path E9 (Hackney). A mineral spring with healing properties used to feed a well here beside the church of St John.

Churchyard Row SE11 (Newington, Southwark). The mediaeval church of St Mary, Newington, stood here; it was demolished in 1876 and rebuilt (opposite Cottington Street) on Kennington Park Road. This second church was burnt in 1941.

Churton Place SW1 (Belgravia, Cit. West.). On the Grosvenor estate; Churton is a village on Grosvenor land in Cheshire.

Cibber Road SE23 (Forest Hill, Lewisham). One of a group taken from the history of the theatre (*see* **Farren Road, Kemble Road** and **Street, Siddons Lane** and **Road** and **Vestris Road**). Colley Cibber (1671–1757) was a good manager, a talented comedian and a prolific playwright. He excelled in comic eccentric parts: Fondlewife, Sparkish, Lord Foppington, Sir Courtly Nice. His attempts at fine verse and tragedy were less successful and earned him some contemporary derision.

Cicely Road (Peckham, Southwark). *See* **Cerise Road**.

Circus EC3 (Cit. Lond.). This was part of a development designed by

George Dance the Younger in 1767–70. The street originally approached a small circus forming the S end of Vine Street.

Circus Mews W1 (Marylebone, Cit. West.). Leads from Enford Street which was originally called Circus Street, since it was intended to lead to a circus; that part of the development, however, was never completed.

Circus Road NW8 (St John's Wood, Cit. West.). Intended (c1803) as an approach to a new residential estate – smaller than Regent's Park but on similar lines – of outer and inner circles. The estate was never built.

Cirencester Street W2 (Paddington, Cit. West.). *See* **Woodchester Square**.

City Road EC1 (Finsbury, Islington). New direct route to the City of London from Islington and the N, opened from Islington to Old Street in 1761.

Clabon Mews SW1 (Chelsea, Ken. Chel.). Built on the Cadogan estate; John Clabon was the family solicitor at the time of building (1875).

Clapham High Street SW4 (Clapham, Lambeth). The high or principal street of Clapham, called Cloppaham in the 9th century, meaning the homestead belonging to Cloppa.

Clapham Manor Street SW4 (Clapham, Lambeth). The manor of Clapham was held from the king before the Norman Conquest, but there is no record of a manor house at this early date. In the 15th century it was held by relations of the poet John Gower, and their manor house was rebuilt by Bartholomew Clarke in the 16th century. Henry Atkins, physician to James I, bought it in

1616; the Atkins family and their descendants the Atkins-Bowyers still held it in the 19th century. The house stood W of the N end of this street (*see* **Turret Grove**).

Clapham Park Road SW4 (Clapham, Lambeth). Approaches the estate of Clapham Park, laid out by Thomas Cubitt on the former Bleak Hall Farm from 1834.

Clarehall Place SE16 (Rotherhithe, Southwark). Half the manor of Rotherhithe passed to Richard de Clare, Earl of Hertford, by his marriage with Amicia, daughter of the Earl of Gloucester, in *c*1180. The de Clare family held it until Gilbert de Clare died childless in 1314 (killed at the battle of Bannockburn) and his sisters divided the estate. One of them, Elizabeth de Burgh, refounded Clare College, Cambridge, the 'House or Hall of Clare'. In 1730 the college became patron of the living of St Mary, Rotherhithe.

Clare Market WC2 (Aldwych, Cit. West.). Site of a butchers' market set up on land belonging to the Earl of Clare; the earl had a house nearby in the 17th century (*see* **Houghton Street**).

Clarence Crescent SW4 (Clapham Park, Lambeth). *See* **King's Avenue** for this and **Clarence Road**.

Clarence Road E5 (Hackney). Named from an inn here called *The Duke of Clarence*, in compliment to George III's second son, who became William IV (1830–7).

Clarence Terrace NW1 (Regent's Park, Cit. West.). Part of John Nash's Regent's Park scheme (*see* **Regent Street**). The terrace is named from the Regent's brother William, Duke of Clarence (*see* **Clarence Road**). **Clarence Gardens** is nearby, **Clarence Gate** approaches. **Clarence**

Way in Camden Town is also named after him.

Clarendon Place W2 (Bayswater, Cit. West.). *See* **Bathurst Street** for this and **Clarendon Close** and **Mews**.

Clarendon Road W11 (Notting Hill, Ken. Chel.). Named in 1861, in place of a number of separately named groups which included Clarendon Terrace and Clarendon Villas. The contemporary Lord Clarendon was Foreign and Colonial Secretary 1853–8.

Clarens Street SE6 (Forest Hill, Lewisham). *See* **Helvetia Street**.

Clareville Grove SW7 (Kensington, Ken. Chel.). Built in the 1880s on the site of a house called 'Clareville Cottage' which stood on Old Brompton Road. **Clareville Street** adjoins.

Clarges Street W1 (Mayfair, Cit. West.). Laid out in the late 17th century by the owner of the land, Sir Walter Clarges. **Clarges Mews** adjoins.

Clarke's Mews W1 (Marylebone, Cit. West.). One William Clarke held the property on lease in the 18th century.

Clark's Place EC2 (Cit. Lond.). Probably a corruption of 'clerks'. The hall and almshouses of the Parish Clerks' Company stood here, after their incorporation under Henry III (1216–72). John Stow, in his *Survey of London* of 1598, describes it as next to the Angel, inside the walls, and next to the SE side of Bishopsgate. The company's property was confiscated under Henry VIII *c*1540. They later acquired a new hall in Vintry.

Clark Street E14 (Stepney, T. Ham.). Named in 1873, possibly from W. Clark, Metropolitan Board of Works representative for St George's in the East.

Claude Road SE15 (Peckham, Southwark). Built on the Crespigny estate (*see* **De Crespigny Park**). This area was developed mainly in the 1870s under Sir Claude Raul Champion de Crespigny. The family was of Huguenot extraction, and **Huguenot Road** adjoins.

Claude Street E14 (Isle of Dogs, T. Ham.). Claude Lyon-Bowes (or Bowes-Lyon) (1824–1904), Earl of Strathmore and Kinghorne, who was also Lord Glamis, owned land here and on the site of **Glamis Road**, Shadwell. He was the grandfather of Queen Elizabeth the Queen Mother.

Claverton Street SW1 (Pimlico, Cit. West.). *See* **Kinnerton Street**.

Clave Street E1 (Wapping, T. Ham.). Thomas Clave, parish benefactor, gave £50 to Wapping in 1635. This name was introduced to commemorate him; the original street here was King Edward Street, built on land belonging to the Bridewell (*see* **Bridewell Place**), a foundation of Edward VI, and leading to King Edward's Stairs on the river bank.

Claybrook Road W6 (Fulham, Hammersmith). From the name of a villa, now demolished, which stood in Fulham Palace Road.

Claylands Road SW8 (Vauxhall, Lambeth). Originally led to brick-clay fields on part of the Vauxhall manor estate. The fields were sold in 1801 and drained for building (*see* **Fentiman Road**).

Clayton Road SE15 (Peckham, Southwark). Sir William Clayton owned the land *c*1830.

Clayton Street SE11 (Kennington, Lambeth). Commemorates the Clayton family who, beginning with Sir Robert Clayton, leased parts of the manor of Kennington from the Duchy of Cornwall from 1661 until 1834.

Cleaver Street SE11 (Kennington, Lambeth). Approaches **Cleaver Square**, both built on land belonging to Mary Cleaver (*d*1797) and her daughter Mary Ann Cleaver, who surrendered it in 1815 (*see* **Bowden Street**). The square was built from 1789.

Clem Attlee Court SW6 (Fulham, Hammersmith). Commemorates Clement Richard Attlee, Labour Prime Minister 1945–51, who died in 1967.

Clement's Inn WC2 (Cit. West.). Inns of Court near to St Clement's Church, a Danish foundation of the 12th century, and St Clement's Well which was probably older than the church. St Clement was bishop of Rome; he was martyred (*c*100) by being thrown into the sea with an anchor tied to his neck. An 'inn' was originally a large town house; many of them were taken by lawyers who set up their chambers there and preserved a word which had otherwise fallen out of use, except in the sense of a public inn.

Clenston Mews (Marylebone, Cit. West.). On the Portman estate *see* **Portman Square**). The family held property near Winterbourne Clenston in Dorset.

Clephane Road N1 (Islington). *See* **Douglas Road**.

Clere Street EC2 (Shoreditch, Islington). Named from the nearby well of St Agnes le Clere, otherwise called Dame Annis the Cleare (*see* **Bath Place**).

Clerkenwell Close EC1 (Clerkenwell, Islington). *See* **Clerkenwell Road**. The 'close' was formerly part of the precincts of the convent of St Mary.

Clerkenwell Road EC1 (Clerkenwell, Islington). A Victorian improvement that completely dislocated the old settlement of Clerkenwell. The name means 'the clerks' well'; it refers to a holy well where members of the Parish Clerks' Company used to perform miracle plays on religious feast days. The well still exists beneath premises in Farringdon Road. **Clerkenwell Green**, N of this road, is the original centre of the village which lay between two religious foundations: the convent of St Mary (*see* **Clerkenwell Close**) and the English headquarters of the Knights of St John of Jerusalem (*see* **St John Street**).

Cleveland Place SW1 (St James's, Cit. West.). Adjoins the site of Cleveland House, St James's Square, bought by the Duke of Cleveland in 1720 and owned by his descendants until 1891. It was demolished in 1895.

Cleveland Row SW1 (St James's, Cit. West.). Originally adjoined a house which Charles II gave to Barbara, Duchess of Cleveland, in 1670. The house passed to the dukes of Bridgewater in 1730 and to the Marquis of Stafford in 1803.

Cleveland Square W2 (Paddington, Cit. West.). Probably named from the builder. The square was laid out in the 1850s when a builder called William Cleveland was active in the area. **Cleveland Gardens** and **Terrace** adjoin.

Cleveland Street W1 (Euston Road, Camden/Cit. West.). Bounds the estate of the manor of Tottenhall held by the Fitzroy family. The name commemorates the founder of their house, Barbara Palmer (née

Villiers), mistress of Charles II. She was Viscountess Castlemaine, and Duchess of Cleveland. The latter title left the family when her grandson died without an heir in 1774.

Cleveland Way E1 (Stepney, T. Ham.). Commemorates the Wentworth family, lords of the manor of Stepney from 1550 and earls of Cleveland from 1626–67.

Cleve Road NW6 (W Hampstead, Camden). Kentish place name: built by the Powell-Cotton family of Quex Park, Birchington, Kent.

Clifford's Inn EC4 (Cit. Lond.). Site of the 'inn' or town house of Robert Clifford, granted to him by Edward II (1307–27). After Clifford's death it was leased to lawyers. The last house on the site was demolished in 1935 (*see* **Clement's Inn**).

Clifford Street W1 (Mayfair, Cit. West.). Built from 1718 on land belonging to the third Earl of Burlington, who was also Lord Clifford and Baron Clifford of Lanesborough. Much of his fortune came from his ancestress Elizabeth Clifford.

Clifton Gardens W9 (Paddington, Cit. West.). Probably named from the fashionable district of Bristol, newly famous for Brunel's suspension bridge. **Clifton Road** adjoins. **Bristol Gardens** is named by association.

Clink Street SE1 (Southwark). The Clink was a prison run by the church to house troublesome customers of the Bankside brothels. The building in Clink Street was the second (the first was nearer to Winchester Walk) and was burnt down in 1780. The origin of the word 'clink' is obscure.

Clipstone Street W1 (Cit. West.). *See* **Carburton Street**.

Clissold Road N16 (Stoke Newington, Hackney). Approaches Clissold Park, acquired as a public park in 1889, and formerly the garden of Clissold House. The house was built *c*1800 and was later owned by the Rev. Mr Clissold, who named it. **Clissold Crescent** approaches.

Cliveden Place SW1 (Belgravia, Cit. West./Ken. Chel.). Part of the Grosvenor Belgravia estate, the Grosvenor family acquired Cliveden House, Buckinghamshire, in 1868 and sold it to William Waldorf Astor in 1893.

Cloak Lane EC4 (Cit. Lond.). Derivation unknown: the former name recorded in John Stow's *Survey of London* of 1598 is Horseshoe-bridge Street, from a bridge over the Walbrook which has since been demolished. 'Cloak Lane' first appears in *c*1677.

Cloth Fair EC1 (Cit. Lond.). St Bartholomew's Fair, important to the cloth trade, was held here and on the surrounding land annually, from the founding of St Bartholomew's Hospital in the 12th century until 1855.

Clothier Street E1 (Cit. Lond.). Named by association with local dealers in old clothes. A clothes market flourished here from 1875.

Cloth Street EC1 (Cit. Lond.). A Victorian street named by association with nearby **Cloth Fair**.

Cloudesley Square N1 (Islington). Richard Cloudesley held a field on this site and left the income from it to charity in 1517. **Cloudesley Street** approaches.

Clowders Road SE6 (Perry Hill, Lewisham). An old name of the farm later called 'Perry Hill'. The farm was once occupied by Abraham Clowders, who died in 1686. He is buried at St Mary's parish church, Lewisham. The road was built on the farm's land.

Cluny Place SE1 (Bermondsey, Southwark). Part of the site of the mediaeval abbey of St Saviour's, Bermondsey, which until 1381 was owned by and administered from the Benedictine abbey of Cluny.

Clydesdale Road W11 (Notting Hill, Ken. Chel.). Commemorates the veteran soldier Colin Campbell, Lord Clyde of Clydesdale, whose part in suppressing the Indian mutiny (1857–8) made him a hero to his contemporaries.

Coach and Horses Yard W1 (Mayfair, Cit. West.). The *Burlington Arms* public house here was originally called *The Coach and Horses*.

Coate Street E2 (Bethnal Green, T. Ham.). Built on part of the former Coate's Farm, which covered much of Bethnal Green in the early 19th century. The farm house stood between the present Gosset Street and Bethnal Green Road, near Squirries Street.

Cobden Street E14 (Poplar, T. Ham.). *See* **Bright Street**.

Coborn Road E3 (Bow, T. Ham.). Mrs Prisca or Priscilla Coborn, Coburn or Colborne was a benefactor to the original parish of Stepney (which included this area) and to Bow in particular. By her will of 1701 she left a fund for the benefit of seamen's widows, to be taken from the income of her manor of Covill Hall, White Roding, Essex. She also left an annuity to the clergy and poor of Bow, and money for a schoolmaster and his wife to teach 50 poor children. These were supported by land here, N of Bow Road. The school was built W of Old Ford Road.

Cobourg Road SE5 (Peckham, Southwark). *See* **Cobourg Street**. The British royal link with the house of Cobourg was strengthened by the marriage of Edward, Duke of Kent, to the Dowager Princess of Leiningen in 1818; she was sister to Prince Leopold and to the Duke of Saxe-Coburg and Saalfeld, whose son Albert was marked down from birth as the future husband of the Kents' own daughter Victoria.

Cobourg Street NW1 (Euston, Camden). Commemorates the marriage of Princess Charlotte, only child of George IV, to Prince Leopold of Saxe-Coburg in 1816. The name appears in English as Cobourg and Coburg. Both the princess and the marriage were extremely popular; her death in childbirth (of a stillborn child) in 1817 was seen as a national disaster.

Cochrane Street NW8 (St John's Wood, Cit. West.). Admiral Lord Cochrane (1775–1860) lived at Hanover Lodge in Regent's Park from 1832. He was a successful, ingenious and unorthodox commander, but his career suffered from friction between himself and the Admiralty. He was convicted of a stock-exchange swindle in 1814 and, after a period of bitter opposition to the government, went to Chile to lead the Chilean navy against Spain. The rest of his adventurous career was mainly spent abroad; he returned to England following a free pardon given at the accession of William IV in 1830.

Cock Lane EC1 (Cit. Lond.). This could have been a lane where cockerels were reared for market, or a place of cock-fighting.

Cockpit Steps SW1 (Cit. West.). Site of the royal cockpit, a circular

building like a small theatre, for staging cock-fights. The building appears on a panorama made by the Dutch artist John Kip *c*1710–20.

Cockpit Yard WC1 (Bloomsbury, Camden). Site of an 18th-century cock-fighting pit.

Coin Street SE1 (Lambeth). On a part of the Duchy of Cornwall estate which was developed as Prince's Town from 1815, and so-called from the current Duke of Cornwall, the Prince Regent. This street was called Prince's Street until 1893, when it was changed to avoid confusion with other 'Prince's' streets. The origin of the new name is unknown.

Coke Street E1 (Bethnal Green, T. Ham.). The Rev. Edward F. Coke was vicar of St James the Great, Bethnal Green Road, from the 1850s onwards for more than 40 years (*see* **Redchurch Street**).

Colbeck Mews SW7 (Kensington, Ken. Chel.). Probably built by the Colbeck family; the Rev. William Colbeck is recorded as owning land in Kensington in 1849.

Colby Road SE19 (Dulwich, Southwark). Edmund Colby was a 17th-century fellow of nearby Dulwich College.

Cold Bath Square EC1 (Clerkenwell, Islington). Built on part of Cold Bath Fields, so named from a spring discovered in 1697 and used as a medicinal cold bath. The square was built during the early 18th century.

Cold Blow Lane SE14 (New Cross, Southwark). Named from Coldblow Farm, which stood near the junction with the present Juno Way. On the tithe map of 1844 the farm covers about 130 acres.

Coldharbour E14 (Blackwall, T.

Ham.). Commemorates a house called 'Coldharbour' in Blackwall which is thought to have been the residence of Sir John Pulteney (of Coldharbour in Upper Thames Street). Sir John was lord of the manor of Poplar in the 14th century (*see* **Coldharbour Lane**).

Coldharbour Lane SE5, SW9 (Camberwell, Lambeth). Originally a country lane; the meaning of the name is obscure, but it may mean a wayside shelter. The original hamlet of Cold Harbour is recorded in the 14th century as a manor occupied by the Vaughan family. It stood on and around the present Loughborough Junction.

Colebert Avenue E1 (Stepney, T. Ham.). *See* **Amiel Street**.

Colebrooke Row N1 (Islington). One of the manors of Islington (Highbury) consisted of the present Highbury area and a detached portion in S Islington. James Colebrooke acquired the manor in 1723. Colebrooke Row was built *c*1768 (*see* **Eade Road**).

Colegrove Road SE15 (Peckham, Southwark). Properly Colegrave. David Colegrave was a churchwarden of St Giles's, Camberwell, in 1875. The parish included Peckham.

Coleherne Road SW10 (Earl's Court, Ken. Chel.). A house at the junction of Redcliffe Gardens and Brompton Road, called 'Coleherne Court', was demolished in the late 19th century and replaced by flats of the same name. The house is thought to have been built *c*1700.

Colehill Lane SW6 (Fulham, Hammersmith). Site of Colehill House, built on the present Fulham Palace Road *c*1770. The place was called Colyshill or Coleshill, probably from a personal name, in

the 15th century.

Coleman Fields N1 (Islington). Built on fields called Great Coleman and Little Coleman, from an early proprietor.

Coleman Road SE5 (Camberwell, Southwark). The architect W.G. Coleman designed St George's school nearby.

Coleman Street EC2 (Cit. Lond.). First recorded in the 12th century; the derivation of the name is uncertain. It may be the name of a local land or property owner, or it may record the site of an early church dedicated to St Coleman, who was Abbot of Lindisfarne and champion of the Celtic Church in its disputes with Rome. He died in 676.

Coleridge Close SW8 (Battersea, Wandsworth). Commemorates the poet Samuel Taylor Coleridge (1772–1834), author of *Khubla Khan* and *The Rime of the Ancient Mariner*.

Colet Gardens W14 (Hammersmith). John Colet, Dean of St Paul's Cathedral, founded St Paul's School in 1510. The school moved to this site in 1880. The street was built along the line of an old lane called Cow Lane, from the *Red Cow* inn.

Coley Street WC1 (Holborn, Islington). Henry Coley (1633–*c*95), astrologer and mathematician, lived in Baldwin's Gardens, Gray's Inn Road. He published *Claris Astrologiae Elimata* in 1669, and also published a regular almanack, as well as inheriting an established almanack from his adoptive father William Lilly.

Colfe Road SE23 (Forest Hill, Lewisham). The Rev. Abraham Colfe was vicar of Lewisham 1610–57, and was outstanding for his work for the parish. He successfully resisted the enclosure of Westwood and Sydenham commons, and he refounded and endowed a free grammar school. He owned a field here called the Great Ozey Field.

Collamore Avenue SW18 (Earlsfield, Wandsworth). Built partly on the site of a large house called 'Collamore'.

College Crescent NW3 (Swiss Cottage, Camden). *See* **Eton Avenue**.

College Cross N1 (Barnsbury, Islington). Crosses the rear of the college built for the Church Missionary Society. The college and streets were built on the former Cooke's Field, which Thomas Cubitt bought in 1822, and of which he sold a portion to the College.

College Lane NW5 (Kentish Town, Camden). The College of St John the Evangelist, Cambridge, acquired this land by the will of William Platt in 1637. The estate lay E of Highgate Road and extended S from Ingestre Road, approximately to the line of Falkland Road. Other street names on the estate have college associations (*see* **Lady Margaret Road**).

College Mews SW1 (Cit. West.). *See* **Great College Street**.

College Road SE19, SE21 (Dulwich, Southwark). Passes Dulwich College, built in 1614 as a boys' school and almshouses, and endowed with the income of Dulwich manor in 1620 (*see* **Alleyn Park**).

College Street EC4 (Cit. Lond.). With **College Hill**, bounds the church of St Michael Royal which was rebuilt as a collegiate church by Richard Whittington, Lord Mayor in 1419. The college of clergy was suppressed under Edward VI. The church was formerly called St Michael Paternoster Royal, or church of the rosary-

makers (paternosterers) by La Reole. College Street was called Paternoster Street, where the rosary-makers worked, and College Hill was Royal Street (*see* **Tower Royal**).

Collingham Gardens SW5 (Kensington, Ken. Chel.). *See* **Knaresborough Place** for this and **Collingham Place** and **Row**.

Collingwood Street E1 (Bethnal Green, T. Ham.). Admiral Collingwood entered the navy as a volunteer in 1761, when he was 11, and served in N America, the West Indies and the Mediterranean before winning public acclamation at the battle of Cape St Vincent in 1797. He became a Rear Admiral in 1804, in which capacity he fought at Trafalgar under Nelson (*see* **Trafalgar Square**).

Collinson Street SE1 (Borough, Southwark). A Victorian street commemorating a family active in parish affairs. Edward Collinson was the first representative of St George the Martyr parish to the Metropolitan Board of Works, which was established in December 1855.

Collin's Yard N1 (Islington). Leads N off Islington Green. Sam Collins took the *Lansdowne Arms* inn on Islington Green in 1862 and ran it as a variety theatre; it was later known as Collins Music Hall. It was rebuilt in the 1890s.

Colls Road SE15 (Peckham, Southwark). Benjamin Colls of Camberwell was a successful builder active in S London in the 1860s.

Collyer Place SE15 (Peckham, Southwark). Commemorates a popular minister of nearby Hanover Chapel, who served from 1801 for over 40 years.

Colombo Street SE1 (Southwark). Built on part of the mediaeval manor called Paris Garden. Alexander Colombo was bailiff of the manor 1859–63.

Colonnade WC1 (Bloomsbury, Camden). Formerly a Georgian colonnade of shops with a pillared arcade.

Colston Road SW14 (Mortlake, R. upon T.). Commemorates Edward Colston, philanthropist, of Bristol, who lived in a house on the present Lower Richmond Road, Mortlake. In 1720 he left money for the support of a local school. The house was demolished *c*1860.

Columbia Road E2 (Bethnal Green, T. Ham.). Formerly Crabtree Row, from crab-apple trees, and renamed in 1875 after the opening of Columbia Square and Columbia Market in 1862 and 1869 respectively. These probably compliment the new Crown colony of British Columbia, constituted in 1858 and amalgamated with Vancouver Island Colony in 1866. The united colony became a province of the Dominion of Canada in 1871.

Colville Gardens W11 (Notting Hill, Ken. Chel.). Probably commemorates General Charles Colville, veteran of the Napoleonic Wars, who commanded with distinction in the Peninsular campaign and at Cambray. He died in 1843.

Colville Place W1 (Tottenham Court Road, Camden). Built by John Colvill or Colville, carpenter, who began the street in 1766.

Colwell Road SE22 (E Dulwich, Southwark). Properly Coldwell, a Derbyshire place name, as **Melbourne Grove**.

Comber Grove SE5 (Camberwell, Southwark). Commemorates a missionary to the Congo called

Thomas Comber, who was born in Camberwell.

Comeragh Road W14 (Baron's Court, Hammersmith). *See* **Palliser Road**.

Comet Place SE8 (Deptford, Lewisham). The *Comet* was a ship built at Deptford shipyards in 1822. **Comet Street** adjoins.

Commercial Dock Passage SE16 (Rotherhithe, Southwark). A dock called the Great West Dock was built here by the first Duke of Bedford and the Howland family in 1700; the duke's grandson had married Elizabeth Howland. The dock was leased by the South Sea Company in 1725 with a view to reviving the Greenland fisheries, and it was called Greenland Dock. This project coming to nothing, the dock changed hands until it was enlarged and reopened as the Commercial Dock in 1809. Further expansion followed until the whole Surrey Commercial group filled the area between Rotherhithe Street and Plough Way. All these docks are now closed.

Commercial Road E1, E14 (Stepney, T. Ham.). Built in 1804 as a new direct route for commercial traffic between the City of London and the new East India and West India Docks. **Commercial Street**, Spitalfields, was made to link this road with routes to the N.

Commercial Way SE15 (Peckham, Southwark). The road bridged the Peckham branch of the Surrey Commercial Dock Company's Surrey Canal (now closed) which helped the establishment here of many small businesses. In the 19th century the street was called Commercial Road, the name replacing an earlier sequence of 35 names extending down the length of the street; two of these were

Commercial Place and Commercial Terrace.

Commonfield Passage SW17 (Tooting, Wandsworth). This name preserves one of the old field names of Tooting Graveney parish.

Commonwealth Avenue W12 (Shepherd's Bush, Hammersmith). *See* **Australia Road**.

Como Road SE23 (Forest Hill, Lewisham). *See* **Vestris Road**.

Compton Road N1 (Canonbury, Islington). In 1570 the manor of Canonbury passed to the merchant Sir John Spencer, called 'Rich Spencer'. In 1594 his daughter Elizabeth eloped with Lord Compton, who became Spencer's heir. The Comptons became earls (1618) and later marquises of Northampton. The Northampton estate has **Compton Avenue, Compton Street** and **Northampton Square** and **Street**.

Comus Place SE17 (Walworth, Southwark). One of three local names taken from 17th-century drama. The poet John Milton wrote two dramatic works: *Comus*, a masque (1634), and the verse tragedy *Samson Agonistes* (1671) (*see* **Congreve Street** and **Massinger Street**).

Conder Street E14 (Stepney, T. Ham.). The name of a builder active in E London from the 1850s.

Conduit Mews W2 (Bayswater, Cit. West.). *See* **Spring Street**. The conduit pipes to the City of London from Ox Close nearby passed the S end of this street. **Conduit Place** is nearby.

Conduit Street W1 (Regent Street, Cit. West.) Crosses the former Conduit Mead held by the

Corporation of the City of London from the 15th century, to safeguard a conduit taking water to the City. This water supply is first mentioned in 1236, the source being in the present Stratford Place. More springs nearby were railed in and protected for the City in 1355.

Congreve Street SE17 (Walworth, Southwark). One of three local names taken from 17th-century drama. William Congreve (1670–1729) continued writing into the 18th century, but his social and sexual satires were the culmination of the 17th-century Restoration drama (*see* **Comus Place** and **Massinger Street**).

Coniger Road SW6 (Fulham, Hammersmith). Revival of an old place name. Coniger or Conigre was a plot of land belonging to Fulham manor.

Connaught Square W2 (Bayswater, Cit. West.). Connaught House, SE of the square, was owned by the royal house of Hanover and named from a family title, Duke of Connaught. The house was occupied by Caroline, Princess of Wales, after her separation from Prince George in 1796. **Connaught Place** and **Street** approach.

Consort Road SE15 (Peckham, Southwark). *See* **Albert Bridge Road**. Formerly Albert Road, as running S from Queen's Road. The name was changed because there were many other 'Albert' street names. The road was built along the line of an old lane called Cow Walk.

Cons Street SE1 (Lambeth). The Royal Victoria Coffee Music Hall nearby, otherwise called the 'Old Vic', was opened by an association headed by Emma Cons in 1880. Her aim was reform – family entertainment and coffee in place of bawdy jokes and gin (*see* **Baylis Road**).

Conway Street W1 (Euston, Camden). *See* **Hertford Place**.

Coomer Place SW6 (Fulham, Hammersmith). From a resident maker of tobacco pipes in the 19th century.

Cooper's Road SE1 (Old Kent Road, Southwark). Formerly one of a pair, with Astley Road (now abolished), and named in 1868 in honour of the surgeon Sir Astley Paston Cooper.

Cooper's Row EC3 (Cit. Lond.). Named in the 18th century from a property owner. The earlier name was Woodruffe Lane, of which the derivation was not known, but may have been from an earlier owner or trader.

Copeland Road SE15 (Peckham, Southwark). Chief Justice Copeland lived in Camberwell and is recorded as subscribing to a building fund for Hanover Chapel, when the premises were enlarged between 1741 and 1757.

Copenhagen Place E14 (Limehouse, T. Ham.). N extension of a short street leading to the 19th-century Copenhagen Oil Mills and Wharf on the Limehouse Cut.

Copenhagen Street N1 (Islington). Built across the former Copenhagen Fields, an area of general resort and public assemblies attached to Copenhagen House. The house became a tea-house after the Restoration, and the derivation of its name is uncertain. It is thought to have been the refuge of the Danish ambassador during the plague outbreak of 1665, or the home of a 17th-century Danish merchant. It was demolished in 1856.

Cope Place W8 (Kensington, Ken. Chel.). Sir Walter Cope, Chamberlain of the Exchequer to James I, bought the manor of West Towne, Kensington, in 1591. He built the house which was later known as 'Holland House'. He bought two other Kensington manors – Notting Barns (which he resold) and Abbot's Kensington (*see* **St Mary Abbot's Place**) in 1599, and the fourth manor, Earl's Kensington, in 1609.

Copleston Road SE15 (Camberwell, Southwark). One of a group commemorating eminent churchmen. Edward Copleston (1776–1849) was Bishop of Llandaff. His friend Richard Whateley was Archbishop of Dublin 1831–63; **Whateley Road** is in E Dulwich. Reginald Heber became prebendary of St Asaph in 1812 and Bishop of Calcutta in 1822; **St Asaph Road** is in Nunhead and **Heber Road** is in E Dulwich. Robert Lowth was Bishop of London (*d* 1787). **Lowth Road** is in Camberwell.

Copley Park SW16 (Streatham Common, Lambeth). *See* **Braxted Park**.

Copperas Street SE8 (Deptford, Greenwich). The first English factory producing copperas was set up in Queenborough, Kent, when the copperas stone was found on the Isle of Sheppey. In the 17th century a noted works was established in Deptford by Sir Nicholas Crisp (*see* **Crisp Road**). The stones, also called sulphur stones, were exposed, laid out in beds 100 feet long, until they had broken down into a nitrous earth. Water which percolated this earth was boiled to produce crystals. The smell produced by the process is said to have been revolting.

Copperfield Street SE1 (Southwark). *See* **Dickens Square**. Charles Dickens's novel *David Copperfield* was published in 1850, and is considered his most autobiographical novel.

Copthall Avenue EC2 (Cit. Lond.). This street replaced the N end of Bell Alley, which ran from Coleman Street across the line of the modern Moorgate to the point now called **Copthall Buildings** and then N to London Wall. Named by association with Copthall Buildings and Copthall Close, which it approached.

Copthall Buildings EC2 (Cit. Lond.). These were originally approached by Copthall Court, which is now gone, and which ran N from Throgmorton Street – beside the Draper's Hall. A 'copt' hall was a crested hall.

Coptic Street WC1 (Bloomsbury, Camden). Formerly Duke Street, from the dukes of Bedford who owned the land. The street was renamed in 1894. The British Museum nearby had recently acquired an important collection of manuscripts from the Egyptian or Coptic Christian Church.

Coram Street WC1 (Bloomsbury, Camden). In 1741 Captain Thomas Coram bought part of Lamb's Conduit Fields in order to set up a foundling hospital. Coram was born at Lyme Regis and spent much of his youth in America. He had returned to England and settled in London by 1720. The plight of small children abandoned in the streets moved him to work for the establishment of a refuge for them, a task which took him 20 years of persuasion and agitation. The hospital moved to Berkhamsted in 1926, but the land is still called Coram's Fields.

Corbet Court EC3 (Cit. Lond.). Named after a 17th-century property owner.

Cord Way E14 (Isle of Dogs, T. Ham.). Built across part of the 19th-century Universe Ropeworks.

Cork Street W1 (Mayfair, Cit. West.). Built from 1718 on land leased by Richard Boyle, Third Earl of Burlington and Fourth Earl of Cork (*see* **Boyle Street**).

Corney Road W4 (Chiswick, Hounslow). Corney House (demolished), which stood at the SE end of this street, was the home of Sir William Russell in the 16th century. He is the ancestor of the dukes of Bedford.

Cornflower Terrace SE22 (Dulwich, Southwark). Named by association with nearby Dulwich College, whose scholars wear cornflowers on Founder's Day.

Cornhill EC3 (Cit. Lond.). The derivation is uncertain, but it is a very old name. It was possibly a place where a corn-market was held; it has also been suggested that corn was grown there, since it would have been prudent for the City to have a food supply within its walls.

Cornmill Lane SE13 (Lewisham). *See* **Mill Road**.

Cornthwaite Road E5 (Clapton, Hackney). The Rev. Thomas Cornthwaite (*d* 1799) was vicar of Hackney parish (which then included Clapton) for 46 years. His daughter Anne (*d* 1831) married into the local family of Powell (*see* **Powell Road**).

Cornwall Gardens SW7 (Kensington, Ken. Chel.). Compliments Prince Albert Edward, Prince of Wales and Duke of Cornwall (*see* **Prince of Wales Drive**). Surrounding streets were given Cornish place names by association: **Launceston Place** and **Kynance Mews** and **Place**.

Cornwall Road SE1 (Lambeth). Built in 1815, as a widening and lengthening of the former Green Lane. The land on which the street was built is a detached portion of the manor of Kennington, which belongs to the Duchy of Cornwall (*see* **Black Prince Road**).

Cornwall Terrace NW1 (Regent's Park, Cit. West.). Part of John Nash's Regent's Park scheme (*see* **Regent Street**). The Prince Regent was also Duke of Cornwall. **Cornwall Terrace Mews** adjoins.

Corporation Row EC1 (Clerkenwell, Islington). Formerly Cut-Throat Lane, and renamed after the opening there of the New Corporation Workhouse *c*1665. The workhouse later became a school for poor children.

Corunna Road SW8 (Battersea, Wandsworth). Commemorates an action in the Peninsular campaign of the Napoleonic Wars. British forces under Sir John Moore had been attacking Napoleon's lines of communication. Heavily outnumbered, Moore decided to evacuate his men and, in January 1809, brought them to Corunna (La Coruña) on the N coast of Spain. He was killed during the evacuation. Charles Wolfe's poem *The Burial of Sir John Moore at Corunna* was extremely popular.

Cosmo Place WC1 (Bloomsbury, Camden). This leads off Southampton Row on the Duke of Bedford's estate. John Russell, Sixth Duke of Bedford, married in 1803 Georgiana Gordon, grand-daughter of Cosmo, Marquis of Huntly and Duke of Gordon. **Huntley Street** lies W of Gower Street.

Cosser Street SE1 (Lambeth). A local family name. Walter Cosser had a timber yard in Stangate Street (which lay E of this area) in 1805. Cosser and Sons were timber

merchants on Belvedere Wharf in 1841, moving to Acre Wharf by 1845. At the same time Andrew Cosser, builder, was established in York Road.

Cosway Street NW1 (Marylebone, Cit. West.). Commemorates the painter Richard Cosway (*d* 1821) who was born in Tiverton, Devonshire, and lived in Marylebone. Cosway was best known for his miniatures.

Cotham Street SE17 (Walworth, Southwark). The Rev. George Cotham was vicar of St John's church nearby in the 1860s.

Cottage Place SW3 (Brompton, Ken. Chel.). Originally a row of mews cottages serving Brompton Square.

Cottington Street SE11 (Lambeth). Laid out on part of the manor of Kennington. Sir Francis Cottington (afterwards Lord Cottington) held part of the manor on lease. He was a diplomat and adviser to James I, and also to Charles I who made him Lord Treasurer in 1643. **Cottington Close** is nearby.

Cotton Street E14 (Poplar, T. Ham.). Joseph Cotton (1745–1825) was a deputy master of Trinity House from 1803 and a director of the East India Company 1795–1823. He acted as chairman of the newly-formed East India Docks Company, from 1803, and he held land in Poplar and Limehouse.

Coulson Street SW3 (Chelsea, Ken. Chel.). Built on part of the former Colvill's Nursery, which was left to Thomas Coulson of Clerkenwell in the mid-19th century. The trustees responsible for developing the estate were John Anderson of Chelsea and Stroud Lincoln of Brompton. **Anderson** and **Lincoln** Streets adjoin.

Counter Court SE1 (Borough, Southwark). Corruption of 'Compter court': the mediaeval parish church of St Margaret which stood here was closed *c*1540 and the buildings used partly as a courtroom and partly as a prison or compter (*see* **St Margaret's Court**).

Counter Street SE1 (Tooley Street, Southwark). *See* **Counter Court**. The Borough Compter was later moved to this spot from St Margaret's church.

Countess Road NW5 (Kentish Town, Camden). *See* **Lady Margaret Road**.

County Grove SE5 (Camberwell, Southwark). Local historians associate this with **Flodden Road**.

Courtfield Gardens SW5 (Kensington, Ken. Chel.). Site of the Courtfield, a field connected with the manorial court of Earl's Court (*see* **Earl's Court Road**).

Courthill Road SE13 (Lewisham). A mediaeval place name of Lewisham manor, possibly the customary site of the manorial court.

Court Lane SE21 (Dulwich, Southwark). Originally approached (at the N end) a houses and estate called 'Dulwich Court'. The Court belonged to Bermondsey Abbey before the dissolution of the monasteries *c*1539. Thomas Calton acquired it from Henry VIII at the suppression of the abbey; Sir Francis Calton mortgaged it away in 1602, and it came into the possession of Edward Alleyn (*see* **Alleyn Park**). **Calton Avenue** approaches.

Courtnell Street W2 (Paddington, Cit. West.). Commemorates Reuben Courtnell Greatorex, architect and member of a building company active in local development from *c*1850.

Cousin Lane EC4 (Cit. Lond.). The house of William Cousin or Cosin, early 14th-century sheriff of the City, stood here.

Coutts Road E3 (Mile End, T. Ham). *See* **Burdett Road**.

Covent Garden WC2 (Cit. West.). Corruption of 'Convent garden', being part of the 40-acre herb and vegetable garden belonging to the Abbey of St Peter, Westminster, from *c*1200 and possibly earlier. The land passed to the Russell family, earls of Bedford, who laid out the streets from 1631. Covent Garden itself was designed by Inigo Jones as a piazza; in 1670 the fifth Earl of Bedford obtained a licence for a flower, fruit and vegetable market.

Coventry Street W1 (Cit. West.). Henry Coventry, Secretary of State to Charles II in 1672–9, lived here (in the former Shaver's Hall; *see* **Shaver's Place**) for most of his term of office. The rest of the street had been built up by 1682. **New Coventry Street** is an E continuation built *c*1845.

Cowcross Street EC1 (Clerkenwell, Islington). Route on which the cattle were driven to W Smithfield. John Stow's *Survey of London* of 1598 says the street also had 'sometime' a mediaeval cross near its junction with St John Street.

Cowden Street SE6 (Bellingham, Lewisham). Part of the mediaeval manor of Lewisham which belonged to the abbots of Ghent (*see* **Ghent Street**). When they acquired the manor in 1044 it included small plots of land in the Weald of Kent, some of which were in Cowden parish.

Cowley Street SW1 (Cit. West.) *See* **Barton Street**.

Cowper Road N16 (Shacklewell,

Hackney). *See* **Shakespeare Walk**.

Cowper Street EC2 (Finsbury, Islington). John and Frederick Cowper, proprietors of a city warehouse, owned much of the property here from the 1830s.

Cox's Walk SE21 (Dulwich Common, Southwark). Cut by Francis Cox, landlord of the *Green Man*, Dulwich, in 1730, as a path through what was then a 50-acre wood. He was obliged to leave a certain depth of trees unfelled on either side of his lane.

Crabtree Lane SW6 (Fulham, Hammersmith). Originally approached Crabtree Close, a holding with cottages and crab-apple trees. A house is recorded there in the 16th century.

Crace Street NW1 (St Pancras, Camden). As **Inwood Place**, commemorates the company of interior designers and decorators who worked on St Pancras New Church nearby, in 1880. Frederick Crace (1779–1859) had become celebrated through his interior designs for the Brighton Pavilion. He was also a noted collector of London maps and topographical pictures.

Cramer Street W1 (Marylebone, Cit. West.). The German-born violinist Wilhelm Cramer (*d* 1799) was an associate of Johann Christian Bach, on whose invitation he came to London and settled in St Marylebone. He is buried in the old St Marylebone burial ground, now a public garden, nearby. Cramer had a distinguished career as a soloist; his son Johann Baptist Cramer was an equally successful pianist, and also a composer.

Cranbourn Street WC2 (Cit. West.). Built from *c*1670 on land belonging to the Earl of Salisbury, who was also

Viscount Cranbourn or Cranborne; he took his title from a property in Dorset (*see* **Cecil Court**).

Cranley Gardens SW7 (Kensington, Ken. Chel.). Laid out on land belonging to the Earl of Onslow, who was also Viscount Cranley of Cranley in Surrey. **Cranley Mews** adjoins, **Cranley Place** is nearby (*see* **Onslow Square**).

Cranworth Gardens SW9 (Stockwell, Lambeth). The Rt Hon. Lord Cranworth was Lord High Chancellor in 1856, about the time that this street was built.

Craven Hill W2 (Bayswater, Cit. West.). Site of the 17th-century house and estate of that name belonging to the Earl of Craven. The earl was noted for his concern for the victims of the plague, in 1665, and for his devotion to the ex-queen Elizabeth of Bohemia, sister of Charles I and mother of Prince Rupert of the Rhine. **Craven Hill Gardens**, **Craven Road** and **Craven Terrace** adjoin.

Craven Street WC2 (Strand, Cit. West.). Built on land belonging to William Craven, Third Baron Craven of Hampstead Marshall, *c*1730.

Crawford Passage EC1 (Clerkenwell, Islington). An old path, formerly called Pickled Egg Walk, from its tavern, *The Pickled Egg*, of which Peter Crawford was landlord from 1760.

Crawford Street W1 (Marylebone, Cit. West.). On the Portman estate (*see* **Portman Square**). The family held property at Tarrant Crawford in Dorset. **Crawford Place** adjoins.

Crebor Street SE22 (Dulwich, Southwark). Site of Crebor Villa, now demolished.

Creechurch Lane EC3 (Cit. Lond.). Corruption of Christchurch Lane: the Priory of Holy Trinity Christchurch stood on the site before the dissolution of the monasteries (*see* **Duke's Place**).

Creed Lane EC4 (Cit. Lond.). *See* **Amen Corner.**

Creekside SE8 (Deptford, Lewisham). Runs alongside Deptford Creek. The head of the creek lay beside the junction with Church Street. The S end of this lane was formerly called Slaughterhouse Lane.

Cremer Street E2 (Shoreditch, Hackney). Commemorates Sir William Randal Cremer, MP for Haggerston 1885–95 and secretary of the International Arbitration League. He was awarded the Nobel Peace Prize in 1903.

Cremorne Road SW10 (Chelsea, Ken. Chel.). Cremorne House stood here, belonging to Thomas Dawson, Viscount Cremorne. After the death of Viscountess Cremorne in 1825 the grounds became a stadium for boxing and athletics. In 1846 they were reopened as a public pleasure garden. The garden closed in 1877 and the site was built up. **Stadium Street** adjoins.

Crescent Wood Road SE26 (Dulwich, Southwark). *See* **Low Cross Wood Lane.**

Cresswell Gardens SW5 (Kensington, Ken. Chel.). Built on the site of Cresswell Lodge, built for William Cresswell on land leased from the Gunter estate in 1813.

Cressy Road NW3 (Hampstead, Camden). *See* **Agincourt Road.**

Crewdson Road SW9 (Brixton Road, Lambeth). Built on land belonging to

a Mr Crewdson in 1888.

Crew Street E14 (Isle of Dogs, T. Ham.). *See* **Capstan Square.**

Cripplegate Street EC2 (Cit. Lond.). Originally approached the Cripplegate or Crepel Gate in the N wall of the City; 'crepel' is from the Latin and means a covered way. The name was corrupted to 'Cripplegate' after reports that the body of St Edmund the Martyr, when brought through the gate, had miraculously cured cripples who sat beside it. The gate was near the ruins of St Alphage's church on London Wall.

Crispin Street E1 (Spitalfields, T. Ham.). Derivation unknown. Built from 1668 along the E wall of the old artillery ground, the builders being William Savill, carpenter, and John Pike, bricklayer.

Crisp Road W6 (Hammersmith). Brandenburgh House, which stood at the E end of this road, was built for Sir Nicholas Crisp or Chrisp, city merchant in African trade and lifelong supporter of the royalist cause. He died in 1665 and is buried at St Paul's, Hammersmith, which he helped to build (*see* **Queen Caroline Street**).

Croftdown Road NW5 (Highgate, Camden). From a house here called 'Croft Lodge'.

Crompton Street W2 (Paddington, Cit. West.). *See* **Hall Place.**

Cromwell Avenue W6 (Hammersmith). The Town Brewery on Hammersmith Creek was founded by Joseph Cromwell in 1780 and survived into the late 19th century. It stood on the site of the present Town Hall.

Cromwell Road SW5, SW7 (Kensington, Ken. Chel.).

Commemorates Oliver Cromwell, Lord Protector of England 1653–8 (actual head of state from 1649). He was succeeded by his son Richard, who resigned in 1659. His fourth son Henry is supposed to have lived in a former manor house named 'Cromwell House', which stood on the site of the present Queensberry Place. **Cromwell Place** and **Mews** adjoin.

Crooked Billet Yard E2 (Hoxton, Hackney). Site of the *Crooked Billet* inn, recorded in the early 19th century.

Crosby Square EC3 (Cit. Lond.). Site of Crosby Hall, built for Sir John Crosby, sheriff of the city, in 1466. After his death it was owned by Richard III (1483–5) and briefly by Sir Thomas More (*d* 1535). The house was taken down in 1908, the great hall being saved and re-erected in Danvers Street, Chelsea, on what was formerly Sir Thomas More's garden.

Crossfield Street SE8 (Deptford, Lewisham). Remnant of an old path across the fields from Deptford village to Greenwich.

Cross Keys Court EC2 (Cit. Lond.). Site of a house on London Wall called 'Cross Keys' in the reign of Elizabeth I; whether this was a tavern or a private house is not known.

Cross Keys Square EC1 (Cit. Lond.). Recorded in 1677 as Cross Key Court, presumably from a hanging sign. Scheduled for demolition at the time of writing.

Cross Lane EC3 (Cit. Lond.). The sense is 'cutting across'; it was formerly called Fowle Lane, meaning foul or dirty.

Crosswall EC3 (Cit. Lond.). Crosses the line of the mediaeval City Wall

between the Tower and Aldgate. Remains of the Roman wall were found nearby, beneath America Square.

Crouch End Hill N8 (Hornsey, Haringey). Rises to Crouch End, a hamlet with a 'crouch', 'cruce' or standing cross. Any small group of houses forming a hamlet some distance from the main settlement in the parish was often called an 'end'.

Crowder Street E1 (Whitechapel, T. Ham.). Commemorates G. Crowder, member of the vestry of the parish of St George's in the East in the 1890s. Other members commemorated are: R.S. Sly (*see* **Sly Street**); R.C. Hellings, in **Hellings Street**; and G. Tillman, in **Tillman Street**.

Crown Court WC2 (Covent Garden, Cit. West.). From the sign of an inn called *The Crown*, now demolished, which stood on the corner with Russell Street.

Crowndale Road NW1 (Camden Town, Camden). Built on land belonging to the dukes of Bedford, who also held land at Crowndale, near Tavistock, Devon.

Croxted Road SE21, SE24 (Dulwich, Lambeth/Southwark). Called Crock Strete or Croke Strete in the 14th and 15th centuries, it had become Crocksted Lane by 1594. Possibly from 'crock' meaning a pot or vessel, whether made, sold or found there, or from a word meaning crooked.

Crucifix Lane SE1 (Bermondsey, Southwark). *See* **Holyrood Street**.

Cruden Street N1 (Islington). Commemorates Alexander Cruden (*d* 1770), compiler of the *Concordance to the Holy Scriptures*.

Cruikshank Street WC1 (Islington).

The artist George Cruikshank (1792–1878) lived in adjoining Amwell Street. He was first a political cartoonist in the tradition of Gillray, and later concentrated on book illustration, notably for the work of Dickens.

Crutched Friars EC3 (Cit. Lond.). The Friary of the Holy Cross was founded towards the end of the 13th century and stood nearby in Hart Street. The monks wore a cross as an emblem, and were known as the 'crossed' or 'crutched' order. The friary was dissolved under Henry VIII, c1539.

Crystal Palace Parade SE19 (Sydenham, Southwark). The Crystal Palace, which housed the Great Exhibition in Hyde Park in 1851, was taken down and a new, larger version was erected here in 1854. It was burnt down in 1936; its park remains as a sports centre (*see* **Paxton Place**).

Cuba Street E14 (Isle of Dogs, T. Ham.). Built during development following the opening of the West India Docks here in 1802. **Havannah Street** and **Tobago Street** nearby are from other West Indian names. Two from the East India Company's field also appear, in **Malabar Street** and **Manilla Street**.

Cubitt Street WC1 (Gray's Inn Road, Camden). The builder Thomas Cubitt, responsible for much of London's development in the mid-19th century, built this street. It was originally named Arthur Street and was later renamed in his honour. His building works stood nearby ⁻in Gray's Inn Road after 1815.

Culford Gardens SW3 (Chelsea, Ken. Chel.). *See* **Caversham Street**.

Culling Road SE16 (Rotherhithe, Southwark). One of the family names

of the Carr-Gomm family who held the manor of Rotherhithe (*see* **Gomm Road**).

Cullum Street EC3 (Cit. Lond.). Commemorates Sir John Cullum, 17th-century sheriff of the City, who owned property here.

Culross Street W1 (Mayfair, Cit. West.). On the Grosvenor estate, and formerly named 'Northop' from a family property in Flintshire. It was renamed in 1899, for reasons unknown.

Culverhouse Gardens SW16 (Streatham, Lambeth). Built on a field called Culverhouse Close in the 16th century, from a pigeon-cote which presumably stood there.

Culvert Road SW11 (Battersea, Wandsworth). Together with **Rowditch Lane** and **Heathwall Street**, testifies to the nature of the land before it was built up. Battersea's farm and market-garden land was flat, wet, and crossed by water-courses draining the higher ground of Clapham into the Thames.

Cumberland Crescent W14 (North End, Hammersmith). Site of a house called 'Cumberland Lodge'.

Cumberland Gate W1 (Marble Arch, Cit. West.). Formerly Tyburn Gate, renamed in honour of Prince William, Duke of Cumberland, brother of George III and victor of the battle of Culloden in 1746. **Great Cumberland Place** approaches.

Cumberland Terrace NW1 (Regent's Park, Camden). Built as part of John Nash's Regent's Park scheme (*see* **Regent Street**) and named from the Prince Regent's brother, Ernest Augustus, Duke of Cumberland. The duke died in 1851. **Cumberland Market** is nearby. **Cumberland Mews** and **Place** adjoin.

Cunard Street SE5 (Peckham, Southwark). Named in 1869, presumably in honour of the shipowner Sir Samuel Cunard, who died in 1865.

Cundy Street SW1 (Pimlico, Cit. West.). Part of the Grosvenor estate, to which Thomas Cundy was appointed surveyor in 1821; he, his son and his grandson controlled the development of the estate until 1890.

Cunningham Place NW8 (St John's Wood, Cit. West.). *See* **Lyons Place**. The Rev. J.W. Cunningham, vicar of Harrow, was elected a governor of Harrow School in 1818. This street is on the school's land.

Cureton Street SW1 (Cit. West.). The Rev. William Cureton (1808–64) was a canon of Westminster 1849– 64. He was assistant keeper of manuscripts at the British Museum 1837–49, and was a noted scholar of Arabic and Syriac.

Curlew Street SE1 (Bermondsey, Southwark). John Curlew, miller, rented the nearby mill at St Saviour's Dock (*see* **Mill Street**, Bermondsey) in 1536; the mill belonged to Bermondsey Abbey.

Cursitor Street EC4 (Chancery Lane, Cit. Lond./Cit. West.). Site of the office of Cursitor or Coursitor established here in the 16th century; the cursitors served Chancery writs.

Curtain Road EC2 (Shoreditch, Hackney). Formerly the W boundary of a close or small pasture belonging to the priory of Holywell, mentioned in 1537 and called (for unknown reasons) Curtain or Curten close. The Curtain Playhouse was built on this close in 1577 and named after it. It was the second theatre to be opened in London. The first – called simply 'The Theatre' – was also in Curtain Road.

Curtis Street SE1 (Bermondsey, Southwark). William Curtis (1746– 99), botanist and apothecary, laid out his first botanical garden between here and the present Crimscott Street, before beginning his large garden in Lambeth Marsh. Curtis wrote a study of London plants, *Flora Londinensis*.

Curwen Road W12 (Hammersmith). The Rev. John Curwen (1816–80) introduced the 'Look and Say' method of teaching reading in 1839, and was an advocate of the Tonic Sol-fa method of teaching singing. He founded a Tonic Sol-fa college at Forest Gate, which opened in 1879.

Curzon Street W1 (Mayfair, Cit. West.). Built in the early 18th century on land belonging to Sir Nathaniel Curzon. The land was called the Brook Field; it covered the SW corner of Mayfair and was the site of the annual May Fair, which began as a cattle market in 1686 and became general.

Cut, The SE1 (Lambeth, Lambeth/ Southwark). Made as The New Cut *c*1820, being newly cut through open country called Lambeth Marsh.

Cuthbert Street W2 (Paddington, Cit. West.). *See* **Hall Place**.

Cuthill Road SE5 (Camberwell, Southwark). Built on part of a market garden belonging to a 19th-century nurseryman called Cuthill.

Cutler Street E1 (Cit. Lond.). The Cutlers' Company owned property here in the 18th century, when the W end of the street was so-named. The section running SE was renamed by association in 1906.

Cygnet Street E1 (Bethnal Green, T. Ham.). Named by association with **Swanfield Street** and the *White Swans* tavern recorded in Little Bacon Street in 1805.

Cyrena Road SE22 (Dulwich, Southwark). Named from a fossil shell discovered in Dulwich: *Cyrena dulwichiensis*.

Czar Street SE8 (Deptford, Lewisham). Peter the Great, Czar of Russia, stayed at Deptford in 1698 studying the dockyards (*see* **Sayes Court Street**).

D

Dacre Street SW1 (Victoria, Cit. West.). Joan, Baroness Dacre, married Sir Richard Fiennes in 1446. In 1458 the king accepted him as Lord Dacre, known as Lord Dacre of the South. Their descendants lived at Stourton House, on the site of the present Dacre and Tothill Streets. Gregory Fiennes (*d* 1594) married Anne Sackville, who founded almshouses in Tothill Fields after her husband's death.

Dagmar Road SE25 (Camberwell, Southwark). Built as part of a small development by a local builder called Purkiss, who leased land from the free grammar school in 1863. A local historian suggests that Dagmar was a member of his family, as **Grace's Road** and **Maude Road** adjoining.

Dagnall Street SW11 (Battersea, Wandsworth). Edward Dagnall died in 1881, leaving £100 to be spent on bread which was to be distributed to poor widows every December.

Daleham Gardens NW3 (Hampstead, Camden). *See* **Canfield Gardens**. The Maryon-Wilson family held property at Daleham in Sussex.

Dale Road NW5 (Kentish Town, Camden). Commemorates Canon Thomas Dale, vicar of St Pancras 1846–60; he was popular as a poet and as a preacher.

Dalgarno Gardens W10 (N Kensington, Hammersmith/Ken. Chel.). Built *c*1887; commemorates the Rev. Arthur Dalgarno Robinson, who built three local churches. He was the first incumbent of St Clement's, Treadgold Street, and worked ceaselessly for the poor of the surrounding slums from 1860 until his death in 1899.

Dalling Road W6 (Hammersmith). *See* **Bulwer Street**.

Dallington Street EC1 (Clerkenwell, Islington). Commemorates the Rev. Sir Robert Dallington, Master of Sutton's Charterhouse hospital 1624–7 (*see* **Great Sutton Street**).

Dalston Lane E8 (Hackney). Old lane leading to Dalston. The name is from OE 'Dāl's Tun', meaning Dal's settlement, and in mediaeval records it appears as Dorleston. The original hamlet lay at the N end of the present Queensbridge Road.

Dame Street N1 (Islington). *See* **Packington Street**.

Danby Street SE15 (Camberwell, Southwark). Chosen in 1873 to replace 19 separately-named groups, of which three were Danby Cottages, Danby Terrace and Danby Villas. Danby may have been the builder of these three.

Dancer Road SW6 (Fulham, Hammersmith). Nathaniel Dancer or Dauncer left a fund for the poor of Fulham in 1656; the money was to be paid out of two acres of land near High Elms, SW of this road. The Dancer family still held a market garden here in the 19th century.

Dane Street WC1 (Holborn, Camden). Built on land held by the church of St Clement Danes, Aldwych, since 1522. The income is used to endow parish charities. The land extends across Eagle Street towards High Holborn.

Daneville Road SE5 (Camberwell, Southwark). The Princess of Wales had visited Camberwell shortly before the road was named in 1872. Her father, Prince Christian of Schleswig-Holstein-Sonderburg-Glücksburg, was appointed heir to the Danish throne by the Treaty of London (1852) and became king of Denmark in 1863.

Daniel's Road SE15 (Nunhead, Southwark). Henry Daniels served on Camberwell vestry in the 1860s.

Dan Leno Walk W6 (Hammersmith). Dan Leno was part owner of the nearby Granville Theatre. His real name was George Galvin, and he was born in St Pancras *c*1861. He became the most famous comedian of his day, especially as a pantomime dame. He played every Christmas pantomime at Drury Lane in 1888–1903. He died in 1904.

Dante Road SE11 (Newington, Lambeth/Southwark). Commemorates the Italian poet Dante Alighieri (*d* 1321), author of *The Divine Comedy*. Henry Barlow, a Dante scholar, suggested the name (*see* **Barlow Street**).

Danube Street SW3 (Chelsea, Ken. Chel.). Formerly Little Blenheim Street, it was renamed by association (Blenheim battle-field being on the River Danube). A descendant of the first Duke of Marlborough lived nearby (*see* **Marlborough Street**).

Danvers Street SW3 (Chelsea, Ken. Chel.). Sir John Danvers built a house here in 1623 (demolished *c*1720). Sir John acquired land that had been part of Sir Thomas More's estate.

D'Arblay Street W1 (Soho, Cit. West.). The writer Fanny Burney, Madame D'Arblay, lived nearby at 50 Poland Street (demolished) for ten years of her childhood, 1760–70. The street was renamed in her honour in 1909.

Darling Road SE4 (Deptford, Lewisham). Commemorates Lord Darling, MP for Deptford 1888–97.

Darrell Road SE22 (Dulwich, Southwark). Part of the original parish of St Giles, Camberwell; Sir Marmaduke Darrell married Ann Clappham of Camberwell at St Giles's church in 1621.

Dartmouth Park Hill NW5, N19 (Kentish Town, Camden). An estate lying W of this street and traversed by **Dartmouth Park Road** belonged to the Nicoll family from *c*1650. Frances Nicoll married William Legge, Second Earl of Dartmouth, in 1755. The Legges inherited the estate through Frances, and it became known as the Dartmouth Park estate.

Dartmouth Road SE23, SE26 (Forest Hill, Lewisham). Built on land owned by the Legge family, earls of Dartmouth (*see* **Legge Street**).

Dartmouth Street SW1 (Cit. West.). William Legge, First Earl of Dartmouth and Viscount Lewisham, was one of the first residents of nearby Queen Square (now Queen Anne's Gate) when it was built in 1704. **Lewisham Street** adjoins.

Dartnell Road SE5 (Peckham, Southwark). Built by Thomas Dartnell of Croydon in 1881–2.

Darvall Square SW18 (Wandsworth). Commemorates a French Huguenot immigrant who settled in Wandsworth and is buried in the Huguenot Burial Ground nearby. **Darvall Street** links it with **Delaporte Square**, named for the same reason.

Dassett Road SE27 (Knight's Hill, Lambeth). Built next to a large house on Knight's Hill called 'Burton Dassett'.

Datchelor Place SE5 (Camberwell, Southwark). The Mary Datchelor Girls' School in Grove Lane was founded through a charity set up in 1726 by the will of Mary Datchelor. The will provided for a day school 'for the education of girls of middle class' in the City of London. By 1871 so few eligible girls lived in the City that the conditions were changed and the school reopened in Camberwell in 1877.

Davenant Street E1 (Whitechapel, T. Ham.). Ralph Davenant was rector of Whitechapel 1668–81; he was appointed directly by Charles II, of whom he was a favourite. He left a bequest to establish the Davenant Schools.

Davies Street W1 (Mayfair, Cit. West.). The Grosvenor estate was formed from land in the dowry of Mary Davies, who married Sir Thomas Grosvenor in 1677, when she was 12. She was the heiress to the Audley properties which consisted of c100 acres in Mayfair and the much more extensive manor of Ebury (*see* **Ebury Street**).

Dawes Road SW6 (Fulham, Hammersmith). This is a local family name; the street is called Dawes Lane in the 16th century, while a William Dawe is recorded as living in Fulham in the 13th century. Sir Abraham Dawes was a prominent 17th-century property owner.

Dawes Street SE17 (Walworth, Southwark). James Arthur Dawes was the first mayor of the new Borough of Southwark in 1899, having been chairman of Newington vestry. The new borough comprised the civil parishes of St Mary, Newington, St George the Martyr, St Saviour, and Christchurch.

Dawnay Road SW18 (Wandsworth). Commemorates Sir Archibald Dawnay who was mayor of Wandsworth 1908–18. **Dawnay Gardens** adjoins.

Dawson Place W2 (Notting Hill, Ken. Chel.). Built c1852–3 on land belonging to the Dawson family; they inherited it from John Silvester Dawson, an 18th-century brewer.

Dean Bradley Street SW1 (Cit. West.). The Rev. George Granville Bradley (1821–1903) was Dean of Westminster 1881–1902. The dean is appointed by the crown; together with the canons (acting as a corporate body, the Dean and Chapter) he is responsible for the government of the abbey, its fabric and finances. He has personal responsibility for the form and order of services, and he decides who shall be baptised, married and buried in the abbey. Dean Bradley was a former schoolmaster (Rugby and Marlborough) and Master of University College, Oxford, in 1870–81.

Deanery Street W1 (Cit. West.). Formerly Dean and Chapter Street; Westminster Abbey owned the land when the street was built c1737.

Dean Farrar Street SW1 (Cit. West.). The Rev. Frederick William Farrar, schoolmaster and writer, was rector of nearby St Margaret's, Westminster, and a canon of Westminster 1876–95. He was also Dean of Canterbury 1895–1903. His novel *Eric, or Little by Little* was very successful (*see* **Dean Bradley Street**).

Dean Ryle Street SW1 (Cit. West.). The Rev. Herbert Edward Ryle (1856–1925) was an Old Testament scholar and former Cambridge don. He was Bishop of Exeter 1901–3, Bishop of Winchester 1903–11 and Dean of Westminster 1911–25 (*see* **Dean Bradley Street**).

Dean's Court EC4 (Cit. Lond.). The residence of the deans of St Paul's Cathedral was built here *c*1670 (*see* **Dean Bradley Street**).

Dean Stanley Street SW1 (Cit. West.). The Rev. Arthur Penrhyn Stanley was Dean of Westminster 1864–81. He is noted for his conviction that the Abbey should be 'the sanctuary, not of any private sect, but of the English people' (*see* **Dean Bradley Street**).

Dean Street W1 (Soho, Cit. West.). First recorded in 1678, it was built by Frith, who continued its development in the 1680s. The derivation is unknown.

Dean's Yard SW1 (Cit. West.). The house of the deans of Westminster Abbey is here (*see* **Dean Bradley Street**).

Dean Trench Street SW1 (Cit. West.). The Rev. Richard Chevenix Trench (1807–86) was Dean of Westminster from 1856, and instituted public evening worship in the nave. He became Archbishop of Dublin in 1864 (*see* **Dean Bradley Street**).

De Beauvoir Road N1 (Hackney). The manor of Bammes or Balmes (*see* **Balmes Road**) passed to Richard de Beauvoir of Guernsey, who died in 1708. **De Beauvoir Crescent** and **Square** adjoin.

De Crespigny Park SE5 (Camberwell, Southwark). The family of Champion de Crespigny, Huguenot refugees, settled in Camberwell *c*1695 and built a house called 'Champion Lodge' in 1717; it was demolished in 1841 (*see* **Champion Hill** and **Cerise Road**).

Deerhurst Road SW16 (Streatham, Lambeth). Commemorates Lord Deerhurst, afterwards Earl of Coventry, who bought the manor house of the Howland family *c*1800 (*see* **Tooting Bec Road**). The house and grounds lay between Streatham High Road and Streatham Common North. Deerhurst replaced the house with a villa called 'Coventry Park'.

Dee Street E14 (Poplar, T. Ham.). *See* **Leven Road**.

Defoe Road N16 (Stoke Newington, Hackney). The novelist Daniel Defoe (*d* 1731) lived here at the corner with Church Street, Stoke Newington. Here he wrote his most popular book, *Robinson Crusoe*, in 1719.

Dekker Road SE21 (Dulwich, Southwark). Commemorates the Elizabethan dramatist Thomas Dekker, author of *The Shoemakers' Holiday* (1599). Dekker's main inspiration was London city life. He was a prolific writer, both alone and in collaboration, much of his work going to the theatre manager Philip Henslowe, who bought him out of the debtors' prison more than once. Named by association with Edward Alleyn (*see* **Alleyn Park**).

Delancey Street NW1 (Camden Town, Camden). Built from 1795 by James Delancey of Marylebone, on land which he leased from the Fitzroy family, lords of the manor of Tottenham Court.

Delaporte Square SW18 (Wandsworth). *See* **Darvall Square**.

De Laune Street SE17 (Kennington, Southwark). The De Laune family of Doddington, Kent, owned land here from *c*1780 which they developed. Their estate was sold in small lots between 1913 and 1953 (*see* **Doddington Grove**).

Delhi Street N1 (King's Cross, Islington). *See* **Havelock Street**.

Dean's Yard

De Morgan Road SW6 (Fulham, Hammersmith). Commemorates William de Morgan (*d* 1917), artist potter prominent in the Arts and Crafts Movement, who worked in Fulham.

Denbigh Road W11 (Notting Hill, Ken. Chel.). Built by W.K. Jenkins, a property developer of Welsh origin who frequently used Welsh place names for his streets. **Denbigh Close** is nearby. **Denbigh Terrace** adjoins.

Dene Close SE4 (Brockley, Lewisham). Ralph de Dene was a member of a religious sect, the Premonstratensians, which was established at Ottham, Sussex, by 1150. Their Ottham land being infertile, they obtained land in Brockley (*see* **St Norbert Road**).

Denman Road SE15 (Peckham, Southwark). Commemorates Thomas, Baron Denman (1779–1854), who was made Attorney General in 1830. This is one of a group of Peckham names taken from the legal profession.

Denman Street W1 (Soho, Cit. West.). Built *c*1675 and originally called Queen Street in compliment to Catherine of Braganza, consort of Charles II. Renamed in honour of Lord Denman (*see* **Denman Road**) who was born there.

Denmark Hill SE5 (Camberwell, Lambeth/Southwark). Traditionally the place where Queen Anne's consort, Prince George of Denmark (*d* 1708), was accustomed to hunt; it was then a wooded hill rising above marsh ground (*see* **Dog Kennel Hill**).

Denmark Street WC2 (Charing Cross Road, Camden). A short street popularly known as Tin Pan Alley, named in honour of Prince George of Denmark (*see* **Denmark Hill**). **Denmark Place** runs parallel.

Dennett's Road SE14 (New Cross, Lewisham). A Lewisham builder called Dennett was active in S London in the 1860s and onwards. **Dennett's Grove** adjoins.

Denny Street SE11 (Kennington, Lambeth). Commemorates the Rev. Edward Denny, former vicar of St Peter's, Upper Kennington Lane.

Dents Road SW11 (S Battersea, Wandsworth). Built 1881–2 on a small estate surrounding a mansion called 'Dents House' from the Dent family who owned it. The house is now demolished. Adjoining **Gorst Road** (1883–4) records the name of a former occupier of the house, Sir John Eldon Gorst.

Denyer Street SW3 (Chelsea, Ken. Chel.). Elizabeth Denyer (*d* 1824) was a benefactor to the parish of St Luke's, Chelsea.

Deptford Church Street SE8 (Deptford, Lewisham). The original parish of St Nicholas was divided in 1730 into two. A new church was built here and dedicated to St Paul.

Deptford High Street SE8 (Deptford, Lewisham). The high or principal street of Deptford, called Depeford in the early middle ages, from the 'deep ford' across the River Ravensbourne near its entry into the Thames.

Derby Gate SW1 (Whitehall, Cit. West.). **Cannon Row** crossing this street was relinquished by the canons of St Stephen's *c*1539; it was then built up with private mansions, one of which was built by William, Lord Derby, *c*1600.

Derby Street W1 (Mayfair, Cit. West.). Off **Curzon Street**. The Curzons named it in honour of their home county, Derbyshire.

Dericote Street E8 (Hackney). Named in 1883 to commemorate Arthur Dericote, a prominent Hackney resident.

Dermody Road SE13 (Lewisham). The Irish-born poet Thomas Dermody (1775–1802) is buried in Lewisham parish church. His talent fought unsuccessfully against his dissipation, and he died in poverty.

Deronda Road SE24 (Tulse Hill, Lambeth). Commemorates the novel *Daniel Deronda* which was the last work of Mary Ann Evans, called George Eliot (1819–80). She also wrote the historical romance *Romola*, and **Romola Road** adjoins.

Derry Street W8 (Kensington, Ken. Chel.). From Derry and Toms department store, first opened in Wright's Lane in 1862 by Charles Derry and his brother-in-law Charles Toms.

Derwent Grove SE22 (E Dulwich, Southwark). *See* **Melbourne Grove**.

Desenfans Road SE21 (Dulwich, Southwark). The Dulwich Art Gallery (*see* **Gallery Road**) was established to house the collection of Noel Desenfans (*d* 1807).

De Vere Gardens W8 (Kensington, Ken. Chel.). Aubrey de Vere (or de Ver, from Ver in Normandy) acquired the manor of Kensington after the Norman Conquest. The family of de Vere, who were created earls of Oxford in 1155, held the manor until 1526.

Devereux Court WC2 (Essex Street, Cit. West.). Part of the site of Essex House, the Tudor London house of the Devereux family, earls of Essex (*see* **Essex Street**).

Devonshire Road W4 (Chiswick, Hounslow). The dukes of Devon-

shire owned nearby Chiswick House for over a century (*see* **Duke Road**).

Devonshire Row EC2 (Cit. Lond.). Leads to **Devonshire Square**, built on the site of a town house belonging to the dukes of Devonshire, which they held until 1670 (*see* **Cavendish Court**).

Devonshire Street W1 (Marylebone, Cit. West.). The Cavendish family, of which one branch became dukes of Devonshire, were related by marriage to John Holles, Duke of Newcastle, who bought the Marylebone estate in 1708. Holles was son-in-law to Henry Cavendish, Duke of Newcastle (*d* 1691), and was granted his father-in-law's title in 1694. **Devonshire Close**, **Mews** and **Place** adjoin.

De Walden Street W1 (Marylebone, Cit. West.). Built on the Duke of Portland's Marylebone estate, which passed to a sister of the fifth duke, Baroness Howard de Walden, in the 1880s.

Dewar Street SE15 (Peckham Rye, Southwark). Named in 1876, this probably commemorates John Dewar, inventor of the vacuum flask.

Dewey Road N1 (Islington). W.F. Dewey was the first Town Clerk of the Borough of Islington, having previously served as Vestry Clerk since the 1880s.

Dewey Street SW17 (Tooting, Wandsworth). Planned in 1898; between April and December that year Spain was at war with the USA. In an action off the Spanish-held Philippines, the American Admiral Dewey destroyed a Spanish squadron without loss of American life. After similar American successes in Cuba peace was signed; Spain ceded Cuba, the Philippines, Guam and Puerto Rico.

Diamond Street SE15 (Peckham, Southwark). Traditionally, a diamond was the source of the builder's capital.

Dickens Square SE1 (Southwark). The novelist Charles Dickens (*d* 1870) spent part of his boyhood in Southwark while his parents were held for debt in the Marshalsea Prison (*see* **Marshalsea Road**). The novelist and characters from his novels (particularly those with a Southwark setting) are commemorated in a group of local street names.

Dickens Street SW8 (Battersea, Wandsworth). A commemorative street named in 1877; the novelist (*see* **Dickens Square**) had died in 1870. James Knowles, the architect (1831–1908) who designed this estate, was a man of wide interests and active in the world of letters. He edited the *Contemporary Review* 1870–7, and then founded his own review, *Nineteenth Century*.

Digby Road E9 (Homerton, Hackney). Charles Digby, by his will of 1812, left £300 in trust for the poor of Hackney parish.

Dilke Street SW3 (Chelsea, Ken. Chel.). Sir Charles Wentworth Dilke (*d* 1869) of Sloane Street was a friend of the Prince Consort and an organiser of the Great Exhibition of 1851. His son became Conservative MP for the new constituency of Chelsea in 1868.

Dingley Road EC1 (Finsbury, Islington). Commemorates Charles Dingley, who proposed the building of the adjacent City Road in 1756. **Dingley Place** adjoins.

Distaff Lane EC4 (Cit. Lond.). Originally ran from Old Change to Friday Street along the present line of Cannon Street. Little Distaff Lane (the present Distaff Lane) ran off it.

The street housed mediaeval suppliers of the distaff, a cleft stick holding raw wool or flax, which was basic to all spinning, whether by hand or with a wheel.

Distillery Lane W6 (Fulham, Hammersmith). The Hammersmith Distillery was established at the river end of this lane in 1857 on the site of Brandenburgh House (*see* **Queen Caroline Street**). The place was on the border between Fulham and Hammersmith. The Haig (whisky) and Booth (gin) families used it in partnership. It was later used for processing chemicals.

Dixon Road SE14 (New Cross, Lewisham). Commemorates a local benefactor, Thomas Dixon, who left a bequest to Christ's Hospital, to be used for charity, in 1579.

Doby Court EC4 (Cit. Lond.). Probably named from a property owner. Before 1800 it was called Maidenhead Court, as leading off the then Maiden Lane, now Skinners Lane.

Dock Street E1 (Whitechapel, T. Ham.). Built as an approach to the London Docks which were opened in 1805. They were built by the City of London Corporation as competition for the New West India complex at Millwall. The London Docks originally handled wine, spirits, tobacco and rice. This street was formerly a narrow way along what is now its W side; it was widened during the extensive post-war redevelopment of this area.

Doctor Johnson Avenue SW17 (Streatham, Wandsworth). Commemorates Dr Samuel Johnson, the scholar and lexicographer who frequently stayed at Streatham during the period 1766–82 (*see* **Thrale Road**).

Docwra's Buildings N1 (Newington Green, Hackney). A mid-Victorian Street (1857) built by Docwra and Sons.

Doddington Grove SE17 (Kennington, Southwark). The De Laune family of Doddington, Kent, owned land here (*see* **De Laune Street**).

Doggett Road SE6 (Catford, Lewisham). Commemorates the actor Thomas Doggett (*d* 1721), founder of the annual Thames watermen's race for Doggett's Coat and Badge.

Dog Kennel Hill SE22 (Denmark Hill, Southwark). Traditionally the site of kennels owned by Prince George of Denmark, who kept hounds here (*see* **Denmark Hill**). The name may be older. Land owned by Edward Alleyn (*see* **Alleyn Park**) is recorded in the 17th century as Kennels, Kennold's Acre or Kennoldes Croft. An alternative theory is that 'Dog-Kennel' is a corruption of 'De Canel' from a Monsier de Canel who once lived on the hill.

Dolben Street SE1 (Southwark). Built as part of a new scheme of streets linking the lately-opened Blackfriars Bridge with St George's Fields, *c*1778. The street was originally called George Street; it was renamed to commemorate John Dolben, Bishop of Rochester, who consecrated nearby Christchurch in 1671. The original line of the street was E from Blackfriars Road.

Dolman Street SW4 (Brixton, Lambeth). Frederick Dolman was a member of the London County Council for Brixton, 1901–7.

Dombey Street WC1 (Bloomsbury, Camden).Named in 1936 to commemorate Charles Dickens's novel *Dombey and Son*. This particular novel has no local significance, but Dickens lived in nearby Doughty Street for some years. This street was formerly called East Street, in relation to New North Street.

Domett Close SE5 (Denmark Hill, Southwark). Alfred Domett was Prime Minister of New Zealand and a friend of the poet Browning (*see* **Browning Close**).

Domingo Street EC1 (Finsbury, Islington). *See* **Timber Street**.

Dominion Street EC2 (Finsbury, Islington). Originally South Street, as leading to South Place, it was renamed in 1938 from 'Dominion House' on the corner with South Place.

Domville Grove SE5 (Peckham, Southwark). Domvilles were solicitors to the Champion de Crespigny estate in Camberwell, developed during the latter half of the 19th century (*see* **Champion Hill**).

Donne Place SW3 (Chelsea, Ken. Chel.). A modern street name which may commemorate the metaphysical poet John Donne (1572–1631).

Doric Way NW1 (Eversholt Street, Camden). Formerly the E end of Drummond Street, which was broken by SE extensions to Euston Station in the 1960s. The station was opened in 1838. The architects Philip and Philip Charles Hardwick (father and son) designed an approach of great grandeur, with a monumental Greek Doric portico and flanking lodges in the same style. These were demolished during the 1960s expansion. The Doric Order of column and entablature developed in mainland Greece from *c*630 BC; it was the most austere and massive style of Greek architecture.

Dorrington Street EC1 (Holborn, Camden). Corruption of Dodding-ton: Robert Grenville (*d* 1676) who lived in Brooke Street married Anne Doddington. His Brooke Street house was demolished after his death (*see* **Brooke Street**).

Dorrit Street SE1 (Southwark). *See* **Dickens Square**. Charles Dickens's novel *Little Dorrit* draws deeply on his knowledge of Southwark and of the Marshalsea Prison.

Dorset Rise EC4 (Cit. Lond.). Leads to Dorset Buildings, part of the site of Salisbury Court (*see* **Salisbury Square**). After dissolution of the monasteries in 1536–9 Salisbury Court passed to Thomas Sackville, Earl of Dorset, and became known as 'Dorset House'. It has since been demolished.

Dorset Square NW1 (Marylebone, Cit. West.). Built on the estate of the Portman family who held consider-able property in Dorset. **Dorset Close** is nearby, **Dorset Street** is to the S (*see* **Portman Square**).

Dorville Crescent W6 (Hammer-smith). Approaches **Ravenscourt Park**. John Dorville of Soho Square bought Ravenscourt in 1765. He began selling land for building de-velopment in the 1780s.

Doughty Street WC1 (Bloomsbury, Camden). Built from 1792 on land belonging to Henry Doughty of Bed-ford Row. The Doughty family had acquired their Bloomsbury estate through Sir Edward Doughty on whom it was settled. The estate ran N from the parish boundary and W from Gray's Inn Road. It was bounded on two sides by the Coram Foundling Hospital estate and some of its streets were built in conjunction with the latter's development. **Doughty Mews** runs parallel.

Douglas Road N1 (Islington). Built on land belonging to the second Marquis of Northampton, who married Margaret Douglas-Maclean-Clephane. **Clephane Road** is nearby.

Douro Place W8 (Kensington, Ken. Chel.). Commemorating the creation of the title of Baron Douro for the Duke of Wellington, following his ac-tion on the River Douro (which flows from Spain into Portugal) during the Peninsular campaign of 1808–14.

Dovehouse Street SW3 (Chelsea, Ken. Chel.). A revival of an old place name. Dovehouse Close lay on the site of the present Paulton's Square. It was a small field containing the dove-cotes of Chelsea manor. A mediaeval manor had no resources to support grazing animals in the winter, so pigeons were an essential source of fresh meat. Their raids on crops were often a source of friction between lord and tenant.

Dove Mews SW5 (Kensington, Ken. Chel.). Remnant of old country path called Dove Lane, leading from Ken-sington High Street (S of Kensington Palace) to the Old Brompton Road.

Dover House Road SW15 (Roe-hampton, R. upon T.). This origin-ally approached Dover House which was built in the 18th century for Lord Dover, and stood at the S end of this road. **Dover Park Drive**, which crosses the grounds, runs parallel.

Dove Road N1 (Canonbury, Isling-ton). Commemorates a family of Islington builders. The firm originally consisted of four brothers, three of whom formed Dove Brothers as a partnership in 1862. They built many churches and schools, including many in this area. F.L. Dove was London County Council member for North Islington from 1910.

Dover Street W1 (Mayfair, Cit.

West.). Clarendon House, which stood here, was demolished in 1683. Part of the site was leased by Lord Dover, who built this street.

Dowgate Hill EC4 (Cit. Lond.). Site of an early route to a watergate and wharf at the confluence of the River Thames and the Walbrook; recorded in the 12th century as Duuegate. 'Duue' is from an OE word meaning dove, and might be literally that or a personal name.

Dowlas Street SE5 (Camberwell, Southwark). Site of part of Dowlas Common. This commonland was attached to that part of the manor of Camberwell which passed to the family of De Uvedale or De Ovedale in 1305. Dowlas is a corruption of De Ovedales or Dovedales, as the manor came to be called.

Downham Road N1 (De Beauvoir Town, Hackney). Built on the De Beauvoir estate which was at one time owned by the Rev. Peter Beauvoir of Downham Hall, Essex; he held it at the time of his death in 1821.

Downham Way (Lewisham). Named in 1924. The road runs through the estate called Downham after Lord Downham, president of the Local Government Board and an important influence on local authority housing schemes after World War I.

Downing Street SW1 (Whitehall, Cit. West.). Built in the late 17th century on land belonging to Sir George Downing. Sir Robert Walpole, England's first Prime Minister (1721), lived at no. 10 and it remained the official residence of the Prime Minister thereafter.

Downshire Hill NW3 (Hampstead, Camden). Wills Hill served in Lord North's administration of 1779–82 as Secretary of State for the South. He

was created Marquis of Downshire in 1789.

Downs Road E5 (Hackney). Passes Hackney Downs, common land where there had been winter grazing rights since the middle ages. William Robinson, in his *History and Antiquities of Hackney* of 1842, reports a tendency to plough up the Downs, and they were later saved from the threat of building and preserved as public open space.

Down Street W1 (Mayfair, Cit. West.). Built during 1720–30 by John Downes, bricklayer.

Dowrey Street N1 (Islington). *See* **Cloudesley Square**. Dowrey is a corruption of Docwra. Sir Thomas Docwra (*d* 1527), Prior of the Knights of St John of Jerusalem from 1502, was an executor of Richard Cloudesley's will.

D'Oyley Street SW1 (Chelsea, Ken. Chel.). Built on the estate inherited from Sir Hans Sloane (*see* **Sloane Street**) by his daughters, Elizabeth, Countess Cadogan, and Sarah Stanley. Sarah's daughters, inheriting in their turn, were Sarah D'Oyley and Anne Ellis. **Ellis Street** adjoins.

Dragoon Road SE8 (Deptford, Lewisham). Approaches the site of Deptford Royal Dockyards (later the Foreign Cattle Market), embarkation point for troops serving overseas. The dockyards were a royal station from 1513 until they closed in 1869.

Drake Road SE4 (Deptford, Lewisham). Part of the sub-manor of Brockley which passed by marriage from the Wickham family (*see* **Wickham Road**) to the Drakes in the 1780s. Anne and Mary Wickham married respectively Thomas and John Drake of Shardeloes in

Buckinghamshire (*see* **Tyrwhitt Road**).

Drapers Gardens EC2 (Cit. Lond.). Runs behind Throgmorton Street where the Drapers' Company established their guildhall in 1543; they bought the house of Thomas Cromwell, Secretary of State to Henry VIII, after his execution. Cromwell had extended the gardens northwards by stealing his neighbours' land, according to John Stow (*Survey of London*, 1598), and 'no man durst go to argue the matter'.

Draycott Avenue SW3 (Ken. Chel.). Maria Draycott married Sir Francis Shuckburgh of Blacklands House in 1825. The house, which stood at the corner of Draycott Avenue and **Draycott Place**, has been demolished.

Drayton Gardens SW10 (Kensington, Ken. Chel.). The derivation of the name Drayton, which the street shares with its public house, is not known. 'Gardens' appears all over Kensington. The borough, before development, was filled with market gardens, nursery gardens and landscape gardeners, and had been since the 17th century at least.

Drewstead Road SW16 (Streatham, Lambeth). Built on the Streatham estate of Beriah Drew, who bought the manor of Leigham Court in 1836. The road was first called Leigham Court Road West; it was changed in the 1860s.

Driffield Road E3 (Bow, T. Ham.). Commemorates the Rev. George Townsend Driffield, rector of St Mary's, Bow, for over 30 years until his retirement in the 1880s.

Driver Street SW8 (Battersea, Wandsworth). John Driver had a market garden on Battersea marshes in 1805.

Droitwich Close SE26 (Sydenham, Lewisham). *See* **Wells Park Road**.

Druce Road SE21 (Dulwich, Southwark). Commemorates the family who acted for several generations as legal advisers to nearby Dulwich College, owners of this land.

Druid Street SE1 (Bermondsey, Southwark). Built as a short turning off Neckinger in 1871; the inspiration of the name is unknown. The first resident was Henry Hepworth, 'beer retailer'; he might have had an establishment called the 'Druid's Arms' or 'Druid's Head', but there is no evidence of it.

Drury Lane WC2 (Cit. West, Camden). An old road, recorded in 1199 as 'old' and called variously Aldwychestrate in the 13th century and Fortescu Lane. In the 16th century it came to be called Drury Lane after Sir William Drury, who built his house at the S end.

Dryden Street WC2 (Covent Garden, Cit. West.). Commemorates the poet and playwright John Dryden (1631–1700), Poet Laureate in 1670, whose verse dramas were produced at the Theatre Royal, Drury Lane, from 1663, and occasionally at the Duke's Theatre.

Du Cane Court SW17 (Balham, Wandsworth). Commemorates the Du Cane family who acquired the manor of Balham in 1701.

Du Cane Road W12 (Hammersmith). Runs across the front of Wormwood Scrubs prison and commemorates Sir Edmund Du Cane (1830–1903), Major-General in the Royal Engineers and prison reformer. He was surveyor-general of prisons from 1869 and was responsible for the transfer of all local prisons to the control of central government. He

Downing Street

also set up an identification register of habitual offenders.

Duchess of Bedford's Walk W8 (Holland Park, Ken. Chel.). A house on the site of the present Holland Park school belonged to the Duke and Duchess of Bedford from c1820. **Bedford Gardens** approaches.

Duchess Street W1 (Marylebone, Cit. West.). Built on the estate of the dukes of Portland and named by association.

Duchy Street SE1 (Lambeth). Built as Duke Street in 1815 on land belonging to the Duchy of Cornwall (*see* **Cornwall Road**). **Duchy Place** gives off it.

Dufour's Place W1 (Soho, Cit. West.). Paul Dufour obtained a building lease from the Pulteney family and built this street from 1721 (*see* **Great Pulteney Street**).

Duke of Wellington Place SW1 (Hyde Park, Cit. West.). Nearby Apsley House was the London house of the duke from 1817 (*see* **Wellington Road**, **Square** and **Street**).

Duke of York Street SW1 (St James's, Cit. West.). Built as part of a scheme of streets leading to **St James's Square**, and named after James, Duke of York, brother to Charles II.

Duke Road W4 (Chiswick, Hounslow). Chiswick House, nearby, bought by the first Earl of Burlington in 1628, passed by marriage to the dukes of Devonshire in the mid-18th century. They occupied it until 1892.

Duke's Place EC3 (Cit. Lond.). The Priory of Holy Trinity near Aldgate was given to Sir Thomas Audley at the dissolution of the monasteries under Henry VIII (1509–47). Audley built a house (now demolished) on the site which was left to his son-in-

law, the Duke of Norfolk.

Duke's Road WC1 (Bloomsbury, Camden). The remnant of a road built by the dukes of Bedford running N from Bedford House, Russell Square. The road was an early (1760s) northward extension of the development on the Bedford estate.

Duke Street W1 (St James's, Cit. West.). First recorded in 1673, it was built on the Earl of St Albans' estate and the name compliments James Stuart, the Duke of York and later James II.

Duke Street Hill SE1 (London Bridge, Southwark). Commemorates Arthur Wellesley, First Duke of Wellington (*see* **Wellington Road**). That stretch of Borough High Street between London Bridge and Southwark Street was briefly called Wellington Street.

Dulwich Village SE21 (Dulwich, Southwark). Called Dilwihs in the 10th century, meaning the meadow where dill grows.

Dulwich Wood Avenue SE19 (Dulwich, Southwark). Dulwich woods, now built over, extended for several miles and were part of the forest of North Wood (*see* **Norwood High Street**). Before clearance for building began in the 19th century the woods stretched from this site to the S end of Lordship Lane. There are numerous 'Wood' street names in Dulwich.

Duncannon Street WC2 (Cit. West.). *See* **Agar Street**.

Duncan Street N1 (Islington). *See* **Camperdown Street**. Neighbouring **Nelson Place** and **Vincent Terrace** (*see* **Napier Street**) also commemorate naval heroes.

Dundas Road SE15 (Peckham,

Southwark). Named in 1871 after Sir Thomas Dundas, art collector.

Dunford Road N7 (Holloway, Islington). Named in 1865, and probably laid out by Dunfords, N London builders active in the 1860s.

Dunn Street E8 (Shacklewell, Hackney). Began as Dunn's Cottages, and was possibly built by a builder called Dunn who was active in N London in the 1850s onwards.

Dunraven Street W1 (Mayfair, /Cit. West.). Windham Thomas Wyndham-Quin, Earl of Dunraven (1841–1926), lived here. He was an enthusiastic yachtsman and an America's Cup competitor.

Dunstan's Road SE22 (E Dulwich, Southwark). A large house called 'Dunstan's Hern' stood on Forest Hill Road S of this road; **Dunstan's Grove** was called Herne Grove, and **Cornflower Terrace** was Herne Terrace.

Dunster Court EC3 (Cit. Lond.). Corruption of Dunstan's Court, in which form it appears in 1677. The derivation is obscure, the court appears to have no connection with St Dunstan's church and the name probably refers to a proprietor or tradesman.

Duntshill Road SW18 (Wandsworth). Commemorates a local property recorded in the 16th century as Dunshill or Duntshill.

Durham House Street WC2 (Strand, Cit. West.). Site of the mediaeval London palace belonging to the bishops of Durham. The house was leased to the Earl of Pembroke in

1641, and after the Restoration of 1660 it was demolished and replaced by streets of small houses which rapidly became slums.

Durham Place SW3 (Chelsea, Ken. Chel.). Next to the site of Durham House, a Tudor or Jacobean house of unknown history; it was demolished and replaced by a 19th-century house of the same name.

Durham Terrace W2 (Paddington, Cit. West.). Named from the neighbouring *Durham Castle* public house. **Sunderland Terrace**, from a county Durham place name, was named by association.

Durweston Street W1 (Marylebone, Cit. West.). On the Portman estate (*see* **Portman Square**). The family also held property at Durweston village in Dorset.

Dutch Yard SW18 (Wandsworth). Part of the original village centre of Wandsworth, where Dutch settlers established the manufacture of pans and kettles in the 17th century.

Dylways SE5 (E Dulwich, Southwark). Revives an ancient form of 'Dulwich'.

Dymock Street SW6 (Fulham, Hammersmith). Humphry Dymock was a tenant of the house called 'Rosamund's', W of Parsons Green, in 1527. Cressy Dymock, possibly of the same family, founded a College of Husbandry in Fulham in the middle of the 17th century.

Dyott Street WC1 (St Giles, Camden). Records Simon Dyott, local resident named in a survey of 1676.

E

Eade Road N4 (Seven Sisters Road, Hackney). In 1783 Jonathon Eade bought a lease of the manor of Stoke Newington from Lady Abney. In 1791 he acquired a life interest in the adjoining manor of Highbury from Sir George Colebrooke. The Eades were granted a 99-year renewal of their lease of Stoke Newington in 1814.

Eagle Court EC1 (Clerkenwell, Islington). Properly Egle. The Commanderie of Egle in Lincolnshire was formed by the Order of Knights of St John of Jerusalem in the 14th century when their possessions were augmented by much land formerly belonging to the suppressed order of Knights Templar. The Bailiff of Egle was and is one of the most important officers of the Order of St John, and the bailiff's house stood here. (*See* **St John Street**).

Eagle Street WC1 (Holborn, Camden). Named from the sign of an inn recorded here in the 18th century.

Eaglet Place E1 (Mile End, T. Ham.). From the *Golden Eagle* public house, recorded nearby in 1830.

Eardley Road SW16 (Streatham, Lambeth). Commemorates the Rev. Mr Stenton-Eardley (*d* 1883), for many years rector of the Church of Immanuel, Streatham Common.

Earlham Street WC2 (Seven Dials, Camden). Called Earl Street in 1691, altered to avoid confusion with other 'Earl' street names. It is not thought to have complimented any particular earl.

Earl Road SE1 (Old Kent Road, Southwark). *See* **Shorncliffe Road.**

Earl's Court Road W8, SW5 (Ken. Chel.). The de Vere family, earls of Oxford, were lords of the manor until 1526 and held manorial courts here, in a house near the present Earl's Court Station. Their manor was known as Earl's Kensington. **Earl's Court Gardens** and **Square** adjoin (*see* **Earl's Terrace**).

Earlsferry Way N1 (Caledonian Road, Islington). *See* **Carnoustie Drive**.

Earl's Terrace W8 (Kensington, Ken. Chel.). The de Vere family gave part of their manor of Kensington to the Abbey of Abingdon (*see* **St Mary Abbot's Place**) and the part remaining to them was known as Earl's Kensington, Aubrey de Vere having been created Earl of Oxford in 1155. **Earl's Walk** is nearby (*see* **Earl's Court Road**).

Earlstoke Street EC1 (Clerkenwell, Islington). Properly Earlstone, this street was built on land belonging to the first Marquis of Northampton, who married Maria Smith of Earlstone Park, Wiltshire (*see* **Compton Road**).

Earnshaw Street WC2 (Holborn, Camden). The watchmaker Thomas Earnshaw (1749–1829) worked here, at 119 High Holborn. He invented the cylindrical balance spring and the detached detent escapement.

Earsby Street W14 (North End, Hammersmith). Commemorates William Earsby of The Washes Farm, North End, trustee of parish charities in 1654 and 1655, and benefactor to the parish. In 1664 he left the income from five acres in Fulham Fields to buy clothing for 'six poor widows of good character'. The Earsby family held The Washes until 1702.

Easley's Mews W1 (Marylebone, Cit. West.). Abraham Easley is recorded as owning this land in the mid 18-century.

East Arbour Street E1 (Stepney, T. Ham.). *See* **Arbour Square**.

Eastbourne Terrace W2 (Bayswater, Cit. West.). Named by association with adjacent **Westbourne Terrace**.

Eastcastle Street W1 (Oxford Street, Cit. West.). *See* **Great Castle Street**.

Eastcheap EC3 (Cit. Lond.). Early London had two main food and commodity markets, the west and the east 'cheap', from OE 'chepe', a market. The western market was in Cheapside, the eastern one was here.

East Harding Street EC4 (Cit. Lond.). Agnes Harding or Hardinge left property in this area to the Goldsmiths' Company in 1513. **West Harding Street** is nearby.

East India Dock Road E14 (Poplar, T. Ham.). Approached a dock built W of Leamouth Road for the East India Company in 1806, and now closed. The **East India Dockwall Road** bounded the export basin.

Eastlands Crescent SE21 (Dulwich, Southwark). Site of a house called 'Eastlands', now demolished.

Eastminster E1 (Whitechapel, T. Ham.). The mediaeval Cistercian abbey of Eastminster stood nearby, on the site of the former Royal Mint buildings in East Smithfield. It was founded by Edward III (1327–77) as the East Minster of St Mary of Graces.

Easton Street WC1 (Clerkenwell, Islington). Built on land belonging to the first Marquis of Northampton who also held property at Easton Maudit, Northamptonshire (*see* **Compton Road**).

East Smithfield E1 (Whitechapel, T. Ham.). First recorded in the 12th century as open land adjoining Tower Hill, a gift to the Priory of Holy Trinity from the Knights' Guild who held Portsoken (*see* **Portsoken Street**). For the derivation *see* **Smithfield**.

East Street SE17 (Walworth, Southwark). Self-explanatory, as running E from Walworth Road. The E end (beyond present Blackwood Street) was formerly East Lane, which extended to present Elsted Street. Beyond that was Bedford Place, leading to Old Kent Road. The present Dawes Street was called North Street and South Street, by association.

East Tenter Street E1 (Whitechapel, T. Ham.). Built on part of the former space called Goodman's Fields, which became a tenter ground (*see* **Tenter Ground**) in the early 18th century. **North**, **South** and **West Tenter** Streets adjoin, marking the edges of the ground.

Eastway E9 (Hackney Wick, Hackney). Named as part of a main route leading E out of London into Essex.

Eaton Square SW1 (Belgravia, Cit. West.). Part of the Grosvenor family's Belgravia estate; Eaton Hall in Cheshire is the family seat. **Eaton Mews** and **Place** adjoin.

Eatonville Road SW17 (Tooting, Wandsworth). Probably a compliment to F. Eaton, who served on Wandsworth Borough Council from 1906.

Ebbsfleet Road NW2 (W Hampstead, Camden). Kentish place name; built by the Powell-Cotton family of Quex Park, Birchington, Kent.

Ebor Street E1 (Bethnal Green, T. Ham.). Originally called York Street in honour of James, Duke of York, in 1676. By 1799 it had become Old York Street. As London filled with 'York' street names it was altered to Ebor, from Eboricum, the Roman name for the city of York.

Ebury Bridge Road SW1 (Pimlico, Cit. West.). Approaches Ebury Bridge, which originally crossed the stream flowing S from the Chelsea Waterworks (on the site of the present Victoria Station). The waterworks later became the head of the Grosvenor Canal, which is now closed (*see* **Ebury Street**).

Ebury Street SW1 (Pimlico, Cit. West.). This land was part of the Saxon manor of Eye, later called Eyburgh or Ebury, which probably extended S from the present Bayswater Road to the Thames, between the Westbourne and Tyburn streams. The manor passed to the Abbey of Westminster after the Norman Conquest; in 1536 it passed to Henry VIII and the manors of Hyde (*see* **Hyde Park Corner**) and Neat, Pimlico, were separated from it. The manor was later acquired by the Audleys and through them by the Grosvenors (*see* **Audley Street**). A Grosvenor became Baron Ebury during the 19th century.

Eccleston Place SW1 (Belgravia, Cit. West.). Part of the Grosvenor estate, and named from Eccleston in Cheshire where the family held property. **Eccleston Bridge** and **Street** adjoin; **Eccleston Square** is nearby.

Edenhurst Avenue SW6 (Fulham, Hammersmith). Former name of Hurlingham Lodge nearby.

Edge Street W8 (Kensington, Ken. Chel.). Built beside land belonging to Andrew Edge, who bought it from the West Middlesex Water Works Company in 1825. The street originally approached the company's reservoir which lay in the angle of Campden Hill Road and Kensington Place.

Edgware Road W2 (Paddington, Cit. West.). Road leading to Edgware, called Aegceswer in the 10th century and Eggeswera in the 12th; the name means the weir of Ecgi.

Edis Street NW1 (Primrose Hill, Camden). Colonel Robert Edis was London County Council member for St Pancras South from 1889. He was also a distinguished architect.

Edith Grove SW10 (Fulham Road, Ken. Chel.). Laid out on land belonging to the Gunter family (*see* **Gunter Grove**). Edith Gunter died in 1849 at the age of seven. **Edith Road**, **Terrace** and **Villas** are nearby.

Edmund Street SE5 (Camberwell, Southwark). John Edmunds or Edmonds, a market-gardener of New Cross, acquired land here from the Bowyer family and developed it.

Edwardes Square W8 (Kensington, Ken. Chel.). Elizabeth Rich, daughter and heiress of the second Earl of Holland, of Holland House, married Francis Edwardes of Haverfordwest. Holland House passed to their son William Edwardes in 1721.

Edwards Lane N16 (Stoke Newington, Hackney). Named from Job Edwards, active as a local builder and developer *c*1700.

Edward Street SE14 (Deptford, Lewisham). A Victorian modernisation of an old lane called Loving Edward's Lane. The new version, with **Alexandra Street** turning off it, possibly commemorates the marriage of Edward, Prince of Wales (later Edward VII) and Princess Alexandra in 1863.

Effra Road SW2 (Lambeth). Built in 1810 on land previously called Effra Farm. **Effra Parade** is nearby. The farmland, originally called Heathrow Manor, stretched N to Coldharbour Lane and S to Dulwich Road. The River Effra flowed through it; rising in Streatham and Dulwich, its combined streams flowed NW up the line of Croxted Road, Dulwich Road and Dalberg Road. It ran parallel to Brixton Road up to Kennington and thence into the Thames through Vauxhall Creek.

Egerton Gardens SW3 (Kensington, Ken. Chel.). *See* **Onslow Square**. **Egerton Crescent**, **Place** and **Terrace** adjoin.

Elba Place SE17 (Walworth, Southwark). One of a group of streets from the period of the Napoleonic Wars. Napoleon was exiled, briefly, on the island of Elba in 1814–15.

Elder Street E1 (Spitalfields, T. Ham.). *See* **Blossom Street**.

Eldon Grove NW3 (Hampstead, Camden). As **Eldon Street** (Cit. Lond.). Here, on the former Lord Rosslyn's estate, it is Lord Eldon's high reputation as a judge which is commemorated (*see* **Rosslyn Hill**).

Eldon Road W8 (Kensington, Ken. Chel.). Originally this road ran beside a large house called 'Eldon Lodge', then a solitary mansion.

Eldon Street EC2 (Cit. Lond.).

Commemorates John Scott, created Earl of Eldon in 1799. He was Solicitor General in 1788, Attorney General 1793 and Lord Chancellor 1801–7 and 1807–27. He was known as a firm opponent of radicalism.

Electric Avenue SW9 (Brixton, Lambeth). Opened in the late 19th century as a shopping street specially equipped with ample electric light for late shopping.

Elephant and Castle SE11 (Newington, Southwark). The *Elephant and Castle Inn* (*c*1760) opened in a former smithy on an island site at the junction of roads to Walworth, Kennington and Lambeth. It was rebuilt twice. The island site disappeared in the building of the present interchange. The device of an elephant carrying a castle howdah is recorded in England in the 15th century. It appeared in the arms of the Royal Africa Company, incorporated in 1588, and became more widely known when it was adopted by the Cutlers' Company in 1642. **Elephant Road** is nearby.

Elephant Lane SE16 (Rotherhithe, Southwark). Led to Elephant Stairs on the river bank. The name is recorded in the mid-18th century and probably derives from an inn sign.

Elfindale Road SE24 (Herne Hill, Southwark). Named from a nearby house (demolished) called 'Elfindale' or 'Elfendale'.

Elfrida Crescent SE6 (Bellingham, Lewisham). *See* **King Alfred Avenue**.

Elgar Street SE16 (Rotherhithe, Southwark). Formerly Lower York Street, the remnant of a patriotically-named group of the early 19th century (*see* **Ainsty Street**). Renamed in 1873 (too early for the composer Edward Elgar, who was then only 16).

Elgin Avenue W9 (Maida Vale, Cit. West.). Commemorates James Bruce, Eighth Earl of Elgin (1811–63). A distinguished public servant, he was made Governor-General of Canada in 1848 and was notably successful in implementing the recommendations of Lord Durham (his father-in-law) to bring about a greater degree of Canadian independence. This street was named in 1862, when he was appointed Viceroy of India. **Elgin Crescent** is also named after him.

Elia Street N1 (Islington). The author Charles Lamb (*d* 1834) lived nearby, at Colebrooke Cottage, from 1823–7. 'Elia' was his pseudonym, adopted in 1820.

Elizabeth Close W9 (Paddington, Cit. West.). *See* **Browning Close**.

Elizabeth Street SW1 (Belgravia, Cit. West.). On the Grosvenor estate; Richard Grosvenor, Second Marquis of Westminster, married Elizabeth Leveson-Gower, daughter of the Duke of Sutherland, in 1819. **Elizabeth Bridge** adjoins.

Elliott's Court EC4 (Cit. Lond.). Uncertain derivation. It is recorded in 1677 as Ellis Court, in 1708 as Elliott's Court.

Ellis Street SW1 (Chelsea, Ken. Chel.). *See* **D'Oyley Street**.

Elm Court EC4 (Cit. Lond.). One of the courts of the Inner Temple. It was formerly called Elm-Tree Court, which is self-explanatory.

Elm Lane SE6 (Perry Hill, Lewisham). The house called 'The Elms' here was the farmhouse attached to Place House, a local estate. The farm was tenanted by a family called Sabin at the time of development (*c*1870), and the lane was formerly called Sabin's Lane.

Elm Park Gardens SW10 (Chelsea, Ken. Chel.). In 1586 the parish of Chelsea planted a ring of nine elms here to commemorate a visit by Elizabeth I. The queen is said to have taken shelter from the rain under an elm nearby (*see* **Queen's Elm Square**). **Elm Park Road** approaches.

Elm Place SW7 (Chelsea, Ken. Chel.). *See* **Elm Park Gardens**.

Elms Mews W2 (Bayswater, Cit. West.). Formerly an old lane called Elms Lane, from trees growing there, it became a Victorian mews opposite the Marlborough Gate into Hyde Park, and the Marlborough Gate stables still exist there.

Elms Road SW4 (Clapham, Lambeth). Approaches the S side of Clapham Common, where formerly stood two large groups of elms. The common was noted for its elm trees, many of which were planted by local residents in the late 18th and early 19th centuries. **Elms Crescent** adjoins.

Elmwood Road SE24 (Dulwich, Southwark). A house on Half Moon Lane called 'Elm Lodge' was noted for an enormous elm tree, about 35 feet round the trunk. By *c*1900 it had become a hollow shell, and a source of great local interest and curiosity as to how many people could sit inside it.

Elphinstone Street N5 (Highbury, Islington). Possibly commemorates James Elphinstone, critic, author, philologist and translator, who lived in Islington from 1787.

Elsiemaud Road SE4 (Lewisham). *See* **Amyruth Road**.

Elsynge Road SW18 (Battersea, Wandsworth). Henry ·Elsynge was born in Battersea in 1598, and became a noted writer and traveller.

His best-known work, based on his researches while Clerk to the House of Commons, is *The Ancient Method and Manner of Holding Parliaments in England*. He died in 1654.

Elvaston Place SW7 (Kensington, Ken. Chel.). Built on land held by the Stanhope family, whose seat was at Elvaston in Derbyshire. They held the titles of Earl of Harrington and Viscount Petersham. **Petersham Mews** and **Place** adjoin (*see* **Harrington Road**).

Ely Place EC1 (Holborn, Camden). Built in 1772 on the site of the London palace of the Bishops of Ely, who were forced to give up their property in the late 16th century. They did retain some rights, and Ely Place was known for many years as a sanctuary where the police might not make an arrest.

Elysium Street SW6 (Fulham, Hammersmith). Site of a cottage called 'Elysium Cottage' from the ancient Greek name for a paradise. Its more down-to-earth occupant was toll-gate keeper on the King's Road.

Elystan Place SW3 (Chelsea, Ken. Chel.). Ancient Welsh family name of Lord Cadogan (*see* **Cadogan Square**). The Cadogans claimed descent from Prince Cadwgan of Gwynedd (*d* 1112). **Elystan Street** adjoins.

Emerald Street WC1 (Bloomsbury, Camden). So named in 1885; it was formerly Green Street, a street name so common as to cause confusion and necessitate a change.

Emerson Street SE1 (Bankside, Southwark). Commemorates Thomas Emerson (*d* 1595), parish benefactor. The American poet Ralph Waldo Emerson thought that he was probably descended from Thomas.

Emery Hill Street SW1 (Cit. West.). Commemorates Emery Hill, former benefactor to parish charities.

Emery Street SE1 (Lambeth). Formerly Short Street, renamed in 1893 by association with the nearby mills (*see* **Oakey Lane**).

Emmanuel Road SW12 (Streatham, Lambeth). Built on land belonging to Emmanuel College, Cambridge.

Emma Street E2 (Hackney). *See* **Pritchard's Road**.

Emperors' Gate SW7 (Kensington, Ken. Chel.). Commemorates the League of the Three Emperors (Austria–Hungary, Germany and Russia) to maintain peace in E Europe. Francis Joseph of Austria, William I of Prussia and Czar Alexander II met in September 1872 and agreed informally to take united action in the event of subversion. This agreement having lapsed by 1878, Bismarck, German Foreign Minister, negotiated a formal league in 1881.

Empress Place SW6 (Lillie Road, Hammersmith). The Empress Hall stadium opened here in 1937.

Empress Street SE17 (Walworth, Southwark). Formerly Prince's Street; as this was an extremely common name it was changed in 1869. As Queen Victoria was not proclaimed Empress of India until 1877, the inspiration may have been the Empress Eugénie of France. She had visited England and made a favourable impression on the queen and people alike.

Endell Street WC2 (St Giles, Camden). Named in 1846 to commemorate James Endell Tyler, who was rector of St Giles 1826–51. Originally Bowl Yard (built before 1680) from an inn called *The Bowl*, it was improved *c*1683 and called Belton Street, from the Lincolnshire seat of the owner, Sir John Brownlow. It became Hanover Street *c*1746.

Endsleigh Gardens WC1 (Bloomsbury, Camden). Part of the Duke of Bedford's estate. Endsleigh was the name of his property at Tavistock in Devon (*see* **Tavistock Square**). **Endsleigh Place** and **Street** adjoin.

Enford Street W1 (Marylebone, Cit. West.). On the Portman estate (*see* **Portman Square**). The family held property at Enford village in Dorset.

England's Lane NW3 (Primrose Hill, Camden). Corruption of 'Ing-land', from OE 'ing', a strip of meadow-land. The meadows lay immediately beyond **Belsize Park**. They remained as such until development began in the mid-19th century.

Englefield Road N1 (De Beauvoir Town, Hackney/Islington). Built on the De Beauvoir estate. Richard de Beauvoir, who built St Peter's parish church for the estate, lived at Englefield House near Pangbourne in Berkshire.

Ennismore Gardens SW7 (Knightsbridge, Cit. West.). Built on land belonging to Lord Listowel and named from a family title. William Hare of Ennismore, County Kerry, was created Baron Ennismore in 1800, and Viscount Ennismore and Listowel in 1816. He became Earl of Listowel in 1822. **Ennismore Mews** and **Street** approach.

Ensign Street E1 (Whitechapel, T. Ham.). Formerly Well Street, from adjacent Well Close Square. A well-known sailors' home established here in 1835 may have inspired the new name.

Epple Road SW6 (Fulham, Hammersmith). *See* **Bradbourne Street**.

Epworth Street EC2 (Finsbury, Islington). Named in honour of John Wesley, founder of Methodism, who was born at Epworth (then in Lincolnshire) in 1703 and whose London chapel and house (now the Wesley Museum) are round the corner in City Road.

Erasmus Street SW1 (Cit. West.). Commemorates the Dutch scholar Erasmus who came to England in 1498; he became the mainspring of N European intellectual life.

Erconwald Street W12 (Hammersmith). Erconwald or Erkenwald was Bishop of London in the late 7th century, and brother to St Ethelburga. This street lies in the manor of Hammersmith which was held by the bishops of London.

Errington Road W9 (Westbourne Green, Cit. West.). Probably commemorates the civil engineer John Edward Errington (1806–62). Although he is best known for his work on railways in Scotland and N England he also built three bridges across the Thames: Kew, Kingston and Richmond. He is buried at Kensal Green.

Esparto Street SW18 (Wandsworth). Named by association with a paper-mill nearby on the River Wandle. Esparto is a mediterranean grass, one of the raw materials of good paper.

Essex Road N1 (Islington). Part of a main route into Essex; formerly called Lower Street (*see* **Upper Street**) and – NE of Cross Street – Newington Green Lane, as leading to Newington Green.

Essex Street WC2 (Strand, Cit. West.). Site of the town house belonging to the earls of Essex. It had been bought by the Earl of Leicester and passed to his stepson Robert Devereux, Earl of Essex (*see* **Devereux Court**). He was beheaded for treason in 1601; most of the house was pulled down and the street built in the 1680s. **Little Essex Street** adjoins.

Estreham Road SW16 (Streatham, Lambeth). Records 'Estraham', the form of the name 'Streatham' found in the *Domesday Book*.

Etherstone Green SW16 (Streatham, Lambeth). Built on the site of a house and grounds called 'Etherstone'. **Etherstone Road** approaches.

Eton Avenue NW3 (Primrose Hill, Camden). Built on land belonging to the Provost and Fellows of Eton College, who formerly held a large estate at Primrose Hill, including the hill itself. **Eton College Road**, **Eton Road** and **Eton Villas** are all nearby.

Ettrick Street E14 (Poplar, T. Ham.). *See* **Leven Road**.

Euston Road NW1 (Camden). That part of the New Road (the N bypass of 1757) which crossed ground belonging to the Duke of Grafton, and named after his son, Lord Euston (of Euston in Suffolk). **Euston Square** adjoins.

Evangelist Road NW5 (Kentish Town, Camden). Built on land belonging to the College of St John the Evangelist, Cambridge (*see* **College Lane**).

Evelyn Gardens SW7 (Kensington, Ken. Chel.). *See* **Onslow Square**.

Evelyn Street SE8 (Deptford, Lewisham). Commemorates the 17th-century diarist John Evelyn (1620–1706), who lived at Deptford and whose descendants owned large

areas of it, including the line of this street. Evelyn's house, Sayes Court, was lent to Czar Peter the Great (*see* **Sayes Court Street**).

Evelyn Yard W1 (Soho, Cit. West.). Built in the 18th century by a family called Evelyn from St Clare, Kent. They were connected with the family of the diarist (*see* **Evelyn Street**).

Eversholt Street NW1 (St Pancras, Camden). Originally the name was applied only to the N end which lay on land belonging to the dukes of Bedford: Eversholt is the nearest village to the Bedford seat, Woburn Abbey. The name was later extended S down the length of the street.

Exbury Road SE6 (Catford, Lewisham). Part of the estate of Lord Forster, and named from a Hampshire village near his country seat.

Exchange Court WC2 (Strand, Cit. West.). Mid-17th-century alley from Maiden Lane to the Strand. Originally it opened on to the Strand opposite an exchange, or covered court of shops, which stood on the S side of the Strand here until *c*1738.

Exeter Street WC2 (Strand, Cit. West.). Site of a house built by Lord Burleigh in the 16th century and later owned by his son, who became Earl of Exeter. This street and Burleigh Street were laid out when the house was demolished in 1676.

Exhibition Road SW7 (Kensington, Ken. Chel./Cit. West.). This road and its surrounding complex of colleges, museums and halls was laid out as a cultural centre in the 1860s. The land was bought with the profit from the Great Exhibition held nearby in 1851 (*see* **Prince Consort Road**).

Exmouth Market EC1 (Clerkenwell,

Islington). Formerly Exmouth Street; commemorates Edward Pellen, Admiral Lord Exmouth (*d* 1833), distinguished for his service in the Napoleonic Wars and for the destruction of the Algerian fleet in 1816. (The ruler of Algiers had broken a treaty which abolished the enslavement of Christian prisoners.) The street became a barrow boys' market in the late 19th century.

Eynham Road W12 (Wormwood Scrubs, Hammersmith). The ancient manor of Wormholt Barns was divided into two in the 18th century: Wormholt and Eynham. Further division occurred in 1812 when the government acquired a large section including the site of the prison.

Eyot Gardens W6 (Chiswick, Hammersmith). Approaches the river bank near Chiswick Eyot (pronounced 'ate'), a small island in the Thames. Eyot is from an OE word meaning an islet.

Eyre Court NW8 (St John's Wood, Cit. West.). The Eyre family acquired St John's Wood in 1732 when Henry Eyre, City of London merchant, bought it from Lord Chesterfield. The *Eyre Arms* – an inn, ballroom, theatre and pleasure-garden combined – stood here until 1928.

Ezra Road SE5 (Camberwell, Southwark). In the present Harvey Street stood the Ezra Independent Chapel, named from the Old Testament prophet. Many Jews returned to Jerusalem from exile in Babylon with authority from King Cyrus to rebuild the temple. A later Persian king, Artaxerxes, sent Ezra the priest to Jerusalem to enrich the temple and to purify the practice of religion.

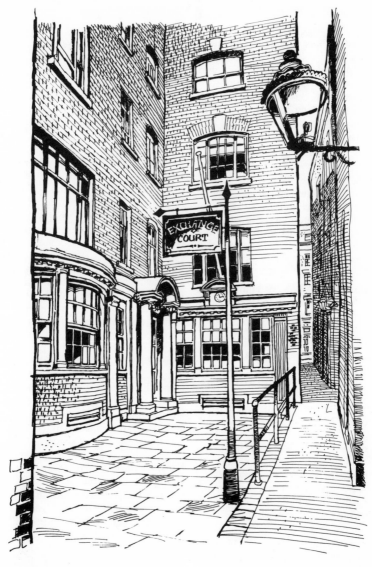

Exchange Court

F

Fairchild Place EC2 (Shoreditch, Hackney). Thomas Fairchild, a Hoxton gardener, died in 1729 and left money for an annual sermon to be preached on 'The Wonderful Works of God in Creation'. Fairchild was an outstanding botanist and had a particular interest in developing hybrid varieties.

Fairclough Street E1 (Whitechapel, T. Ham.). Named in 1869, possibly after T.M. Fairclough who was active in local government and later (c1880) represented the parish of St George in the East on the Metropolitan Board of Works.

Fairfax Road NW6 (W Hampstead, Camden). Renamed in 1870, from Victoria Road. Possibly it commemorates General Fairfax, Third Baron Fairfax (1612–71), commander-in-chief under Cromwell of the Parliamentarian army during the Civil War of 1642–9. Two modern streets attached to this road are named from Parliamentarian victories: Marston Moor (1644) and Naseby (1645). The latter was Fairfax's decisive defeat of Charles I; he opposed, however, any action designed to bring the king to sentence of death, refused to take part in his trial and resigned his command following Charles's execution.

Fairfield Road E3 (Bow, T. Ham.). Crosses the site of an annual fair which flourished until the middle of the 19th century.

Fairfield Street SW18 (Wandsworth). A field called the Fair Field (site of an occasional visiting fair) lay between the present York Road and the railway. It was built over in the later 19th century.

Fairhazel Gardens NW6 (Hampstead, Camden). *See* **Canfield Gardens**. Fairhazel is the name of a Sussex property held by the Maryon-Wilson family.

Fairholt Street SW7 (Knightsbridge, Cit. West.). The artist and scholar Frederick William Fairholt (1814–66) lived in Montpelier Square. He was best known as an engraver and illustrator and as an antiquarian collector.

Fair Street SE1 (Bermondsey, Southwark). Formerly Horselydown Fair Street, from the site of a regular fair held on the open grazing land of Horselydown (*see* **Horselydown Lane**).

Falconberg Court W1 (Soho, Cit. West.). Leads to **Falconberg Mews**, formerly attached to Falconberg House which belonged to Oliver Cromwell's son-in-law Thomas Belasye, Lord Fauconberg (*d* 1700). The house was demolished in 1924.

Falcon Close SE1 (Southwark). Commemorates the nearby *Falcon* tavern which stood on Bankside, N of the junction with Hopton Street. The inn is recorded from 1541 until 1808. It was later pulled down and the property was developed as the Falcon Drawing Dock. The nearby Falcon Glass Factory in Hopton Street is named from it, and the name was revived in the *Castle and Falcon*, an inn recorded at Bank End in 1890.

Falcon Court EC4 (Cit. Lond.). From 'the sign of the Falcon, Fleet

Street', recorded as the address of a printer in 1565. The falcon was a popular emblem for inn and shop signs.

Falcon Road SW11 (Wandsworth). Formerly Falcon Lane, from the Falcon Brook which ran N beside Wandsworth Common to ponds by Battersea Rise, and then NW to the Thames at York Place.

Falkland Road NW5 (Kentish Town, Camden). *See* **Ascham Street**.

Fann Street EC1 (Cit. Lond./ Islington). Extension E of the former Fann's Alley (recorded 1677 and 1746) off Aldersgate Street. This was probably named from a property owner or resident tradesman.

Fanshaw Street N1 (Hoxton, Hackney). Named in 1878, this was formerly two streets of which the eastern was East Street and the western Robert Street (*see* **Aske Street**). The new name possibly commemorates a family called Featherstonehaugh (often pronounced Fanshawe) who held land here in the 18th century and owned nearby Pimlico House.

Faraday Close N7 (Barnsbury, Islington). *See* **Faraday Street**. The scientist was an elder at the Sandemanian chapel on the corner with Bride Street, 1862-7.

Faraday Street SE17 (Newington, Southwark). Commemorates the scientist Michael Faraday (1791–1867), born at Newington. Faraday became famous for his discovery of magneto-electricity and his explorations into the nature of electric power and magnetic force.

Fareham Street W1 (Soho, Cit. West.). Formerly Titchfield Street, this was built in 1736 on the Soho estate of the Duke of Portland, who

was also Marquis of Titchfield in Hampshire. The street was renamed in 1950 after Titchfield's neighbouring village of Fareham.

Farmer's Road SE5 (Camberwell, Lambeth/Southwark). Fragment of an old lane from Kennington Common to Camberwell Green, called Farmer's Lane. Richard Farmer established a vitriol works on the site of the present Kennington Park Gardens c1796. The road ran SE from this point, and the Farmers later obtained more land along its route, leased from the Bowyer-Smijth estate.

Farm Lane SW6 (Fulham, Hammersmith). Chayham's Farm here is recorded as belonging to Robert de Chayham in the reign of Edward II (1307–27). A farmhouse at the E corner of the lane survived until c1814.

Farmstead Road SE6 (Bellingham, Lewisham). Built on land which was formerly part of Bellingham Farm.

Farm Street W1 (Mayfair, Cit. West.). Built on land which was formerly part of Hay Hill farm (*see* **Hay Hill**).

Farquhar Road SE19 (Gipsy Hill, Southwark). Thomas Farquhar was chairman of the Crystal Palace Company at the time of the removal to Sydenham (*see* **Crystal Palace Parade**).

Farren Road SE23 (Forest Hill, Lewisham). One of a group taken from the history of the theatre (*see* **Cibber Road**, **Kemble Road** and **Street**, **Siddons Lane** and **Road**, and **Vestris Road**). Elizabeth Farren (1759–1829) was a popular actress who retired from the stage on her marriage to the Earl of Derby.

Farrier Street NW1 (Camden Town).

A modern renaming of the E end of Clarence Way, which approaches Royal College Street and the Royal Veterinary College. A farrier is a shoeing-smith, but the word was formerly used to denote a horse doctor.

Farringdon Street EC4 (Cit. Lond.). Built in the 1760s as Fleet Market, covering the course of the River Fleet N of Ludgate Hill. The street runs through the middle of Farringdon Ward and was renamed from the ward in the early 19th century. The ward is named from Sir William de Farnedon, a 13th-century sheriff. The continuation, **Farringdon Road**, was cut through numerous older lanes in 1856.

Farthing Alley SE1 (Bermondsey, Southwark). The surviving one of two narrow passages called Halfpenny Alley and Farthing Alley, from their size.

Fashion Street E1 (Spitalfields, T. Ham.). Corruption of the surname Fossan; the street was built in the 1650s on ground belonging to Thomas Fossan, citizen and skinner, and Lewis Fossan, citizen and goldsmith.

Fauconberg Road W4 (Chiswick, Hounslow). Runs through Sutton manor, approaching Sutton Court (now demolished). The house and manor were acquired on lease by Thomas, Lord Fauconberg, in 1676. A later Lord Fauconberg assigned the lease to Richard, Earl of Burlington, in 1727 (*see* **Falconberg Court**).

Featherstone Street EC1 (Finsbury, Islington). Built on land belonging to the Featherstone family. Matthew Featherstone is recorded as the owner in 1732.

Fellbrigg Road SE22 (Dulwich,

Southwark). Named from Felbrigg Hall, Norfolk seat of the Wyndham family who intermarried with the Bowyers (*see* **Bowyer Place**).

Fellows Road NW3 (Primrose Hill, Camden). *See* **Eton Avenue**.

Fenchurch Street EC3 (Cit. Lond.). Derives from OE 'fen' or 'faen', a fen or marshy place, and was formerly called Fanchurch Street, or the street past the church on marshy ground. **Fen Court** and **Fenchurch Avenue** are nearby.

Fendall Street SE1 (Bermondsey, Southwark). Richard Fendall owned an estate here at his death in 1739. It was left to his son Richard (*d* 1753) and his daughters Elizabeth (*d* 1795) and Ann. The estate was built up by George Choumert, Elizabeth's son-in-law (*see* **Choumert Road**).

Fentiman Road SW8 (Vauxhall, Lambeth). Built in 1838 on land belonging to John Fentiman. Fentiman bought parts of the former clay-fields, which had been used as a source of brick-earth for local development, drained them and built on them.

Ferdinand Street NW1 (Chalk Farm, Camden). Built on the estate of the Fitzroy family, barons Southampton. Commemorates Ferdinand Fitzroy, Second Baron, who was then lord of the manor.

Fernsbury Street WC1 (Finsbury, Islington). Named in 1912: Fernsbury was thought to have been an early variant of Finsbury (*see* **Finsbury Circus**).

Fern Street E3 (Bow Common, T. Ham.). *See* **Blackthorn Street**.

Fetter Lane EC4 (Cit. Lond.). Corruption of mediaeval Fewter Lane, meaning idlers' lane.

Ffinch Street SE8 (Deptford, Lewisham). A local family name. Ffinches are recorded as parish benefactors in 1730 and 1813. The Rev. Benjamin Sanderson Ffinch was rector of St Paul's, Deptford, 1834–74.

Field Place EC1 (Islington). Self-explanatory: the fields in question surrounded Goose Farm (*see* **Goose Yard**) until the early 19th century.

Field Road W6 (Fulham, Hammersmith). Built on part of a former area of market gardens. In the 18th century this area extended from the present Fulham Palace Road to North End Road and was called Fulham Field.

Field Street WC1 (Gray's Inn Road, Camden). Built from 1767 on land called Battle Bridge Field (*see* **Battle Bridge Road**).

Filmer Road SW6 (Fulham, Hammersmith). From a family connected with nearby Munster House. The Powells held the house from c1613. In 1666 Thomas Hinson, nephew of Sir Edward Powell, married Mary Filmer.

Finborough Road SW10 (W Brompton, Ken. Chel.). *See* **Petyward**.

Finch Lane EC3 (Cit. Lond.). Formerly Fink Lane or Fink's Lane, from a local merchant family who founded the mediaeval church of St Benet Fink in Threadneedle Street. The church has since been demolished.

Finchley Road NW11, NW2, NW3, NW8 (Camden/Cit. West.). Road to Finchley, derived from OE 'Finchleah', the glade or open place where finches are found.

Findhorn Street E14 (Poplar, T.

Ham.). *See* **Leven Road**.

Finsbury Circus EC2 (Cit. Lond.). Built on part of the Saxon 'burgh' or settlement belonging to one Finn. **Finsbury Square** and **Finsbury Pavement** (Islington district) are nearby, the latter being originally a paved walk made in 1777 across the marshy land N of the City.

Firbank Road SE15 (Peckham, Southwark). Built on land which belonged to a Mr Firbank in the 1870s.

Firhill Road SE6 (Bellingham, Lewisham). From a house on the N side of Southend Lane belonging to the Leathersellers' Company and called 'Firhill'.

First Street SW3 (Chelsea, Ken. Chel.). *See* **Hasker Street**.

Fisher Street WC1 (Holborn, Camden). Built on the former Red Lion Fields (*see* **Red Lion Square**) which belonged to Thomas Fisher from 1596, together with the *Red Lion Inn*, Holborn. The Fisher family sold the land to Nicholas Barbon for building in 1684.

Fisherton Street NW8 (Lisson Grove, Cit. West.). Named from a village near Salisbury, Wiltshire, the street having originally been a part of **Salisbury Street**.

Fishmongers' Hall Street EC4 (Cit. Lond.). The guild of fishmongers first established their guildhall here in 1310; the present building is 19th-century.

Fish Street Hill EC3 (Cit. Lond.). Originally led down to the approach to mediaeval London Bridge which lay downstream of the present bridge. This approach was called New Fish Street when the fishmongers moved their trade from

Queenhithe to Billingsgate in the time of Edward I (1272–1307). They were then carrying their fish into the City up this route; Old Fish Street (now vanished) was their former route from Queenhithe. The Billingsgate fish market has now moved to the Isle of Dogs.

Fitzalan Street SE11 (Lambeth). Commemorates Thomas Fitzalan or Fitz Alan, Archbishop of Canterbury, who was banished by Richard II in 1397. His brother Richard Fitzalan, Earl of Arundel and Surrey, held land nearby until his execution, also in 1397. The Fitzalan estate in Lambeth later passed to the dukes of Norfolk who held it until *c*1555 (*see* **Lambeth Palace Road**).

Fitzhardinge Street W1 (Marylebone, Cit. West.). *See* **Upper Berkeley Street**.

Fitzjohn's Avenue NW3 (Hampstead, Camden). *See* **Canfield Gardens**. The Maryon-Wilson family owned Fitzjohn's Farm in Essex.

Fitzmaurice Place W1 (Mayfair, Cit. West.). *See* **Lansdowne Row**.

Fitzneal Street W12 (Wormwood Scrubs, Hammersmith). Richard Fitzneale or Fitz Nele was Bishop of London 1189–98. John Stow, in his *Survey of London* of 1598, says he 'took great pains about the building of St Paul's church'. The bishops of London held Hammersmith manor.

Fitzroy Park N6 (Highgate, Camden). Approached Fitzroy House (demolished in 1828) across its park. The house was built *c*1786 for the Fitzroy family who held land in N London (*see* **Fitzroy Road**).

Fitzroy Road NW1 (Chalk Farm, Camden Town). Built on land belonging to the Fitzroy family, barons Southampton, who bought

the manor in 1786. The Southampton estate here extended N up to Malden Road and SE to Mornington Crescent.

Fitzroy Square W1 (Euston, Camden). Built on land belonging to the Duke of Grafton, whose family name this is. Another branch of the family became barons Southampton and owners of land in Kentish Town, Camden Town and Chalk Farm. **Fitzroy Court**, **Mews** and **Street** are nearby.

Flamborough Street E14 (Stepney, T. Ham.). A Yorkshire place name, chosen by association with neighbouring York Square. The square was named after Frederick, Duke of York (Queen Victoria's uncle), and this street was originally called York Street East. **Yorkshire Road** approaches.

Flask Walk NW3 (Hampstead, Camden). A medicinal spring nearby was given to the village of Hampstead by the then lord of the manor in 1698. Taverns in this lane sold flasks of spring water to eating houses in the City of London.

Flaxman Court W1 (Soho, Cit. West.). Commemorates the residence in Wardour Street of the neoclassical sculptor and artist John Flaxman (1755–1826).

Flaxman Terrace WC1 (St Pancras, Camden). The artist John Flaxman (*see* **Flaxman Court**) is buried in nearby St Pancras churchyard.

Fleet Road NW3 (Hampstead, Camden). Line of the upper River Fleet, which rises on Hampstead Heath and runs S (*see* **Fleet Street**).

Fleet Street EC4 (Cit. Lond.). Approaches the course of the River Fleet which flows S from Hampstead to the Thames at Blackfriars. The

Fish Street Hill

river is now channelled underground, and it passes under Ludgate Circus at the E end of this street.

Fleetwood Street N16 (Stoke Newington, Hackney). Site of Fleetwood House, demolished in 1872. Charles Fleetwood (*d* 1692) married Oliver Cromwell's daughter Bridget as her second husband. He already had a son and daughter by a previous marriage. The son, Smith Fleetwood, married Mary Hartopp of Stoke Newington. This house was built by the Hartopps, and it became known as Fleetwood House after the marriage.

Fleur de Lis Court EC4 (Cit. Lond.). Uncertain derivation; probably named from the sign of a shop or an inn which is now demolished.

Fleur de Lis Street E1 (Spitalfields, T. Ham.). *See* **Blossom Street**.

Flitcroft Street WC2 (St Giles, Camden). Commemorates Henry Flitcroft who was the architect of the new parish church of St Giles-in-the-Fields, built 1731–3.

Flodden Road SE5 (Camberwell, Southwark). Camberwell was originally in the county of Surrey. It was the Earl of Surrey who led the attack at the battle of Flodden (1513) when the English defeated a combined Scottish and French force. The First Surrey Rifles Headquarters opened in this street in 1865.

Flood Street SW3 (Chelsea, Ken. Chel.). Commemorates Mr L.T. Flood, Victorian benefactor to St Luke's parish, Chelsea. This street was originally called Pound Lane, from the village pound at the S end. **Flood Walk** adjoins.

Floral Street WC2 (Covent Garden, Cit. West.). Formerly Hart Street, from the *White Hart* inn which stood on Long Acre from 1632, with a frontage and access on to Hart Street. Originally ending W of Conduit Court, the street was extended in 1861–5 and renamed in 1895 from the adjacent Floral Hall. Hall and street were named by association with the Covent Garden flower market.

Flower and Dean Street E1 (Spitalfields, T. Ham.). Built in the 1650s by John Flower and Gowen Deane, Whitechapel bricklayers, on land belonging to the Fossan brothers (*see* **Fashion Street**).

Foley Street W1 (Marylebone, Cit. West.). Lord Foley's house originally formed the S limit of Portland Place; it was taken down when John Nash built a S extension to Portland Place and continued its line in Langham Place, which he did as part of his Regent Street and Regent's Park scheme *c*1825. Foley Street and Langham Street were originally Foley Place, an approach to the house.

Folgate Street E1 (Shoreditch, Hackney). *See* **Norton Folgate**.

Foliot Street W12 (Wormwood Scrubs, Hammersmith). Gilbert Foliot was Bishop of London 1163–86. This is one of a set of names commemorating bishops of London; the manor of Hammersmith belonged to the diocese.

Folly Wall E14 (Isle of Dogs, T. Ham.). The 'Folly' which stood here was a tavern with gardens beside the sea-wall. It is recorded in the late 18th century. The wall would have been part of the defensive dyke which went all around the Isle of Dogs, and which is remembered in names like Millwall and Blackwall.

Ford Mill Road SE6 (Bellingham, Lewisham.). A watermill formerly stood by a ford here through the River Ravensbourne.

Ford Place SW11 (Battersea, Wandsworth). A wide ford crossing the Thames between Battersea and Chelsea is traditionally held to have been in use since before the Roman occupation of Britain. It is thought to have been approximately where Battersea Bridge stands.

Fordwych Road NW2 (W Hampstead, Camden). Kentish place name; built by the Powell-Cotton family of Quex Park, Birchington, Kent.

Foreman Court W6 (Hammersmith). Henry Foreman served on Hammersmith Borough Council from 1912, and became mayor.

Foreshore SE8 (Deptford, Lewisham). *See* **Capstan Square**.

Forest Hill Road SE22, SE23 (Honor Oak, Lewisham/Southwark). Runs S towards the area first called Forest Hill in 1797, being part of the great North Wood which extended across N Surrey.

Fore Street EC2 (Cit. Lond.). Recorded in the 14th century as Le Forstrete, the street before or in front of the City Wall.

Formosa Street W9 (Paddington, Cit. West.). Sir George Young of Formosa Place, Berkshire, married into the family of William Praed (*see* **Praed Street**) in the 1830s.

Forset Street W1 (Marylebone, Cit. West.). Edward Forset or Forsett, who died *c*1630, was given a lease of the surrounding manor of Tyburn by Elizabeth I in 1583. He was granted the manor by James I in 1611. He was a surveyor of the department of works and, as a JP, examined the conspirators to the 'gunpowder plot'

of 1603. The manor passed ultimately to his great-grandson John Austen, who sold it in 1710.

Fortess Road NW5 (Kentish Town, Camden). Runs through a former close or small field called the Forties which was part of the mediaeval Cantelowes manor.

Fort Road SE1 (Bermondsey, Southwark). Named from a fort built nearby by Parliamentarian forces in 1642–3. The fort stood by the present Old Kent Road, guarding one of the main routes to London from the SE.

Fort Street E16 (Spitalfields, T. Ham.). Replaced an earlier Fort Street which ran from W to NE across what is now Spitalfields Market, and was built on part of the old artillery ground (*see* **Artillery Lane**). The Fort was the armoury. The present Fort Street is the S remnant of the former Duke Street, which was built from 1682 and named after James, Duke of York (*see* **Steward Street**).

Fortune Green Road NW6 (W Hampstead, Camden). Runs N to a small green so named. This is an old place name of uncertain derivation.

Fortune Street EC1 (Finsbury, Islington). The Fortune Theatre was established on the corner with Golden Lane in 1599; it was managed by Edward Alleyn and Philip Henslowe. The theatre survived until the Civil War; it was closed in 1648.

Foscote Mews W9 (Paddington, Cit. West.). *See* **Rundell Road**.

Foster Lane EC2 (Cit. Lond.). Foster is a mediaeval corruption of the name of St Vedast, whose church stands at the S end. Vedast was a 6th-century bishop of Arras.

Foubert's Place W1 (Soho, Cit. West.). Major Henry Foubert (*d*

1743) established a military and equestrian school on the S side of a passage between the present Regent Street and Kingly Street. The passage was named after him, and in 1882 the name was extended along the former Tyler Street, Tyler Court and the E–W arm of Marshall Street to make the present Foubert's Place.

Foulis Terrace SW7 (Brompton, Ken. Chel.). Commemorates Sir Henry Foulis, an early 19th-century benefactor to the Brompton Hospital, who presented the hospital chapel.

Founders' Court EC2 (Cit. Lond.). Off Lothbury, mediaeval centre of the metal-founders' craft. The Founders' Company had their guildhall here until 1853.

Fountain Drive SE19 (Dulwich, Southwark). Leads off Crystal Palace Parade opposite a drinking fountain. The provision of public drinking fountains, with a free supply of pure water, was a Victorian achievement, a special society being formed for the purpose.

Fountain Street E2 (Bethnal Green, T. Ham.). An inn called *The Fountain* is first recorded here on Virginia Row *c*1826.

Fournier Street E1 (Spitalfields, T. Ham.). Commemorates George Fournier, local benefactor of Huguenot extraction, who left a bequest for the poor of Spitalfields in 1834.

Fowler Street (Islington). The Fowler family were lords of the manor of Barnsbury, Islington, from 1539–1656.

Fownes Street SW11 (Battersea, Wandsworth). John Fownes established a glove factory in Falcon Road in 1777. The works, grounds

and his own house (Poplar House) occupied most of this side of the road. In *c*1840 the business was moved to a former silk factory (*see* **York Place**) and the Falcon Road site was built upon. The company later moved to Worcester.

Fox and Knot Street EC1 (Cit. Lond.). The *Fox and Knot* tavern stood in Fox and Knot Court, which led W out of Cow Lane into Chick Lane, and is recorded *c*1740. There is no record of what the sign looked like; it may have been a symbol of the joining of two taverns, *The Fox* and *The Knot*. The knot appears in heraldry; the arms of the Silkthrowers' Company (1630) had three knots of silk, and the arms of the Long-Bow String Makers' Company had a knot of bowstrings. Alternatively there may be a link with the sign of the nearby *Fox and Anchor*: a fox entwined in a knot of anchor cable.

Fox Close E1 (Stepney, T. Ham.). *See* **Amiel Street**.

Fox Court EC1 (Holborn, Camden). Named from a tavern, possibly Elizabethan, which stood on the site of the *Havelock* public house.

Foxley Road SW9 (Kennington, Lambeth). Built in the 19th century on part of Lambeth Wick manor which was leased to Baron Holland of Foxley (*see* **Wickwood Street**).

Frampton Park Road E9 (Hackney). William and Thomas Frampton, whose house was here, were trustees of the new chapel of St John in Well Street in 1809. The property is marked 'Frampton' on a map of 1731, and the family kept it until it was built upon in the late 19th century.

Frampton Street NW8 (Lisson Grove, Cit. West.). Commemorates Sir George Frampton, sculptor (*d*

1928); his best-known work is probably the statue of Edith Cavell in St Martin's Place.

Francemary Road SE4 (Lewisham). *See* **Amyruth Road**.

Francis Chichester Way SW11 (Battersea, Wandsworth). Commemorates the English aviator and yachtsman (1901–72) with a long record of solo flights and single-handed voyages.

Francis Street SW1 (Victoria, Cit. West.). Continuation of an original small street owned by Francis Wilcox in 1806; **Wilcox Place** adjoins.

Frank Dixon Close SE21 (Dulwich, Southwark). A modern street commemorating a post-war governor of Dulwich College. **Frank Dixon Way** adjoins.

Frankfurt Road SE24 (Herne Hill, Southwark). Built on the site of a large house on Herne Hill called 'Frankfurt Villa'.

Franklin Square W14 (W. Kensington, Hammersmith). Commemorates H.W. Franklin, president of the National Union of Railwaymen 1951–3.

Franklin's Row SW3 (Chelsea, Ken. Chel.). Commemorates an 18th-century Chelsea family who held property nearby.

Fransfield Grove SE26 (Sydenham, Lewisham). Commemorates (with **Kelvin Grove** and **Panmure Road**) an occasion during the Crimean War. Navvies who had been engaged in putting up the new Crystal Palace at Sydenham in 1854 were sent to the Crimea as a labour force. Before embarking they were inspected on Sydenham Hill by Lords Fransfield, Kelvin and Panmure, the latter being Secretary of State for War.

Frederick Close W2 (Bayswater, Cit. West.). Sir John Frederick of Burwood, Surrey, leased this area from the Bishop of London, lord of the manor of Paddington, in 1741. The estate was developed by his family. **Burwood Place** is nearby.

Frederick's Place EC2 (Cit. Lond.). Site of the house of Sir John Frederick, Lord Mayor of London in 1662.

Frederick Street WC1 (Gray's Inn Road, Islington). Built on the Gough-Calthorpe estate (*see* **Calthorpe Street**). The fourth (1790–1868) and fifth (1826–93) barons Calthorpe were both called Frederick.

Freedom Street SW11 (Battersea, Wandsworth). *See* **Reform Street**.

French Ordinary Court EC3 (Cit. Lond.). Site of an 'ordinary' or eating house opened before 1677 to serve the French community living in London.

Freston Road W11 (N Kensngton, Hammersmith). *See* **Latimer Road**.

Frewin Road SW18 (Wandsworth). Built on land belonging to Magdalen College, Oxford. A royalist Anglican divine with the Puritan name of Accepted Frewin or Frewen (1588–1664) was President of Magdalen 1626–44 and Archbishop of York 1660–4.

Friars' Close SE1 (Southwark). From nearby **Blackfriars Road**.

Friar Street EC4 (Cit. Lond.). Originally approached the monastery of the Dominican or Black Friars (*see* **Blackfriars Lane**).

Friary Road SE15 (Peckham, Southwark). From a Franciscan monastery and school here.

Friday Street EC4 (Cit. Lond.). The street leading to the stalls of fishmongers trading in the food markets of Cheapside in the early middle ages; the name refers to the practice of buying and eating fish on Fridays, the day when the street would be particularly busy. The Roman Catholic observance of Friday as a fast day was general in England before the Reformation. The street originally extended N of Cannon Street up to Cheapside. S of it lay Old Fish Street (now vanished) up which the fish was carried from the landing place at Queenhithe. The trade moved from Queenhithe to Billingsgate in the reign of Edward I (1272–1307) (*see* **Fish Street Hill**).

Frideswide Place NW5 (Kentish Town, Camden). On the estate of Christchurch Cathedral, Oxford, of which St Frideswide is patron. The saint was a Saxon princess with a vocation to religious life. She sought refuge in Oxford to escape an unwanted suitor, King Algar. She founded a convent there which was the forerunner of Christchurch (*see* **Caversham Road**).

Friend Street EC1 (Goswell Road, Islington). Commemorates George Friend, a scarlet-dyer and parish benefactor. In 1780 he founded the free clinic called the Finsbury Dispensary which later stood here (1870–1936) (*see* **Paget Street**).

Friern Road SE22 (Dulwich, Southwark). The surrounding area was called Friern manor, held until the dissolution of the monasteries (*c*1539) by the Friars of Halliwell Priory. 'Friern' is an antique form of the genitive plural. Friern Manor House, now demolished, lay NE of the present Goodrich Road, between Barry Road and Crebor Street.

Frith Street W1 (Soho, Cit. West.). Laid out by Richard Frith, late 17th-century property developer, who took a lease for building on Soho Fields in 1677.

Frognal   NW3   (Hampstead, Camden). Course of the Frognal Brook which ran S from Hampstead Heath by **Frognal Rise**. **Frognal Gardens**, **Lane** and **Way** adjoin.

Froude Street SW8 (Battersea, Wandsworth). Compliments the English historian James Anthony Froude (1818–94). He published his *History of England from the Fall of Wolsey to the Spanish Armada* in 1869, in 12 volumes. He was noted for a superb literary style and some provocative judgments.

Frying Pan Alley E1 (Spitalfields, T. Ham.). Named from a shop sign. The frying pan was an emblem used by braziers and ironmongers.

Fulbourne Street E1 (Whitechapel, T. Ham.). Commemorates Hugh de Fulbourne, recorded as rector of Whitechapel in 1329.

Fulham Palace Road W6, SW6 (Fulham, Hammersmith). Fulham Palace, at the S end, was the private residence of the bishops of London until 1972. The date of the first palace on the site is unknown. The present building was begun for Bishop Fitzjames (1506–22); it is now leased by Hammersmith Borough and used for a variety of purposes.

Fulham Park Gardens SW6 (Fulham, Hammersmith). A house called 'Fulham Park House' was recorded in use as a school in the early 19th century. It was designed in the 18th century by the architect Henry Holland. It later came to be called 'High Elms House'.

Fulham Road SW3, SW6, SW10

(Hammersmith/Ken. Chel.). Road to Fulham, called Fulanham in the 8th century, the 'ham' (OE, 'home') of Fulla.

Fuller Street E2 (Bethnal Green, T. Ham.). Commemorates John Fuller (*d* 1592), judge and church warden of Stepney parish church. The parish at that time included the hamlet of Bethnal Green, which Fuller represented. He lived at Bishop's Hall, and created a charity for almshouses in Stepney and Shoreditch parishes.

Fulwood Place WC1 (Holborn, Camden). Built on land belonging to Sir George Fulwood, a member of Gray's Inn from 1589. It was originally a S approach to Gray's Inn.

Furmage Street SW18 (Wandsworth). Built on land owned by William Furmage Palmer in 1898.

Furnival Street EC4 (Cit. Lond.). Furnival's Inn nearby was the town house of Sir Richard Furnival in the late 14th century. Like several other 'inns' or great town houses it was leased to lawyers (*see* **Clement's Inn**).

Furzedown Drive SW17 (Streatham, Wandsworth). Built on part of the former Furzedown Park estate, named from the nearby 'Furze down', or gorse common, now part of Tooting Graveney Common. **Furzedown Road** approaches. The estate was owned in the late 19th century by the Seely family. **Seely Road** is nearby.

Furze Street E3 (Bow Common, T. Ham.). *See* **Blackthorn Street**.

G

Gainsborough Gardens NW3 (Hampstead, Camden). The third Earl of Gainsborough was lord of the manor of Hampstead in the late 17th century. He gave the nearby Hampstead Wells for the good of the parish in 1698.

Gainsford Street SE1 (Bermondsey, Southwark). This appears as Black's Fields on a map of 1769. The Gainsford family later held this land (originally the property of the Order of Knights of St John of Jerusalem).

Gaisford Street NW5 (Kentish Town, Camden). Built on land which had belonged to the Dean and Chapter of Christchurch Cathedral, Oxford, since 1735. The dean at the time of development was Thomas Gaisford (1779–1855).

Galen Place WC1 (Bloomsbury, Camden). Commemorates the Greek physician Claudius Galen (130–200); named by association with the Pharmaceutical Society whose examination hall was built here.

Gallery Road SE21 (Dulwich, Southwark). Passes the art gallery attached to Dulwich College. The gallery was designed in 1817 by Sir John Soane to house a collection of paintings originally made for Stanislaus, King of Poland (1764–95) and bequeathed to the college by Sir Francis Bourgeois (*d* 1810). The collection had been acquired, on the fall of the Polish king, by Desenfans (*see* **Desenfans Road**).

Galley Wall Road SE16 (Bermondsey, Southwark). Approached a place called the Gallow Wall in a record of the reign of Henry VII (1485–1509). An old lane which was briefly, in the 19th century, called Manor Road, being a boundary of the manor of Rotherhithe.

Gambetta Street SW8 (Battersea, Wandsworth). In honour of Léon Michel Gambetta, a French republican politician who was among the founders of the republic of 1870. He acted in sole command for five months during the Franco-Prussian war, and came to popular attention in England by escaping from the siege of Paris in a balloon. He led the government 1879–82.

Garbutt Place W1 (Marylebone, Cit. West.). Named in 1894 after William Garbutt, St Marylebone vestry clerk and later the first Town Clerk of the borough.

Garden Road NW8 (St John's Wood, Cit. West.). Crosses the original Great Garden Field, presumably a market garden plot.

Garden Street E1 (Stepney, T. Ham.). *See* **King John Street**.

Gardners' Lane EC4 (Cit. Lond.). Uncertain, probably the name of a property owner. In the 18th century the street was also called Dunghill Lane.

Gardnor Road NW3 (Hampstead, Camden). Thomas Gardnor bought Gardnor House here in 1749, and the Gardnor family afterwards acquired a large Hampstead estate, including the site of this road.

Gard Street EC1 (Finsbury, Islington). One Gard was vice president of the Orphan Working

128

Garlick Hill

School which stood in nearby City Road 1773–1847.

Garfield Road SW11 (Battersea, Wandsworth). Named in 1882, and probably commemorates President Garfield of the United States of America, who took office in March 1881. He was shot by an assassin in July of the same year, and died of his wounds on 19 September.

Garlick Hill EC4 (Cit. Lond.). Led down to the mediaeval Garlick Hythe, or wharf where garlick was landed, on the Thames.

Garlinge Road NW2 (W Hampstead, Camden). Kentish place name; built by the Powell-Cotton family of Quex Park, Birchington, Kent.

Garnault Place EC1 (Islington). Built c1825 on land belonging to the New River Company (see **Myddelton Square**). Samuel Garnault (d 1827) was treasurer to the company. **Garnault Mews** is nearby.

Garratt Lane SW17, SW18 (Wandsworth). Runs S from Wandsworth village to the former hamlet of Garratt or Garretts, around Garratt Green. This was referred to in 1535 as an estate belonging to Merton Priory; after the dissolution of the priory c1539 Elizabeth I granted it with nearby Dunsford manor to her favourite Robert Dudley, Earl of Leicester. He sold it to Sir William Cecil, and it was afterwards held by the Smith and Brodrick families. **Garratt Terrace** adjoins.

Garrett Street EC1 (Finsbury, Islington). Named in 1898 at the suggestion of the parish vestry Works Committee, which included a member called Garrett.

Garrick Street WC2 (Covent Garden, Cit. West.). Built 1859–61, this street commemorates the 18th-century actor-manager David Garrick (d 1779). Garrick lived in various lodgings in the Covent Garden area before moving to Southampton Street in 1749.

Garway Road W2 (Westbourne Grove, Cit. West.). Built by W.K. Jenkins, a developer who also held property in Herefordshire. Garway is a village in the county, near the Monmouthshire border.

Gasholder Place SE11 (Vauxhall, Lambeth). Gas, after some early experiments, was first used for street-lighting in London in 1814, in Piccadilly. The manufacture of coal gas was important in Vauxhall and Nine Elms from 1833, when the London Gas-Light Company opened its works in Vauxhall Walk. (By 1860 the company had expanded on to a 17-acre site at Nine Elms; in 1865 ten workmen were killed and surrounding houses destroyed when one of the Nine Elms gasholders blew up.) This smaller group has become a landmark associated with the Oval Cricket Ground; it was originally used by the Phoenix Gas Works which stood upstream of Vauxhall Bridge.

Gaskell Street SW4 (Clapham, Lambeth). Named in 1909 after T. Penn Gaskell, London County Council member for Clapham.

Gassiot Road SW17 (Tooting, Wandsworth). Commemorates Charles Gassiot of Tooting, recorded as a former benefactor to St Bartholomew's Hospital.

Gate Street WC2 (Lincoln's Inn, Camden). Called Yeates Street on a map of 1746, which indicates a personal name – Yeates or Gates – of owner or builder.

Gateway SE17 (Camberwell,

Southwark). Off the Walworth Road at its S end, where formerly stood the turnpike gate at the beginning of the Camberwell Road. This street replaces another slightly further S and called Camberwell Gate.

Gatliff Road SW1 (Pimlico, Cit. West.). Commemorates Charles Gatliff, secretary and driving force of the Metropolitan Association for Improving the Dwellings of the Industrious Classes, founded 1841 and chartered 1846. The association concentrated on the better-paid skilled workman as the ideal tenant for its model blocks of flats.

Gauden Road SW4 (Clapham, Lambeth). Commemorates the Gauden family who held land in Clapham in the 17th century. The estate (between the present Cedars Road and The Chase) belonged to Sir Dennis Gauden (*d* 1688) before passing to the Hewer family.

Gautrey Road SE15 (Peckham, Southwark). Commemorates Thomas Gautrey, who was an alderman of Camberwell Borough from 1903.

Gayfere Street SW1 (Cit. West.). Thomas Gayfere, resident of Smith Square, was a master mason who worked on the restoration of the Henry VIII chapel in Westminster Abbey from 1807–23.

Gaynesford Road SE23 (Brockley, Lewisham). Built on part of the ancient manor of Brockley; the manor was held by John Gaynesford in the 16th century.

Geary Street N7 (Islington). Mrs Ann Geary left £50 to be invested for the poor of the parish of Islington, the income to be spent on bread. The money was put into South Sea Annuities in 1728.

Gee Street EC1 (Finsbury, Islington). Built from 1784 by Osgood Gee, descendant of two families (the Gees and the Osgoods) owning the ground.

Geffrye Street E2 (Shacklewell, Hackney). Runs beside the Geffrye Museum, Shoreditch. Sir Robert Geffrye, ironmonger and Lord Mayor of London 1685–6, left money to endow almshouses which were built in 1715. The buildings are now open as a museum of furniture, furniture-making having been an important local trade in the past.

Geldart Road SE15 (Peckham, Southwark). Edmund Martin Geldart was a local Unitarian minister from 1844 until 1885.

Geoffrey Road SE4 (Brockley, Lewisham). Geoffrey de Say, one of the barons who presented the *Magna Carta* to King John in 1215, held the surrounding area of Brockley (*see* **Sayes Court Street**).

George and Catherine Wheel Alley EC2 (Spitalfields, T. Ham.). Combination of the yards of two inns, *The George* and *The Catherine Wheel*. An inn with the combined name is recorded in 1810.

George Court (Strand, Cit. West.). *See* **Buckingham Street**.

George Inn Yard SE1 (Borough, Southwark). *The George* is the only one of Southwark's many coaching inns to survive. Parts of the present building are 17th century. The inn is recorded in 1542 and is almost certainly older than that. It originally extended all round the yard. The name refers to St George.

George Lane SE13 (Lewisham). From *The George* public house, at the junction with Lewisham High Street. The old inn was removed here during the 18th century from a Tudor house near the parish church; the latter was later known as 'Sion House'.

George's Road N7 (Holloway, Islington). Built *c*1800 by George Pocock, who was paying a compliment either to himself or to the king (George III). **Wells Yard** nearby originally approached a deep well which was dug at Pocock's expense in 1809. The well, near the S end of what is now Geary Street, cost him £2,000 and was intended as a water supply for his new streets which were not served by the New River Company. A company supply was introduced almost as soon as Pocock's scheme went into operation, and he lost heavily.

George Street W1 (Marylebone, Cit. West.). Built in the 1760s and named after the reigning king George III, who came to the throne in 1760.

George Yard EC3 (Cit. Lond.). Leads to the rear of the *George and Vulture*, an 18th-century chop house in Castle Court; its name presumably represents the merging of two earlier establishments.

George Yard W1 (Mayfair, Cit. West.). John George, glazier, leased land here in the early 18th century and was involved in local building. It is not certain, but it is probable, that he built this yard.

Georgina Gardens E2 (Bethnal Green, T. Ham.). Christian name of the Baroness Burdett-Coutts (*see* **Angela Gardens** and **Baroness Road**).

Geraldine Street SE11 (St George's Road, Southwark). Adjoins the Geraldine Mary Harmsworth Park, presented to the London County Council in 1930 by Lord Rothermere, and named after his mother.

Gerrard Street W1 (Shaftsbury Avenue, Cit. West.). Built *c*1682 on land belonging to Charles, Baron Gerard. Gerard House stood at nos. 34 and 35 (burnt down in 1887). The form 'Gerrard' came into use during the 19th century. **Gerrard Place** adjoins.

Gertrude Street SW10 (Chelsea, Ken. Chel.). Hans Sloane's grand-daughters, Anne Ellis and Sarah D'Oyley, left their part of his estate to a second cousin; he married Lady Gertrude Howard, and had a son who married Laura Webber of Tedworth in Hampshire. **Tedworth Gardens** and **Square** are nearby (*see* **Sloane Street**).

Ghent Street SE6 (Bellingham, Lewisham). *See* **King Alfred Avenue**. The Abbot of Ghent held Lewisham (and Greenwich) until 1414, when Henry V took them and settled them on a Carthusian abbey of his own foundation at Shene. Both manors passed to Henry VIII in 1531.

Gibbon Road SE15 (Nunhead, Southwark). Charles Gibbon, the first editor of the *South London Press*, lived in Camberwell.

Gibbon Walk SW15 (Putney, R. upon T.). Commemorates the historian Edward Gibbon who was brought up in Putney; his father, also Edward Gibbon, bought a house called 'Lime Grove' at the bottom of Putney Hill in 1736.

Gibbs Avenue SE19 (W Norwood, Lambeth). Commemorates Alderman Sir Charles Gibbs (*d* 1924), six times mayor of Lambeth. **Gibbs Close** and **Square** adjoin.

Gibson Close E1 (Stepney, T. Ham.). *See* **Amiel Street**.

Gibson Square N1 (Islington). Built on land belonging to Thomas Milner

George Yard EC3

Gibson's estate; the square was developed from 1828 on land which was formerly market gardens and nurseries. **Milner Square** is nearby.

Giles Coppice SE19 (Dulwich, Southwark). *See* **Low Cross Wood Lane**.

Gilkes Crescent SE21 (Dulwich, Southwark). Commemorates Arthur Gilkes, Master of nearby Dulwich College 1885–1914.

Gilpin Avenue SW14 (Sheen, R. upon T.). Commemorates W.S. Gilpin (*d* 1843), gardener and landscape designer in the picturesque tradition, who lived at Palewell Lodge, E Sheen.

Gilston Road SW10 (W Brompton, Ken. Chel.). On the Gunter estate (*see* **Gunter Grove** and **Talgarth Road**). Gilston was the name of a family property.

Giltspur Street EC1 (Cit. Lond.). Thought to be the place where spurriers (makers of spurs) worked, probably advertising themselves with the sign of a gilt spur.

Gipsy Hill SE19 (Norwood, Lambeth/Southwark). Formerly famous for a large colony of gipsies, who are recorded as living in the woods between the present Gipsy Hill and **Gipsy Road** from the 17th century.

Girdler's Road W14 (Brook Green, Hammersmith). Built on land owned by the Girdlers' Company.

Gladstone Street SE1 (St George's Road, Southwark). The Victorian statesman William Ewart Gladstone served four terms as Liberal Prime Minister between 1868 and 1894. This street was named in 1875, when Liberal Southwark mourned his electoral defeat in 1874 and replacement by the Conservative Disraeli. Gladstone became Liberal leader in 1866, after eight years as an innovative Chancellor of the Exchequer. In his early ministries he carried through unprecedented programmes of reform, but in later years he became entrammelled in the question of Irish Home Rule, and his popularity suffered from his handling of the Sudanese and Boer Wars. He died in 1898.

Glamis Road E1 (Shadwell, T. Ham.). *See* **Claude Street**.

Glasshill Street SE1 (Southwark). Recalls the proliferation of glass-works in 19th-century Southwark, and possibly their heaps of material. This is a modern name for the former Hill Street.

Glasshouse Fields E1 (Stepney, T. Ham.). Site of an 18th-century glassworks, producing crown-glass.

Glasshouse Street W1 (Piccadilly Circus, Cit. West.). Probably named from a glass factory. The extraction of saltpetre from night-soil is mentioned (as causing an insufferable nuisance) in the 1690s, and the *Survey of London* offers the suggestion that it may have been wanted for glass-making.

Glasshouse Walk SE11 (Vauxhall, Lambeth). Led to the old Vauxhall Glassworks which were demolished when the Albert Embankment was built 1866–70. The works were started in the 1670s, under the patronage of the Duke of Buckingham, by Dawson, Bowles and Co. This firm introduced Venetian techniques and craftsmen, and operated here until 1780.

Glasshouse Yard EC1 (Clerkenwell, Islington). Site of a 17th-century glass factory which is recorded in 1677.

Glazbury Road W14 (Baron's Court, Hammersmith). On the Gunter family's estate (*see* **Gunter Grove**). Glazbury was the name of a family property.

Glebe Place SW3 (Chelsea, Ken. Chel.). Built on part of the glebeland of the parish of St Luke (*see* **Camberwell Glebe**).

Glebe Road SW13 (Barnes, R. upon T.). *See* **Camberwell Glebe**.

Gledhow Gardens SW5 (Kensington, Ken. Chel.). On the Gunter estate (*see* **Gunter Grove**). The wife of Colonel Sir Robert Gunter came from Gledhow Hall, Yorkshire.

Gledstane's Road W14 (Baron's Court, Hammersmith). *See* **Palliser Road**.

Glengall Causeway E14 (Isle of Dogs, T. Ham.). Lady Glengall owned a large area of the Isle of Dogs in the mid-19th century (*see* **Glengall Grove**). The Grove originally extended right across the Isle (along the present Tiller Road) to this point.

Glengall Grove E14 (Isle of Dogs, T. Ham.). Developed by William Cubitt, brother of the great builder Thomas Cubitt, on land bought from the Countess of Glengall *c*1840. Lady Glengall, who married into the Irish peerage in 1834, was formerly Miss Margaret Lauretta Mellish, daughter and co-heir of William Mellish, a multi-millionaire and government contractor of Woodford, Essex. **Mellish Street** is nearby. The Earl of Glengall was also Viscount and Baron Cahir. **Cahir Street** lies to the SW off Ferry Road. **Glengall Road** and **Terrace** in Peckham are also named from the countess's property.

Glentworth Street NW1 (Marylebone, Cit. West.). Commemorates Lord Glentworth, an Irish peer who

was created Earl of Limerick in 1803. He was a strong supporter of the union of England and Ireland, and one of the original 28 Irish peers in the parliament of the United Kingdom. He lived for a time in Marylebone.

Gliddon Road W14 (Baron's Court, Hammersmith). *See* **Talgarth Road**.

Globe Road E1, E2 (Bethnal Green, T. Ham.). Runs N from the *Old Globe* public house which was built at the corner with Mile End Road. The street is part of an old route from the Bishop of London's manor house in Bethnal Green to the church of St Dunstan's, Stepney, the only parish church until 1734. The *Globe* became the *Old Globe* when the *New Globe* opened near the Grand Union Canal.

Globe Street SE1 (Southwark). The *Globe* inn on Great Dover Street is first recorded in 1826, and was probably named in memory of the Globe Theatre on Bankside.

Gloucester Gate NW1 (Regent's Park, Camden). Built as part of John Nash's Regent's Park scheme (*see* **Regent Street**). The gate is named after the Regent's sister, Princess Mary, Duchess of Gloucester. **Gloucester Avenue** approaches.

Gloucester Place NW1, W1 (Marylebone, Cit. West.). Commemorates Prince William, brother of George III, created Duke of Gloucester in 1764. His son William, also Duke of Gloucester, married his cousin the Princess Mary (*see* **Gloucester Gate**).

Gloucester Road SW7 (Kensington, Ken. Chel.). The Duchess of Gloucester, sister-in-law of George III, built Orford Lodge on the site of the present Stanhope Gardens. This road was then called Hogmore Lane; it and the house were renamed after the duchess's death. The house was demolished in 1853 (*see* **Canning Place**).

Gloucester Square W2 (Bayswater, Cit. West.). *See* **Connaught Place**. The Duke of Gloucester who was both cousin and brother-in-law to George IV was also Earl of Connaught.

Gloucester Terrace W2 (Bayswater, Cit. West.). Together with **Gloucester Gardens**, named by association with Gloucester Square (*see* above).

Gloucester Walk W8 (Kensington, Ken. Chel.). Queen Anne lived at Campden House on this site with her son, the Duke of Gloucester, from 1691–6; the duke died in 1700, aged 11.

Gloucester Way EC1 (Islington). *See* **Hardwick Street**.

Glyn Road E5 (Homerton, Hackney). Built on land belonging to the Glyn family. The estate also covered the area of present Coopersale and Roding Roads. The Glyns are recorded as holding land in Hackney in 1745; this development is late Victorian.

Goat Street SE1 (Bermondsey, Southwark). The *Goat* tavern in Horselydown is recorded in 1672; it appears again as 'The Goat Tavern, Queen Street' in 1809 (Queen Street being the present Queen Elizabeth Street).

Godfrey Street SW3 (Chelsea, Ken. Chel.). Probably built on a plot belonging to John Godfrey, corn-chandler, who owned land beside the King's Road at the time of building (*c*1835).

Godliman Street EC4 (Cit. Lond.). Formerly Paul's Chain, from a chain barrier which stopped traffic going across the churchyard of St. Paul's Cathedral during services. After *c*1700 the street was called variously Godliman or Godalmin Street; this is thought to be derived from a surname connected with Godalming in Surrey.

Godman Road SE15 (Peckham, Southwark). On the Crespigny estate (*see* **De Crespigny Park**). Major General Richard Godman married into the Champion de Crespigny family *c*1870.

Godolphin Road W12 (Shepherd's Bush, Hammersmith). Sir William Godolphin (*d* 1696), scholar and diplomat, became ambassador to Spain in 1671 and embraced the Catholic faith. Money left by him for charity was used to buy land near St James's, Westminster. The income from this was later applied to education, and the Godolphin School for Boys opened in Hammersmith in 1856 (in Great Church Lane). The school closed in 1900 and the Godolphin and Latymer Girls' School was opened in its place in 1906, a joint venture with the Latymer foundation (*see* **Latimer Road**).

Golden Fleece Court EC3 (Cit. Lond.). Named from the sign of an old inn, now demolished.

Golden Lane EC1, EC2 (Cit. Lond./ Islington). Called Goldynglane and Goldynggeslane in the 14th century. The derivation is probably from an early property owner called Golding.

Golden Square W1 (Soho, Cit. West.). Probably a corruption of 'gelding'; the site was a field called Gelding's Close when the land was farmed in the 17th century. The square was laid out in 1670.

Goldhawk Road W6, W12 (Hammersmith). John Goldhawk of Sands End held various plots of land in the original parish of Fulham, which included modern Hammersmith in his lifetime (14th century). His farm lay S of Dawes Road, Fulham. The Goldhawk family are still recorded as property owners in the 15th century, and are mentioned in connection with a 'fosse' (dyke) and a 'merssh' (marsh).

Golding Street E1 (Whitechapel, T. Ham.). *See* **Hessel Street**.

Goldington Crescent NW1 (Camden Town, Camden). Built on land belonging to the dukes of Bedford, who also held property at Goldington in Bedfordshire. **Goldington Street** approaches.

Goldney Road W9 (Paddington, Cit. West.). *See* **Rundell Road**.

Goldsmith Road SE15 (Peckham, Southwark). The poet and playwright Oliver Goldsmith taught at the school attached to a dissenters' meeting house in Meeting House Lane, Peckham, in 1717.

Goldsmiths' Row E2 (Haggerston, Hackney). Almshouses built by the Goldsmiths' Company formerly stood on the W side, near the junction with Audrey Street. They were built in the 18th century on part of what was then called Milkwives' Bridge Field.

Goldsmith Street EC2 (Cit. Lond.). The hall of the Goldsmiths' Company was first established in nearby Foster Lane in 1339; Goldsmiths' Row ran parallel to this street along Cheapside.

Goldsworthy Gardens SE16 (Rotherhithe, Southwark). Lieutenant-General Philip Goldsworthy (*d* 1801) inherited the manor of Rotherhithe from his aunt Martha Gashry in 1777. He was appointed equerry to George III in 1788 and was MP for Wilton.

His sister, a governess to the royal children, inherited the manor after him and left it to a friend, Miss Gomm (*see* **Gomm Road**).

Gomm Road SE16 (Rotherhithe, Southwark). Miss Gomm (*see* **Goldsworthy Gardens**) inherited the manor of Rotherhithe in 1816. The Gomm family held it until 1875 when, on the death of Field Marshal Gomm, it passed to a related family called Carr-Gomm.

Gondar Gardens NW6 (W Hampstead, Camden). *See* **Asmara Road**.

Gonson Street SE8 (Deptford, Greenwich). Benjamin Gonson and Admiral William Gonson were treasurers to the navy in the 16th century. Both lived in Deptford.

Goodge Street W1 (Tottenham Court Road, Camden). John Goodge acquired land here, part of some meadows called Crab Tree Field and Walnut Tree Field, when the leaseholder, William Beresford, died in 1718. Goodge, a carpenter, married the widow Ann Beresford; he died in 1748 and his nephews Francis (*d* 1771) and William (*d* 1778) inherited the estate, which passed on William's death to a nephew, Samuel Foyster.

Goodman Street E1 (Whitechapel, T. Ham.). Built on the E side of Goodman's Fields, which were approached over **Goodman's Stile** (*see* **Goodman's Yard**).

Goodman's Yard E1 (Whitechapel, T. Ham.). John Stow's *Survey of London* of 1598 says that a farm here, belonging to the nuns of the covent of St Clare (*see* **Minories**), was worked by a farmer called Goodman in the mid-16th century, and was subsequently owned by his son.

Goodwin Road W12 (Shepherd's Bush, Hammersmith). Nicholas Goodwin was a benefactor to the parish by his will of 1727.

Goose Yard EC1 (Islington). Site of a former farmhouse called 'Goose Farm'; it became an apartment house in the 1820s, housing staff and performers from the Sadler's Wells Theatre. It was later demolished.

Gophir Lane EC4 (Cit. Lond.). Called Gofairelane in the 14th century; Gofaire was a mediaeval surname.

Gordon Court W12 (Wormwood Scrubs, Hammersmith). Probably commemorates Leslie Gordon, Town Clerk of Hammersmith from c1913.

Gordon House Road NW5 (Kentish Town, Camden). Built c1806 along a footpath S of Gordon House, an 18th-century academy which is now demolished. The footpath ran W beside the River Fleet.

Gordon Road SE15 (Peckham, Southwark). Named in 1875, and probably in honour of General Charles Gordon, who was at the time Governor of Central Africa. Gordon came to public attention in 1864 when he was sent to help suppress a rebellion against the Qing dynasty in China, and to protect British trading interests which were threatened by it. His upright character and Christian faith maintained his popularity (*see* **Khartoum Road**).

Gordon Street WC1 (Bloomsbury, Camden). Leads to **Gordon Square**, both being on the Bedford estate. The sixth duke of Bedford married, as his second wife, the granddaughter of the Duke of Gordon (*see* **Cosmo Place**).

Gore Road E9 (S Hackney, Hackney). Part of the approaches to Victoria Park, and possibly named after Charles Gore, one of the Commissioners for Improving the Metropolis. The commission was replaced by the Metropolitan Board of Works in 1856.

Gore Street SW7 (Kensington, Ken. Chel.). *See* **Kensington Gore**.

Goring Street EC3 (Cit. Lond.). Formerly Castle Court, from a 17th-century inn. Renamed in 1885.

Gorst Road SW11 (S Battersea, Wandsworth). *See* **Dents Road**.

Gorsuch Place E2 (Shoreditch, Hackney). Commemorates Thomas Talbot Gorsuch, surgeon and local benefactor, who left money for the poor of Shoreditch in 1820. **Gorsuch Street** adjoins.

Gosling Way SW9 (S Lambeth, Lambeth). Formerly Gosling Road, and probably named after H. Gosling, alderman of London County Council from 1900.

Gosterwood Street SE8 (Deptford, Lewisham). Named from Gosterwood Manor Farm, on the Evelyn family's Wotton estate (*see* **Evelyn Street**).

Gough Square EC4 (Fleet Street, Cit. Lond.). Owned by Richard Gough (*d* 1728) who was a wool-merchant and father of Sir Henry Gough (*see* **Calthorpe Street**). Richard Gough bought an estate of fields off the Gray's Inn Road in 1706, and this was later developed as the Gough-Calthorpe estate, including **Gough Street**.

Gower Street WC1 (Bloomsbury, Camden). Part of the Bedford estate; the fourth Duke of Bedford married the daughter of the first Earl Gower.

Gower Court, **Mews** and **Place** adjoin.

Gracechurch Court EC3 (Cit. Lond.). *See* **St Benet's Place**.

Gracechurch Street EC3 (Cit. Lond.). In the middle ages it was called Garscherch Street, Grass Church Street and Gracious Street. The only thing that emerges with any certainty is that it had both grass and church. It may have been a church by a place where a grass, hay and corn market was held, or possibly a church in a grassy place. Eilert Ekwall, in his *Street Names of the City of London* (1954), suggests that the church may have been a primitive early building with a turf roof.

Grace's Alley E1 (Whitechapel, T. Ham.). Approaches part of the site of the Abbey of St Mary Grace, or St Mary of Graces (*see* **Eastminster**).

Grace's Road SE5 (Camberwell, Southwark). *See* **Dagmar Road**.

Grafton Road NW5 (Kentish Town, Camden). Built on land belonging to the manor of Tottenhall which was held at the time by the Fitzroy family; the head of the family was the Duke of Grafton.

Grafton Street W1 (Mayfair, Cit. West.). Built on land belonging to the dukes of Grafton, who had a town house nearby on New Bond Street in the early 18th century. The house later became the Clarendon Hotel and was demolished in 1877.

Grafton Way WC1, W1 (Euston, Camden). Built on land belonging to the dukes of Grafton who held the manor of Tottenhall. They inherited it from Isabella Bennet, daughter and heiress of the Earl of Arlington (*see* **Bennet Street**). She was married to Henry Fitzroy, natural son of Charles II and Barbara Villiers (*see* **Cleveland Street**). Henry was created First Duke of Grafton and his brother Charles became Duke of Cleveland. **Grafton Mews** approaches.

Graham Road E8 (Dalston, Hackney). The Graham family owned pieces of land throughout the borough of Hackney in the 19th century. Graham House stood N of Dalston Lane and S of Montague Road.

Graham Terrace SW1 (Belgravia, Cit. West.). Built on land leased from the Grosvenor estate by William Graham of Ebury Street in 1822.

Granada Street SW17 (Tooting Broadway, Wandsworth). The Granada Cinema here was built in 1931 in Venetian–Gothic style. Designed by Komisarjevsky, it was London's most spectacular picture-palace. It closed as a cinema in 1973.

Granby Terrace NW1 (Hampstead Road, Camden). Commemorates Lieutenant-General John Manners, Marquis of Granby, son of the third Duke of Rutland and son-in-law of the sixth Duke of Somerset. As a commander in the Seven Years War (1756–63) he won great acclaim for successful tactics – spectacular cavalry charges and stormings of defended positions – which appealed to the public imagination.

Grandison Road SW11 (Battersea, Wandsworth). *See* **Bolingbroke Walk**. Oliver St John, who obtained Battersea Manor from Charles I, was Viscount Grandison.

Grange Lane SE21 (Dulwich, Southwark). From a house here called 'The Grange' (*see* **Grange Road**).

Grangemill Road SE6 (Lewisham). The Grange Mill was a 15th-century mill here on the River Pool.

Grangemill Way adjoins (*see* **Grange Road**).

Grange Road SE1 (Bermondsey, Southwark). The W end marks the site of the mediaeval grange attached to the Abbey of Bermondsey. A grange is a group of barns associated with a great house, a monastery or an estate. **The Grange** adjoins, with **Grange Walk** and **Yard**.

Grantham Place W1 (Mayfair, Cit. West.). Built by John Grantham, builder and property developer, in the 1780s; he built the street on his own brick-field.

Granville Place W1 (Marylebone, Cit. West.). Probably named after Granville George Leveson-Gower, Earl Granville, a Victorian politician who was three times Foreign Secretary. When the street was named in 1864 he was Lord President of the Council.

Granville Square WC1 (Clerkenwell, Islington). Built on the Lloyd Baker estate (*see* **Lloyd Baker Street**). Thomas Lloyd Baker married Mary Sharpe, niece of the anti-slavery campaigner Granville Sharpe (1735–1813). **Granville Street** approaches.

Grape Street WC2 (St Giles, Camden). Formerly Vine Street, and probably the site of an early vineyard attached to the hospital of St Giles. A property called 'The Vyne', belonging to the hospital, stood here in the 16th century.

Gravel Lane E1 (Cit. Lond.). Originally ran E from Houndsditch with a branch N to New Street; an old path, so-called from the character of the ground.

Gravel Street E1 (Wapping, T. Ham.). Off Garnet Street which was called New Gravel Lane in the 18th century. The present Wapping Lane was Old Gravel Lane. They were routes for carrying sand and gravel. The Admiralty (from 1535) and, later, Trinity House were both permitted to take gravel and sand for ballast from the riverside. This indicates that the supply was ample, enough for regular removal inland as well.

Graveney Road SW17 (Tooting, Wandsworth). Part of the mediaeval manor of Tooting Graveney, so called because the Graveney or Gravenell family held it from the Abbot of Chertsey in the 12th and 13th centuries.

Gravesend Road W12 (Wormholt Park, Hammersmith). Richard Gravesend was Bishop of London 1280–1303, and Stephen Gravesend was Bishop 1319–38. The manor of Hammersmith formerly belonged to the diocese of London.

Gray's Inn Road WC1 (Camden). Passes Gray's Inn Square and Gray's Inn Gardens where stood the inn or town house of Lord Gray of Wilton, which was leased to lawyers in the 16th century (*see* **Clement's Inn**).

Gray's Yard W1 (Marylebone, Cit. West.). Built by Edward Gray, scavenger, on land leased from Sir Thomas Edwardes in the late 18th century. Edwardes originally planned to build distinguished streets to link up with the Cavendish Harley estate. This plan was ruined by the intrusion of Stratford Place, and he was obliged to let small areas. The W end of Wigmore Street was formerly Edwardes Street.

Great Bell Alley EC2 (Cit. Lond.). Formerly Bell Alley, which ran across the line of the modern Moorgate, along the line of Telegraph Street and N to London Wall. The street was named from the sign of an inn, now demolished.

Great Castle Street W1 (Oxford Street, Cit. West.). Built behind land belonging to an Oxford Street inn, *The Castle*, which is now demolished. **Eastcastle Street**, E of it, was named by association; it was formerly called Little Castle Street.

Great Chapel Street W1 (Soho, Cit. West.). Approached a French Protestant (Huguenot) chapel which was built at the corner with Sheraton Street (then Little Chapel Street) in 1694.

Great Church Lane W6 (Hammersmith). Originally approached the parish church of St Paul, Hammersmith, built as a chapel of ease for Fulham parish in 1631. Hammersmith became a parish in 1834, and the present church is Victorian. It has been cut off from Great Church Lane by the huge roundabout under Hammersmith Flyover.

Great College Street SW1 (Cit. West.). Leads to Westminster School, properly St Peter's College, Westminster. **Little College Street** and **College Mews** adjoin.

Great Cumberland Place W1 (Marble Arch, Cit. West.). *See* **Cumberland Gate**.

Great Dover Street SE1 (Southwark). Built under an act of 1809 to improve and re-route the N section of Kent Street, which originally extended to Long Lane. The remnant of Kent Street is now called the Old Kent Road, leading into the county of Kent and, ultimately, to Dover.

Great Eastern Street EC2 (Shoreditch, Hackney). Built in 1875 as part of a through route for traffic from N into E London, which was mainly going to the docks.

Great George Street SW1 (Cit.

West.). Built in 1750 and named for the reigning king George II (1727–60). **Little George Street** adjoins.

Great Guildford Street SE1 (Southwark). Suffolk Place at the S end of this street was left to Lady Jane Guildford in 1510 by Sir Thomas Brandon. Sir Thomas's nephew Charles, later Duke of Suffolk, acquired it from her in exchange for an annuity (*see* **Great Suffolk Street**). The name has a double significance, since Southwark was in the county of Surrey when the street was formed, and Guildford is the county town.

Great James Street WC1 (Bloomsbury, Camden). Built by the Doughty family in association with James Burgess (*see* **Doughty Street**).

Great Marlborough Street W1 (Regent Street, Cit. West.). Commemorates John Churchill, First Duke of Marlborough, Captain-General of the English army 1702–12. **Little Marlborough Street** adjoins.

Great Maze Pond SE1 (Southwark). Formerly led to a pond belonging to the mediaeval manor called the Maze, which covered the area now between Tooley Street and Snowsfields. The manor is recorded by that name in 1386; the land had formerly belonged to the Abbot of Battle (*see* **Battle Bridge Lane**) and included his garden maze and fishponds. By 1650 the manor was covered in dwellings, many of them in bad repair and declining into slums.

Great Newport Street WC2 (Charing Cross Road, Cit. West.). *See* **Little Newport Street**.

Great New Street EC4 (Cit. Lond.). *See* **New Street Square**.

Greatorex Street E1 (Whitechapel,

T. Ham.). Dan Greatorex became minister of St Paul's Seamen's Church, Dock Street, in the 1860s, and stayed for nearly 40 years.

Great Ormond Street WC1 (Bloomsbury, Camden). Built *c*1690 and probably commemorates James Butler, First Duke of Ormonde (*d* 1688), Royalist commander in the Irish campaigns of the Civil War, and created a duke by a grateful Charles II.

Great Percy Street WC1 (Islington). *See* **Percy Circus**.

Great Peter Street SW1 (Cit. West.). Named from St Peter, patron of Westminster Abbey, on whose land the street was built. Formerly the section between St Anne's Street and Tufton Street was Little Peter Street.

Great Portland Street W1 (Marylebone, Cit. West.). Originally Portland Street, built in the mid-18th century on land belonging to the dukes of Portland. **Little Portland Street** crosses it.

Great Pulteney Street W1 (Soho, Cit. West.). Built 1719–20 on land which Sir William Pulteney leased from the Crown. The family, later earls of Bath, held extensive London estates. 'Great' compares with Little Pulteney Street (*see* **Brewer Street**).

Great Queen Street WC2 (Covent Garden, Camden). Laid out in the early 17th century and named in compliment to the royal family. 'Great' is in contrast to Little Queen Street, which formerly adjoined.

Great Russell Street WC1 (Bloomsbury, Camden). *See* **Russell Square**.

Great St Helen's EC3 (Cit. Lond.). St Helen (*c*250–330) was the wife of the Roman emperor Constantius and the mother of Constantine; she became a Christian in 312. A mediaeval tradition held that she was of British origin. The church of St Helen, Bishopsgate, is known to have been within the jurisdiction of St Paul's Cathedral *c*1150; the date of its foundation is unknown. A Benedictine nunnery was established there in *c*1210. The convent buildings were acquired by the Leathersellers' Company after the dissolution of the monasteries *c*1539; their present guildhall was built on the site.

Great St Thomas Apostle EC4 (Cit. Lond.). The mediaeval church of St Thomas the Apostle stood here.

Great Scotland Yard SW1 (Cit. West.). Site of the London house used by visiting kings of Scotland until the 13th century. Cardinal Wolsey, Archbishop of York, bought it *c*1514 to add to the adjacent York Place which was his London house. In 1829 the office of the Police Commissioners was opened in Whitehall with a rear police station opening on to the Yard; the name remained attached to the Metropolitan Police Force when they moved to new premises on the embankment in 1890 and again to Victoria Street in 1967.

Great Smith Street SW1 (Cit. West.). Sir James Smith built this street *c*1700; he was a member of the family which built Smith Square. **Little Smith Street** adjoins.

Great Suffolk Street SE1 (Southwark). Commemorates Suffolk Place, London house of Charles Brandon, Duke of Suffolk and brother-in-law to Henry VIII. The house stood N of the junction of this street with Borough High Street; it was demolished in 1557 (*see* **Mint Street**). The street was built up in the late 18th century and was formerly known as Dirty Lane.

Great Sutton Street EC1 (Clerkenwell, Islington). Thomas Sutton, Master of Ordnance to Elizabeth I, established the school at the nearby Charterhouse in 1611.

Great Swan Alley EC2 (Cit. Lond.). Approach from Coleman Street to an inn called *The Swan*, and formerly divided as Great and Little Swan Alleys. It predates Moorgate Street which was built across it.

Great Titchfield Street W1 (Marylebone, Cit. West.). Built on the estate of the dukes of Portland who were also barons of Titchfield in Hampshire.

Great Tower Street EC3 (Cit. Lond.). First recorded in the 13th century, leads to the Tower of London, of which the first part was built by William I (1066–87).

Great Trinity Lane EC4 (Cit. Lond.). The parish church of Holy Trinity (now demolished) stood at the junction of this lane and **Little Trinity Lane**.

Great Turnstile WC1 (Lincoln's Inn Fields, Camden). A 17th-century turnstile gate into Lincoln's Inn stood here.

Great Winchester Street EC2 (Cit. Lond.). An Augustinian monastery nearby (*see* **Austin Friars**) was acquired by Sir William Powlet, Lord Treasurer, after the dissolution of the monasteries *c*1539. He left it to his son Lord Winchester, who called it 'Winchester House'.

Great Windmill Street W1 (Soho, Cit. West.). A windmill stood in the present Ham Yard in the 16th century, in what was formerly Windmill Field; the field was laid out in streets from *c*1660, and the mill is thought to have gone by 1700. 'Great' compares with the former Little Windmill Street, now **Lexington Street**.

Greaves Place SW17 (Tooting, Wandsworth). The Rev. Richard Greaves of Deddington, Oxford-shire, was patron of the living of Tooting Graveney parish. In that capacity he laid the foundation stone of the new parish church in 1831, having subscribed £400. He bought the advowson on behalf of his nephew, Richard Wilson Greaves, who was rector 1844–67.

Greek Street W1 (Soho, Cit. West.). Greek Orthodox refugees from Turkish rule came here in the late 17th century; a Greek Orthodox church was built for them on the site of the present St Martin's School of Art.

Green Arbour Court EC1 (Cit. Lond.). Originally connected Old Bailey and Seacoal Lane, with a large courtyard midway. The court was truncated by Holborn Viaduct Station which it now approaches. It is recorded in 1637 as Green Arbour, possibly from an inn.

Greenaway Gardens NW3 (Hampstead, Camden). Kate Greenaway (1846–1901), writer and illustrator of children's books, lived in Hampstead. Her books and pictures glorified childhood as a golden age.

Greenberry Street NW8 (St John's Wood, Cit. West.). Leads to **Barrow Hill Road**; Green Berry Hill was an old name for Barrow Hill.

Greencoat Place SW1 (Cit. West.). The Green Coat School which stood nearby was founded in 1636 in a building properly called St Margaret's Hospital. The school became part of the United Westminster Schools in 1874. The building was demolished in 1877 for an extension to the Army and Navy Stores. **Greencoat Row** adjoins.

Green Dragon Court SE1 (Southwark). Site of an inn of that name, recorded as such in 1542 and previously as 'Cobham's Inn'. Part of this house became St Saviour's Grammar School in 1562; the school continued on approximately the same site until 1838.

Green Dragon Yard E1 (White-chapel, T. Ham.). The *Green Dragon Inn* here is recorded in 1746.

Greenhill's Rents EC1 (Smithfield, Islington). From the property owner; John Greenhill applied, unsuccess-fully, for a market on his land in 1736. 'Rents' are properties built to be rented out.

Green Hundred Road SE15 (Peckham, Southwark). Revival of an early place name. The Green Hundred was a plot of land held by the Gardyner family (*see* **Bellenden Road**). The derivation of its name is unknown.

Greenland Place NW1 (Camden Town, Camden). Built by a local builder, Augustine Greenland, from *c*1790. **Greenland Road** and **Street** adjoin.

Green Lanes N16, N4, N8 (Stoke Newington, Hackney). An old route; the name is self-explanatory, from a green or grass track.

Greenside Road W12 (Shepherd's Bush, Hammersmith). The land next to this road was formerly called Starch Green.

Green Street W1 (Mayfair, Cit. West.). Built by John Green on land owned by the Grosvenor estate in the 1720s.

Greenwell Street W1 (Great Portland

Street, Cit. West.). The name of a family active in local government; a modern street name.

Greenwood Place NW5 (Highgate Road, Camden). From Thomas Greenwood, landlord of the *Bull and Gate* tavern on Highgate Road from 1786.

Greenwood Road E8 (Hackney). Possibly laid out by Greenwoods, builders active in E London from the 1860s.

Grendon Street NW8 (Lisson Grove, Cit. West.). *See* **Paveley Street**. Walter Grendon was Grand Prior of the Order of Knights of St John of Jerusalem in England, 1400–16.

Grenville Place SW7 (Kensington, Ken. Chel.). Borders the estate formerly held by Lord Holland, who inherited it from Sir Walter Cope and his wife Dorothy Grenville (*see* **Cope Place**).

Grenville Street WC1 (Bloomsbury, Camden). Built *c*1792, and named in honour of William Wyndham Grenville, Baron Grenville (1759–1834). He was Speaker of the House of Commons in 1789, Home Secretary later in that year and president of the Board of Control in 1790. He served as Foreign Secretary 1791–1801, under his cousin William Pitt the Younger, and he became Prime Minister after Pitt's death in 1806.

Gresham Street EC2 (Cit. Lond.). Sir Thomas Gresham (*d* 1579), merchant, royal agent and founder of the Royal Exchange, endowed his own house in Bishopsgate as Gresham College. This was demol-ished in 1768 and a new Gresham College opened in 1833 on what was then Lad Lane (W) and Cat Eaton Street (E). Cat Eaton is a 16th-century corruption of mediaeval

Catteten, Catten or Catte Street (street of cats, significantly placed behind the Cheapside food market). These two streets were altered and reopened as Gresham Street in 1845.

Gresse Street W1 (Tottenham Court Road, Camden/Cit. West.). The N part lay on land attached to a house bought by Peter Gaspard Gresse from the Hassell family in 1752. Gresse built the N part of the street from 1768; the S portion already existed under another name. Peter Gaspard Gresse was Swiss.

Greville Place NW6 (Kilburn, Camden). Built on part of the grounds of the former Kilburn Priory. The priory lands belonged (at the time of building) to Fulke Greville Howard, who developed them c1820 in association with Thomas Mortimer of the Albany, Piccadilly. **Mortimer Crescent** and **Place** adjoin.

Greville Street EC1 (Holborn, Camden). Approached a house bought in 1619 by Fulke Greville, Lord Brooke (*see* **Brooke Street**).

Greycoat Place SW1 (Cit. West.). The Grey Coat Hospital was founded in 1698 as a school for poor children and moved here in 1701.

Grey Eagle Street E1 (Spitalfields, T. Ham.). A *Grey Eagle* tavern nearby in Brick Lane is recorded in the 17th century.

Greyfriars Passage EC1 (Cit. Lond.). The Franciscans or Greyfriars (from the colour of their habits) set up a community in Cornhill in 1225 and were later given land on the N side of Newgate Street. There they founded the monastery of Christchurch, which became Christ's Hospital, a school for poor children, in 1552. The school moved to Horsham in 1902.

Greyhound Road W6, W14 (Fulham, Hammersmith). From the *Greyhound* inn, mentioned in the early 19th century and since rebuilt.

Greystoke Place EC4 (Cit. Lond.). Formerly Black Raven Alley, from an inn sign. Called Greystock Place c1810, from a property owner.

Greyswood Street SW16 (Furzedown, Wandsworth). Built on or near a small wood called Grey's Wood in the 18th century; the identity of Grey is unknown.

Grimwade Crescent SE15 (Nunhead, Southwark). Built by one Grimwade in the 1870s.

Grindal Street SE1 (Lambeth). Part of the manor of Lambeth belonging to the archbishops of Canterbury. Archbishop Grindal held office 1575–83.

Grinling Place SE8 (Deptford, Lewisham). John Evelyn, Deptford landowner of Sayes Court, first recommended the woodcarver Grinling Gibbons (1648–1720) to Charles II.

Grittleton Road W9 (Westbourne Green, Cit. West.). The Neelds of Grittleton, Wiltshire, held this land from 1820 (*see* **Rundell Road**). They named **Braden Street**, **Lanhill Road**, **Sevington Street** and **Surrendale Place** from family properties.

Grocers' Hall Court EC2 (Cit. Lond.). The Grocers' Company had their first charter in 1428, having previously been called Pepperers. They bought their first guildhall here in the same year. **Grocers' Hall Gardens** adjoins.

Grosvenor Gate W1 (Mayfair, Cit. West.). Sir Richard Grosvenor (*d* 1732) made a gate here into Hyde

Park, for his tenants on the Grosvenor Mayfair estate.

Grosvenor Place SW1 (Belgravia, Cit. West.). Boundary of the Grosvenor estate (*see* **Belgrave Square**), continued by **Grosvenor Gardens** and **Lower Grosvenor Place**. **Grosvenor Crescent** approaches.

Grosvenor Road SW1 (Pimlico, Cit. West.). The Grosvenor estate on the old manor of Ebury includes Pimlico and this road along the Thames embankment across the mouth of the former Grosvenor Canal. The canal was built in 1725 and improved by Lord Grosvenor in 1824; it is now closed.

Grosvenor Square W1 (Mayfair, Cit. West.). The most important development on the estate inherited by the Grosvenor family (*see* **Davies Street**). The square was built *c*1720–55. **Grosvenor Street** and **Upper Grosvenor Street** were built as approaches to it. (*See* **Blackburne's Mews**.)

Grotto Court SE1 (Southwark). Site of Finch's Grotto Garden, a pleasure ground opened in 1760 by Thomas Finch. The garden was closed in 1773, and the ground was bought by the parish in 1777.

Grotto Passage W1 (Marylebone, Cit. West.). Part of the site of an extensive shell-grotto devised by John Castle and opened in 1738 as a public amusement. The grotto was closed *c*1760.

Grove Hill Road SE5 (Camberwell, Southwark). Built on the site of an 18th-century estate called Grove Hill, noted for its plantations. **Camberwell Grove** (*see* **Camberwell Road**) marks the avenue which approached the house. **Grove Park** and **Lane** adjoin.

Grove Park Road W4 (Chiswick, Hounslow). Laid out as a residential development by the Duke of Devonshire (*see* **Duke Road**) who acquired the estate of Grove House. **Grove Park Gardens** and **Terrace** adjoin. The duke owned Burlington House nearby, and had leased Sutton manor on the death of Richard, Lord Burlington, in 1727.

Grove Road E3 (Mile End, T. Ham.). An old lane running N from Mile End through the groves on the site of the present Victoria Park.

Grove Street SE8 (Deptford, Lewisham). A new, wide street along the line of the former Grove Street Hill, Victoria Street and Albert Street. Queen Victoria had visited the Royal Naval Victualling Yards here in 1858.

Grummant Road SE15 (Peckham, Southwark). From John Grummant, 19th-century property owner and Camberwell vestryman.

Grundy Street E14 (Poplar, T. Ham.). Uncertain: one Thomas Grundy of Poplar was working as a carpenter and joiner in 1805, and may have begun the first houses of this street.

Gubyon Avenue SE24 (Herne Hill, Lambeth). Built in the late 19th century on land belonging to the Gubbins family, and given a composite name including part of their own.

Guildhouse Street SW1 (Pimlico, Cit. West.). When named (in 1936) this street ran to the rear of a building called the Guild House in Eccleston Square.

Guilford Street WC1 (Bloomsbury, Camden). Frederick North, Second Earl of Guilford or Guildford, Lord North and Eighth Baron Guilford

(1732–92), was usually known in political life as Lord North. He was Prime Minister 1770–82. This street was built from 1792 on the estate of the Thomas Coram Foundling Hospital (*see* **Coram Street**); Lord North was president of the hospital from 1771 until his death.

Guinness Court NW8 (Primrose Hill, Camden). Dwellings were built here by the Guinness Trust for workers' housing in the 1960s. The trust was founded by Edward Guinness, Lord Iveagh, who gave Kenwood House on Hampstead Heath to the London County Council in 1925.

Gulliver Street SE16 (Rotherhithe, Southwark). Jonathon Swift's character Captain Lemuel Gulliver retired to Rotherhithe after his travels in Lilliput and Brobdingnag.

Gunstor Road N16 (Stoke Newington, Hackney). Possible corruption of Gunston. Thomas Gunston bought the lease of the manor of Stoke Newington in 1699; he had been acquiring land in the parish since 1684. In 1700 he died, and the lease of the manor (which was owned by St Paul's Cathedral) passed to his sister, Mary, wife of Sir Thomas Abney.

Gun Street E1 (Spitalfields, T. Ham.). Part of the site of the Tasel Close Artillery Yard (*see* **Artillery Lane**), which is described by John Stow in his *Survey of London* of 1598: '. . . whereunto the gunners of the Tower do weekly repair . . . and there levelling certain brass pieces of great artillery against a butt of earth . . . discharge them for their exercise'.

Gunter Grove SW10 (West Brompton, Ken. Chel.). On the Gunter family estate, which they began to acquire *c*1800 when James

Gunter bought the first plot of land. Much of the development was done by 1860–80 by Colonel Sir Robert Gunter (*see* **Barkston Gardens**).

Gunterstone Road W14 (Baron's Court, Hammersmith). *See* **Gunter Grove**.

Gunthorpe Street E1 (Whitechapel, T. Ham.). Commemorates John Gunthorpe (*d* 1498), rector of St Mary, Whitechapel, 1471–2. He was Dean of Wells, a royal chaplain, ambassador and keeper of the Privy Seal.

Guthrie Street SW3 (Chelsea, Ken. Chel.). Commemorates the army surgeon George James Guthrie (1785–1856), noted for his improvements to practical surgery on the battlefield. A book on the treatment of gunshot wounds, especially where amputation was required, was published in 1814 and enlarged and revised through three editions.

Gutter Lane EC2 (Cit. Lond.). Corruption of Guthrun's Lane, a name which records an early landowner, probably Danish.

Guy Street SE1 (Southwark). Thomas Guy, publisher, was a governor of St Thomas's hospital which lay on the N side of St Thomas's Street. In 1721 he took land on the S side and built an annex. This he endowed, and enabled it to function as a separate hospital. The first patients were admitted in 1726.

Gwendwr Road W14 (Baron's Court, Hammersmith). *See* **Gunter Grove** and **Talgarth Road**. Gwendwr was the name of the Gunter family's Breconshire estate.

Gwynne Place WC1 (King's Cross Road, Islington). Nell Gwynne, mistress of Charles II (1660–85), traditionally lived in Bagnigge House which stood W of King's Cross Road opposite this street. The house later became the spa and pleasure garden called Bagnigge Wells.

H

Haberdasher Street N1 (Hoxton, Hackney). Robert Aske's Haberdashers' School and almshouses were founded nearby in 1690–6 (*see* **Aske Street**).

Hackney Road E2 (Shoreditch and Bethnal Green, Hackney/T. Ham.). Road leading to Hackney, which is called Hakney in a 13th-century reference. The name contains the OE word meaning an island, and is thought to mean either Haca's Island or 'the island at the bend'; either meaning refers to the River Lea.

Hack Street E14 (Poplar, T. Ham.). Name of an E London builder who was active from the 1850s.

Haddonhall Street SE1 (Southwark). Approached Haddon Hall, a mission hall named after the evangelist Charles Haddon Spurgeon (*see* **Spurgeon Street**).

Hadleigh Street E2 (Stepney, T. Ham.). An Essex place name, by association with Braintree Street adjoining. **Hadleigh Close** is nearby.

Haggerston Road E8 (Kingsland Road, Hackney). Approaches the former hamlet of Haggerston (surrounding the present Haggerston Park), called Hergotestane in the *Domesday Book*. The name means 'Heregod's Stone'.

Haldane Place SW18 (Southfields, Wandsworth). Richard Burdon Haldane, created Viscount Haldane in 1912, sat as a Liberal MP 1885–1911 and became War Secretary in 1905. He created the General Staff in 1906 and the Territorial Army in 1907. Despite his achievement in

mobilising the British Expeditionary Force at the outbreak of World War I he was attacked in the press as pro-German and forced out of public life in 1915. The attack was based on his knowledge of German life and culture.

Half Moon Court EC1 (Cit. Lond.). Named from the sign of an inn, now demolished.

Half Moon Lane SE24 (Dulwich, Southwark). An old lane, named from the *Half Moon* inn at the W end, by Stradella Road.

Half Moon Street W1 (Cit. West.) Named from the sign of an inn at the corner with Piccadilly.

Haliday Walk N1 (Kingsland, Islington). Sir Henry Mildmay (*see* **Mildmay Park**) married Ann, daughter of Alderman William Haliday, who died in 1623 and left his daughter his estate of Newington Green. Mildmay's own possessions were confiscated at the Restoration in 1660, but this estate had been his wife's property and it remained in the Mildmay family after her death.

Halkin Street SW1 (Belgravia, Cit. West.). Part of the Grosvenor family's estate. Halkin or Halkyn Castle in Flintshire was a family house until 1912. **Halkin Arcade, Mews** and **Place** and **West Halkin Street** are nearby.

Hallam Street W1 (Marylebone, Cit. West.). The historian Henry Hallam (1777–1859) lived in Wimpole Street. He published *A View of the State of Europe during the Middle Ages* in

1818, and at once gained a reputation as an interpretative historian. His son Arthur Hallam (*d* 1833) was the friend mourned in Tennyson's poem, *In Memoriam*.

Hall Place W2 (Paddington, Cit. West.). Edward Hall married Elizabeth Crompton, heiress to this and surrounding land, in 1773. They and their family lived at Paddington Green until the development of the estate by their grandson Cuthbert Hall and his wife, the former Sarah Howell, from 1858. The streets laid out were named Hall Place, **Cuthbert Street, Crompton Street, Adpar Street** and **Newcastle Place**; Cuthbert's mother came from Adpar near Newcastle Emlyn.

Hall Road NW8 (St John's Wood, Cit. West.). Begun from 1820 as a group of expensive villas built near the junction with Grove End Road by William Hall, a local builder.

Hall Street EC1 (City Road, Islington). Built in 1822 by Joseph and James Hall.

Halsbury Road W12 (Shepherd's Bush, Hammersmith). Lord Halsbury was Lord High Chancellor in Lord Salisbury's government of 1886–92. The street was named in 1890.

Halsey Street SW3 (Chelsea, Ken. Chel.). *See* **Moore Street.**

Halton Road N1 (Barnsbury, Islington). The Halton family were lords of the manor of Barnsbury from 1656–1754. Sir William Halton of Samford, Essex, married Ursula Fisher, who inherited the manor from her father Thomas Fisher. The Halton's manor house stood at the S end of this street.

Hamilton Place W1 (Piccadilly, Cit. West.). Built on ground belonging to

the ranger of Hyde Park in the reign of Charles II (1660–85); his name was Hamilton. The Ranger's Lodge formerly stood on the site of Apsley House.

Hamilton Square SE1 (Southwark). Commemorates Lord Claud Hamilton, chairman of the Metropolitan Association for Improving the Dwellings of the Industrious Classes, in 1874.

Hamilton Terrace NW8 (Maida Vale, Cit. West.). *See* **Lyons Place.** C. Hamilton was governor of Harrow School in 1829, and this street is on school land. **Hamilton Close** and **Gardens** are nearby.

Hamlets Way E3 (Mile End, T. Ham.). The borough of Tower Hamlets is named from the group of Tudor hamlets which owed service to the lieutenant of the Tower of London, and were obliged to raise a force for the defence of the Tower. In the 16th century the lieutenant could call on men from 21 hamlets: Bethnal Green, Blackwall, Bow, Bromley, East Smithfield, Hackney, Limehouse, Mile End, Norton Folgate, Old Ford, Poplar, Ratcliff, Saint Katherine's, Shadwell, Shoreditch, Spitalfields, Tower Liberty Within, Tower Liberty Without, Trinity Minories, Wapping and Whitechapel.

Hammersmith Bridge Road W6 (Hammersmith). Built as an approach to Hammersmith Bridge which was begun in 1825.

Hammersmith Road W6, W14 (Hammersmith). Road to Hammersmith: the name means 'the smithy where hammers were forged.'

Hammond Street NW5 (Kentish Town, Camden). The Rev. Dr Robert Smith of Caversham owned this land at his death in 1716. He left it to his housekeeper Mrs Margaret Hammond for her lifetime, and afterwards to Christchurch, Oxford. The street was laid out after Mrs Hammond's death in 1735.

Hampden Gurney Street W1 (Marylebone, Cit. West.). Commemorates the Rev. John Hampden Gurney, highly regarded rector of St Mary's, Bryanston Square, 1847–62.

Hampstead Road NW1 (Camden). Road leading to Hampstead: the name derives from an OE word meaning a homestead.

Ham Yard W1 (Soho, Cit. West.). The *Lyric Tavern* on the corner with Great Windmill Street was originally an inn called *The Ham*, first recorded in the early 18th century.

Hanbury Street E1 (Spitalfields, T. Ham.). The nearby 'Black Eagle' brewery belonging to Truman, Hanbury, Buxton and Co. is first recorded as belonging to Joseph Truman in 1683. Sampson Hanbury joined the company c1800. This street was formerly Brown's Lane, from a large holding of property there by William and Jeffrey Brown or Browne c1649.

Handel Street WC1 (Bloomsbury, Camden). Commemorates the composer George Frederick Handel (1685–1759), one-time organist to the chapel of the Thomas Coram Foundling Hospital on whose land the street was built. Handel was also a benefactor to the hospital: he donated the MS of *Messiah*.

Handley Road E9 (S Hackney, Hackney). Commemorates the Rev. Henry Handley Norris, first rector of St John of Jerusalem, South Hackney, which church he served from its foundation as a chapel of ease (*see* **Church Crescent**). A

popular and generous rector, he gave land here for a church school.

Hanging Sword Alley EC4 (Cit. Lond.). Probably named from the sign of an inn or shop which is now demolished.

Hankey Place SE1 (Southwark). Donald Hankey was a prominent student member of the Oxford and Bermondsey Club, an Edwardian welfare mission established in a former Wesleyan chapel which is now demolished.

Hannen Road SE27 (West Norwood, Lambeth). Sir James Hannen, later Baron Hannen (1821–94), was born in Peckham and is buried in the South Metropolitan Cemetery, West Norwood. He became a judge in 1868 and was made a Lord of Appeal in Ordinary in 1891.

Hanover Park SE15 (Peckham, Southwark). The Hanover Chapel (demolished) stood E of the junction of Rye Lane and Peckham High Street. It was built in 1817 for an already existing congregation of nonconformists who had named their assembly after the reigning royal house. Hanoverian kings, since 1714, had ensured the safety of the Protestant succession and the Protestant faith. 'Park' denotes an open, well-planted, villa-and-garden style of building. Nearby Highshore Road was formerly Hanover Street.

Hanover Square W1 (Oxford Street, Cit. West.). Laid out from 1713 by the Earl of Scarborough, strong supporter of the House of Hanover and the Protestant succession. **Hanover Street** approaches (*see* **St George Street**).

Hanover Terrace NW1 (Regent's Park, Cit. West.). Built as part of John Nash's Regent's Park scheme (*see* **Regent Street**). The royal family were also the rulers of Hanover in Germany. Queen Anne died without an heir in 1714 and the next in line was George, Elector of Hanover, a descendant of James I of England and VI of Scotland. The Hanoverians were at first unpopular; they appeared entirely German and relatively uninterested in British affairs. It took the threatened restoration of the Stuarts to give the Hanoverians some virtue in the nation's eyes. **Hanover Gate** and **Mews** adjoin.

Hansler Road SE22 (E Dulwich, Southwark). Variation on Henslowe (*see* **Henslowe Road**), whose name appears on contemporary documents in a variety of spellings.

Hanson Street W1 (Marylebone, Cit. West.). The Cleveland Street block of the Middlesex Hospital Medical School was opened in 1887 by the Lord Mayor, Sir Reginald Hanson (*d* 1905).

Hans Place SW1 (Chelsea, Ken. Chel.). Sir Hans Sloane died in 1753; part of his land was leased to the architect Henry Holland who laid out Hans Place, Sloane Street and Cadogan Square. **Hans Crescent** and **Road** are nearby (*see* **Sloane Street**).

Hanway Place W1 (Oxford Street, Camden/Cit. West.). Thomas Hanway, a commissioner of the Royal Navy, owned this land in the early 18th century and left it to his nephew, the Rev. James Altham. The latter's son James Hanway Altham was in possession of it by 1796. The Hanways were related to Jonas Hanway, also appointed a Royal Navy commissioner in 1762 but mainly noted for his work on behalf of children in the care of the workhouse.

Harben Road NW6 (Swiss Cottage, Camden). Henry Harben was first

mayor of the borough of Hampstead in 1899. He was also London County Council member for Hampstead from 1889.

Harbinger Road E14 (Isle of Dogs, T. Ham.). The iron passenger sailing-ship *Harbinger* was built for Anderson, Anderson and Co. in 1876, for the Australian trade. Fast, comfortable and popular with passengers, she sailed between London and Adelaide and later between London and Melbourne. She was sold to a Russian owner for the Baltic trade in 1897.

Harbledown Road SW6 (Fulham, Hammersmith). *See* **Bradbourne Street**.

Harcourt Street W1 (Marylebone, Cit. West.). John Harcourt bought part of the manor of Lilestone, W Marylebone, in the late 18th century and lived at the manor house which stood here (*see* **Lilestone Street**).

Harcourt Terrace SW10 (Earl's Court, Ken. Chel.). Probably from the Rev. Leveson Vernon Harcourt, a business associate of the Gunter family, on whose land this street was built (*see* **Gunter Grove**).

Hardel Rise SW2 (Tulse Hill, Lambeth). The Hardel family owned land in Tulse Hill in the 14th century. Their holdings passed to the hospital of St Thomas the Martyr, Southwark, in 1352.

Harder's Road SE15 (Peckham, Southwark). Built on land owned by a Mr Harder in the late 19th century; originally there were several named groups of houses including Harder's Place. The name was extended along the whole road in 1893.

Hardwick Street EC1 (Clerkenwell, Islington). Built on the Lloyd Baker estate, when the land was owned by

Thomas Lloyd Baker of Hardwick Court, Gloucester. **Gloucester Way** is nearby.

Hardwidge Street SE1 (Bermondsey, Southwark). Local family name; a James Hardwidge is recorded in the late 18th century as needlemaker to Queen Charlotte, as appears on a tablet in Bermondsey parish church. He left a bequest to the parish in 1812.

Hare Court EC4 (Cit. Lond.). Part of the lawyers' complex called The Temple; Nicholas Hare (*d* 1557), Master of the Rolls to Mary I, lived here.

Hare Place EC4 (Cit. Lond.). Formerly Ram Alley, site of Hare House which is recorded in 1594 as bequeathed to the parish of St Dunstan's-in-the-West. Ram Alley had acquired a bad name as a sanctuary for criminals, and the name was changed for a pleasanter association.

Harewood Avenue NW1 (Marylebone, Cit. West.). On the Portman estate (*see* **Portman Square**). Edward Berkeley Portman (1799–1888) married Emma Lascelles, daughter of the second Earl of Harewood, in 1827.

Haringey Park N8 (Hornsey, Haringey). The ancient manor house of Haringey stood nearby; it was demolished in *c*1870 and the site built over. This street was built across the park surrounding the house.

Harleyford Road SE11 (Kennington, Lambeth). Built *c*1818 on land leased to the Clayton family (*see* **Clayton Street**); their country house was at Harleyford in Buckinghamshire. **Harleyford Street** is nearby.

Harley Street W1 (Marylebone, Cit. West.). Built *c*1730–75 on land

belonging to the Duke of Portland and inherited from his wife, the former Lady Margaret Cavendish Harley.

Harmood Street NW1 (Kentish Town, Camden). Built on land which had been a field, leased to the Harmood family by the lord of the manor *c*1800. **Harmood Place** adjoins.

Harp Alley EC4 (Cit. Lond.). Now a court between Farringdon Street and St Bride Street, first recorded in 1654 as a much longer court. The W end, to Shoe Lane, was demolished and replaced by St Bride Street. The name probably derives from an inn sign.

Harper Road SE1 (Southwark). A modern name, of unknown origin, replacing the name 'Union Road' which was common enough to cause confusion. The street was built up from *c*1827; before that it was a country lane called Horsemonger Lane, from horse-dealing.

Harp Lane EC3 (Cit. Lond.). Lane leading to a building known as 'The Harp', which was once a brewhouse.

Harpur Street WC1 (Holborn, Camden). Laid out in the early 18th century on land belonging to Peter Harpur of Bedford. Harpur was able to endow a school in Bedford with the income from his London properties.

Harriet Street SW1 (Sloane Street, Cit. West.). Built in the 1830s on land belonging to the Lowndes family. Harriet Lowndes was the mother of the landowner William Lowndes. **Harriet Walk** adjoins.

Harrington Road SW7 (Kensington, Ken. Chel.). The Earl of Harrington was a former owner of nearby Cromwell House, which was demolished in 1853, and also the owner of this estate. **Harrington Gardens** approaches.

Harrington Square NW1 (Camden Town, Camden). Built on land belonging to the dukes of Bedford. The seventh Duke of Bedford (1788–1861) married Anna Maria Stanhope, daughter of the third Earl of Harrington.

Harrington Street NW1 (Hampstead Road, Camden). Built on the Fitzroy estate; Caroline Fitzroy, daughter of the second Duke of Grafton, married William Stanhope, second Earl of Harrington, in 1746. **Stanhope Street** is nearby.

Harrison Street WC1 (Gray's Inn Road, Camden). Built from 1818 on land owned by the Harrison family. The first holding was acquired by Daniel Harrison in 1739. The family were brickmakers and much of the land was used for digging brick-earth.

Harris Street SE5 (Camberwell, Southwark). Probably after the family of builders, Harris of Camberwell, who operated widely in S London in the 1870s and 1880s and were also active in local affairs.

Harrowby Street W1 (Marylebone, Cit. West.). Lord Harrowby, in 1820, invited members of Lord Liverpool's Tory cabinet to dinner. The radical extremists called the Cato Street Conspirators, having advance knowledge of this, planned to murder them all. The plan came to nothing; the conspirators were arrested in adjoining **Cato Street**, five were hanged and five transported.

Harrow Place E1 (Cit. Lond.). Probably named from the sign of a harrow over a metal-worker's shop.

Harrow Road W2, W9, W10, NW10 (Cit. West.). Road leading to Harrow: the name means 'the place

of the pagan shrine', and comes from OE 'Hearga'.

Hartland Road NW1 (Camden Town, Camden). See **Hawley Road**. The Buck family came from Hartland in N Devon.

Hartshorn Alley EC3 (Cit. Lond.). Named from the sign of a tavern, the *Hart's Horn*, now demolished.

Hart Street EC3 (Cit. Lond.). Called Herthstrete in the 14th century and Hertstrete in the 15th. The name perhaps indicates a connection with hearthstones.

Harvey Street N1 (Hoxton, Hackney). The Harvey family was connected by marriage to the Pitfield family, who held land here from 1648 until 1917.

Harwood Road SW6 (Fulham, Hammersmith). Built in the late 19th century on land belonging to the Harwood family, market gardeners. **Harwood Terrace** is nearby.

Hasker Street SW3 (Chelsea, Ken. Chel.). Built c1845 for the Rev. George Hasker, who inherited land here from his father. He had first built **First Street** in 1845 and some of the land had also been leased to a builder called Bull. **Bull's Gardens** is nearby.

Hastings Street WC1 (Bloomsbury, Camden). See **Leigh Street**.

Hatcham Park Road SE14 (Lewisham). The Saxon manor of Hatcham was called Hacchesham, meaning the homestead of Hacca. Its ownership is first recorded in 1086, and last in the mid-18th century. A map of 1744 shows Hatcham House, moated and with extensive grounds, near this road.

Hatherley Grove W2 (Bayswater,

Cit. West.). Built on land leased by Charles Hatherley, surgeon, in 1870.

Hatherley Street SW1 (Cit. West.). William Page Wood, Baron Hatherley (1801–81), was Lord Chancellor from 1868 until 1872. He was a resident of the parish of St Margaret's and was actively concerned with parish affairs.

Hatton Garden EC1 (Holborn, Camden). Laid out in 1659 on land belonging to the Hatton family; the site had formerly been the garden of Ely Place, London house of the bishops of Ely. The bishops were forced by Elizabeth I to cede part of their property to Sir Christopher Hatton in 1576. Hatton acquired the rest on the death of Bishop Cox in 1581. The gardens were extensive and famous for roses and fruit. **Hatton Place** and **Wall** are adjacent (*see* **Ely Place**).

Haunch of Venison Yard W1 (Mayfair, Cit. West.). Named from an 18th-century inn, now demolished.

Havannah Street E14 (Isle of Dogs, T. Ham.). *See* **Cuba Street.**

Havelock Street N1 (King's Cross, Islington). Commemorates General Sir Henry Havelock who, with General Sir James Outram, was active in suppressing the Indian Mutiny of 1857–8. Havelock was noted for his relief of Delhi and Cawnpore. **Delhi** and **Outram** Streets run parallel.

Havil Street SE5 (Peckham, Southwark). Havil House, home of a family of that name, stood on the corner with Peckham High Road until its replacement by the Town Hall. The street was formerly called Workhouse Lane, from the Camberwell Workhouse on the site of the present hospital.

Hawes Street N1 (Islington). Commemorates Dr William Hawes of Islington, who founded the Royal Humane Society in 1774. He died in Islington in 1808.

Hawke Road SE19 (Norwood, Lambeth). Named in 1872, and probably laid out by John Hawke of New Cross, a builder active in S London in the 1860s and 1870s.

Hawkesbury Road SW15 (Putney, Wandsworth). Part of the Putney Park estate. Charles Jenkinson, First Earl of Liverpool and First Baron Hawkesbury (1727–1808), had a house W of Putney Park Lane.

Hawkesfield Road SE23 (Lewisham). Built on land, formerly farmland, recorded since the 17th century as Hawkes Field. It is not known whether this refers to an occupier, or to the habitat of hawks, but the former is more likely.

Hawley Road NW1 (Camden Town, Camden). Built on land belonging to the Hawley family of Leybourne, Kent, in the middle of the 19th century. **Hawley Crescent** and **Street** are nearby. Sir Joseph Hawley, who was responsible for much of the development, had a partner, George Stucley Buck, who inherited an interest from his father Lewis Buck. **Buck Street** and **Stucley Place** adjoin; **Lewis Street** is to the N.

Hay Currie Street E14 (Poplar, T. Ham.). Sir Edmund Hay Currie, of Currie's distilleries, was chairman of Beaumont's Trustees and active in the work of establishing the People's Palace (*see* **Beaumont Square**). The Currie family was also instrumental in providing church schools in this area.

Haydon Square E1 (Whitechapel, T. Ham.). Properly Heydon, and first recorded as such in 1677. Captain

John Heydon was Master of the Ordnance 1627–42, and lived in the Minories, where he had an interest in the development of this square and of **Haydon Street** and **Walk**.

Hayes Place NW1 (Marylebone, Cit. West.). Developed by Francis Hay of Hayes, in Middlesex, from 1819 (*see* **Hay's Lane**).

Hay Hill W1 (Mayfair, Cit. West.). Built on land belonging to a farm of that name. In the 16th century it is recorded as Aye Hill, from the Aye Brook which bounded it; in the 1690s it appears as Hay Hill, a farm held by Lord Berkeley. **Hay's Mews** and **Hill Street** are nearby.

Hayles Street SE11 (St George's Road, Southwark). Built on land left to Lambeth parish by the Hayles family and called Hayles Estate (*see* **West Square**).

Haymarket SW1 (Cit. West.). Site of a market where hay was sold as fodder until 1830.

Haymerle Road SE15 (Peckham, Southwark). In honour of Baron Heinrich von Haymerle, Austro–Hungarian minister at the Congress of Berlin in 1878. He was Prime Minister and Foreign Minister of the dual monarchy 1879–80.

Hayne Street EC1 (Cit. Lond/Islington). The premises of Haynes, timber merchants and woodworkers, formerly occupied the corner with Long Lane. The street was renamed in 1871, having been formerly Charterhouse Street.

Hay's Lane SE1 (Tooley Street, Southwark). Approaches Hay's Wharf, where the Hay family first acquired property (a brewery) in 1651, and gradually extended their activities as wharfingers and warehousemen. The last Hay,

Francis, died in 1838.

Hay's Mews W1 (Mayfair, Cit. West.). *See* **Hay Hill**.

Hayward's Place E1 (St John Street, Islington). Built *c*1845 on land belonging to James Hayward, ironmonger, of Aylesbury Street.

Hazelbourne Road SW12 (Balham, Lambeth/Wandsworth). Built on the site of a large house on Balham Hill called 'Hazelbourne'.

Hazlitt Road W14 (Shepherd's Bush, Hammersmith). Commemorates the English essayist William Hazlitt (1778–1830).

Headfort Place SW1 (Belgravia, Cit. West.). Thomas Taylour, Marquis of Headfort, had a house at 46 Belgrave Square where he died in 1894.

Headlam Street E1 (Bethnal Green, T. Ham.). Commemorates the Rev. Stuart Headlam (1847–1924), radical founder of the Anglo-Catholic Guild of St Matthew. Headlam was a pioneer of education for poor children in E London. His guild, which began in 1877, was an agency of Christian socialism and general reform.

Healey Street NW1 (Kentish Town, Camden). Commemorates Francis Healey, local representative on the Metropolitan Board of Works in the 1860s.

Heathcote Street WC1 (Bloomsbury, Camden). On the Foundling Hospital estate (*see* **Coram Street**). Michael Heathcote was a governor of the hospital from 1810.

Heathfield Terrace W4 (Hammersmith). George Augustus Eliott, Lord Heathfield, Baron Heathfield of Gibraltar, lived for a time S of Turnham Green. As Governor of

Gibraltar (1776–90) he defied a four-year siege by Spain and France (1779–83) and won great popularity at home. He died in 1813. **Heathfield Gardens** approaches.

Heathman's Road SW6 (Fulham, Hammersmith). J.H. Heathman served on Fulham Borough Council from 1906.

Heathstan Road W12 (Wormwood Scrubs, Hammersmith). Heathstan or Heahstan was Bishop of London in the early 10th century. This is one of a group commemorating early bishops; the manor of Hammersmith belonged to the diocese of London.

Heathwall Street SW11 (Battersea, Wandsworth). Follows part of the course of the Heathwall Ditch, a watercourse along the slopes of Clapham draining the marshy meadows of Longhedge Farm. It ran along the side of the Kingston road and drained the higher ground into the Thames at two points – Battersea Creek and Nine Elms. It became a nuisance as an open sewer, and is now covered.

Heaton Road SE15 (Peckham, Southwark). Heaton's Folly was built nearby *c*1800 by a Mr Heaton who, according to Lysons' *Environs of London*, wished to provide employment for the local poor. The folly consisted of a building in fantastic style, with a tower, on a lake island.

Heaver Road SW11 (Battersea, Wandsworth). Named in 1879, and possibly laid out by Heaver and Coates, builders active in the 1870s.

Hebdon Road SW17 (Tooting, Wandsworth). Sir John Hebdon (1621–70), diplomat and envoy to Russia, lived in Tooting and is commemorated in the parish church.

Heber Road SE22 (E Dulwich, Southwark). *See* **Copleston Road**.

Heckfield Place SW6 (Fulham, Hammersmith). The novelist Frances Trollope (1780–1863) had a house nearby called 'Heckfield Lodge'; her father had been vicar of Heckfield in Hampshire. Having visited America, she achieved success with *Domestic Manners of the Americans* in 1832. She wrote travel books and novels, always emphasising the broadly comic aspects of life.

Heckford Street E1 (Ratcliff, T. Ham.). Commemorates a Victorian local doctor noted for his care of sick children in poor families.

Heddon Street W1 (Soho, Cit. West.). Built from 1726 on the Pulteney estate; William Pulteney held property at Heddon in Yorkshire (*see* **Great Pulteney Street**).

Hellings Street E1 (Wapping, T. Ham.). *See* **Crowder Street**.

Helmet Row EC1 (Finsbury, Islington). Built on land belonging to the Ironmongers' Company, whose arms incorporated a helmet (*see* **Lizard Street**).

Helvetia Street SE6 (Forest Hill, Lewisham). An old name for Switzerland, still in use. The surrounding group of streets is named from Swiss towns: **Clarens Street**, **Neuchâtel Road**, **Nyon Grove** and **Vevey Street**.

Hemming Street E1 (Bethnal Green, T. Ham.). Said to commemorate Edward Hemming, who represented Bethnal Green (then a hamlet) on the first select vestry of the parish of Stebunhithe (Stepney) in 1589.

Hemus Place SW3 (Chelsea, Ken.

Chel.). Commemorates William Hemus Raynor, who was active in developing the Cadogan estate.

Henchman Street W12 (Wormwood Scrubs, Hammersmith). Humphrey Henchman was Bishop of London 1663–75 and, as such, held the manor of Hammersmith.

Henderson Road SW18 (Wandsworth). John Young Henderson was a member of the original Wandsworth Borough Council from 1900.

Hendre Road SE1 (Old Kent Road, Southwark). On the Rolls family estate (*see* **Rolls Road**). John Alan Rolls, First Baron Llangattock (1837–1912), lived at The Hendre, Monmouthshire (*see* **Marcia Road**).

Heneage Lane EC3 (Cit. Lond.). Leads to Heneage Place off **Bevis Marks**. A house there belonging to the Abbot of Bury was acquired at the dissolution of the abbey (*c*1539) by Thomas Heneage.

Heneage Street E1 (Spitalfields, T. Ham.). Built on the Osborn estate (*see* **Chicksand Street**). Heneage Finch was the second wife of Sir George Osborn.

Henniker Mews SW3 (Chelsea, Ken. Chel.). Built on part of Chelsea Park where a family called Henniker-Wilson had a house. The house was demolished *c*1876.

Henrietta Mews WC1 (Bloomsbury, Camden). On the Foundling Hospital estate (*see* **Coram Street**). Henrietta, wife of Sir Stephen Gaselee, Vice-President of the hospital, died in 1838 and was buried in the hospital chapel, as were her husband and their two daughters. All died between 1838 and 1841.

Henrietta Place W1 (Marylebone,

Cit. West.). John Holles, Duke of Newcastle, bought the Marylebone estate in 1708. His daughter Henrietta was also his heiress.

Henrietta Street WC2 (Covent Garden, Cit. West.). Laid out for the fourth Earl of Bedford by Inigo Jones in 1631, and named after Henrietta Maria, consort of the reigning king Charles I.

Henry Prince Estate SW18 (Southfields, Wandsworth). Alderman Henry Prince (*d* 1936) was active on the housing committee of the Borough of Wandsworth and was responsible for much of the council's building programme.

Henshaw Street SE17 (Walworth, Southwark). A firm of builders active in the 1860s. They built Pocock Brothers' works in Southwark Bridge Road in 1868, and this street at about the same time.

Henslowe Road SE22 (E Dulwich, Southwark). The Elizabethan theatre manager Philip Henslowe was associated with Edward Alleyn (*see* **Alleyn Park**).

Henty Walk SW15 (Putney, Wandsworth). The novelist G.A. Henty (1832–1902), who wrote immensely popular adventure stories for boys, lived in Putney.

Herbal Hill EC1 (Clerkenwell Road, Camden/Islington). Originally part of a herb garden attached to the palace of the bishops of Ely (*see* **Ely Place**).

Herbert Crescent SW1 (Chelsea, Ken. Chel.). Commemorates Sir Herbert Stewart, investor in the development of Sir Hans Sloane's estate (*see* **Hans Place**).

Herbert Street NW5 (Kentish Town,

Camden). Built by Vincent Herbert in the 1850s.

Herbrand Street WC1 (Bloomsbury, Camden). Built on the Bedford estate; the eleventh Duke of Bedford (*d* 1940) was Herbrand Arthur Russell.

Hercules Road SE1 (Lambeth). Philip Astley, circus owner, who opened Astley's Amphitheatre near Westminster Bridge in 1779, built himself a house near the junction of this road and Westminster Bridge Road. He called it 'Hercules Hall' after one of his favourite acrobatic acts, 'The Strength of Hercules'. The house was demolished in 1841.

Hereford Road W2 (Westbourne Grove, Cit. West.). Built by W.K. Jenkins, a developer who held property in Herefordshire.

Hereford Square SW7 (Kensington, Ken. Chel.). Originally lay at the rear of a large house called 'Hereford Lodge', which was demolished in the 1880s for the building of Brechin Place.

Hermes Street N1 (Pentonville, Islington). The Swiss doctor and chemist Francis de Valangin built a house here in 1772 and called it 'Hermes Hill' after Hermes Trismegistus, said to be the first chemist.

Hermitage Wall E1 (Wapping, T. Ham.). A hermitage is recorded here in the 14th century, when it was occupied by a friar, John Ingram. In the 15th century it became a public brew-house; in the 18th century and later it was known as the Red Lion Brewery. The wall was part of the river wall.

Hermit Place NW6 (Kilburn, Camden). *See* **Kilburn Priory**. The original cell was inhabited by Godwyn, a hermit.

Hermit Street EC1 (St John Street, Islington). A hermitage and oratory was founded nearby in 1511 by the Hospital of St John of Jerusalem at Clerkenwell. The land passed into secular ownership at the dissolution of the monasteries *c*1539; it was later bought by Dame Alice Owen as the site of her almshouses and school (*see* **Owen Street**).

Herne Hill SE24 (Lambeth/ Southwark). Possibly from a word meaning heron or heronry; the surrounding country was originally marsh, and the haunt of wildfowl.

Herrick Street SW1 (Cit. West.). Commemorates Robert Herrick (1591–1674), clergyman and cheerful poet, who lived for a time in St Ann's Street nearby.

Hertford Place W1 (Euston, Camden). Built on the Fitzroy estate. Isabella Fitzroy, daughter of the second Duke of Grafton, became Baroness Conway and Marchioness of Hertford. **Conway Street** is nearby.

Hertford Street W1 (Mayfair, Cit. West.). From an 18th-century inn, now demolished, named after the Seymours, who were dukes of Somerset and also marquises of Hertford.

Hesperus Crescent E14 (Isle of Dogs, T. Ham.). The iron passenger sailing-ship *Hesperus* (1,777 tons) was built for Anderson, Anderson & Co. and launched in 1873. She sailed between London and Australia, mainly as a cadet ship, until she was sold to the Russian government in 1899 and renamed *Grand Duchess Maria Nikolaevna*.

Hessel Street E1 (Stepney, T. Ham.). Commemorates Phoebe Hessel

(1713–1821), called 'the Stepney Amazon', who, in the tradition of Sweet Polly Oliver, joined the army to be near her lover. **Golding Street** is named after him. She died at Brighton where she was famous for her great age and her stories of her exploits as a private in the ranks.

Hichisson Road SE15 (Nunhead, Southwark). J.G. Hichisson was active in Camberwell's local government. He was a vestryman in the 1890s and later served on the Borough Council, of which he became an alderman.

Highbury Park N5 (Highbury, Islington). Formerly Cream Hall Road, leading to a dairy farm. Most of this area supplied London with milk. The road became a 'park' in the course of residential development by Thomas Cubitt after 1820 (*see* **Hanover Park**).

Highbury Place N5 (Highbury, Islington). Highbury is the 'high burgh', the manor on the height as opposed to neighbouring Tollington. Early earthworks are recorded on Highbury Hill. The immediate area has ten **Highbury** street names, of which **Highbury Grange** marks the site of a popular 18th-century tea-garden called Highbury Barn.

Highgate Hill N6 (Highgate, Islington). Hill leading up to the high gate, the toll gate built by the bishops of London *c*1280, and now demolished.

High Holborn WC1 (Holborn). *See* **Holborn.**

High Timber Street EC4 (Cit. Lond.). Corruption of 'timber hythe' or timber wharf. Wood, originally brought to the city by waggon from surrounding woodlands and sold by Cheapside (*see* **Wood Street**), was later brought by river, as being more convenient for unwieldy loads, and landed at wharves beside this street. The first reference to this is in 1272.

Hill Farm Road W10 (N Kensington, Ken. Chel.). Built on land formerly part of a farm of that name.

Hillman Street E8 (Hackney). J. Hillman served on Hackney Borough Council from 1912.

Hill Road NW8 (St John's Wood, Cit. West.). Follows an old lane leading to a field called the Hill Field.

Hill Street W1 (Mayfair, Cit. West.). *See* **Hay Hill**.

Hilly Fields Crescent SE4 (Lewisham). The open space called Hilly Fields was made into a public recreation ground in 1896; the older name is **Vicar's Hill**.

Hinde Street W1 (Marylebone, Cit. West.). Built in the 1770s on land belonging to Jacob Hinde who had inherited it through his wife, Anne Thayer.

Hindrey Road E5 (Hackney). Commemorates Phillis Hindrey, a local benefactor who left £200 to be invested for the parish poor in accordance with her will of 1794.

Hippodrome Place W11 (Notting Hill, Ken. Chel.). Part of the site of the Hippodrome racecourse, 1837–41; the mound of St John the Evangelist's church, St John's Gardens, was part of a grandstand.

Hitherwood Drive SE19 (Dulwich, Southwark). *See* **Low Cross Wood Lane.**

Hoadly Road SW16 (Streatham, Lambeth). Commemorates the Rev. Benjamin Hoadly or Hoadley, rector of Streatham 1710–23. As Bishop of Bangor he was known as a controversialist. He died in 1761.

Hobart Place SW1 (Belgravia, Cit. West.). The family of Robert Hobart, Lord Hobart and Fourth Earl of Buckinghamshire (1760–1816), lived in Grosvenor Place. He served as Colonial Secretary 1801–5, and Hobart, Tasmania, was named after him in 1804.

Hobbes Walk SW15 (Putney, R. upon T.). The philosopher and political theorist Thomas Hobbes, author of *Leviathan* in 1651, lived for a time in Putney as a tutor in the Earl of Devonshire's household. The Dowager Countess of Devonshire had bought Putney Park House *c* 1650 and the family lived there until *c* 1689 (*see* **Putney Park Lane**).

Hogarth Court EC3 (Cit. Lond.). The artist William Hogarth lodged at the *Elephant Tavern* in Fenchurch Street *c* 1725. Murals which he painted there were later removed and preserved (*see* **Hogarth Lane**).

Hogarth Lane W4 (Chiswick, Hounslow). The artist William Hogarth (1697–1764) lived in this lane from 1749 for some 15 years. He painted a series of narrative moral satires, of which the best-known are *The Rake's Progress* and *Marriage à la Mode*, which he also engraved. These were very popular in his own time; his portraits were not greatly liked but their qualities proved the more enduring and influential.

Holbein Place SW1 (Chelsea, Ken. Chel/Cit. West.). The German artist Hans Holbein came to London 1526–8 and painted Sir Thomas More and his family at their house in Chelsea.

Holborn EC1 (Camden). The 'bourne or stream in the hollow', referring to the Fleet (*see* **Fleet Street**). This road led W from the valley of the stream to gain higher ground as **High Holborn**. In 1869 the low-lying stretch was raised and carried across the valley on **Holborn Viaduct**.

Holford Place WC1 (Islington). Built on land belonging to the New River Company. The Holford family served the company in the 18th century. **Holford Street** is nearby.

Holland Grove SW9 (S Lambeth, Lambeth). Built in the 19th century on part of the manor of Lambeth Wick, which was leased to Baron Holland of Foxley (*see* **Wickwood Street**).

Holland Park Avenue W11 (Kensington, Ken. Chel.). Holland House and its park lie S of this road. The house was built in 1605–7 for Sir Walter Cope. It passed by marriage to Henry Rich, who was made Earl of Holland in 1624. The title died out and the house passed, again by marriage, to William Edwardes (*see* **Edwardes Square**). Henry Fox, who had been created Baron Holland in 1763, bought it in 1768. The house was demolished during an air-raid in World War II.

Holland Street W8 (Kensington, Ken. Chel.). Approaches Holland Park. This street was formerly called Parson's Yard, since it ran N of the parsonage house by St Mary Abbot's church. The parsonage house was also known as the 'Manor House'; it may have been the mediaeval manor house of Abbot's Kensington.

Hollen Street W1 (Soho, Cit. West.). Built 1715–16, partly on a lease from the Duke of Portland, by Allen Hollen.

Holles Street W1 (Marylebone, Cit. West.). John Holles, Duke of Newcastle, bought the Marylebone estate, then parkland and open country, in 1708. This street was part of an early development around Cavendish Square, laid out from c1717.

Holloway Road N19, N7 (Islington). Road to Holloway; the name means the place with the 'hollow' or sunken road.

Holly Bush Hill NW3 (Hampstead, Camden). A *Hollybush Inn* is recorded here in the 18th century, named from the tree or trees growing there. Nearby are **Holly Hill**, **Walk** and **Vale**.

Holly Lodge Gardens N6 (Highgate, Camden). Holly Lodge, the large house which was the original centre of this estate, was presumably named from a grove of trees. It was the home of the Victorian millionairess and philanthropist Baroness Burdett-Coutts (*d* 1906).

Hollywood Road SW10 (Earl's Court, Ken. Chel.). The Hollywood Brewery stood on the corner with Fulham Road until the 1880s.

Holmes Road NW5 (Kentish Town, Camden). Built on farmland occupied in the late 18th century by Richard Holmes; he laid out the street from c1790.

Holyrood Street SE1 (Bermondsey, Southwark). The Holy Rood or Cross of Bermondsey, which was in the church of Bermondsey Abbey, was a favourite object of pilgrimage before the Reformation. After the dissolution of the abbey c1539, Sir Thomas Pope (*see* **Pope Street**) took the Rood out of the church and set it up on Horselydown at the E end of what came to be called **Crucifix Lane**. It was removed and destroyed in St Paul's churchyard in 1559.

Holywell Lane EC2 (Shoreditch, Hackney). Site of the former Holywell Priory in Shoreditch, which

was dedicated to St John the Baptist. The priory precincts extended N from this lane to **Bateman's Row**; the house, with other monasteries, came to an end at the dissolution c1539. **Holywell Row** is nearby.

Homefield Road W4 (Chiswick, Hounslow). Runs S to the Home Field, now a recreation ground. This is a remnant of a field attached to the Prebendal Manor of Chiswick, of which the manor house stood at the corner of Chiswick Mall and Chiswick Lane until 1875.

Homer Street W1 (Marylebone, Cit. West.). Built on land belonging to John Harcourt; his neighbour Edward Homer suggested this name and two others – **Cato Street** and **Virgil Place** – sufficiently classical to disguise his motive.

Homerton High Street E9 (Hackney). The high or principal street of Homerton, called Hummington in the 10th century, which means the village of Humma's people.

Homestall Road SE22 (Peckham, Southwark). Runs N to Peckham Rye Park which, when opened in 1894, surrounded an existing property called Homestall Farm.

Honduras Street EC1 (Finsbury, Islington). *See* **Timber Street**.

Honey Lane EC2 (Cit. Lond.). Place where the honey-sellers set up their stalls at the mediaeval food market along Cheapside.

Honor Oak Road SE23 (Lewisham). Runs N to Oak of Honour Hill, the oak having been honoured by Elizabeth I who is said to have sat under it on May Day, 1602. **Honor Oak Park** and **Rise** adjoin.

Hook's Road SE15 (Peckham, Southwark). Edward Hook was

Holly Bush Hill

Camberwell vestry clerk in the 1840s.

Hop Gardens WC2 (Covent Garden, Cit. West.). *See* **Covent Garden**. The name records part of the abbey's gardens devoted to growing hops.

Hopkins Street W1 (Soho, Cit. West.). One Richard Hopkins held a building lease here from 1709.

Hopping Lane N1 (Canonbury, Islington). Old name for a lane along the route of the present St Paul's Road. A plot of land at the E end – on the site of St Paul's Place – appears as 'The Hoppinge' in a survey of 1611. The derivation is uncertain.

Hopton Street SE1 (Southwark). Commemorates Charles Hopton, by whose endowment almshouses were built here in 1752. Formerly the S arm of the street was Green Walk, from the grassy path which preceded it; the E arm was Holland Street, from the nearby Paris Garden manor house which came to be known as 'Holland's Leaguer'. The house (now demolished) had become a gaming house in the 17th century. A robust local history of 1632 tells how the landlady, Dame Holland, was besieged or beleaguered by the peace officers.

Horatio Street E2 (Bethnal Green, T. Ham.). Formerly Nelson Street; to avoid confusion with others, the Admiral's Christian name was used.

Horder Road SW6 (Fulham, Hammersmith). Built on land belonging to George Henry Horder.

Horniman Drive SE23 (Forest Hill, Lewisham). Approaches the Horniman Museum, founded in 1890 by Frederick John Horniman, and based on his own collection of objects acquired by his company in its trade with China and the East. The Horniman family went into the tea

trade in 1826.

Hornsey Road N19, N7 (Holloway, Haringey/Islington). Road to Hornsey: the name is a corruption of Haringeie (early 13th century) through Haringesheye (later 13th century) and Harnesey to Hornsey (16th century). The original name continued to be applied to the manor house which survived until *c*1870 (*see* **Haringey Park**).

Horse and Dolphin Yard W1 (Shaftesbury Avenue, Cit. West.). Adjoined an inn called the *Horse and Dolphin* which is recorded here in the late 17th century and was probably older; it stood, altered and enlarged, until 1890 when it was rebuilt as the *Macclesfield*.

Horseferry Road SW1 (Cit. West.). A ferry carrying men and horses over the Thames between the end of this road and Lambeth is first recorded in the 16th century; it ceased to run when Lambeth Bridge opened in 1750.

Horse Guards Avenue SW1 (Whitehall, Cit. West.). Leads to the quarters of the Horse Guards, established on the opposite side of Whitehall in 1663. **Horse Guards Road** bounds the other side of the Guards' parade.

Horselydown Lane SE1 (Bermondsey, Southwark). Corruption of Horsey Down, recorded as Horsemead or Horsedune in 1206, when five acres of horses' grazing was sold to the Order of Knights of St John of Jerusalem. Part of the grazing land belonged to Bermondsey Abbey, who sold it to the parish of St Olave in 1553 (the abbey then being in private hands). The parish endowed St Olave's Grammar School with this land.

Horsley Street SE17 (Walworth,

Horse Guards Avenue

Southwark). Commemorates Dr Samuel Horsley, polemical writer, controversial preacher and rector of Newington from 1759.

Horsman Street SE5 (Kennington, Southwark). L.C. Horsman was a member of the Newington vestry, which administered this area, in the 1890s.

Horton Street SE13 (Lewisham). Named in 1865; Horton is a local family name. A memorial of 1866 in St Mary's, Lewisham, commemorates the mother of Benjamin Horton. H.B. Horton served on the Lewisham District Board of Works in the 1890s, and later on Lewisham Borough Council.

Hosier Lane EC1 (Cit. Lond.). A mediaeval lane where hosiers (stocking suppliers) lived and traded, selling not only stockings but tights and woollen underclothing.

Houghton Street WC2 (Aldwych, Cit. West.). Built c1655 by John Holles, Second Earl of Clare and Second Baron Houghton, who also built **Clare Market** and Clare House nearby. His ancestor Sir William Holles acquired this land in 1528. His son became Duke of Newcastle (*see* **Holles Street**).

Houndsditch EC3 (Cit. Lond.). Built beside the broad channel or ditch dug along the E boundary of the City c1200. The ditch was gradually filled in and built over, but it originally extended along the N wall of the City as well, as far as the Barbican. John Stow, in the *Survey of London* of 1598, suggests that the 'hounds' were dead dogs thrown into the ditch. However it is not clear why this one should have been so named, since every ditch in mediaeval London must have been similarly abused. It is more likely that the hounds were hunting dogs kennelled on the far

side of this channel. The monk Fitzstephen's famous description of 12th-century London says that the citizens hunted with dogs in 'densely wooded thickets, the coverts of game . . .' in the 'great forest' which lay N and E. Hound is from OE 'hund', which was specifically a hunting dog; the ordinary city mongrel 'dog' is from OE 'docga'.

Howard Place SW1 (Victoria, Cit. West.). *See* **Carlisle Place**.

Howard Road N16 (Stoke Newington, Hackney). The prison reformer John Howard was born in Hackney in 1727 and later lived in Church Street, Stoke Newington.

Howitt Road NW3 (Hampstead, Camden). Commemorates William and Mary Howitt, 19th-century authors of books on travel and history, including *Northern Heights of London*. The Howitts were associated with both Hampstead and Highgate.

Howland Street W1 (Tottenham Court Road, Camden). Built on land belonging to the dukes of Bedford. Elizabeth Howland married Wriothesley Russell, later Second Duke of Bedford, in 1695. The dukes, on this marriage, received the additional title of Baron Howland of Streatham (*see* **Tooting Bec Road**).

Howlett's Road SE24 (Herne Hill, Southwark). Howlett's Acre was a plot of land in Dulwich which was left for the benefit of the poor of Camberwell by a member of the Bowyer family (*see* **Bowyer Place**).

Howley Place W2 (Paddington, Cit. West.). *See* **Porteus Road**. William Howley was Bishop of London 1813–28.

Hows Street E2 (Shoreditch, Hackney). A Victorian street named after William Hows who was one of

Shoreditch's first representatives on the Metropolitan Board of Works when it was founded in December 1855.

Hoxton Market N1 (Hoxton, Hackney). Local leaseholders obtained a licence for a market here in 1687; it was to sell foodstuffs on Tuesdays and Saturdays. The plan came to nothing and the intended market-place became a residential square.

Hoxton Street N1 (Hoxton, Hackney). Street leading through Hoxton, called Hochestone in the *Domesday Book*, meaning the village belonging to Hoc.

Hubbard Road SE27 (W Norwood, Lambeth). N.W. Hubbard of Herne Hill served on the Lambeth vestry in the 1890s and later became an alderman of the London County Council.

Huddart Street E3 (Poplar, T. Ham.). Joseph Huddart, of the East India Company and Trinity House (1741–1816), was noted for his work on techniques of navigation and charting. He invented an improved type of cable. He was technical adviser to the East India Docks Company.

Huggin Hill EC4 (Cit. Lond.). Called Hoggen Lane in the 14th century, meaning the lane where hogs were kept.

Hugh Street SW1 (Pimlico, Cit. West.). Part of the Grosvenor family's Pimlico estate; Hugh is a recurring Christian name in the family, from Hugh Lupus (*see* **Lupus Street**).

Hugon Road SW6 (Fulham, Hammersmith). Built on land owned by the Taylor family, and named after their son Hugon Taylor. Their other son Stephen Dale Taylor is commemorated in **Stephendale Road**.

Huguenot Road SE15 (Peckham, Southwark). *See* **Claude Road**.

Huguenot Place SW18 (Wandsworth). Huguenots, Protestant refugees from religious persecution in France, settled in Wandsworth in the late 17th century and pioneered market-gardening there, especially the raising of asparagus (*see* **Nantes Passage**).

Hull Street EC1 (Finsbury, Islington). Properly Hulls; built by William Hulls of Shoreditch in the late 18th century.

Humphrey Street SE1 (Old Kent Road, Southwark). Formerly Gloucester Place, in honour of Humphrey, Duke of Gloucester (1391–1447), brother to Henry V, who had a palace at Greenwich. A patron of learning, he was also a strong supporter of the war with France, in which he held a command under his brother. He died shortly after being charged with high treason, and was generally supposed to have been murdered by the 'peace with France' faction.

Hungerford Lane WC2 (Charing Cross, Cit. West.). Site of the 15th-century town house of the Hungerford family. Their descendants established the Hungerford market there in 1682; it was demolished in 1863 to make way for Charing Cross station.

Hunsdon Estate E5 (Hackney). *See* **Brooke Road**.

Hunter Street WC1 (Bloomsbury, Camden). Passes the School of Medicine and commemorates John Hunter (1728–93), surgeon and anatomist, governor of St George's Hospital, royal surgeon. He is regarded as the father of scientific surgery. His brother William Hunter had a school of anatomy in Great Windmill Street.

Huntingfield Road SW15 (Roehampton, Wandsworth). Sir Joshua Vanneck of Huntingfield in Suffolk was created Baron Huntingfield in 1796. He was a City of London merchant and a Tory MP for Dunwich. He married Maria Thompson of Roehampton.

Huntley Street WC1 (Bloomsbury, Camden). *See* **Cosmo Place**.

Hunt's Court WC2 (Cit. West.). Samuel Hunt, carpenter, worked here in the late 17th century. He obtained a lease of the sites for 21–3 Leicester Square *c*1672.

Huntsworth Mews NW1 (Marylebone, Cit. West.). *See* **Bickenhall Street**.

Hurlbutt Place SE17 (Newington, Southwark). James Hurlbutt founded the New Building of the Fishmongers' Almshouses (otherwise called St Peter's Hospital) in Newington Butts. The 'old building' had been completed in 1636.

Hurlingham Road SW6 (Fulham, Hammersmith). Approached Hurlingham Park, laid out on the former Hurlingham Fields, of which the

derivation is unknown (*see* **Ranelagh Avenue**).

Hutchings Street E14 (Isle of Dogs, T. Ham.). Formerly approached Hutchings's wire-rope and cable factory.

Hyde Lane SW11 (Battersea, Wandsworth). An old lane formerly running to Surrey Lane beside Hyde House.

Hyde Park Corner SW1 (Cit. West.). Hyde was one of three manorial estates given to Westminster Abbey after the Norman Conquest of 1066. Henry VIII acquired them in 1536, sold two and kept Hyde as a private deer-park; it was opened to the public by James I.

Hyde Road N1 (Hoxton, Hackney). The remnant (now in two parts) of a lane which approached a field called The Hyde, and recorded as such in 1540. A hyde or hide was a unit of land about 100 acres.

Hydethorpe Road SW12 (Streatham Hill, Lambeth). Built *c*1900 on a farm recorded as The Hide in 1284 and later as Hyde's Farm, on the Falcon Brook.

I

Ibbott Street E1 (Stepney, T. Ham.). *See* **Amiel Street**.

Idol Lane EC3 (Cit. Lond.). Called Idle Lane in the 17th century, and St Dunstan's Hill in the 16th. 'Idle' may be a personal name, or it may imply loiterers, c.f. **Fetter Lane**.

Ilchester Place W14 (Kensington, Ken. Chel.). Lord Ilchester bought Holland House in 1874; he died in 1905. Lady Ilchester lived there until 1935.

Iliffe Street SE17 (Newington, Southwark). Dr Iliffe was the Medical Officer of Health for Newington in the 1860s. **Iliffe Street Yard** adjoins.

Imperial Road SW6 (Fulham, Hammersmith). The gas works established here in the mid-19th century were originally called the Imperial Gas Works.

India Street EC3 (Cit. Lond.). Formerly George Street; renamed in 1913 when the surrounding area consisted of the tea warehouses of the East and West India Docks Company. The same company's eastern trade gave the name to **Rangoon Street** nearby.

India Way W12 (Shepherd's Bush, Hammersmith). *See* **Australia Road**.

Ingelow Street SW9 (Battersea, Wandsworth). Commemorates the poet Jean Ingelow (1820–97), author of *High Tide on the Coast of Lincolnshire* (*see* **Dickens Street**).

Ingestre Place W1 (Soho, Cit. West.). Formerly two streets, New Street which is self-explanatory and Husband Street from Thomas Husbands who held a building lease from 1701. In 1852 an artisan block was built here under the patronage of Lord Ingestre, and the streets were renamed in 1868.

Ingestre Road NW5 (Kentish Town, Camden). *See* **Chetwynd Road**.

Ingham Road NW6 (W Hampstead, Camden). Laid out by the National Standard Land Mortgage and Investment Company, of which Edward Ingham was manager.

Inglebert Street EC1 (Islington). *See* **Myddelton Square**. The practical engineering of the New River scheme was first devised by William Inglebert in 1607.

Inigo Place WC2 (Covent Garden, Cit. West.). Part of the Covent Garden development designed for the Earl of Bedford by Inigo Jones from 1631. Jones was the forerunner of English classicism in architecture.

Inkerman Road NW5 (Kentish Town, Camden). Commemorates the battle of Inkerman, fought on 5 November 1854 during the Crimean War (*see* **Alma Grove**).

Insurance Street WC1 (Clerkenwell, Islington). Named in 1916 from Insurance House, office of the Insurance Committee of the county of London.

Inverness Terrace W2 (Bayswater, Cit. West.). Probably compliments the Duchess of Inverness, formerly Lady Cecilia Buggin (widow of Sir George Buggin and daughter of the

Earl of Arran) who married Augustus Frederick, Duke of Sussex and Earl of Inverness, in 1831. The marriage was ecclesiastically but not legally valid since the consent of Parliament (required in the Royal Marriage Act) was not obtained. Lady Cecilia was created Duchess of Inverness in her own right in 1840, and after 1843 she lived at Kensington Palace.

Inwood Place NW1 (St Pancras, Camden). Commemorates Henry William Inwood (1794–1843), architect of neighbouring St Pancras New Church, which was built 1819–22. Inwood lived nearby in Euston Square, 1822–36, and later in Eversholt Street.

Ireland Yard EC4 (Cit. Lond.). William Ireland, haberdasher, had a house here in the 16th century; the building was formerly the gatehouse of Blackfriars Priory (*see* **Blackfriars Lane**). William Shakespeare bought Ireland's house in 1613.

Iron Mill Road SW18 (Wandsworth). Formerly led to Iron Mill Place, the site of a foundry near the River Wandle, opposite the end of Mapleton Road.

Ironmonger Lane EC2 (Cit. Lond.). Leads to the place where the ironmongers traded beside the mediaeval Cheapside market.

Ironmonger Row EC1 (Finsbury, Islington). Built on land belonging to the Ironmongers' Company, bequeathed to them in 1527 by Thomas Mitchell or Michell, ironmonger and citizen.

Irving Street WC2 (Cit. West.). Commemorates the actor Henry Irving, who died in 1905. Originally built in 1670 as Green Street, leading to a bowling green E of Leicester Square.

Islington High Street N1 (Islington). The high or principal street of Islington; the name is from OE 'Gislandun', meaning Gisla's hill. The High Street was originally so-called as far N as **Islington Green**.

Islip Street NW5 (Kentish Town, Camden). The Rev. Robert South of Caversham owned this land and left it ultimately to Christchurch, Oxford. He had been rector of Islip in Oxfordshire from 1678. The streets were laid out after his death.

Ivanhoe Road SE5 (Camberwell, Southwark). From Sir Walter Scott's novel of that name. Scott's immense popularity inspired a number of Camberwell street names, mainly from the novels *Waverley*, *Old Mortality* and *The Heart of Midlothian*.

Ivatt Place W14 (W Kensington, Hammersmith). Built on a former goods yard of the London, Midland and Scottish Railway. H.G. Ivatt was Chief Mechanical Engineer to the company 1945–6, and afterwards filled the same post in British Railways.

Ivy Bridge Lane WC2 (Strand, Cit. West.). The Ivy Bridge (presumably covered in ivy) crossed a sunken way which may have been an old watercourse running down to the Thames. The bridge had been demolished by 1600.

Ivyday Grove SW16 (Streatham, Lambeth). Preserves a 16th-century Streatham place name.

Ixworth Place SW3 (Chelsea, Ken. Chel.). *See* **Caversham Street**.

J

Jacob Street SE1 (Bermondsey, Southwark). Site of the 19th-century rookery called Jacob's Island, with houses and warehouses overhanging a broad, filthy ditch that was once a stream running into the Thames. Dickens described it in *Oliver Twist*. The identity of Jacob is not known.

Jago Walk SE5 (Camberwell, Southwark). Named in 1960 after Richard Jago, poet.

Jamaica Road SE1, SE16 (Bermondsey, Southwark). A Jacobean house in Cherry Garden Street, called 'Jamaica House' and named from the island which became a British colony in 1655, survived until *c*1860. In the late 17th century it was part of a pleasure garden.

James Street WC2 (Covent Garden, Cit. West.). Built from 1635 and named from Prince James, younger son of the reigning king Charles I.

Janeway Street SE16 (Bermondsey, Southwark). A nonconformist clergyman, James Janeway (*d* 1674) preached at a meeting house built for him in Jamaica Row. The chapel was built after the indulgence to nonconformists had been granted in 1672, and it was later wrecked by soldiers when the indulgence was withdrawn.

Jarvis Road SE22 (E Dulwich, Southwark). Commemorates Henry Jarvis, architect and surveyor to Camberwell vestry in the 1860s.

Jeffreys Street NW1 (Camden Town, Camden). Nicholas Jeffreys acquired the lease of the surrounding land in 1670. His grand-daughter Elizabeth Jeffreys married Charles Pratt, later Lord Camden. Much of the development of Camden Town was carried out by their son John Jeffreys Pratt, Marquis Camden (1759–1840).

Jennings Road SE22 (E Dulwich, Southwark). The Rev. H.E. Jennings of St Clement's, E Dulwich, served on Camberwell Borough Council from 1906.

Jephson Street SE5 (Camberwell, Southwark). Alexander Jephson, his son Thomas and Thomas's son the Rev. William Jephson were masters of Camberwell Free Grammar School and active in local good works from 1700.

Jerdan Place SW6 (Fulham, Hammersmith). William Jerdan (1782–1869) was a journalist and regular visitor to Fulham. He edited *The Sun* (1813–17) and the *Literary Gazette* (1817–50). As a working reporter in 1812 he was present when Perceval, the Prime Minister, was shot and he was one of those who seized the murderer, Bellingham.

Jermyn Street SW1 (St James's, Cit. West.). Built on land granted by Charles II to Henry Jermyn, Earl of St Albans, in 1661 (*see* **St James's Square**).

Jerningham Road SE14 (New Cross, Lewisham). Edward Jerningham (1727–1812) was a minor poet; the adjacent **Waller Road** and **Kitto Road** commemorate another minor poet, Edmund Waller (1606–87), and religious writer, John Kitto (1804–54), respectively.

Jerome Street E1 (Spitalfields, T.

Ham.). Commemorates William Jerome, vicar of Stepney from 1537 until his execution in 1540; he had been active in the work of the Reformation and was burnt as a heretic.

Jerrard Street SE13 (Lewisham). Local family name; Jerrards were builders active in Lewisham and beyond in the 1880s. William Jerrard served on the Lewisham District Board of Works in the 1890s, and became one of the first Lewisham Borough councillors.

Jerusalem Passage EC1 (Clerkenwell, Islington). Near to the Hospital of the Knights of St John of Jerusalem (*see* **St John Street**). The *St John of Jerusalem* inn stood at the N end until 1760.

Jewry Street EC3 (Cit. Lond.). Formerly Poor Jewry Lane, from an ancient settlement of Jews who were not, unlike those near the Guildhall, prosperous (*see* **Old Jewry**). The parish of St James's, Duke's Place, became once more an area of Jewish settlement in the 17th century, and Ashkenazi refugees increased the numbers again after *c*1750.

Johanna Street SE1 (Lambeth). Possibly commemorates Johanna Serres, grand-daughter of Dominic Serres of Waterloo Road, a painter and entrepreneur who subscribed to the building of the Coburg Theatre opposite, later called the 'Old Vic'. Johanna lived in Gibson Street, now Baylis Road, in the 1830s. She became famous by her attempt, through her mother, to claim the title of Duchess of Lancaster.

John Adam Street WC2 (Strand, Cit. West.). Formerly John Street, and part of the Adelphi development built by John and Robert Adam *c*1768. This street was balanced by Robert Street (*see* **Adelphi Terrace**).

John Campbell Road N16 (Kingsland, Hackney). John Campbell was minister of Kingsland Independent Chapel from 1804. He was a missionary, popular preacher and local benefactor.

John Carpenter Street EC4 (Cit. Lond.). John Carpenter, Town Clerk of London in 1442, gave lands and rents to the corporation for the education of boys. The City of London School was founded here in 1834 as the successor to Carpenter's project.

John Fisher Street E1 (Whitechapel, T. Ham.). Commemorates John Fisher, Bishop of Rochester, executed on Tower Hill in 1535. Fisher and Thomas More (*see* **Thomas More Street**) refused to take the oath of allegiance to Henry VIII. The oath implied acceptance of Henry as supreme head of the Church in England, and recognition of the religious validity of his divorce from Katharine of Aragon and remarriage to Anne Boleyn. This street was formerly called Glasshouse Street, from a glass factory near the S end.

John Islip Street SW1 (Cit. West.). John Islip joined the Abbey of Westminster in 1480 and became Abbot in 1500.

John Prince's Street W1 (Oxford Street, Cit. West.). John Prince was surveyor to the Cavendish-Harley estate during the building of Cavendish Square and the surrounding streets from 1717.

John Ruskin Street SE5 (Walworth, Southwark). Commemorates the Victorian scholar and critic John Ruskin (1819–1900) who attended the Congregational Chapel here as a boy.

Johnson's Court EC4 (Cit. Lond.).

Jerusalem Passage

Named from an early property owner; a Johnson family lived here in the 16th century and Dr Samuel Johnson, by coincidence from 1765 to 1776.

Johnson's Place SW1 (Pimlico, Cit. West.). Laid out by John Johnson of Millbank, who acquired the site from Messrs Hunter and Bramah in 1817.

Johnson Street E1 (Stepney, T. Ham.). Uncertain; possibly commemorates the Johnson family, shipowners. Sir Henry Johnson of Bradenham, Buckinghamshire, married Martha, Lady Wentworth in 1703. The Wentworths had formerly been lords of the manor of Stepney. The Johnsons also became local property owners, with docks at Millwall.

John Spencer Square N1 (Islington). The manors of Canonbury and Clerkenwell were held in the 16th century by John Spencer, a City merchant called 'Rich Spencer'. His daughter and heiress Elizabeth eloped with William, Lord Compton (*see* **Compton Road**).

John Street WC1 (Bloomsbury, Camden). Built by the Doughty family in association with John Blagrave, carpenter, from 1754. **John's Mews** runs parallel.

Jonathon Street SE11 (Vauxhall, Lambeth). Jonathon Tyers, father and son, owned the nearby Spring Gardens (*see* **Spring Gardens** and **Tyers Street**).

Joubert Street SW11 (Battersea, Wandsworth). *See* **Reform Street**.

Jubilee Place SW3 (Chelsea, Ken. Chel.).Built *c*1810 to commemorate the Golden Jubilee of George III (1760–1820).

Jubilee Street E1 (Stepney, T. Ham.). N extension of a short street called Jubilee Place, built off the new Commercial Road and named to commemorate the Jubilee of George III in 1810.

Judd Street WC1 (Euston Road, Camden). Built on land belonging to the Skinners' Company, to whom it was presented by Sir Andrew Judd in 1572. Judd vested the land in the company as trustees for Tonbridge School in Kent. **Tonbridge Street** runs parallel.

Judges' Walk NW3 (Hampstead, Camden). Traditionally held to be a promenading place for justices who fled here from the City during the plague of 1665.

Juer Street SW11 (Battersea, Wandsworth). Henry Juer owned extensive market-garden land here on the S bank, where he grew fruit. He died in 1874, leaving a bequest for the aged poor of the parish.

Junction Place W2 (Praed Street, Cit. West.). The nearby wharf of the Grand Union Canal was originally the terminus of the Grand Junction Canal.

Junction Road N19 (Tufnell Park, Islington). Built *c*1811 to make a junction or link between Kentish Town and Holloway Road.

Juxon Street SE11 (Lambeth). Commemorates William Juxon, Archbishop of Canterbury 1660–3, who rebuilt the Great Hall of Lambeth Palace (*see* **Lambeth Palace Road**). The street was formerly called Mill Street, from a windmill which stood here in the 18th century.

K

Kean Street WC2 (Covent Garden, Cit. West.). Commemorates the 19th-century actor Edmund Kean who appeared at Drury Lane theatre, where he was exceptionally successful in Shakespeare. His first triumph was as Shylock in *The Merchant of Venice* in 1814. He died in 1833, aged about 46.

Keats Grove NW3 (Hampstead, Camden). The poet John Keats lived at Wentworth Place in this street 1818–20. The house is now the Keats Museum.

Keeley Street WC2 (Covent Garden, Camden). Robert Keeley (1793–1869), actor, was born in Carey Street. Famous in comedy and pathos, he appeared at the Covent Garden theatre 1822–32, at Drury Lane and at the Lyceum, Wellington Street, of which he and his wife were co-managers 1844–7.

Keen's Yard N1 (St Paul's Road, Islington). From Henry Keen, builder, who traded here *c*1860.

Kelly Street NW1 (Kentish Town, Camden). Built by John Kelly *c*1850.

Kelvin Grove SE26 (Sydenham, Lewisham). *See* **Fransfield Grove**.

Kemble Road SE23 (Forest Hill, Lewisham). One of a group taken from the history of the theatre (*see* **Cibber Road, Farren Road, Siddons Lane** and **Road** and **Vestris Road**; *see also* **Kemble Street**).

Kemble Street WC2 (Covent Garden, Cit. West.). Commemorates the Kemble family, active in the theatre, and particularly Drury Lane, in the 18th and 19th centuries. Roger Kemble (1721–1802), actor-manager, married Sarah Ward who bore him eight talented children. Of these, Sarah became famous as Mrs Siddons; John Philip was an actor and manager of Drury Lane from 1788. The others were Stephen, Fanny, Elizabeth, Anne, Henry and Charles.

Kendall Place W1 (Marylebone, Cit. West.). Formerly ran to the rear of William Kendall's property in Manchester Street; Kendall was an 18th-century builder and timber merchant.

Kendal Street W2 (Bayswater, Cit. West.). Uncertain; there is a possible reference to Prince Leopold of Saxe-Coburg, popular husband of the Princess Charlotte (*d* 1817). The *Complete Peerage* refers to the possibility that the king intended to create him Duke of Kendal; it quotes a report in the *Annual Register* to the effect that the title had been conferred in 1816, but says that it was never official.

Kenlor Road SW17 (Tooting, Wandsworth). Built by a Mr *Ken*sett and a Mr Tay*lor*.

Kennet Road W9 (Paddington, Cit. West.). On land developed by two Wiltshire families, the Goldneys of Chippenham and the Neelds of Grittleton. The River Kennet rises near Chippenham and flows E to join the Thames at Reading.

Kennet Wharf Lane EC4 (Cit. Lond.). Approached a wharf recorded as Kennet's Wharf, from the name of the owner, in 1799.

Kennington Lane SE11 (Lambeth).
Road through Kennington; the name
is from OE 'Chenintune', meaning
the settlement of Chena's people.
Kennington Road is nearby.

Kennington Oval SE11 (Lambeth).
Surrounds The Oval cricket ground,
named from its shape and opened for
cricket in 1845. **Oval Way**
approaches.

Kennington Park Road SE11 (Lambeth). Originally part of the Roman
Stane Street (from Chichester to
London), this road was built up from
c1770 as a series of short terraces with
separate names. It was renamed as a
continuous street after Kennington
Common, which it passes, had been
enclosed in 1852 and made into a
public park (*see* **Kennington Lane**).

Kennington Road SE1, SE11
(Lambeth). *See* **Kennington Lane**.
This road was made as a turnpike in
the late 18th century to relieve the
congestion of traffic coming S from
the new Westminster Bridge. It was
at first called the New Road.

Kenrick Place W1 (Marylebone, Cit.
West.). William Kenrick (*d* 1779),
lecturer and writer, gave lectures at
the nearby Marylebone Gardens. He
was noted for the ease with which he
produced articles and lectures on an
enormous variety of topics, for his
unscrupulous behaviour and for the
intense loathing which he appears to
have inspired in his contemporaries.

Kensal Road W10 (N Kensington,
Ken. Chel.). Road to Kensal Green;
Kensal is a corruption of Kingisholte,
the 13th-century name which means
'the king's wood'.

Kensington Church Street W8
(Kensington, Ken. Chel.). Leads S to
St Mary Abbot's parish church, a
12th century foundation. The present
building (1872) is by Sir George

Gilbert Scott (*see* **St Mary Abbot's
Place**).

Kensington Gore SW7 (Kensington,
Cit. West.). *See* **Kensington High
Street**. The word 'gore' is from OE,
and means a stretch of woodland.

Kensington High Street W8, W14
(Ken. Chel.). High or principal street
of Kensington; the name means the
settlement or 'town' of Cynesige. The
place name appears frequently in
street names of the borough.

Kensington Palace Gardens W8
(Kensington, Ken. Chel.). Runs
beside Kensington Palace, formerly
Nottingham House, which William
III bought from the Earl of
Nottingham in 1689. The house was
rebuilt by Wren. The use of the
palace as a royal residence has had an
enormous effect on Kensington,
from the days when it was called a
'court suburb' to its present status as
Royal Borough.

Kent House Road SE26 (Sydenham,
Lewisham/Bromley). A large house
called 'Kent House' is marked near
the S end of this road on a map of
1809.

Kentish Buildings SE1 (Southwark).
Thomas Kentish owned property
here in 1684, but the property was
then called Christopher Alley, site of
the courtyard of the *Saint
Christopher* inn recorded here in
1542. The name Kentish was revived
in the early 19th century.

Kentish Town Road NW1, NW5
(Camden). Approaches Kentish
Town; the name is from OE and
means the settlement of the men of
Kent. Some scholars think 'Kent'
refers to the county. Some think it
refers to the old, common British
river-name of Kent or Cant which
may here have been applied to the
River Fleet.

Keats Grove

Kenton Road E9 (Hackney). Commemorates Benjamin Kenton, vintner (1719–1800), who, among many philanthropic bequests, gave land here to Sir John Cass's charity. **Cassland Road** adjoins.

Kenton Street WC1 (Bloomsbury, Camden). *See* **Kenton Road**. Kenton was also a benefactor to the Thomas Coram Foundling Hospital, on whose land the street was built.

Kent Terrace NW1 (Regent's Park, Cit. West.). Built as part of John Nash's Regent's Park scheme (*see* **Regent Street**). Named after the Regent's brother Edward, Duke of Kent (*d* 1820), father of Queen Victoria. **Kent Passage** adjoins.

Kent Yard SW7 (Knightsbridge, Cit. West.). To the rear of Kent House, so-called because it was once occupied by the Duke of Kent (*see* **Kent Terrace**).

Kenway Road SW5 (Kensington, Ken. Chel.). Part of an old path from Earl's Court to Kensington, along the line of the present Marloes Road. Possibly this is a contraction of Kensington Way.

Kenwood Close NW3 (Hampstead, Finchley). Opposite the gates of Ken Wood House, recorded in the 16th century as Canewood, and sometimes written Caen Wood or Kentwode. The present house belonged to Lord Mansfield, for whom it was rebuilt by Robert Adam in 1767 (*see* **Mansfield Road**).

Keppel Row SE1 (Southwark). Augustus Keppel (1725–86) became Admiral of the Fleet and was created First Viscount Keppel in 1782.

Keppel Street WC1 (Bloomsbury, Camden). Part of the Bedford estate. Keppel was the maiden name of the fourth Duchess of Bedford.

Kerry Road SE14 (Deptford, Lewisham). *See* **Arklow Road**.

Keyse Road SE1 (Bermondsey, Southwark). Thomas Keyse established a tea-garden and spa nearby in the 1760s (*see* **Spa Road**).

Keyworth Street SE1 (Newington, Southwark). Lance-Corporal Leonard Keyworth, of the 24th battalion, London Regiment, was awarded the VC in 1915 for 'most conspicuous bravery at Givenchy on the night of 25–26 May, 1915 . . . During this very fierce encounter L.-Corpl. Keyworth stood fully exposed for two hours on the top of the enemy's parapet and threw about 150 bombs amongst the Germans, who were only a few yards away'.

Khartoum Road SW17 (Tooting, Wandsworth). Named in 1898; Khartoum was founded in 1823 after the Sudan had been conquered by Egypt. In 1885 General Charles Gordon, in the service of the then British administration in Egypt, was besieged and killed at Khartoum by Sudanese Moslem forces under Mohammed Ahmed, called 'The Mahdi', or Messiah. Gordon's death caused an outcry in Britain. Kitchener's subsequent victory over the Sudanese at Omdurman (1898), which restored Khartoum and the Sudan to Anglo-Egyptian rule, was seen as 'Gordon avenged'.

Khyber Road SW11 (Battersea, Wandsworth). *See* **Cabul Road**.

Kidderpore Avenue NW3 (Hampstead, Camden). *See* **Cannon Hill** for this and **Kidderpore Gardens**.

Kidron Way E9 (S Hackney, Hackney). Named by association with a local Jewish community which bought land here for a burial ground *c*1788. It was in the gorge of the brook Kidron or Kedron, flowing

Kensington Gate, Gloucester Road

from Jerusalem to the Dead Sea, that Josiah, king of Judah, destroyed the images of pagan gods.

Kilburn High Road NW6 (Brent/ Camden). Main road through Kilburn, called Keneburne in the 12th century and Keleburne in the 13th. The name is from OE 'cylenburne', a stream by a kiln.

Kilburn Priory NW6 (Kilburn, Camden). Site of the Priory, founded as a hermitage in the early 12th century and dissolved by Henry VIII in 1539. The building stood near the present railway line. **Priory Road** and **Terrace** approach.

Kildare Gardens W2 (Bayswater, Cit. West.). Built by one Thomas Fitzgerald in the 1850s and given an Irish place name. **Kildare Terrace** approaches, and Fitzgerald also built **Leinster Gardens**, **Square** and **Terrace**. He may have intended a compliment to the noble family of Fitzgerald, dukes of Leinster and marquises of Kildare.

Kilkie Street SW6 (Fulham, Hammersmith). Named from a village in County Clare, home of the builder John Madigan.

Killowen Road E9 (Hackney). Charles Russell, Baron Russell of Killowen (1832–1900), was MP for South Hackney 1885–94 and Lord Chief Justice for 1894.

Kimberley Avenue SE15 (Nunhead, Southwark). Named in 1867, probably in honour of the Earl of Kimberley, Liberal politician.

Kimber Road SW18 (Southfields, Wandsworth). Commemorates Sir Henry Kimber, MP for Wandsworth from 1885 for over 20 years.

King Alfred Avenue SE6 (Bellingham, Lewisham). Alfred the Great, king of England 871–99, was lord of the manor of Lewisham. **Athelney Street** records the Isle of Athelney, where he took refuge and gathered his forces against the Danes; **Elfrida Crescent** his heiress, Countess of Flanders, who gave the manor to the Abbey of St Peter at Ghent; her sons are recorded in **Arnulf Street** and **Adolf Street**.

King and Queen Street SE17 (Walworth, Southwark). Approximately on the line of two early 19th-century streets: N was a crescent called Queen Street which ran S from present Browning Street; S was King Street which extended to East Street.

King David Lane E1 (Upper Shadwell, T. Ham.). From the *King David* tavern, recorded here 1741–65. 'King David' signs first became popular in the 17th century.

King Edward Street EC1 (Cit. Lond.). Made in 1843 as a rebuilding of the old shambles called Stinking Lane; named after Edward VI, under whom the Greyfriars monastery beside Stinking Lane was turned into Christ's Hospital for poor children (*see* **Greyfriars Passage**).

King Edward Walk SE1 (Lambeth/ Southwark). Edward VI granted land here, later called Brick Close, to the City of London in 1550. The King Edward School or House of Occupation, for instructing poor children in useful skills, moved nearby c1815.

King Henry's Road NW3 (Primrose Hill, Camden). Built on land which formerly belonged to Eton College, founded in 1440 by Henry VI. **King's College Road** is nearby (*see* **Eton Avenue**).

King Henry's Walk N16 (Newington Green, Hackney). There was a royal hunting lodge at Newington Green nearby, which was used by Henry VIII (1509–47). The Earl of Northumberland held property at Newington Green which he is said to have given to the king. Northumberland had previously written from his Newington Green house to Thomas Cromwell, Secretary of State, denying that he had ever entertained any idea of marriage with Anne Boleyn, Henry's second queen.

Kinghorn Street EC1 (Cit. Lond.). Renamed 1885 as a variant on the former name King Street (recorded 1799) which had become all too common.

King John's Court EC2 (Shoreditch, Hackney). This is possibly a corruption of St John, the court having once been part of the buildings of the Holywell Priory of St John the Baptist; alternatively, King John (*d* 1216) may have used apartments at the Priory.

King John Street E1 (Stepney, T. Ham.). Site of a house on Stepney Green which was called locally 'King John's Palace', although no connection with the king has been established. The house was called 'The Great Place' and is recorded from the early 14th century until the late 18th, when it became the Spring Garden Coffee House. **Garden Street** is to the rear. This may have been the house belonging to Henry le Waleys (*see* **Waley Street**).

Kingly Street W1 (Regent Street, Cit. West.). Built from 1686 on the line of the old pathway, and named King Street in compliment to James II. The street was renamed in 1906, probably to avoid confusion with other 'King' streets. **Kingley Court** runs parallel.

King's Arms Court E1 (Whitechapel, T. Ham.). The *King's Arms* tavern is recorded here in 1746.

King's Arms Yard EC2 (Cit. Lond.). This led E from Coleman Street to an inn called the *King's Arms* in 1677 and the *King's Head* in 1666. The yard predates Moorgate Street, which was built across it.

King's Avenue SW4, SW12 (Clapham Park, Lambeth). The N end (beyond Crescent Lane) was formerly Loat's Road, from John Loat, a builder who owned land to the E of it and also had brickyards in Acre Lane. The S end was South Road and the middle, King's Road, after William IV (1830–7). The king was formerly Duke of Clarence, and **Clarence Crescent** and **Road** adjoin. This is all part of the Clapham Park estate originally laid out by Thomas Cubitt in the 1830s.

King's Bench Street SE1 (Southwark). The King's (or Queen's) Bench Prison was established in Borough High Street in the 13th century and moved to a site here in 1758. The new prison grounds were bounded by Southwark Bridge Road, Borough Road and Great Suffolk Street (*see* **Queen's Buildings**).

King's Bench Walk EC4 (Temple, Cit. Lond.). Built in the 17th century as an extension to the Temple community of lawyers, and housing lawyers of the King's Bench.

King's College Road NW3 (Swiss Cottage, Camden). On the Eton College estate (*see* **Eton Avenue**). Eton's founder Henry VI (1422–61) also founded King's College, Cambridge.

Kingscote Street EC4 (Cit. Lond.). Formerly King Edward Street, after Edward VI (*see* **Bridewell Place**). Renamed 1885 to avoid confusion with King Edward Street, Newgate.

King's Cross Road WC1 (Camden). Formerly Bagnigge Wells Road, because of the local Bagnigge Wells tea-gardens which closed *c*1840 (*see* **Gwynne Place**). The area around the present King's Cross Station, which this road approaches, was named from a statue of George IV which was put up at the cross-roads outside.

Kingsgate Place NW6 (Kilburn, Camden). Kentish place name; built by the Powell-Cotton family of Quex Park, Birchington, Kent. **Kingsgate Road** adjoins.

King's Head Court EC3 (Cit. Lond.). Named from the sign of an inn, now demolished.

King's Head Yard (Southwark). Led to the *King's Head*, a mediaeval inn which before the Reformation was called the *Pope's Head*. It was burnt down in 1676, rebuilt and demolished in 1885.

Kingshold Road E9 (Hackney). Commemorates the ancient manor belonging to the Knights of St John of Jerusalem (*see* **St-John's Church Road**). It was acquired by the Crown at the dissolution of the monasteries *c*1539, and came to be known as Kingshold, or the King's holding.

Kingsland High Street E8 (Kingsland, Hackney). High or principal street of a former hamlet in the king's hunting lands. Henry VIII had a hunting lodge at Newington Green (*see* **King Henry's Walk**). **Kingsland Gate** marks an old entrance, and **Kingsland Road** approaches.

Kingsley Street SW11 (Battersea, Wandsworth). On the Shaftesbury estate of model houses for artisans. Charles Kingsley (1819–79) was a social reformer as well as a novelist.

King's Mews WC1 (Theobald's Road, Camden). The adjoining E end of **Theobald's Road** was formerly King's Way.

Kingsmill Terrace NW8 (St John's Wood, Cit. West.). Built on land belonging to Kingsmill Eyre, who inherited it from his brother Henry Samuel Eyre in 1754.

King Square EC1 (Finsbury, Islington). Originally a proper square, and named after George IV in 1820.

King's Road SW3, SW10, SW6 (Chelsea, Ken. Chel.). Formerly 'The King's Private Road' which led from St James's Palace and the then Buckingham House along a royal route to Hampton Court. The road became a public highway in 1830 (*see* **New King's Road**).

King's Scholars Passage SW1 (Cit. West.). Built on the former Tothill Fields on land belonging to Westminster Abbey, and named after the King's Scholars of Westminster School.

King's Terrace NW1 (Camden Town, Camden). Named in honour of George III (1760–1820)

King Street EC2 (Cit. Lond.). Part of a new straight route from the Guildhall to the river, cut through after the Great Fire of 1666 and named as a compliment to Charles II (*see* **Queen Street** and **Prince's Street**).

King Street SW1 (St James's, Cit. West.). Built as part of a scheme of streets leading to **St James's Square** and named after Charles II (1660–85).

King Street WC2 (Cit. West.). Laid out as part of the Covent Garden development for the fourth Earl of Bedford by Inigo Jones in 1631. Named after the reigning king Charles I.

King Street W6 (Hammersmith). The main road to Brentford and the West, called King Street from 1794 as was customary for a principal thoroughfare.

Kingsway WC2 (Aldwych, Camden/ Cit. Lond.). Begun in 1899 and completed in 1906; named in honour of Edward VII (1901–10).

Kingswear Road NW5 (Highgate, Camden). From a Devonshire town facing Dartmouth across the River Dart; named by association with Dartmouth Park nearby.

Kingswood Drive SE19 (Dulwich, Southwark). *See* **Low Cross Wood Lane**.

King William Street EC4 (Cit. Lond.). Cut through from the Royal Exchange to London Bridge between 1829 and 1835 and named from William IV (1830–7). A new London Bridge was built in 1831, slightly upstream of the old one, and the street was designed as an approach to it.

Kinnerton Street SW1 (Belgravia, Cit. West.). On the Grosvenor family's estate and named from a village in Cheshire, the county where the family seat is. Other Cheshire names in Belgravia are **Minerva Mews**, **Claverton Street**, **Beeston Place** and **Churton Place**.

Kirby Street EC1 (Hatton Garden, Camden). Built on land belonging to the Hatton family. Christopher Hatton was created Baron Hatton of Kirby in 1643.

Kirton Gardens (Bethnal Green, T. Ham.). A modern name probably commemorating the Rev. Andrew Kirton, vicar of St Andrew's, Viaduct Street, in the 1860s, 1870s and 1880s.

Kirwyn Way SE5 (Kennington, Lambeth). A modern name reviving the name of a 17th-century property owner on Kennington Lane: Benjamin Kirwyn.

Kitcat Terrace E3 (Bow, T. Ham.). Commemorates the Rev. Henry James Kitcat, former rector of St Mary's, Bow.

Kitson Road SW13 (Barnes, R. upon T.). *See* **Church Road**.

Kitto Road SE14 (New Cross, Lewisham). *See* **Jerningham Road**.

Knapmill Road SE6 (Lewisham). A water-mill called the knapmill or chapmill stood nearby on the River Ravensbourne in the 14th century.

Knapp Road E3 (Bow, T. Ham.). Built on land belonging to the Knapp family. Eleanor Knapp is recorded as owning it when land was needed for Tower Hamlets cemetery in 1841.

Knaresborough Place SW5 (Kensington, Ken. Chel.). Yorkshire place name associated with the landowners, the Gunter family of Wetherby, Yorkshire. Other county place names are recorded nearby in **Bramham Gardens**, **Collingham Gardens**, **Place** and **Row**, **Laverton Place** and **Mews**, **Slaidburn Street**, **Westgate Terrace** and **Wharfedale Street** (*see* **Gunter Grove**).

Knatchbull Road SE5 (Camberwell, Lambeth/Southwark). Built from *c*1820 on land which passed to Sir Wyndham Knatchbull Wyndham in 1762 and later to his uncle Sir Edward Knatchbull. Sir Edward sold it to the Minet family in 1770 (*see* **Minet Road**).

Knightrider Street EC4 (Cit. Lond.). Only a short length remains of the mediaeval street running from **Tower Royal** to St Andrew-by-the-Wardrobe. John Stow's *Survey of*

London of 1598 says that supposedly the knights who had armed themselves at the Tower Royal rode this way to the W gates of the City and out to the tournament ground of Smithfield. The Tower Royal is not recorded as a royal possession until *c*1370, and the other royal wardrobe, by St Andrew's, was not bought until 1359. The name is recorded in 1322; the elements of 'knight' and 'riding' are clear, but the derivation is obscure. There may be a reference to an early form of civic procession.

Knightsbridge SW1, SW7 (Cit. West.). Obscure: called Cnighte-briga in the 12th century. The bridge is that over the Westbourne, which runs S at the present Albert Gate. No particular knight is recorded in association with it. Sir Walter Besant, in his *Survey of London North* of 1903, suggests an association with the name of the adjoining manor of Neyt or Neat.

Knight's Hill SE27 (West Norwood, Lambeth). Runs through one of the properties belonging to the Knight family in the 16th century. This one they held from the manor of Lambeth, the second area (SE of Brockwell Park) they held as a detached portion of the manor of Leigham Court, Streatham.

Kynance Mews SW7 (Kensington, Ken. Chel.). *See* **Cornwall Gardens** for this and **Kynance Place**.

L

Lackington Street EC2 (Finsbury, Islington). James Lackington (1746–1815) ran the 'Temple of the Muses' bookshop (the biggest in London) on the corner of Finsbury Square. He was noted in his time as an eccentric character and a very successful bookseller.

Lacy Road SW15 (Putney, R. upon T.). John Lacy, clothworker of the City of London, had a house on the river bank nearby where he entertained Elizabeth I (1558–1603). It was demolished in the early 19th century.

Ladbroke Grove W10, W11 (Ken. Chel.). Richard Ladbroke acquired two farms N of Notting Hill Gate in the mid-18th century. These were laid out in streets from c1820, by which time they were owned by his great-nephew James Weller Ladbroke (*d* 1847). There are seven other 'Ladbroke' street names on the estate.

Lady Margaret Road N19, NW5 (Kentish Town, Camden). Built on the St John's College estate (*see* **College Lane**). The college was founded by Lady Margaret Beaufort, Countess of Richmond and Derby. **Countess Road** adjoins. College benefactors include Lord Burghley, Roger Lupton and Sarah, Lady Somerset. **Burghley** and **Lady Somerset** Roads and **Lupton Street** are nearby (*see* **Ascham Street**).

Lady Somerset Road NW5 (Kentish Town, Camden). *See* **Lady Margaret Road**.

Ladywell Road SE13 (Lewisham). Originally approached a settlement called Ladywell, from the ancient well which stood in this road (near Ladywell Station) until its source was drained away by sewage schemes for new building development in the 19th century. The name is not thought to be ancient; it is first mentioned in the 1790s.

Lafone Street SE1 (Bermondsey, Southwark). Alfred and Henry Lafone headed the Bermondsey company of Boutcher, Mortimore and Co., leather factors. Alfred Lafone was MP for Bermondsey 1886–92 and 1895–1900.

Lakeside Road W14 (Hammersmith). The 'lakes' in this area were flooded pits left by the extraction of brick-earth. Brick-making was an early and extensive industry in Hammersmith.

Lambert Street N1 (Barnsbury, Islington). Samuel Lambert was active in local government in Islington for over 25 years. He was a member of the original Islington Borough Council (1900) on which he represented Barnsbury Ward.

Lambeth Hill EC4 (Cit. Lond.). Formerly Lambert or Lambart Hill, named after a former property owner.

Lambeth Palace Road SE1 (Lambeth). Passes Lambeth Palace, official residence of the archbishops of Canterbury, who acquired the manor of Lambeth from the bishops of Rochester in 1197.

Lambeth Road SE1 (Lambeth). Road leading to Lambeth; the name may mean the lamb hythe, or wharf where lambs were shipped, or it may mean a loamy or silted harbour.

Lamble Street NW5 (Kentish Town, Camden). Renamed in 1887. The original road ran E from the now demolished Lismore Circus and was called Circus Road East; it may have been rebuilt *c*1887 by Lambles, builders active in N London in the 1880s.

Lamb Lane E8 (Hackney). *See* **Sheep Lane**.

Lamb's Conduit Street WC1 (Theobald's Road, Camden). The conduit or conducting channel was built in the 16th century by William Lamb to bring fresh water from the fields N of the City. It was demolished in 1746. Lamb was a Free Brother of the Clothworkers' Company, but his profession was choral music, and he served as a Gentleman of the Chapel to Henry VIII. He was a benefactor to the parish of St Giles's, Cripplegate, and to many charities. He died in 1577.

Lamb's Passage EC1 (Finsbury, Islington). Formerly Great Swordbearers' Alley; renamed from a resident called Thomas Lamb, a buckram stiffener, who owned property here (Lamb's Buildings) and lived in the alley until 1813.

Lamb Walk SE1 (Bermondsey Street, Southwark). The 'Lamb' or 'Holy Lamb' inn in Bermondsey Street is recorded in the 1650s.

Lammas Road E5 (S Hackney, Hackney). Approaches Well Street Common and refers to pasturing rights on common land. After Lammas, or 'loaf-mass', when the first fruits of the harvest were brought to church, local residents had the right of pasture on the common.

Lamont Road SW10 (Chelsea, Ken.

Chel.). Possibly from John Lamont, wine merchant, who held land in this area in the 1870s.

Lancaster Gate W2 (Bayswater, Cit. West.). Opposite to the Lancaster Gate into Hyde Park, which was named in compliment to the royal Duchy of Lancaster. **Lancaster Terrace** is nearby.

Lancaster Grove NW3 (Hampstead, Camden). Built on the estate surrounding Belsize manor house. The manor was granted to Westminster Abbey by Edward II (1307–27) on condition that mass should be said daily for the souls of Edmund, Duke of Lancaster, and Blanche his wife. **Lancaster Drive** adjoins.

Lancaster Place WC2 (Strand, Cit. West.). Site of part of the Savoy Palace, originally owned by Peter of Savoy and passing to the earls of Lancaster in the late 13th century. The earldom became a dukedom in 1351 and the Savoy was held by the most famous of the dukes of Lancaster, John of Gaunt, when it was sacked and blown up during the peasants' revolt of 1381 (*see* **Savoy Street**).

Lancaster Road W11 (Notting Hill Gate, Ken. Chel.). *See* **Cambridge Square**. The Lancastrian Countess of Richmond, mother of Henry VII (1485–1509) owned the manor of Notting Hill. She was the great-grand-daughter of John of Gaunt (*see* **Lancaster Place**).

Lancelot Place SW7 (Knightsbridge, Cit. West.). *See* **Trevor Square**.

Landcroft Road SE22 (Dulwich, Southwark). A revival of an old place name. Landcroft was a plot of land in Friern manor.

Landells Road SE22 (Dulwich,

Southwark). Ebenezer Landells (1808–60) was the engraver and illustrator who first conceived the idea of *Punch* magazine. The first issue came out in 1841.

Landon Place SW1 (Chelsea, Ken. Chel.). The poet Letitia Elizabeth Landon (1802–38) was born in Hans Place nearby. She wrote numerous popular poems and articles and some fiction, and was known to her readers as 'L.E.L.'.

Lanfranc Street SE1 (Lambeth). Part of the manor of Lambeth belonging to the archbishops of Canterbury. Archbishop Lanfranc held office 1070–89.

Langford Place NW8 (St John's Wood, Cit. West.). One William Langford held the surrounding manor of Lilestone *c*1330, and was commemorated in this street name in 1867.

Langham Place W1 (Oxford Circus, Cit. West.). Built *c*1820 around the boundaries of a large house belonging to Sir James Langham. **Langham Street** approaches.

Langley Street WC2 (Covent Garden, Camden). Sir Roger Langley is recorded as owning property here on the N side of Long Acre in 1718.

Lang Street E1 (Stepney, T. Ham.). *See* **Amiel Street**.

Langthorn Court (Cit. Lond.). First recorded in the late 18th century, built or owned by one Langthorn.

Langton Rise SE23 (Dulwich, Lewisham/Southwark). John Langton was a 19th-century Camberwell vestryman.

Langton Street SW10 (Chelsea, Ken. Chel.). Built from *c*1855 on land held

by Thomas Langton, timber merchant.

Langtry Road NW8 (Kilburn, Camden). Formerly the W end of Alexandra Road, after Queen Alexandra, consort to Edward VII (1901–10). It became famous as the home of Lillie Langtry, one of Edward's mistresses.

Lanhill Road W9 (Westbourne Green, Cit. West.). *See* **Grittleton Road**.

Lansbury Gardens E14 (Poplar, T. Ham.). George Lansbury (1859–1940) was a member of Poplar Borough Council in 1921 when the Borough defied the London County Council and refused to levy the rates; their case was that in the post-war slump Poplar could not produce the money. The Borough was sued by the County; Lansbury and others were imprisoned for six weeks. The action produced a general and successful campaign to lessen the rate burden for poorer boroughs. Lansbury, Christian Socialist and pacifist, was editor of the *Daily Herald* 1919–23, a member of the Labour Government of 1929–31 and leader of the Labour Party 1932–5.

Lansdowne Crescent W11 (Notting Hill, Ken. Chel.). Built in the 1840s by Richard Roy and Pearson Thompson who, in laying out Notting Hill, imitated Thompson's development at Lansdowne and Montpellier, Cheltenham. **Lansdowne Mews**, **Rise**, **Road** and **Walk** are nearby.

Lansdowne Row W1 (Mayfair, Cit. West.). Runs to the rear of Lansdowne House (demolished) on the S side of Berkeley Square, which was built by Robert Adam in 1765 and became the town house of William Petty, First Marquis of Lansdowne. Petty's father (who took the name of Petty) was born John

Fitzmaurice, son of the Earl of Kerry. **Fitzmaurice Place** is nearby.

Lansdowne   Terrace   WC1 (Bloomsbury,   Camden).   Commemorates William Petty, First Marquis of Lansdowne (*see* **Lansdowne Row**). He served as Home Secretary in 1782 and Prime Minister 1782–3.

Lant   Street   SE1   (Southwark). Thomas   Lant   began   building development of the former Suffolk Place estate in 1702; Lant Street was laid out in 1770 after his death and named after him (*see* **Great Suffolk Street**).

Larkhall   Rise   SW4   (Clapham, Lambeth). From the *Larkhall* tavern here, said to be named from an early licensee who kept cages of larks. **Larkhall Lane** approaches.

Latchmere Road SW11 (Battersea, Wandsworth).   Commemorates   a common   called   Latchemere   and Lachemoor in the 16th century, a tautologous name since 'lache' means the same as 'mere'. About 16 acres of the common were enclosed and let out in smallholdings in the mid-19th century. The road at that time was called Pig Hill. The whole common was later built upon.

Latham Street E14 (Limehouse, T. Ham.). Named in 1876, formerly Richard Street. It may have been rebuilt by Lathams, builders and engineers active in N and E London in the 1870s.

Latimer   Road   W10,   W11   (N Kensington,   Hammersmith/Ken. Chel.). In 1624 Edward Latymer or Latimer left money to establish a free school, originally for eight poor boys, in Hammersmith. Latimer was born at Freston in Suffolk, and **Freston Road**   is   nearby.   The   Latymer Foundation school was united with the Godolphin School in 1906 (*see*

Godolphin Road).

Lauderdale   Road   W9   (Paddington, Cit. West.). Probably commemorates Admiral Lord Lauderdale, Admiral of the Fleet. The road was named in 1875, when he was living at Lancaster Gate.

Laud   Street   SE11   (Lambeth).   By association with nearby Lambeth Palace   and   Lambeth   manor, belonging to the archbishops of Canterbury. Archbishop Laud held office from 1633 until his execution by Parliament in 1644.

Launcelot   Street   SE1   (Lambeth). The builder and architect Launcelot or Lancelot Holland developed the area between Westminster Bridge and Waterloo Bridge in the 1820s.

Launceston Place W8 (Kensington, Ken. Chel.). *See* **Cornwall Gardens**.

Launch Street E14 (Isle of Dogs, T. Ham.). *See* **Capstan Square**.

Laurence Pountney Lane EC4 (Cit. Lond.). Site of the mediaeval church dedicated to St Lawrence (*see* **Lawrence Lane**) and built by Sir John Poultney, four times Lord Mayor during   the   1330s.   His   house, Poultney's Inn, stood between this land and Suffolk Lane; he bought it and all its surrounding property in 1335 and leased it to Humfrey de Bohun, Earl of Hereford and Essex, in 1348, for the annual rent of a rose at midsummer.

Laurier   Road   NW5   (Highgate, Camden). *See* **Dartmouth Park Hill**. This was formerly Lewisham Road, Viscount Lewisham being one of the Earl of Dartmouth's titles. The name was   changed   in   1937   to   commemorate Sir Wilfred Laurier, first French-Canadian Prime Minister of Canada (1896–1911).

Lavender Hill SW11 (Battersea, Wandsworth). The area was known from the 18th century for its market gardens growing lavender. Nearby **Lavender Road** originally led off the W side of Falcon Road, where **Lavender Terrace** lies opposite.

Lavengro Road SE27 (W Norwood, Lambeth). Commemorates George Borrow's autobiographical book *Lavengro* of 1849. Borrow had a lifelong interest in gipsies or 'Rommany Chals'. His success in mastering the Rommany language earned him the name of 'Lavengro' or 'word-smith'. **Rommany Road** is nearby (*see* **Gipsy Hill**).

Laverton Place SW5 (Kensington, Ken. Chel.). *See* **Knaresborough Place** for this and **Laverton Mews**.

Lawford Road NW5 (Kentish Town, Camden). Built on a small estate belonging to the Earl of Dartmouth, *c*1860. John Lawford was the earl's land agent and was in charge of development. Adjoining **Patshull Road** and **Sandall Road** are named from properties belonging to the earl.

Lawley Street E5 (Clapton, Hackney). The Rev. the Hon. Algernon Lawley, Prebendary of St Paul's Cathedral, was vicar of St John's parish church, Hackney, from 1907.

Lawn Lane SW8 (Vauxhall, Lambeth). Crosses the site of The Lawn, a short terrace of houses built in 1791 and so-called from the grass plot in front. The terrace was demolished when Vauxhall Park was made in 1889–90.

Lawrence Lane EC2 (Cit. Lond.). The church of St Lawrence Jewry (i.e. the church dedicated to St Lawrence and situated in the Jewry) stands opposite in Gresham Street. St Lawrence was a Roman deacon who was martyred in 258; legend says he was roasted on a gridiron.

Lawrence Road E3 (Bow, T. Ham.). *See* **Parnell Road**.

Lawrence Street SW3 (Chelsea, Ken. Chel.). The Lawrence family owned Chelsea manor house from the mid-16th century until 1725.

Laxton Place NW1 (Euston, Camden). Developed by George Laxton, baker, from 1806.

Layard Road SE16 (Rotherhithe, Southwark). Austen Henry Layard, traveller, diplomat and archaeologist, was MP for Southwark 1860–70. **Layard Square** adjoins.

Laycock Street N1 (Islington). Built on land formerly part of Laycock's dairy-farm. Richard Laycock died in 1834. The farm was purchased by a Mr Flight and much of it built over.

Laystall Street EC1 (Clerkenwell, Camden). Led to the laystall or refuse heap nearby (*see* **Mount Pleasant**).

Layton Road N1 (Islington). Possibly commemorates John Layton, vestry clerk of the parish of St Mary, Islington, in the 1860s.

Layton's Buildings SE1 (Southwark). Built up from 1761 by Benjamin Powell and Edward Layton, on the site formerly occupied by the King's Bench Prison (*see* **King's Bench Street**).

Lea Bridge Road E11 (Hackney). Made *c*1750 as an improvement of the former Mill Fields Lane, then the principal route over the River Lea into Essex, from Hackney.

Leadenhall Street EC3 (Cit. Lond.) Leaden Hall (the roof was lined with lead) was built as a house for Sir

Hugh Neville *c*1320; by 1450 it had become a market and that part of Cornhill on which it stood had been renamed.

Leake Street SE1 (Lambeth). Dr John Leake was the founder of the General Lying-in Hospital which opened near Westminster Bridge in 1767 and moved to York Road in 1828.

Leamore Street W6 (Hammersmith). Built on open ground formerly called Leamore Fields which, in the 18th century, extended N from King Street, Hammersmith, to Shepherd's Bush.

Leather Lane EC1 (Holborn, Camden). Called Le Vrunelane in the 13th century and Loverone Lane in the 14th, and probably named from a local merchant whose name could have been a later form of OE 'Leofrun'. The street name was later corrupted to Liver and, finally, to Leather.

Leathermarket Street SE1 (Bermondsey, Southwark). *See* **Tanner Street**. The dressers and sellers of leather had congregated near the Bermondsey tanneries since the 17th century; they originally sold their goods in the City of London, until this market was opened in 1833.

Lebanon Road SW18 (Wandsworth). Approaches Lebanon Gardens, site of a large house called 'Lebanon House', from a fine cedar of Lebanon in the garden.

Lecky Street SW3 (Brompton, Ken. Chel.). The historian William Lecky (1838–1903) lived at 38 Onslow Gardens nearby.

Ledbury Road W11 (Westbourne Park, Cit. West./Ken. Chel.). Built from the S end on ground developed for the Ladbroke estate (*see*

Ladbroke Grove) by W.H. Jenkins and his relation W.K. Jenkins. The Jenkins family also held property in Herefordshire and were of Welsh origin. The town of Ledbury lies between Hereford and the Malvern Hills.

Lee's Place W1 (Mayfair, Cit. West.). One Robert Lee or Lees was the first owner of *The Two Chairmen* public house which stood at the corner with North Audley Street. He also held property in the Place.

Leeway SE8 (Deptford, Lewisham). *See* **Capstan Square**.

Lefevre Road E3 (Old Ford, T. Ham.). In the late 18th century Lefevres are recorded here as brewers and maltsters, while another branch of their enterprise was established in Limehouse.

Legge Street SE13 (Lewisham). Family surname of the viscounts Lewisham (created 1711). The manor of Lewisham came to the Legge family in 1673 when Raynold Graham, citizen and draper who bought it in 1640, conveyed it to his wife's nephew George Legge. The family, as active supporters of the house of Stuart, were punished by William III and restored to favour under Queen Anne. It was she who created George's son William Viscount Lewisham and Earl of Dartmouth in 1711.

Leicester Court WC2 (Cit. West.). Named in 1936 by association with Leicester Square. Formerly Ryder's Court, from Richard Ryder, who held the building lease from 1692.

Leicester Square WC2 (Cit. West.). Robert Sidney, Second Earl of Leicester, bought the land between Wardour/Witcomb Streets and the present Charing Cross Road in 1630 (one plot) and 1648. He built

Leicester House on the N side of the present square in 1635; the square was laid out in front of it in 1670.

Leigham Court Road SW16 (Streatham, Lambeth). Runs through the ancient manor of Leigham Court, Streatham. The early history of the manor is obscure, but it consisted of Balham Hamlet and part of Streatham. In 1165 it is mentioned as having been granted to Bermondsey Abbey by Henry I. In 1610 it came to the Howland family, who already held the manor of Tooting Bec. From their heirs, Sir Walter Roberts and his daughter Jane, it passed by marriage to George, Duke of St Albans in 1752. It was sold to Lord Thurlow (*see* **Thurlow Park Road**) in 1789. **Leigham Court Avenue** and **Vale** adjoin.

Leigh Hunt Street SE1 (Southwark). Commemorates the writer Leigh Hunt, who spent the years 1812–14 in nearby Horsemonger Lane Gaol (S side of Harper Road). He had referred to the Prince Regent as 'This Adonis in loveliness . . . a corpulent man of fifty'.

Leigh's Place EC1 (Holborn, Camden). *See* **Baldwin's Gardens**.

Leigh Street WC1 (Bloomsbury, Camden). Named from Leigh near Tonbridge, Kent; reflects the Kentish associations of Sir Andrew Judd (*see* **Judd Street**) as do **Bidborough**, **Hastings**, **Sandwich** and **Thanet** Streets and **Mabledon Place**.

Leighton Road NW5 (Kentish Town, Camden). Sir David Leighton inherited a part share in the Torriano estate (*see* **Torriano Avenue**). He married Isabella, daughter of Honoria Torriano, and came into the property in 1844. He renamed this street and nearby **Leighton Crescent** and **Grove**.

Leinster Gardens W2 (Bayswater, Cit. West.). *See* **Kildare Gardens** for this and **Leinster Square** and **Terrace**.

Leman Street E1 (Whitechapel,T. Ham.). Built *c*1690 on land belonging to the Leman family. Their founder Sir John Leman (1544–1632) was alderman of the Portsoken Ward of the City of London from 1605; he was Lord Mayor 1616–17. He set up a trust for the poor of the parish of St Botolph Without Aldgate, and gave to it his property called Blue Anchor in the Minories.

Lennox Gardens SW1 (Kensington, Ken. Chel.). *See* **Onslow Square**.

Leonard Street E16 (Shoreditch, Hackney/Islington). Named from its original E section within the parish of St Leonard, Shoreditch. St Leonard was a 6th-century Frankish hermit who inspired a wide mediaeval cult as the patron of prisoners and pregnant women.

Leopold Street E3 (Bow Common, T. Ham.). Prince Leopold, Duke Albany (1853–84) and fourth son of Queen Victoria, opened Leopold House here, one of Dr Barnardo's homes for destitute children.

Leo Street SE15 (Peckham, Southwark). Said to be a humorous reference to a 19th-century vestryman called Washington Lyon.

Lettsom Street SE5 (Camberwell, Southwark). Dr John Coakley Letsom or Lettsom lived at Grove Hill House in the early 19th century (*see* **Grove Hill Road**).

Levehurst Way SW4 (Stockwell, Lambeth). Until 1543 the lords of the manor of Stockwell (the Leigh family) also held the manor of Levehurst in Norwood.

Levendale Road SE23 (Lewisham).

Commemorates a local landowner of the 15th century, John Levendale.

Leven Road E14 (Poplar, T. Ham.). Built on the estate of the Mackintosh family and given a Scottish name like most of its neighbours (*see* **Bromley Hall Road**). The other streets nearby with Scottish place or river names are: **Aberfeldy**, **Ailsa**, **Blair** (from Blair **Athol**), **Dee**, **Ettrick**, **Findhorn**, **Lochnagar**, **Nairn**, **Spey**, **Teviot** and **Zetland** Streets.

Leverett Street SW3 (Chelsea, Ken. Chel.). Commemorates James Leverett, a benefactor to the parish who died in 1660.

Lever Street EC1 (Finsbury, Islington). *See* **Ratcliff Grove**. This street was renamed in 1861; the reason for the new name is unknown.

Leverton Street NW5 (Kentish Town, Camden). *See* **Torriano Avenue**. Thomas Leverton Donaldson was land agent for the Torriano estate and organised development in the 1860s.

Lewen's Court EC1 (Finsbury, Islington). Part of the Ironmongers' estate given to the company by Thomas Mitchell (*see* **Ironmonger Row**). Thomas Lewen was Master of the Ironmongers' Company *c*1527 and left a bequest to build almshouses here.

Lewisham High Street SE13 (Lewisham). High or principal street of Lewisham, called Levesham in the *Domesday Book*. The name derives from OE Leofsa's home.

Lewisham Street SW1 (Cit. West.). *See* **Dartmouth Street**.

Lewis Street NW1 (Camden Town, Camden). *See* **Hawley Road**.

Lexington Street W1 (Soho, Cit. West.). Formerly Little Windmill Street, and renamed in 1885 by the Sutton family who had inherited the Pulteney estate; a Sutton became Baron Lexington or Lexinton in 1645 (*see* **Great Pulteney Street** and **Great Windmill Street**).

Leybourne Road NW1 (Camden Town, Camden). Built on land belonging to the Hawley family of Leybourne, Kent, in the mid-19th century. **Leybourne Street** is nearby (*see* **Hawley Road**).

Lidiard Road SW18 (Wandsworth). Commemorates John Lidiard who became first mayor of Wandsworth on the formation of the borough. He had previously served on the Wandsworth Board of Works.

Lidlington Place NW1 (Camden Town). *See* **Oakley Square**.

Lightfoot Road N8 (Hornsey, Haringey). The 17th-century Bible scholar John Lightfoot (*d* 1675) lived in Hornsey.

Ligonier Street EC2 (Bethnal Green, T. Ham.). Commemorates Jean Louis Ligonier (1680–1770), Field Marshal and Earl Ligonier. He went to Dublin as a Protestant refugee from France in 1697, and joined Marlborough's army, in which he had a distinguished career. In 1720 he became colonel of an Irish regiment, the 8th or Black Horse, later called the 7th Dragoon Guards. He was one of a number of Huguenot refugees to win distinction in exile; this street is one of a group with Huguenot associations (*see* **Nantes Passage**).

Lilestone Street NW8 (Lisson Grove, Cit. West.). The manor of Lilestone, the W half of Marylebone, is recorded in the *Domesday Book*.

Lillie Road SW6 (Fulham, Hammersmith/Ken. Chel). Sir John

Lillie (1790–1868) was a soldier who served in the Peninsular Campaign against Napoleon and later with Portuguese forces in support of Queen Maria. In later life he was concerned with the creation of this road.

Lillington Gardens Estate SW1 (Pimlico, Cit. West.). *See* **Tachbrook Street**.

Limehouse Causeway E14 (Limehouse, T. Ham.). A raised, made-up road across marshy land at Limehouse, called Limeostes in the 15th century, from the oasts or kilns burning lime.

Limes Grove SE13 (Lewisham). Built on land attached to a house called 'The Limes' (demolished *c*1895), a 17th-century house visited by John Wesley.

Lime Street EC3 (Cit. Lond.). An old name meaning the place where there were lime kilns. Its 12th-century name is Limstrate.

Lincoln's Inn Fields WC2 (Camden). Adjoining Lincoln's Inn, the great town house or 'inn' of the Lacy family, earls of Lincoln, which was leased to lawyers in the 14th century (*see* **Clement's Inn**).

Lincoln Street SW3 (Chelsea, Ken. Chel.). *See* **Coulson Street**.

Lindfield Gardens NW3 (Hampstead, Camden). *See* **Canfield Gardens**. The Maryon-Wilson family held property at Lindfield, Sussex.

Lingham Street SW9 (Stockwell, Lambeth). The Rev. John F. Lingham was rector of St Mary, Lambeth, in the 1850s. Stockwell was part of St Mary's parish.

Linnell Road SE5 (Camberwell, Southwark). Henry Linnell served on Camberwell vestry in the 1860s.

Lisle Street WC2 (Cit. West.). The W end was built 1682–3 on part of the gardens of Leicester House; it was extended E beyond Leicester Place 1792–5. The street is named after Philip, Viscount Lisle, who succeeded to the earldom of Leicester in 1677 (*see* **Leicester Square**).

Lisson Grove NW1, NW8 (Cit. West.). Corruption of Lilestone Grove, a grove in the manor of Lilestone. **Lisson Street** is nearby (*see* **Lileston Street**).

Litchfield Street WC2 (Charing Cross Road, Cit. West.). Built from 1684, derivation uncertain. An adjoining street called Grafton Street was built *c*1684 and demolished for the construction of Charing Cross Road. If, as seems probable, this was named after Henry Fitzroy, Duke of Grafton (son of Charles II and Barbara Villiers), then Litchfield Street may have been named after his brother-in-law Edward Lee, Earl of Litchfield.

Little Albany Street NW1 (Regent's Park, Camden). *See* **Albany Street**.

Little Argyll Street W1 (Oxford Circus, Cit. West.). *See* **Argyll Street**.

Little Boltons, The SW10 (Kensington, Ken. Chel.). *See* **Boltons, The**.

Little Britain EC1 (Cit. Lond.). The earliest form, in the 14th century, was Brettonestrete, later Britten Street and then Little Britaine Street. Robert le Bretoun inherited property in that part of the street by St Botolph's church in 1274. The street was under threat of demolition at the time of writing.

Little Chester Street SW1 (Belgravia, Cit. West.). *See* **Chester Square**.

Little College Street SW1 (Cit. West.). *See* **Great College Street**.

Little Dorrit Court SE1 (Southwark). *See* **Dickens Square**. Charles Dickens's novel *Little Dorrit* relies heavily on his knowledge of Southwark and the Marshalsea prison.

Little Essex Street WC2 (Strand, Cit. West.) *See* **Essex Street**.

Little George Street SW1 (Cit. West.). *See* **Great George Street**.

Little Green Street NW5 (Highgate Road, Camden). Leads off Highgate Road which was formerly called Green Street, as passing Kentish Town Green, now the SE corner of Parliament Hill Fields.

Little Marlborough Street W1 (Cit. West.). *See* **Great Marlborough Street**.

Little Newport Street WC2 (Charing Cross Road, Cit. West.). Mountjoy Blount, Earl of Newport (Isle of Wight), lived from 1633 in a house which extended along the N side of the street. Before that the street was part of Military Street, a path from St Martin's Lane to the Military Ground which occupied the site of Gerrard Street, Macclesfield Street and Gerrard Place 1616–61. This was a drilling ground for a company of volunteers. Lord Newport bought land N of his house in 1634, extending his estate to the present West Street and Cambridge Circus. The land was sold for building in 1682 and the house demolished. This and **Great Newport Street** formed Newport Street before it was divided by the construction of Charing Cross Road. **Newport Court** and **Place** adjoin.

Little New Street EC4 (Cit. Lond.). *See* **New Street Square**.

Little Portland Street W1 (Marylebone, Cit. West.). *See* **Great Portland Street**.

Little Russell Street WC1 (Bloomsbury, Camden). *See* **Russell Square**.

Little Sanctuary SW1 (Cit. West.). **See Broad Sanctuary**.

Little Smith Street SW1 (Cit. West.). *See* **Great Smith Street**.

Little Trinity Lane EC4 (Cit. Lond.). *See* **Great Trinity Lane**.

Liverpool Grove SE17 (Walworth, Southwark). Built in 1827 and named as for **Liverpool Street**.

Liverpool Road N1, N7 (Islington). Formerly called the Back Road, as running N behind the main route through Islington; it was renamed in 1826 as for **Liverpool Street**.

Liverpool Street EC2 (Cit. Lond.). Made in 1829 and named after Lord Liverpool, Conservative Prime Minister 1812–27. The street was an improvement of Old Bethlem, a lane across the site of the Bethlehem Hospital for the Insane ('Bedlam') which stood here from 1247 until 1675, when it was moved to Moorfields outside London Wall. It was moved again *c*1819 to St George's Fields, Southwark, where part of the building still forms the main block of the Imperial War Museum. The hospital was moved for a third time to Addington, Surrey, in 1926.

Livonia Street W1 (Soho, Cit. West.). Formerly Bentinck Street, and built in 1736 on the estate of William Bentinck, Duke of Portland. The street was renamed in 1894 by

Lincoln's Inn

association with nearby **Pland Street**.

Lizard Street EC1 (Finsbury, Islington). Built on land belonging to the Ironmongers' Company and marked with their arms, which are supported by two salamanders, popularly called lizards.

Lloyd Baker Street WC1 (Clerkenwell, Islington). Built on an estate belonging to the Lloyd Baker family in the early 19th century; formerly Baker Street. **Lloyd Square** and **Street** adjoin.

Lloyd Square WC1 (Clerkenwell, Islington). *See* **Lloyd Baker Street**.

Loampit Hill SE13 (Lewisham). The original loam pit was on the SW side of the hill, at the top. **Loampit Vale**, at the bottom of the hill, adjoins.

Lochnagar Street E14 (Poplar, T. Ham.). *See* **Leven Road**.

Loddiges Road E9 (Hackney). Conrad Loddiges bought a nursery-garden here in 1771. He specialised in cultivating exotic plants and acclimatising them to grow in British gardens. The nursery continued as an important breeding centre for introduced species until c1850.

Lofting Road N1 (Islington). Commemorates John Lofting or Loftingh (*d* 1742), a Dutchman who became a British subject in 1688; he invented and manufactured a type of fire-engine and later (c1694) set up factories, of which one was in Islington, to make thimbles.

Lolesworth Street E1 (Spitalfields, T. Ham.). John Stow in his *Survey of London* of 1598 says of the priory and hospital of St Mary Spital: 'the bounds thereof . . . extendeth . . . to the bishop of London's field, called Lollesworth, on the east'. The field, lying next to the priory, was by Stow's time called Spital or Spittle Field. He says it was dug for brick clay c1576, when 'many earthen pots, called *urnae*, were found full of ashes, and burnt bones of men, to wit, of the Romans that inhabited there'.

Lollard Street SE11 (Lambeth). Formerly East Street, after a branch of the Clayton family(*see* **Clayton Street**); renamed to commemorate the persecution of Lollards by the archbishops of Canterbury from 1382. Lollards followed the religious teaching of John Wycliffe (*d* 1384), a forerunner of Protestantism. Their name (applied by their enemies) came from a Dutch word meaning one who mumbles or talks nonsense. **Lollard Place** is nearby (*see* **Lambeth Palace Road**).

Loman Street SE1 (Southwark). Built on the site of a pool recorded on 18th-century maps as Loman's Pond.

Lombard Lane EC4 (Cit. Lond.). Recorded in 1732 as Lombard Street and probably altered to avoid confusion with the other. The derivation is possibly from a personal name.

Lombard Street EC3 (Cit. Lond.). Site of the wool market held by the Italian merchants from Lombardy who bought English wool from the 13th century onwards. This was the nucleus of an Italian merchant community in this street, of whom the most prominent were merchant bankers.

Lombardy Place W2 (Bayswater, Cit. West.). Modern street possibly named in association with Poplar Place adjoining, the Lombardy being the best-known type of poplar tree in England.

London Street EC3 (Cit. Lond.). Named not from the city but from an 18th-century property owner. **New**

London Street is a later extension.

London Street W2 (Paddington, Cit. West.). The bishops of London once held the manor of Paddington.

London Wall EC2 (Cit. Lond.). A modern street replacing one which ran along the line of the N wall of the City. The E section between Old Broad Street and Moorgate still bears some relation to the position of the wall.

Long Acre WC2 (Covent Garden, Cit. West.). The long acre was originally part of the gardens of Westminster Abbey (*see* **Covent Garden**). John Russell, First Earl of Bedford, bought it in 1552. The street was laid out in 1615.

Longdown Road 'SE6 (Bellingham, Lewisham). Commemorates a local field name, as do the nearby **Randlesdown** and **Swallands** Roads. Randlesdown field is also recorded as Riddlesdown.

Longhedge Street SW11 (Battersea, Wandsworth). A farm here is recorded as Long Hedge Farm in 1647, when the area was rural. **Sheepcote Lane** is nearby. The farm was enclosed, probably in the 18th century, by a long hedgerow along what is now the Battersea Park Road. The farmhouse, which stood on the present junction of Queenstown and Silverthorne Roads, survived until 1965. The area was still open farmland (179 acres) in 1860, before the Parktown estate was built.

Long Lane EC1 (Cit. Lond.). Recorded as such in the 16th century; self-evident.

Longmead Road SW17 (Tooting, Wandsworth). Commemorates an early Tooting field name.

Longridge Road SW5 (Kensington,

Ken. Chel.). *See* **Edwardes Square**. This is one of a number of streets nearby with Pembrokeshire and Cardiganshire place names. The others are: **Marloes Road**, **Nevern Place**, **Road** and **Square**, **Pennant Mews**, **Penywern Road**, **Philbeach Gardens**, **Templeton Place** and **Trebovir Road**.

Longshore SE8 (Deptford, Lewisham). *See* **Capstan Square**.

Longstaff Road SW18 (Wandsworth). Commemorates Dr George Longstaff, London County Councillor for Wandsworth 1889–1904.

Lonsdale Road W11 (Westbourne Grove, Ken. Chel.). Named after the earls of Lonsdale. William Lowther, Second Earl (*d* 1872), was Chairman of the Metropolitan Roads Commission. Hugh Lowther, Fifth Earl, was the 'sporting earl' who gave the Lonsdale Belt award for boxing. He succeeded to the title in 1882.

Lord Hill's Road W2 (Westbourne Green, Cit. West.). Rowland Hill, First Viscount Hill (1772–1842), lived at Westbourne Place, a house near Westbourne Green. **Lord Hill's Bridge** is nearby. He became popular following a distinguished army career in the Napoleonic Wars. He served in the Mediterranean from 1796 to 1802, in the Peninsular campaign of 1808–14 and at Waterloo in 1815. He was General Commander-in-Chief of the army 1828–42.

Lord Napier Place W6 (Chiswick, Hammersmith). Commemorates Field Marshal Lord Napier of Magdala (1810–90). He served for many years in India, but it was a campaign in Ethiopia in 1868 that made him a popular hero. King Theodore of Ethiopia held British prisoners at Magdala; Napier's attack destroyed Magdala and secured their release.

Lordship Lane SE22 (Dulwich, Southwark). Refers to the lordship of the manor of Dulwich.

Lordship Place SW3 (Chelsea, Ken. Chel.). Refers to the lordship of the manor of Chelsea (*see* **Chelsea Manor Street**).

Lordship Road N16 (Hackney). Refers to the lordship of the manor of Stoke Newington. Given by the king to St Paul's Cathedral in 940, it was held on lease by the Abney family from 1700 to 1782. Their manor house stood on the site of the present Abney Park. The earlier manor house (demolished in 1695) stood on the site of the present **Lordship Terrace** which was built as Church Row *c*1700–10. The house E of Edward's Lane called 'the manor house' was used as the manorial courtroom after 1695.

Lorrimore Square SE17 (Walworth, Southwark). Built *c*1856 at the SW edge of the former Lorrimore (or Lower-moor) Common, enclosed in 1769. **Lorrimore Road** approaches.

Lothbury EC2 (Cit. Lond.). The 'burgh' or enclosed area belonging to Lotha's or Hlothere's people. Hlothere as a personal name was known in the 7th century.

Lots Road SW10 (Chelsea, Ken. Chel.). Built across the lots of land attached to the manor of Chelsea, and over which the manor's inhabitants held grazing rights which were distributed among them by drawing lots.

Loubet Street SW17 (Tooting, Wandsworth). Named in 1899 when Emile Loubet was President of France.

Loudoun Road NW8 (St John's Wood, Cit. West.). In 1871 the name was applied to the whole road, having previously applied only to one group of houses near the S end: Loudoun Villas, which were built in the 1840s. The name possibly compliments the second Marquis of Hastings and his family, who were the object of strong public sympathy at that time. Francis Rawdon Hastings, First Marquis, married Lady Flora Mure Campbell, Countess of Loudoun, in 1804. Their unmarried daughter Lady Flora Hastings suffered from an enlarged liver. Queen Victoria, who disliked Lady Flora, expressed and disseminated the view that her swollen shape indicated pregnancy. Lady Flora was subjected to medical examination to prove that she was not and could not be pregnant. After considerable distress and humiliation she died, in 1839. Her mother died in 1840 and both were buried at Loudoun Castle. Lady Flora's brother, who succeeded his father as second Marquis of Hastings and his mother as seventh Earl of Loudoun, died in 1844. He had connections with Marylebone; his son had been baptised in the parish church in 1832.

Loughborough Road SW9 (Brixton, Lambeth). Henry Hastings, created First Baron Loughborough in 1643, lived at Loughborough House, which was probably built for him. The house stood at the junction with the present Akerman, Claribel and Evandale Roads. Loughborough was a Royalist commander in the Civil War of 1642–8. He wished, through a private act of parliament, to make the River Effra navigable from Brixton Causeway to the Thames, but he died in 1667 with his project unrealised. The house became a school and was demolished *c*1854.

Lough Road N7 (Islington). Commemorates Mr T. Lough, MP for Islington from 1900.

Louisa Street E1 (Stepney, T. Ham.). On the Beaumont estate and, with **Maria Street**, probably from a family Christian name (*see* **Beaumont Square**).

Lovat Lane EC3 (Cit. Lond.). Formerly Love Lane, said to be a corruption of mediaeval Lucas Lane, from the owner of the land.

Love Lane EC2 (Cit. Lond.). John Stow in his *Survey of London* of 1598 says this was the haunt of prostitutes.

Low Cross Wood Lane SE21 (Dulwich, Southwark). Preserves the name of a woodland area here before building began. Dulwich Woods were extensive and included numerous small copses and spinneys. Other similar names preserved are **Crescent Wood Road**, **Peckarman's Wood**, **Woodland Road**, **Giles Coppice**, **Kingswood Drive**, **Hitherwood Drive** and **Bluebell Close**.

Lower Grosvenor Place SW1 (Belgravia, Cit. West.). *See* **Grosvenor Place**.

Lower James Street W1 (Soho, Cit. West.). Named from James Axtell, joint owner of the land on which Golden Square and its adjoining streets were built from 1673. **Upper James Street** continues NW of the square.

Lower John Street W1 (Soho, Cit. West.). Named from John Emlyn, joint owner of Golden Square (*see* **Lower James Street**). **Upper John Street** continues NW of the square.

Lower Marsh SE1 (Lambeth). This part of N Lambeth was marshland until it was drained for building in the early 19th century. This street is continued in **Upper Marsh**. The antiquarian J. Tanswell, writing on Lambeth in 1858, says: 'Fifty years ago Lower Marsh was considered a rural retreat; leading from it were numberless pretty walks with pollard willows on each side . . .'.

Lower Regent Street SW1 (Cit. West.). *See* **Regent Street**.

Lower Thames Street EC3 (Cit. Lond.). *See* **Upper Thames Street**.

Lowndes Square SW1 (Knightsbridge, Ken. Chel.). Built on land belonging to the Lowndes family, who owned the first plot of land beyond the stream which bounded the Grosvenors' Belgravia estate. **Lowndes Street** approaches.

Lowth Road SE5 (Camberwell, Southwark). *See* **Copleston Road**.

Lubbock Street SE14 (New Cross, Lewisham). Named in 1899 after Sir John Lubbock, former chairman of the London County Council. He was also an MP, and in that capacity introduced the law establishing bank holidays. They were known as 'St Lubbock's Days' consequently.

Lucas Street SE8 (Deptford, Lewisham). Local family name (*see* **St John's Vale**). This street originally ran S off Garden Row (now Albyn Road) and did not extend to Lewisham Way.

Ludgate Hill EC4 (Cit. Lond.). The hill running up, originally, through the Ludgate into the City. The gate stood here at the junction with Old Bailey; it was an old one, rebuilt in the 13th and 16th centuries and demolished in 1760. Its name derives from OE 'Ludgeat' or 'Ludgaet', a postern gate.

Lugard Road SE15 (Peckham, Southwark). General the Rt Hon. Sir Edward Lugard was Under-Secretary at the War Department 1861–71. He served in the Afghan

Wars in 1842, in India and in Persia. He died in 1898.

Lukin Street E1 (Shadwell, T. Ham.). An early 19th-century street, part of an extensive development following the opening of the Commercial Road. It was originally called Lucas Street, after the developer.

Lumley Street W1 (Mayfair, Cit. West.). On the Grosvenor estate. Victor, Earl Grosvenor and son of the first Duke of Westminster, married Sibell Lumley in 1874. She was the daughter of the Earl of Scarborough; as Earl Grosvenor predeceased his father she never became Duchess of Westminster.

Lupton Street NW5 (Kentish Town, Camden). *See* **Lady Margaret Road**.

Lupus Street SW1 (Pimlico, Cit. West.). Part of the Grosvenor estate; Hugh Lupus Grosvenor was Third Marquis and First Duke of Westminster (*d* 1899).

Luttrell Avenue SW15 (Putney, Wandsworth). One of the family names of Lord Westbury on whose land the street was built. Richard Luttrell Pilkington Bethell succeeded to the title in 1875.

Lutwyche Road SE6 (Forest Hill, Lewisham). Revival of an early local surname: one Lutwyche is recorded as a local property owner in 1852.

Luxford Street SE16 (Rotherhithe, Southwark). Probably laid out by Humphris and Luxford, builders active in S London from *c* 1860.

Lyall Avenue SE21 (Dulwich, Southwark). Sir Alfred Comyn Lyall was a 19th-century governor of Dulwich College.

Lyall Street SW1 (Belgravia, Cit.

West.). Turns off Chesham Street (*see* **Chesham Place**) and begins on the Lowndes estate although it extends into Grosvenor property. Charles Lyall was business partner to William Lowndes and trustee to the Lowndes estate.

Lyford Road SW18 (Earlsfield, Wandsworth). Probably built by G. Lyford, builder, active in this area from the 1880s.

Lyndhurst Gardens NW3 (Hampstead, Camden). *See* **Lyndhurst Grove**, Peckham, The Hampstead group also has **Lyndhurst Road** and **Terrace**.

Lyndhurst Grove SE15 (Peckham, Southwark). Commemorates John Singleton Copley, son of the artist, who was created Baron Lyndhurst. A lawyer, he was Solicitor General 1819–24, Attorney General 1824–6 and Lord Chancellor in 1827. **Lyndhurst Way** adjoins.

Lynwood Road SW17 (Tooting, Wandsworth). Built on the site of a house called 'Lynwood' on Upper Tooting Road.

Lyons Place NW8 (St John's Wood, Cit. West.). John Lyon of Preston (1514–92) founded Harrow School and endowed it with the income from an estate here. The estate stretched NW towards the lands of Kilburn Priory. Streets on the land are named from school governors.

Lyon Street N1 (Caledonian Road, Islington). Formerly Lion Street, it was changed to avoid confusion with numerous other 'Lion' street names.

Lysons Walk SW15 (Putney, R. upon T.). The topographer Daniel Lysons (1762–1834), author of the survey *Environs of London*, was curate of Putney in the 1790s.

Lytcott Grove SE22 (E Dulwich, Southwark). Colonel Thomas Lytcott (*d* 1666) was a resident of St Giles's parish, Camberwell, which then included E Dulwich. His death is recorded in St Giles's church; he died of plague, his wife, four sons and two servants having died of it in 1665.

M

Mabledon Place WC1 (Euston Road, Camden). *See* **Leigh Street**.

Macaulay Road SW4 (Clapham, Lambeth). Zachary Macaulay, former Governor of Sierra Leone, settled at 5 The Pavement, Clapham, and joined the 'Clapham Sect' as an anti-slavery campaigner (*see* **Thornton Road**). His son, the future Lord Macaulay, historian, grew up and went to school in Clapham. **Macaulay Square** adjoins.

Macbeth Street W6 (Hammersmith). Robert Macbeth was minister of the New Meeting House in George Yard from 1853.

Macclesfield Road EC1 (Finsbury, Islington). Runs beside a stretch of the City Road Basin (now closed) on the Regent's Canal. The fourth Earl of Macclesfield was a director of the canal company from 1812 and chairman from 1816 until 1842.

Macclesfield Street W1 (Shaftesbury Avenue, Cit. West.). *See* **Gerrard Street**. Charles, Baron Gerard, was created Earl of Macclesfield in 1679. This street, which was built *c*1684, approached his house from the N.

McDermott Road SE15 (Peckham, Southwark). One Bryan McDermott owned this land *c*1830.

McDowall Road SE5 (Camberwell, Southwark). Built by A. McDowall of Paulet Road and named in 1887.

Macfarren Place NW1 (Regent's Park, Cit. West.). Runs beside the Royal Academy of Music, of which Sir George Alexander Macfarren (1813–87), composer of opera and

oratorio, was principal from 1875. He had taught at the Academy 1837–46 and from 1851.

Mackennal Street NW8 (St John's Wood, Cit. West.). Commemorates Sir Bertram Mackennal, Australian sculptor (1863–1931), a resident of St John's Wood. He designed the coinage for the reign of George V (1910–36).

Mackenzie Road N7 (Islington). The Rev. William Mackenzie was incumbent of St James's Anglican church (corner of Liverpool Road and Chalfont Road) for some 30 years until *c*1872.

McKerrell Road SE15 (Peckham, Southwark). On the Crespigny estate (*see* **De Crespigny Park**). Sir Claude Champion de Crespigny married a Miss McKerrell in 1872. Their country house was at Maldon in Essex, and **Maldon Close** is off Grove Lane.

Mackeson Road NW3 (Hampstead, Camden). The Rev. Charles Mackeson (1843–99) took charge of the Church of the Good Shepherd in Savernake Road in 1885. During the following ten years he worked zealously for a new church, the foundation stone of which he laid in 1892. The church was consecrated as All Hallows in 1901.

Macklin Street WC2 (Covent Garden, Camden). Commemorates the 18th-century actor Charles Macklin who appeared at Drury Lane Theatre.

Macks Road SE16 (Bermondsey, Southwark). Built on a former market garden belonging to John Mack.

Maclise Road W14 (Shepherd's Bush, Hammersmith). Commemorates the painter Daniel Maclise (1806–70), noted for historical subjects in the grand manner. His most famous painting is *The Death of Nelson*.

Macquarie Way E14 (Isle of Dogs, T. Ham.). The iron passenger sailing-ship *Melbourne* (1,857 tons) was built at Blackwall for the Australian trade by R. and H. Green and launched in 1875. She made regular voyages to Melbourne, Victoria, until 1887, and then to Sydney. Her name was changed to *Macquarie* in 1888 (after the Australian river). She was considered an outstanding passenger and cargo ship. She was later bought by a Norwegian company and called the *Fortuna*, and she ended as a coal-hulk in Sydney harbour.

Maddams Street E3 (Bromley, T. Ham.). George Maddams represented Bromley on the Poplar District Board of Works in the 1890s. He became one of the first Poplar borough councillors.

Maddock Way SE17 (Walworth, Southwark). Commemorates the nurseryman James Maddock, who grew exotic flowers in his Walworth gardens and wrote about them in his *Florists' Directory or Treatise on the Culture of Flowers* in 1792. The botanists of his time, including Curtis (*see* **Curtis Street**), had great respect for Maddock, whom they visited in search of rare specimens.

Maddox Street W1 (New Bond Street, Cit. West.). Built on part of the Maddox estate. William Maddox, City of London merchant, bought land here *c*1620; it was developed by his descendants.

Magdalen Road SW18 (Earlsfield, Wandsworth). Built on land belonging to Magdalen College, Oxford. Adjoining streets are named from scholars and benefactors of the college.

Magdalen Street SE1 (Bermondsey, Southwark). Magdalen College, Oxford, was founded by William of Waynflete, Bishop of Winchester. He lived at Winchester House, Southwark, and endowed the college with local property. **Bursar Street** adjoins, and **Shand Street** was formerly College Street.

Magpie Alley EC4 (Whitefriars, Cit. Lond.). An inn here called the *Magpie* is recorded in 1761.

Maguire Street SE1 (Bermondsey, Southwark). Probably commemorates the Rev. Dr Robert Maguire (1826–90), who was rector of St Olave's, Southwark, from 1875. He was a noted controversialist, of militant anti-Catholic views.

Maida Vale W9 (Cit. West.). Commemorates the victory of Sir John Stuart's forces over the French at Maida, in Spain, in 1806 during the Napoleonic Wars. **Maida Avenue** adjoins.

Maiden Lane WC2 (Covent Garden, Cit. West.). An old pathway, first recorded by this name in 1636. The derivation is not known; it may have been named from an inn or shop sign depicting 'The Maiden' or 'The Maid's Head'.

Maitland Park Road NW3 (Chalk Farm, Camden). Site of the Orphan Working School (*see* **Pickard Street**) which moved here in 1847; Ebenezer Maitland was its treasurer in the 1820s. The school has since moved to Reigate.

Malabar Street E14 (Isle of Dogs, T. Ham.). *See* **Cuba Street**.

Malden Crescent NW1 (Kentish Town, Camden). Built on part of the Fitzroy estate belonging to the barons Southampton. They also owned property at Malden in Surrey. **Malden Place** and **Road** adjoin. **Southampton Street** approaches.

Maldon Close SE5 (Camberwell, Southwark). *See* **McKerrell Road**.

Malet Street WC1 (Bloomsbury, Camden). Part of the estate of the dukes of Bedford. Sir Edward Baldwin Malet (1837–1908), diplomat, married lady Ermyntrude Sackville Russell, daughter of the ninth Duke of Bedford, in 1885. He was ambassador in Berlin at the time.

Mall, The SW1 (Cit. West.). Laid out as a course for the game of pall-mall which was fashionable in the reign of Charles II. The first course, the present **Pall Mall**, had been abandoned and built up as a street. This later course became a thoroughfare when the game went out of fashion.

Mallord Street SW3 (Chelsea, Ken. Chel.). The painter Joseph William Mallord Turner (1775–1851) had a house on the river in Chelsea, where he died.

Mallory Close SE4 (Brockley, Lewisham). Commemorates the Rev. Thomas Mallory, vicar of St Nicholas, Deptford, 1644–59. In 1661, as the incumbent of a City church, he was one of 24 independents who signed the *Renunciation and Declaration of the Congregational Churches* and was put out of his church (St Michael's, Crooked Lane) under the Act of Uniformity, 1662.

Mallory Street NW8 (Lisson Grove, Cit. West.). *See* **Paveley Street**. Robert Mallory was Grand Prior of the Order of Knights of St John of Jerusalem in England 1433–40.

Mallow Street EC1 (Finsbury, Islington). Commemorates Mallow Field, presumably named from wild mallow plants, one of the three open fields belonging to the manor of Finsbury, recorded in 1567.

Malpas Road SE4 (Brockley, Lewisham). On the Tyrwhitt-Drake estate; Malpas is a small town in Cheshire where a member of the family was rector of the parish church (*see* **Drake Road**).

Maltravers Street WC2 (Strand, Cit. West.). Built on part of the site of Arundel House (*see* **Arundel Street**). Henry Fitzalan, Earl of Arundel (*d* 1580), was also Baron Maltravers. The title remained with the Fitzalan family.

Malt Street SE1 (Old Kent Road, Southwark). Probably from a 19th-century brewery which stood nearby.

Managers Street E14 (Isle of Dogs, T. Ham.). This street approached a wharf which belonged to a local government board in the 19th century, the Managers of the Metropolitan Asylum District.

Manchester Street W1 (Marylebone, Cit. West.). Approaches **Manchester Square**, laid out around Manchester House (1776) which was the London house of the dukes of Manchester.

Manciple Street SE1 (Southwark). One of a group taken from Geoffrey Chaucer's *Canterbury Tales*; the manciple or maunciple (a purveyor) was one of the group of pilgrims who set out from the *Tabard* inn at Southwark.

Mandarin Street E14 (Limehouse, T. Ham.). *See* **Oriental Street**.

Mandeville Place W1 (Marylebone, Cit. West.). Approaches **Manchester Square** through Hinde Street. The Duke of Manchester was also Viscount Mandeville.

Mandeville Street E5 (Clapton, Hackney). Bernard Mandeville (*d* 1733) was a writer and social satirist who lived in Hackney. The most famous of his books was the satire *The Fable of the Bees*.

Manette Street W1 (Soho, Cit. West.). Charles Dickens set part of his novel *A Tale of Two Cities* in a house on the corner of this street and Greek Street. The former was later renamed after the Manette family of the novel.

Manilla Street E14 (Isle of Dogs, T. Ham.). *See* **Cuba Street**.

Manor Avenue SE4 (Brockley, Lewisham). Built across land which was originally part of Brockley Manor farm, and was later used as market-garden land. There is doubt as to whether mediaeval Brockley was a manor in the full sense, but it was treated as one and it comprised land in Lewisham and Deptford. The Deptford portion passed to the Crown in 1529, and was held separately after that (*see* **Wickham Road**).

Manor Fields SW15 (Putney, R. upon T.). The manor of Putney had three common fields: Thames Field, Park Field (which lay E of Putney Park; *see* **Putney Park Lane**) and Basin Field E of Putney Hill.

Manor Place SE17 (Walworth, Southwark). Walworth Manor. which stood here (at the junction with Penton Place), was the principal dwelling of a Saxon manor granted to

Christ Church Priory, Canterbury, in 1052. The house was demolished in 1856 and what remained of the manorial estate was bought from the Church Commissioners in the 1950s by the London County Council.

Manor Road N16 (Stoke Newington, Hackney). Refers to the manor of Stoke Newington (*see* **Lordship Road**). Nearby Abney Park Cemetery is on the site of the manor house which belonged to the Abney family, lords of the manor from 1700.

Manresa Road SW3 (Chelsea, Ken. Chel.). Approached Trafalgar (now Chelsea) Square; Manresa is a Spanish place name.

Mansell Street E1 (Whitechapel, Cit. Lond./T. Ham.). *See* **Leman Street**. William Leman (*d* 1667) married Rebecca Prescot (*see* **Prescot Street**). Their son married Mary Mansell, of a Welsh family; their grandson Mansell Leman married Lucy Alie in 1683. The Alies also held a local estate (*see* **Alie Street**). In the 18th century this name applied only to that part of the street between Alie Street and Prescot Street.

Mansfield Road NW3 (Hampstead, Camden). Marked the S boundary of the estate of Lord Mansfield who lived at Kenwood House. The street was laid out *c* 1806.

Mansfield Street W1 (Marylebone, Cit. West.). *See* **Ogle Street**.

Manstone Road NW2 (W Hampstead, Camden). Kentish place name; built by the Powell-Cotton family of Quex Park, Birchington, Kent.

Mantell Street N1 (Islington). The area was known as the Mantell's or Mantel's when it was given to the hospital of St John of Jerusalem (*see* **St John Street**) in the reign of Henry

II (1154–89); the name was a corruption of a former owner's name, Geoffrey de Mandeville. Mandeville was a member of the order of Knights Templar; his tomb effigy may be seen in the Temple Church. By contemporary account he was guilty of great cruelty during the civil war of 1139–52.

Mantus Close E1 (Stepney, T. Ham.). *See* **Amiel Street**. **Mantus Road** approaches.

Manwood Road SE4 (Lewisham). Commemorates a local landowner of the 16th century, Sir Roger Manwood (1525–92), judge.

Maple Street W1 (Tottenham Court Road, Camden). Commemorates Sir John Maple (1845–1903), London County Council member for St Pancras South 1895–1901. He was the son of John Maple, founder of the Tottenham Court Road furniture shop; as well as being active in politics he was a noted breeder of racehorses.

Marchant Street SE14 (Deptford, Lewisham). W.F. Marchant was an early member of Deptford Borough Council; he became mayor *c* 1914.

Marchmont Street WC1 (Bloomsbury, Camden). Commemorates Hugh Hume, Third Earl of Marchmont (1708–94), a governor of the nearby Coram Foundling Hospital.

Marcia Road SE1 (Old Kent Road, Southwark). On the Rolls estate (*see* **Rolls Road**). Georgiana Marcia Maclean, of Morvaren, married John Allen Rolls, First Baron Llangattock. Their son Charles Stewart Rolls was the motorist, aviator and engineer who joined with Henry Royce in 1904 to build the first Rolls-Royce.

Marcilly Road SW18 (St John's Hill,

Wandsworth). Marie Claire des Champs de Marcilly became the mistress and then the second wife of Henry St John, Second Viscount Bolingbroke (*see* **Bolingbroke Walk**).

Maresfield Gardens NW3 (Hampstead, Camden). *See* **Canfield Gardens**. The Maryon-Wilson family also held property at Maresfield in Sussex.

Mare Street E8 (Hackney). Called Merestreet in the 15th century, from an OE word meaning an edge or boundary.

Margaret Street W1 (Marylebone, Cit. West.). Built *c* 1730 on land belonging to Edward Harley, Earl of Oxford, and named after his daughter, Lady Margaret Cavendish Harley.

Margaretta Terrace SW3 (Chelsea, Ken. Chel.). *See* **Phene Street**. Margaretta was the name of Dr Phene's wife.

Margery Street WC1 (Clerkenwell, Islington). Formerly Margaret Street, recording a name in the family of the Marquis of Northampton on whose land it was built (*see* **Compton Road**).

Margravine Road W6 (Fulham, Hammersmith). The Margravine and Margrave of Brandenburg-Anspach bought the former home of Sir Nicholas Crisp (*see* **Crisp Road**) in 1792 and called it 'Brandenburg House'. The Margravine lived on in the house after her husband's death. **Margravine Gardens** adjoins.

Marian Street E2 (Haggerston, Hackney). *See* **Pritchard's Road**.

Maria Street E14 (Stepney, T. Ham.). *See* **Louisa Street**.·

Marigold Alley SE1 (Upper Ground,

Southwark). The *Marygold Inn* is recorded here in 1761.

Market Place W1 (Oxford Street, Cit. West.). The Oxford Market was opened here in 1732 as part of the Cavendish Square development; the land belonged to the Earl of Oxford. **Market Court** and **Street** approach.

Market Road N7 (Caledonian Road, Islington). Runs beside the site of the Metropolitan Cattle Market which moved from Smithfield and opened here in 1855. The cattle market closed in 1963 (*see* **Pedlars' Way**).

Markham Square SW3 (Chelsea, Ken. Chel.). Site of part of Box Farm, farmed by the Markham Evans family from the 16th to the 19th centuries. The farmhouse was demolished in 1900. **Markham Street** approaches.

Mark Lane EC3 (Cit. Lond.). Called Marthe Lane in the 13th century, Martlane in the 14th and Marke Lane in the 16th. The original name is possibly a form of 'Martha's Lane'.

Marlborough Grove SE1 (Old Kent Road, Southwark). The E side of the Old Kent Road was originally a series of groups of houses with fine-sounding names, either patriotic or aristocratic or, as in this case, both. Examples are Gloucester, Windsor, Nelson and Burlington. This street led off Marlborough Place (*see* **Marlborough Place**, Cit. West.).

Marlborough Place NW8 (St John's Wood, Cit. West.). Commemorates John Churchill, First Duke of Marlborough, Captain-General of the English army 1702–12. **Marlborough Hill** adjoins (*see* **Marlborough Road**).

Marlborough Road SW1 (St James's, Cit. West.). Runs beside Marlborough House, built in 1711 for Sarah Churchill, Duchess of Marlborough, confidante of Queen Anne. The house belonged to the dukes of Marlborough until the lease reverted to the Crown in 1817.

Marlborough Street SW3 (Chelsea, Ken. Chel.). Charles Spencer (1706–58), son of the third Earl of Sunderland and Anne Churchill, was Third Duke of Marlborough; he lived, towards the end of his life, near Chelsea Common nearby.

Marloes Road W8 (Kensington, Ken. Chel.). *See* **Longridge Road**.

Marmora Road SE22 (Peckham Rye, Southwark). From a group inspired by the Crimean War of 1854–6 (*see* **Alma Grove**). **Mundania Road** and **Therapia Road** are named from two towns by the sea of Marmora. Therapia or Tarabya is a health resort named from the Greek *therapeuo*, to look after or cure. **Scutari Road** is named from the base where Florence Nightingale set up her hospital.

Marsden Road SE15 (Camberwell, Southwark). George William Marsden was clerk to Camberwell vestry in the 1860s.

Marsden Street NW5 (Kentish Town, Camden). Developed by Thomas Marsden in the 1850s.

Marshall Gardens SE1 (Southwark). Built on land belonging to a charitable trust, Marshall's Charity. The street was built in the late 18th century. John Marshall of Newcomen Street, in his will of 1627, left money for various charitable purposes, including a sum to establish Christ Church parish in the manor of Paris Garden.

Marshall Street W1 (Soho, Cit. West.). Built 1735–6 on land held by the Earl of Craven, whose Berkshire seat was at Hampstead Marshall.

Marshalsea Road SE1 (Southwark). Commemorates the Marshalsea Prison which stood on the E side of Borough High Street; it is recorded from 1294 as a prison for offenders to be tried by the King's Knights Marshal, and was also later used by the Marshal of the Court of King's Bench. By the early 19th century it had become a debtors' prison.

Marsham Street SW1 (Cit. West.). Sir Robert Marsham (*d* 1703) inherited this land from Sir Richard Tufton in 1631. The estate included Tufton Street and the site of **Romney Street**, named after Sir Robert's son Robert, Baron Romney (created 1716).

Marsh Hill E9 (Hackney). Overlooks and approaches Hackney Marshes, acquired as a public recreation ground in 1892, and formerly grazing marshes in the valley of the River Lea.

Marsland Road SE17 (Walworth, Southwark). John Marsland, builder, developed local property including parts of **Lorrimore Square** in the 1850s. A later member of the family was the first London County Council member for Walworth in 1889.

Martin Lane EC4 (Cit. Lond.). Named from the church of St Martin, pulled down in 1820. The churchyard remains as a garden.

Mart Street WC2 (Covent Garden, Cit. West.). Led originally to the market held in the square of **Covent Garden**.

Marylands Road W9 (Westbourne Green, Cit. West.). The 'Marylands' (bounded SW by the present Shirland Road) were granted to the Abbot of St Mary's, Abingdon, by Aubrey de Vere in the 11th century; a grant of lands in Kensington was made at the

same time (*see* **St Mary Abbot's Place**).

Marylebone High Street W1 (Cit. West.). High or principal street of Marylebone: the name is a corruption of 'Mary-burn'. This district was originally called Tyburn, from Tyburn hamlet which became deserted in the 14th century. A new hamlet grew up around the church of St Mary which stood further N and actually on the banks of the Tyburn stream; this became known as St Mary Burn or Bourne (meaning a stream). **Marylebone Lane**, **Mews**, **Passage**, **Road** and **Street** are nearby.

Mary Terrace NW1 (Camden Town, Camden). Developed by one William Maryon from 1828.

Masbro Road W14 (Brook Green, Hammersmith). Joseph Crookes, born at Masbro' in Yorkshire, bought Brook Green Farm in the 19th century and called the farmhouse 'Masbro' House'. His wife was born at Aynhoe in Northumberland. **Aynhoe Road** is nearby.

Mason's Avenue EC2 (Cit. Lond.). The Masons' Company had a guildhall here from 1463. The mediaeval building was destroyed in the Great Fire of 1666; the hall was then rebuilt; and the company sold that 17th-century building in 1865.

Mason Street SE17 (Old Kent Road, Southwark). Runs beside the school for the deaf; the Rev. H.C. Mason was co-founder of the first school for the deaf and dumb, set up in Bermondsey in 1792 and removed here in 1809.

Mason's Yard SW1 (St James's, Cit. West.). Originally West Stable Yard, a mews for Duke Street and St James's Square. The yard was occupied 1717–*c*1740 by the family of Henry Mason, victualler.

Massinger Street SE17 (Walworth, Southwark). One of three local names taken from 17th-century drama. Philip Massinger wrote comedy and romantic drama, his best-known play being *A New Way to Pay Old Debts* (1625). He is buried in Southwark Cathedral. (*See* **Congreve Street** and **Comus Place**.)

Masthouse Terrace E14 (Millwall, T. Ham.). A Mast House stood S of this point and was approached by the 19th-century Devonshire Terrace.

Matham Grove SE22 (E Dulwich, Southwark). On the Dulwich College Estate, and possibly influenced by the nearby College Art Gallery. Jacobus (1571–1631) and Theodore (1606–60) Matham were Dutch engravers.

Matthew Parker Street SW1 (Cit. West.). Commemorates Matthew Parker, Archbishop of Canterbury 1559–75, a strongly independent champion of the Church of England and reviser of the *Thirty-nine Articles* of Anglican doctrine.

Matthews Street SW11 (Battersea, Wandsworth). *See* **Reform Street**.

Matthias Road N16 (Stoke Newington, Hackney/Islington). The Anglican church of St Matthias, at the junction with Wordsworth Road, was consecrated in 1853. It was the scene of anti-ritualist rioting in 1867.

Maude Road SE5 (Camberwell, Southwark). *See* **Dagmar Road**.

Maunsel Street SW1 (Victoria, Cit. West.). Built on part of the former Tothill Fields; John Maunsel or Mansell is recorded as holding the manor of Tothill in 1256. He was perhaps the most important of Henry III's advisers, and extremely rich from his estimated 300 benefices. He was driven out of England in 1263 when the barons under Simon de Montfort rose against the king; he died in France in 1265.

Maurice Street W12 (Wormwood Scrubs, Hammersmith). Maurice was Bishop of London 1085–1107, during which time St Paul's Cathedral was burnt and the foundations laid for a new building. The bishops of London held the manor of Hammersmith.

Mawbey Road SE1 (Old Kent Road, Southwark). Built on land belonging to Erasmus Mawbey, who lived on the opposite side of the Old Kent Road. He appears in a directory of 1841 as a cow-keeper, and as a butcher in 1845. **Mawbey Place** adjoins.

Mawbey Street SW8 (S Lambeth, Lambeth). Sir Joseph Mawbey (1730–98) inherited the copyhold of large areas in the manor of Kennington from his uncle, a Vauxhall distiller called Joseph Pratt (*see* **Pratt Walk**). He became Sheriff of Surrey and MP for Southwark; his estates were sold off in separate lots from 1819.

Maxwell Road SW6 (Fulham, Hammersmith). Built in the late 19th century on land belonging to the Maxwell family of Moore Park, Waterford, in Ireland. **Moore Park Road** and **Waterford Road** adjoin.

Mayfield Road E8 (Kingsland Road, Hackney). Built on a former field which is recorded as The Mayfield in 1557, probably from may or hawthorn hedges.

Mayflower Street SE16 (Rother-hithe, Southwark). A modern name, chosen to commemorate the *Mayflower* which carried settlers to America in 1620. Formerly Prince's Street, one of a local group of royally-inspired names from the early 19th century (*see* **Ainsty Street**). The captain of the *Mayflower*, Christopher Jones, lived in Rotherhithe and is buried in St Mary's churchyard. His first mate and a part-owner of the ship were also Rotherhithe men. Traditionally, the ship was berthed at Rotherhithe before her voyage.

Mayow Road SE23, SE26 (Sydenham, Lewisham). An estate extending across the present Sydenham Road end, S of Mayow Park, belonged *c*1800 to Major Mayow Wynell Mayow; it remained in his family until development began in the 1870s.

Maysoule Road SW11 (Battersea, Wandsworth). Commemorates a local Baptist minister, the Rev. Israel May-Soule, who was active in the education of the poor until his death in the 1870s. He continued a campaign which began with the work of Joseph Hughes (*d* 1833) and a local family of benefactors named Tritton.

Mazenod Avenue NW6 (S Hampstead, Camden). From the Roman Catholic church of the Oblates of Mary Immaculate, a French society founded in 1826 by Eugène de Mazenod.

Meadowbank NW3 (Chalk Farm, Camden). Built on meadow land; the neighbouring farms of Rugmere and Chalcot were predominantly meadow and other pasture land before development.

Meadow Road SW8 (Vauxhall, Lambeth). Built up in the early 19th century on meadows belonging to the Caron House estate. **Meadow Place** approaches.

Meard Street W1 (Soho, Cit. West.). Built from 1722 by John Meard the younger, carpenter. It was Meard who built the spire for the new church of St Anne, Soho, in 1718.

Mecklenburgh Square WC1 (Bloomsbury, Camden). Laid out in the late 18th century with **Brunswick Square**. Named after George III's consort, Queen Charlotte, who had been Princess Charlotte of Mecklenburg-Strelitz.

Medburn Street NW1 (St Pancras, Camden). *See* **Aldenham Street**. Platt also endowed the school with land at Medburn Farm, Hertfordshire.

Medcalf Place N1 (Pentonville Road, Islington). Built in 1819 by one Robert Medcalf.

Medlar Street SE5 (Camberwell, Southwark). A fruit-tree name by association with the former name, Orchard Row. In the late 19th century there was still an orchard near the E end.

Medway Street SW1 (Cit. West.). Built on land belonging to the Dean and Chapter of Westminster Abbey. Between 1663 and 1802 the deans of Westminster were also bishops of Rochester, a town and diocese at the mouth of the River Medway in Kent.

Meeting House Lane SE15 (Peckham, Southwark). Traditionally the site of the first dissenters' congregation in Peckham; their meeting house is said to have been built there in 1657.

Melbourne Grove SE22 (E Dulwich, Southwark). One of a group of Derbyshire place names chosen by E.J. Bailey of Lordship Lane, who developed his own land here between 1873 and 1885. The other streets are **Ashbourne Grove**, **Chesterfield Grove**, and **Derwent Grove**, from the river.

Melbury Road W14 (Kensington, Ken. Chel.). Laid out on land belonging to Holland House after it was bought by Lord Ilchester in 1874;

Melbury was his country house. **Melbury Court** adjoins.

Melbury Terrace NW1 (Marylebone, Cit. West.). *See* **Broadstone Place**.

Melcombe Street NW1 (Marylebone, Cit. West.). Built on the estate of the Portman family who also held a property called Melcombe in Dorset (*see* **Portman Square**).

Mellish Street E14 (Isle of Dogs, T. Ham.). *See* **Glengall Grove**.

Mellitus Street W12 (Wormwood Scrubs, Hammersmith). Mellitus or Miletus was consecrated first Bishop of London by St Augustine in 604. The diocese of London has a long association with Hammersmith manor, which it later owned.

Melon Place W8 (Kensington Church Street, Ken. Chel.). Laid out across land formerly called the Melon Ground, which may once have been part of the gardens of adjoining Sheffield House (*see* **Sheffield Terrace**).

Melon Road SE15 (Peckham, Southwark). Built on land formerly belonging to the manor house of Peckham, a garden known as the Melon Ground.

Memel Street EC1 (Finsbury, Islington). *See* **Timber Street**.

Menelik Road NW2 (W Hampstead, Camden). *See* **Asmara Road**.

Merceron Street E1 (Bethnal Green, T. Ham.). Joseph Merceron, a silk-weaver of Huguenot extraction, dominated local affairs through the Bethnal Green parish vestry (of which he was treasurer) from 1788. He was convicted of corruption and imprisoned in 1818, but had returned to public life by 1830.

Mercer Street WC2 (Covent Garden, Camden/Cit. West.). Runs S into the former Elm Close, a field acquired by the Mercers' Company in the 14th century; the field extended along the N side of Long Acre from St Martin's Lane to Drury Lane.

Meredith Street EC1 (Clerkenwell, Islington). Built by one Meredith who owned a building lease here together with a co-developer, whose name is recorded in **Whiskin Street**.

Meredyth Road SW13 (Barnes, R. upon T.). *See* **Church Road**.

Meretone Close SE4 (Lewisham). Commemorates an ancient name for Deptford: Meretun or Méreton is given by a local historian as a Saxon name for the town.

Merlin Street WC1 (Clerkenwell, Islington). Named from the *New Merlin's Cave*, a tavern nearby. A magician's or 'Merlin's' cave was a popular attraction in 18th-century taverns and pleasure gardens; the first one was made in the gardens of the royal palace at Richmond.

Mermaid Court SE1 (Southwark). In 1720 this is recorded as Mermaid Alley, running S of the Marshalsea Prison and named from the sign of an inn; it led through to a bowling green (*see* **Bowling Green Place**).

Merrick Square SE1 (Southwark). Christopher Merrick bought most of the area now bounded by Borough High Street, Great Dover Street, Falmouth Road and Harper Road in 1605. In 1661 his son (also Christopher) conveyed it to the Brethren of Trinity House (*see* **Trinity Street**).

Merritt Road SE4 (Brockley, Lewisham). Named in 1879; a builder called Merritt of Merritt and Ashby was active in S London at the time.

Merton Lane N6 (Highgate, Camden). From a large house here called 'Merton Lodge'.

Merton Rise NW3 (Swiss Cottage, Camden). Built on the Eton College estate (*see* **Eton Avenue**). Henry VI (1422–61) endowed the college with this land and also with land belonging to Merton Priory.

Methwold Road W10 (N Kensington, Ken. Chel.). Commemorates William Methwold, a 17th-century benefactor; by his will of 1652 a charity was set up for the poor women of the parish.

Meymott Street SE1 (Southwark). Built on part of the mediaeval manor called Paris Garden, of which W.J. Meymott wrote an account in 1881. He was a solicitor, and from 1863 steward of the manor, as were previous Meymotts: John Gilbert from 1828 and Edward from 1850.

Micawber Street N1 (Shepherdess Walk, Hackney). In Charles Dickens's novel *David Copperfield*, Mr Micawber is portrayed as living in adjacent Windsor Terrace.

Middlesex Passage EC1 (Cit. London.). Said to be the site of a mansion called 'Middlesex House', which was still standing in 1720; the passage is recorded as Middlesex Court in 1746.

Middlesex Street E1 (Cit. Lond./T. Ham.). Part of the boundary between the City of London and the old county of Middlesex, which existed when the street was so named c1830. A popular name, Petticoat Lane, is recorded from 1602; before that it was Hog Lane. The name of 'Petticoat' derives from an old-clothes market held in the lane regularly; this name has proved so persistent as to render 'Middlesex Street' more or less redundant.

Middle Temple Lane EC4 (Cit. Lond.). The Order of Knights Templar set up a hall, church and headquarters on the surrounding land c1180. The order was dissolved, with charges of necromancy, in 1312; their property here was later leased to lawyers. Originally there were three building complexes called Inner, Middle and Outer Temple; the first two still exist, the latter was sold and built up by 1600.

Middleton Road E8 (Dalston, Hackney). Built on land owned by Sir John Middleton, who held an estate here c1850.

Midland Road NW1 (St Pancras, Camden). Runs beside St Pancras Station, opened as their London terminus by the Midland Railway Company in 1868. The approaching lines were cut, to great public consternation, through the burial grounds of St Pancras old church and St Giles. They also destroyed about 3,000 houses of a slum called Agar Town. This street was formerly Skinner Street, as built on land belonging to the Skinners' Company (*see* **Judd Street**).

Midmoor Road SW12 (Streatham Hill, Lambeth). Built on a field formerly called Midmoor Field.

Mildmay Park N1 (Newington Green, Islington). Centre of a group of streets of this name near Newington Green. The Mildmay family were lords of the manor of Stoke Newington. Sir Walter Mildmay (*d* 1589) was a privy councillor to Elizabeth I. Sir Henry Mildmay was one of the judges at the trial of Charles I in 1649 (*see* **Haliday Walk**).

Mile End Road E1, E3 (T. Ham.). Road from the City of London to Mile End, the hamlet at the end of the first mile. The hamlet lay around

Middle Temple Lane

the present junction of Mile End Road and Globe Road.

Miles Lane EC4 (Cit. Lond.). Contraction of St Michael's Lane, from the mediaeval church of St Michael (now demolished) which stood here.

Milford Lane WC2 (Strand, Cit. West.). An old name, the origin is unknown; it was possibly the site of a watermill on a small, fast stream running down into the Thames through a ford. Small watercourses were a feature of the Strand area in the middle ages.

Milk Street EC2 (Cit. Lond.). Place where the dairymen congregated to sell produce at the mediaeval food market along Cheapside.

Milkwood Road SE24 (Brixton, Lambeth). Part of the Milk Wood, woodland belonging to the manor of Lambeth Wick. The woods were cut down in the 17th century and the area was built up from 1869 (*see* **Wickwood Street**).

Milk Yard E1 (Wapping, T. Ham.). An old name from an 18th-century or earlier cow-keeper and milk-seller.

Millbank SW1 (Cit. West.). The watermill belonging to the Abbey of St Peter, Westminster, stood near the present junction of Millbank and Great College Street, at the N end of the 'bank' or embankment of the river. The mill is last recorded in the mid-17th century.

Miller's Avenue E8 (Shacklewell, Hackney). A 19th-century street built – with adjoining **Miller's Terrace** – on land belonging to the Miller family.

Miller Street NW1 (Camden Town, Camden). Built by a N London builder, John Miller, from 1811.

Mill Hill Road SW13 (Barnes, R. upon T.). A windmill on a hilly part of the common is recorded here in 1443.

Milligan Street E14 (Isle of Dogs, T. Ham.). Robert Milligan, City of London merchant, was one of the principal founders of the West India Docks. He died in 1809.

Mill Lane NW6 (W Hampstead, Camden). A windmill stood at the W end; it was burnt down in 1861.

Millman Street WC1 (Bloomsbury, Camden). Built in the 1680s by Sir William Millman or Milman of Great Ormond Street. He later (1697) bought property in Chelsea (*see* **Milman's Street**).

Mill Road SE18 (Lewisham). Approached a flour mill on the Ravensbourne, burnt down *c*1924. **Cornmill Lane** approaches.

Mill Row N1 (Shoreditch, Hackney). Built on a field called Millfield, part of which formerly belonged to Holywell Priory (*see* **Holywell Lane**).

Millstream Road SE1 (Bermondsey, Southwark). A stream running into the Thames (*see* **Mill Street**) followed this course, originally as far inland as Bermondsey Abbey. The stream was covered over in the 1850s.

Mill Street W1 (Mayfair, Cit. West.). Built on a field called Mill Field, from a nearby windmill which is recorded beside the Tyburn stream here in 1622.

Mill Street SE1 (Bermondsey, Southwark). Site of a watermill belonging to the Abbey of St Saviour, Bermondsey, at St Saviour's Dock, where the mill stream came out into the Thames.

Millwall Dock Road E14 (Isle of

Dogs, T. Ham.). The low-lying Isle of Dogs, once called Stepney Marsh, was once bounded by a river wall of earth along which were seven windmills. A dock basin S of this street was formerly known as the Millwall Outer Dock.

Milman's Street SW10 (Chelsea, Ken. Chel.). Sir William Millman or Milman (*d* 1713) owned a house here on the estate formerly belonging to Sir Thomas More (*d* 1535).

Milner Square N1 (Islington). *See* **Gibson Square**.

Milner Street (Chelsea, Ken. Chel.). *See* **Moore Street**.

Milton Court Road SE14 (Deptford, Lewisham). On the Evelyn family estate (*see* **Evelyn Street**). Milton Court was the family's Surrey seat.

Milton Road SE24 (Brixton, Lambeth). *See* **Shakespeare Road** for this and **Milton Grove**, Shacklewell.

Milton Street EC2 (Cit. Lond.). Renamed in the 1820s from the owner of the building lease. The street was formerly Grub Street, from an early mediaeval property owner called Grub or Grubbe.

Milward Street E1 (Whitechapel, T. Ham.). Named in 1911 from a ward in the nearby London Hospital.

Mincing Lane EC3 (Cit. Lond.). A convent of nuns or 'minchins' held property here; they sold it to a branch of the Clothworkers' Guild in 1455, and the Guildhall was built here.

Minera Mews SW1 (Belgravia, Cit. West.). *See* **Kinnerton Street**.

Minet Road SW9 (Camberwell, Lambeth). Hughes Minet bought land here from Sir Edward Knatchbull (*see* **Knatchbull Road**) in

1770. He was the grandson of a Huguenot refugee, Isaac Minet of Calais.

Ming Street E14 (Limehouse, T. Ham.). *See* **Oriental Street**. The Ming dynasty ruled China from 1368 until 1644.

Minories EC3 (Cit. Lond.). The Little Sisters (or Sorores Minores) were an order of nuns founded by St Clare of Assisi in 1215, and vowed to poverty. They established their convent here in 1293. Their church became a parish church in 1538, was rebuilt in the 18th century and demolished in 1958.

Minster Road NW2 (W Hampstead, Camden). Kentish place name; built by the Powell-Cotton family of Quex Park, Birchington, Kent.

Mint Street SE1 (Southwark). Suffolk Place here (demolished in 1557) was used as a royal mint *c*1545–51, Henry VIII having acquired it from the Duke of Suffolk (*see* **Great Suffolk Street**). The name 'Mint' in the 17th, 18th and 19th centuries referred to this street and all the surrounding narrow lanes on the old site.

Mitcham Lane SW16 (Lambeth/Wandsworth). Old lane leading to Mitcham; the name is from OE 'Micel-ham', the great homestead. **Mitcham Road** also approaches.

Mitchell Street EC1 (Finsbury, Islington). *See* **Ironmonger Row**.

Mitre Court EC2 (Cit. Lond.). Named from the *Mitre Inn* which stood round the corner in Wood Street.

Mitre Street EC3 (Cit. Lond.). Leads to **Mitre Square**, and both were named from the *Mitre* tavern, now demolished, which stood near

Aldgate. The inn is first mentioned in 1636.

Moat Place SW9 (Stockwell, Lambeth). Site of part of the moat surrounding the manor house of Stockwell. Stockwell became a manor c1300; the date of the first manor house is unknown, but the last one was demolished c1755. Its chapel (S of the moat) survived into the 19th century.

Modder Place SW15 (Putney, Wandsworth). Named in 1900 after an action on the Modder River, Orange Free State, during the Boer War.

Molesworth Street SE13 (Lewisham). Commemorates Bevil Molesworth, a local benefactor who in 1630 left a property in Lewisham, the *Castle* inn, to charity and the sum of ten shillings for a sermon.

Monck Street SW1 (Cit. West.). Henry Monck, parish benefactor, made a gift of a tobacco box to the Overseers of the Poor of Westminster in 1713. The box and its inscribed silver plates have been preserved.

Monclar Road SE5 (Herne Hill, Southwark). Comte Amédée de Ripert-Monclar was an associate of the poet Browning (*see* **Browning Close**).

Moncrieff Street SE15 (Peckham, Southwark). Sir Alexander Moncrieff (1829–1906) was a soldier and engineer. He invented 'Moncrieff Pits' and types of carriage for siege and fortress guns.

Monkwell Square EC2 (Cit. Lond.). Site of mediaeval Monkwell Street, recorded in the 12th century as Mukewellestrate, in the 13th as Mogwellestrate and in the 16th as Mugwelstrete. The name probably

refers to a well belonging to an owner called Muca or Mucca.

Monmouth Place W2 (Westbourne Grove, Cit. West.). Built by W.K. Jenkins, a property developer of Welsh origin who frequently used place names from Wales or the Welsh border. **Monmouth Road** adjoins.

Monmouth Street WC2 (Soho, Cit. West.). Commemorates the Duke of Monmouth, natural son of Charles II, who had a house in Soho Square. His unsuccessful rebellion against James II led to his execution in 1685.

Montacute Road SE6 (Lewisham). William de Montacute, later first Earl of Salisbury, held the surrounding manor of Catford from 1331. A favourite of Edward III, he received grants of land as a reward for the murder of Mortimer, unpopular favourite of the Queen Mother, Isabella of France. He gave the manor to the Church c1340, and died in 1344.

Montague Avenue SE4 (Lewisham). The Lewisham portion of the manor of Catford belonged in 1621 to the daughters of Brian Annesley (*see* **Polsted Road**) who sold it in that year to Edward Montague of Boughton. Montague's family held it until his great-grandson John, Duke of Montague, sold it in 1717 to James Craggs, Postmaster General.

Montague Close SE1 (Southwark). The cloisters and convent belonging to the priory of St Mary Overie (on the site of the present Southwark Cathedral) passed to Sir Anthony Browne in 1545, after the dissolution of the monasteries. His son and heir was created Viscount Montague and the priory house, which stood against the N wall of the church, became known as 'Montague House'. Lord Montague sold it in 1625.

Montague Court EC1 (Cit. Lond.). Approached the mansion belonging to Ralph, First Earl and Third Baron Montague of Boughton, created an earl in 1689. The house lay E of Little Britain and S of Bartholomew Close. The E part of Cox's Court was formerly called Montague Place.

Montague Place WC1 (Bloomsbury, Camden). Montague House was built c1675 for Lord Montague, and stood on the site of the present British Museum. It was burnt down in 1686 and rebuilt, and the trustees of the British Museum bought it to house the original collection in 1754. The museum has been gradually enlarged and the old building had disappeared by 1850. **Montague Street** adjoins.

Montagu Square W1 (Marylebone, Cit. West.). Begun 1810 to the rear of Montagu House, a vast mansion at the E end of Upper Berkeley Street built c1780 for Elizabeth Montagu, famous for her salons. **Montagu Street**, **Upper Montagu Street** and **Montagu Place** approach; **Montagu Mansions**, **Mews** and **Row** are nearby.

Montclare Street E2 (Bethnal Green, T. Ham.). *See* **Camlet Street**.

Montefiore Street SW8 (Battersea, Wandsworth). On the Park Town estate of which Philip Flower (*see* **St Philip's Street**) was the main promoter. His son Cyril, later Lord Battersea, married Constance de Rothschild, daughter of Sir Anthony de Rothschild. Lady Battersea's mother had been a Montefiore.

Montpelier Square SW7 (Knightsbridge, Cit. West.). From the French resort famous for its air, and fashionable in the 1830s when this square was built. **Montpelier Place**, **Terrace** and **Walk** adjoin.

Montrose Place SW1 (Belgravia, Cit.

West.). Crosses the rear of the house in Belgrave Square belonging to the Duke of Montrose and retained by Caroline, Duchess of Montrose, until her death in 1894.

Monument Street EC3 (Cit. Lond.). Passes the monument designed by Sir Christopher Wren to commemorate the Great Fire of London in 1666. The column is 202ft high and stands 202ft away from the place where the fire began.

Moore Park Road SW6 (Fulham, Hammersmith). *See* **Maxwell Road**.

Moore Street SW3 (Chelsea, Ken. Chel.). Built on land inherited in 1829 by the children of Richard Moore of Hampton Court. **Halsey Street** is named from a son who changed his name to Halsey on marriage; **Milner Street** is from a daughter who married Colonel Charles Milner.

Moorfields EC2 (Cit. Lond.). The moorfields consisted of a stretch of marshy ground which began here, outside the Moor Gate (*see* **Moorgate**). They were crossed by a causeway in 1415 and drained in 1527. The fields began to be built upon after the Great Fire of 1666. **Moor Lane** has the same derivation.

Moorgate EC2 (Cit. Lond.). A late 18th-century street leading to the site of the Moor Gate in the N wall of the City, so named because it gave on to the moor beyond. The Moor Gate was demolished c1760, and the street was built to take advantage of the new broader way through the wall.

Moorhouse Road W2 (Paddington, Cit. West.). Commemorates the Rev. James Moorhouse, vicar of St James's, Paddington, 1868–76.

Moor Lane EC2 (Cit. Lond.). *See* **Moorfields**.

Mora Street EC1 (Finsbury, Islington). Commemorates the Prebend of Mora, or the Moor, a part of Finsbury belonging to St Paul's Cathedral, the income of which supported one prebendary canon of the cathedral. The Prebend of Mora included Cayton Street and the area bounded S by Lever Street, N by the City Road and W by Central Street. The St Paul's prebends date from before 1066.

Moravian Place SW10 (Chelsea, Ken. Chel.). Lindsey House on this site was occupied 1751–70 by a Moravian religious community led by Count Zinzendorf; their burial ground remains.

Moreland Street EC1 (Finsbury, Islington). Commemorates a family of builders prominent in parish affairs. John Moreland was a builder and bricklayer trading from Goswell Street in 1805. Joseph Moreland was the first representative of St Luke's parish on the Metropolitan Board of Works in 1855, and there were two Morelands serving on St Luke's vestry in 1885 when the street was named.

Moreton Place SW1 (Pimlico, Cit. West.). *See* **Tachbrook Street** for this and **Moreton Street** and **Terrace**.

Morgan Street E3 (Bow, T. Ham.). *See* **Tredegar Square**.

Morley Street SE1 (Waterloo Road, Lambeth/Southwark). Samuel Morley was a benefactor of the Royal Victoria Coffee Music Hall (*see* **Cons Street**), which he rescued financially in 1884. Evening classes in association with the theatre were expanded and a college established in 1889 as Morley College; in 1923 it was moved to Westminster Bridge Road, opposite this street.

Mornington Avenue W14 (W

Kensington, Hammersmith). *See* **Mornington Crescent**. Lord Mornington had a shooting lodge in Hammersmith.

Mornington Crescent NW1 (Camden Town, Camden). Commemorates Richard Wellesley, Earl of Mornington, eldest brother of the Duke of Wellington, Governor-General of Bengal 1797–1805. He was also Marquis Wellesley. After returning from India, where he extended British power by military campaigns, he served as Foreign Secretary 1809–12 and was appointed Lord Lieutenant of Ireland in 1821. **Mornington Place** and **Street** adjoin; **Mornington Terrace** approaches.

Morocco Street SE1 (Bermondsey, Southwark). Named by association with the local leather trade, from workers in Morocco leather.

Morpeth Terrace SW1 (Victoria, Cit. West.). *See* **Carlisle Place**.

Morris Road E14 (Poplar, T. Ham.). Built on land belonging to a Mr Morris, and named in 1860.

Morshead Road W9 (Paddington, Cit. West.). Sir John Morshead married a daughter and co-heiress of the Frederick family (*see* **Frederick Close**). The family held Paddington manor. **Warwick Avenue** is named from his daughter-in-law, the former Jane Warwick.

Mortimer Crescent NW6 (Kilburn, Camden). *See* **Greville Place** for this and **Mortimer Place**.

Mortimer Market WC1 (Tottenham Court Road, Camden). Originally built as a food and general market by Hans Winthrop Mortimer in 1768.

Mortimer Street W1 (Marylebone, Cit. West.). Edward Harley, Earl of Oxford and Mortimer, inherited the surrounding estate through his wife Lady Henrietta Holles. This street was laid out from c1730.

Mortimer Terrace NW5 (Kentish Town, Camden). Richard Mortimer lived at 39 Kentish Town Road in 1803, when he let out 28 acres to the rear on building leases. Lismore Circus (now demolished) and the surrounding streets were laid out on his land.

Morton Place SE1 (Lambeth). Commemorates Cardinal John Morton, Archbishop of Canterbury (d 1500), for whom the great gateway to Lambeth Palace nearby was built c1490.

Morwell Street WC1 (Bloomsbury, Camden). Built on the Russell estate. John Russell (1485–1555) held two of the family's early estates at Morwell and Werrington in Devonshire. **Werrington Street** in Somers Town is a N extension across Russell land of Lord Somers's Clarendon Street; eventually the name was given to the whole of the former Clarendon Street as well.

Moscow Road W2 (Bayswater, Cit. West.). This and other streets in Edward Orme's development around Orme Square were designed in 1816 and commemorated the recent visit to London of Czar Alexander I, who had defeated Napoleon in the Moscow campaign.

Mossop Street SW3 (Chelsea, Ken. Chel.). Commemorates the Irish actor-manager Henry Mossop, a potentially great tragedian whose career was spoilt by an unmanageable temperament and by financial problems. He died c1774, aged about 44.

Motcomb Street SW1 (Belgravia, Cit. West.). Part of the Grosvenor Belgravia estate. Motcomb was the Dorset home of Richard Grosvenor, Second Marquis of Westminster (d 1869).

Mount Adon Park SE22 (Lordship Lane, Southwark). Built on the site of a house called Adon Mount; the 'mount' is thought to have been part of an early British camp (see **Overhill Road**).

Mountfort Crescent N1 (Barnsbury, Islington). Site of a Roman fort where an emblem of the 20th Legion was found in 1842. **Roman Way** approaches.

Mount Mills EC1 (Goswell Road, Islington). Successive 'mounts' have been raised on the site; the first, probably natural, supported a windmill. This was replaced by a chapel called the Mount of Calvary, built for Katharine of Aragon, queen to Henry VIII until 1533, after which date the chapel was demolished and replaced by another mill. Cromwellian troops established a raised, fortified battery here in 1642; victims of the Great Plague were buried here in 1665 and the site was finally used as a rubbish heap before being levelled c1750.

Mount Pleasant EC1, WC1 (Clerkenwell, Camden/Islington). Local wit: this lane originally led to a huge mound of refuse and cinders at the junction with Gray's Inn Road. There was a second mound on part of Coldbath Fields (now occupied by the General Post Office) which was largely cleared away when Coldbath Fields Prison was built in 1794. The first mound is said to have been used up in the rebuilding of Moscow after 1812.

Mount Pleasant Road SE13 (Lewisham). From a house called 'Mount Pleasant' which stood here on Lewisham High Street.

Mount Street W1 (Mayfair, Cit. West.). Ran across the Mount Field, so-called from Oliver's Mount, a fortification set up, probably on the site of the present Carpenter Street, by Oliver Cromwell's forces in the Civil War of 1642–8. **Mount Row** runs parallel.

Mount Terrace E1 (Whitechapel, T. Ham.). Site of Whitechapel Mount, an artificial hill made partly from rubble collected after the Great Fire of 1666, and partly from earth displaced when London threw up defensive ramparts in the Civil War of 1642–8.

Mount Vernon NW3 (Hampstead, Camden). General Charles Vernon bought property here in 1785, on a hilly site.

Mowlem Street E2 (Bethnal Green, T. Ham.). Named in 1884 when Mowlems, civil engineering contractors, were already active in building streets, paving them and constructing sewerage systems.

Moxon Street W1 (Marylebone, Cit. West.). Formerly Paradise Street, from the old public burial ground at the W end, now a garden. The name was changed in 1937 to avoid confusion with other 'Paradise' street names. Moxon was the name of an apartment block in the street.

Mulberry Street E1 (Whitechapel, T. Ham.). Recalls an attempt to grow mulberry trees, on which to breed silk worms for the local silk-weaving industry; the industry began to decline in the second half of the 19th century.

Mulberry Walk SW3 (Chelsea, Ken. Chel.). Lord Wharton's Park, said to have been part of the estate belonging to Sir Thomas More, lay here. It was planted with mulberry trees in 1721 as part of a project to produce silk (*see* **Park Walk**).

Mulgrave Road SW6 (Fulham, Hammersmith). Edmund Sheffield, Earl of Mulgrave (*d* 1646), lived in Hammersmith. He was one of the signatories to the agreement founding the church of St Paul in Hammersmith as a chapel of ease for Fulham in 1631. His epitaph describes his 'valiant services' against the *Armada* in 1588. A later Lord Mulgrave (*d* 1831) occupied Little Mulgrave House, which lay S of this road.

Mulready Street NW8 (Marylebone, Cit. West.). Commemorates the artist William Mulready (1786–1863), genre and narrative painter who did much work designing children's books; he was also the designer of the first penny-post envelope.

Mumford Court EC2 (Cit. Lond.). First recorded as Munford's Court (1677) and Montford's Court (1720). Named from the builder or property owner.

Mundania Road SE22 (Peckham Rye, Southwark). *See* **Marmora Road**.

Munden Street W14 (Hammersmith). The Munden family lived at Colehill Cottage (*see* **Colehill Lane**) in Fulham, which Richard Munden, mariner, bought in 1667. The family lived there until *c* 1720.

Mund Street W14 (W Kensington, Hammersmith). Built by Eli Griffin and Ed*mund* Wood. Eli Street ran N from this street before re-development.

Munster Road SW6 (Fulham, Hammersmith). Munster House which stood here was demolished in 1895. The name is probably a corruption of Mustowe, from an old word for a meeting place.

Munster Square NW1 (Regent's Park, Camden). Part of John Nash's Regent's Park scheme (*see* **Regent Street**). The Regent's brother the Duke of Clarence was also Earl of Munster.

Murdock Street SE15 (Old Kent Road, Southwark). At the entrance to the South Eastern Gas Works; William Murdock, Scottish engineer and inventor, discovered coal-gas which he began distilling in the 1790s. He first used it successfully for lighting in 1803.

Muschamp Road SE15 (Peckham Rye, Southwark). Named from the Muschamp family, prominent in Camberwell and Peckham from *c*1500 to *c*1670 when their estates were bought by Sir Thomas Bond. There is a Muschamp memorial window in the church of St Giles, Camberwell.

Muscovy Street EC3 (Cit. Lond.). In the 16th century English merchants trading in Russia as The Muscovy Company were encouraged by Elizabeth I. They had a charter in 1555 from Mary I, and were given a monopoly of trade with Russia which lasted until 1698.

Museum Street WC1 (Bloomsbury, Camden). Approaches the main entrance of the British Museum; the collection dates from 1753, the building on this site from 1823.

Muswell Hill N10 (Haringey). Approaches the place known for its 'mossy well or spring' on a hill.

Myatt Road SW9 (Camberwell, Lambeth). Myatt's Fields nearby were named from Joseph Myatt, tenant and market-gardener. The fields were given to the London County Council as public open space by William Minet in 1889.

Myddelton Square EC1 (Islington). Sir Hugh Myddelton devised and engineered the New River which was cut from Hertfordshire to nearby New River Head in 1609–13 to increase the water supply for London's growing population. The New River now ends in reservoirs in Stoke Newington. **Myddelton Street** is nearby.

Mylne Street EC1 (Islington). Built on land belonging to the New River Company (*see* **Myddelton Square**). Robert Mylne (*d* 1811) was architect, surveyor and engineer to the company and also architect of the first Blackfriars Bridge (1760–9); his son William Chadwell Mylne (*d* 1863) was architect and engineer to the company and also architect of St Mark's church, Myddelton Square, in 1827.

N

Nag's Head Court EC1 (Golden Lane, Islington). The *Nag's Head Inn* here is recorded in 1761.

Nairne Grove SE24 (Camberwell, Southwark). Named from a Camberwell family; Captain Nairne (*d* 1866) was in the service of the East India Company and a director of Pacific and Orient Lines. As a midshipman he had fought at Copenhagen under Nelson in 1801. His son Perceval Nairne, solicitor, was an active churchman, and a School Board manager. He was Honorary Secretary of the Green Coat School Charity from 1869. He was knighted in 1915 and died in 1921.

Nairn Street E14 (Poplar, T. Ham.). *See* **Leven Road**.

Nankin Street E14 (Limehouse, T. Ham.). *See* **Oriental Street**.

Nansen Road SW11 (Battersea, Wandsworth). Commemorates Fridtjof Nansen (1861–1930), Norwegian explorer and politician. He led the first expedition across Greenland (1888). In 1895 he travelled further N across polar ice than any previous explorer, reaching 86°14′. Returning to Norway as a popular hero, he entered politics and worked for Norwegian independence from Sweden. When this was achieved (1905) he was the first Norwegian ambassador to London.

Nantes Passage E1 (Spitalfields, T. Ham.). The Edict of Nantes (1598) ensured religious freedom for French Protestants, called Huguenots. Its revocation in 1685 caused many more Huguenots to leave France than had

left since the 16th century. A large community of Huguenot weavers, mainly engaged in the manufacture of patterned silks, grew up in Spitalfields, an area which had already received Flemish Protestant weavers a century before (*see* **Wheeler Street**).

Napier Avenue SW6 (Fulham, Hammersmith). Mark Francis Napier lived at Little Mulgrave House from 1879.

Napier Place W14 (Kensington, Ken. Chel.). Built on the estate surrounding Holland House, acquired by the Fox family in 1768. Caroline Fox married General Sir William Napier, grandson of the second Duke of Richmond, in 1812. Active in the Peninsular Campaign against Napoleon, he published his *History of the War in the Peninsula and in the South of France* in a number of volumes 1828–40. **Napier Close** and **Road** adjoin.

Napier Street SE8 (Deptford, Lewisham). Commemorates Admiral Sir Charles Napier (1786–1860), active in the cause of the queen of Portugal, for whom he won a victory off Cape St Vincent in 1833. **Napier Grove**, Shoreditch, also commemorates him.

Nash Street NW1 (Regent's Park, Camden). John Nash, architect (1752–1835), designed the terraces surrounding Regent's Park as well as the original **Regent Street**.

Nassau Street W1 (Marylebone, Cit. West.). Formerly Suffolk Street, and renamed *c*1818. William V of Orange-Nassau, Prince of Nassau (a small German state) and hereditary Stadtholder of the Netherlands from 1751, was the son of an English princess. In 1795 he fled from the invading French forces to England. In 1815 the Nassau family fortunes were restored when his son, who succeeded him as Prince of Nassau, was also created King of the United Netherlands· and Grand Duke of Luxembourg.

Navarino Road E8 (Hackney). From a sea battle of 1827 during the Greek War of Independence. British, French and Russian ships under Vice-Admiral Codrington destroyed the Turkish fleet in Navarino Bay, in the Morea. **Navarino Grove** adjoins.

Navarre Street EC2 (Bethnal Green, T. Ham.). One of a group with Huguenot associations (*see* **Nantes Passage**). Louis I de Bourbon, Prince de Condé, was a leader of French Protestants. His brother became king-consort of Navarre in N Spain, and his nephew Henry became Henry III of Navarre. After long religious wars Henry became king of France as Henry IV in 1589. He later renounced his Protestant faith and became a Catholic.

Neal Street WC2 (Covent Garden, Camden/Cit. West.). Commemorates Thomas Neale who laid out the Seven Dials circus in 1693; the column in the centre (now removed) had seven facets, each with a dial or face.

Neate Street SE5 (Peckham, Southwark). From the landowner as recorded c1830.

Neathouse Place SW1 (Pimlico, Cit. West.). The original settlement at Pimlico was a group of cottages called the 'Neat Houses'; in the late 17th century they began to provide entertainment for young blades going to the amusement gardens at Ranelagh and Vauxhall (*see* **Pimlico Road**).

Neckinger SE1 (Bermondsey, Southwark). An ancient stream, the Neckinger, ran from Bermondsey Abbey and beyond to the Thames; it is said to have been navigable as far as the abbey. It was one of several tidal streams which provided the water supply for the local tanneries in the 17th century. In 16th-century records it appears as Neckercher; it has been suggested that this derives from neckerchief, describing the stream's looping course.

Nella Road W6 (Fulham, Hammersmith). The name of the builder – Allen – in reverse.

Nelson Passage EC1 (Finsbury, Islington). Off Mora Street, which was formerly called Nelson Street in honour of Admiral Nelson (*see* **Nelson Square**).

Nelson Place N1 (Islington). *See* **Duncan Street**.

Nelson Square SE1 (Southwark). Commemorates Admiral Lord Nelson, killed at the battle of Trafalgar, 21 October 1805. Active in the Mediterranean since the beginning of the French wars, Nelson had contributed to the victory of Cape St Vincent in 1797 and had gone on to destroy the French fleet at Aboukir in 1798. He defeated the Napoleonic forces again at Copenhagen in 1801 and was sent back to the Mediterranean in 1803, where he blockaded the French fleet in Toulon. Trafalgar was the culminating battle, after the French had escaped from the Toulon blockade and joined Spanish ships at Cadiz.

Nepaul Road SW11 (Battersea, Wandsworth). From the Himalayan kingdom which is now normally spelt

Nepal. Named by association with **Cabul Road** and in reflection of British interests in N India and the Himalayan states at the time (1880).

Neptune Street SE16 (Rotherhithe, Southwark). From the *Neptune* public house, recorded here in the 1830s and reflecting local maritime interests.

Netherfield Road SW17 (Tooting, Wandsworth). Built on farmland, of which this plot was a field called the Netherfield.

Netherhall Gardens NW3 (Hampstead, Camden). *See* **Canfield Gardens**. The Maryon-Wilson family held a Sussex property by this name.

Netherton Grove SW10 (Kensington, Ken. Chel.). Built on land belonging to the Gunter family (*see* **Gunter Grove**). Netherton is a place name from Yorkshire, the home county of Colonel Sir Robert Gunter.

Neuchâtel Road SE6 (Forest Hill, Lewisham). *See* **Helvetia Street**.

Nevern Place SW5 (Kensington, Ken. Chel.). *See* **Longridge Road** for this and **Nevern Road** and **Square**.

Nevill Road N16 (Stoke Newington, Hackney). Named in 1863; a builder called William Nevill of Highbury was active at the time.

New Bond Street W1 (Mayfair, Cit. West.). *See* **Old Bond Street.**

New Bridge Street EC4 (Cit. Lond.). Made in 1765 when Blackfriars Bridge, to which it leads, was newly built. The street covers the Fleet river and its banks S from Ludgate Circus, the site of the old Fleet Bridge. The Fleet river N of the Fleet Bridge had been covered in 1737.

New Burlington Street W1 (Mayfair,

Cit. West.). *See* **Old Burlington Street** for this and **New Burlington Mews** and **Place**.

Newbury Street EC1 (Cit. Lond.). Formerly New Street, a 17th-century street which was renamed to avoid confusion *c*1890.

Newcastle Close EC4 (Cit. Lond.). Now a cul-de-sac E from Farringdon Street; before Holborn Viaduct station was built it was a route to the old Seacoal Lane and was called Castle Street, probably from an inn sign; this was changed to the New Castle Close.

Newcastle Court EC4 (Cit. Lond.). Site of a house belonging to the Duke of Buckingham in 1677; this passed to a City alderman, John Lethulier. By 1732 the house was recorded as demolished and replaced by a small development called 'Castle's New Court'.

Newcastle Place W2 (Paddington, Cit. West.). *See* **Hall Place**.

Newcastle Row EC1 (Clerkenwell, Islington). Built in the 1790s on the site of Newcastle House. The convent of St Mary, Clerkenwell, which stood here, passed to the Cavendish family at the dissolution of 1539. William Cavendish was made Duke of Newcastle in 1664, and the main house of the convent became known as Newcastle House.

New   Cavendish   Street W1 (Marylebone, Cit. West.). *See* **Cavendish Square**.

New Change EC4 (Cit. Lond.). Modern street replacing (on a slightly different line) the street called Old Change, the site of a Plantagenet royal exchange where plate and bullion were received to be minted as coins.

New Charles Street EC1 (Goswell Road, Islington). Formerly adjoined Charles Street which was named in 1682 after Charles II.

New Church Road SE5 (Peckham, Southwark). Approaches the church of St George, built for a new parish formed in 1825 (*see* **St George's Way**).

Newcombe Gardens SW16 (Streatham, Lambeth). Adjoins **Pendennis Road**, both named from popular novels by William Makepeace Thackeray (*d* 1863). Both novels were originally published in instalments, *The Newcombes* 1853–5 and *Pendennis* 1848–50.

Newcomen Street SE1 (Southwark). Developed from an inn-yard leading to the *Axe and Bottle*. By the 17th century this yard contained a number of small tenements. Mrs Jonathon Newcomen left property here in 1675 to pay for a local charity. The Newcomen Charity let out building leases from 1677, but the street proper was not begun until 1736. In 1774 the street was called King Street, since the old *Axe and Bottle* had gone and the main inn on what was now a through road to Snow's Fields was *The King's Head*. In 1879 the street was renamed after the Newcomen charity.

New Compton Street WC2 (Soho, Cit. West.). *See* **Old Compton Street**.

New Court EC4 (Cit. Lond.). Built off St Swithin's Lane *c*1700 and named as a new development.

Newcourt Street NW8 (St John's Wood, Cit. West.). Originally New Street, one of many, and altered to avoid confusion.

New Coventry Street WC2 (Cit. West.). *See* **Coventry Street**.

New Cross Road SE14 (Lewisham). Approaches the important crossroads at the place now called New Cross; this was the junction of the main route from London into Kent (down the Old Kent Road) and a cross-route from Greenwich into Surrey through Camberwell.

Newell Street E14 (Poplar, T. Ham.). Commemorates James Edgar Newell, Stepney borough councillor 1903–30.

New End NW3 (Hampstead, Camden). An early 18th-century hamlet so-called to distinguish it from the older settlements at N, S and W 'ends' of the parish.

Newgate Street EC1 (Cit. Lond.). Led to the New Gate which was made to take the extra traffic during the building of St Paul's Cathedral in 1087. Mediaeval gatehouses, being strongly fortified, were often used as prisons or lock-ups, and Newgate had become a prison by the time of King John (1199–1216). It was taken down in the 1770s when a new prison building was built on the S side of the street; this was demolished in 1902 to make way for the Central Criminal Court.

Newick Road E5 (Clapton, Hackney). *See* **Powell Road**.

Newington Butts SE11 (Newington, Lambeth/Southwark). Led to the 'butts' between main roads at the NE end of this street; the name first appears in 1512, and is thought to describe, not archers' butts but an odd, triangular bit of land. Newington means 'new village'; this village was new *c*1200.

Newington Causeway SE1 (Newington, Southwark). Road to the former village of Newington (*see* **Newington Butts**). Originally part of the Roman Stane Street (from

Chichester to London) and forming the only firm crossing of the marshes which covered the area betwen the present New Kent Road and Great Dover Street. The street was first called 'Causeway' in the 18th century.

Newington Green N1, N16 (Islington). Original green of a hamlet at the S end of Newington parish (*see* **Stoke Newington High Street**).

New Inn Passage WC2 (Aldwych, Cit. West.). The New Inn, new by comparison with **Clement's Inn** which is nearby, was opened for chancery lawyers c1490.

New Inn Yard EC2 (Shoreditch, Hackney). Originally ran from Shoreditch High Street W to the present New Inn Broadway (formerly Holywell Court), and served an inn built on part of the former Holywell Priory. **New Inn Square** and **Street** are nearby.

New Kent Road SE1 (Walworth, Southwark). Laid out from 1751 as a continuation of St George's Road to make a link with the **Old Kent Road**.

New King's Road SW6 (Fulham, Hammersmith). Route followed by the court from the 17th century onwards as the most direct way from London to Hampton Court Palace; they crossed the river by a ferry at the point where Putney Bridge now stands.

New King Street SE8 (Deptford, Lewisham). Replaces King Street and adjoins Prince Street. Royal visits to Deptford were frequent while the town had a royal dockyard; the yard was open from 1513 until 1869.

New London Street EC3 (Cit. Lond.). *See* **London Street**.

Newman's Row WC2 (Lincoln's Inn, Camden). Formerly Partridge Alley, probably from a sign. The street was built by Arthur Newman from 1657, on a building lease transferred to him from William Newton (*see* **Newton Street**).

New North Road N1 (Islington). Built c1812–13 as a new route to the north between Old Street and Highbury.

New North Street WC1 (Theobald's Road, Camden). *See* **Old North Street**.

New Oxford Street WC1 (St Giles, Camden). Cut in 1845–7 through slum lanes around St Giles, to link **Oxford Street**, which it extended, with Holborn.

New Park Road SW2 (Clapham, Lambeth). Ran along the SE boundary of what was then the new Clapham Park estate, developed from 1830 by Thomas Cubitt.

Newport Place WC2 (Shaftesbury Avenue, Cit. West.). *See* **Little Newport Street**. Before the formation of Shaftesbury Avenue in 1883–6 the N end was called Hayes Court; it was built c1683 by Nicholas Barbon, whose wife was the former Margaret Hayes.

New Quebec Street W1 (Marylebone, Cit. West.). *See* **Old Quebec Street**.

New Road E1 (Whitechapel, T. Ham.). So-called when newly laid out c1740–60 along the line of 17th-century Civil War ramparts (*see* **Cannon Street Road**).

New Row WC2 (Covent Garden, Cit. West.). Originally New Street, from the time of building in 1635–7 as a new replacement for a narrow alley.

New Spring Gardens Walk SE11 (Vauxhall, Lambeth). Site of part of the Vauxhall Spring Gardens or Vauxhall Gardens; a 'spring' was a plantation. Vauxhall Gardens opened c1660 as a pleasure garden. It became disreputable in time but, at its best, it was an extravagantly splendid place with tree-lined promenades, ornate follies, music, banquets and spectacular entertainments. The gardens closed in 1859.

New Square WC2 (Lincoln's Inn, Camden). Called Lincoln's Inn New Court in 1720, and Little Lincoln's Inn in 1682 when it was added to the existing courts.

New Street EC2 (Cit. Lond.). So-called when newly built as a rebuilding of a former alley in the 18th century (off Bishopsgate).

New Street Square EC4 (Cit. Lond.). Originally part of New Street which was new in the mid-17th century; New Street ran W out of Shoe Lane along the present **Little New Street**, and then N through the present square. **Great New Street** originally ran N along the W side of the square. **New Street Hill** approaches.

Newton Street WC2 (Covent Garden, Camden). Runs N from Great Queen Street, which was built c1635 by William Newton of Bedfordshire; Newton, a speculative builder, also laid out Lincoln's Inn Fields.

New Union Street EC2 (Cit. Lond.). First recorded in 1848, formerly a narrow court called Gun Alley, of which the derivation is unknown. The union in this case was between the two adjacent streets, Moor Lane and Moorfields.

Nicholas Glebe SW17 (Tooting Graveney, Wandsworth). Built on the glebe or clergy land of St Nicholas parish church which stands nearby at the S end of **Church Lane**. The church is first referred to in 1086 as having four acres of land (*see* **Nicholas Lane** and **Camberwell Glebe**).

Nicholas Lane EC4 (Cit. Lond.). The parish church of St Nicholas Acon stood on the corner with Lombard Street. Acon is a corruption of Haakon, the Danish patron for whom the church was built, probably in the 11th century. St Nicholas was a Bishop of Myra imprisoned for his faith by the Roman Emperor Diocletian (284–305). He became the patron saint of Russia and of the young, his name being corrupted in England to Santa Claus.

Nichol's Square E2 (Hackney Road, Hackney). Commemorates a resident, John Nichols (*d* 1826), author, editor of the *Gentleman's Magazine*; his son John (*d* 1863) became its proprietor.

Niederwald Road SE26 (Forest Hill, Lewisham). From a German property owner. Forest Hill had a large German community in the late 19th century. A German Lutheran church was founded in Dacres Road in 1875. Dietrich Bonhoeffer was pastor of the church 1933–5. He returned to Germany, where he opposed National Socialism; he was shot in a concentration camp on 9 April 1945.

Nigel Playfair Avenue W6 (Hammersmith). The actor-manager Sir Nigel Playfair (1874–1934) staged extremely successful revivals of classic drama at the Lyric Theatre, Hammersmith, after 1920. The best known is *The Beggar's Opera* (1920).

Nightingale Lane SW4, SW12 (Clapham Common, Wandsworth). A former country lane noted for the song of nightingales. **Nightingale Walk** adjoins.

Nile Terrace SE15 (Peckham, Southwark). *See* **Trafalgar Avenue**.

Nine Elms Lane SW8 (Battersea, Wandsworth). An old lane which formerly ran across open country past nine elm trees, on the route to Battersea Fields from Vauxhall.

Noble Street EC2 (Cit. Lond.). Probably the surname of an early property owner.

Noel Street W1 (Soho, Cit. West.). Built on the estate of William Bentinck, Duke of Portland, in the 1740s. The duke's mother was the former Lady Elizabeth Noel; she was responsible for the development of the estate during the duke's minority.

Norbroke Street W12 (Wormwood Scrubs, Hammersmith). Michael Norbroke or Northburgh was Bishop of London 1355–61 and, as such, held the manor of Hammersmith.

Norcroft Gardens SE22 (Dulwich, Southwark). Revival of an old place name. Norcroft or Northcroft was a small plot of land in Dulwich manor.

Norland Square W11 (Notting Hill, Ken. Chel.). Corruption of Northland; formerly called the North Lands or N portion of the manor of Abbot's Kensington. **Norland Place** approaches, **Norland Road** is nearby.

Normand Road W14 (Fulham, Hammersmith). Approaches Normand Park, part of the estate of Normand House, built 1664 and used as a hospital and a lunatic asylum. The house is now demolished.

Norman Street EC1 (Finsbury, Islington). Built on land leased by the Ironmongers' Company to William Norman, bricklayer, in 1759. **Norman's Buildings** adjoin.

Norris Street SW1 (St James's, Cit. West.). Godfrye Norris in 1661 obtained a lease of property here from the Earl of St Albans's trustees; this consisted of a yard with four houses and the site of the future St James's Market.

Northampton Square EC1 (Clerkenwell, Islington). Built *c*1800 on land belonging to the Marquis of Northampton. **Northampton Buildings**, **Road** and **Row** are nearby (*see* **Compton Road**).

Northampton Street N1 (Canonbury, Islington). *See* **Compton Road**. **Northampton Grove** and **Park** are nearby.

North Audley Street W1 (Mayfair, Cit. West.). Part of the estate laid out on land belonging to Lord Grosvenor in 1720–50. The Grosvenors acquired the Mayfair estate through the marriage of Sir Thomas Grosvenor to Mary Davies, heiress of Hugh Audley (*see* **Davies Street**). **South Audley Street** adjoins.

Northburgh Street EC1 (Clerkenwell, Islington). Built on land formerly part of the Charterhouse monastery, founded in London by Michael de Northburgh, Bishop of London, in 1371 (*see* **Charterhouse Street**).

North End Road W14, SW6 (North End, Hammersmith). Led from Fulham to a hamlet called the North End (i.e. of the parish of Fulham) which lay approximately at the junction with the present Lillie Road.

Northfields SW18 (Wandsworth). Built on the North Field, one of the former common fields of the mediaeval village of Wandsworth: **Southfields Road** lies on the South Field, S of the village street (present West Hill and Wandsworth High Street).

Northington Street WC1 (Theobald's Road, Camden). Commemorates Robert Henley (*d* 1772) Lord Chancellor 1761–6 and Lord President of the Council, who was created Viscount Henley and Earl of Northington in 1764.

North Pole Road W10, (N Kensington, Hammersmith/Ken. Chel.). From the *North Pole* public house here, a 19th-century tavern.

North Row W1 (Mayfair, Cit. West.). Northernmost street in the Grosvenor estate.

North Street SW4 (Clapham, Lambeth). Runs N from Clapham old town; formerly Nag's Head Lane, from the public house at the junction with Wandsworth Road.

North Tenter Street E1 (Whitechapel, T. Ham.). *See* **East Tenter Street**.

Northumberland Alley EC3 (Cit. Lond.). Site of Northumberland House, London house of the Percies, earls of Northumberland, in the 15th century; in the 16th it was let out in tenements.

Northumberland Avenue WC2 (Charing Cross, Cit. West.). Site of Northumberland House, built *c*1605 for the Earl of Northampton and later passing by marriage to the earls of Northumberland. The house was demolished in the 1870s.

Northumberland Park N17 (Haringey). At the junction of this road and High Road, Tottenham, stood the Black House which was owned by Sir Hugh Smithson, ancestor of the Duke of Northumberland.

Northwick Terrace NW8 (St John's Wood, Cit. West.). *See* **Lyons Place**. John Rushout, Second Baron

Northwick (*d* 1859), was a governor of Harrow School from 1801.

Norton Folgate E1 (Shoreditch, Hackney). Site of the North Tun or north town – north of the city, that is – belonging to the Folgate family. **Folgate Street** adjoins.

Norwood High Street SE27 (Norwood, Lambeth). The high or principal street of Norwood, called Northwode in the 13th century. The North Wood extended across what was then N Surrey.

Notley Street SE5 (Camberwell, Southwark). Changed in 1889 from John Street and John's Terrace. John Notley, builder, flourished in S London in the 1860s, and later Notleys served as Camberwell vestrymen.

Nottingham Court WC2 (Covent Garden, Camden). Heneage Finch, created Earl of Nottingham in 1681, had a house in the parish, in Great Queen Street, where he died. A lawyer of the Inner Temple, he was Solicitor General in 1660, Attorney General 1670–3 and Lord Chancellor from 1675. He died in 1682. His son Daniel, Second Earl of Nottingham, was First Lord of the Admiralty 1680–4.

Nottingham Street W1 (Marylebone, Cit. West.). Built on the estate of the dukes of Portland who also held properties in Nottinghamshire. **Bingham Place**, from a Nottinghamshire village, is named by association.

Notting Hill Gate W11 (Ken. Chel.). Formerly part of the Uxbridge Road; renamed from a turnpike gate. Notting Hill is 'the hill belonging to Cnotta's people'.

Nuding Close SE13 (Lewisham). Originally Nuding Street, it became

Nuding Road in 1896. Henry Nuding sat on the Greenwich District Board of Works in the 1890s.

Nugent Terrace NW8 (St John's Wood, Cit. West.). Commemorates Field Marshal Sir George Nugent (1757–1849); he served in the American War of Independence and, on his return, was able to combine an army career with politics. He was MP for Buckingham 1790–1800 and 1819–32, mainly through the patronage of the first Marquis of Buckingham, to whom he was related.

Nun Court EC2 (Cit. Lond.). Probably from the builder; first recorded in 1720.

Nunhead Lane SE15 (Peckham, Southwark). Approaches Nunhead Green, so-called from a 17th-century (and probably earlier) inn called *The Nun's Head*. **Nunhead Grove** also approaches.

Nursery Row SE17 (Walworth, Southwark). *See* **Townley Street**.

Nutbrook Street SE15 (Peckham Rye, Southwark). Revival of an old local field name.

Nutford Place W1 (Marylebone, Cit. West.). On the Portman estate. The Portmans held property at the village of Nutford in Dorset (*see* **Portman Square**).

Nutley Terrace NW3 (Hampstead, Camden). *See* **Canfield Gardens**. The Maryon-Wilson family held property at Nutley in Sussex.

Nuttall Street N1 (Hoxton, Hackney). Named in 1878 in place of King's Road and Axe's Place. This street has had a sequence of names. The first-known is Webbe's Lane or White Hart Lane, in the 16th century. It is possible that Webbe was a landlord of the *White Hart* inn there. In the 17th century it was certainly named from a tenant of the *White Hart* called Haddon. In the 18th century it was called Dirty Lane. King's Road was a patriotic improvement of this; the other names are obscure.

Nyon Grove SE6 (Forest Hill, Lewisham). *See* **Helvetia Street**.

O

Oakeshott Avenue N6 (Highgate, Camden). John Oakeshott lived in Highgate in the 1870s; he was a doctor, a member of the local Scientific and Literary Institute.

Oakey Lane SE1 (Lambeth). Site of the Wellington Mills, now demolished, built for the manufacture of emery paper in 1873 by J. Oakey and Sons.

Oakfield Court N8 (Crouch End, Haringey). Built on the S side of an old manorial field called the Oak Field.

Oakhill Avenue NW3 (Hampstead, Camden). Together with **Oak Hill Park** and **Oak Hill Way**, this is the site of a mediaeval oak wood belonging to the manor of Hampstead.

Oakley Place SE1 (Old Kent Road, Southwark). Built to the rear of a terrace called Oakley Terrace on the Old Kent Road; the terrace was built c1844 but the derivation of its name is not known. The builder was Gurney of Lambeth.

Oakley Square NW1 (Camden Town, Camden). Built on the estate belonging to the dukes of Bedford; Oakley is a village in Bedfordshire, as is Lidlington, where the dukes held property. **Lidlington Place** is nearby.

Oakley Street SW3 (Chelsea, Ken. Chel.). Part of the manor of Chelsea, and built when the manor was owned by the Earl of Cadogan, who was also Lord Cadogan of Oakley. An earl of Cadogan had married the daughter of Hans Sloane, and inherited part of Sloane's estate in 1753 (*see* **Sloane Street**).

Oakmead Road SW12 (Balham, Wandsworth). Built next to the site of a large house called 'Oakmead'.

Oaks Avenue SE19 (Gipsy Hill, Lambeth). The woods covering Gipsy Hill until the 18th century were mainly of pollarded oak.

Oak Tree Road NW8 (St John's Wood, Cit. West.). Follows an old lane which led to a field called the Oak Tree Field.

Oak Village NW5 (Gospel Oak, Camden). A small residential centre near a large oak on the parish boundary between Hampstead and St Pancras, the 'gospel' oak. Names like Gospel Oak indicate particular points on the Rogation Day procession around the parish when, at certain points on the boundaries, the Gospel or Epistle would be read and prayers would be said.

Oakwood Court W14 (Kensington, Ken. Chel.). Built on the site of a house called 'Oak Lodge' which stood on Addison Road.

Oat Lane EC2 (Cit. Lond.). This is recorded in the 16th century as Oatelane, the lane where oats were sold.

Observatory Gardens W8 (Kensington, Ken. Chel.). The astronomer Sir James South built an observatory here in 1826, on what was then part of the garden of Phillimore House (*see* **Phillimore Gardens**).

Occupation Road SE17 (Walworth, Southwark). Formerly an access to a strip of land occupied, for cultivation, by a villager of the manor of Walworth; occupation rights and right of access had to go together.

Odger Street SW11 (Battersea, Wandsworth). *See* **Reform Street**.

Oglander Road SE15 (Camberwell, Southwark). The Grymes family of Peckham were connected by marriage to Sir John Oglander. Thomas Grymes, MP and Deputy Lieutenant of Surrey, married Margaret Moore. Her sister Frances married Sir John in 1606.

Ogle Street W1 (Marylebone, Cit. West.) Built on land belonging to the dukes of Portland who inherited it, by marriage, from Henry Cavendish, Duke of Newcastle, Baron Ogle and Viscount Mansfield. **Mansfield Mews** and **Street** are nearby.

Oil Mill Lane W6 (Hammersmith). On the site of a factory here; East Indian Products opened the Albert Mills for processing oil-seeds *c*1900.

Okeburn Road SW17 (Tooting, Wandsworth). The surrounding manor of Tooting Bec belonged to the Abbey of Bec Hellouin, Normandy, from the 12th century to the 15th; the abbey also held land in Wiltshire, the manor of Okeburn (*see* **Tooting Bec Road**).

Old Bailey EC4 (Cit. Lond.). Street along the old bailey or outwork attached to the City wall; it was called simply The Bailey until the 15th century.

Old Barge House Alley SE1 (Upper Ground, Southwark). *See* **Barge House Street**.

Old Barrack Yard SW1 (Belgravia, Cit. West.). Formerly approached an infantry barracks in Wilton Place, in use before the establishment of Wellington Barracks in Birdcage Walk.

Old Bond Street W1 (Mayfair, Cit. West.). Built *c*1686 on part of the site of the mansion belonging to Edward Hyde, Lord Clarendon, which was demolished in 1683. Sir Thomas Bond was a member of the consortium which developed the land. The street was called Bond Street until its northern continuation was built as **New Bond Street** in 1700–20.

Old Broad Street EC2 (Cit. Lond.). Formerly called Bradestreet (13th century) or the broad street. The mediaeval street extended from the Stocks Market (on the site of the present Mansion House) up the present Threadneedle Street to London Wall; the continuation as far as Liverpool Street was called New Broad Street, a name now transferred to a side street.

Old Brompton Road SW5, SW7 (Kensington, Ken. Chel.). *See* **Brompton Road**.

Old Burlington Street W1 (Mayfair, Cit. West.). Part of the Burlington estate which was laid out between *c*1720 and 1740 on land belonging to the third Earl of Burlington. **New Burlington Street** is nearby, with **New Burlington Mews** and **Place**. **Burlington Gardens** is the name applied to the improved form of an existing lane when the estate was laid out.

Old Castle Street E1 (Whitechapel, T. Ham.). From the *Castle Inn*, which stood in Whitechapel from the 1630s until *c*1730, and was later referred to as the 'Old Castle'.

Old Cavendish Street W1 (Marylebone, Cit. West.). *See* **Cavendish Square**.

Old Change Court EC4 (Cit. Lond.). Built on the site of the S end of the street called Old Change (*see* **New Change**).

Old Church Road E1 (Stepney, T. Ham.). Originally extended N from Commercial Road to Stepney Way, opposite St Dunstan's Church.

Old Church Street SW3 (Chelsea, Ken. Chel.). Chelsea Old Church at the S end of this street is first recorded in the late 13th century. A new parish church dedicated to St Luke was built in 1819.

Old Compton Street W1 (Soho, Cit. West.). Begun in 1677; probably compliments Henry Compton, Bishop of London, who was active in establishing the new parish church of St Anne, Soho, from 1676. **New Compton Street** extends E.

Old Court Place W8 (Kensington, Ken. Chel.). Part of Kensington was called 'The Old Court Suburb' after George III (1760–1820) moved the court away to St James's Palace and Buckingham House. The suburb comprised the immediate surroundings of Kensington Palace, once the court but now the old court.

Old Ford Road E2, E3 (T. Ham.). *See* **Roman Road**.

Old Gloucester Street WC1 (Theobald's Road, Camden). Called Gloucester Street until 1873; approached Queen Square which commemorates Queen Anne. The queen's longest-surviving son was the Duke of Gloucester (1689–1700).

Old Jewry EC2 (Cit. Lond.). Site of a Saxon settlement of Jews, near to the Saxon royal palace which stood near the present Guildhall, and under whose protection the Jews would have settled. Jewish money-lenders could come to London only with royal permission.

Old Kent Road SE1, SE15 (Southwark). The first route from London Bridge to Kent and the Channel ports. London Bridge was the City's only river crossing and the beginning of all routes to the S until the 18th century. Chaucer's pilgrims travelled down the Old Kent Road in the 14th century: pubs along the road had names like 'The Kentish Drover', from the herds of fat cattle driven in to market from Kentish pastures. The importance of this road in linking London to the S coast is enormous (*see* **Great Dover Street**).

Old Manor Yard SW5 (Earl's Court, Ken. Chel.). Site of the mediaeval manor house of Earl's Kensington (*see* **Earl's Court Road**).

Old Marylebone Road NW1 (Marylebone, Cit. West.). *See* **Marylebone High Street**. This old track led from the manor of Lilestone, W Marylebone, to Bayswater, and was formerly called Watery Lane.

Old Mitre Court EC4 (Cit. Lond.). From the *Mitre* tavern here, known to have been frequented by Dr Johnson (1709–84).

Old Montague Street E1 (Whitechapel, T. Ham.). Built c1700 on land belonging to Edward Montague of Horton, Northants, and later his widow Elizabeth. The family was related to the earls of Manchester (*see* **Wentworth Street**).

Old Nichol Street E2 (Bethnal Green, T. Ham.). Site of a field called the Nicholas Field which was part of the mediaeval convent of St John the Baptist, Holywell. The site was built upon during the 17th and 18th centuries and became the centre of a criminals' and outcasts' rookery known as The Nichol. It was mainly to destroy this place that the Arnold Circus development was designed by the London County Council in the 1890s.

Old North Street WC1 (Holborn, Camden). N approach to Red Lion Square; **New North Street** continues N.

Old Palace Yard SW1 (Cit. West.). The Old Palace at Westminster was built by Edward the Confessor c1050 and stood where the Houses of Parliament stand. The palace was greatly altered and extended during the middle ages; the Great Hall which still survives was built 1097–9 and re-roofed c1397. The palace was abandoned as a royal residence by Henry VIII (1509–47); most of it was burnt down in 1834.

Old Paradise Street SE11 (Lambeth). Formerly Paradise Row, a name once commonly given to streets approaching or passing churchyards and burial grounds. The recreation ground E of this street was a burial ground originally; the ground was cleared and the tombstones placed around the walls.

Old Park Avenue SW12 (Clapham Common, Wandsworth). Built on the site of a large house called 'Old Park House'.

Old Pye Street SW1 (Cit. West.). Sir Robert Pye was MP for Westminster under Charles I (1625–49). A street crossing on the line of the present Perkins Rents and Abbey Orchard Street was called New Pye Street.

Old Quebec Street W1 (Marylebone, Cit. West.). The old Quebec Chapel, built here in 1787 to commemorate the earlier battle of Quebec, was used as an army chapel; it was demolished in 1912 and the Church of the Annunciation built on the site. **New Quebec Street** approaches.

Old Queen Street SW1 (Cit. West.). The original street built to approach Queen Square (now **Queen Anne's Gate**) in 1704.

Old Seacoal Lane EC4 (Cit. Lond.). *See* **Seacoal Lane**.

Old Street EC1 (Finsbury, Islington/ Hackney). Formerly called Ealde Street, from OE 'ealde' meaning 'old'; the road is thought to have been a Roman road, part of a route through Bethnal Green to the ford on the River Lea (*see* **Roman Road**).

Old Swan Wharf EC4 (Cit. Lond.). Named from a 14th-century inn, *The Old Swan*, destroyed in the Great Fire of 1666 and afterwards rebuilt. **Old Swan Lane** approaches.

Old Town SW4 (Clapham, Lambeth). Original village of Clapham which grew up around the manor house (*see* **Clapham Manor Street**). The old parish church was by Rectory Road.

Oley Place E1 (Stepney, T. Ham.). Part of an estate belonging to Clare College, Cambridge. The Royalist clergyman Barnabas Oley (1602–86) was president of the college, and largely responsible for its rebuilding from 1638.

O'Meara Street SE1 (Southwark). Commemorates Daniel O'Meara, a priest attached to St George's Roman Catholic Cathedral (*see* **Thomas Doyle Street**).

Ommaney Road SE14 (New Cross, Lewisham). Commemorates Admiral Sir John Ommaney (1773– 1855), active in the battle of Navarino (*see* **Navarino Road**).

Onslow Gardens SW7 (Kensington, Ken. Chel.). Laid out in the mid-19th century on land belonging to the Earl of Onslow. **Onslow Square** adjoins.

Onslow Square SW7 (Kensington, Ken. Chel.). This was part of an 84-acre site left in trust for charity. The trustees perpetuated their names in the streets built upon it. The other streets are: **Cranley Gardens**, after Viscount Cranley, son of Lord Onslow; **Evelyn Gardens**, after the Hon Rev. John Evelyn; **Sydney Close** and **Mews**, after Viscount Sydney; **Sumner Place**, after William Sumner; **Walton Street** , after George Walton Onslow; **Lennox Gardens,** after Charles Lennox, Sixth Duke of Richmond; **Egerton Gardens**, after the Hon. Francis Egerton; **Pelham Crescent** and **Street**, after Henry Pelham, Earl of Chichester. The charity was that set up by Henry Smith, with the original aim of ransoming Christian captives of Turkish pirates.

Oppidans Road NW3 (Primrose Hill, Camden). Built on the Eton College estate (*see* **Eton Avenue**). Oppidans, from the Latin word for town, refers to those Eton College boys that live in the town of Eton.

Orange Street WC2 (Cit. West.). Built 1695–6 as a shorter street between the present Charing Cross Road and St Martin's Street, and named in honour of the ruling house. The present W section was built in 1673 and called James Street after James, Duke of York (later James II). It was during the so-called Bloodless Revolution of 1689 that the Stadtholder of the United Provinces of the Netherlands, William of Orange, was proclaimed king in James's place.

Orchard Place E14 (Poplar, T. Ham.). An inn here called *The Orchard House* gave its name to the whole area W of the River Lea mouth. The inn was demolished *c*1850.

Orchardson Street NW8 (Lisson Grove, Cit. West.). Commemorates the artist Sir William Quiller Orchardson, one-time local resident, who died in 1910.

Orchard Street W1 (Marylebone, Cit. West.). Built on land owned by the Portman family who also held property at Orchard Portman in Somerset (*see* **Portman Square**).

Orde Hall Street WC1 (Holborn, Camden). Mr Orde Hall was a long-serving chairman of the Holborn District Board of the Metropolitan Board of Works. The Metropolitan Board, which preceded the London County Council, began operating in 1856 and was wound up in 1889.

Ordnance Hill NW8 (St John's Wood, Cit. West.). Named from the Royal Horse Artillery barracks here, ordnance being an older term for artillery.

Oriel Place NW3 (Hampstead, Camden). From a Georgian house here, now demolished, which had an oriel window. The oriel, a windowed recess projecting from the wall of a building and usually supported on corbels, was a feature of mediaeval buildings which the 18th-century Gothick style of architecture revived.

Oriental Street E14 (Limehouse, T. Ham.). Chinatown, Limehouse, was settled by Chinese seamen arriving on the tea-trade vessels of the 19th century. Most had sailed with the East India Company. Chinatown was virtually a separate community until World War II. Nearby streets are: **Amoy Place, Canton Street, Mandarin Street, Ming Street, Nankin Street** and **Pekin Street**.

Orme Square W2 (Bayswater, Cit. West.). Laid out in 1816 by Edward Orme, who also built Moscow Road and St Petersburgh Place nearby.

Ormonde Gate SW3 (Chelsea, Ken. Chel.). Built on the site of Ormonde House, the 18th-century home of the Duchess of Ormonde.

Ormond Yard SW1 (St James's, Cit. West.). James Butler, First Duke of Ormonde, had a house on the N side of St James's Square (nos. 9, 10 and 11) adjoining this yard, which he bought in 1682. The second duke conveyed the house to his brother the Earl of Arran on his impeachment as a Jacobite in 1715.

Orsman Road N1 (Hoxton, Hackney). W.J. Orsman founded the Costermongers' Mission in Hoxton Street *c*1880. In 1889 he became London County Council member for Haggerston.

Osbert Street SW1 (Cit. West.). Osbert of Clare, in Suffolk, was prior of the abbey of St Peter's, Westminster from 1136.

Osborn Street E1 (Whitechapel, T. Ham.). The Osborn family inherited the Montague estate (*see* **Old Montague Street**) in the early 19th century. Sir Algernon Osborn was active in local development *c*1904, when he built **Strype Street**.

Oseney Crescent NW5 (Kentish Town, Camden). Built on land inherited by the Dean and Chapter of the cathedral of Christchurch, Oxford, who also had property at Oseney.

Osiers Road SW18 (Wandsworth). Laid out on former osier beds by the Thames which belonged to the parish. Osiers are a type of willow. An osier bed was an important parish asset in the middle ages and later, as the uses of osier rods were many. Not only were they used to make all kinds of baskets as well as hurdles and waggon-sides, but they were extensively used in building. Nearly

all small mediaeval houses had timber frames filled in with woven panels. often of willow, which were daubed with earth plaster.

Osmund Street W12 (Wormwood Scrubs, Hammersmith). Osmund was Bishop of London 802–11 (*see* **Bentworth Road**).

Osnaburgh Street NW1 (Regent's Park, Camden). Part of John Nash's Regent's Park development (*see* **Regent Street**). The regent's brother Frederick, Duke of York and Albany, also held the bishopric of Osnaburgh which had been given to him in his cradle. **Osnaburgh Terrace** adjoins.

Ospringe Road NW5 (Kentish Town, Camden). On the estate belonging to St John's College, Cambridge (*see* **College Lane**). The college was endowed with property at Ospringe, Kent, and at Little Raveley in the former county of Huntingdonshire. **Raveley Street** is nearby.

Ossington Buildings W1 (Marylebone, Cit. West.). Built on land inherited by Charlotte, Viscountess Ossington (*d* 1889), co-heiress of the Cavendish Harley estate (*see* **Ossington Street**).

Ossington Street W2 (Bayswater, Cit. West./Ken. Chel.). Commemorates Viscount Ossington, Speaker of the House of Commons, who died in 1873.

Ossory Road SE1 (Old Kent Road, Southwark). Presumably commemorates Thomas Butler (1634–80). Earl of Ossory and son of the first Duke of Ormonde. Known as Gallant Ossory, he died young and much regretted. John Evelyn the diarist (*see* **Evelyn Street**) said he was 'a brave soldier, a virtuous courtier, a loyal subject, an honest man, a bountiful master and a good Christian'.

Ossulston Street NW1 (St Pancras, Camden). Named c1807, and revives the name of the Saxon Hundred of Ossulston in the county of Middlesex; the Hundred included all the land later incorporated in the London County Council area and lying N of the Thames. The stone is thought to have been a Roman marker; it stood on the site of the present Marble Arch and was appropriated as a territorial mark by a Saxon called Oswulf or Oswald.

Outram Street N1 (King's Cross, Islington). *See* **Havelock Street**.

Outwich Street EC3 (Cit. Lond.). Oteswich or Ottewich, meaning 'Otho's dwellings', was the early mediaeval name for the area of London surrounding the church of St Martin which stood at the E end of Threadneedle Street. A surname arose from this area and is recorded as Oteswich; Outwich is probably a corruption of this name, a citizen who held property in the street.

Oval Road NW1 (Camden Town, Camden). Intended as the centre of an oval development comprising two crescents: Gloucester Crescent was built in the 1830s but its corresponding crescent was finished off by the opening of the railway line in the 1840s.

Oval Way SE1 (Lambeth). *See* **Kennington Oval**.

Overhill Road SE22 (Lordship Lane, Southwark). Built on Ladlands Hill, a natural hill further built up and defended as an early British camp. It is thought to have been used later as a Roman fort on the road S from London and Camberwell. **Underhill Road** goes round the hill.

Owen Street EC1 (St John Street, Islington). Dame Alice Owen founded ten almshouses and a school here in 1609. This fulfilled a vow that she would make a thanks-offering for the preservation of her life when, as a young woman, she had been accidentally shot at by archers practising in Islington fields. An arrow passed through her hat.

Oxendon Street SW1 (Cit. West.). Robert Baker, tailor, who built Piccadilly Hall, left a daughter and heiress Mary (*d* 1638) who married Sir Henry Oxenden. Oxenden acquired a life-interest in the development of the Baker estate, including this street.

Oxenford Street SE15 (Camberwell, Southwark). Commemorates the playwright John Oxenford (1812–77) who was born nearby in Camberwell. His plays began with *My Fellow Clark* and *A Day Well Spent* in 1835; he wrote about 70 in all, as well as opera libretti. He was drama critic of *The Times* from 1850.

Oxford Circus W1 (Cit. West.). Named from **Oxford Street**. Formerly Regent Circus, being part of John Nash's scheme for a new route up **Regent Street** to Regent's Park.

Oxford Court EC4 (Cit. Lond.). A large house here, formerly Church property, belonged to the earls of Oxford in the 16th century.

Oxford Square W2 (Bayswater, Cit. West.). *See* **Cambridge Square**.

Oxford Street W1 (Cit. West.). Formerly Tyburn Road, as leading to Tyburn Gibbet which stood on the site of the mediaeval hamlet of Tyburn near present Marble Arch. The street was developed from c1720 as part of an estate belonging to the Earl of Oxford, Edward Harley.

P

Pace Place E1 (Stepney, T. Ham.). Richard Pace, vicar of Stepney 1519–27, became Secretary of State to Henry VIII. He returned to Stepney in retirement and was buried in St Dunstan's parish church.

Packington Street N1 (Islington). Built on an estate bequeathed to the Clothmakers' Company by Dame Anne Packington; her will of 1559 left the company the copyhold of 23 acres in the St Paul's prebend manor. **Dame Street** is nearby.

Padbury Court E2 (Bethnal Green, T. Ham.). A modern name, probably commemorating the Rev. Joseph F. Padbury, priest of St Mary's and St Michael's Roman Catholic church in Commercial Road in the 1860s and 1870s.

Paddenswick Road W6 (Hammersmith). Corruption of Palyngswick, the name of the mediaeval manor estate through which the road ran. The manor belonged to Alice Perrers (*d* 1401) mistress of Edward III (*see* **Perrers Road**). The site of the house is now in Ravenscourt Park. The old name comes from OE 'Palyngewyk', meaning the farm of Palla's people.

Paddington Green W2 (Cit. West.). The original village green of Paddington; the name means Pedda's or Paeda's settlement.

Paddington Street W1 (Marylebone, Cit. West.). Remnant of an old way from the parish church of St Marylebone to Paddington village.

Page Street SW1 (Cit. West.).

William Page was head of nearby Westminster School 1814–19.

Paget Street EC1 (Goswell Road, Islington). Sir James Paget (1814–99) was elected surgeon to the free clinic in **Friend Street** in 1841. He was probably the most distinguished surgeon and pathologist of his day, and was surgeon-extraordinary to Queen Victoria from 1858.

Pagnell Street SE14 (New Cross, Lewisham). Possibly a corruption of Paganell. Under Henry III (1216–72) the Abbot of Ghent granted his manors of Lewisham and Greenwich to Robert de Baunton of Lee and his heirs. Baunton's daughter Juliana, her husband William de Paganell and their son Fulke were the immediate heirs.

Pakenham Street WC1 (Gray's Inn Road, Islington). Built by the third Lord Calthorpe (*see* **Calthorpe Street**) who held an estate at Pakenham and another at Ampton, both in Suffolk. **Ampton Street** is nearby.

Palace Court W2 (Bayswater, Cit. West.). Named from nearby Kensington Palace, which lies S.

Palace Gate W8 (Kensington, Ken. Chel.). Approaches the Palace Gate into Kensington Gardens and the grounds of Kensington Palace.

Palace Street SW1 (Victoria, Cit. West.). *See* **Buckingham Palace Road**.

Palatine Road N16 (Stoke Newington, Hackney). Protestant refugees from the German state called the Palatinate were accepted by the parish and settled here in 1709.

Palewell Park SW14 (Sheen, R. upon T.). Site of a house, Palewell Lodge (*see* **Gilpin Avenue**).

Palissy Street E2 (Bethnal Green, T. Ham.). One of a series, around Arnold Circus, commemorating the Huguenot connection with this area (*see* **Nantes Passage**). Bernard Palissy was a potter and enameller of Huguenot faith. He worked in Paris from 1566 under the patronage of the royal family, making ware decorated with natural forms: fish, reptiles, leaves etc, modelled from life. He glazed his pots in exceptionally rich colours.

Palliser Road W14 (Baron's Court, Hammersmith). On an estate developed by Sir William Palliser, inventor of guns and other weapons, MP for Taunton from 1880 until his death in 1882. Sir William was the son of Wray Palliser of Comeragh, County Waterford, in Ireland. He had two brothers: John, an explorer who travelled in N America, and Wray Gledstane, a naval officer. In 1868 Sir William married Anna Perham. **Comeragh Road**, **Gledstane's Road** and **Perham Road** are on the estate.

Pall Mall SW1 (Cit. West.). Laid out in the late 17th century on the site of an alley where the game of pall-mall (similar to croquet) had been played (*see* **Mall, The**).

Palmer Place N7 (Holloway Road, Islington). S. Lewis, in his *History and Topography of Islington*, says Palmer was a treasurer of Christ's Hospital. Local benefactors, including Dame Alice Owen, entrusted Christ's Hospital with the payment of alms in the parish of St Mary, Islington. These payments were made by the Christ's Hospital treasurer.

Palmerston Road NW6 (W Hampstead, Camden). Commemorates the Victorian statesman Henry John Temple, Viscount Palmerston, who died in 1865. He is best remembered as Foreign Secretary (1830–41, 1846–51) and Prime Minister (1855 and 1859–65). His early work for the protection of independent states was followed by a later period when diplomacy was replaced by gunboats. **Palmerston Road** in Sheen runs through the family estate of Temple Grove which he inherited.

Palmer Street SW1 (Cit. West.). The Rev. James Palmer founded almshouses here in 1656; they were demolished and incorporated into the Westminster United Almshouses in 1881.

Pancras Lane EC4 (Cit. Lond.). The mediaeval church of St Pancras stood here, in what was formerly called Needlars Lane (*see* **Pancras Road**).

Pancras Road NW1 (St Pancras, Camden). Passes the old church of the parish of St Pancras. The saint was a Roman Christian martyred at the age of 14 for defying the emperor Diocletian. **St Pancras Way** approaches. This and Pancras Road together form an old route called The King's Road from Gray's Inn and the City to Hampstead and Highgate.

Panmure Road SE26 (Sydenham, Lewisham). *See* **Fransfield Road**.

Panton Street SW1 (Cit. West.). Built 1671 for Colonel Thomas Panton, property speculator.

Panyer Alley EC4 (Cit. Lond.). A brewhouse here called the Panyer (basket) is recorded in the 15th century.

Paradise Road SW4 (Stockwell, Lambeth). Built on part of a seven-acre field of the old manor of Stockwell, called Paradise field (*see* **Paradise Street**).

Paradise Street SE16 (Bermondsey, Southwark). A house called 'Paradise' is recorded as standing here in 1631; the street was called Paradise Row in the 18th century. Paradise usually referred either to a closed garden or to a burial place.

Paradise Walk SW3 (Chelsea, Ken. Chel.). Leads off **Royal Hospital Road** which was originally Paradise Row (*see* **Paradise Street**).

Paragon Road E9 (Hackney). Named from a 19th-century terrace of houses at the NE end called The Paragon.

Paragon Row SE17 (Walworth, Southwark). *See* **Searles Road**. This street was built leading E off Rodney Road, with nothing but open ground between it and the Paragon Crescent on New Kent Road.

Pardoner Street SE1 (Southwark). Commemorates the Pardoner, one of Chaucer's pilgrims who travelled from the *Tabard Inn* in Southwark to Canterbury. The mediaeval pardoner sold the Church's pardons for sins, one of numerous financial transactions which paved the way for the rise of Protestantism.

Pardon Street EC1 (Clerkenwell, Islington). The Pardon Chapel and Churchyard lay S of Great Sutton Street and N of the Charterhouse. Ralph de Stratford, Bishop of London, bought the land in 1349 to provide a consecrated burial ground for victims of the Black Death and a place of prayer for the pardon and repose of their souls. The impact of the Black Death on London can hardly be exaggerated; the churchyard is said to have received 200 bodies daily, most of whom had died without receiving the last rites. The place later became a burial ground for suicides and those dying by execution.

Parfrey Street W6 (Fulham, Hammersmith). Developed by Smith, Parfrey and Co. of Fulham Palace Road.

Paris Garden SE1 (Southwark). The mediaeval manor of Wideflete or Wythefleet (willow stream) was also called Paris or Parish Garden. Edward II took the 'mills of Widflete with a garden called the Paris Garden' from the Knights Templar in 1313. The derivation is obscure, but is possibly from Old French *pareil*, an enclosure. The land extended S from the river to the present Boundary Row and Surrey Row. The manor house and its immediate grounds became a pleasure garden in the 16th century (*see* **Hopton Street**).

Park, The N6 (Hornsey, Haringey). Part of the site of Hornsey Great Park, the estate surrounding the manor house of Hornsey. The house belonged to the bishops of London until the 16th century; it was called 'Hornsey Park' or 'Hornsey Lodge'. **Bishop's Road** and **Bloomfield Road** adjoin.

Park Crescent W1 (Regent's Park, Cit. West.). Leads to **Park Square**, part of John Nash's Regent's Park scheme (*see* **Regent Street**).

Parker Street WC2 (Covent Garden, Camden). Called Parker's Lane in the 17th century from Philip Parker, a local resident; he is mentioned in a survey of 1625.

Park Hall Road SE21 (Dulwich, Lambeth/Southwark). Hall Place, manor house of Dulwich manor, stood here until its demolition (for building development) in 1882.

Parklands Road SW16 (Furzedown, Wandsworth). Built on the site of a house of that name.

Park Lane W1 (Mayfair, Cit. West.). Bounds Hyde Park, which was enclosed as a royal park by Henry VIII (1509–47) and opened to the public by James I (1603–25). **Park Street** runs parallel. The street was once a lane directly overlooking the park; the dual carriage-way which has destroyed this relationship is modern.

Park Place Gardens W2 (Paddington, Cit. West.). Together with Park Place Villas, sole evidence of a Victorian residential building scheme for a 'park' style of development; it seems that it never materialised (*see* **Hanover Park**).

Park Square W1 (Regent's Park, Cit. West.). *See* **Park Crescent.**

Park Street SE1 (Southwark). Built on the park of the bishops of Winchester which lay W of Winchester House (*see* **Winchester Walk**). The street incorporates an old path called Maid Lane (derivation unknown) which ran parallel to Bankside and another called Deadman's Place (running S and SE) which crossed a burial ground now part of the Anchor Brewery site.

Park Walk SW10 (Chelsea, Ken. Chel.). Runs along the W boundary of Lord Wharton's Park, which stretched between the present King's Road and Fulham Road and covered about 40 acres. The park survived into the 18th century (*see* **Mulberry Walk**). **Park Gardens** adjoins.

Parliament Court E1 (Spitalfields, T. Ham.). Unknown, built in the 1680s on part of the old artillery ground (*see* **Artillery Lane**) and recorded as Parliament Alley in 1746. This may reflect a tradition that Parliamentary forces first enlisted London troops on the artillery ground at the beginning of the Civil War in 1642.

Parliament Hill NW3 (Hampstead, Camden). Leads to a hilly part of Hampstead Heath said to have been a rallying point for the Chartist movement. The People's Charter of 1838 advocated, among other things, annual parliaments, universal male suffrage, vote by ballot and reform of the status and qualifications of MPs. Another tradition says that the supporters of Guy Fawkes gathered here, in 1605, in the hope of watching Parliament burn.

Parmiter Street E2 (Bethnal Green, T. Ham.). Thomas Parmiter, by his will of 1681, gave his estates in Suffolk to provide six almshouses and a school for ten children at Bethnal Green. These were built *c*1722 at Cambridge Heath on land later bought by the Great Eastern Railway Company. Almshouses were built in this road in 1838, together with a school which moved to Approach Road in 1887. The charity owned considerable property in the Cambridge Heath area.

Parnell Road E3 (Bow, T. Ham.). Named in 1873, probably from the Rev. Richard Parnell of St Stephen's Anglican church, Tredegar Road. He was succeeded in the 1880s by the Rev. Thomas Ranger Lawrence. **Lawrence Road** is nearby. **St Stephen's Road** approached the church.

Parry Street SW8 (Vauxhall, Lambeth). Sir Thomas Parry, Chancellor of the Duchy of Lancaster (*d* 1616), held Copt Hall, a house next to Vauxhall manor house nearby.

Parsifal Road NW6 (W Hampstead, Camden). Named in 1882 from

Wagner's last opera, *Parsifal*, which was performed in that year.

Parson's Green SW6 (Fulham, Hammersmith). A green named from a rectory or parsonage which stood on the W side, first recorded in the late 16th century but probably older. **Parson's Green Lane** approaches.

Passfield Drive E14 (Poplar, T. Ham.). Commemorates Sidney Webb, Lord Passfield (1859–1947), Labour politician who was president of the Board of Trade in 1924 and Colonial Secretary 1929–31. In his early political career he was a member of the London County Council, advocating what he called 'municipal socialism'. He and his wife Beatrice, whom he married in 1892, had great influence on radical socialism. **Passfield Road** adjoins.

Passmore Street SW1 (Belgravia, Cit. West.). Built from 1833 by Richard Passmore of Bourne Street, on lease from the Grosvenor estate.

Paternoster Row EC4 (Cit. Lond.). The makers of paternosters or rosary beads traded here before the Reformation, part of a large body of ecclesiastical purveyors around St Paul's Cathedral.

Pater Street W8 (Kensington, Ken. Chel.). Commemorates the Victorian writer Walter Pater (1839–94) who lived nearby. His best-known work was *Essays on the Renaissance* (1873).

Patshull Road NW5 (Kentish Town, Camden). *See* **Lawford Road**.

Paulton's Square SW3 (Chelsea, Ken. Chel.). Built on land inherited from Hans Sloane by his daughters of whom one, Sarah, married George Stanley of Paultons in Hampshire (*see* **Sloane Street**).

Paveley Street W1 (Lisson Grove, Cit. West.). Built on what was once an estate belonging to the Order of Knights of St John of Jerusalem (*see* **St John's Wood High Street**). Richard de Paveley was Grand Prior of the order in England 1315–21; John de Paveley was Grand Prior 1358–71.

Pavement, The SW4 (Clapham, Lambeth). An old name for a stretch of road which was noted as a paved way in the early 17th century.

Pavilion Road SW1 (Chelsea, Ken. Chel.). The architect Henry Holland developed land on Sir Hans Sloane's estate. He began in 1777 by building his own house, 'The Pavilion', as a project for the Brighton Pavilion.

Paxton Place SE27 (Gipsy Hill, Lambeth). Commemorates Joseph Paxton, supervisor of the Duke of Devonshire's gardens at Chatsworth, who conceived the idea of a vast glass building with an iron frame to house the Great Exhibition of 1851. His 'Crystal Palace' was removed to nearby Sydenham in 1854; it was the most extraordinary building of its age, covering 19 acres and reaching a height of over 100 feet. Paxton's design was a further development of the lily house he had built at Chatsworth for the giant South American water lily *Victoria regia*. This lily house is thought to have been inspired by his study of the lily itself and the ribbed structure of its leaf. There is also a **Paxton Terrace** in Pimlico.

Peabody Avenue SW1 (Pimlico, Cit. West.). The American banker George Peabody gave £150,000 in 1862 for the housing of the poor of London. Controversy was rife as to whether or not the resulting Peabody Trust housed the really poor, or only the better-washed and well-organised. The trust is now considered to have made more contribution to housing the genuinely poor than most similar organisations. The first Peabody Buildings were in Spitalfields in 1863. By 1900 they were all over central London and the inner suburbs. The tenancies were subject to strict regulations and the blocks were barrack-like.

Peacock Street SE17 (Newington, Southwark). The *Peacock* tavern in Newington Butts existed before 1761. It was possibly connected with the Peacock Brewery in Gravel Lane (now Great Suffolk Street), Southwark.

Peak Hill SE26 (Sydenham, Lewisham). A polite corruption of the old place name for this neighbourhood: Pig Hill. **Peak Hill Avenue** and **Gardens** adjoin.

Pearfield Road SE23 (Perry Vale, Lewisham). *See* **Perry Hill**.

Pearscroft Road SW6 (Fulham, Hammersmith). Revival of an old place name. Pearscroft or Pesecroft was a plot of land in Fulham manor.

Pearson Street E2 (Hoxton, Hackney). Site of a market and nursery-garden belonging to a Mr Pearson, noted in the 1790s as specialising in anemones and other flowers. The *Annual Register*, quoting a report of 1791, says: 'he has no greenhouse, yet has abundance of myrtles and striped philareas [ornamental grasses] with oranges and other greens, which he keeps safe enough under sheds, sunk a foot within ground and covered with straw'.

Pear Tree Court EC1 (Clerkenwell, Islington). Recorded in 1685, probably from a tree and not from a sign, since the area was at that time rural.

Peartree Street EC1 (Finsbury, Islington). Named from pear trees; built *c*1725 on what was formerly an area of orchards, gardens and fields.

Peckarman's Wood SE26 (Dulwich, Southwark). *See* **Low Cross Wood Lane**.

Peckham High Street SE15 (Peckham, Southwark). The high or principal street of Peckham, called Pecheham in the *Domesday Book*; 'ham' is home or dwelling in OE, and Peche may be a personal name, or it may be derived from OE 'peac', meaning a hill.

Peckham Hill Street SE15 (Southwark). *See* **Peckham High Street**. A Mrs Hill bought the manor of Bredinghurst *c*1732; her manor house stood here until it was demolished for building development in 1797.

Peckham Park Road SE15 (Peckham, Southwark). *See* **Peckham High Street** and above. The estate of parkland surrounding the manor house was called Peckham Park, and it extended across the line of this street.

Peckham Rye SE15, SE22 (Peckham, Southwark). *See* **Peckham High Street**. Rye is from OE 'rithe', a brook. **Rye Lane** approaches.

Pedlars' Way N7 (Caledonian Road, Islington). The general or Pedlars' Market which was held here flourished until World War II; it has been revived in Bermondsey, where it is still referred to as the 'Caledonian' market.

Peerless Street EC1 (Finsbury, Islington). Site of the Peerless Pond, an 18th-century bathing place; the name is thought to be a euphemistic corruption of 'perilous' pond.

Pekin Street E14 (Limehouse, T. Ham.). *See* **Oriental Street**.

Pelham Crescent SW7 (Kensington, Ken. Chel.). *See* **Onslow Square** for this and **Pelham Street**.

Pellatt Road SE22 (E Dulwich, Southwark). Apsley Pellatt senior founded the Falcon Glass House in Southwark in the late 18th century; his son, also Apsley (1791–1823), invented a type of glass cameo. A later Apsley continued the development of art glass and architectural glass, and also served as MP for Southwark 1852–7.

Pelter Street E2 (Bethnal Green, T. Ham.). Named in 1905 to revive the name of a 16th-century landowner; formerly Willow Walk.

Pemberton Row EC4 (Cit. Lond.). Derivation unknown; recorded as such on a map of 1746.

Pembridge Crescent W11 (Notting Hill, Ken. Chel.). Laid out by W.H. and W.K. Jenkins, property developers of Welsh extraction; W.K. Jenkins also held land in Herefordshire, and frequently used Welsh border names for his streets. Pembridge is a Herefordshire village near Kington. **Pembridge Gardens**, **Mews** and **Place**, **Road**, **Square** and **Villas** are nearby.

Pembroke Road W8 (Kensington, Ken. Chel.). *See* **Edwardes Square**. Francis Edwardes came from Haverfordwest in Pembrokeshire. **Pembroke Gardens**, **Square**, **Villas** and **Walk** adjoin.

Pemell Close E1 (Stepney, T. Ham.). *See* **Amiel Street**.

Pendennis Road SW16 (Streatham, Lambeth). *See* **Newcombe Gardens**.

Penfold Street NW1, NW8 (Lisson Grove, Cit. West.). Commemorates the Rev. George Penfold, incumbent of three Marylebone churches in succession: Brunswick Chapel, Christ Church and finally (from 1828) Trinity Church. **Penfold Place** adjoins.

Pennack Road SE15 (Peckham, Southwark). Built by Charles Pennack in the 1870s.

Pennant Mews W8 (Kensington, Ken. Chel.). *See* **Longridge Road**.

Pennethorne Close E9 (S Hackney, Hackney). The architect James Pennethorne, pupil of John Nash, designed nearby Victoria Park which opened in 1845.

Pennyfields E14 (Limehouse, T. Ham.). The Penny Field is recorded here in 1663, and was probably named from a nominal rent.

Penry Street SE1 (Old Kent Road, Southwark). John Penry, a Welsh preacher, helped to found the Independent Congregation in 1592. This was a body which had separated from the established Church of England. The Congregation had followers and a meeting place in Southwark. Their stand against the established Church was considered treasonable. Penry was executed in 1593 at St Thomas à Waterings, a halting place nearby on the Old Kent Road (*see* **Shorncliffe Road**).

Pensbury Place SW8 (Clapham, Lambeth). Traditionally marks the site of a house in Wandsworth Road once occupied by the Quaker William Penn (1644–1718), founder of Pennsylvania. **Pensbury Street** runs parallel.

Penton Place SE17 (Walworth, Southwark). Henry Penton, who held the lease of Walworth Manor (*see* **Manor Place**), let building leases on his land from 1774; this street was one of the first to be built.

Pentonville Road N1 (Islington). The area on either side of the road was developed from *c*1773 by Henry Penton as a new residential district. The road was formerly the NE end of the New Road which was made from Paddington to Islington in 1765. **Penton Rise** and **Street** adjoin.

Penywern Road SW5 (Kensington, Ken. Chel.). *See* **Longridge Road**.

Pepys Road SE14 (New Cross, Lewisham). *See* **Pepys Street**. Reflects the connection between the navy and the Deptford–New Cross area, which was influenced by the Deptford royal dockyards from the 16th century until the mid-19th.

Pepys Street EC3 (Cit. Lond.). Samuel Pepys (*d* 1703), diarist and Naval Secretary, worked in the Navy Office (now demolished) which stood on this site; his house was here also. Pepys's *Diary* covers the years 1660–9.

Perceval Avenue NW3 (Hampstead, Camden). Spencer Perceval (1762–1812), lived at Belsize House which stood S of Belsize Avenue nearby. He was Chancellor of the Exchequer in Lord Portland's Tory government from 1807, and succeeded Portland as Prime Minister in 1809. He was shot dead in the lobby of the House in 1812; his assassin was John Bellingham, who had a grievance against the government.

Percival Street EC1 (Clerkenwell, Islington). Formerly Perceval Street; built on land belonging to the Marquis of Northampton and named from his cousin, Spencer Perceval (*see* **Perceval Avenue**).

Percy Circus WC1 (Islington). Built on land belonging to the New River

Company. Robert Percy Smith (1770–1845), lawyer and MP, and his son Robert Vernon Smith (1800–73), Baron Lyvedon, were both directors of the company. Robert Percy Smith was a governor of the company 1827–45, and was largely responsible for its sound financial structure. **Great Percy Street** approaches and **Vernon Rise** adjoins, with **Vernon Square**.

Percy Street W1 (Tottenham Court Road, Camden/Cit. West.). Built from 1764–70, mainly by William Franks who also developed much of Charlotte Street and Rathbone Street. The contemporarily celebrated Percy is Sir Hugh Smithson, who took the name in 1750. He inherited property from a relation, Hugh Smithson of Tottenham (*see* **Northumberland Park**) in 1740; in the same year he became MP for Middlesex and married Elizabeth Seymour, grand-daughter of Josceline Percy, Eleventh Earl of Northumberland. Elizabeth inherited the Percy property and her husband received the title of Earl of Northumberland in 1750. In 1762 he became Lord Chamberlain to Queen Charlotte and Lord Lieutenant of Middlesex. He was created Duke of Northumberland in 1766.

Perham Road W14 (Baron's Court, Hammersmith). *See* **Palliser Road**.

Perkin's Rents SW1 (Cit. West.). Recorded in the late 17th century by this name: tenements paying rent to a landlord called Perkin or Perkins.

Perrers Road W6 (Hammersmith). Alice Perrers (*d* 1401), mistress of Edward III, held the nearby manor of Palyngswick (*see* **Paddenswick Road**).

Perrin's Lane NW3 (Hampstead, Camden). John Perrin owned taverns in Hampstead village in the 1720s, the first recorded member of a family which gradually added to its Hampstead estate. This lane was built on their land. **Perrin's Walk** is opposite.

Perry Hill SE23 (Lewisham). Built on land formerly belonging to a farm of that name (*see* **Clowders Road**). Perry comes from an OE word for pear; this was the farm with the pear orchards on a hill. **Perry Rise** and **Vale** adjoin.

Perry's Place W1 (Oxford Street, Cit. West.). Richard Perry was a property owner here in 1790 and may be the source of the name. As a thoroughfare the place is the remnant of an old track from the Soho area to St Marylebone old parish church.

Peterborough Court EC4 (Cit. Lond.). The abbots of Peterborough had a town house here until the dissolution of the monasteries *c*1539.

Peterborough Road SW6 (Fulham, Hammersmith).   Peterborough House stood near the NE corner. Formerly Villa Carey, it passed during the 17th century to Thomas Carey's son-in-law Viscount Mordaunt, younger son of the Royalist Earl of Peterborough. A later earl rebuilt the house, and it was finally demolished *c*1900 (*see* **Avalon Road**).

Petersham Mews SW7 (Kensington, Ken. Chel.). *See* **Elvaston Place** for this and **Petersham Place**.

Peter's Hill EC4 (Cit. Lond.). Remnant of a lane which once led from St Paul's churchyard to join Thames Street by the small mediaeval church of St Peter, which is now demolished.

Peter's Lane EC1 (Clerkenwell, Islington). Named from an inn which stood here: *St Peter's Keys*.

Peter Street W1 (Soho, Cit. West.).

Derivation uncertain, but the *Survey of London* reports a factory nearby in the 17th century where saltpetre was extracted, and considers it likely that this street approached it.

Petley Road W6 (Fulham, Hammersmith).   Richard Petley owned land in the Wild Mead, part of the town meadow, from 1519.

Peto Place NW1 (Regent's Park, Camden). The Regent's Park Chapel which gives on to this street was founded by Sir Samuel Morton Peto (1809–89). He was a railway contractor, engineer and Liberal politician. He was also a Baptist and a generous benefactor to his sect.

Petticoat Square E1 (Cit. Lond.). Adjoins **Middlesex Street**.

Petty France SW1 (Cit. West.). A Little France or French settlement here is mentioned by John Stow in his *Survey of London* of 1598.

Petyt Place SW3 (Chelsea, Ken. Chel.). Petyt House opposite was built as a school, parish hall and vestry room by William Petyt, lawyer (1636–1707).

Petyward SW3 (Chelsea, Ken. Chel.). The Petyward or Pettiward family held several small properties in Chelsea and Brompton, at least from the late 17th century. They also had a country seat in Suffolk called Finborough Hall. **Finborough Road** runs beside Brompton cemetery.

Phene Street SW3 (Chelsea, Ken. Chel.). Commemorates Dr Phene, a Victorian enthusiast who pioneered the planting of London streets with trees; he lived at 32 Oakley Street.

Philbeach   Gardens   SW5 (Kensington, Ken. Chel.). *See* **Long-ridge Road**.

Phene Street

Philip Road SE15 (Peckham, Southwark). On the Crespigny estate (*see* **De Crespigny Park**). Named in 1868 from Philip Champion de Crespigny.

Phillimore Gardens W8 (Kensington, Ken. Chel.). Built on land belonging to the Phillimore family, who first began granting building leases on their land in 1788. **Phillimore Place** and **Walk** adjoin.

Philpot Lane EC3 (Cit. Lond.). Site of the house of Sir John Philpot, 14th-century mayor of the City.

Philpot Street E1 (Stepney, T. Ham.). Commemorates the prominent local family of Philpot or Philipot; Sir George Philpot of Mile End was a member of Stepney parish vestry and was possibly descended from the family of Philipot who were lords of the secondary manor of Mile End in the 15th century.

Phoebeth Road SE4 (Lewisham). *See* **Amyruth Road**.

Phoenix Place WC1 (Clerkenwell, Camden/Islington). The Phoenix Iron Foundry, now closed, stood at the S end.

Phoenix Street WC2 (Charing Cross Road, Camden). Named from the sign of an inn, now demolished, which stood in Stacey Street.

Piccadilly W1 (Cit. West.). Robert Baker, a tailor, built a house, Piccadilly Hall, in 1612 at the S end of the present Great Windmill Street. It is probable, but not certain, that the house was christened by local wits, in reference to the pickadils (collars or hem trimmings) which made Baker's fortune.

Piccadilly Circus W1 (Cit. West.). Designed in 1819 by John Nash as part of his scheme of streets from Regent's Park to Carlton House; it was originally a circus and has since been distorted by new development. The place marked the approximate site of Pickadilly Hall or Piccadilly Hall (*see* **Piccadilly**).

Pickard Street EC1 (City Road, Islington). Site of the Orphan Working School (removed to Maitland Park, Hampstead, in 1847; *see* **Maitland Park Road**) which was founded by a clergyman called Pickard in 1754 and moved here from Hoxton *c*1770.

Pickle Herring Street SE1 (Tooley Street, Southwark). One of the older wharves on the Thames, used for shipping cargoes of pickled herrings, lies here.

Pickwick Road SE21 (Dulwich, Southwark). Mr Pickwick, in Charles Dickens's novel *The Pickwick Papers* (1837), was associated with the surrounding area of Dulwich village.

Pickwick Street SE1 (Southwark). One of a group of names commemorating Charles Dickens and his novels (*see* **Dickens Square** and **Pickwick Road**).

Picton Place W1 (Marylebone, Cit. West.). Lieutenant-General Sir Thomas Picton (1758–1815) lived in Wigmore Street N of this street. He served with distinction in the Peninsular Campaign of the Napoleonic Wars, and was killed at Waterloo in 1815.

Piggot Street E14 (Limehouse, T. Ham.). Built on land belonging to the Piggot family: Paynton and Francis Piggot are recorded as holding it in 1858.

Pilgrimage Street SE1 (Southwark). Commemorates the pilgrimage described in Geoffrey Chaucer's

Canterbury Tales as beginning at the *Tabard Inn* in Southwark.

Pilgrim's Lane NW3 (Hampstead, Camden). James Pilgrim held land here in 1787 as a tenant of the manor of Hampstead.

Pilgrim Street EC4 (Cit. Lond.). First recorded in 1799, and of uncertain derivation. It appears as Blackfriars, from the surrounding area, in 1677, Stonecutters Alley in 1746 and Little Bridge Street in 1758, as approaching the old Fleet Bridge at Ludgate Circus. 'Pilgrim' is too late to have a religious connotation; it may be the name of a property owner.

Pimlico Road SW1 (Chelsea and Pimlico, Cit. West./Ken. Chel.). Approaches Pimlico, a name for the village which developed at Neat-house (*see* **Neathouse Place**); the Neathouse cottages, near the present Victoria Station, became inns and places of entertainment after the Restoration in 1660. A man called Ben Pimlico was known for brewing a special beer in the 16th century (*see* **Pimlico Walk**). One of the Neathouse inns may have been known as a 'Pimlico house', or a house selling Pimlico beer; alternatively the name may be a slang term for a house of entertainment similar to Pimlico's in Hoxton.

Pimlico Walk N1 (Hoxton, Hackney). Ben Pimlico is praised in a 16th-century pamphlet as an inn-keeper who brewed good beer in Hoxton. Pimlico House stood here, and was famous as a place of entertainment for citizens making an excursion across the fields from London.

Pindar Street EC2 (Bishopsgate, Cit. Lond./Hackney). Leaves Bishops-gate across the site of a house belonging to Sir Paul Pindar, a City merchant and diplomat who had it built in 1599. The elaborate timber façade of the house is preserved in the Victoria and Albert Museum.

Piper Close N7 (Caledonian Road, Islington). This and **Watkinson Road** are two modern streets commemorating members of the first Islington Borough Council: William Piper and Frederick Watkinson both represented Thornhill Ward.

Pitfield Street N1 (Hoxton, Hackney). Developed through building leases from 1683, beginning on a field at the S which comprised 10 acres N of Old Street and was called the Pitfield, presumably from pits left by digging for brick-earth. (The arrival in Hoxton of a property-owning family called Pitfield is coincidental.)

Pitt's Head Mews W1 (Mayfair, Cit. West.). An inn, now demolished, stood at the corner with Stanhope Row and was called the *Pitt's Head*. William Pitt the Elder is commemorated in **Chatham Street** in Walworth. William Pitt the Younger followed his father as a dominant figure in British politics from 1784 until his premature death at 47; his already failing health collapsed after Napoleon's victory at Austerlitz in 1806.

Pitt Street W8 (Kensington, Ken. Chel.). Built on the estate of Campden House which Stephen Pitt bought in 1751. The estate remained the property of the Pitt family into the 20th century.

Plato Road SW2 (Clapham, Lambeth). *See* **Aristotle Road**.

Platt Street NW1 (St Pancras, Camden). Built *c*1848–53 on land belonging to the Brewers' Company, to whom it had been given by Richard

Platt, brewer and citizen of London, in 1575.

Playhouse Yard EC4 (Cit. Lond.). Richard Burbage opened the Blackfriars Playhouse here in 1600. The Blackfriars monastery had been dissolved *c*1539, and years later the Master of the royal chapel choirboys rented part of the premises where his boys gave public performances of plays they were to put on at court. James Burbage, father of Richard, turned part of the monastery into a proper theatre which was outside City jurisdiction; here the boys, re-formed as an acting company, began a new series of productions. Theatres were not allowed in any area under the City's authority; they were feared as centres of vice, riot and infection (*see* **Burbage Close**).

Plender Street NW1 (Camden Town, Camden). Commemorates William Plender, created First Baron Plender in 1931; he was a distinguished accountant active in government service.

Pleydell Street EC4 (Cit. Lond.). Formerly Silver Street, it became known as Pleydell Street *c*1848, by association with adjoining **Bouverie Street**; by this date the family name of the earls of Radnor was Pleydell-Bouverie.

Plimsoll Street E14 (Poplar, T. Ham.). Samuel Plimsoll was responsible for the Merchant Shipping Act of 1876 which greatly reduced dangerous practices in the loading of merchant ships. The Plimsoll line painted on the hull indicates the safe waterline when loaded.

Plough Court EC3 (Cit. Lond.). Runs S from Lombard Street; recorded as Plough Yard in 1720, and named from the sign of a plough which may have belonged to an inn or

to an ironmonger.

Plough Place EC4 (Fetter Lane, Cit. Lond.). The 'Plough' or 'Plow' is recorded as an eating house in the 16th century, when it was granted to Thomas Bartlett or Bartlet, King's Printer, by Edward VI (1547–53). **Bartlett's Passage**, immediately N, formerly led to a later family property called Bartlett's Buildings. Bartlett also owned property E of New Fetter Lane in **Bartlett Court**.

Plough Road SW11 (Battersea, Wandsworth). The Plough Inn on the corner with St John's Hill is recorded in the early 18th century when the area was farmland. The last of Battersea's farms was not built over until the 1860s.

Plough Way SE16 (Rotherhithe, Southwark/Lewisham).   Replaces Plough Road, a 19th-century road named from *The Plough*, an inn built beside the Surrey Canal bridge E of Yeoman Street.

Plough Yard EC2 (Shoreditch, Hackney). The *Plough Inn* 'in Shorditch' is recorded in 1669 and Plough Yard which approached it appears *c*1800.

Plumtree Court EC4 (Cit. Lond.). Originally ran S from Holborn, and recorded in 1720; it is uncertain whether it was named from a tree or a sign.

Pocock Street SE1 (Southwark). A local family name. Thomas Pocock started a shoe-leather business in 1815, and later expanded it into a wholesale footwear trade. G. Pocock was District Surveyor responsible for roads in the 1860s, and in 1876 A. Pocock represented the parish on the Metropolitan Board of Works.

Poland Street W1 (Soho, Cit. West.). The victory of Polish forces over the

Turks in 1683 was commemorated by a public house called *The King of Poland* which stood at the NW corner of this street.

Pollard Close E16 (Holloway, Islington). A modern name commemorating James Pollard, engraver, who was born at Spa Fields and worked in Holloway. The traffic on the Holloway Road inspired many of his most famous scenes of the coaching age of the 1820s and 1830s.

Pollard Row E2 (Bethnal Green, T. Ham.). *See* **Wellington Street** for this and **Pollard Street**.

Pollen Street W1 (Mayfair, Cit. West.). Built on land belonging to the Pollen family who had inherited the former Maddox estate (*see* **Maddox Street**).

Polsted Road SE6 (Lewisham). Henry Polsted of Chilworth had a share in the manor of Catford from 1548, when it was granted to him and to William More. Francis Polsted sold it to Brian Annesley *c*1578.

Polygon Road NW1 (St Pancras, Camden). Runs N of the former Polygon, an experimental development of 32 houses built so as to form a 16-sided block. The building was put up *c*1794 by Jacob Leroux and Job Hoare.

Pomeroy Street SE14 (New Cross, Southwark/Lewisham). Named in 1874, replacing 23 named groups of houses, one of which was Pomeroy Place. Edwin Pomeroy, member of the original Bermondsey Borough Council, lived in New Cross and it is possible that Pomeroy Place was built by his family.

Pond Mead SE21 (Dulwich, Southwark). Originally the site of a village pond which was filled in, leaving a property called 'The Pond House'

beside it; the house gave its name to this road.

Pond Place SW3 (Chelsea, Ken. Chel.). Approached ponds used by beasts grazing on Chelsea Common; the common extended S from Fulham Road, E from Sydney Street; it was built over from 1790.

Pond Street NW3 (Hampstead, Camden). Called Pound Street on 18th-century maps, presumably from a village cattle pound at what is now called South End Green, or possibly on the small green called Hampstead Green at the top of Pond Street.

Pond Yard SE1 (Southwark). Crosses the site of the King's Pike Garden, one of three fish farms, each containing several ponds, which lay along Bankside in the 16th century; some of them had mediaeval monastic origins.

Ponsonby Place SW1 (Pimlico, Cit. West.). *See* **Bessborough Gardens** for this and **Ponsonby Terrace**.

Ponsonby Road SW15 (Roehampton, Wandsworth). Family name of the earls of Bessborough (*see* **Bessborough Gardens**).

Pont Street SW1 (Brompton, Ken. Chel.). Built *c*1830, a period when this and the Knightsbridge area had a distinctly French flavour; this may have produced the French *pont* for a road that bridged the Westbourne stream.

Poole Road E9 (S Hackney, Hackney). Valentine Poole of Old Ford, by his will of 1664, left the income of a plot of land called the Butfield, in Hackney, to support the poor of Hackney parish. **Valentine Road** adjoins.

Pope's Head Alley EC3 (Cit. Lond.). Named from the *Pope's Head Tavern* which stood here. The land was granted to Florentine merchants in the papal service in 1318, and the tavern is first mentioned as *The Pope's Head* in 1415.

Pope Street SE1 (Bermondsey, Southwark). Sir Thomas Pope bought Bermondsey Abbey from Sir Robert Southwell, Master of the Rolls, in 1540. The abbey had been granted to Southwell at the dissolution of the monasteries in 1537. Pope built Bermondsey House on the site, and held the manor of Bermondsey until 1555.

Poplar Grove W6 (Shepherd's Bush, Hammersmith). From a house called 'The Poplars'.

Poplar Place W2 (Bayswater, Cit. West.). An early development in then rural Bayswater, and named from its trees.

Poppins Court EC4 (Cit. Lond.). Originally Poppinjay Court, a popinjay or parrot appearing on a sign here. The popinjay was the crest of Cirencester Abbey which owned a town house here in the 14th century.

Porchester Place W2 (Bayswater, Cit. West.). *See* **Southwick Street** for this and **Porchester Street**.

Porden Road SW2 (Brixton, Lambeth). Leads off Brixton Hill opposite the church of St Matthew, consecrated in 1824 and designed by the architect Charles Porden.

Porteus Road W2 (Paddington, Cit. West.). Dr Beilby Porteus was Bishop of London 1787–1808. Edward VI (1547–53) gave the manor of Paddington to the then Bishop of London and his successors; the bishops also held the curacy of St Mary's church, Paddington.

Portland Mews W1 (Soho, Cit.

West.). Leads off D'Arblay Street which was built *c*1735 on an estate belonging to the second duke of Portland and was originally called Portland Street.

Portland Place W1 (Marylebone, Cit. West.). Built *c*1773 on land belonging to the dukes of Portland. The second duke had married the heiress to this estate, Lady Margaret Cavendish Harley, daughter of the Earl of Oxford, in 1734.

Portman Square W1 (Marylebone, Cit. West.). Part of the manor of Lilestone in W Marylebone passed to the Portman family of Orchard Portman, Somerset, *c*1550. The square was laid out by Henry William Portman from *c*1760; **Portman Street** approaches, and **Portman Close** is nearby.

Portobello Road W11 (Notting Hill, Ken. Chel.). Formerly Portobello Lane, which led past Portobello Farm; the farm was named in honour of Admiral Vernon's capture of Portobello, Panama, in 1739.

Portpool Lane EC1 (Gray's Inn Road, Camden). A mediaeval manor, recorded as belonging to the Priory of St Bartholomew in West Smithfield, is called Purtepol in the early 13th century, and probably derived from 'Purta's pool'. The manor stretched N from Holborn up the present Gray's Inn Road, and included the present Gray's Inn.

Portsea Mews W2 (Bayswater, Cit. West.). *See* **Southwick Street** for this and **Portsea Place**.

Portsmouth Road (Putney, Wandsworth). Remaining fragment of the old London to Portsmouth road which crossed Putney Heath, leaving Putney Hill and joining the Kingston Road through the present Norstead

Place. The Kingston Road has now superseded it.

Portsmouth Street WC2 (Lincoln's Inn, Camden). Traditionally the site of a house belonging to Louise de Kérouaille, mistress of Charles II who created her Duchess of Portsmouth. Her pro-Catholic intrigues made her unpopular.

Portsoken Street E1 (Whitechapel, T. Ham.). The Portsoke was the early mediaeval 'soke' immediately outside the 'port' or gate of the City of London. Sokes were small areas which enjoyed certain freedoms and privileges. This one was granted to a group of knights in the 10th century (*see* **St Katharine's Way**).

Portugal Street WC2 (Lincoln's Inn, Cit. West.). Named after the Restoration of 1660 in honour of Charles II's Portuguese queen, Catharine of Braganza.

Post Office Court (Cit. Lond.). On the site of the present Post Office nearby (junction of Lombard Street and King William Street) stood a 17th-century house which became London's first General Post Office (1705) and, later, the Mail Coach Office.

Potters' Fields SE1 (Bermondsey). Leads to part of the river bank so-called from finds of Roman pottery on the site.

Pottery Lane W11 (N Kensington, Ken. Chel.). Led to a settlement of potters who worked here in the early 19th century making cheap earthenwares and tiles. The settlement extended up the present Walmer Road and westward across the N boundary of the Norland estate. Pig-keeping was introduced later, and 'The Potteries' became the name of a foul-smelling slum district with an appalling death rate.

Pottery Street SE16 (Rotherhithe, Southwark). Thomas Dearne 'brown-stone potter' is recorded at work here in 1805.

Poultry EC2 (Cit. Lond.). The place where the poulterers had their stalls, at the end of the mediaeval food-market along Cheapside.

Powell Road E5 (Clapton, Hackney). The Powell family are recorded as owning land in Hackney in 1745. Baden Powell of Stamford Hill was major of the local militia in 1803. His son, the Rev. Baden Powell of Newick, was born at Stamford Hill in 1796. In 1840 he gave land here (known as the Strawberry Gardens) as the site for St James's church, of which another Powell became vicar. The Rev. Baden Powell's son was Robert Baden-Powell (1857–1941), founder of the Boy Scout Movement. **Newick Road** approaches.

Powis Place WC1 (Bloomsbury, Camden). Site of Powis House (demolished and now replaced by the Hospital for Sick Children), built *c*1706 for William Herbert, Second Marquis of Powis (*c*1665–1745). The marquis had sold his previous house in Lincoln's Inn Fields in 1705. His parents having been staunch Catholic supporters of James II, for whose cause they took considerable risks, Powis was twice imprisoned and once outlawed under William III, James's Protestant successor. He was not restored to his estates until 1722, by which time he was too poor to enjoy them.

Poynder's Road SE4 (Clapham, Lambeth). Runs along the NE boundary of land held by Thomas Poynder, of the Poynder family of building contractors, in the 1830s. **Poynder's Gardens** was built on his ground. Poynder's Road was built as part of Thomas Cubitt's Clapham

Park estate, widening an existing lane with Poynder's agreement.

Praed Street W2 (Paddington, Cit. West.). Built on land bought by the Grand Junction Canal Company, whose canal (now the Grand Union Canal) runs to the N. The first chairman of the Grand Junction Company was William Praed.

Pratt Street NW1 (Camden Town, Camden). Charles Pratt, created Earl Camden in 1786, inherited the area later called Camden Town through his wife (*see* **Jeffreys Street**). He began to let building leases in 1790.

Pratt Walk SE11 (Lambeth). Formerly Pratt Street; built by Sir Joseph Mawbey in 1775 and named after his mother's family (*see* **Mawbey Street**).

Prebend Street N1 (Islington). Built on land which was a prebend belonging to the canons of St Paul's Cathedral (*see* **Mora Street**). **St Paul Street** is linked to it by **Canon Street**; **Rector Street** and **Bishop Street** are named by association. The Islington prebendary is Saxon in origin; by the time this estate was built in the mid-19th century it covered the only Islington land still owned by St Paul's.

Prentis Road SW16 (Streatham, Lambeth). Family name of the estate owner on whose land this road was built.

Prescot Street E1 (Whitechapel, T. Ham.). *See* **Leman Street**. Alexander Prescot, citizen and goldsmith, Alderman of the City of London 1611–12 and Sheriff 1612–13, had a son called Edward, citizen and salter. Edward's daughter Rebecca Prescot married Sir William Leman (*d* 1667). Both families, Lemans and Prescots, held land locally.

Prescott Place SW4 (Clapham, Lambeth). Probably commemorates Colonel Prescott who in 1803 took command of the local volunteer force, the Clapham Armed Association, which was formed to meet the threat of French invasion during the war of 1793–1815.

Preston's Road E14 (Isle of Dogs, T. Ham.). Built across land belonging to Sir Robert Preston, who held property here in the early 19th century.

Price's Street SE1 (Southwark). Extension of Price's Buildings, Gravel Lane (now Great Suffolk Street), built in the 18th century by one Price. By 1805 there were four Prices trading in the immediate neighbourhood, including two running inns in Gravel Lane.

Prideaux Place WC1 (Islington). Built on land belonging to the New River Company. Arthur R. Prideaux became a director of the company in 1889.

Priestfield Road SE23 (Perry Hill, Lewisham). Built across a mediaeval field called the Priest Field (derivation unknown) which is recorded as belonging to Walter Bronger in the time of Henry VII (1485–1509) and later formed part of the Leathersellers' Company estate.

Priest's Bridge SW15 (Barnes, R. upon T.). Bridge over the Beverley Brook, built on land belonging to the dean and canons of St Paul's Cathedral who held the manor of Barnes from 1086, and probably before.

Primrose Hill EC4 (Cit. Lond.). Renamed in the late 18th century when the area was completely urban, and 'Primrose' is more likely to have been a builder than a flower. The same applies to **Primrose Street**,

Norton Folgate. The hill was formerly called Salisbury Court, as approaching **Salisbury Square**.

Primrose Hill Road NW3 (Camden). Approaches Primrose Hill, formerly called Barrow Hill but known as Primrose Hill from the 16th century because of the flowers that grew there. The hill was obtained for the public as an open space in the mid-19th century, having been previously owned by Eton College.

Prince Albert Road NW8 (Primrose Hill, Camden/Cit. West.). Renamed (from Primrose Hill Road) to commemorate Albert of Saxe-Coburg (*see* **Albert Bridge Road**).

Prince Arthur Road NW3 (Hampstead, Camden). Prince Arthur, Duke of Connaught and son of Queen Victoria, opened the nearby Sailors' Orphan Girls' School and Home on Greenhill Road, in 1869.

Prince Consort Road SW7 (Kensington, Cit. West.). Prince Albert (*see* **Albert Bridge Road**) inspired and advised on the acquisition of this land as the most suitable use of profits from his Great Exhibition of 1851; it was to be laid out as a complex of educational, scientific and cultural institutions.

Princelet Street E1 (Spitalfields, T. Ham.). Originally Princes Street when it was built 1718–24; this is more likely to have been a suggestion of dignity than a compliment to the future George II. In 1893, the number of 'Prince' street names being too great, this one was renamed.

Prince of Wales Drive SW11 (Battersea, Wandsworth). Made as an approach to Battersea Park (opened 1858) and named from Albert Edward, Prince of Wales.

Adjoining **Alexandra Avenue** was named following his marriage in 1863 to Princess Alexandra of Schleswig-Holstein-Sonderburg-Glücksburg. He became Edward VII in 1901.

Prince of Wales Road NW5 (Kentish Town, Camden). Renamed in honour of the Prince of Wales (*see* **Prince of Wales Drive**). The E and earliest section was formerly called Grafton Place (*see* **Grafton Road**).

Prince of Wales Terrace W8 (Kensington, Ken. Chel.). One of a group with royal names (*see* **Prince of Wales Drive**). **Albert Place**, **Victoria Grove** and **Victoria Road** are nearby. The Prince was the eldest son of Queen Victoria and Prince Albert. **Prince's Gardens** and **Prince's Gate** are also named after him.

Prince's Square W2 (Bayswater, Cit. West.). Commemorates Prince Albert, consort of Queen Victoria (*see* **Albert Bridge Road**).

Prince's Street EC2 (Cit. Lond.). Laid out after the Great Fire of 1666 and named as a compliment to the royal family, as were **Queen Street** and **King Street**.

Prince's Street W1 (Mayfair, Cit. West.). Runs E from Hanover Square, and named in compliment to the royal family, the house of Hanover (*see* **Hanover Square** and **Terrace**).

Princeton Street WC1 (Holborn, Camden). Formerly Prince's Street, but not thought to commemorate any particular prince. Changed to avoid having too many 'Prince' street names.

Printer Street EC4 (Cit. Lond.). Properly Printer's Street. The surrounding area between Shoe Lane and Fetter Lane is traditionally a centre of printing since the 16th century (*see* **Bartlett Court**).

Printing House Square EC4 (Cit. Lond.). Originally part of the Blackfriars monastery (*see* **Blackfriars Lane**), a complex of buildings was occupied in the 17th century by tenants including the King's Printers, Norton and Bill. The official press moved to Gough Square in 1769 and in 1784 John Walter bought their premises for his own press. He began printing the *Daily Universal Register* there in 1785 and changed its name to *The Times* in 1788.

Prior Bolton Street N1 (Canonbury, Islington). Commemorates the prior of St Bartholomew's Priory, Smithfield, for whom Canonbury Tower was built (*see* **Canonbury Road**).

Priory Road NW6 (Kilburn, Camden). *See* **Kilburn Priory** for this and **Priory Terrace.**

Priory Street E3 (Bromley, T. Ham.). Part of the site of the priory of Bromley St Leonards, a Benedictine convent established before the Norman Conquest. Being at the W end of the ford across the River Lea to Stratford, it was often called Stratford-at-Bow, whence it has been confused with the Cistercian abbey at Stratford on the E bank. The most likely date of its foundation is *c*960, when St Dunstan, an admirer of the Benedictine Rule, was Bishop of London and lord of the manor of Stepney (which included Bromley). The priory was dissolved in 1535.

Priory Walk SW10 (W Brompton, Ken. Chel.). On the Gunter family's estate (*see* **Gunter Grove**). The family also owned Abergavenny Priory.

Priscilla Road E3 (Bow, T. Ham.). *See* **Coborn Road**.

Pritchard's Road E2 (Cambridge Heath, Hackney/T. Ham.). Built on an estate belonging to the Pritchard family in the early 19th century. The estate stretched N to Duncan Road and E to the line of Sheep Lane. It includes family Christian names in **Ada**, **Emma** and **Marian** Streets.

Procter Street WC1 (Holborn, Camden). The poet Bryan Waller Procter (1787–1874) lived in Red Lion Square. He knew Byron, Leigh Hunt and Lamb, and tended to imitate them in his more serious work; he is best remembered for his songs.

Province Street N1 (Islington). Formerly Provence Street, from the name of a field near the site which appears on a parish map of 1735.

Provost Road NW3 (Primrose Hill, Camden). *See* **Eton Avenue**.

Prowse Place NW1 (Camden Town, Camden). Possibly commemorates Rear Admiral Sir William Prowse of St Pancras parish, who died in 1826. He commanded the frigate *Sirius* at Trafalgar in 1805.

Pudding Lane EC3 (Cit. Lond.). Puddings in this context are animal guts; the lane was so named in the 16th century because butchers from nearby Eastcheap used to dispose of hogs' offal or puddings there, carting them down to throw them in the river. The street was originally called Rother Lane, from Rothers gate or Retheresgate, a water-gate where cattle were landed.

Puddle Dock EC4 (Cit. Lond.). John Stow in his *Survey of London* of 1598 attributes the name either to a mediaeval wharf owner called Puddle, or to the puddling caused by the custom of watering horses in the river at this point.

Pulton Place SW6 (Fulham, Hammersmith). Possibly commemorates a John Pulton, recorded as 'Constable for Fulham' in 1583.

Purchese Street NW1 (St Pancras, Camden). F. Purchese of Platt Street, a vestryman in the 1890s, was London County Council member for St Pancras East from 1900.

Purdy Street E3 (Bromley, T. Ham.). William Purdy represented Bow on the Poplar District Board of Works in the 1890s. He later became a member of Poplar Borough Council.

Purser's Cross Road SW6 (Fulham, Hammersmith). The junction of Parson's Green Lane and Fulham Road is called Purser's Cross from 1602. The derivation is uncertain; possibly it is a corruption of Purser's Croft, recorded as a smallholding in 1552.

Putney High Street SW15 (Putney, Wandsworth). The main street of Putney, called Potenhithe in the 14th century, from OE 'Puttan-hithe',

meaning the wharf belonging to Putta.

Putney Park Lane SW15 (Putney, Wandsworth). In 1397 the Archbishop of Canterbury is recorded as owning a game park at Putney as part of his manor of Mortlake; this lane marks the E boundary. The park extended over 300 acres; it was part of Mortlake manor until 1548 when it was reserved to the Crown. Richard Weston, Earl of Portland, obtained it in 1634, and it then remained in private hands.

Pyrland Road N5 (Newington Green, Islington). A local builder and developer, Henry Rydon, acquired land in Highbury from the Fellowes estate in 1852. Rydon came from Pyrland Acre in Taunton, Somerset; the house he built here was called 'Pyrland House'.

Pyrmont Grove SE27 (Norwood, Lambeth). In 1882 Queen Victoria's son, Prince Leopold, Duke of Albany and Baron Arklow, married Princess Hélène of Waldeck and Pyrmont. **Waldeck Grove** runs parallel.

Pytchley Road SE22 (Camberwell, Southwark). *See* **Belvoir Road**.

Q

Quaker Street E1 (Spitalfields, T. Ham.). Commemorates a Friends' Meeting House established here c1656. The Society of Friends also founded a boys' school here in 1849; it removed to the corner of Wheeler Street in 1865 and was then called the Bedford Institute, in honour of the Quaker philanthropist Peter Bedford.

Queen Anne's Gate SW1 (Cit. West.). Formerly Queen Square. Approaches the gate into St James's Park named after Queen Anne (1702–14); **Queen Anne's Mansions** adjoins.

Queen Anne Street W1 (Marylebone, Cit. West.). Intended as an approach to a square which was planned and never built; it was to be called Queen Anne Square and it was to be laid out across the line of Portland Place. **Queen Anne Mews** runs parallel.

Queen Caroline Street W6 (Hammersmith). George IV's estranged wife, Caroline, lived at Brandenburgh House after her unsuccessful attempt to be acknowledged as his queen in 1820.

Queen Elizabeth Street SE1 (Bermondsey, Southwark). Formerly Free School Lane, commemorating Elizabeth I's Free Grammar School of St Olave's; the school stood E of St Olave's, Tooley Street, until it was moved (1831) to make way for the new London Bridge. In 1899 the school merged with the Free Grammar School of St Saviour's. The St Saviour's school was set up in 1556–62 (also under Queen Elizabeth) on land which was near St Saviour's church, in Green Dragon Court. In 1560 Henry Leeke, brewer, left a bequest to the school which it was to enjoy unless St Olave's parish set up its own school within two years, in which case the money was to go to them. St Olave's acted promptly.

Queen Elizabeth's Walk N16 (Stoke Newington, Hackney). Elizabeth I visited John Dudley at Stoke Newington Manor House; Dudley held the manor 1571–80 (*see* **Lordship Road**).

Queenhithe EC4 (Cit. Lond.). 'Hithe' is from OE 'hythe' and means a wharf or landing place. Queenhithe was a royal quay built by Ethelred II of Wessex (978–1016); it was called Ethelredshythe until Henry I's queen, Matilda, held it (1100–35).

Queen Margaret's Grove N1 (Kingsland, Islington). Named by association with adjoining King Henry's Walk. Margaret, Queen of Scotland, married the Earl of Angus in 1514, following the death of her husband James IV at the battle of Flodden in 1513. She was sister to Henry VIII, and she and her husband returned to live in England under his protection. There is a local tradition that her daughter, Lady Margaret Lennox, had a house nearby in Hackney.

Queensberry Place SW7 (Kensington, Ken. Chel.). Possibly named after the Marquis of Queensberry who drew up the Queensberry Rules for boxing in 1867.

Queensborough Terrace W2

(Bayswater, Cit. West.). Built on land belonging to the Aldridge family in the 1860s. John Aldridge (*d* 1795) had been MP for Queensborough; his marriage to a rich Bayswater widow founded the family's estate.

Queen's Buildings SE1 (Southwark). Site of the Queen's Bench Prison, called the Queen's Prison in 1842 when it became the only prison for debtors in place of the Fleet and the Marshalsea. The prison was demolished in 1879.

Queen's Club Gardens W14 (Fulham, Hammersmith). The Queen's Club here opened as a lawn tennis club in 1887 and was named after Queen Victoria.

Queen's Crescent NW5 (Kentish Town, Camden). Compliments Queen Victoria (1837–1901).

Queen's Elm Square SW3 (Chelsea, Ken. Chel.). Elizabeth I (1558–1603) sheltered from the rain under an elm tree here when visiting Lord Burleigh at Chelsea (*see* **Elm Park Gardens**).

Queen's Gardens SW1 (The Mall, Cit. West.). Surrounds the memorial to Queen Victoria designed by Sir Thomas Brock in 1901.

Queen's Gate SW7 (Kensington Gardens, Cit. West./Ken. Chel.). Approaches the Queen's Gate into Kensington Gardens, named from Queen Victoria. **Queen's Gate Gardens**, **Mews**, **Place** and **Terrace** adjoin.

Queen's Grove NW8 (St John's Wood, Cit. West.). Named in honour of Queen Victoria, as is **Queen's Terrace** adjoining.

Queen's Head Street N1 (Islington). The 'Queen's Head' was an Elizabethan or Jacobean house. It was much praised for its quality by local historians, and bitterly regretted when it was demolished and replaced in 1829.

Queen's Head Yard SE1 (Southwark). The *Queen's Head Inn* here was demolished in 1886. It is first recorded in the 15th century under the name of the *Cross Keys*.

Queen Square WC1 (Holborn, Camden). Laid out in the early 18th century and named after Queen Anne (1702–14).

Queen's Road SE15, SE14 (Peckham, Southwark). Formerly Deptford Lane, as approaching Deptford; renamed in honour of Queen Victoria (1837–1901).

Queenstown Road SW8 (Battersea, Wandsworth). The section N of Battersea Park Road was originally Victoria Road, approaching what was then called Victoria Bridge (now Chelsea Bridge) after its opening in 1858. The road and the bridge were closely associated with the development of the area around Battersea Park. The S section was called Queen's Road; the name Queenstown was introduced to avoid confusion with Queen's Road, Peckham, and it also reflects the strategic position of the road as the main spine of the Parktown estate (between Silverthorne Road and Stanley Grove).

Queen Street EC4 (Cit. Lond.). Made after the Great Fire of 1666 and named after Charles II's queen Catharine of Braganza. The N section was formerly a lane called Soper Lane, meaning soapers' or soap-makers' lane.

Queen Street W1 (Mayfair, Cit. West.). Built in 1753, when there was no reigning queen or queen consort; George II's queen Caroline of Ansbach had died in 1737. This may be a late tribute to a consort who was somewhat above the common run, or it may be simply a dignified name, indicating a street of quality.

Queensway W2 (Bayswater, Cit. West.). Formerly a lane called Black Lion Lane, from the *Black Lion* tavern which stood there. The lane was widened and improved as a new street in the late 19th century; it was named after Queen Victoria.

Queen's Wood Road N10 (Hornsey, Haringey). *See* **Southwood Lane**.

Queen Victoria Street EC4 (Cit. Lond.). Made in 1871; self explanatory.

Quemerford Road N7 (Upper Holloway, Islington). *See* **Biddestone Road**.

Quex Road NW6 (Kilburn, Camden). Built on land belonging to the Powell-Cotton family of Quex Park, Birchington, Kent, who owned this and another estate in Hampstead/Kilburn.

Quick Street N1 (Islington). Commemorates John Quick, an 18th-century comedian popular with George III.

Quilp Street SE1 (Southwark). *See* **Dickens Square**. The character called Quilp appears in Charles Dickens's novel *Little Dorrit*, which has a Southwark background.

Quorn Road SE22 (Camberwell, Southwark). *See* **Belvoir Road**.

R

Rabbit Row W8 (Notting Hill, Ken. Chel.). An old street of the hamlet of Notting Hill, named from breeders and sellers of rabbits.

Raby Street E14 (Stepney, T. Ham.). The name of a builder active in E London from the 1850s.

Radnor Place W2 (Paddington, Cit. West.). *See* **Bouverie Place**.

Radnor Street EC1 (Finsbury, Islington). Sole remaining street on the estate of the French hospital in Bath Street, built 1718 as a general refuge for French Huguenot (Protestant) refugees. The earls of Radnor were governors of the hospital, which was closed in 1866 and transferred to a new building N of Victoria Park.

Radnor Terrace W14 (Kensington, Ken. Chel.). On the estate which Lady Elizabeth Holland brought to her husband Francis Edwardes; he claimed descent from the earls of Radnor (*see* **Edwardes Square**).

Radnor Walk SW3 (Chelsea, Ken. Chel.). Built on land owned by the Earl of Radnor; the 17th-century Radnor House (demolished) stood at the corner of Flood Street and Royal Hospital Road.

Raglan Street NW5 (Kentish Town, Camden). Commemorates Lord Raglan who, having been second in command to the Duke of Wellington, was appointed Commander-in-Chief of the British Expeditionary Army to the East (i.e. the Crimea) in 1854. He died of Crimean fever, exacerbated by the disasters of the war, in June 1855 (*see* **Alma Grove**).

Railway Avenue SE16 (Rotherhithe, Southwark). The East London Railway Company took over the Thames Tunnel (*see* **Brunel Road**) which runs beside this road. The company acquired it in 1865, and extended it greatly to connect with main railway lines at Shoreditch and New Cross. The S section of their system comes above ground near Surrey Docks Station.

Raine Street E1 (Wapping, T. Ham.). Commemorates Henry Raine, brewer and benefactor to the parish. By his will of 1719 he founded schools to teach and keep 50 boys and 50 girls; he also provided dowries for the girls in the event of their receiving offers of marriage.

Rainsford Street W2 (Bayswater, Cit. West.). Commemorates the Rev. Marcus Rainsford, vicar of St James's, Sussex Gardens, 1904–11.

Raleana Road E14 (Isle of Dogs, T. Ham.). Said to be a composite name including elements of 'Raleigh'; there is a local tradition connecting Sir Walter Raleigh (executed in 1618) with the Coldharbour area (*see* **Raleigh Street**).

Raleigh Street N1 (Islington). Sir Walter Raleigh (1554–1618), explorer, is said to have lived in a house nearby which later became the *Pied Bull* tavern and has since been demolished. Raleigh led unsuccessful attempts to establish a colony in Virginia, although he brought back to England the potato and tobacco plants from America. He was involved in exploration of South America in search of gold, in 1596. A favourite with Elizabeth I, he was accused of treason by her successor James I; his death sentence was commuted to imprisonment from which James released him to lead another gold search on the Orinoco. Raleigh returned empty-handed and was beheaded.

Ramillies Street W1 (Oxford Street, Cit. West.). Commemorates a victory for English forces under the Duke of Marlborough; they defeated the French at Ramillies in Flanders in 1706. **Ramillies Place** adjoins.

Rampart Street E1 (Whitechapel, T. Ham.). Site of ramparts erected by Parliament troops against a Royalist attack on London, during the Civil War of 1642–8 (*see* **Cannon Street Road** and **Mount Terrace**).

Ram Place E9 (Homerton, Hackney). Stephen Ram built a chapel in Homerton in 1723 which was often used for Anglican worship but not connected to the parish. It was called Ram's Chapel. A school was added in 1801.

Rampayne Street SW1 (Cit. West.). Commemorates a parish benefactor called Rampayne, who in 1705 left a fund with which the children of the nearby Grey Coat Hospital, Greycoat Place, could be apprenticed.

Randells Road N1 (York Way, Islington). The Randell family owned a pottery with tile-kilns here in the 19th century (*see* **Tileyard Road**). John Randell gave the site for St Michael's church, consecrated here in 1864.

Randlesdown Road SE6 (Bellingham, Lewisham). *See* **Longdown Road**.

Randolph Avenue W9 (Paddington, Cit. West.). *See* **Porteus Road**. John Randolph was Bishop of London

1809–13. **Randolph Crescent**, **Gardens**, **Mews** and **Road** adjoin.

Ranelagh Avenue SW13 (Barnes, R. upon T.). From the Ranelagh Club in Barn Elms House, which moved here from Ranelagh House in Fulham (where it had been established in 1878) in 1884 (*see* **Ranelagh Avenue**).

Ranelagh Avenue SW6 (Fulham, Hammersmith). The viscounts of Ranelagh (*see* **Ranelagh Grove**) occupied two houses in Fulham after leaving Chelsea; one was Mulgrave House, and the other Ranelagh House, on this site. Both were acquired by Thomas Jones, Sixth Viscount Ranelagh, in 1807.

Ranelagh Bridge W2 (Royal Oak, Cit. West.). The Westbourne stream here flows underground as the Ranelagh Sewer, a name which was first applied to its mouth by Ranelagh Gardens and later extended up the course of the stream.

Ranelagh Grove SW1 (Chelsea, Cit. West.). Richard Jones, Lord Ranelagh, built a house nearby, E of the Chelsea Hospital, in 1690. During the 18th century its gardens became a pleasure ground. **Ranelagh Road** is nearby.

Ranelagh Road SW1 (Churchill Gardens, Cit. West.). Originally led to the New Ranelagh Tea Gardens by the river, named in imitation of the famous Ranelagh Gardens (*see* **Ranelagh Grove**).

Rangoon Street EC3 (Cit. Lond.). *See* **India Street**.

Ranston Street NW1 (Lisson Grove, Cit. West.). *See* **Shroton Street**.

Raphael Street SW7 (Knightsbridge, Cit. West.). Built from 1842 on land belonging to Lewis Raphael.

Ratcliffe Cross Street E1 (Ratcliff, T. Ham.). Runs S towards the former Ratcliffe Cross, a cross-roads which appears on a map of 1769 at the W end of Narrow Street. Ratcliff or Ratcliffe is a corruption of the hamlet's earlier name, Red Cliff.

Ratcliffe Orchard E1 (Ratcliff, T. Ham.). Marks the site of an extensive orchard which appears on a map of 1769 lying between Cable Street and the present N end of this street.

Ratcliff Grove EC1 (Finsbury, Islington). Off Lever Street, of which the E and W ends were formerly (before 1861) called Ratcliff Row and Ratcliff's Mount; they were named after Ratcliff Moffat, a local 18th-century farmer.

Rathbone Place W1 (Oxford Street, Cit. West.). Built by Thomas Rathbone from c1720 on land belonging to the Berners estate (*see* **Berners Street**). **Rathbone Street** approaches and, although on another estate and by another builder some 40 years later, was named by association.

Raul Road SE15 (Peckham, Southwark). *See* **Claude Road**.

Raveley Street NW5 (Kentish Town, Camden). *See* **Ospringe Road**.

Ravenet Street SW11 (Battersea, Wandsworth). Commemorates the French engraver who introduced transfer-printing (from a copper plate) on porcelain or enamel; he produced some of the best-known pieces from the Battersea Enamel factory 1750–c1762.

Raven Row E1 (Stepney, T. Ham.). Changed in 1879 from Raven Terrace, it appears in 1832 as Raven Row, probably from the builder.

Ravenscourt Park W6 (Hammer-smith). Ravenscourt House (bombed in 1941) was built here in the early 18th century; its grounds are the site of the mediaeval manor of Palyngswick (*see* **Paddenswick Road**).

Rawlings Street SW3 (Chelsea, Ken. Chel.). Commemorates Charles Rawlings (*d* 1862), parish benefactor.

Rawson Street SW11 (Battersea, Wandsworth). Probably commemorates Sir A. Cooper Rawson, mayor of the borough of Wandsworth c1919.

Rawstorne Street EC1 (Goswell Road, Islington). Built by Thomas Rawstorne, bricklayer, on land bequeathed to the Owen Schools trustees, c1773 (*see* **Owen Street**).

Raymond Buildings WC1 (Gray's Inn, Camden). Lord Chief Justice Raymond (1673–1733), was called to the bar of Gray's Inn in 1697. He was Solicitor General in the Tory government of 1710–13, Attorney General in 1720 and a Judge of the King's Bench in 1724. He became Lord Chief Justice in 1725 and was noted as impartial and conscientious.

Ray Street EC1 (Clerkenwell, Islington). Called Hockley in the Hole and, at the S end, Town's End Lane. In 1774 the name Ray Street was transferred from an adjacent lane. Ray is a corruption of the earlier 'Rag', from dealers therein.

Rector Street N1 (Islington). *See* **Prebend Street**.

Rectory Grove SW4 (Clapham, Lambeth). Site of the old Clapham Rectory; the parish church of Holy Trinity is first recorded in 1285 and stood near the present St Paul's; it was pulled down and replaced by a new church on the common in 1774–5.

Rectory Road SW13 (Barnes, R. upon T.). *See* **Church Road**.

Rectory Square E1 (Stepney, T. Ham.). Named from the rectory of St Dunstan's parish church nearby. The first recorded church was Saxon but the first recorded rector is William, who held office in 1233. St Dunstan, monk and statesman, was Bishop of London and lord of the manor of Stepney 959–61.

Red Anchor Close SW3 (Chelsea, Ken. Chel.). The Chelsea Pottery, established *c*1740, is thought to have stood on the opposite side of Old Church Street in the angle of Lawrence Street and Justice Walk. The pottery used the mark of a red anchor in 1754–8.

Redan Place W2 (Bayswater, Cit. West.). With **Redan Street**, Shepherd's Bush, and **Redan Terrace**, Camberwell, this is a street name made popular by the Crimean War (*see* **Alma Grove**). A redan is a field-work made to protect a gun position and characterised by its two faces jutting outwards to form a sharp point.

Red Bull Yard EC4 (Cit. Lond.). Formerly approached Red Bull Wharf on the Thames. Both wharf and yard were probably named from the sign of an inn, now gone.

Redchurch Street E2 (Bethnal Green, T. Ham.). The 'red church' was St James the Great (the apostle). During the 1860s the vicar, convinced that many of his parishioners living in sin were doing so because they could not afford the marriage fee, began performing marriage services free of charge. The cost was met from a fund. The response ensured the fame of the 'red church' (*see* **Coke Street**).

Redcliffe Gardens SW10 (Earl's Court, Ken. Chel.). Designed in the 1860s by George Godwin and named from his previous work at Redcliffe in Bristol. **Redcliffe Place**, **Road**, **Square** and **Street** are nearby.

Redcross Way SE1 (Southwark). Passes the site (NE corner with Union Street) of the Redcross Burial Ground, formerly called the Cross Bones Burial Ground, and locally believed to be the cemetery for prostitutes from the 16th-century Bankside brothels. There is no evidence that it was. It was not consecrated ground but it was owned by the Bishop of Winchester and held on lease from him.

Reddin's Road SE15 (Peckham, Southwark). Edmund Reddin was contractor to Camberwell vestry in the 1860s, and an active local builder.

Rede Place W2 (Bayswater, Cit. West.). Commemorates Richard Rede, salter, to whom Henry VIII granted this manor at the dissolution of the monasteries. The Redes held the manor until the 1620s.

Redfield Lane SW5 (Kensington, Ken. Chel.). An old path, formerly approaching a field called the Red Field beside the present Cromwell Road.

Red Lion Court EC4 (Cit. Lond.). Named from the sign of an inn, now demolished.

Red Lion Market EC1 (Cit. Lond.). A *Red Lion Inn* is recorded here *c*1650–70.

Red Lion Row SE17 (Walworth, Southwark). The *Red Lion Inn* which stood here on Walworth Road is first mentioned in 1789.

Red Lion Square WC1 (Holborn, Camden). Built in the late 17th century on land surrounding the *Red*

Lion Inn, which is now demolished. **Red Lion Street** is nearby.

Redman's Road E1 (Stepney, T. Ham.). Captain John Redman was a member of Stepney parish vestry in the 1740s.

Red Place W1 (Mayfair, Cit. West.). A late-Victorian name given in association with adjoining Green Street and inspired by the colour of the buildings.

Red Post Hill SE24, SE25 (Herne Hill, Southwark). An old lane leading from a marker post on Denmark Hill, and recorded as such in the 17th century.

Redriff Road SE16 (Rotherhithe, Southwark). An old corruption of Rotherhithe (*see* **Rotherhithe Street**). In the 17th century the district was commonly known as Redriff.

Reece Mews SW7 (Kensington, Ken. Chel.). Built on land owned by Louisa and Robert Reece in 1869.

Reed's Place NW1 (Camden Town, Camden). Built by a local builder called William Reed, who also lived there, in the 1860s.

Reeves Mews W1 (Mayfair, Cit. West.). Built on land leased from the Grosvenor estate in 1731 by a Mr Reeves.

Reform Street SW11 (Battersea, Wandsworth). One of a group built by Battersea Council and named in 1903, by association with neighbouring **Freedom Street** and the names of radical politicians. The others are: **Odger Street**, after George Odger (1820–77); **Matthews Street**, after William Matthews; **Joubert Street**; and **Burns Road**.

Regency Street SW1 (Pimlico, Cit. West.). Built as part of improved approaches to Vauxhall Bridge, opened by George, Prince Regent, in 1811. **Regency Place** adjoins.

Regent Square WC1 (Bloomsbury, Camden). Built by the Harrison family. The Regency ended in 1820 and the square was not laid out until *c*1824; the Harrisons, however, had formerly made plans and chosen names years in advance of building (*see* **Sidmouth Street**).

Regent Street W1, SW1 (Cit. West.). Made 1813–21 by John Nash as part of a scheme for the Prince Regent; the whole comprised Regent's Park, Regent Street as a grand approach to it and **Lower Regent Street** as the final link with the Prince's residence at Carlton House. The street has since been rebuilt. Regent's Park to the N was intended to be a residential estate, a group of mansions in private parks, and not the open space it is today.

Relf Road SE15 (Peckham Rye, Southwark). Properly Relph, a 19th-century vestryman of Camberwell parish which included this area.

Remnant Street WC2 (Lincoln's Inn, Camden). James Farquharson Remnant, First Baron Remnant (1863–1933), was a lawyer of Lincoln's Inn and London County Council member for Holborn 1892–1900. He was MP for Holborn 1900–28. He lived at Bear Place, Twyford, in Berkshire. **Twyford Place** runs parallel.

Rennie Street SE1 (Southwark). Crosses Stamford Street where the engineer and architect John Rennie lived and worked from 1794 until 1821. He designed and built Southwark Bridge and Waterloo Bridge. His son Sir John Rennie, who built London Bridge, was born in Stamford Street in 1794.

Retreat Place E9 (Hackney). This road originally passed a small estate of almshouses called Robinson's Retreat, which stood on the junction with Mead Place.

Rewell Street SW6 (Fulham, Hammersmith). Approaches the house called 'Sandford Manor' which James Rewell is recorded as occupying in 1788; he ran a pottery there.

Rex Place W1 (Mayfair, Cit. West.). This street was renamed in Latin in 1951; it was formerly King's Mews.

Reynolds Road SE15 (Nunhead, Southwark). Jonathon C. Reynolds was surveyor to Camberwell vestry in the 1860s.

Rhodes Street N7 (Islington). Samuel Rhodes, farmer, held land here in the 1820s. He was the grandfather of Cecil Rhodes (1853–1902) who extended British imperial rule in southern Africa.

Rhodeswell Road E14 (Limehouse, T. Ham.). This is a corruption of Rogues' Well, and the original lane approached Rogues' Well Common, let by Stepney parish to Michael Barks of Rogues' Well House in 1651. The identity of the rogues who frequented the well is unknown. The common was formerly part of the parish Pest House field.

Ribblesdale Road SW16 (Furzedown, Wandsworth). Named in 1901, when Lord Ribblesdale was an alderman of the London County Council.

Richard Street E1 (Stepney, T. Ham.). *See* **Pace Place**.

Richbell Place WC1 (Theobald's Road, Camden). Built in 1710 by John Richbell.

Richborough Road NW2 (W

Hampstead, Camden). Kentish place name; built by the Powell-Cotton family of Quex Park, Birchington, Kent.

Richmond Buildings W1 (Soho, Cit. West.). Built in 1732–3 by Thomas Richmond, carpenter, who built the adjacent S side of **St Anne's Court** in 1735–6. **Richmond Mews** adjoins.

Richmond Terrace SW1 (Whitehall, Cit. West.). Site of a house belonging to the dukes of Richmond which was first built after the Restoration of 1660, rebuilt in the 18th century and burnt down in 1791.

Rich Street E14 (Limehouse, T. Ham.). Charles Rich and Co., coopers, were at work in Church Row, Limehouse, in 1805.

Rickett Street SW6 (Fulham, Hammersmith). James Ricketts owned a wharf here in 1855. The present line of the railway was formerly that of a waterway called (like the other, W of it) the Stanford or Stamford Brook.

Rickman Street E1 (Stepney, T. Ham.). *See* **Amiel Street**.

Ridgmount Street WC1 (Bloomsbury, Camden). Built on land belonging to the dukes of Bedford, who also held property at Ridgmount, Bedfordshire. **Ridgmount Gardens** and **Place** adjoin.

Riding House Street W1 (Great Portland Street, Cit. West.). Formerly Riding House Lane, recorded in the 18th century; the derivation is unknown.

Ridley Road E8 (Hackney). Commemorates Nicholas Ridley, Bishop of London under Edward VI (1547–53), who was martyred as a Protestant under Edward's successor and half-sister Mary I in 1555. He was burnt at the stake.

Ringcroft Street N7 (Islington). Corruption of Ring Cross, the boundary-marker cross of the Knights of St John of Jerusalem; it stood here marking the N limit of their property before the dissolution of the monasteries (*see* **St John Street**).

Ripplevale Grove N7 (Barnsbury, Islington). Sir John French was Commander-in-Chief of the British Expeditionary Force in 1914–15. He was created Earl of Ypres and Ripplevale. This street was named in his honour in 1921; it was formerly Albion Grove, from Thomas Albion Oldfield's tea gardens.

Rivercourt Road W6 (Hammersmith). Rivercourt House was built W of this road *c*1809, on the site of an earlier house. A house built in the grounds, and on the line of this road, became the residence of the Queen Dowager Catharine of Braganza after 1686.

River Place N1 (Islington). Formerly approached the New River, which flowed down the line of Astey's Row (*see* **Myddelton Square**). **River Street** runs beside the former New River Head, the reservoirs at the head of Myddelton's watercourse (*see also* **Amwell Street**).

Robert Adam Street W1 (Marylebone, Cit. West.). Robert Adam, architect, built Home House (1773) and others in Portman Square nearby; he was also active elsewhere in the development of Marylebone.

Robert Close W9 (Paddington, Cit. West.). *See* **Browning Close**.

Robertson Street SW8 (Battersea, Wandsworth). *See* **Broughton Street**. This name possibly compliments Sir

J. Robertson, Prime Minister of New South Wales, Australia. The name was chosen in 1877.

Robert Street WC2 (Strand, Cit. West.). Part of the Adelphi development built by John and Robert Adam *c*1768; it was balanced by John Street (now John Adam Street; *see* **Adelphi Terrace**).

Robinhood Court EC2 (Cit. Lond.). Leads off Milk Street and probably derives from a tavern, now demolished, called the *Robin Hood*. Ballads of Robin Hood were popular from at least 1377. The earliest rhymes mention him in connection with Randolf, Earl of Chester, who flourished *c*1200. By the end of the 15th century he had grown into a popular folk hero with a complete set of followers and exploits; May Day became a festival of Robin Hood.

Robin Hood Yard EC1 (Holborn, Camden). Named from the sign of an inn, now demolished (*see* **Robinhood Court**).

Rochelle Street E2 (Bethnal Green, T. Ham.). Part of the Arnold Circus scheme, named by association with the Huguenot settlement in this area (*see* **Nantes Passage**). After long religious wars in France the port of La Rochelle on the W coast was granted to the Huguenots (Protestants) as a stronghold by the Treaty of Montpellier in 1622. Further conflict between the Huguenots and the Catholic establishment came to a climax when Cardinal Richelieu ordered the siege of La Rochelle in 1627; an English expedition failed to relieve the city, which 'surrendered in 1628. The Huguenot wars ended by treaty in 1629.

Rochester Row SW1 (Cit. West.). This was formerly a private road belonging to the Dean and Chapter of Westminster Abbey, and named from a long-standing connection between the deans of Westminster and the diocese of Rochester in Kent (*see* **Medway Street**). The road became a public thoroughfare *c*1800. **Rochester Street** adjoins.

Rochester Walk SE1 (Southwark). Commemorates a house nearby which belonged to the bishops of Rochester. During the mediaeval and Tudor periods episcopal properties in S London changed hands in a sequence that resembles 'musical chairs'. The bishops of Rochester originally held Lambeth manor. This they conveyed to the archbishops of Canterbury, who built Lambeth Palace. Rochester retained some land in Lambeth for its own use, and built there a house; it later gave this house to Henry VIII in exchange for one at Southwark. The house at Southwark which Henry obtained for Rochester had belonged to the bishops of Winchester. Henry VIII later gave the old Rochester house in Lambeth to the bishops of Carlisle.

Rodmarton Mews W1 (Marylebone, Cit. West.). Named by association with parallel Gloucester Place. Rodmarton is a Gloucestershire village SW of Cirencester.

Rodney Place SE17 (Walworth, Southwark). Commemorates Admiral Rodney, whose victories against the French and Spanish fleets in 1782 helped to ensure that neither country was able to exploit the American War of Independence at the expense of Britain. This area had a group of streets commemorating naval victories. Adjoining **Rodney Road** was originally Trafalgar Road, and Orb Street was Nelson Place.

Rodwell Road SE22 (Dulwich, Southwark). Probably in honour of George Herbert Rodwell, minor composer. His daughter married the son of Landells the engraver (*see* **Landells Road**).

Rogers Road SW17 (Tooting, Wandsworth). Named in 1928. Possibly commemorates John Rogers, benefactor to the parish of Tooting Graveney, who left £200 to be invested for the poor in 1778.

Roger Street WC1 (Gray's Inn Road, Camden). Renamed in 1937 in an attempt to reduce the number of London's 'Henry' streets; in the process the link with the original developer has been lost. The old name, Henry Street, came from the estate owner Henry Doughty.

Rollit Street N7 (Holloway, Islington). Sir Albert Rollit (*d* 1922) was MP for Islington South and a benefactor of the nearby Northern Polytechnic College.

Rolls Passage EC4 (Chancery Lane, Cit. West.). Leads off Chancery Lane on the site of the house where the rolls of Chancery were kept from 1342. John Stow, in his *Survey of London* of 1598, says: 'King Edward III annexed the house of Converts [from Judaism to Christianity] by patent to the office of Custos Rotulorum, or Master of the Rolls, in the fifteenth of his reign'.

Rolls Road SE1 (Old Kent Road, Southwark). The Rolls (originally Rowles) family held land in St George's Fields, in Walworth and along the Old Kent Road. The Rolls Estate Office was built nearby in the Old Kent Road in 1795. John Rolls, cow-keeper, founded this estate. He first rented 10 acres of meadow S of the Old Kent Road in 1775; this belonged to the Bridge House Estates Commissioners of the City of London. In 1786 he took 22 acres round the present Albany Road.

Most of the land was developed after 1840 (*see* **Hendre Road**).

Rolt Street SE8 (Deptford, Lewisham). Peter Rolt was born in Deptford, at Broomfield House in the present Evelyn Street, in 1798. He was a pioneer of iron-clad men o'war and a partner in Brocklebank and Rolt. In 1820 he married the daughter of Thomas Brocklebank, of the General Steam Navigation Company. He died in 1882.

Roman Road E2, E3 (Bethnal Green, T. Ham.). Follows the line of the Roman route from London to Colchester which crossed the River Lea at the place called Old Ford. This 'old' or Roman ford was the only crossing point until the construction of Bow Bridge (*see* **Bow Road**). **Old Ford Road** approaches it along a line further N, leading not only to the ford but also to the hamlet which grew up around it and took its name.

Roman Way N7 (Barnsbury, Islington). *See* **Mountfort Crescent**.

Romborough Way SE13 (Lewisham). A name first recorded in the 13th century, describing part of Lewisham which now lies between Lewisham Park and Hither Green.

Romilly Street W1 (Soho, Cit. West.). Commemorates Sir Samuel Romilly (*d* 1818), legal reformer, who lived in Frith Street.

Rommany Road SE27 ()W Norwood, Lambeth). *See* **Lavengro Road.**

Romney Street SW1 (Cit. West.). *See* **Marsham Street**.

Romola Road SE24 (Tulse Hill, Lambeth). *See* **Deronda Road**.

Ronalds Road N5 (Highbury, Islington). The scientist Sir Francis Ronalds (1788–1873) lived in the adjacent Highbury Terrace, where he conducted the experiments leading to his invention of the electrical telegraph.

Rondu Road NW2 (W Hampstead, Camden). Built by the Powell-Cotton family of Quex Park, Birchington, Kent. Travellers and big-game hunters, they owned properties in Kashmir at Rondu and Skardu. **Skardu Road** runs parallel.

Rood Lane EC3 (Cit. Lond.). John Stow in his *Survey of London* of 1598 says that a rood or cross was set up in the adjacent churchyard of St Margaret Pattens while the church was being rebuilt in the early 16th century; offerings to the shrine at this cross defrayed building expenses. The cross was broken up, as an object of superstition, in 1538.

Rookstone Road SW17 (Tooting, Wandsworth). A large house called 'The Rookery' lay between this and Charlmont Road.

Ropemakers' Fields E14 (Limehouse, T. Ham.). Site of a traditional industry of Limehouse, Ratcliff and Shadwell: making ships' cables and rigging. Individual ropemakers, Risbey and Margetts, are recorded in the 17th century. The 'fields' provided the open space necessary for the long rope-walks where the rope was twisted. Yarns of hemp, jute, sisal or manila were twisted into strands, and the strands then wound round each other, in the opposite direction to the first twist. A hawser has three strands; a cable is made up of three hawsers.

Ropemaker Street EC2 (Cit. Lond.). The name is first recorded in 1672, and indicates a street of ropemakers (*see* **Ropemakers' Fields**). The work here would have been general and not specifically maritime.

Ropery Street E3 (Bow Common, T. Ham.). A 19th-century street built on a rope-walk (*see* **Ropemakers' Fields**) and originally called South Grove. The old name was revived in 1882. When land here was acquired for the Tower Hamlets cemetery in 1841 the rope-walk belonged to Soanes and Son.

Rosary Gardens SW7 (Kensington, Ken. Chel.). Properly Rosery, from a property here in the 18th century; this was a house called 'The Rosery' and a small field called the Rose Haw Field.

Rose Alley EC2 (Bishopsgate, Cit. Lond.). Named from the sign of an inn, now demolished. Bishopsgate was always one of the main exits from the City, and the number of old inns recorded along its length is significant.

Rose Alley SE1 (Southwark). Site of the Elizabethan Rose Theatre, built for Philip Henslowe and first recorded in 1588; it was the first of the Bankside theatres, before the Swan (after 1594), the Globe (1599) and the Hope (1614).

Rosebery Avenue EC1 (Clerkenwell, Camden/Islington). A Victorian street which compliments Lord Rosebery, Liberal politician. He served as Foreign Secretary in Gladstone's government in 1886 and again 1892–4, when he replaced Gladstone as Prime Minister. The street was named in 1889, when he was the first chairman of the London County Council.

Rosemary Road SE15 (Peckham, Southwark). The *Rosemary Branch* at the junction of Southampton Way and Commercial Way is first recorded *c*1700. **Rosemary Gardens** is nearby.

Rosemary Street N1 (Islington). The

Rosemary Branch is mentioned in 1735 as a point near the parish boundary between St Mary, Islington, and St Leonard, Shoreditch. In 1783 a new inn was built on the boundary and the old site became a white lead factory. **Branch Place** is nearby.

Rosemoor Street SW3 (Chelsea, Ken. Chel.). *See* **Caversham Street**.

Rosenau Road SW11 (Battersea, Wandsworth). A compliment to Prince Albert (*see* **Albert Bridge Road**, adjoining). The prince was born at his parents' summer residence, The Rosenau, near Coburg. **Rosenau Crescent** adjoins.

Rosenthal Road SE6 (Lewisham). Built on an estate called Rosenthal which belonged to a Victorian manufacturer of macassar oil.

Rosoman Street EC1 (Clerkenwell, Islington). Commemorates the builder and first manager of the Sadler's Wells Theatre, which replaced Sadler's Music House in 1765. Rosoman also owned the land on which this street was built; it was formerly a footpath past the House of Detention, and was locally known as the Bridewell Walk. Rosoman called his first group of houses Rosoman Row. (The name Sadler's Wells arose from the discovery, in Mr Sadler's Music House, of an ancient well; it was uncovered in 1683 and was thought to have been a holy or healing well.)

Rosslyn Hill NW3 (Hampstead, Camden). Rosslyn House, N of Belsize Lane, belonged to Alexander Wedderburn, Lord Loughborough, Earl of Rosslyn. He was Lord Chancellor from 1795, and very unpopular with his contemporaries.

Rossmore Road NW1 (Marylebone, Cit. West.). Built on the Portman family estate (*see* **Portman Square**); the family also held a property called Rossmore.

Rotherfield Street N1 (Islington). Built on land belonging to J.W. Scott of Rotherfield Park.

Rotherhithe Street SE16 (Southwark). Runs along the Rother Hithe, or the wharf where cattle were shipped (from OE 'rother' or 'rether', cattle). The original stretch of this street ran along the river bank from W of St Mary's church to a point opposite Ratcliff. The SE stretch covers the line of an old rope-walk (*see* **Ropemakers' Fields**). The S end covers part of the former Trinity Street, from Trinity church which stood where Bryan Road now is.

Rotten Row SW7 (Hyde Park, Cit. West.). The name is probably a corruption of 'Route du Roi', the King's Road; Kensington Palace, which it approaches, became the principal royal residence under William III (1689–1702).

Roupell Road SW2 (Norwood, Lambeth). Part of the Roupell Park estate; John Roupell, metal refiner, of Lambeth, bought land from Lord Thurlow's trustees some time after 1810 (*see* **Thurlow Park Road**). Building continued under his son Richard Palmer Roupell and Richard's illegitimate son William who, after managing the S London estate and serving as MP for a Lambeth constituency, was convicted of forgery in 1862 and sentenced to penal servitude for life. He had forged his father's will on finding that the true will did not, as he felt, give him his just reward.

Roupell Street SE1 (Lambeth). Developed in the 1820s by John Roupell, metal refiner, who owned property in the area (*see* **Roupell Road**).

Rouse Gardens SE21 (Dulwich, Southwark). Harold Lindsay Rouse (*d* 1959), Director of the Midland Bank, was educated at Alleyn's school nearby.

Rowcross Street SE1 (Old Kent Road, Southwark). Thomas Rowcross was a benefactor to his parish in Bermondsey, St Mary Magdalene, in 1812.

Rowditch Lane SW11 (Battersea, Wandsworth). *See* **Culvert Road**.

Rowington Close W2 (Paddington, Cit. West.). A Warwickshire place name, chosen by association with the nearby Warwick estate, approached by Warwick Crescent.

Rowland Hill Street NW3 (Hampstead, Camden). Sir Rowland Hill (1795–1879), originator of prepaid flat-rate postage, lived here.

Royal Arcade SW1 (Mayfair, Cit. West.). A shopping arcade off Old Bond Street, called Royal after a visit from Queen Victoria.

Royal Avenue SW3 (Chelsea, Ken. Chel.). This approaches the Royal Hospital on the other side of Burton's Court gardens; the avenue is said to have been designed as part of a royal route from Kensington Palace.

Royal College Street NW1 (Camden Town, Camden). Approaches the Royal Veterinary College which was founded in 1791; the original building was completed in 1792. The college received its royal charter in 1844; it was rebuilt in 1937.

Royal Hospital Road SW3 (Chelsea, Ken. Chel.). Passes the Royal Hospital, founded for old and disabled soldiers in 1682. The hospital was paid for by Sir Stephen Fox, Paymaster General, and Charles II; it was inspired by Louis

XIV's foundation of the Hôtel des Invalides in Paris. The road was formerly called Paradise Row (*see* **Paradise Street**), a name once commonly given in association with a burial ground or an enclosed garden.

Royal Mint Street E1 (Whitechapel, T. Ham.). The Royal Mint, formerly within the Tower of London, was set up at the end of this street in 1811 and remained there until 1968 when it was moved to Llantrisant in S Wales. The old name for this street was Hog Street, recorded in the 16th century. It was Hoggestrete and Heggestrete in the 14th century and Hacchestrete in the 13th; the word comes from OE 'haecc', a hatch-gate or wicket-gate, and refers to such a gate in the City wall by the Tower of London.

Royal Opera Arcade SW1 (Cit. West.). The original theatre on the site occupied by Her Majesty's Theatre opened as an opera house in 1705. It was rebuilt by John Nash in 1818 with colonnades and arcades – of which this one survives – incorporated in it.

Royal Street SE1 (Lambeth). The *Royal George* public house stands on the corner with Carlisle Lane.

Roydon Close SW11 (Battersea, Wandsworth). The Roydon family were formerly lords of the manor of Battersea. Elizabeth I (1558–1603) granted the lease of the manor to Henry Roydon; his daughter Joan, widow of Sir William Holcroft, inherited it and brought it to her second husband Oliver St John, who was able to buy the manor from the Crown in 1627 (*see* **Bolingbroke Walk**).

Ruckholt Road E10 (Hackney/Newham). Described in 1512 as 'the common way which leads from Hackney to Rockholt in Essex'.

Ruddigore Road SE14 (Deptford, Lewisham). Named in 1888 after the Gilbert and Sullivan opera of that name.

Rugby Street WC1 (Holborn, Camden). The founder of Rugby School, Lawrence Sheriff, gave land here in 1567 for the endowment of the school. This street was built *c*1680.

Rumbold Road SW6 (Fulham, Hammersmith). William Rumbold, court official and Surveyor General of Customs, lived in Fulham in 1664. His house stood at Parson's Green. His own family had left Fulham by 1690, but his brother Henry's family had returned, to a different house, by 1735.

Rundell Road W9 (Paddington, Cit. West.). The surrounding area formed part of the manor of Westbourne which was held by Westminster Abbey; the Dean and Chapter leased it to Philip Rundell, who was goldsmith to George III. Development began with later members of the Rundell family; **Goldney Road** and **Chippenham Road** are named after Eleanora Rundell's husband Samuel Goldney of Chippenham. In 1820 the lease was transferred to their co-developers, the Neeld family of Grittleton (*see* **Grittleton Road**). **Foscote Mews** is named from a Goldney family property in Wiltshire.

Rupack Street SE16 (Rotherhithe, Southwark). Approaches the church of St Mary where a tablet commemorates Prince Lee Boo, son of Abba Thulle, Rupack or King of the Pelew Islands. The Rupack received the shipwrecked crew of an East Indiaman with kindness, and sent his son to London in their company. The prince lived with the Wilsons (*see* **Wilson Grove**) in Rotherhithe and died there in 1784.

Rupert Street W1 (Shaftesbury Avenue, Cit. West.). Commemorates Prince Rupert of the Rhine, son of the Elector Palatine (briefly King of Bohemia) and Elizabeth, daughter of James I. He was nephew to Charles I and commanded the Royalist cavalry during the Civil War of 1642–8. He was highly professional in the equipping and training of his men, and an inventive cavalry tactician. Very successful in the early stages of the war, he met his match in Cromwell who was equally professional and a lot more inventive.

Rushcroft Road SW2 (Brixton, Lambeth). Built across the head of the former Rush Common, which extended S approximately to the line of Josephine Avenue and Brixton Water Lane. The common was developed from 1810; 'rush' is an indication of the watery nature of the land.

Rushey Green SE6 (Lewisham). Recorded in the 16th century as Rushet Green, and as Russchetes-lond in the reign of Edward II (1307–27); the name probably comes from marshy ground with small streams and beds of rushes.

Rush Hill Road SW11 (Battersea, Wandsworth). Built on the site of Rush Hill House.

Rushworth Street SE1 (Southwark). Runs parallel to **King's Bench Street**. The lawyer and historian John Rushworth (*d* 1690) spent the last years of his life in the King's Bench Prison. Rushworth made a special study of the workings of Parliament, based on his own verbatim records of proceedings. He was an influential supporter of Parliament during the Civil War of 1642–8. His *Historical Recollections* were published in eight volumes between 1659 and 1701.

Ruskin Walk SE24 (Herne Hill, Southwark). *See* **Brantwood Road**. Approaches the house on Herne Hill where the Victorian scholar and critic John Ruskin lived from 1823; his family moved to Denmark Hill in 1842.

Russell Road W14 (Kensington, Ken. Chel.). Built on the estate surrounding Holland House, centre of the Whig aristocracy in the early 19th century. Lord John Russell (1792–1878), son of the sixth Duke of Bedford, was a friend of Lord and Lady Holland from his youth. A member of the committee which drafted the great Reform Bill of 1832, he was Prime Minister 1846–51 and 1865–6.

Russell's Footpath SW16 (Streatham, Lambeth). The Russell family acquired a Streatham manor by marriage (*see* **Bedford Hill**); the Rev. Lord Wriothesley Russell occupied St Leonard's Rectory, Streatham, in 1831, and Lord John Russell, as his guest, there drafted much of the Reform Bill of 1832.

Russell Square WC1 (Bloomsbury, Camden). Part of the Bloomsbury estate of the Russell family, dukes of Bedford. The Russells moved into Bloomsbury in 1700, having acquired the manor through the marriage of Lord William Russell to the heiress (*see* **Southampton Row**). **Great Russell Street** and **Little Russell Street** are nearby.

Russell Street WC2 (Covent Garden, Cit. West.). Laid out by Inigo Jones in 1631 as part of the Covent Garden scheme for the fourth Earl of Bedford, Francis Russell.

Russia Lane E2 (Bethnal Green, T. Ham.). This is a corruption of an old name which appears as Rushy and Russey; it may be from the state of the ground, or from the original landowner.

Russia Row EC2 (Cit. Lond.). First recorded in 1810, when it ran through Honey Lane Market, presumably as a 'row' of traders as in Leadenhall Market today. The market, which was created on a cleared area after the Great Fire of 1666, closed in 1835. There is no known connection with Russian products or the incorporated body of merchants known as the Russia or Muscovy Company.

Rutherford Street SW1 (Cit. West.). The Rev. William Rutherford was headmaster of nearby Westminster School 1883–1901.

Rutland Gate SW7 (Knightsbridge, Cit. West.). Built on land belonging to the dukes of Rutland, who had a house here in the 18th century. **Rutland Gardens** and **Street** approach.

Rutland Place EC1 (Charterhouse, Islington). After the dissolution of the Charterhouse as a monastery (*see* **Charterhouse Street**), the buildings were granted by Henry VIII to Sir Edward North in 1545. His son Roger, Lord North, sold most of it to the Duke of Norfolk in 1565, keeping this SE part for himself. He died in his house there in 1600; his property was afterwards sold to the Manners family, earls of Rutland, and in 1656 there is a record of plays produced as private entertainment at 'Rutland House' in the Charterhouse. After

receiving a dukedom, the family moved on to the more fashionable Knightsbridge (*see* **Rutland Gate**).

Rutley Close SE17 (Kennington, Lambeth). Originally Rutley Gardens (1869) and probably laid out by Rutleys, builders active in Lambeth in the 1860s and 1870s.

Ryder Street SW1 (St James's, Cit. West.). Probably named from Richard Rider or Ryder (*d* 1683) who was master carpenter to Charles II and is known to have engaged in speculative building, although there is no evidence to link him directly with this street. He was active at the right time, and the surrounding area was built up with royal encouragement (*see* **St James's Square**).

Rydon Street N1 (New North Road, Islington). Henry Rydon took land here from the Church Commissioners and built houses between 1847 and 1852, when the complete streets were sold back to the Church (*see* **Prebend Street**). Henry (*d* 1885) was followed as a developer by his sons Horace (*d* 1910) and Arthur (*d* 1930). (*See* **Pyrland Road**.)

Rye Lane SE15 (Peckham, Southwark). *See* **Peckham Rye**.

Rysbrack Street SW3 (Chelsea, Ken. Chel.). Named in honour of the sculptor Michael Rysbrack, whose work includes a statue of Sir Hans Sloane, completed in 1737 (*see* **Sloane Street**).

S

Sackville Street W1 (Piccadilly, Cit. West.). Edward Sackville, brother of the fifth Earl of Dorset, leased one of the first houses here in 1675.

Saffron Hill EC1 (Holborn, Camden). Originally part of the garden of the bishops of Ely, where they grew saffron crocuses; their palace was at nearby **Ely Place**.

St Alban's Road NW5 (Highgate, Camden). Harriet Mellon, actress, married the banker Thomas Coutts who left her a fortune. In 1827 she married as her second husband the ninth Duke of St Albans, who was 24 years her junior. She died in 1837, leaving her Holly Lodge estate, Highgate, to Thomas Coutts's granddaughter Angela Burdett (*see* **Baroness Road**).

St Alban's Street SW1 (St James's, Cit. West.). Built on land granted by Charles II to Henry Jermyn, Earl of St Albans, in 1661.

St Alban's Terrace W6 (Fulham, Hammersmith). St Alban's mission was established here in 1881, and was dedicated to the first British martyr (*d* 301).

St Alphage High Walk EC2 (Cit. Lond.). Modern elevated footpath past the site of the church of St Alphage by the old London wall, first mentioned in the early 12th century. The saint, who died in 1012, was Archbishop of Canterbury. The first church was built against the Norman city wall; this was pulled down at the dissolution of the monasteries *c* 1539, when the church of the adjacent, newly dissolved priory of Elsing Spital, S of the wall, became the new parish church of St Alphage. There is another church of St Alphage in Greenwich, the scene of his martyrdom. When he refused to impoverish his tenants to ransom himself from the Danes, he was brought into the Danish assembly and pelted with animal bones.

St Andrew's Road W14 (Hammersmith). St Andrew's Mission church was established here in 1868; a permanent church dedicated to the apostle was built in 1874.

St Anne's Court W1 (Soho, Cit. West.). Named from the surrounding parish of St Anne, Soho, created in 1678. A new church was designed by Sir Christopher Wren for the new parish, which was formerly part of St Martin-in-the-Fields. St Anne, Anna or Hannah is mentioned in the 2nd century as the mother of the Virgin Mary.

St Anne Street E14 (Limehouse, T. Ham.). Opposite St Anne's parish church, built as one of the 50 new 'Queen Anne' churches designed to cater for the expanding suburbs of London 1712–30. The architect was Nicholas Hawksmoor, and the new parish was established in 1729. The church was burnt down in 1850 and rebuilt (*see* **St Anne's Court**).

St Ann's Hill SW18 (Wandsworth). Passes St Ann's church, built in 1824 as a chapel of ease to the original Wandsworth parish church of All Saints; the separate parish of St Ann was created in 1847. **St Ann's Crescent** adjoins (*see* **St Anne's Court**).

St Ann's Road SW13 (Barnes, R.

upon T.). Site of an 18th-century house called 'St Ann's' which belonged to a fashionable beauty, Lady Archer, and later to Lord Lonsdale. **Lonsdale Road** approaches.

St Ann's Street SW1 (Cit. West.). A chapel dedicated to St Ann used to stand here but is now demolished. The present St Ann's church is in Old Pye Street and the church in St Ann's Street is dedicated to St Matthew. **St Ann's Lane** runs parallel (*see* **St Anne's Court**).

St Anselm's Place W1 (Mayfair, Cit. West.). Site of St Anselm's church, consecrated in 1896 and demolished in 1938. Anselm, Benedictine abbot of Bec, came to England as Archbishop of Canterbury in 1093 and remained until his death in 1109. He was a staunch defender of the rights of the Church against the claims of William II and Henry I.

St Asaph Road SE4 (Nunhead, Southwark). *See* **Copleston Road**.

St Augustine's Road NW1 (Kentish Town, Camden). In the parish of St Pancras. St Augustine, sent by Pope Gregory to convert the English in 596, is locally associated with St Pancras. Augustine established the first cathedral in Canterbury and became head of the southern province, with powers to set up a northern province based on York. He also founded, in Canterbury, a church which he dedicated to St Pancras.

St Barnabas Street SW1 (Pimlico, Cit. West.). St Barnabas's church was built here 1848–50 as a chapel of ease to the Anglican parish of St Paul's, Knightsbridge; it was noted in its early years as a centre of the ritualistic movement. St Barnabas was a Jewish Cypriot active in the early Church at the time of St Paul,

whom he accompanied on a mission to the Gentiles.

St Benet's Place EC3 (Cit. Lond.) The church of St Benet (the 'grass church', *see* **Gracechurch Street**) stood at the junction of Gracechurch Street and Fenchurch Street, next to this yard. Gracechurch Court is almost opposite. Benet is a contraction of Benedict, from St Benedict of Nursia (*c*480–*c*550), reformer of monastic life.

St Bride Street EC4 (Cit. Lond.). Built *c*1870 and named from St Bride's church on the other side of Fleet Street (*see* **Bridewell Place**).

St Chad's Place WC1 (King's Cross, Camden). Site of St Chad's Well, traditionally held to be a mediaeval holy well with healing properties and certainly used as a medicinal spa in the 18th and early 19th centuries. **St Chad's Street** approaches. Chad (*d* 672) was Abbot of Lastingham and Bishop of Mercia, founder of the diocese of Lichfield.

St Charles Square W10 (N Kensington, Ken. Chel.). St Charles College, a boys' school, formerly in Paddington, moved here in 1874. It was managed by the Oblates of St Charles. The school closed in 1903 and the building became a training college. St Charles Borromeo (1538–84) was Archbishop of Milan, a diocesan and liturgical reformer noted for practical help for his flock.

St Christopher's Place W1 (Marylebone, Cit. West.). Named by Octavia Hill, the reformer, who had rescued it from slum condition and turned it into clean, cheap lodgings. Miss Hill had a special admiration for St Christopher, a 3rd-century martyr. In legends and paintings he appears as a giant, carrying the infant Christ on his shoulder; he is the patron of travellers and is invoked as a protection against sudden death.

St Clare Street EC3 (Whitechapel, T. Ham.) Part of the site of the mediaeval convent of the Little Sisters of St Clare (*see* **Minories**).

St Cross Street EC1 (Holborn, Camden). Originally Cross Street, as crossing the land belonging to the Hatton family (*see* **Hatton Garden**). Cross Street was a common name and it was altered in 1937 to this pseudo-mediaeval name which means Holy Cross.

St Dionis Road SW6 (Fulham, Hammersmith). Formerly Rectory Road, from a rectory on the W side of **Parson's Green**. The church of St Dionis at the E end of the road was consecrated in 1885; it incorporated furnishings from St Dionis Backchurch in Lime Street, City of London, which had been demolished. This Fulham church was built with funds from the sale of the Lime Street site. The population of the City had so shrunk in the late 19th century that many City churches became redundant. This one had been dedicated to St Dionis or Denis, patron saint of France, a Bishop of Paris who was martyred *c*250. The mediaeval cult of the saint grew partly from a mistaken identification with Dionysius, a disciple of St Paul.

St Donatt's Road SE14 (Lewisham). On the Tyrwhitt-Drake family estate. Their seat was at St Donatt's Castle, Glamorgan (*see* **Drake Road**).

St Dunstan's Road W6 (Hammersmith). Built on land belonging to the parish of St Dunstan's-in-the-West, Fleet Street.

St Edmund's Terrace NW8 (Primrose Hill, Camden/Cit. West.). Renamed in 1876, formerly St John's Terrace. St Edmund was a Christian king of East Anglia who was martyred by the Danes in 869. **St Edmund's Close** adjoins.

St Ermin's Hill SW1 (Cit. West.). Uncertain; thought to be a corruption of Hermit's Hill, which name appears on maps of the 17th and 18th centuries. There may be a local traditional memory that the hermit was devoted to St Ermin, or Armel, a 6th-century Welsh monk who founded two monasteries in Brittany. His cult was encouraged in England by Henry VII (1485–1509) of the Welsh house of Tudor, who believed Ermin had saved him from death by shipwreck off the Breton coast. The saint was invoked against fevers, gout and rheumatism.

St Gabriel Street SE11 (Newington, Southwark). St Gabriel's church which stood here was consecrated in 1874 and demolished in 1936. It was dedicated to the archangel Gabriel, angel of the annunciation to the Virgin Mary.

St George's Circus SE1 (Southwark). Opened in 1770 as the central junction of a new pattern of roads leading S from the new Blackfriars Bridge, and dispersing traffic across the former St George's Fields (*see* **St George's Road**).

St George's Fields W2 (Bayswater, Cit. West.). Site of the 18th-century burial ground belonging to the parish of St George's, Hanover Square (*see* **St George's Road**).

St George's Lane EC3 (Cit. Lond.). The mediaeval parish church of St George, now demolished, stood here (*see* **St George's Road**).

St George's Road SE1 (Southwark). This crosses the former common fields belonging to the Borough of Southwark and called St George's Fields from the parish church of St

George the Martyr. The saint, patron of England, was martyred at Lydda in Palestine *c*303. He is thought to have been a soldier. He became popular in England in the middle ages, when his legendary fight with a dragon fitted the contemporary ideal of chivalry.

St George's Square SW1 (Pimlico, Cit. West.). Originally part of the large 18th-century parish of St George's, Hanover Square, which extended to the Thames at its creation in 1724. **St George's Drive** approaches (*see* **St George's Street**).

St George Street W1 (Mayfair, Cit. West.). The Hanover Square area was named in compliment to the royal house of Hanover and the reigning Hanoverian king, George I; the church in the square was dedicated to the king's namesake, St George. This street was at first called George Street, after the king, and was later made to relate to the church instead (*see* **St George's Road**).

St George's Way SE15 (Peckham, Southwark). From the church of St George which was built at the NE corner of the junction with Wells Way in 1825 (*see* **St George's Road**).

St German's Road SE23 (Brockley Rise, Lewisham). Edward Eliot of St German's, created Baron Eliot in 1784, acquired the surrounding Lewisham portion of the manor of Brockley through Elizabeth Craggs, daughter of James Craggs (*see* **Montague Avenue**).

St Giles High Street WC2 (St Giles, Camden). The leper hospital of St Giles was founded and endowed with land here, in what was then open country, by Henry I's queen, Matilda, in 1117. The saint was a hermit of Provence, who died *c*710. His cult was based on a 10th-century legend that he was crippled while protecting a hind from a royal huntsman; he became the patron saint of cripples, and of lepers.

St Giles Road SE5 (Camberwell, Southwark). Crosses land which belonged to the parish church of St Giles, Camberwell. Camberwell had a Saxon church, but this dedication is first recorded in the 12th century. The mediaeval church was burnt down and replaced in 1841 (*see* **St Giles High Street**).

St Helena Road SE16 (Rotherhithe, Southwark). Site of the St Helena Gardens, a public tea-garden which flourished 1770–1881. The reason for its name is obscure.

St Helena Street WC1 (Clerkenwell, Islington). Probably commemorates the defeat and exile of Napoleon I, who was sent to the island of St Helena in 1815 and remained there until his death.

St Helen's Place EC3 (Cit. Lond.). Part of the site of the convent attached to St Helens, Bishopsgate (*see* **Great St Helen's**).

St James's SE14 (New Cross, Lewisham). A temporary church of St James the apostle was established in the Old Kent Road as a district church in 1845. St James's church here was built to replace it and consecrated in 1854. Between 1876 and 1886 the church was notorious as a battlefield for ritualists and Low Churchmen. The ritualist vicar, the Rev. Arthur Tooth, was imprisoned for his defiance of the Public Worship Regulation Act.

St James's Avenue E2 (Bethnal Green, T. Ham.). The Anglican church of St James the Less was built here in the 1840s (*see* **St James's Row**).

St James's Market SW1 (St James's, Cit. West.). Named from the surrounding area (*see* **St James's Square**). This is the site of a general market which flourished here next to the fodder market in the early 19th century.

St James's Road SE14 (Bermondsey, Southwark). Runs through the parish of St James which was separated from the original parish of St Mary Magdalen, Bermondsey, in 1840. The church of St James the apostle lies at the N end.

St James's Row EC1 (Clerkenwell, Islington). Approaches the parish church of St James the Less, originally the church of the convent of St Mary. The present building was completed in 1792. **St James's Walk** adjoins. St James the Less has been identified with James the brother of Christ, and also with a minor apostle.

St James's Square SW1 (Cit. West.). Laid out originally in the 17th century. Charles II (1660–85) favoured St James's Palace and encouraged the development of the surrounding area which was named from it (*see* **St James's Street**). The square was built on land granted by the king to Henry Jermyn, Earl of St Albans, in 1661.

St James's Street SW1 (Cit. West.). Leading to St James's Palace which was built in 1530–40 on the site of St James's hospital for lepers. This hospital, founded in the 13th century, was dedicated to St James the apostle, martyred by Herod Agrippa. A strong mediaeval cult of the saint was based on the legend that his relics had been brought to Compostella, Spain, where his influence was thought to have defended Christian Spain from the Moors. Compostella became an important place of pilgrimage.

St John's Church Road E9 (Hackney). Approaches the parish

church of St John the Evangelist. The church was first dedicated to St Augustine, and is recorded as such in the 13th century. The surrounding Hackney manor was confiscated from the Knights Templar at the suppression of their order in 1312, and was given to the Knights of St John of Jerusalem, who rededicated the church (*see* **Temple Mills Lane** and **St John Street**).

St John's Crescent SW9 (Brixton, Lambeth). Part of the Angell Town estate. John Angell, who died at Stockwell Park in 1784, expressed the wish that a chapel dedicated to his namesake should be built on his land. The site for St John's church was given by his descendant Benedict Angell; the church was built in 1853 at the expense of William Stone of 'The Casino' (*see* **Casino Avenue**). John Angell had also wished to set up a charitable college called St John's; it was to be built in a Stockwell field called Burden Bush, and would accommodate seven decayed gentlemen, two clergymen, one organist, six singing men, 12 choristers, one verger or chapel clerk, one butler, one baker and one groom. This marvellously mediaeval idea never materialised.

St John's Grove N19 (Upper Holloway, Islington). St John's church, at the junction with Holloway Road, was consecrated as a district church of the parish of St Mary, Islington, in 1828.

St John's Hill SW11 (Battersea, Wandsworth). Commemorates the St John family who held the manor of Battersea 1627–c1763. **St John's Road** adjoins (*see* **Bolingbroke Walk** and **Roydon Close**).

St John Street EC1 (Clerkenwell, Islington). The Hospital of St John of Jerusalem was founded c1048. In 1123 the brothers of the hospital formed themselves into the Order of Knights of St John of Jerusalem, a military body whose duty it was to protect and care for pilgrims to the Holy Land. The order set up its English headquarters in Clerkenwell in the early 12th century (*see* **Briset Street**). The church and gatehouse still stand at the junction of this street and Clerkenwell Road; the gatehouse is the headquarters of the St John's Ambulance Brigade for which the order is responsible.

St John's Vale SE8 (Lewisham). St John's church at the SE corner was consecrated in 1855 as a district church; its foundation was largely due to the generosity of a parish benefactor, James John Seymour Spencer Lucas.

St John's Wood High Street NW8 (Cit. West.). The Knights of St John of Jerusalem held the manor of Lilestone from 1312; it included this area which was then woodland. **St John's Wood Court**, **Park**, **Road** and **Terrace** are nearby (*see* **St John Street**).

St Jude's Road E2 (Bethnal Green, T. Ham.). St Jude's Anglican church was built nearby on Old Bethnal Green Road in the 1840s.

St Julian's Farm Road SE27 (Norwood, Lambeth). Part of the site of a farm called Julians which formed part of the 124 acres of the manor of Lambeth, which one James Wall acquired here in 1733. The introduction of 'Saint' is mysterious.

St Katharine's Precinct NW1 (Regent's Park, Camden). The religious community of St Katharine's was removed from the neighbourhood of the Tower of London in 1827, displaced by the construction of St Katharine's Dock, and set up here (*see* **St Katharine's Way**).

St Katharine's Row EC3 (Cit. Lond.). The mediaeval parish church of St Katharine Coleman, now demolished, stood here. Its name indicates that it was dedicated to St Katharine and built for a patron called Colman or Coleman (*see* **St Katharine's Way**).

St Katharine's Way E1 (Whitechapel, T. Ham.). Runs alongside St Katharine's Dock which was created in 1828 on the site of St Katharine's Hospital, a charitable foundation of Queen Matilda, consort of Stephen, in 1148. The religious community of the hospital was moved first to Regent's Park and later to Ratcliff. The cult of St Katharine of Alexandria began in the 9th century, describing the saint as a girl of good family who was martyred for her faith, being broken on the wheel and then beheaded.

This street runs along the line of the former Nightingale Lane, from Cnihten Gild, or Knights' Guild; the Guild held the area E of the City wall which was called the Portsoke (*see* **Portsoken Street**). John Stow, in his *Survey of London* of 1598, describes how 13 Saxon knights received this land in return for service to King Edgar (959–75) 'with the liberty of a guild forever'. Their successors presented it to the priory of Holy Trinity, Aldgate, in 1125.

St Leonard's Street E3 (Bromley, T. Ham.). Site of the priory of Bromley St Leonards (*see* **Priory Street**). After the priory had been dissolved in 1535 the Lady-chapel continued in use as the parish church of St Leonard (*see* **Leonard Street**).

St Leonard's Terrace SW3 (Chelsea, Ken. Chel.). Built by John Tombs, who came from Upton St Leonard's near Cheltenham in Gloucestershire; he also built nearby **Cheltenham Terrace**.

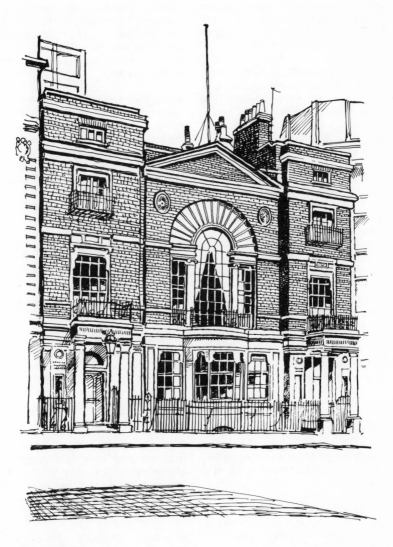

St James's Street

St Loo Avenue SW3 (Chelsea, Ken. Chel.). A Victorian name, possibly commemorating Elizabeth, Countess of Shrewsbury (called 'Bess of Hardwick'), who held property in Chelsea. Before her marriage to the Earl of Shrewsbury she was Lady St Loe.

St Luke's Street SW3 (Chelsea, Ken. Chel.). The new parish church of St Luke the Evangelist was built in 1819 to replace Chelsea Old Church, considered too small and decrepit. Neighbouring **Britten Street** is named from a trustee.

St Margaret's Court SE1 (Southwark). The mediaeval parish church of St Margaret stood nearby. The church was suppressed in 1540 (*see* **Counter Street**). The area continued to be known as St Margaret's Hill. St Margaret (1046–93) was an English princess who fled to Scotland at the Norman Conquest of 1066. She became Queen Consort of Malcolm III in 1069, and began the reorganisation of the Church in Scotland.

This street was renamed in honour of the old parish in 1835; it was formerly Fishmongers' Alley, having belonged to the Fishmongers' Company in the early 16th century.

St Mark's Crescent NW1 (Camden Town, Camden). Approaches the church of St Mark the Evangelist, built 1851–2 and designed by Thomas Little.

St Mark's Rise E8 (Dalston, Hackney). St Mark's church here was consecrated in 1860. The first temporary iron building was destroyed in a storm of 1865 and a stone church replaced it.

St Martin's Close NW1 (Camden Town, Camden). Approaches St Martin's Gardens, originally bought in 1803 as an extra burial ground for the parish of St Martin-in-the-Fields, which was densely populated and had no surplus open space. This close was built on an unused part of the plot in 1854. Following an unpopular attempt by the trustees to build over the actual graves, the rest of the land was taken over by St Pancras parish in 1887 and laid out as a garden (*see* **St Martin's Lane**).

St Martin's Lane WC2 (Cit. West.). A church dedicated to St Martin has stood at the S end of this land since the 11th century, when it was literally 'in the fields', surrounded by the cultivated fields of the monks of Westminster Abbey (*see* **Covent Garden**). The saint, Martin of Tours (*c*316–97), was a Hungarian-born soldier of the Roman imperial army who was discharged on his conversion to Christianity. He became a pioneer of monastic life in Europe. The most popular element of his cult was a story of the saint taking off his cloak and giving it to a beggar.

St Martin's-le-Grand EC1 (Cit. Lond.). The church of St Martin's-le-Grand was founded here in 700, rebuilt in 1056 and demolished in 1538. 'Le Grand' refers to the status and importance of the church (*see* **St Martin's Lane**).

St Martin's Street WC2 (Cit. West.). Built on part of a field called St Martin's Field, from the parish of St Martin-in-the-Fields to which it originally belonged (*see* **St Martin's Lane**).

St Mary Abbot's Place W8 (Kensington, Ken. Chel.). The nearby church of St Mary was given, as part of the manor of Kensington, to the Abbot of Abingdon *c*1100. Geoffrey de Vere, lord of the manor of Kensington, gave the abbey lands which were afterwards known as Abbot's Kensington; this automatically gave the abbot the control of the church.

St Mary at Hill EC3 (Cit. Lond.). Passes the church of that name, St Mary's church on the hill.

St Mary Axe EC3 (Cit. Lond.). The church of St Mary stood here until its demolition in 1561. Its mediaeval name, St Mary at Axe, derived from the sign of an axe hanging outside the next-door building.

St Marychurch Street SE16 (Rotherhithe, Southwark). The nearby parish church of St Mary, Rotherhithe, is first mentioned as such in 1291. The present building dates (with alterations) from 1714.

St Mary's Gardens SE11 (Kennington, Lambeth). Built 1839–41 on land originally given as a source of income for the parish poor of St Mary's parish, Lambeth. **St Mary's Walk** approaches (*see* **Walcot Square**).

St Mary's Path N1 (Islington). The parish church of St Mary, Islington, is first recorded in 1317 and is thought to be older. The mediaeval church was replaced in 1751 on the same site, N of this path.

St Mary's Road SE15 (Peckham, Southwark). Named in 1875 from the newly-built church of St Mary Magdalene.

St Mary's Square W2 (Paddington, Cit. West.). Approaches St Mary's church, Paddington Green. The first church, N of the present building, was a mediaeval chapel of ease; it was demolished c1680 and replaced by the present St Mary's in 1788. It was the sole parish church in Paddington until the consecration of St James's, Sussex Gardens, in 1845.

St Matthew's Road SW2 (Brixton, Lambeth). Approaches the church of St Matthew, the evangelist, consecrated in 1824 (*see* **Porden Road**).

St Matthew's Row E2 (Bethnal Green, T. Ham.). The parish of St Matthew, with its church here, was formed out of the parent parish of Stepney in 1743.

St Matthew Street SW1 (Cit. West.). Renamed in 1864 after St Matthew's church had been built nearby in 1857; the street was formerly Duck Lane, from the practice of rearing ducks.

St Michael's Road SW9 (Stockwell, Lambeth). Approaches St Michael's church, built in 1841 and designed by William Rogers. St Michael the archangel is honoured as champion of the heavenly host against Satan.

St Michael's Street W2 (Bayswater, Cit. West.). A church dedicated to St Michael and All Angels (now closed) was built in parallel Star Street in 1860 (*see* **St Michael's Road**).

St Mildred's Court EC2 (Cit. Lond.). The mediaeval church of St Mildred stood here before its demolition in 1872. The church used to stand over the course of the Walbrook at a spot where the stream had been closed in. The saint was a Saxon princess with a vocation to religious life; she became abbess of Minster-in-Thanet and died c700.

St Norbert Road SE4 (Lewisham). Approaches St Norbert Green, Brockley, where the Premonstratensian Order established itself in the 12th century. St Norbert (1080–1134) was their founder. The monks moved on into Kent c1200.

St Olave's Court EC2 (Cit. Lond.). The mediaeval church of St Olave, first recorded 1181, stood here; the tower of the church, rebuilt after the Great Fire of 1666, remains. The saint was Olaf Haraldsson, king Olaf II of Norway and Norway's patron saint. He was converted to Christianity in 1013 and wished to consolidate Norway as a Christian kingdom. He was overthrown by his enemy Canute II of Denmark and England. He was popular in London because of his attempt to help defend the city against Canute in 1014; it was said that in order to prevent the Danes from entering the city, Olaf and his men had brought down London Bridge.

St Olave's Gardens SE11 (Kennington, Lambeth). Built on land originally given as a source of income for the parish poor of St Olave's parish in Southwark (*see* **St Olave's Court** and **Walcot Square**).

St Olave's Terrace SE1 (Bermondsey, Southwark). *See* **St Olave's Court** and **Tooley Street**. St Olave's Grammar School was founded through a bequest of Henry Leek in 1567 to serve children of the parish of St Olave. The present combined school of St Olave's and St Saviour's parishes stands opposite.

St Pancras Way NW1 (St Pancras, Camden). *See* **Pancras Road**.

St Paul's Avenue SE16 (Rotherhithe, Southwark). St Paul's church was built here in 1850 as a chapel of ease for the parish church of St Mary, Rotherhithe.

St Paul's Churchyard EC4 (Cit. Lond.). Remnant of the extensive churchyard which once surrounded St Paul's Cathedral. The cathedral as it was built in 1087 had a churchyard extending N up Ave Maria Lane to Paternoster Row, through the present Paternoster Square and along the Row to the Cheapside end of New Change; southwards it stretched down Creed Lane to Carter Lane.

St Paul's Road N1 (Islington). St Paul's church at the E end was consecrated as a district church of the parish of St Mary, Islington, in 1828.

St Paul Street N1 (Islington). *See* **Prebend Street**.

St Paul's Way E3 (Bow Common, T. Ham.). St Paul's church nearby was consecrated in 1858, subdividing the parish of St Anne's, Limehouse, which was expanding rapidly. The Victorian church was bombed, and rebuilt in 1958–60.

St Petersburgh Place W2 (Bayswater, Cit. West.). Laid out in 1816 following the visit to London of Czar Alexander I (*see* **Moscow Road**).

St Peter's Close E2 (Bethnal Green, T. Ham.). St Peter's Anglican church here was consecrated in 1840, the first of ten churches built in Bethnal Green in the decade 1840–50; all were named after apostles.

St Peter's Grove W6 (Hammersmith). St Peter's church nearby was consecrated in 1829 and made the centre of a separate parish in 1836. **St Peter's Road**, **Square** and **Villas** adjoin.

St Peter's Street N1 (Islington). St Peter's church was consecrated in 1835; before that the street was called River Lane, from the New River which it bridged (*see* **Myddelton Square**).

St Peter's Terrace SW6 (Fulham, Hammersmith). St Peter's church here was consecrated in 1882.

St Peter's Way N1 (De Beauvoir Town, Hackney). St Peter's church was built NW of De Beauvoir Square and consecrated on St Peter's day in 1841, with a new parish for the De Beauvoir Town estate.

St Philip's Place W2 (Paddington, Cit. West.). From St Philip's church which stood here c1854–94.

St Philip's Road E8 (Dalston, Hackney). The Anglican church of St Philip was built in Richmond Road in 1840, on land granted by Thomas and William Rhodes. An ecclesiastical district was assigned to it in 1848.

St Philip's Street SW8 (Battersea, Wandsworth). St Philip's church here was consecrated in 1870 at the centre of the new Park Town estate. St Philip the apostle was the namesake of Philip Flower (d 1872) merchant of London and Sydney, Australia. He was a chief promoter of the Queenstown Road development, and he paid for the church to be built.

St Philip's Way N1 (Islington). St Philip the Evangelist, Arlington Square, was built c1850 as a district church of St Mary's parish, Islington.

St Quintin Avenue W10 (N Kensington, Ken. Chel.). Built on part of the Notting Barns manor farm, acquired by William St Quintin in 1767, and still held by the St Quintin family at the time of building, in the late 19th century.

St Silas Place NW5 (Kentish Town, Camden). The church of St Silas stood in Shipton Place; described as a mission church, it was consecrated in 1884. In 1912 a new church was built on Prince of Wales Road to replace it. The saint accompanied St Paul on his missionary journeys.

St Simon's Avenue SW15 (Putney, Wandsworth). The Roman Catholic church here is dedicated to St Simon or Simeon Stock (d 1265), sixth general of the Carmelite Order. Born in Kent, he is said to have lived for some 20 years as a hermit, inhabiting the hollow trunk or stock of a tree.

St Stephen's Avenue SW15 (Hammersmith). The surrounding parish of St Stephen was created in 1850 when the new church was consecrated; it consisted of all the old parish of Hammersmith N of Goldhawk Road. In 1871 and 1882 it was further subdivided as the population increased. (*See* **St Stephen's Close**.)

St Stephen's Close NW8 (Primrose Hill, Camden). A church dedicated to St Stephen, the first Christian martyr, formerly stood on Avenue Road.

St Stephen's Gardens W2 (Paddington, Cit. West.). St Stephen's church here was built in 1855 (*see* **St Stephen's Close**).

St Stephen's Road E3 (Bow, T. Ham.). See **Parnell Road**.

St Swithin's Lane EC4 (Cit. Lond.). The church of St Swithin, rebuilt in the 15th century, was bombed during World War II; the churchyard remains as a garden. St Swithin (d 862), a monk of Westminster Abbey, was made Bishop of Winchester in 852. He is traditionally associated with heavy rainfall from 15 July, the date in 971 when his body, against his expressed wish, was moved from the old minster graveyard into the newly-extended cathedral.

St Thomas's Square E9 (Hackney). Built on land held here by the governors of St Thomas's Hospital (*see* **St Thomas's Street**).

St Thomas's Street SE1 (Southwark). A hospital for poor children was founded here by the Prior of Bermondsey in 1213 and dedicated to St Thomas the apostle. At the dissolution of the monasteries in the 16th century it was bought by the City of London and then refounded by Edward VI in 1551. The hospital was forced to move when London Bridge Station was built, since it occupied the N side of St Thomas's Street; its later extension which, as Guy's, had become a separate hospital, was safe on the S side. Arguments as to a suitable site for St Thomas's went on for years; it finally reopened on the Albert Embankment in 1871.

St Thomas's Way SW6 (Fulham, Hammersmith). The Roman Catholic church of St Thomas the apostle was consecrated here in 1849 to serve the Irish community which had begun to settle on the former Fulham Fields in the 1830s.

St Vincent Street W1 (Marylebone, Cit. West.). Passes the school founded by the Sisters of Charity of St Vincent de Paul. The saint was a Gascon priest, chaplain to the rich and influential, who used his position to the benefit of the poor and oppressed, for whom he exercised a devoted care. He founded the sisterhood in 1633.

Sale Place W2 (Paddington, Cit. West.). Richard Sale was clerk and legal adviser to the Grand Junction Canal Company (*see* **Praed Street**) in the 1820s when their land here was built upon.

Salford Road SW2 (Streatham Hill, Lambeth). Built on land belonging to Lees Knowles, then MP for Salford West, near Manchester.

Salisbury Place W1 (Marylebone, Cit. West.). Isaac Salisbury was active as a builder in this area in the early 19th century, when this street was built.

Salisbury Square EC4 (Cit. Lond.). Built on land which had belonged to the bishops of Salisbury before the Reformation; their London house, Salisbury Court, was here (*see* **Dorset Rise**).

Salisbury Street NW8 (Lisson Grove, Cit. West.). Broadley Street was originally named Earl Street and the streets crossing it were given the names of contemporary (1820) earldoms: Carlisle, Exeter and Salisbury. Carlisle Street was altered to Penfold Street and Exeter Street to Ashbridge Street. **Whitehaven Street** was originally Little Carlisle Street, and was given another Cumbrian place name in 1937. **Carlisle Mews** adjoins Penfold Street.

Salmon Lane E14 (Limehouse, T. Ham.). This is an old lane and the name is a corruption of Sermon Lane; it was the way taken by the inhabitants of the hamlet of Limehouse when going to hear the service and sermon at St Dunstan's, Stepney Green. St Dunstan's was the only parish church available to them until St Anne's, Limehouse, was built in 1729.

Salters Court EC4 (Cit. Lond.). The Salters' Company had their guildhall and almshouses here, between this court and Bread Street, until 1600. Prominent salters were buried in the two mediaeval churches in Bread Street, All Hallows and St Mildred's — both now demolished. (*See* **Salters' Hall Court**.)

Salters' Hall Court EC4 (Cit. Lond.). A new guildhall of the Salters' Company was built here in 1600 and bombed in 1941.

Salvador Place SW17 (Tooting Graveney, Wandsworth). A prominent family of the 18th century in Tooting. Francis Salvador headed the list of contributors to the Poor Rate in 1729, and served as joint Overseer of the Poor in 1738. Joseph Salvador acquired land from the manor in 1752, and served as a vestry member in the 1760s; he also gave money to the parish for charity. There are no records of Salvadors in public life after c1770. In 1787 their house is referred to as an academy for young gentlemen.

Samuda Estate E14 (Isle of Dogs, T. Ham.). J. d'Aguilar Samuda was the owner of the shipyard here, which was cut out of the reed beds in the later 19th century and was formerly approached by Samuda Street. Samuda represented the district on the Metropolitan Board of Works in the 1860s.

Sancroft Street SE11 (Lambeth). By association with nearby Lambeth Palace (*see* **Lambeth Palace Road**). Archbishop Sancroft held office 1678–90; he clashed frequently with James II but honour prevented his changing his allegiance to William III in 1688.

Sanctuary Street SE1 (Southwark). *See* **Mint Street**. The surrounding area of the Mint claimed the privilege of sanctuary or protection from arrest for debt, and continued to do so into the 19th century.

Sandall Road NW5 (Kentish Town, Camden). *See* **Lawford Road**.

Sandell Street SE1 (Waterloo Road, Lambeth). New warehouses 'in Short Street, Lambeth, for Mr. Sandell' are recorded as begun in 1861.

Sandford Street SW6 (Fulham, Hammersmith). Led to Sandford Manor, an early 17th-century house said to have been the home of Nell Gwynn. Sandford means a sandy ford (*see* **Sand's End Lane**).

Sandilands Road SW6 (Fulham, Hammersmith). The Rev. R.S.B. Sandilands lived at Ranelagh Lodge nearby in 1823–9 and is commemorated here.

Sandrock Road SE13 (Lewisham). From the nature of the site: land off

Loampit Hill contained sections of Thanet sand as well as rich loam and fossil-bearing clay; there was also an outcrop of chalk. The place had a number of steep drops and deliberate embankments, all because of the nature of the ground and the former extraction workings. The surrounding street names also reflect this.

Sand's End Lane SW6 (Fulham, Hammersmith). The surrounding area was called Sand's End or Sandy End before development; this was from the nature of the ground on the Thames shore around the mouth of Chelsea Creek.

Sandwell Crescent NW6 (W Hampstead, Camden). Built on the site of a large house called 'Sandwell'.

Sandwich Street WC1 (Bloomsbury, Camden). *See* **Leigh Street**.

Sandy Row E1 (Spitalfields, T. Ham.). Formerly ran S from Artillery Lane to Harrow Place. First recorded in 1799, before that it was regarded as part of Petticoat Lane. The name is properly Sandy's Row, after a builder or property owner.

Sanford Street SE14 (Deptford, Lewisham). Built c1878 on land belonging to the Sanford family.

Sansom Street SE5 (Camberwell, Southwark). Built 1879–80 by a Kennington builder, S. Sansom.

Sans Walk EC1 (Clerkenwell, Islington). Local family name. The street was named in 1893 after Edward Sans, then the oldest member of the parish vestry of St James and St John, Clerkenwell.

Saracen's Head Yard EC3 (Aldgate, Cit. Lond.). The *Saracen's Head Inn* is first recorded here c1650.

Sardinia Street WC2 (Lincoln's Inn, Camden). The Sardinian chapel, 1648–1909, was attached to the house of the Sardinian envoy to London; it was said to be the oldest foundation in the city continually used by Roman Catholics. In 1912 Sardinia Street, where it stood, was demolished and replaced by the present street of the same name. The old street lay a little further N.

Sarre Road NW2 (W Hampstead, Camden). Kentish place name; built by the Powell-Cotton family of Quex Park, Birchington, Kent.

Saunders Ness Road E14 (Isle of Dogs, T. Ham.). Saunders Ness is a point on the coast of the Isle of Dogs near the N end of this street.

Savage Gardens EC3 (Cit. Lond.). Sir Thomas Savage is recorded in 1626, living in a house at the S end, on Tower Hill.

Savile Row W1 (Mayfair, Cit. West.). Built from 1732 on land held by the third Earl of Burlington, whose countess was the former Dorothy Savile, daughter of William Savile, Marquis of Halifax.

Savona Street SW8 (Battersea, Wandsworth). One of a group with Mediterranean place names: Savona is a town on the Ligurian coast of Italy near Genoa.

Savoy Street WC2 (Strand, Cit. West.). Site of part of the Savoy Palace built for Peter of Savoy in 1245. The alpine state of Savoy was founded in 1034 on the strategic SE boundary of France. Henry III of England married Eleanor of Provence, the French state neighbouring Savoy, and Peter of Savoy was her uncle. He was one of a train of Provençal and Savoyard nobles and courtiers who came to England in the queen's wake and

established themselves in positions of power. **Savoy Buildings**, **Court**, **Hill**, **Place**, **Row** and **Steps** are nearby.

Sawyer Street SE1 (Southwark). *See* **Dickens Square**. Bob Sawyer appears in Charles Dickens's novel *The Pickwick Papers*, where he is seen as lodging in Lant Street.

Sayes Court Street SE8 (Deptford, Lewisham). Approached an Elizabethan mansion called 'Sayes Court' which stood at the E end of the present recreation ground, and has now been demolished. Deptford manor was known as Sayes after Geoffrey de Say (*d* 1214) who acquired it through his marriage to Alice de Maminot. Says held it until William de Say died in 1375; his daughter Elizabeth inherited it and passed it to her second husband Sir William Heron, who came to have the title of Lord Say.

The house belonged to the diarist John Evelyn, who let it to Czar Peter the Great in 1698. **Czar Street** was built on part of the gardens; they and the house suffered from the Czar, an unruly tenant who wrecked Evelyn's holly hedges by riding through them in a wheelbarrow.

Scala Street W1 (Tottenham Court Road, Camden). The Scala Theatre which stood here was built in 1904 on the site of a former theatre dating from 1772.

Scandrett Street E1 (Wapping, T. Ham.). Commemorates the Rev. John Scandrett, rector of St John's, Wapping, 1900–8.

Scarsdale Place W8 (Kensington, Ken. Chel.). Scarsdale House (demolished) stood on the corner of High Street and Wright's Lane. Built *c*1685 by John Curzon, who was related to Lord Curzon, Viscount Scarsdale.

Scarsdale Road SE5 (Peckham, Southwark). Said to commemorate Prince George of Denmark's association with this area (*see* **Denmark Hill**). Robert Leke, Third Earl of Scarsdale, attended the prince as a gentleman groom.

Scawen Road SE8 (Deptford, Lewisham). On the Evelyn estate (*see* **Evelyn Street**). The original name was Boscawen, a name occurring twice in the Evelyn family. James Boscawen Evelyn, who died at one year old in 1869, was named after his uncle Edmund Boscawen Evelyn.

Scholars Road SW12 (Streatham Hill, Lambeth). *See* **Emmanuel Road**; this name refers to the scholars of Emmanuel College, Cambridge.

Schoolhouse Lane E1 (Ratcliff, T. Ham.). Nicholas Gibson, a prominent City grocer (*d* 1540) held property in Ratcliff. From 1536 he financed the establishment of a school E of this lane, with almshouses and a master's house. His widow Avice (*d* 1554) continued the work, leaving the Coopers' Company as trustees for the charity when she died.

Sclater Street E1 (Bethnal Green, T. Ham.). Commemorates a local family called Slater or Slaughter; the former appears in a property survey of 1659, the latter as owning the adjacent land in 1703.

Scott Ellis Gardens NW8 (Lisson Grove, Cit. West.). Built on the Howard de Walden estate; Scott Ellis was a family name of the lords Howard de Walden (*see* **De Walden Street**).

Scott Lidgett Crescent SE16 (Bermondsey, Southwark). The Rev. J. Scott Lidgett was a Wesleyan minister and warden of the Bermondsey Settlement, Farncombe

Street. The settlement did much educational and philanthropic work in Bermondsey; Scott Lidgett himself was active on the London School Board and a member of the London County council in its early years.

Scovell Road SE1 (Borough, Southwark). Southwark businessmen, Scovells owned warehouses in Tooley Street, including some that were destroyed in the Tooley Street fire of 1861 (*see* **Braidwood Street**).

Scrubs Lane NW10, W10 (Wormwood Scrubs, Hammersmith). Forms the E boundary of Wormwood Scrubs, the 'worm' wood being a wood with snakes, and the 'scrub' being a place of scrubby or sparse growth and bushes.

Scutari Road SE22 (Peckham Rye, Southwark). *See* **Marmora Road**.

Scylla Road SE15 (Peckham, Southwark). On the Crespigny estate (*see* **De Crespigny Park**). Captain Augustus James de Crespigny commanded HMS *Scylla*, and died on board in 1826.

Seacoal Lane EC4 (Cit. Lond.). This was the lane where sea-borne coal was to be had; it would have come by barge up the River Fleet which was navigable as far as **Old Seacoal Lane**; the first of its landing-places, until the late 18th century.

Seager Place E3 (Burdett Road, T. Ham.). J. Renwick Seager represented Mile End as a member of the London County Council from 1900.

Searles Road SE1 (New Kent Road, Southwark). Michael Searles, surveyor to the Rolls estate, built a crescent of houses here, called The Paragon, in 1789–90. They were demolished in 1898, but their gardens remain as a public open space.

Sears Street SE5 (Camberwell, Southwark). James Sears was a vestryman of Camberwell in the 1870s.

Sebastian Street EC1 (Clerkenwell, Islington). Lewis Sebastian, past Master of the Skinners' Company, was chairman of the governors of the then Northampton Polytechnic in 1901; it is now the City University. Four of the 21 governors had to be chosen from the Skinners' Company, on whose estate the college was built.

Sebbon Street N1 (Islington). Local surname; a Mr Sebbon kept the *Angel and Crown* c1750. The inn stood near the corner of present Laycock Street and Upper Street, the N end of which was called Sebbon's Wells Road. Walter and James Sebbon are recorded as stewards of the parish church of St Mary in 1738.

Secker Street SE1 (Lambeth). Part of the manor of Lambeth belonging to the archbishops of Canterbury. Archbishop Secker held office 1758–68.

Sedan Way SE17 (Walworth, Southwark). Replaces Sedan Street which led off Thurlow Street and was named in 1870. The battle of Sedan which was fought in that year was the deciding battle of the Franco-Prussian War. Napoleon III, with 100,000 men, was surrounded by the Prussians and forced to surrender. One result of the war was the French loss of Alsace to Germany. **Alsace Road** is nearby.

Sedding Street SW1 (Chelsea, Ken. Chel.). Runs beside Holy Trinity church, Sloane Street, designed by J.D. Sedding (1838–91).

Sedgwick Street E9 (Homerton, Hackney). Local surname; Harry Sedgwick (*d* 1818) was a prominent resident of Homerton and a benefactor to Hackney parish church. His son Harry Bingley Sedgwick was killed at the siege of Badajoz, during the Peninsular Campaign, in 1811 at the age of 23.

Sedley Place W1 (Mayfair, Cit. West.). Angelo Sedley's furniture store stood at the S end in 1873; Sedley in that year had permission to name the Place.

Seeley Drive SE21 (Dulwich, Southwark). Named in 1885 after Harry Govier Seeley, Assistant Master of nearby Dulwich College.

Seely Road SW17 (Tooting, Wandsworth). *See* **Furzedown Drive**.

Seething Lane EC3 (Cit. Lond.). Called Shyvethenestrat in the 13th century and later Sivethenelane, both from OE 'sifetha', meaning chaff or siftings. It was probably a place where corn was threshed.

Sekforde Street EC1 (Clerkenwell, Islington). Built on land once belonging to Thomas Sekforde (*d* 1588) who left his Clerkenwell estate for the maintenance of an almshouse (*see* **Woodbridge Street**).

Sellincourt Road SW17 (Tooting, Wandsworth). The Sellincourt family lived at Wandsworth Lodge (between the present Trinity and Beechcroft Roads). From c1878 they were influential in developing the congregational churches in Balham and Tooting.

Selous Street NW1 (Camden Town, Camden). The painter Henry Selous (1803–90) and the dramatist Angielo Selous (1812–83) lived in adjacent Bayham Street. Angielo's greatest popular success was *True to the Core*, which was produced at the Surrey Theatre (in what is now Blackfriars Road) in 1866. Henry's best-known painting is probably *The*

Inauguration of the Great Exhibition, 1851.

Selwood Place SW7 (Brompton, Ken. Chel.). Built on the site of Selwood's Nurseries, recorded here in 1712. **Selwood Terrace** adjoins.

Semley Place SW1 (Belgravia, Cit. West.). On the Grosvenor estate. Semley was a property brought to the Grosvenors from the Leveson-Gower family by marriage (*see* **Sutherland Street**).

Senior Street W2 (Paddington, Cit. West.). Built on land belonging to Nassau William Senior, political economist, who bought an estate here in 1847.

Senrab Street E1 (Stepney, T. Ham.). 'Barnes' reversed; the land belonged to W.H. Pemberton Barnes, who had already used his name for **Barnes Street**.

Serjeants Inn EC4 (Cit. Lond.). A house here, next to the Temple, belonged to York Minster until the reign of Henry VIII (1509–47) when it was acquired by the Serjeants-at-Law. The Serjeants moved to Chancery Lane in the 1730s; they were barristers of the highest qualification. All High Court judges were Serjeants-at-Law before 1873.

Serle Street WC2 (Lincoln's Inn, Camden). Built by Henry Serle of Lincoln's Inn from c1683; he also built **New Square**.

Sermon Lane EC4 (Cit. Lond.). This is probably a corruption of Sarmoner's Lane; Adam le Sarmoner is recorded as holding property here in the 13th century.

Seven Dials WC2 (Covent Garden, Camden). *See* **Neal Street**.

Seven Sisters Road N15, N4, N7 (Hackney/Haringey). Road leading to the area around Page Green which was called Seven Sisters, probably from seven elm trees which used to grow on the green.

Sevington Street W9 (Westbourne Green, Cit. West.). Built on land belonging to a family who also held farms in Wiltshire from which this street and **Surrendale Place** are named (*see* **Grittleton Road**).

Seward Street EC1 (Goswell Road, Islington). Built from 1778 by Edward Seward, dyer, who set up his dye works on the corner with Goswell Road.

Seymour Close EC1 (Clerkenwell, Islington). *See* **Aylesbury Street**. Aylesbury House belonged to Robert Bruce, First Earl of Aylesbury, through his countess (Diana, grand-daughter of William Cecil, Second Earl of Exeter) whom he married in 1646. His son Thomas married Elizabeth Seymour, sister of the third Duke of Somerset and descendant of Henry VII.

Seymour Road SW18 (Wandsworth). Formerly Seymour Villas and probably built by Seymours, builders active in South London in the 1860s.

Seymour Street W1, W2 (Marylebone, Cit. West.). Built on the estate of Henry William Portman (*see* **Portman Square**). His mother was the former Anne Seymour, through whom the estate came into his branch of the family.

Shackleton Close SE23 (Forest Hill, Lewisham). The explorer Sir Ernest Shackleton · (1874–1922) lived in Westwood Hill, Sydenham, and was educated at Dulwich College. His most famous expedition was that of 1914–16; he set out for the Antarctic in *Endurance*, which stuck fast in the ice and broke up. Shackleton's party

were marooned; they reached
Elephant Island by sledge and boat,
and there most of the party
remained, living under the upturned
hulls, while Shackleton and a small
group put to sea to find help. They
did so after a journey of some 800
miles.

Shad Thames SE1 (Bermondsey,
Southwark). Some historians suggest
a contraction of 'St John at Thames'.
A manor here, of 24 acres, manor
house and watermills, belonged to
the Priory of St John of Jerusalem,
Clerkenwell, at least from the reign
of Edward I (1272–1307) until
the dissolution of the monasteries
1536–9.

Shadwell Place E1 (Shadwell, T.
Ham.). The place name Shadwell is
from OE 'Sceald' meaning shallow,
and 'well', meaning a stream.

Shaftesbury Avenue W1, WC2
(Camden). Cut in the 1850s to link
New Oxford Street with Piccadilly,
and named in honour of Lord
Shaftesbury (1801–85), industrial
reformer and evangelical churchman.

Shafts Court EC3 (Cit. Lond.). *See*
Undershaft.

Shakespeare Road SE24 (Brixton,
Lambeth). One of two London
streets commemorating William
Shakespeare, dramatist and poet
who died in 1616. The rest of this
Brixton group also commemorate
great English poets: Geoffrey
Chaucer (*d* 1400) in **Chaucer Road**;
John Milton (1608–74) in **Milton
Grove** and **Road**; and Edmund
Spenser (*d* 1599) in **Spenser Grove**
and **Road**.

Shakespeare Walk N16 (Shacklewell,
Hackney). *See* **Shakespeare Road**.
The other names in this Hackney
group of poets include Milton and

Spenser, together with William
Cowper (1731–1800) and William
Wordsworth (1770–1850) in **Cowper
Road** and **Wordsworth Road**
respectively.

Shalfleet Drive W10 (N Kensington,
Ken. Chel.). Named by association
with the surrounding streets, a 19th-
century development by James
Whitchurch of Southampton who
used Hampshire place names.
Shalfleet is on the Isle of Wight, then
part of Hampshire and now a
separate county.

Shand Street SE1 (Bermondsey,
Southwark). Named in 1891 in
honour of Augustus Shand, sail-
maker, former chairman of the St
Olave District Board of Works. He
represented St Olave's ward on the
first Bermondsey Borough Council
and was mayor of the borough in
1905. This street was formerly
College Street (*see* **Magdalen Street**).

Shardeloes Road SE14 (Brockley,
Lewisham). Built on part of Brockley
manor held by the Drake family of
Shardeloes, Buckinghamshire. Nearby **Amersham Road** is named by
association (*see* **Drake Road**).

Shard's Square SE15 (Peckham,
Southwark). Isaac Pacatus Shard
inherited land here, the manor of
Bredinghurst, from his aunt Mrs Hill
in the late 18th century (*see* **Peckham
Hill Street**).

Sharon Gardens E9 (S Hackney,
Hackney). A place name of Israel,
used by association with a local
Jewish community which bought land
here for a burial ground *c*1788. The
fertile plain of Sharon runs N
between Haifa and Tel Aviv (*see*
Kidron Way).

Shaver's Place SW1 (Piccadilly, Cit.
Lond.). Site of a gaming house built
by Simon Osbaldeston, former

barber to the Lord Chamberlain, in the early 17th century. Local wits called it 'Shaver's Hall', the owner having now changed his trade to 'shaving' of a more profitable kind.

Sheen Road (R. upon T.). Leads through Sheen; the name comes from OE 'sceon', meaning a sheltered place. Richmond was also called Sheen before 1485 (*see* **Upper Richmond Road**).

Sheepcote Lane SW11 (Battersea, Wandsworth). *See* **Longhedge Street**. This rural name is a refined revival of the old name 'Sheepgut'.

Sheep Lane E8 (Hackney). Attests to the formerly rural nature of the area, which was pastureland. **Lamb Lane** approaches London Fields from Mare Street, and the top of what is now Broadway Market was called Mutton Lane.

Sheffield Terrace W8 (Kensington, Ken. Chel.). Approached Sheffield House which stood E of Kensington Church Street until 1744. It was probably Elizabethan and was acquired by Edmund Sheffield, Lord Mulgrave, *c*1645. The house was demolished and the grounds used as a brickfield in 1744. A later Sheffield House was built on the site by one Thomas Robinson in the 1790s; this was demolished *c*1854 (*see* **Berkeley Gardens**).

Shelbury Road SE22 (Camberwell, Southwark). The Shelbury family were prominent residents of Camberwell in the 17th century.

Shelford Place N16 (Stoke Newington, Hackney). The Rev. Leonard Shelford, curate of Hackney, became the first incumbent of St Matthew's, Clapton, in 1866. In 1886 he became rector of Stoke Newington.

Shelton Street WC2 (Covent Garden, Camden). William Shelton, by his will of 1672, founded a charity school in the then Parker's Lane (the present Parker Street) for 50 poor children; he also provided for gowns to be given to 20 poor and aged persons.

Shepherdess Walk N1 (Hoxton, Hackney). A tavern called the *Shepherd and Shepherdess* was built *c*1700 at the SE corner of what was then a path across the fields. The tavern was later rebuilt as the *Eagle* public house.

Shepherd Market W1 (Mayfair, Cit. West.). Edward Shepherd, builder (*d* 1747), was responsible for many Mayfair streets from the 1720s. He leased land for development here from Sir Nathaniel Curzon, and in this street he established his market. **Shepherd Mews** and **Street** approach.

Shepherd's Place W1 (Mayfair, Cit. West.). Begun in the 1730s by John Shepherd, plasterer, brother to the founder of **Shepherd Market** (*see* above).

Shepherd's Walk NW3 (Hampstead, Camden). Crosses the former Shepherd's or Conduit Fields, where a spring called the Shepherd's Well fed a stone conduit with exceptionally pure water. This was an important local supply until the late 19th century.

Sheraton Street W1 (Soho, Cit. West.). Commemorates the cabinetmaker and designer Thomas Sheraton who lived nearby in Wardour Street 1793–5 and in this street 1798–1800. This was formerly Little Chapel Street (*see* **Great Chapel Street**).

Sherborne Lane EC4 (Cit. Lond.). This appears in the 16th century as Shirebourne Lane; in the 13th it is called Shitteborwelane, a facetious name for a public privy.

Sherlock Mews W1 (Marylebone, Cit. West.). Commemorates the fictional detective Sherlock Holmes, of 221*b* Baker Street, created by Sir Arthur Conan Doyle.

Sherwin Road SE14 (New Cross, Lewisham). Commemorates a local benefactor, William Sherwin, who gave money for the upkeep and apprenticing of poor boys of Deptford.

Sherwood Street W1 (Soho, Cit. West.). This is a corruption of Sherard; Francis Sherard, lessee of the Pulteney family, developed the property during the 1670s.

Shillibeer Place W1 (Marylebone, Cit. West.). George Shillibeer, coach-builder, began his first omnibus service in London in 1829; his two omnibuses ran from the *Yorkshire Stingo* public house at the junction of Marylebone Road and Old Marylebone Road, and their destination was the Bank.

Shipman Road SE23 (Forest Hill, Lewisham). Commemorates a local benefactor who died in 1842, leaving £4,500 to be used for education and £500 to be invested, and the income spent on coal for poor labourers.

Ship Street SE8 (Deptford, Lewisham). *See* **Vanguard Street**.

Shipton Place NW5 (Kentish Town, Camden). The *Mother Shipton* tavern here was named from a witch of the 15th century who prophesied that when London and Hampstead met, England would fall.

Shoe Lane EC4 (Cit. Lond.). In the 13th and 14th centuries this is called variously Sholane, Sholand and

Scholaunde, as leading to a holding of land shaped like a shoe.

Shoreditch   High   Street   E1 (Shoreditch, Hackney). High or principal street of Shoreditch, called Soredich and Soresdich in the 12th century; in the 13th it is variously Schoredich, Schoresdich, Shordich and Shoresdich. The *Oxford Dictionary of English Place Names* interprets the name as 'ditch leading to the shore', which is possible if, at the time the settlement began, the artificial channels draining this area already ran into the broad channel which was later called the Hounds-ditch; the channel led to the shore of the Thames. Scholars agree that the 'dich' or ditch was an artificial drainage channel distinct from the natural course of the Walbrook, but 'shore' in its various spellings is more difficult. The London County Council's *Survey of London* suggests that the first hamlet here was not connected to the Thames shore, and that 'shore', 'schore' and 'sore' could all indicate an OE word, possibly a personal name. The name in any case reveals the nature of the land N of the City, a marsh which in winter presented vast sheets of ice.

Shore   Road   E9   (S Hackney, Hackney). Site of a mediaeval house owned from 1352 by Nicholas Shordych and John Blanch, and later called 'Shoreditch Place'. **Shore Place** runs parallel.

Shorncliffe Road SE1 (Walworth, Southwark). Leads off the **Old Kent Road** and named from a combination of Kentish place names. Before 1878 this was St Thomas's Road, to commemorate a stopping and watering place called St Thomas à Waterings. Here the stream called the Earl's Sluice, running along the boundary between Southwark and Camberwell, crossed the main road. Chaucer's pilgrims halted here on their way to St Thomas's shrine in Canterbury, and there may have been a wayside shrine to the saint. The stream was later enclosed as a sewer. **Earl Road** lies opposite.

Shorrold's Road SW6 (Fulham, Hammersmith). Corruption of Sherewold, the name of a family recorded as holding property in this area in the 15th century.

Shortlands W6 (Hammersmith). Runs across an early common field of the then parish of Fulham called Shortlands Field; the field extended S from the present Hammersmith Road to Great Church Lane.

Short's Gardens WC2 (Covent Garden, Camden). In the 17th century a large house and gardens stood here, belonging to a family called Short.

Short Street SE1 (Lambeth, Lambeth/Southwark). Built by a local carpenter, Samuel Short, c1820.

Shouldham Street W1 (Marylebone, Cit. West.). Built on land leased from John Harcourt by his step-relation Molyneux Shuldham, Baron Shuldham (c1717–98), naval commander active against the French in the 1750s, and later Governor of Newfoundland (1772–5) and Commander-in-Chief of the North America Station (1775–6).

Shrewsbury Road W2 (Paddington, Cit. West.). Probably named in association with nearby Welsh border place names such as Chepstow and Hereford (*see* **Chepstow Road**, and **Hereford Road** and **Square**).

Shroton Street NW1 (Lisson Grove, Cit. West.). Compliments the Baker family of Shroton, Dorset. William Baker managed farmland in Marylebone on behalf of the

Portman family, and arranged building leases there from 1755. The family became business associates and friends of the Portmans, as well as land agents, and subsequently moved to Ranston at Shroton near Stalbridge in Dorset. Sir Edward Baker owned property in Lisson Green after 1821, including **Ranston**, Shroton and **Stalbridge** Streets, and **Bendall Mews**, named after his brother Sir Talbot Hastings Bendall Baker.

Shrubbery Road SW16 (Streatham, Lambeth). From a large house here called 'The Shrubbery' which at one time was occupied by the rectors of Streatham.

Shuttle Street E1 (Bethnal Green, T. Ham.). *See* **Weaver Street**.

Shuttleworth Street SW11 (Battersea, Wandsworth). Sir James Kay-Shuttleworth established England's first training college for elementary school teachers in Battersea in 1840.

Sicilian Avenue WC1 (Bloomsbury, Camden). An Edwardian exercise in the Italian style, incorporating Sicilian marble.

Sickert Court N1 (Islington). Commemorates the British painter Walter Richard Sickert (1860–1942), who was the main inspiration of the Camden Town Group and the London Group from 1905. He lived in Barnsbury Park and had a studio in Highbury Place. Many of his paintings are of Islington.

Siddons Lane NW1 (Regent's Park, Cit. West.). The actress Sarah Siddons lived in Clarence Gate nearby after 1817, when she had retired from the stage. She made her début at Drury Lane in 1782 and was quickly recognised as a great tragedienne; she was a remarkable

Lady Macbeth. She was born into the theatrical family of Kemble (*see* **Kemble Street**).

Siddons Road SE23 (Forest Hill, Lewisham). One of a group taken from the history of the theatre (*see* **Cibber Road**, **Farren Road**, **Kemble Street** and **Vestris Road**). Commemorates Sarah Siddons (*see* **Siddons Lane**).

Sidmouth Street WC1 (Gray's Inn Road, Camden). Built from 1807, but the Harrison family who owned the land had planned a Sidmouth Street before 1799; it appears on Horwood's map of that date as a projected street. The derivation is probably from the then fashionable Devonshire resort.

Silchester Road W10 (N Kensington, Ken. Chel.). Developed by James Whitchurch of Southampton who used Hampshire place names for his streets. Silchester is a village in N Hampshire, site of a Roman city.

Silk Mills Path SE11 (Lewisham). Formerly led to a silk mill that operated until World War I. This is thought to have been a mediaeval manorial mill called Toddelesmill.

Silk Street EC2 (Cit. Lond.). Built between 1750 and 1799, and probably named from the builder; the street began as a cul-de-sac leading W out of Milton Street, and it was extended into Whitecross Street in 1879. It now lies across the S end of Milton Street and leads E into Moor Lane.

Silver Place W1 (Soho, Cit. West.). Approaches the E end of **Beak Street**.

Single Street E3 (Mile End, T. Ham.). Probably built by a family of builders living in the area. Thomas Single of White Horse Lane was active as a builder *c*1840 and Jabez Single of Whitechapel *c*1860.

Sise Lane EC4 (Cit. Lond.). Corruption of Sythe, since the lane originally led to the mediaeval church of St Sythe, which is now demolished. St Sythe or Osyth was an early English princess with a vocation to religious life. She died *c*700.

Sisters Avenue SW11 (Clapham Common, Wandsworth). Built on the site of a large house and garden which was one of a pair of 18th-century houses called 'The Sisters'.

Skardu Road NW2 (W Hampstead, Camden). *See* **Rondu Road**.

Sketchley Gardens SE16 (Deptford, Lewisham). The Rev. Alexander Everingham Sketchley was vicar of St Nicholas, Deptford, 1836–74.

Skin Market Place SE1 (Southwark). The skin or fur market is shown in 18th-century maps as covering most of the former King's Pike Garden (*see* **Pond Yard**).

Skinners Lane EC4 (Cit. Lond.). Formerly Maiden Lane, probably from the sign of 'The Maiden' over a tavern or a shop; the lane was renamed from the fur-trade, the prevailing trade in the district centred on Queenhithe.

Skinner Street EC1 (Clerkenwell, Islington). Built from *c*1817 on land belonging to the Skinners' Company. The company had been long associated with Clerkenwell, where mediaeval mystery plays were performed at the Skinners' Well on Clerkenwell Green. A Skin Market formerly stood SW of Northampton Square (*see* **Sebastian Street**).

Slaidburn Street SW10 (Kensington, Ken. Chel.). **Knaresborough Place**.

Slingsby Place WC2 (Covent Garden, Camden). Built (contrary to a royal proclamation against new

Sicilian Avenue

building) by Sir William Slingsby in the reign of James I. The land was owned by the Mercers' Company, from whom Slingsby obtained a lease (*see* **Mercer Street**).

Sloane Street SW1 (Chelsea, Ken. Chel.). Sir Hans Sloane, doctor, scholar and natural historian, bought the manor of Chelsea in 1712. After his death his son-in-law Lord Cadogan received part of the estate; he leased land to Henry Holland, architect, who laid out Sloane Street (*see* **Hans Place** and **Cadogan Square**).

Sly Street E1 (Stepney, T. Ham.). *See* **Crowder Street**. R.S. Sly became London County Council member for St George's in the East in 1890.

Smallbrook Mews W2 (Bayswater, Cit. West.). *See* **Brook Mews North**.

Smart's Place WC2 (High Holborn, Camden). An 18th-century street, possibly named from William Smart, who traded here as a carpenter in 1710.

Smithfield EC1 (Cit. Lond.). The name derives from OE 'smethe', meaning smooth, and 'field'. This was the smooth or flat field outside the W wall of the City between Newgate and the Barbican; it was formerly called West Smithfield. Unlike the marshy ground to the N, this was a suitable place for fairs, tournaments and other entertainments. It also became a live-cattle market and remained so until the mid-19th century.

Smith Square SW1 (Cit. West.). Laid out in the 1720s on land belonging to Sir James Smith.

Smith Street SW3 (Chelsea, Ken. Chel.). Built from 1794 by Thomas Smith; **Smith Terrace** adjoins.

Snow Hill EC1 (Cit. Lond.). Called Snore Hill or Snowrehille in the 16th century. The meaning is obscure but it is possibly from an old word meaning 'twist'. The original Snow Hill followed a roundabout route.

Soho Square W1 (Soho, Cit. West.). Named from the surrounding area, formerly open country which belonged to the Hospital of Burton Lazar, Leicestershire, before the dissolution of the monasteries. 'Soho!' is said to have been a hunting cry from this rural past. The square was laid out in 1681 and originally named King's Square, probably after Charles II. **Soho Street** approaches it.

Somali Road NW2 (W Hampstead, Camden). *See* **Asmara Road**.

Somers Crescent W2 (Bayswater, Cit. West.). *See* **Stanhope Place**.

Somerton Road SE15 (Nunhead, Southwark). Site of a house called 'Somerton Lodge', now demolished.

Southampton Buildings WC2 (Bloomsbury, Camden). Site of Southampton House, now demolished. The house was originally built for the bishops of Lincoln in the 12th century; in the mid-16th century it was acquired by the earls of Southampton (*see* **Southampton Row**).

Southampton Row WC1 (Bloomsbury, Camden). Southampton House, town house of the earls of Southampton, stood near the S end, N of the present Bloomsbury Square, in the 16th century. The daughter and heiress of the fourth earl married Lord William Russell (*d* 1683) and it is through this marriage that the Russells acquired Bloomsbury, to which estate they moved in 1700 from their old house on the Strand. **Southampton Place** is nearby (*see* **Southampton Street**).

Southampton Street WC2 (Strand, Cit. West.). *See* **Southampton Row**. This street was the site of Bedford House, built for Edward Russell, Third Earl of Bedford, *c*1586. The family formerly lived at Russell House (otherwise called 'Russell Place' or 'Bedford House') S of the Strand, a building which had belonged to the bishops of Carlisle. Their move to Bedford House in this street was followed in 1700 by a further move to Bloomsbury, made possible by a Russell's marriage to the heiress of the Earl of Southampton's Bloomsbury estate.

South Audley Street W1 (Mayfair, Cit. West.). *See* **North Audley Street**.

South Bolton Gardens SW10 (Kensington, Ken. Chel.). *See* **Boltons, The**.

Southcombe Street W14 (North End, Hammersmith). This may commemorate an accident of 1814, when John Southcombe was killed by the Bath Mail Coach on the Hammersmith Road.

Southfields Road SW18 (Wandsworth). *See* **Northfields**.

Southmead Road SW19 (Putney, Wandsworth). Originally approached a house called 'Southmead', now demolished.

South Place EC2 (Moorfields, Cit. Lond./Islington). Laid out in the 1790s along the S side of Moorfields.

South Tenter Street E1 (Whitechapel, T. Ham.). *See* **East Tenter Street**.

Southwark Bridge Road SE1 (Southwark). Made as an approach to Southwark Bridge which opened in 1819; the bridge was designed by John Rennie (*see* **Southwark Street**).

Southwark Park Road SE16 (Rotherhithe, Southwark). Approaches Southwark Park, opened in the parliamentary borough of Southwark in 1864.

Southwark Street SE1 (Southwark). The place name is derived from an 11th-century form: Suthgeweork, meaning the southern fortification. This refers to Southwark's early role as a defended bridgehead protecting the City of London in the days when London Bridge was the only access point from the S.

Southwick Street W2 (Bayswater, Cit. West.). Robert Thistlethwaite of Southwick Park, Hampshire (*d* 1802), married a daughter and heiress of the Frederick family (*see* **Frederick Close**). Thistlethwaite named nearby **Porchester Place** and **Street**, and **Portsea Mews** and **Place** from his Hampshire properties; his other properties inspired streets on the Fredericks' other estate in Paddington: **Widley Road** and **Wymering Road**. **Southwick Place** and **Mews** adjoin this street.

Southwood Lane N6 (Hornsey, Haringey). Runs S of that section of Hornsey Wood called Highgate Wood and Queen's Wood. Fragments of the great Hornsey Wood, itself a fragment of the primeval great forest of Middlesex, remain as parks in Hornsey, Finsbury, Highgate and Hampstead. **Queen's Wood Road**, **Wood Lane** and **Vale**, and **Woodside Avenue** are nearby.

Spa Field Street EC1 (Clerkenwell, Islington). The Spa Fields surrounded the 18th-century spa S of the present Exmouth Market. The spa closed in 1776; its central Pantheon building became a chapel for the nonconformist sect called the Countess of Huntingdon's Connection.

Spaniard's Road NW3 (Hampstead, Camden). This passes *The Spaniards* inn, but the derivation of the inn's name is unknown.

Spanish Place W1 (Marylebone, Cit. West.). Manchester House, Manchester Square, became the residence of the Spanish Ambassador on the death of the Duke of Manchester in 1788.

Spa Road SE16 (Bermondsey, Southwark). A tea-garden and mineral-water spa opened here in the 1760s; the place became a general pleasure-garden with music and fireworks, in which form it was enjoyed in the 1780s. The gardens closed *c*1805.

Speedwell Place SE8 (Deptford, Lewisham). Replaces the former Speedwell Street which ran parallel to Deptford High Street; named from a ship with Deptford connections.

Speedy Place WC1 (Bloomsbury, Camden). The Speedy family were landlords of the *Golden Boot* in what was then Lucas Street and is now called Cromer Street. The tavern, which predates the streets, is recorded in the 18th century.

Spencer Park SW18 (Battersea, Wandsworth). John, Viscount Spencer, later Earl Spencer, bought Battersea manor *c*1763; the family retained it into the 20th century, also acquiring land in Wandsworth manors: Downe (1792) and Allfarthing (1816).

Spencer Place SW1 (Victoria, Cit. West.). Named from George Spencer, early 19th-century landlord.

Spencer Rise NW5 (Kentish Town, Camden). *See* **Chetwynd Road**.

Spencer Street EC1 (Clerkenwell, Islington). Built on land belonging to the Marquis of Northampton (*see* **Percival Street**).

Spenser Road SE24 (Brixton, Lambeth). *See* **Shakespeare Road** for this and **Spenser Grove**, Shacklewell.

Spenser Street SW1 (Cit. West.). The poet Edmund Spenser, author of *The Faerie Queen* (*d* 1599) lived in Westminster and is buried in the Abbey.

Spert Street E14 (Ratcliff, T. Ham.). Sir Thomas Spert, first Master of Trinity House after its incorporation in 1514, was a Stepney seaman. He was Master of Henry VIII's ship *Henry Grace à Dieu*, familiarly known as the *Great Harry*.

Spey Street E14 (Poplar, T. Ham.). *See* **Leven Road**.

Spital Square E1 (Spitalfields, T. Ham.). The 'spital' or hospital and priory of St Mary which became the centre of Spitalfields were founded by Walter and Rosia Brune *c*1200. The site was later taken by the Spitalfields Market.

Sprimont Place SW3 (Chelsea, Ken. Chel.). Commemorates Nicholas Sprimont, director of the Chelsea porcelain factory in Lawrence Street until his retirement in 1769.

Springall Street SE15 (Peckham, Southwark). From a builder of that name who was active locally in the 1870s.

Springfield E5 (Clapton, Hackney). Site, with Springfield Park, of a large Victorian house and grounds called 'Springfield' and belonging to the Jacomb family. The house was built in a field of that name. **Spring Field**, **Springfield Hill** and **Lane** adjoin.

Springfield Avenue N10 (Muswell

Hill, Haringey). *See* **Wellfield Avenue**.

Springfield Lane NW6 (Kilburn, Camden). A former field here contained a spring near the corner of Kilburn High Road and Belsize Road; the water was noted as medicinal in the 18th century. The little spa that developed around it was called Kilburn Wells.

Springfield Rise SE26 (Upper Sydenham, Lewisham). *See* **Wells Park Road**.

Springfield Road NW8 (St John's Wood, Cit. West.). Follows an old lane which led to a field called Springfield Meadow.

Spring Gardens SW1 (Cit. West.). The 17th-century pleasure ground called Spring Gardens lay across the line of this street; it was closed after the Restoration of 1660. The garden is thought to have been a simple park laid out with plantations; later taste was for something more elaborate (*see* **New Spring Gardens Walk**).

Spring Mews W1 (Marylebone, Cit. West.). Runs behind Montague Mansions, formerly Spring Street, from a pond called the Spring Pond because it was spring-fed.

Springrice Road SE13 (Lewisham). Commemorates Sir Thomas Spring Rice (1790–1866), Whig politician, whose family held property in Lewisham. He was Chancellor of the Exchequer in Lord Melbourne's government of 1835–9.

Spring Street W2 (Bayswater, Cit. West.). Nearby (NW corner of Craven Road and Westbourne Terrace) were formerly the springs of Ox-Lease or Ox-Close, which were granted to the City of London as a water supply in 1439 and fed the City's conduit system from 1471. The

supply continued in use until 1812. The main spring was called the Roundhead.

Spring Vale Terrace W14 (Shepherd's Bush, Hammersmith). Revival of an old local field name.

Springwell Close SW16 (Streatham, Lambeth). Approaches the medicinal spring called Streatham Spa Well, discovered in 1660. **Springwell Road** adjoins.

Spurgeon Street SE1 (Great Dover Street, Southwark). The Baptist preacher Charles Haddon Spurgeon (1834–92) lodged in adjoining Great Dover Street 1854–6; he was minister of a Baptist chapel in Southwark from 1854 and also preached in the Surrey Gardens Music Hall in Walworth which he filled to capacity. The Metropolitan Tabernacle at the Elephant and Castle was built for him; it opened in 1861. Spurgeon was one of the greatest orators among Victorian evangelists.

Spurling Road SE22 (E Dulwich, Southwark). Henry Spurling served on Camberwell vestry in the 1860s.

Spurstowe Road E8 (Hackney). The Rev. Dr William Spurstowe (*d* 1665), founded and endowed almshouses for six poor widows. In 1662 he was ousted from the living of Hackney for nonconformity; although no longer the incumbent, he continued to live in the parish until his death, and attracted many sympathisers.

Stacey Street WC2 (Shaftesbury Avenue, Camden). Built in the 17th century on land which had belonged to James Stacey in the 16th; Stacey had two houses there, one on either side of what was then a footpath.

Stackhouse Street SW3 (Chelsea, Ken. Chel.). Possibly commemorates Thomas Stackhouse, theologian and author of a widely-read, three-volume *New History of the Holy Bible from the Beginning of the World to the Establishment of Christianity* in 1737. He is recorded as living in Chelsea in the 1740s.

Stacy Path SE5 (Camberwell, Southwark). Thomas Stacy or Stacey (*d* 1527), was vicar of St Giles, Camberwell, 1505–26.

Stadium Street SW10 (Chelsea, Ken. Chel.). The grounds of Cremorne House, which stood here, became a boxing and athletic stadium in 1832 (*see* **Cremorne Road**).

Stafford Place SW1 (Cit. West.). Built along the boundary of a house called 'Tart Hall', home of Viscount Stafford who was executed on a charge of high treason in 1680.

Stafford Street W1 (Mayfair, Cit. West.). Built on land leased by Margaret Stafford after the demolition of Clarendon House in 1683 (*see* **Old Bond Street**).

Stag Place SW1 (Victoria, Cit. West.). The S section is the site of the Stag Brewery, now demolished, which belonged to Watneys from 1837. The original brewers were Greenes, a house of mediaeval origin brewing beer for the Abbey of St Peter, Westminster. They moved to this site in 1607; the stag was a device in their coat of arms.

Staining Lane EC2 (Cit. Lond.). Called Staningelane in the 12th century, from OE 'Staeninga haga'. In the 10th century the adjoining area was a 'haga' belonging to the people at Staines. The definition of 'haga' can occupy scholars for pages; simply, a 'haga' appears to have been a part of the City under the jurisdiction of a Saxon settlement elsewhere.

Stainsbury Street E2 (Bethnal Green, T. Ham.). Renamed from Stainborough Street in 1860, possibly after Conant Stainsbury who held land in E London, including some along the line of Burdett Road, in 1858. The similar **Stainsby Road**, Limehouse, may be a contraction of his name.

Stainsby Road E4 (Limehouse, T. Ham.). *See* **Stainsbury Street**.

Stainton Road SE6 (Lewisham). Passes Mountsfield Park, site of a house where the entomologist Henry Tibbats Stainton (1822–92) lived.

Stalbridge Street NW1 (Lisson Grove, Cit. West.). *See* **Shroton Street**.

Stamford Brook Road W6 (Hammersmith). The Stamford Brook rose NE of Gunnersbury Park and flowed past the green here into Ravenscourt Park, whence it turned S into Hammersmith Creek, now built over. **Stamford Brook Avenue** approaches.

Stamford Hill N16 (Hackney). Corruption of Sanford, its 13th-century name, meaning the hill approaching the sandy ford.

Stamford Street SE1 (Southwark, Southwark/Lambeth). Runs W from the parish of Christchurch, which has a connection with the town of Stamford, Lincolnshire. John Marshall (*see* **Marshall Gardens**) came from Stamford before living in Southwark. In addition to his benefaction to Christchurch parish, he left money to maintain a poor scholar of Stamford or Southwark at university.

Stamp Place E2 (Bethnal Green, T. Ham.). Commemorates Timothy Stamp, who represented Mile End and Bethnal Green on the vestry of Stepney parish in the 17th century.

Stanhope Gardens SW7 (Kensington,

Ken. Chel.). Family name of the earls of Harrington (*see* **Harrington Road**). John, First Lord Stanhope of Harrington, held the adjoining manor of Chelsea in the 16th century. **Stanhope Mews**, **East** and **West**, adjoin.

Stanhope Gate W1 (Mayfair, Cit. West.). Originally led from the mansion built for Philip Stanhope, Fourth Earl of Chesterfield, into Park Lane. Lord Chesterfield occupied the house from 1749 (*see* **Chesterfield Street**). **Stanhope Row** is nearby.

Stanhope Place W2 (Bayswater, Cit. West.). Built on the Frederick estate (*see* **Frederick Close**). Arthur Stanhope was a trustee of the estate after the death of Selina Frederick's husband in 1802. The other trustee was Thomas Somers Cocks, and **Somers Crescent** is nearby.

Stanhope Street NW1 (St Pancras, Camden). *See* **Harrington Street**.

Stanier Close SW5 (W Kensington, Hammersmith). Sir William Stanier was Chief Mechanical Engineer of the London Midland and Scottish Railway 1932–44. Among the classes of locomotive he introduced were the *Black Fives* (1934), *Jubilee* (1935) and *Coronation* (1937). This is one of a group of streets built on former goods yards of the company.

Stanley Grove SW8 (Battersea, Wandsworth). Originally Stanley Street, on Philip Flower's Park Town estate. Flower was a businessman active in London and in Sydney, Australia. This street is thought to commemorate Owen Stanley, captain of HMS *Rattlesnake*, the vessel which protected Australian wool ships. He was brother to Dean Stanley (*see* **Dean Stanley Street**) and he died in Sydney in 1850.

Stanley Street SE8 (Deptford,

Lewisham). J.J. Stanley served on Deptford Borough Council from 1912.

Stannary Street SE11 (Kennington, Lambeth). On the Duchy of Cornwall's manor of Kennington. Stannary towns are those with jurisdiction over the Cornish and Devonian metal-mining areas. The steward of the Stannary Courts is an officer of the Duchy of Cornwall.

Stanstead Road SE6, SE23 (Catford, Lewisham). A corruption of a 17th-century name for this road, an old lane called variously Stanyhurst or Stoneyhurst Lane; the name probably derives from a property along the route called Stoneyhurst or the stony wood.

Staple Inn WC1 (Holborn, Camden). First recorded in 1333 as Stapledhall, which would mean a pillared hall, from OE 'stapel', a post or pillar. The building became an inn or great town house and was taken by lawyers of the court of Chancery in 1529 (*see* **Clement's Inn**). The tradition that the hall is connected with the wool merchants, 'merchants of the Staple', is without foundation.

Stapleton Hall Road N4 (Hornsey, Haringey). The Hall near the NW end is recorded in 1577 and was rebuilt or enlarged by Sir Thomas Stapleton of Grey's Court, Oxfordshire, in 1609. It became an inn in 1765, later a farm house, and in the 1880s it was used as the local Conservative Club premises.

Starboard Way E14 (Isle of Dogs, T. Ham.). *See* **Capstan Square**.

Starcross Street NW1 (Euston, Camden). Formerly Exmouth Street (*see* **Exmouth Market**); renamed in order to avoid confusion with the latter, and given the name of a place associated with the Devonshire resort of Exmouth. Starcross faces Exmouth across the Exe estuary.

Star Road W14 (Fulham, Hammersmith). From the *Seven Stars* public house here.

Stationers' Hall Court EC4 (Cit. Lond.). The Stationers' Company received its charter in 1557; its first hall was destroyed in the Great Fire of 1666; the present hall dates from c1675 with later alterations.

Stayners Road E1 (Mile End, T. Ham.). Stayner and Son, builders, worked from the Mile End Road in the 1840s and later.

Steele's Road NW3 (Chalk Farm, Camden). The 18th-century essayist Sir Richard Steele had a cottage at the junction with Haverstock Hill. Steele edited *The Tatler* magazine 1709–11, and wrote most of it. He then worked with Joseph Addison on *The Spectator*.

Stephendale Road SW6 (Fulham, Hammersith). *See* **Hugon Road**.

Stephenson Way NW1 (Euston, Camden). Approaches Euston Station, planned by Robert Stephenson (1803–59), civil engineer and only son of the locomotive designer George Stephenson (1781–1848).

Stephen Street W1 (Tottenham Court Road, Camden). *See* **Gresse Street**. Gresse built this street with a business partner called Stephen Lemaistre, who was probaly Swiss like himself. **Stephen Mews** runs parallel.

Stepney Causeway E1 (Stepney, T. Ham.). Remnant of a raised made-up road approaching Stepney Green from Ratcliff Highway across low-lying, marshy ground.

Stepney High Street E1 (Stepney, T.

Ham.). The high or principal street of Stepney; the place name appears in the 11th century as Stybbanhithe, meaning the hithe or wharf belonging to Stybba. **Stepney Way** approaches.

Sterling Street SW7 (Knightsbridge, Cit. West.). Captain Edward Sterling (1773–1847) and his son John (1806–44), both writers, lived in Knightsbridge.

Sternhall Lane SE15 (Peckham Rye, Southwark). Site of a large house called 'Sternhall' which is now demolished.

Sterry Street SE1 (Southwark). Probably built by the Sterry family of The Borough; Richard and then Anthony Sterry traded as oilmen between 1780 and 1800.

Stevenage Road SW6 (Fulham, Hammersmith). The Stevenage family lived at Sand's End in the late 17th and early 18th centuries. Lieutenant Colonel William Stevenage of the Coldstream Guards died in 1709, his son William five weeks after him and his widow, Lucy, in 1713.

Steward Street E1 (Spitalfields, T. Ham.). Originally Stuart Street, built from 1682 and named in compliment to the royal house of Stuart by whom the building lease was granted; the ground had formerly been used by the officers of the Tower (*see* **Artillery Lane**).

Stewart's Grove SW3 (Chelsea, Ken. Chel.). Built from 1827 on land leased from Chelsea manor by William Stewart.

Stewart Street E14 (Isle of Dogs, T. Ham.). Site of a firm of engineers and ship-repairers established in the early 19th century. John Stewart of Limehouse owned the Blackwall Iron Works and Canal Dry Dock.

Stillington Street SW1 (Cit. West.). Commemorates Robert Stillington (*d* 1491), Bishop of Bath. He served as Lord Chancellor under Edward IV. After Edward's death in 1483 it was Stillington who told Parliament that he had married the late king to Lady Eleanor Butler before his marriage to his queen, Elizabeth Woodville, which had taken place while Lady Eleanor was still alive. The king's sons by Elizabeth Woodville were therefore illegitimate; these were the two princes who later disappeared, presumably murdered, in the Tower of London.

Stirling Road SW9 (Stockwell, Lambeth). Uncertain: possibly built by Thomas Stirling, a builder active in the Camberwell and Stockwell area in the 1840s.

Stock Orchard Crescent N7 (Upper Holloway, Islington). *See* **Biddestone Road** for this and **Stock Orchard Street**.

Stockwell Green SW9 (Stockwell, Lambeth). The original village green at Stockwell, a place name which appears as Stokewell in the 12th century; it derives from OE 'stoc', meaning wood, and 'well', meaning a stream.

Stockwell Park Road SW9 (Stockwell, Lambeth). Crosses the site of Stockwell Park, open land belonging to Stockwell manor house which stood on the green. The land was built over in the mid-19th century (*see* **Stockwell Green** and **Moat Place**).

Stoke Newington Church Street N16 (Stoke Newington, Hackney). The date of the original church N of this street is unknown; it was rebuilt by William Patten in 1563 and extensively altered after that. The new church, S of the street, was consecrated in 1858 (*see* **Stoke Newington High Street**).

Stoke Newington High Street N16 (Stoke Newington, Hackney). High or principal street of Stoke Newington. The first part of the name is from OE 'stoc', meaning wood, and Newington is given as Newtowne in the *Domesday Book*. The place was the new town in the woods. **Stoke Newington Road** approaches.

Stokesley Street W12 (Wormwood Scrubs, Hammersmith). John Stokesley or Stokeley was Bishop of London 1529–39; the manor of Hammersmith belonged to the diocese of London.

Stonecutter Street EC4 (Cit. Lond.). Street of the stone-cutters or workers in stone, first recorded in 1720. There were formerly four other 'stone-cutter' street names in the City, a testament to continuous expansion and stone building from the Great Fire of 1666 onwards.

Stonefield Street N1 (Barnsbury, Islington). On the site of a stony field called The Stonefield, and recorded as such in 1735.

Stonells Road SW11 (S Battersea, Wandsworth). Built from 1865–7 by a local builder called Stonell.

Stones End Street SE1 (Southwark). Runs beside the point on Borough High Street where the mediaeval paved road came to an end; the 'stones' extended S for some distance from the end of London Bridge, and were probably the successors to a Roman paved street. The paved section was maintained for as far as was practicable, to the beginning of **Newington Causeway**.

Stoney Lane E1 (Cit. Lond.). Originally ran W from Middlesex Street to Cock and Hoop Yard, off

Houndsditch. The yard was removed and the street extended to Houndsditch in 1899; this extension is the only part that remains. The name comes from the character of the ground.

Stoney Street SE1 (Southwark). Formerly Stony Lane, from ancient stone paving; the N end was cut through the gardens of Winchester House to link Clink Street˙with the existing S end.

Stonhouse Street SW4 (Clapham, Lambeth). Commemorates Sir James Stonhouse, rector of Clapham 1753–92.

Storey's Gate SW1 (Cit. West.). A keeper called Storey had charge of the birds in St James's Park under Charles II; he had a lodge at the corner of the present Great George Street and Horse Guards Road.

Stories Road SE5 (Camberwell, Southwark). The Rev. John and the Rev. Thomas Storie, local preachers, held property here c1830.

Stothard Street E1 (Stepney, T. Ham.). *See* **Amiel Street**.

Stourcliffe Street W1 (Marylebone, Cit. West.). *See* **Broadstone Place**.

Stowage SE8 (Deptford, Lewisham). Originally the site of the storage rooms, sail lofts and rigging stores belonging to the East India Company; the land was bought by the company in the early 17th century.

Strafford Street E14 (Isle of Dogs, T. Ham.). *See* **Byng Street**.

Straker's Road SE15 (Peckham Rye, Southwark). Samuel Straker was a 19th-century Camberwell vestryman.

Strand WC2 (Cit. West.). Named from the strand or shore of the River

Thames, which the street traversed. The river was considerably wider before the 19th-century embankments; the remains of river walls and water-gates belonging to old houses along the Strand are sometimes over 100 feet from the present water-line.

Stranraer Way N1 (Caledonian Road, Islington). *See* **Carnoustie Drive**.

Stratford Place W1 (Oxford Street, Cit. West.). A house belonging to the Corporation of the City of London on the then Conduit Mead (City watersource), was granted on lease to Edward Stratford; under his occupation the site was developed as a street c1775.

Strathearn Place W2 (Bayswater, Cit. West.). Named in 1938 in association with nearby Connaught Place. The Duke of Connaught and Strathearn, Prince Arthur, third son of Queen Victoria, died in September 1938.

Stratton Street W1 (Mayfair, Cit. West.). Built on land formerly belonging to Lord Berkeley of Stratton and sold for building in 1684 (*see* **Berkeley Street**).

Streatham High Road SW16 (Streatham, Lambeth). High or principal road through Streatham; the name means the homestead on the Roman street, or paved road.

Streatham Street WC1 (Bloomsbury, Camden). Built on the estate of the dukes of Bedford who were also Barons Howland of Streatham, with considerable Streatham property.

Strutton Ground SW1 (Victoria, Cit. West.). Corruption of Stourton, from the name of the Dacre family's house, Stourton House (*see* **Dacre Street**).

Strype Street E1 (Spitalfields, T. Ham.). John van Strype (*d* 1648) was a silk-weaver of Spitalfields; his son the Rev. John Strype (1643–1737), historian, compiled a revised version of John Stow's *Survey of London* and brought it up to date (1720). The street was built on the site of Strype's Yard; the name had been corrupted to Tripe Yard.

Stucley Place NW1 (Camden Town, Camden). *See* **Hawley Road**.

Stukeley Street WC2 (Covent Garden, Camden). Commemorates the eccentric antiquary the Rev. Dr William Stukeley (1687–1765), resident in Holborn. He was rector of St George the Martyr, Queen Square, from 1748.

Sturdy Road SE15 (Peckham, Southwark). Built on land belonging to Daniel Sturdy.

Sturmer Way N7 (Upper Holloway, Islington). *See* **Biddestone Road**.

Styles Gardens SW9 (Stockwell, Lambeth). Part of the site of Styles or Stiles Farm which belonged to the Angell family and was developed as Angell Town in the 1850s (*see* **Angell Road**).

Suffolk Lane EC4 (Cit. Lond.). A house here called the 'Manor of the Rose' belonged to the dukes of Suffolk; they sold it to the Merchant Taylors, to use as a school, in 1560.

Suffolk Place SW1 (Haymarket, Cit. West.). In 1614 Thomas Howard, Earl of Suffolk, acquired Northumberland House; his stable yards were on this site (*see* **Northumberland Avenue**).

Sugar Loaf Walk E2 (Bethnal Green, T. Ham.). Possibly from a public house called the *Sugar Loaf*. Sugar-refining was one of the principal industries in E London in the 19th century. It flourished mainly, but not only, in Whitechapel and much of it was in the hands of German immigrants.

Sugden Road SW11 (Lavender Hill, Wandsworth). Built *c*1867 when a Mr W. Sugden held property in Battersea, including a house in Battersea Bridge Road, built for him in 1863.

Sulivan Road SW6 (Fulham, Hammersmith). Mr Sulivan of Broom House, which stood on the opposite side of Broomhouse Lane, founded the Elizabeth Free School here in 1855.

Sumner Place SW7 (Kensington, Ken. Chel.). *See* **Onslow Square**.

Sumner Street SE1 (Southwark). Built in 1839 to link Southwark Bridge Road and Great Guildford Street, and afterwards extended W over the former Maid Lane. Named from John Sumner, Bishop of Winchester (*see* **Winchester Walk**). The diocese of Winchester owned the land, and the bishop had given a site for a new building to house St Saviour's Grammar School.

Sunderland Terrace W2 (Paddington, Cit. West.). *See* **Durham Terrace**.

Sun Street EC2 (Shoreditch, Hackney). Originally ran W off Bishopsgate Without, where the *Sun* inn is recorded from *c*1650. **Sun Street Passage** separates Broad Street Station from Liverpool Street Station which obliterated the early street.

Surrendale Place W9 (Westbourne Green, Cit. West.). *See* **Grittleton Road**.

Surrey Mount SE23 (Forest Hill, Lewisham). Site of a house called

'Surrey Mount' because it stood on the border between that county and Kent. The house belonged to Frederick Horniman (*see* **Horniman Drive**); it was demolished in 1969.

Surrey Row SE1 (Southwark). Leads off Blackfriars Road which was originally called Great Surrey Street, since it led over Blackfriars Bridge into the county of Surrey which, before the formation of the County of London, extended N to the Thames.

Surrey Square SE17 (Walworth, Southwark). Built as a terrace with a rectangular garden before it, and named from the county it stood in (*see* **Surrey Row**). The terrace was laid out by Michael Searle in 1795–6; it is not known whether he ever intended to complete it as a square.

Surrey Street WC2 (Strand, Cit. West.). Part of the site of the former Arundel House owned by the Howard family, whose various branches held the dukedom of Norfolk and the earldoms of Arundel and Surrey (*see* **Arundel Street**).

Surr Street N7 (Lower Holloway, Islington). Commemorates Thomas Skinner Surr, a local poet and novelist whose work was published between 1797 and 1815.

Sussex Gardens W2 (Bayswater, Cit. West.). Prince Augustus Frederick, brother of George IV, was created Duke of Sussex in 1801. He died in 1843, when these streets were built. **Sussex Mews**, **Place** and **Square** are nearby.

Sussex Place NW1 (Regent's Park, Cit. West.). Part of John Nash's Regent's Park scheme and named after the Regent's brother Augustus, Duke of Sussex (*see* **Regent Street** and **Sussex Gardens**).

Sussex Place W2 (Hammersmith).

Commemorates Prince Augustus Frederick, Duke of Sussex, who had a house in Hammersmith and laid the foundation stone of Hammersmith Bridge (*see* **Sussex Gardens**).

Sutherland Place W2 (Bayswater, Cit. West.). Built on or adjoining land owned in 1843 by Lucy Sutherland, who held part of the former Westbourne Farm.

Sutherland Street SW1 (Pimlico, Cit. West.). Part of the Grosvenor estate. Two members of the Grosvenor family married into the family of Leveson-Gower, dukes of Sutherland: Richard, Second Marquis of Westminster (*see* **Elizabeth Street**) and Hugh Lupus, the first Duke, whose first wife was his cousin Constance Leveson-Gower. **Sutherland Row** adjoins.

Sutton Court Road W4 (Chiswick, Hounslow). Passes Sutton Court, site of Sutton Court manor house which is now demolished. **Sutton Lane** nearby is an old thoroughfare through the manor (*see* **Fauconberg Road** and **Sutton Row**).

Sutton Place E9 (Homerton, Hackney). Sutton House nearby was built for Thomas Sutton, Master of Ordnance to Elizabeth I and founder of Charterhouse School (*see* **Great Sutton Street**).

Sutton Row W1 (Soho, Cit. West.). Thomas, Lord Fauconberg (*d* 1700), had a town house here on the corner with Soho Square; his country house was the Chiswick manor house of Sutton Court.

Swain's Lane N6 (Highgate, Camden). Called Swayne's Lane in the 15th century, it later appears as Swine Lane. Swain is from OE 'swān', a swineherd.

Swallands Road SE6 (Bellingham, Lewisham). *See* **Longdown Road**.

Swallow Street W1 (Piccadilly, Cit. West.). Built in 1671 to run N from Piccadilly across a field called Swallow Close, after Thomas Swallow who leased it from the Crown *c*1538. The street was later extended to meet an older highway which ran N along the present line of Regent Street to Oxford Street. This older road was then also called Swallow Street or Great Swallow Street; the present **Swallow Passage** and **Swallow Place** off Oxford Street were originally the N end of Great Swallow Street.

Swanfield Street E2 (Bethnal Green, T. Ham.). Built along an old lane which ran S across open ground called the Swan Fields, and recorded as such in 1769.

Swan Street SE1 (Great Dover Street, Southwark). Named from the sign of an inn, now demolished, which stood at the N end.

Swan Walk SW3 (Chelsea, Ken. Chel.). Originally led to the *Swan Inn*, which stood on the river bank and was famous as the finishing post of the watermen's race for Doggett's Coat and Badge. The inn was demolished when the Chelsea embankment was built.

Swan Yard N1 (Highbury, Islington). A *Swan* tavern is recorded here in the early 17th century.

Swedeland Court E1 (Cit. Lond.). First recorded in 1677 as Swedeland Alley. There were three other similar names implying Swedish colonies, one next to a Lutheran church on the

site of the present Mansion House underground station.

Swedenborg Gardens E1 (Whitechapel, T. Ham.). The Swedish philosopher Emanuel Swedenborg (1688–1772) was buried in the Swedish church which stood here until its demolition in 1921.

Sweeney Crescent SE1 (Bermondsey, Southwark). D. Sweeney served on Bermondsey Borough Council from 1912.

Swinburne Road SW15 (Putney, Wandsworth). Commemorates the poet Algernon Swinburne (*d* 1909) who lived at 'The Pines', Putney Hill, from 1879.

Swinton Street WC1 (Gray's Inn Road, Camden). Built by James Swinton, who bought the land from Sir Henry Gough in 1773. **Swinton Place** adjoins (*see* **Gough Square**).

Sycamore Street EC1 (Finsbury, Islington). Named by association with nearby **Timber Street**.

Sydenham Road SE26 (Sydenham, Lewisham). Runs through Sydenham, called Shippenham in the 14th century and Chipeham in the 13th; this is possibly from an OE personal name, Cippa, and means Cippa's homestead.

Sydney Close SW3 (Kensington, Ken. Chel.). *See* **Onslow Square** for this and **Sydney Mews**.

Symons Street SW3 (Chelsea, Ken. Chel.). On the Cadogan estate inherited from Sir Hans Sloane. A carpenter, Samuel Symons, was involved in developing Sir Hans's estate in the 1770s.

T

Tabard Street SE1 (Southwark). Renamed in 1877 to commemorate the *Tabard Inn* which stood further N on Borough High Street; surrounding streets commemorate the pilgrims of Geoffrey Chaucer's *Canterbury Tales* who met at the *Tabard* and travelled to Canterbury down this road, originally the N part of Kent Street (*see* **Great Dover Street** and **Talbot Yard**).

Tabernacle Street EC2 (Finsbury, Hackney/Islington). Commemorates George Whitfield's Methodist tabernacle, built here in the 1740s. The street was formerly called Windmill Street or Windmill Hill, after three mills which were set up there on the slopes of a massive rubbish tip.

Tachbrook Street SW1 (Pimlico, Cit. West.). Henry Wise (*d* 1738) was gardener to William III, Anne and George I. He bought land here in 1713: **Charlwood Street** is named from his estate in Surrey; **Moreton Place**, **Street** and **Terrace**, and **Lillington Gardens Estate** are named from his estates near Tachbrook in Warwickshire; Tachbrook Street and **Warwick Row**, **Square** and **Way** are named by association. Wise lived at Warwick Priory.

Tadema Road SW10 (King's Road, Ken. Chel.). In honour of Sir Lawrence Alma-Tadema (1836–1912), Dutch-born artist who worked in England from *c*1870. His best work was inspired by classical antiquity which he revived with sensuous realism and a clear, Mediterranean light.

Talbot Court EC3 (Cit. Lond.). Named from the sign of an inn, the *Tabard* or *Talbot*, which is now demolished.

Talbot Road W2, W11 (Notting Hill, Ken. Chel/Cit. West.). Built on part of Portobello Farm which Charles Henry Talbot bought in 1755. His descendants the Misses Talbot sold land here for building between 1852 and 1864.

Talbot Yard SE1 (Southwark). The *Talbot* inn, the name being a corruption of Tabard, from the device on the sign, is recorded here in 1306 and became famous as the meeting place of Chaucer's Canterbury pilgrims. The mediaeval building is thought to have survived into the 17th century. That built *c*1629 was demolished in 1875.

Talfourd Road SE15 (Peckham, Southwark). Commemorates Thomas Talfourd, judge, writer and MP; his tragedy *Ion* (1836) was a great success.

Talgarth Road W6, W14 (Hammersmith). Built on land owned by the Gunter family (*see* **Gunter Grove**). They also held an estate at Talgarth, Breconshire. **Gliddon**, **Gwendwr** and **Trevanion** Roads, also named from Welsh family properties, are nearby. **Gunterstone Road** was named by association.

Tallis Street EC4 (Cit. Lond.). Passes the former premises of the Guildhall School of Music and Drama (now at the Barbican Arts Centre), and commemorates the 16th-century English composer Thomas Tallis. Tallis (*d* 1585) was an organist of the Chapel Royal, a post he shared with his pupil William Byrd.

Talwin Street E3 (Bromley, T. Ham.). Commemorates Elizabeth Talwin, a parish benefactor. By her will of 1795 she left £1,600 to found a charity providing bread and coals for the poor. A family called Talwin or Talwyn were active in trade in Bromley at the time; Talwyn Lloyd and Co. were calico printers working at Bromley Hall in the 1780s, and they are later recorded as Talwyn and Foster (*see* **Bromley Hall Road**).

Tamworth Street SW6 (Fulham, Hammersmith). The surrounding manor of Wandon (*see* **Wandon Road**) was held by John Tamworth of Parson's Green (*d* 1569), privy councillor to Elizabeth I.

Tanner Street SE1 (Bermondsey, Southwark). Approaches the Bermondsey Leather Market and marks the site of tanneries concentrated in Bermondsey since the 17th century. Tanning, a process considered too smelly for the confined spaces of the City of London, was forced S of the river. Bermondsey had the necessary supplies of pure water. This street was built as a wider improvement of an old way called Five Foot Lane, from its dimensions (*see* **Leathermarket Street**).

Tannsfield Road SE26 (Sydenham, Lewisham). Revives the name of a local property recorded in the early 17th century.

Tappesfield Road SE15 (Peckham, Southwark). Henry Tappesfield married Susan Muschamp of Peckham (*see* **Muschamp Road**).

Tarling Street E1 (Stepney, T. Ham.). This appears on maps of 1832 and 1855 as Terling Street, and may have been named from the builder.

Tasker Road NW3 (Hampstead, Camden). Approaches St Dominic's Priory, built largely through the generosity of Helen Ann Tasker, benefactor to the Roman Catholic Church. She was made a countess of the Pontifical States in 1870 and died in 1888.

Taunton Place NW1 (Marylebone, Cit. West.). Built on the Portman estate (*see* **Portman Square**). The family comes from Orchard Portman, near Taunton in Somerset.

Tavistock Square WC1 (Bloomsbury, Camden). Part of the estate of the dukes of Bedford; named from the family's estate at Tavistock in Devonshire from which the duke's heir takes his title of Marquis of Tavistock. **Tavistock Place** adjoins.

Tavistock Street WC2 (Covent Garden, Cit. West.). *See* **Tavistock Square**. Covent Garden was laid out for the Russell family, earls of Bedford who later became dukes of Bedford, in the 1630s.

Taviton Street WC1 (Bloomsbury, Camden). *See* **Tavistock Square**. The Devonshire properties of the dukes of Bedford included Taviton.

Tayport Close N1 (Caledonian Road, Islington). *See* **Carnoustie Drive**.

Tedworth Gardens SW3 (Chelsea, Ken. Chel.). *See* **Gertrude Street** for this and **Tedworth Square**.

Teignmouth Close SW4 (Clapham, Lambeth). Lord Teignmouth, former Governor-General of India, was a member of the 'Clapham Sect' of evangelical reformers (*see* **Thornton Road**). He lived in Clapham Park Road *c*1802–8. He became the first president of the British and Foreign Bible Society in 1799.

Telegraph Road SW15 (Putney,

Wandsworth). Approaches the site of an Admiralty semaphore station put up in 1796.

Telegraph Street EC2 (Cit. Lond.). Renaming of part of the former Bell Alley after the telegraph department of the General Post Office had been set up there (*see* **Great Bell Alley**).

Telferscot Road SW12 (Streatham, Lambeth). Built on an estate so named because of Telfer's Cot or Telford's Cottage which stood on it. **Telford Avenue** adjoins.

Telford Avenue SW2 (Streatham, Lambeth). *See* **Telferscot Road**.

Telford Terrace SW1 (Pimlico, Cit. West.). Commemorates the engineer Thomas Telford (1757–1834). Born in Dumfriesshire, the son of a shepherd, he trained as a mason and became a surveyor of roads. He is considered among the greatest of road-builders and his bridges were outstanding. The road surfaces he devised were further developed by another Scottish engineer, John McAdam.

Téméraire Street SE16 (Rotherhithe, Southwark). The warship *Téméraire*, 98 guns, fought at Trafalgar in 1805 and became the subject of a popular ballad, *The Fighting Téméraire*. In 1838 she was towed by tug to Rotherhithe (the scene painted by J.M.W. Turner) and broken up in Beatson's yard. Some of the timber was used to furnish St Paul's chapel nearby.

Temple Avenue EC4 (Cit. Lond.). *See* **Middle Temple Lane** for this and **Temple Lane**.

Temple Mills Lane E15 (Hackney/Waltham Forest). Nearby stood watermills belonging to the Order of Knights Templar, who held a manor in E Hackney 1233–1312 (*see* **Wick Road**).

Temple Sheen SW14 (Sheen, R. upon T.). *See* **Sheen Road**. Sir William Temple, philosopher, essayist and diplomat in the reign of Charles II (1660–85), James II (1685–8) and William III (1689–1702), lived here at a house called 'Temple Grove'.

Templeton Place SW5 (Kensington, Ken. Chel.). *See* **Longridge Road**.

Templewood Avenue NW3 (Hampstead, Camden). Built on land belonging to farms called Great Templewood and Little Templewood; the derivation is uncertain.

Tenison Court W1 (Regent Street, Cit. West.). Approaches the Anglican church of St Thomas, Kingly Street, which was named in 1869 and was formerly Tenison's Chapel. The chapel was built in 1702 on land bought by Dr Thomas Tenison, Archbishop of Canterbury.

Tenison Way SE1 (Lambeth). A Tenison Street was built in 1824 on land belonging to the archbishops of Canterbury (*see* **Lambeth Palace Road**). This was named after Archbishop Tenison (*see* **Tenison Court**) who gave Lambeth a school and a burial ground beside Old Paradise Street. Tenison Street disappeared in redevelopment and the name was transferred to this new road.

Tenniel Close W2 (Bayswater, Cit. West.). Commemorates the Victorian illustrator Sir John Tenniel (1820–1914). He is best remembered for his cartoons for *Punch* magazine and his illustrations to Lewis Carroll's *Alice in Wonderland*.

Tennis Street SE1 (Southwark). Led originally to tennis courts laid out on open recreation land at the rear of the High Street taverns.

Tennyson Street SW8 (Battersea, Wandsworth). The poet-laureate Alfred Tennyson bought houses in Queenstown Road and Battersea Park Road in 1871. Tennyson was a friend of James Knowles, the Clapham architect who designed the surrounding Park Town estate (*see* **Dickens Street**).

Tenter Ground E1 (Whitechapel, T. Ham.). Part of a tenter ground used by cloth-makers until the 1820s, when it was built over. The cloth was fixed to hooks and stretched out on frames to shape and dry it after it had been through the fulling mill. This ground extended from the present White's Row to Wentworth Street.

Tent Street E1 (Bethnal Green, T. Ham.). Part of ground formerly used as a tenter ground (*see* **Tenter Ground**).

Terrick Street W12 (Wormwood Scrubs, Hammersmith). Richard Terrick was Bishop of London in 1764 and, as such, held the manor of Hammersmith.

Teviot Street E14 (Poplar, T. Ham.). *See* **Leven Road**.

Thackeray Street W8 (Kensington, Ken. Chel.). Leads from Young Street where William Makepeace Thackeray, the novelist, lived and where he wrote *Vanity Fair* in 1848 and *The History of Henry Esmond* in 1852.

Thanet Street WC1 (Bloomsbury, Camden). *See* **Leigh Street**.

Thavie's Inn EC1 (Cit. Lond.). Site of the great town house or inn of John Thavie, 14th-century armourer. The house was bombed during World War II.

Thayer Street W1 (Marylebone, Cit. West.). Anne Thayer inherited this land from her father Thomas Thayer; the street was built in the 1770s after the estate had passed to her husband Jacob Hinde.

Theatre Street SW11 (Clapham, Wandsworth). The Shakespeare Theatre was built on this site on Lavender Hill *c*1910.

Theberton Street N1 (Barnsbury, Islington). Named from the Suffolk country seat of Thomas Milner Gibson (*see* **Gibson Square**).

Theobald's Road WC1 (Holborn, Camden). Part of the route used by Stuart kings to the royal hunting lodge at Theobalds in Hertfordshire. Originally there was an approach to it from High Holborn called King's Gate, the W end of the street was Theobald's Row and the E end was The King's Way. 'Theobalds' was extended along the whole road, including the E end which by that time was called King's Road, in 1878.

Therapia Road SE22 (Peckham Rye, Southwark). *See* **Marmora Road**.

Theresa Road W6 (Hammersmith). Theophilus Walford built Theresa Terrace in 1780 and named it after his daughter; the name was later transferred to this road.

Thermopylae Gate E14 (Isle of Dogs, T. Ham.). The clipper *Thermopylae*, 991 gross tons, was launched in 1868. She was built for George Thompson and Sons of Aberdeen, for whom she consistently broke speed records on runs to Melbourne, Australia. She also made fast voyages carrying tea from the East. Only the *Cutty Sark* had comparable overall performance. *Thermopylae* was berthed in the West India Docks, Millwall. In 1890 she was sold to a Canadian company and later she passed to the Portuguese government as a training ship, the *Pedro Nuñez*. She was sunk in 1907.

Thessaly Road SW8 (Battersea, Wandsworth). One of a group with Mediterranean place names; named from a region of Greece between the Pindus Mountains and the Aegean.

Thirleby Road SW1 (Cit. West.). Thomas Thirleby was made Bishop of Westminster in 1541; the diocese was created after the dissolution of the Abbey of St Peter, Westminster, and the abbey became its cathedral. According to John Stow, in his *Survey of London* of 1598, Thirleby was 'first and last bishop there who, when he had impoverished the church, was translated to Norwich . . .' in 1550, when the bishop was replaced by a dean.

Thistle Grove SW10 (Brompton, Ken. Chel.). An old name, describing the type of land here on what was formerly the W edge of Brompton Heath.

Thomas Doyle Street SE1 (Southwark). Father Doyle was leader of the committee responsible for the building of St George's Roman Catholic Cathedral nearby. The foundations were laid in 1841, the church was open for worship in 1848 and the completed cathedral was consecrated in 1894.

Thomas More Street E1 (Wapping, T. Ham.). Commemorates Sir Thomas More, Chancellor to Henry VIII, who resigned in 1532 because he did not accept Henry as supreme head of the Church of England, and refused to condone the king's plans for divorce and remarriage. In 1534 he refused to swear to the Act of Succession because it implied Henry's supremacy and denied the authority of the Pope; he was beheaded on nearby Tower Hill, for treason, in 1535. In 1935 he was canonised by the Roman Catholic Church.

Thornbury Road SW2 (Brixton, Lambeth). Built on the site of a house called 'Thornbury'. The same applies to **Thorncliffe Road** nearby.

Thorncliffe Road SW2 (Brixton, Lambeth). *See* **Thornbury Road**.

Thorney Street SW1 (Cit. West.). Commemorates Thorney Island, an isolated piece of firm ground, covered in briars, which was bounded E by the Thames and elsewhere by the Tyburn Brook and its surrounding marshes. A monastic community was set up there after the conversion of the Saxons, possibly replacing a Romano-British church, and flourished intermittently. The present Westminster Abbey was consecrated there in 1065.

Thornhaugh Street WC1 (Bloomsbury, Camden). Part of the estate of the dukes of Bedford, who also hold the title of Baron Russell of Thornhaugh.

Thornhill Square N1 (Barnsbury, Islington). Developed from *c*1820 by George Thornhill, who owned an estate of 26 acres here.

Thornton Place W1 (Marylebone, Cit. West.). Built on the Portman estate (*see* **Portman Square**). The seventh Viscount Portman had a sister, Emma, who married the eleventh Earl of Leven and Melville. The earl's mother was a Thornton.

Thornton Road SW12 (Clapham, Lambeth). John Thornton (1720–90), supporter of the evangelical movement, lived in Clapham where his father Robert Thornton had settled. John Thornton and his sons Henry and Samuel befriended and worked with the early evangelicals such as William Cowper and John Newton and, later, William Wilberforce. Wilberforce did much of his work against slavery from Henry Thornton's house. The family and their fellow reformers were called the 'Clapham Sect'. **Thornton Avenue** and **Gardens** adjoin.

Thorpebank Road W12 (Shepherd's Bush, Hammersmith). A large house nearby, which is now demolished, was called 'Thorpebank'.

Thorpewood Avenue SE26 (Lewisham). Derived from Wood Thorpe, and built on the site of a house so-called.

Thrale Road SW16 (Streatham, Lambeth). Runs parallel to one side of the kitchen garden of Streatham Place, a house on the edge of the common owned by the brewer Henry Thrale (*see* **Thrale Street**). Here he and his wife entertained Johnson, Boswell and Garrick 1766–81. The house was demolished in 1863.

Thrale Street SE1 (Southwark). Passes the Anchor Brewery, first recorded in the 17th century. It was managed by Ralph Thrale from 1728 and later owned by his son Henry Thrale (*d* 1781) who, with his wife Hester, is famous as the friend of Samuel Johnson.

Thrawl Street E1 (Spitalfields, T. Ham.). Properly Thrall, built from 1658 by Henry Thrall or Thrale.

Threadneedle Street EC2 (Cit. Lond.). Called Three Needle Street in the 16th century and later corrupted by the natural association between 'needle' and 'thread'. The original three needles would have been a sign outside a shop, probably indicating a maker of needles.

Three Colts Lane E2 (Bethnal Green, T. Ham.). From the sign of an inn

recorded here in the early 19th century, on the Cambridge Heath Road. **Three Colt Street** in Limehouse is named from an inn recorded in 1720.

Three Cups Yard WC1 (Holborn, Camden). Originally a yard to the rear of an inn called *The Three Cups* which was approached from Holborn. The writer John Strype in 1720 describes it as large 'and of a considerable resort for Persons that come to town, having great conveniences of Coach Houses and Stables'.

Three Kings Yard W1 (Mayfair, Cit. West.). Named from the sign of an inn, now demolished.

Three Mill Lane E3 (Bromley, T. Ham./Newham). Leads to the Mill Meads, site of a group of three watermills on the River Lea which are first mentioned *c*1300.

Three Oak Lane SE1 (Bermondsey, Southwark). The *Three Oaks Inn* is recorded here in 1761.

Three Tuns Court SE1 (Southwark). Built to approach the *Three Tuns* tavern, recorded here in 1845 and demolished before 1900.

Throgmorton Street EC2 (Cit. Lond.). This is first recorded in the 16th century as Throckmorton Street; Sir Nicholas Throckmorton or Throgmorton (*d* 1571) was a courtier and diplomat, but his connection with the street is not known. **Throgmorton Avenue** was built as an approach in 1876.

Thurland Road SE16 (Bermondsey, Southwark). In 1710 Thomas Trappes left the manor of Bermondsey to his niece Elizabeth, who married Edward Thurland in 1711. The Thurlands lived at

Bermondsey House nearby 1711–17, and then sold the manor.

Thurloe Square SW7 (Kensington, Ken. Chel.). John Thurloe, secretary to Oliver Cromwell, obtained land here in the mid-17th century. His descendant Harris Thurloe Brace (*d* 1799) left it to a godson who laid out the square and surrounding streets (*see* **Alexander Square**). **Thurloe Place** and **Street** approach.

Thurlow Park Road SE21 (Tulse Hill, Lambeth). Edward Thurlow, later Lord Thurlow, acquired Knight's Hill House and 100 acres of land E of the present Norwood Road in 1772. Knight's Hill itself, the Wall estate in Lambeth, the manor of Leigham Court, Streatham, and Levehurst manor were added by 1795. Thurlow built a mansion near the present junction of this road and Elmcourt Road in 1792–5; he disliked it and never lived there, and it was demolished after his death and the land laid out in streets. Lord Thurlow was Solicitor General 1770–1, Attorney General 1771–8 and Lord Chancellor 1778–92. He was described as coarse, vigorous, intelligent and powerful in debate.

Tibbatts Road E3 (Bromley, T. Ham.). Named in 1878, possibly in connection with the family of Tibbatts, shipbuilders of Fore Street, Limehouse.

Tileyard Road N7 (York Way, Islington). On a small area of high ground here, called the Belle Isle, potteries flourished in the early 19th century. They made simple earthenwares, including tiles.

Tiller Road E14 (Isle of Dogs, T. Ham). *See* **Capstan Square**.

Tillett Way E2 (Bethnal Green, T. Ham.). Commemorates Ben Tillett, pioneer of dockers' unions. As secretary of the Dock, Wharf, Riverside and General Workers' Union he led the dock strike of 1889 and that of 1911. He was a Labour MP 1917–24 and 1929–31. The strike of 1889 achieved a rate of 6d. and hour an 8d. for overtime (instead of 5d. and 6d. respectively) and the end of the system under which men were abitrarily chosen for work by sub-contractors. It was mainly Tillett's presentation of the dockers' case that ensured the support of influential men.

Tillman Street E1 (Stepney, T. Ham.). *See* **Crowder Street**.

Tilloch Street N1 (Caledonian Road, Islington). The scientist Alexander Tilloch (*d* 1825) lived in Barnsbury Street. Born in Glasgow, he was also a writer and the founder of the *Philosophical Magazine* in 1797.

Tillotson Street E1 (Stepney, T. Ham.). Built on land belonging to Clare College, Cambridge. John Tillotson (1630–94) was a controversial Archbishop of Canterbury from 1689 and a fellow of Clare from 1651.

Tilney Court EC1 (Old Street, Islington) From Ann Tilney, who owned it in 1771 when it was described as 'new built'.

Tilney Street W1 (Mayfair, Cit. West.). Built on land granted to John Tilney or Tylney by Lord Berkeley of Stratton in the mid-18th century.

Timber Street EC1 (Finsbury, Islington). Built by a timber merchant, who developed the surrounding area with trade-associated names, *c*1810. **Baltic Street** refers to the Baltic softwood trade, mainly fir; **Memel Street** was named from a timber-exporting Baltic port and **Honduras Street** and **Domingo Street** from Honduras and

San Domingo, which were sources of mahogany.

Tinworth Street SE11 (Vauxhall, Lambeth). Near the site of Doulton's Lambeth Potteries. George Tinworth (1843–1913) was a noted modeller of relief panels, mainly on biblical subjects, for Doulton. He joined the company in 1867.

Titchfield Road NW8 (Primrose Hill, Cit. West.). Built on a small, detached part of the Duke of Portland's estate, which extended W to St John's Wood High Street and E to Ormonde Terrace (*see* **Great Titchfield Street**).

Tite Street SW3 (Chelsea, Ken. Chel.). Commemorates the Victorian architect Sir William Tite (*d* 1873); as a member of the Metropolitan Board of Works he was active in the creation of the Chelsea embankment. Buildings he designed elsewhere included the Royal Exchange, Cornhill.

Tobago Street E14 (Isle of Dogs, T. Ham.). *See* **Cuba Street**.

Tokenhouse Yard EC2 (Cit. Lond.). Site of a 17th-century token house, an office issuing tokens for business use during a shortage of coin.

Tollington Park N4 (Holloway, Islington). Site of an estate called Tollington Park. Tollington or Tolenton was a manor acquired from Alice de Barowe in 1271 by the Knights of St John of Jerusalem. The manor house on what is now Hornsey Road was abandoned in favour of one at Highbury. **Tollington Road** is nearby.

Tolmers Square NW1 (Euston, Camden). Named after a village in Hertfordshire near the source of the New River. The New River Company formerly held this land; they had a reservoir here which was closed in 1860.

Tonbridge Street WC1 (Bloomsbury, Camden). *See* **Judd Street**.

Tonsley Hill SW18 (Wandsworth). Site of a large house and grounds called 'Tonsley Hall'. The grounds extended to Fairfield Street; the house was demolished *c*1850. **Tonsley Place**, **Road** and **Street** adjoin.

Took's Court EC4 (Cit. Lond.). Uncertain, probably the name of a builder or property owner who appears variously as Tuke (1746), Tucker (1720) and Duck (1677).

Tooley Street SE1 (Southwark). Corruption of St Olave Street; the mediaeval church of St Olave (commonly corrupted to 'St Towles') stood by the Thames at the junction of this street and Duke Street Hill. The saint was associated with London Bridge (*see* **St Olave's Court**).

Tooting Bec Road SW17 (Tooting, Wandsworth). Runs NW to Tooting Bec, one of the mediaeval mayors of Tooting (*see* **Tooting High Street**). Between 1066 and 1086 Richard de Tonbridge, Lord of Clare, granted this manor to the abbey of Bec Hellouin in Normandy. The abbey held it through an English cell, Ogbourne Priory. In *c*1404 this priory's possessions were granted to a son of Henry IV. The manor eventually passed to Sir Giles Howland in 1599. His great-granddaughter Elizabeth Howland married Wriothesley Russell, heir of the Duke of Bedford, in 1695, and the manor passed to the Russells.

Tooting High Street SW17 (Tooting, Wandsworth). High or principal street of Tooting, called Totinge in the 7th century, which means the place of Tota's people.

Topham Street EC1 (Clerkenwell, Islington). 'Topham the Strong Man' performed feats of strength here in 1741, to celebrate a victory of Admiral Vernon at Carthagena, Spain. A well-known entertainer, Topham died in 1749.

Topsfield Road N8 (Crouch End, Haringey). Preserved the name of a sub-manor with a manor house at Crouch End Broadway. This sub-manor of Topsfield was formed from the manor of Hornsey.

Torriano Avenue NW5 (Kentish Town, Camden). Joshua Prole Torriano inherited land here in 1793. He laid out this street and two others later called **Leighton Road** and **Leighton Grove. Torriano Cottages** adjoins.

Torrington Square WC1 (Bloomsbury, Camden). Built on the estate of the dukes of Bedford. The sixth duke married Georgiana Byng, daughter of Lord Torrington. **Torrington Place** approaches.

Tothill Street SW1 (Cit. West.). Originally led to a stretch of open land called Tothill Fields; the derivation is uncertain.

Tottenham Court Road W1 (Camden). Leads to the former court or hall of the manor of Tottenham or Tottenhale. In the 13th century this manor is called Totenhale, meaning Tota's hall. It later became confused with Tottenham in N London, with which it had no connection. In 18th-century maps the area immediately N of the present Euston Road is called Tottenham Court, and the manor house or hall stood at the SE corner of Hampstead Road. The Fitzroy family inherited the manor of Tottenhall by marriage with the heiress of Lord Arlington (*see* **Grafton Way**).

Tottenham Lane N8 (Haringey). Leads to Tottenham, which is called Toteham in the *Domesday Book*; the name means Tota's homestead.

Totterdown Street SW17 (Tooting, Wandsworth). Built across fields formerly called Totterdown Fields; the derivation is uncertain.

Toulmin Street SE1 (Southwark). Local family name; Captain Toulmin commanded the Christchurch Volunteer Association (1798–1803). Samuel Toulmin was a governor of St Thomas's Hospital 1805–7; Toulmins had a soap factory in Gravel Lane at that time.

Tower Hill EC3 (Cit. Lond.). The Tower of London was begun in 1078, with the White Tower, and several times enlarged. It was used as a fortress, a royal mint and a royal residence until, in the 16th century, it had come to be used extensively as a prison for offenders against the state; these were brought from their trial by water (for fear of trouble in the streets) to the Traitors' Gate. In consequence, Tower Hill became a place of execution.

Tower Royal EC4 (Cit. Lond.). Site of a mediaeval tower which had become a royal lodging by the time of Richard II (1377–99), although Royal is a corruption of Ryole or Réole. The building was originally 'the Réole tower', since it belonged to French wine merchants from La Réole.

Tower Street WC2 (Covent Garden, Camden). Named from the sign of an inn, now demolished.

Townley Road SE22 (Dulwich, Southwark). From the family of Edward Alleyn (*see* **Alleyn Park**), as is nearby **Woodwarde Road**. John Townley was Alleyn's grandfather;

Joan Woodwarde was Alleyn's first wife.

Townley Street SE17 (Walworth, Southwark). Built on the nursery-gardens belonging to E.W. Townley, gardener, seedsman and land surveyor. **Nursery Row** is nearby.

Townmead Road SW6 (Fulham, Hammersmith). Runs across the former river meadows attached to the 'town' of Fulham and called the Town Mead. A map published in 1813 shows the mead extending E from Broomhouse Lane to Chelsea Creek. The land was built over in the late 19th century; this main street of the development was built from 1879.

Townsend Street SE17 (Old Kent Road, Southwark). Runs beside the school for the deaf of which the Rev. John Townsend was co-founder with Henry Cox Mason. Townsend, a nonconformist minister, set up the first school for the deaf and dumb in Grange Road, Bermondsey, in 1792; the school moved to this site in 1809.

Toynbee Street E1 (Whitechapel, T. Ham.). Toynbee Hall was founded in 1884 as an Oxford and Cambridge University mission for social and educational work. The founder-warden was the Rev. Canon Samuel Augustus Barnett of St Jude's, Whitechapel. The centre was named in memory of the historian Arnold Toynbee who died in 1881.

Tracey Street SE11 (Kennington, Lambeth). In 1775 James Tracey left £300 to build a boys' school, and land was given by the mayor of Walworth. The building stood next to the Drapers' Almshouses in Newington.

Tradescant Road SW8 (S Lambeth, Lambeth). Site of a house belonging to John Tradescant (d 1638) and John his son (d 1662), both gardeners and collectors with an interest in coins,

medals and natural history; their collection formed the nucleus of the Ashmolean Museum in Oxford. Their house was demolished and the street built c1880 (see **Walberswick Street**).

Trafalgar Avenue SE15 (Peckham, Southwark). See **Trafalgar Square**. A house at the corner with the Old Kent Road, built by John Rolls in 1780, became the Lord Nelson public house after Nelson's death; three small streets (Brontie Street, Aboukir Street and Victory Place) originally lay S of Waite Street. They commemorated one of Nelson's titles (Duke of Brontë in Sicily), his victory at Aboukir, otherwise called the battle of the Nile, in 1798, and his flagship HMS Victory. **Nile Terrace** adjoins.

Trafalgar Square WC2, SW1 (Cit. West.). Laid out in 1830 on land which had formerly been a royal mews and stables. The square commemorates Admiral Nelson's victory over the French and Spanish fleets at the battle of Trafalgar in 1805. Napoleon had intended the invasion of England, but first needed to secure the English Channel. The English had prevented any enemy approach to the Channel by a two-year blockade of French-controlled ports. Trafalgar was the final French attempt to break the blockade, although by the time the fleet was ready to move out of Cadiz Napoleon had already changed his mind and instructed them to head S into the Mediterranean. They were engaged off Cape Trafalgar and destroyed.

Trafalgar Street SE17 (Walworth, Southwark). Built in 1806 (see **Trafalgar Square**).

Transept Street NW1 (Marylebone, Cit. West.). See **Chapel Street**.

Trebeck Street W1 (Mayfair, Cit.

West.). Commemorates the Rev. Dr Trebeck, rector of St George's, Hanover Square, who suppressed Keith's chapel here in 1754. The chapel was the scene of thousands of irregular marriages.

Trebovir Road SW5 (Kensington, Ken. Chel.). *See* **Longridge Road**.

Treby Street E3 (Mile End, T. Ham.). George Treby administered a portion of the manor of Stepney 1674–6.

Tredegar Square E3 (Bow, T. Ham.). Built *c*1835 on land belonging to the first Baron Tredegar, Charles Morgan Robinson Morgan (1792–1875). He was MP for Brecknock and served as High Sherriff of both Monmouth and Breconshire at different times. He was created Baron Tredegar in 1859. **Tredegar Road** and **Terrace** approach; **Morgan Street** runs to the N.

Tregunter Road SW10 (W Brompton, Ken. Chel.). On the Gunter family's estate (*see* **Gunter Grove**). Tregunter was a family property in Breconshire.

Treherne Court SW17 (Tooting, Wandsworth). Mr Treherne was a resident of Tooting Graveney, active in the Tooting Graveney Common Preservation Society which saved the common for the public. The society fought a long battle (*c*1863–72) against the lord of the manor.

Tresham Crescent W1 (Lisson Grove, Cit. West.). *See* **Paveley Street**. Thomas Tresham was Grand Prior of the Order of Knights of St John of Jerusalem in England from 1557 until its suppression in 1559. The order was not revived in England until 1831. **Tresham Street**, Hackney, was also built on land belonging to the Knights of St John (*see* **St John's Church Road**).

Trevanion Road W14 (Hammersmith). *See* **Talgarth Road**.

Treveris Street SE1 (Southwark). Commemorates Peter Treveris, a Southwark printer active *c*1500–30.

Treviso Road SE23 (Forest Hill, Lewisham). *See* **Vestris Road**.

Trevithick Street SE8 (Deptford, Lewisham). Commemorates Richard Trevithick (1771–1833), Cornish engineer who was a pioneer of high-pressure steam engines suitable for use in locomotives. It was Trevithick who built the first steam-driven passenger vehicle in 1801. Before 1889 this street was called Armada Street.

Trevor Square SW7 (Knightsbridge, Cit. West.). Site of the home of Sir John Trevor (1637–1717), judge. Speaker of the House of Commons, he was expelled from the House in 1695 for accepting a bribe, but no similar accusation could be brought against him in his work as a judge. This square, with approaching **Trevor Place** and **Street**, were built by Lancelot Edward Wood in the 1820s. **Lancelot Place** is nearby.

Trilby Road SE23 (Forest Hill, Lewisham). Named in 1896 after the novel *Trilby* by George du Maurier.

Trim Street SE14 (Deptford, Lewisham). *See* **Arklow Road**.

Trinity Church Passage EC4 (Cit. Lond.). Approaches the site of Holy Trinity church, now demolished, which was built in 1827 as a chapel of ease to St Bride's; the church stood at the S end of Great New Street.

Trinity Church Square SE1 (Southwark). Laid out from 1825 on land belonging to Trinity House, and surrounding Holy Trinity church, built also on Trinity House land in

1823–4 (*see* **Trinity Street** and **Trinity Square**).

Trinity Gardens SW9 (Brixton, Lambeth). Leads to the Trinity almshouses, originally Trinity Asylum, founded in 1822 by Thomas Bailey for 'pious aged women'.

Trinity Road SW17, SW18 (Wandsworth). The church of the Holy Trinity, Upper Tooting, was built in 1855 and the parish formed in the same year. **Trinity Crescent** adjoins.

Trinity Square EC3 (Cit. Lond./T. Ham.). Laid out in front of Trinity House, the headquarters of the corporation responsible for pilotage, buoys and lighthouses. The corporation was first formed in the 15th century, and its full name is the Brotherhood of the Most Glorious and Undivided Trinity.

Trinity Street SE1 (Southwark). Leads to Trinity Church Square, and both were built on land belonging to the corporation of Trinity House, to whom it was given in 1661 as a source of income for seamen, their widows and orphans. The estate was built up from 1813.

Triton Square NW1 (Euston, Camden). A modern square named after a Greek sea-god, son of Poseidon and half human, half dolphin. He is often depicted blowing on a shell to control the movement of the sea.

Trott Street SW11 (Battersea, Wandsworth). Named in 1868; a builder called Trott was active in S London at the time.

Trump Street EC2 (Cit. Lond.). Uncertain, first recorded in 1746. A Duke Street is recorded along the same route in 1720. 'Trump' as an 18th-century name is more likely to

be that of a builder or proprietor than of a product or trade (like trumpet-maker).

Tryon Street SW3 (Chelsea, Ken. Chel.). Commemorates Vice-Admiral Tryon, drowned in 1893 when his flagship HMS *Victoria* collided with HMS *Camperdown* off Tripoli. Tryon had ordered both ships, leading parallel lines, to turn inwards and invert their course; there was not enough room for this manoeuvre.

Tudor Place W1 (Tottenham Court Road, Camden). Formerly Black Horse Yard, from an inn and stable-yard. The land was held copyhold 1819–80 by Elizabeth Mary Jones, who married George Tudor.

Tudor Street EC4 (Cit. Lond.). Runs W from New Bridge Street across the site of the Tudor palace of Bridewell, built for Henry VIII in 1522 (*see* **Bridewell Place**).

Tufnell Park Road N19, N7 (Tufnell Park, Islington). Serves a park-style development built on part of the manor of Barnsbury which was held by the Tufnell family. The Haltons (*see* **Halton Road**) left an entail by which the manor ultimately came to George Forster Tufnell in 1797.

Tufton Street SW1 (Cit. West.). Built by Sir Richard Tufton, who died in 1631.

Tugela Street SE6 (Perry Hill, Lewisham). Commemorates an action on the Tugela River, Natal, in 1900, during the second Boer War.

Tulse Hill SW2 (Lambeth). Leads S to the former Tulse Hill Farm, centre of an estate held by the Tulse family in the 17th century. **Upper Tulse Hill** adjoins. The roads were laid out between 1814 and 1821 by Dr Thomas Edwards.

Tunbridge Court SE26 (Sydenham, Lewisham). *See* **Wells Park Road**.

Tunnel Road SE16 (Rotherhithe, Southwark). This marks the S end of the Thames Tunnel (*see* **Brunel Road**).

Turks Row SW3 (Chelsea, Ken. Chel.). An 18th-century name, probably from a coffee-house. Turkish coffee inspired many 'Turk's Head' coffee-houses.

Turnagain Lane EC4 (Cit. Lond.). Recorded in the 13th century as Wendageyneslane and in the 15th as Turneagayne Lane; a cul-de-sac or lane in which one must turn and go back. Originally the street led down to the River Fleet.

Turner's Alley EC3 (Cit. Lond.). Properly Turners' Alley; the Turners' Company had a hall in Philpot Lane, which this alley approached, until 1737.

Turney Road SE21 (Dulwich, Southwark). George Turney served on Camberwell vestry in the 1860s.

Turnmill Street EC1 (Clerkenwell, Islington). Called Trimullstrete in the 14th century, meaning Three Mill Street, after three watermills on the River Fleet.

Turpentine Lane SW1 (Pimlico, Cit. West.). This lane led to an early 19th-century white lead works (Renny's) which was removed *c*1850 when the area was developed by Thomas Cubitt. The lane was then already called Turpentine Lane, from the previous manufacture there of turpentine.

Turquand Street SE17 (Walworth, Southwark). The Rev. Paul James Turquand was minister of York Street (now Browning Street) Independent Chapel in the 1860s, 1870s and 1880s.

Turret Grove SW4 (Clapham, Lambeth). The manor house, Clapham, had an octagonal turret at one corner which became a local landmark. The house was turned into a school in 1749 and was later demolished (*see* **Clapham Manor Street**).

Turtle Road SW17 (Summerstown, Wandsworth). Possibly built by F.R. Turtle who was active as a builder in S London in the 1870s and 1880s.

Turville Street E2 (Bethnal Green, T. Ham.). *See* **Camlet Street**.

Twyford Place WC2 (Lincoln's Inn, Camden). *See* **Remnant Street**.

Tyburn Way W1 (Oxford Street, Cit. West.). Passes the site of the former place of execution, Tyburn gallows. A gibbet stood here permanently from 1220–1759 and temporarily thereafter until 1783 when it was moved to Newgate prison. The old hamlet of Tyburn (deserted by 1400) is Tiburne in the *Domesday Book*, meaning a boundary stream, or the place where the boundary is a stream.

Tyers Street SE11 (Vauxhall, Lambeth). Jonathon Tyers, father and son, were the proprietors and managers of the Spring Gardens, otherwise called Vauxhall Gardens, which crossed the S end of this street. The family ran the Gardens 1728–92. **Tyers Terrace** is nearby. (*See* **New Spring Gardens Walk**).

Tylney Avenue SE19 (Dulwich, Southwark). By association with Edward Alleyn (*see* **Alleyn Park**). Edmund Tylney was Master of the Revels to Elizabeth I.

Tyndale Terrace N1 (Islington). Built

*c*1792 on land held from the manor as copyhold by Colonel Tyndale.

Tyrrell Road SE22 (Dulwich, Southwark). Sir James Tyrrell (*d* 1718) was educated in Camberwell. He was known for his writing on the constitution and the law.

Tyrwhitt Road SE4 (Brockley, Lewisham). Thomas Drake, co-owner of the manor of Brockley, took the name of Tyrwhitt on receiving a legacy, and became known as Tyrwhitt-Drake (*see* **Drake Road**).

Tysoe Street EC1 (Clerkenwell, Islington). Built on land belonging to the Marquis of Northampton who had a seat at Compton Wynyates, Tysoe.

Tyssen Street E8 (Dalston Lane, Hackney). Francis Tyssen bought the manor of Lordshold in 1697, and a house at Shacklewell which became known as the Manor House. The manor remained in the Tyssen family until *c*1794, when it passed to William George Daniel, who married the Tyssen heiress Amelia. Their descendants took the name of Tyssen.

U

Udall Street SW1 (Cit. West.). Approaches Westminster School playing fields. The playwright, scholar and schoolmaster Nicolas Udall (1505–56) became headmaster of Westminster in 1554, after a chequered career. He is the author of *Ralph Roister Doister*, the earliest English stage comedy.

Ulster Terrace NW1 (Regent's Park, Cit. West.). Part of John Nash's Regent's Park scheme (*see* **Regent Street**). The Regent's brother the Duke of York was also Earl of Ulster. **Ulster Place** is nearby.

Ulverscroft Road SE22 (Dulwich, Southwark). Revival of an old place name; Ulverscroft was a plot of land in Friern manor.

Ulysses Road NW6 (W Hampstead, Camden). *See* **Achilles Road**.

Underhill Road SE22 (Dulwich, Southwark). *See* **Overhill Road**.

Undershaft EC3 (Cit. Lond.). The 'shaft' was a maypole which used to stand, every May Day, on the nearby corner of Leadenhall Street and St Mary Axe. The church of St Andrew on the same corner became known as St Andrew Under Shaft. The use of the maypole was forbidden after May Day riots in 1517. Undershaft is approached from Leadenhall Street by **Shafts Court**.

Union Street SE1 (Southwark). The earliest (E) part was laid out in 1781. 'Union' was once among the commonest London street names, particularly in the 18th century and the early 19th. Sometimes the sense was literal: the street effected the union of two points or routes. Sometimes the inspiration was patriotic: the Acts of Union (England and Scotland, 1707, and Great Britain and Ireland, 1801) produced streets so named, and taverns called *Union Flag* (in Whitechapel) or *Union Arms* (in Holborn). A third and later derivation is from the presence of a Union Workhouse, that is, one built by two or more parishes which had formed a union to administer the poor laws.

University Street WC1 (Bloomsbury, Camden). Approaches University College London, founded in 1828; it became the nucleus of London University.

Unwin Close SE15 (Peckham, Southwark). Formerly Unwin Road, named in 1873. It was probably laid out by Unwins, builders active in S London from *c*1860.

Upbrook Mews W2 (Bayswater, Cit. West.). *See* **Brook Mews North**.

Upland Road SE22 (Dulwich, Southwark). Revival of an old local field name.

Upper Berkeley Street SW1 (Marylebone, Cit. West.). Built on the Portman estate (*see* **Portman Square**). Henry William Berkeley changed his surname to Portman when he inherited the estate from his mother's family. His father William Berkeley was related to the Viscount Fitzhardinge. **Fitzhardinge Street** continues E of Portman Square. (*See* **Seymour Street**).

Upper Grosvenor Street W1

(Mayfair, Cit. West.). *See* **Grosvenor Square**.

Upper Ground SE1 (Lambeth, Lambeth/Southwark). Line of early earth ramparts forming solid raised ground between the river and the marshland behind; originally called Narrow Wall, it was rebuilt as Commercial Road in 1815 as far E as Broadwall, the rest being called Upper Ground Street. The extension of the latter name along the whole length is modern (1938).

Upper James Street W1 (Soho, Cit. West.). *See* **Lower James Street**.

Upper John Street W1 (Soho, Cit. West.). *See* **Lower John Street**.

Upper Marsh SE1 (Lambeth). *See* **Lower Marsh**.

Upper Montagu Street W1 (Marylebone, Cit. West.). *See* **Montagu Square**.

Upper Richmond Road SW14 (Wandsworth). Leads to Richmond, which was called Sheen until the reign of Henry VII (1485–1509). The 13th-century Sheen Palace was rebuilt for Henry and in his honour the palace and its surrounding royal manor was renamed. Before his accession he was Earl of Richmond in Yorkshire. The Yorkshire place name derives from a Norman landowner called Richemont (*see* **Sheen Road**).

Upper Street N1 (Islington). Named in relation to **Essex Road** which was formerly called Lower Street as far as its junction with Cross Street. The two streets passed through upper and lower Islington village.

Upper Thames Street EC4 (Cit. Lond.). Formerly (with its continuation, **Lower Thames Street**) just called Thames Street and thought to be the waterfront of Roman London.

Upper Tulse Hill SW2 (Lambeth). *See* **Tulse Hill**.

Upper Wimpole Street W1 (Marylebone, Cit. West.). *See* **Wimpole Street**.

Upper Woburn Place WC1 (Bloomsbury, Camden). *See* **Woburn Place**.

Urswick Road E9 (Hackney). Commemorates the Rev. Christopher Urswick (*d* 1521), vicar of Hackney. His house stood here.

Uxbridge Street W8 (Kensington, Ken. Chel.). The adjoining main road, now called Notting Hill Gate, was part of the Uxbridge Turnpike; its continuation beyond Shepherd's Bush is still called Uxbridge Road, as leading to Uxbridge, the bridge of the Wixan people.

V

Vale, The SW3 (Chelsea, Ken. Chel.). Built on land attached to a house called 'Vale Grove' in Old Church Street. The house is now demolished.

Valentine Road E9 (Hackney). *See* **Poole Road**.

Vale Royal N7 (Islington). A name commemorating an ancient land ownership; this area, before 1540, belonged to the religious community of the Blessed Virgin Mary in the Vale Royal. The Vale is in Cheshire and is so called because it was a royal hunting ground.

Valette Street E9 (Hackney). Built on land once held by the Order of Knights of St John of Jerusalem (*see* **St John's Church Road**). John Parisot de la Valette was Grand Master of the order, and famous as the commander of Malta during the great siege by the Turks in 1565. The city of Valetta, built on the site of the battle, was named after him.

Vallance Road E1, E2 (Whitechapel, T. Ham.). Named in 1896, replacing Baker's Row, Nottingham Street and White Street. The office of the Whitechapel Board of Guardians stood here then, and the Clerk to the Board at the time was W. Vallance.

Vandon Street SW1 (Cit. West.). Cornelius Vandon or Van Dun, 16th-century yeoman of the guard, founded almshouses for eight poor women in Petty France, to which **Vandon Passage** connects.

Vandy Street EC2 (Shoreditch, Hackney). Joseph Vandy was a church-warden of St Leonard's, Shoreditch, and a member of Shoreditch vestry, in the 1890s.

Vane Close NW3 (Hampstead, Camden). Site of Vane House, the Soldiers' Daughters' School, now demolished. This was originally the home of Sir Harry Vane (*see* **Vane Street**). Sir Harry's house was demolished in 1858 and its successor *c*1971.

Vane Street SW1 (Cit. West.). Adjoins the playing fields of Westminster School where Sir Harry Vane the younger (1613–62) was a pupil. A Puritan and Parliamentarian, he was frequently at odds with Cromwell and was not party to the execution of Charles I in 1649. He was nevertheless executed for high treason under the restored Stuart monarchy in 1662.

Vanguard Street SE8 (Deptford, Lewisham). One of three remaining names (with **Ship Street** and **Admiral Street**) from a set commemorating Admiral Nelson's victories. HMS *Vanguard* was Nelson's flagship at the battle of the Nile in 1798. The street was formerly two, called Nelson and Nile Streets. Cranbrook Street was Victory Street, from Nelson's flagship at Trafalgar (*see* **Trafalgar Avenue** and **Square**).

Varndell Street NW1 (Regent's Park, Camden). Commemorates S.E. Varndell, architect, who succeeded John Nash as surveyor of the Regent's Park development (*see* **Regent Street**).

Vassall Road SW9 (Brixton Road, Lambeth). Built in the 19th century on part of Lambeth Wick manor.

Baron Holland, lessee of the manor, adopted his wife's family name of Vassall in 1800 (*see* **Wickwood Street**).

Vauxhall Bridge Road SW1 (Pimlico, Cit. West.). Built as an approach to Vauxhall Bridge which opened in 1816.

Vauxhall Walk SE11 (Vauxhall, Lambeth). Formerly approached the Vauxhall Pleasure Gardens which occupied the site of Falkeshall, the manor house of Falke de Breaute who died in 1226. **Vauxhall Street** is nearby.

Venables Street NW8 (Lisson Grove, Cit. West.). Commemorates the Rev. Edward Venables (*d* 1891), rector of Christ Church, Bell Street.

Vencourt Place W6 (Hammersmith). From a large house called 'Vencourt House'.

Venn Street SW4 (Clapham, Lambeth). John Venn (*d* 1813) was rector of Clapham and a leading member of the evangelistic movement in the Church of England. He was one of the founders of the Church Missionary Society and the main inspiration of the 'Clapham Sect' (*see* **Thornton Road**).

Verdun Road SW13 (Barnes, R. upon T.). Southernmost point of the trench-line on the Western Front during World War I. The 'Battle of Verdun' lasted for most of 1916.

Vere Street W1 (Oxford Street, Cit. West.). Built *c*1730 on land belonging to the Harley family, earls of Oxford, and named in compliment to the De Vere family who held the earldom from 1155 until the death of the childless twentieth earl in 1703. The De Veres had been lords of the manor of Tyburn (Marylebone) *c*1200.

Verney Road SE16 (N Peckham, Southwark). F.W. Verney was London County Council member for Peckham from 1900.

Vernon Place WC1 (Bloomsbury, Camden). Commemorates Elizabeth Vernon, Countess of Southampton, an ancestor of Lady Rachel Wriothesley who married Lord William Russell (*see* **Southampton Row**).

Vernon Rise WC1 (Islington). *See* **Percy Circus** for this and **Vernon Square**.

Vernon Street W14 (North End, Hammersmith). The Vernon Investment Association owned and developed much of this area.

Verran Road SW12 (Balham, Wandsworth). Named in 1872; probably laid out by Rowe and Verran, builders active in the 1870s.

Verulam Street WC1 (Gray's Inn Road, Camden). Opposite Verulam Buildings, Gray's Inn. The scholar, lawyer and writer Francis Bacon, Lord Verulam, had chambers in Gray's Inn from 1597 until his death in 1626. Bacon published his first *Essays* in 1597 and his *Advancement of Learning* in 1605. His political career brought him to the post of Lord Chancellor in 1618, a height from which he fell in 1621, on a charge of corruption. His philosophical and scientific work had a lasting influence.

Vestris Road SE23 (Forest Hill, Lewisham). One of a group taken from the history of the theatre (*see* **Cibber Road**, **Farren Road**, **Kemble Road** and **Street** and **Siddons Lane** and **Road**). Lucia Bartalozzi (1797–1856) married Auguste Vestris in 1813 and retained his name professionally after his death and her remarriage. Her second husband was the actor Charles Mathews. Madame Vestris excelled in vivacious singing parts and in producing extravagant comedy and musical burlesque. **Treviso** and **Como** Roads record her birthplace at Treviso, near Como.

Vestry Road SE5 (Peckham, Southwark). Opposite the Town Hall, which was built as the parish Vestry Hall in 1873. Vestries, so called from their original meeting-place, were the bodies of local administration which preceded the borough councils. Camberwell vestry administered Camberwell, Peckham and Dulwich. There is a **Vestry Street** in Shoreditch.

Vevey Street SE6 (Forest Hill, Lewisham). *See* **Helvetia Street**.

Viaduct Street E2 (Bethnal Green, T. Ham.). Originally ran S to the railway line from Liverpool Street to Bethnal Green, which is carried above the streets on a viaduct. **Viaduct Place** adjoins.

Vicarage Gate W8 (Kensington, Ken. Chel.). Laid out in 1877 across the site of the vicarage of St Mary Abbot's church.

Vicar's Close E15 (S Hackney, Hackney). *See* **Christchurch Close**.

Vicar's Hill SE13 (Lewisham). Built in the 1880s on part of the glebe land belonging to the vicars of Lewisham. During the 19th century many churches applied for the right to build on their glebe land in order to increase their income.

Vicar's Road NW5 (Kentish Town, Camden). *See* **Dale Road**.

Victoria Avenue EC2 (Cit. Lond.). Named in 1901, the year of Queen Victoria's death.

Victoria Embankment SW1, WC2,

EC4 (Cit. West.). Completed in 1870 to control the Thames and to contain an improved sewerage system which would intercept foul drainage before it reached the river. Named from the reigning queen.

Victoria Grove W8 (Kensington, Ken. Chel.). *See* **Prince of Wales Terrace**.

Victoria Park Road E9 (S Hackney, Hackney). Approaches Victoria Park, laid out as a public park on land bought for the purpose in 1840; the money was raised by the sale of Crown properties and the park was named after the reigning queen.

Victoria Road W8 (Kensington, Ken. Chel.). This small area, W of Palace Gate, was laid out as Kensington New Town from 1837, the year of Queen Victoria's accession. This street was built on the line of an old way called Love Lane. Greater London has over 20 'Victoria' street names from her long reign of 1837–1901. The queen's strong convictions, unequivocally expressed, at times embarrassed her ministers. Her personal qualities and code of conduct restored the lost prestige of the Crown and set the tone for a whole generation.

Victoria Street SW1 (Cit. West.). Made in 1850–1 (*see* **Victoria Road**).

Victory Place SE17 (Walworth, Southwark). Leads off Rodney Road, formerly Trafalgar Road. HMS *Victory* was Nelson's flagship at the battle of Trafalgar in 1805.

Vigo Street W1 (Mayfair, Cit. West.). Named after the Spanish port, on Spain's Atlantic coast, where combined Dutch and English fleets sank Spanish treasure ships in 1702.

Villiers Street WC2 (Strand, Cit.

West.). George Villiers, Duke of Buckingham (*d* 1628), acquired the former York House (*see* **York Buildings**) on this site in 1617. His son sold it as a development site in the 1670s on condition that his name and titles be commemorated in the streets to be built (*see* **Buckingham Street**).

Vincent Square SW1 (Cit. West.). Dr William Vincent (*d* 1815) was Dean of Westminster and headmaster of nearby Westminster School. The square became a recreation ground for the school. **Vincent Street** approaches it.

Vincent Terrace N1 (Islington). *See* **Napier Street**.

Vince Street EC1 (Shoreditch, Hackney). A local property owner called Vince is recorded in the 15th century.

Vinegar Yard SE1 (Bermondsey, Southwark). Vinegar distilling was a common local trade from the 18th century onwards.

Vine Hill EC1 (Clerkenwell Road, Camden). Site of the vineyard of the bishops of Ely who had extensive grounds N of their palace in **Ely Place**. They gave up most of this property in the 16th century.

Vine Street EC3 (Cit. Lond.). Recorded in 1720 as Vine Yard; the derivation is uncertain. It may come from the name of an inn, or it may record the existence of a vineyard belonging to the convent of St Clare in the Minories before the Reformation.

Vine Street W1 (Piccadilly, Cit. West.). Originally ran S from Warwick Street to Piccadilly; probably named from *The Vine* inn which stood here in the early 18th century.

Vine Street Bridge EC1 (Clerkenwell, Islington). Bridge over the railway line from Farringdon, made in Vine Street which approached **Vine Hill**.

Vine Yard SE1 (Borough, Southwark). Probably from the sign of an inn here called *The Bunch of Grapes* which is recorded in 1809.

Vine Yard SE1 (Tooley Street, Southwark). The *Vine* tavern is recorded here in 1761.

Vineyard Walk EC1 (Clerkenwell, Islington). Site of a vineyard here which survived into the 18th century and was probably established by the mediaeval Clerkenwell Priory. **Vineyard Mews** adjoins.

Viney Road SE13 (Lewisham). A modern street commemorating a local nonconformist minister, the Rev. Josiah Viney, secretary of the Lewisham Congregational School.

Vintners Place EC4 (Cit. Lond.). French wine merchants or vintners settled on the river bank near Queenhithe in the 10th century; the area became known as The Vintry. The merchants had established their hall here by 1446; the present Vintners' Company guildhall is on the corner with Upper Thames Street.

Violet Hill NW8 (St John's Wood, Cit. West.). Remnant of a mediaeval path known for its violets. The way led originally from Lisson Green to Kilburn Priory.

Virgil Place W1 (Marylebone, Cit. West.). Named by association with nearby **Homer Street**.

Virginia Road E2 (Bethnal Green, T. Ham.). In the 18th century the E end was called Virginia Row; the rest was Castle Street, probably from an inn sign. The derivation of Virginia is unknown.

Virginia Street E1 (Whitechapel, T. Ham.). The first expedition to the colony of Virginia set out from Blackwall in 1606, and some of the pioneer settlers are thought to have come from nearby Stepney and its neighbouring hamlets.

Viscount Street EC1 (Cit. Lond.). From nearby **Brackley Street** and formerly called Charles Street. Two sons of the family of Egerton, viscounts Brackley, both called Charles, died as children at Bridgewater House here. The first died in 1623 and the second was burnt in 1687 in a fire which destroyed the house. A third Charles, born in 1725, died in 1731.

Vivian Grove SE15 (Peckham, Southwark). On the Crespigny estate (*see* **De Crespigny Park**). Lord Vivian married Eliza Champion de Crespigny.

Vyner Street E2 (Cambridge Heath, T. Ham.). Although just beyond the boundary of Hackney, this commemorates the Vyner family, former lords of the Hackney manor of Kingshold. Sir Robert Vyner was a City of London goldsmith who became Lord Mayor; he made the coronation regalia for Charles II in 1660. His son Sir Thomas lived at the Black and White House (*see* **Bohemia Place**) which he enlarged in 1662. Vyners held the manor until 1695.

W

Waghorn Street SE15 (Peckham Rye, Southwark). Before the cutting of the Suez Canal Thomas Waghorn (1800–50) established a reliable overland link between Port Said and Suez as part of a steamer route from Europe to India. Coal was carried by camel train across the desert.

Waite Street SE15 (Peckham, Southwark). John Waite is recorded as tenant of the land c1830.

Waithman Street EC4 (Cit. Lond.). Commemorates Robert Waithman, Alderman of Farringdon Without from 1818 and Lord Mayor of London 1823–4. He died in 1833.

Wakefield Street WC1 (Bloomsbury, Camden). The inn called *The Pindar of Wakefield* stood on the W side of Gray's Inn Road, near Harrison Street, until its destruction in a storm in 1724. The inn was rebuilt E of the Gray's Inn Road, N of Swinton Street. The property gave its name to the surrounding area, but the derivation is obscure.

Wakeling Street E14 (Ratcliff, T. Ham.). The school at Ratcliff was endowed by a benefactor called Wakeling, who gave to it the income of an estate at Edmonton (*see* **Schoolhouse Lane**).

Wakley Street EC1 (Finsbury, Islington). Commemorates the reformer Thomas Wakley (1795–1862), trained as a doctor and surgeon, who founded *The Lancet* in 1823 as a means to reforming the medical profession, and the administration of public health. Wakley was MP for Finsbury 1835–52, and was coroner for Middlesex from 1839. He gained great popularity for his integrity and strenuous opposition to the abuse of power.

Walberswick Street SW8 (S Lambeth, Lambeth). The family of John Tradescant who lived on this site came from Walberswick in Suffolk (*see* **Tradescant Road**).

Walcot Square SE11 (Kennington, Lambeth). Built in 1837–9 on land bought by Edmund Walcot or Walcott in 1657 and left by him to parish charities. This square was named after the benefactor; other properties built on the land were named after the recipient parishes, St Mary's, Lambeth, and St Olave's, Southwark.

Walcott Street SW1 (Cit. West.). Commemorates the Rev. M.E.C. Walcott, curate of St Margaret's, Westminster 1847–50. Walcott wrote a history of the church in 1847 and *Westminster, Memorials of the City* in 1849.

Waldeck Grove SE27 (Norwood, Lambeth). *See* **Pyrmont Grove**.

Waldram Crescent SE23 (Forest Hill, Lewisham). Named in 1878 as Waldram Road, and probably laid out by Waldrams, builders active in the 1870s.

Waley Street E1 (Stepney, T. Ham.). Commemorates Henry le Waleys or Waleis, mayor of London in 1273, 1281–3 and 1298. He is said to have established the stocks market at the present junction of Poultry and Queen Victoria Street, and to have received Edward I, who held a

parliament in Waleys' Stepney house
c1299. The house is thought to have
been at Stepney Green.

Walham Grove SW6 (Fulham,
Hammersmith). The old village
centre at the cross-roads of Dawes
Road, Fulham Broadway and North
End Road was originally called
Walham Green or Wandon Green,
from a mediaeval manor of Wandon
or Wansdowne (*see* **Wandon Road**).

Wallbutton Road SE4 (New Cross,
Lewisham). Named in 1878 from a
Deptford surname. Wallbuttons
were builders in this area from the
1860s, and Mr R. Wallbutton is
recorded as chairman of the local
Conservative association in the
1880s.

Waller Road SE14 (New Cross,
Lewisham). *See* **Jerningham Road**.

Wallgrave Road SW5 (Earl's Court,
Ken. Chel.). Built from 1860 on land
owned by Charles Wallgrave.

Walnut Tree Walk SE11 (Lambeth)
Originally a lane through the fields,
noted for walnut trees. The street was
built up from 1755.

Walpole Gardens W4 (Turnham
Green, Hounslow). Horace
Walpole, builder of the 'Gothick'
castle at Twickenham called
'Strawberry Hill' (c1753), used the
Pack Horse here on his journeys to
and from London. Walpole was a
writer and antiquarian whose best-
known work is the Gothic novel *The
Castle of Otranto*. He was the fourth
son of Sir Robert Walpole, Prime
Minister 1721–42 (*see* **Walpole
Street**).

Walpole Street SW3 (Chelsea, Ken.
Chel.). Commemorates Sir Robert
Walpole, First Earl of Orford (1676–
1745), who became England's first
Prime Minister in 1721. Walpole is

said to have lodged here before
taking a lease on Walpole House
(part of the Royal Hospital
Infirmary) in 1723. Walpole first
entered Parliament in 1700 and first
held office (as Secretary for War) in
1708. He was Paymaster General at
the time of the South Sea Bubble
investment market collapse, and his
efficient handling of it greatly
increased his influence. He
dominated politics until he was
forced to resign, on an issue of war
with Spain, in 1742.

Walton Street SW3 (Kensington,
Ken. Chel.). Named after George
Walton Onslow (*see* **Onslow Square**).
Walton Place adjoins.

Walworth Road SE17 (Walworth,
Southwark). Road leading to
Walworth; the place name is
recorded as Wealawyrth in the 10th
century, meaning 'the farmstead of
the Britons'.

Wandle Road SW17 (Wandsworth).
The nearby River Wandle (running N
to the Thames, W of Garratt Lane) is
named from the original settlement
at Wandsworth, and not the other
way about. In the 14th century the
river is recorded as an important
route into Surrey, and the first shops
and businesses in Wandsworth grew
up along its banks. In the early 17th
century it is mentioned as a valuable
fishery, especially for trout (*see*
Wandsworth High Street).

Wandon Road SW6 (Fulham,
Hammersmith/Ken. Chel.). Part of
the mediaeval manor of Wandon,
Wansdon or Wansdowne. The
existence of a family called Wandon
is recorded in the 13th century, but
the bounds of their manor are
uncertain. **Wansdown Place** is
nearby.

Wandsworth High Street SW18
(Wandsworth). High or principal

street of Wandsworth, called Wendlesworth in the 7th century and Wandleswurde in the 12th. The name means 'Wendel's farmstead'. **Wandsworth Road** approaches from the NE.

Wanley Road SE5 (Camberwell, Southwark). Nathaniel Wanley was an associate of the poet Browning (*see* **Browning Close**).

Wansdown Place SW6 (Hammersmith). *See* **Wandon Road**.

Wapping High Street E1 (Wapping, T. Ham.). Principal street of Wapping, called Wapping atte wase in the 14th century, 'wase' being an OE word for mud. The derivation of this place name is uncertain, but it is thought to be connected to OE 'wapol', meaning bubble or froth – that is, a squelchy, watery place. **Wapping Lane** approaches.

Wapping Wall E1 (Wapping, T. Ham.). *See* **Wapping High Street**. The wall was built from St Katharine's to Shadwell in the reign of Elizabeth I. The last of a succession of mediaeval embankments (the first was made by the manor of Stepney in the 13th century) had finally been destroyed by a strong tide in the 1560s. The wall was built up piecemeal from 1580. The Commissioners of Sewers recommended that individual householders should be encouraged to take land and build houses along the length of the wall, and that they should be responsible for building and maintaining it. This was done, and it ensured the development of Wapping at a time when Crown policy was against suburban growth in general.

Wardour Street W1 (Soho, Cit. West.). Formerly Colman Hedge Lane, bounding a field called Colman Hedge Close. The street was built up in the late 17th century by the

Wardour family who had bought the land in 1631. The lane formed the N end of Wardour Street; the present street S of Brewer Street was originally called Prince's Street (to match parallel **Rupert Street**) and was renamed in 1878.

Wardrobe Place EC4 (Cit. Lond.). Site of the King's Wardrobe, a house bought in 1359 to store ceremonial robes. The building was burnt down in the Great Fire of 1666. **Wardrobe Terrace** is on the same site.

Warham Street SE5 (Lambeth). By association with the see of Canterbury, which owned Lambeth manor; Archbishop Warham held office 1504–32.

Warneford Street E9 (S Hackney, Hackney). Flight Lieutenant R.A.J. Warneford of the Royal Naval Air Service was awarded the Victoria Cross in 1915; he destroyed a German Zeppelin airship by bombing it, at 6,000 feet, from a Morane monoplane. Warneford was killed shortly afterwards, on a test flight.

Warner Place E2 (Bethnal Green, T. Ham.). Probably commemorates Warner and Sons, one of the longest-surviving companies in the local silk industry. Warners went on weaving silk in Bethnal Green until 1895, when they moved to Braintree.

Warner Street EC1 (Clerkenwell, Islington). An old footpath through Coldbath Fields, built up from c1724, by which time the land belonged to Robert Warner and Walter Baynes (*see* **Baynes Court**).

Warren Street W1 (Euston, Camden). Built on land belonging to Charles Fitzroy, created Lord Southampton in 1780, who held the manor of Tottenhall. He married Anne Warren.

Warwick Avenue W2, W9 (Paddington, Cit. West.). *See* **Morshead Road**.

Warwick Court WC1 (Holborn, Camden). Site of the town house of Robert Rich, Baron Rich, created Earl of Warwick in 1618. Rich was a soldier and a lawyer of Gray's Inn. His first wife was Penelope Devereux, daughter of the Earl of Essex and the inspiration of Sir Philip Sydney's sonnet sequence, *Astrophel and Stella*. The house was given up and demolished when the earl's descendant Robert Rich, Earl of Warwick, Earl Holland, Baron Rich and Baron Kensington, came to prefer Holland House in Kensington; he died in 1675 (*see* **Warwick Gardens**).

Warwick Gardens W14 (Kensington, Ken. Chel.). Near Holland House; Sir Henry Rich, son of the Earl of Warwick and later Lord Holland, inherited Holland House through his wife. Their son Robert succeeded to the title of Earl Holland and also to his grandfather's title as Fifth Earl of Warwick.

Warwick House Street SW1 (Cit. West.). Formerly approached Warwick House, built 1663–5 for Sir Philip Warwick (1609–83). The house was sold to the Prince of Wales in 1792 and demolished in 1827 when Carlton Mews was built for the prince's new Carlton House.

Warwick Lane EC4 (Cit. Lond.). Passes Warwick Square where the Nevilles, earls of Warwick, had a London house in the 15th century.

Warwick Row SW1 (Pimlico, Cit. West.). *See* **Tachbrook Street** for this and **Warwick Square** and **Way**.

Waterford Road SW6 (Fulham, Hammersmith). *See* **Maxwell Road**.

Watergate EC4 (Cit. Lond.). Site of the water-gate on to the old Thames foreshore from the Bridewell Palace (*see* **Bridewell Place**).

Watergate Walk WC2 (Strand, Cit. West.). The Water Gate built for the Duke of Buckingham as an entrance from the river to York House is preserved here in Victoria Embankment gardens. The gate was built *c*1625 (*see* **Villiers Street**).

Waterloo Road SE1 (Lambeth, Lambeth/Southwark). Made as an approach to Waterloo Bridge which was opened in 1817 and named in honour of the allied victory over Napoleon at Waterloo in 1815.

Waterlow Road N19 (Highgate, Islington). Nearby Waterlow Park, Highgate, belonged to Sir Sydney Waterlow as his private estate; he opened it to the public as a park in 1889.

Water Street WC2 (Strand, Cit. West.). This street runs S from Maltravers Street to the old water-line of the Thames, before the building of the embankment.

Watkinson Road N7 (Caledonian Road, Islington). *See* **Piper Close**.

Watling Street EC4 (Cit. Lond.). This street was called Athelingestrate in the 13th century, meaning the Saxon prince's street. The name was later corrupted by association with the better-known Roman road called Watling Street. Which Saxon prince held land here is not known (*see* **Addle Hill**).

Watson Close N16 (Newington Green, Hackney). Archdeacon John James Watson (*d* 1839) was the last vicar of the old parish of Hackney before its subdivision in 1825. He then became the first rector of the new parish. His brother Joshua

Watson (*d* 1854) was locally active in the church and in charitable work.

Watson's Mews W1 (Marylebone, Cit. West.). Built by John Watson on land leased from John Harcourt in the 1790s.

Waverley Place NW8 (St John's Wood, Cit. West.). Commemorates the 'Waverley' novels of Sir Walter Scott. Scott died in 1832 and the street was built shortly afterwards. His novel *Waverley*, published in 1814, was the first of a series of historical novels; the sequence came to be called after the first.

Waverley Road W2 (Westbourne Green, Cit. West.). *See* **Waverley Place** for this and **Waverley Terrace** and **Walk**.

Waverton Street W1 (Mayfair, Cit. West.). Built on the Grosvenor estate; the Grosvenor family also held property at Waverton in Cheshire.

Waylett Place SE27 (Norwood, Lambeth). Harriet Waylett (1798–1851), an actress, is buried in the nearby South Metropolitan Cemetery. After successful provincial work and a short period at the Adelphi, London, she appeared at Drury Lane in 1824 and later at the Haymarket. She was a popular soubrette.

Waynflete Street SW18 (Earlsfield, Wandsworth). Built on land belonging to Magdalen College, Oxford, which was founded by William of Waynflete in 1458.

Weaver Street E1 (Bethnal Green, T. Ham.). Reflects the main industry of the area during the early 19th century, when silk weaving gradually expanded from Spitalfields across to Bethnal Green. The last colony of weavers, active until 1939, was E of Bethnal Green on the site of the present Cranbrook Estate. **Shuttle Street** adjoins.

Webb's Road SW11 (S Battersea, Wandsworth). Begun on the grounds of a large house (demolished) which had belonged in the early 19th century to a City of London merchant called Webb.

Wedderburn Road NW3 (Hampstead, Camden). Built on the grounds of Rosslyn House (*see* **Rosslyn Hill**).

Weech Road NW6 (W Hampstead, Camden). *See* **Burgess Hill**.

Weighhouse Street W1 (Mayfair, Cit. West.). The King's Weigh House Chapel came to this site in 1891 from premises in Little Eastcheap above the King's Weigh House there. Before the opening of the chapel the street was called Robert Street, after Robert, Second Earl Grosvenor, who died in 1845. The original name was Chandler Street, from the prevailing trade. Various trades were restricted on the Grosvenor estate, but restrictions were not uniformly applied and tallow chandlers had flourished in this street well into the 19th century (*see* **Binney Street**).

Weir Road SW12 (Clapham, Lambeth). Originally Grove Road, built on the site of a large field called Friday Grove, belonging to the Kymer family. The road was renamed when the hospital here was named after Sir Benjamin Weir.

Welbeck Street W1 (Marylebone, Cit. West.). Built on part of the Cavendish–Harley estate after its acquisition by the second Duke of Portland. Welbeck Abbey was the Duke's Nottinghamshire seat. **Welbeck Way** approaches.

Wellclose Square E1 (Whitechapel,

T. Ham.). Built c1694 on an open field called Well Close.

Weller Road SE14 (New Cross, Lewisham). *See* **Jerningham Road**.

Weller's Court NW1 (King's Cross, Camden). Built in 1788 by Richard and William Weller of Portpool Lane.

Weller Street SE1 (Southwark). *See* **Dickens Square**. The character of Sam Weller appears in Charles Dickens's novel *The Pickwick Papers* which came out in 1837 and was an immediate success.

Wellfield Avenue N10 (Muswell Hill, Haringey). Site of mediaeval wells recorded as belonging to the Order of Knights of St John of Jerusalem, Clerkenwell. **Springfield Avenue** nearby is also so named. The order built a chapel to Our Lady of Muswell and also owned land at Muswell Hill which they ran as a dairy farm. They gave up the property c1540.

Wellfield Road SW16 (Streatham, Lambeth). Crosses the former field surrounding Streatham Spa Well, discovered in 1660 and used as a medicinal spring. **Wellfield Walk** approaches.

Wellington Road NW8 (St John's Wood, Cit. West.). Named in honour of the victories of the Duke of Wellington, particularly those of the Napoleonic Wars which ended at Waterloo in 1815. Arthur Wellesley, First Duke of Wellington, was born in 1769 and went into the army in 1787. He held command in India, where he was successful against Tipu Sahib, from 1799. After the Napoleonic Wars he entered politics and was ultimately Prime Minister 1828–30 when, being opposed to electoral reform, he was forced to resign. He was Commander-in-Chief

of the army 1827–8 and 1842–52. He died in 1852.

Wellington Square SW3 (Chelsea, Ken. Chel.). *See* **Wellington Road**. The duke's brother, the Hon. Rev. Dr Wellesley, became rector of Chelsea in 1805.

Wellington Street E16 (Bethnal Green, T. Ham.). Site of an early 19th-century pond called the Wellington Fishery, recorded in 1815 as well stocked with fish and described as near **Pollard Row**, so-called from pollarded trees.

Wellington Street WC2 (Covent Garden, Cit. West.). A 19th-century street commemorating Arthur Wellesley, Duke of Wellington (*see* **Wellington Road**). The section between the Strand and Tavistock Street was newly built as Wellington Street; the N section was formerly Charles Street, part of the Covent Garden scheme of 1631 and named in honour of Charles I.

Wells Crescent SE5 (Camberwell, Southwark). Site of ancient wells of the parish of Camberwell; the wells are considered not to have influenced the naming of Camberwell, for which *see* **Camberwell Road**.

Wells Park Road SE26 (Sydenham, Lewisham). Passes Sydenham Wells Park which, with adjoining **Springfield Rise**, marks the site of Sydenham Wells. The wells are recorded in the 17th century, offering saline spa water. **Tunbridge Court** and **Droitwich Close**, recollecting other spas, adjoin.

Wells Rise NW8 (Primrose Hill, Cit. West.). Approaches Barrow Hill Reservoir, and the original name of the street was Wells Road. 'Wells' is not quite 'reservoir' but it sounds better.

Wells Street W1 (Oxford Street, Cit. West.). Originally a track running N from the present Oxford Street to fields farmed by George Wells; Wells was the occupier when Josias Berners bought the estate in 1654. **Wells Mews** adjoins (*see* **Berners Street**).

Well Street E9 (Hackney). An old street named from a well or mineral spring which has now disappeared.

Wells Way SE5 (Camberwell, Southwark). James Wells, builder (with his partner Berriman) of St George's church here, lived in Camberwell 1803–53.

Wells Yard N7 (Holloway, Islington). *See* **George's Road**.

Well Walk NW3 (Hampstead, Camden). Site of a medicinal spring which was popular in the 18th century and turned Hampstead, for a while, into a spa (*see* **Gainsborough Gardens** and **Flask Walk**).

Weltje Road W6 (Hammersmith). Site of a house on the Upper Mall owned by the German chef Weltje, who formerly worked for the Prince Regent at Carlton House.

Wenlock Road N1 (Hoxton, Hackney). Runs beside the Wenlock Basin of the Regent's Canal. This stretch of the canal was cut through land which once belonged to the prebend of Wenlock Barn, one of 13 prebends or estates belonging to St Paul's Cathedral and supporting the cathedral canons. This prebend is recorded as Wenlock Barn in the 12th century.

Wentworth Mews E3 (Mile End, T. Ham.). Thomas, Lord Wentworth, Lord Chamberlain, acquired the manor of Stepney in 1550; it had formerly belonged to the bishops of London, and they had surrendered it

to Edward VI (*see* **Wentworth Street**).

Wentworth Street E1 (Spitalfields, T. Ham.). S boundary of an estate owned by Thomas Wentworth, Earl of Cleveland and lord of the manor of Stepney, who sold it in 1640 to Henry Montague, Earl of Manchester. The Wentworths continued to hold the rest of Stepney manor until 1720.

Werrington Street NW1 (Somers Town, Camden). *See* **Morwell Street**.

Wesley Street W1 (Marylebone, Cit. West.). Charles Wesley (1707–88) is buried in the churchyard of the old Marylebone parish church in Marylebone High Street (the church has been demolished). Charles Wesley, author of many hymns, was the younger brother of John Wesley, founder of Methodism.

West Arbour Street E1 (Stepney, T. Ham.). *See* **Arbour Square**.

Westbere Road NW2 (W Hampstead, Camden). Kentish place name; built by the Powell-Cotton family of Quex Park, Birchington, Kent.

Westbourne Park Road W2, W11 (Westbourne Green, Cit. West.). Laid out as a residential park approaching the old hamlet of Westbourne Green which stood around the site of the present Royal Oak station. **Westbourne Gardens**, **Grove**, **Grove Terrace**, **Park Mews**, **Park Villas**, **Passage** and **Villas** are nearby (*see* **Westbourne Terrace**).

Westbourne Terrace W2 (Bayswater, Cit. West.). The Westbourne, or West Stream, flowed S from Hampstead and Kilburn approximately down the line of the present Shirland Road, through Westbourne Green and S down the line of adjacent Gloucester Terrace into the Serpentine. Leaving Hyde Park again, it ran S under the 'Knight's Bridge' and down the W boundary of the Grosvenor Belgravia estate to the Thames. The stream is now covered in. **Westbourne Crescent** and **Street** adjoin.

Westcote Road SW16 (Streatham Park, Wandsworth). Opposite **Thrale Road.** William Henry Lyttelton, Lord Westcote (1724–1808), was a friend of the Thrales and a visitor to Streatham Park.

Westcroft Square W6 (Hammersmith). Built on part of the site of a large pasture called West Croft on the Pallingswick (later Ravenscroft) estate.

West End Lane NW6 (W Hampstead, Camden).Runs N through the hamlet of West End, named from its position at the W end of Hampstead parish. The hamlet lay approximately at the junction with Fortune Green Road.

Westfields Avenue SW13 (Barnes, R. upon T.). Land here is recorded as the West Field in 1481.

West Gardens E1 (Shadwell, T. Ham.). Recorded in 1813 as West's Gardens, having been built by one West.

Westgate Street E8 (Hackney). Runs SW from Mare Street at The Triangle, a broad junction where once stood the Westgate toll-gate.

Westgate Terrace SW10 (Kensington, Ken. Chel.). *See* **Knaresborough Place**.

West Halkin Street SW1 (Belgravia, Cit. West.). *See* **Halkin Street.**

West Harding Street EC4 (Cit. Lond.). *See* **East Harding Street**.

West India Dock Road E14 (Limehouse, T. Ham.). Approaches the India and Millwall Docks, formerly called the West India Dock and opened by the West India Company in 1802. Until then, the City of London and individual wharf owners provided landing places for dutiable cargoes on a group of 20 Legal Quays between London Bridge and the Tower. Berths were inadequate, delays long, security was impossible and pilfering systematic. Warehousing for perishable goods was unsatisfactory. The West India complex was built after strong opposition from the City, and the City corporation later retaliated with its own London Dock (*see* **Dock Street**). The new docks in the Isle of Dogs covered 295 acres, with strong, extensive warehousing and high walls for security. Customs inspection became relatively easy and the docks' position was equally convenient for import and export. The East India Company followed this example, on a smaller scale and further E, in 1806.

Westminster Bridge Road SE1 (Lambeth). Made as an approach to the new Westminster Bridge which was opened in 1750.

Westmoreland Buildings EC1 (Cit. Lond.). Site of the town house of the earls of Westmoreland, demolished in *c*1760. The Neville family lost this title with the attainder of Charles Neville ·in 1571. The last Neville claimant died in 1636, but the title was revived and given to Francis Fane (who had married a Neville) in 1624.

Weston Rise WC1 (Pentonville, Islington). Built during the 1790s by John Weston of Penton Rise.

Weston Street SE1 (Southwark). Built on land belonging.to one John Webbe Weston, who owned the manor of the Maze in the early 19th century (*see* **Great Maze Pond**).

West Square SE11 (St George's Road, Southwark). Built from 1794 on land belonging to the West family. This area, called St George's Fields, consisted of many small plots under different ownership, survivors of a mediaeval system of open-field farming.

West Tenter Street E1 (Whitechapel, T. Ham.). *See* **East Tenter Street**.

Westwood Hill SE26 (Sydenham, Lewisham). *See* **Dulwich Wood Avenue**.

Wetherby Gardens SW5 (Kensington, Ken. Chel.). *See* **Barkston Gardens** for this and **Wetherby Place**.

Weymouth Street W1 (Marylebone, Cit. West.). Built on land belonging to the dukes of Portland. Elizabeth Bentinck, sister of the third duke (1738–1909), was Viscountess Weymouth.

Wharfedale Street SW10 (Kensington, Ken. Chel.). *See* **Knaresborough Place**.

Wharf Road N1 (Hoxton, Islington/Hackney). Runs beside the wharfs of the City Road and Wenlock Basins on that reach of the Grand Union Canal called the Regent's Canal, opened in 1820.

Wharncliffe Gardens NW8 (Lisson Grove, Cit. West.). The development of the Great Central Railway terminus, goods yards and sidings at Marylebone destroyed many houses and displaced c3,000 people. The Wharncliffe Dwellings Company built blocks here which compensated for some of the loss. The company was headed by Edward Stuart-Wortley-Mackenzie, Third Baron and First Earl Wharncliffe, chairman of the Great Central Railway Company. Lord Wharncliffe died in 1899.

Whateley Road SE22 (E Dulwich, Southwark). *See* **Copleston Road**.

Wheatlands Road SW17 (Tooting, Wandsworth). Commemorates an 18th-century resident of Tooting called Richard Wheatlands.

Wheatley Street W1 (Marylebone, Cit. West.). Francis Wheatley, portrait painter and illustrator of *The Cries of London* was a resident of Marylebone; he died in 1801.

Wheeler Street E1 (Spitalfields, T. Ham.). Sir George Wheeler or Wheler (1650–1722) provided a chapel and burial ground fronting on Tabernacle Yard, now Nantes Passage, to serve the immigrant French Protestant community. The building was adopted by the Church of England in 1842 and consecrated as St Mary's chapel of ease; it was closed in 1911, the district having become mainly Jewish after a fresh wave of immigration. This street originally extended S of Commercial Street to join Lamb Street beside the chapel.

Wheelwright Street N7 (Caledonian Road, Islington). Charles Apthorp Wheelwright was a prominent citizen who commanded the re-formed Loyal Islington Volunteers 1803–6.

Whetstone Park WC2 (Lincoln's Inn, Camden). Built by William Whetstone in 1636.

Whiskin Street EC3 (Clerkenwell, Islington). *See* **Meredith Street**.

Whitby Street E1 (Bethnal Green, T. Ham.). Off **Ebor Street**. This was formerly called Little York Street; it was changed to another Yorkshire place name in 1911.

Whitcher Place NW1 (Camden Town, Camden). Built on land leased from Lord Camden by John Whitcher in 1864.

Whitechapel Road E1 (Whitechapel, T. Ham.). The road to the white chapel, or the chapel of St Mary Matfelon which was built in white stone c1250. The chapel became the parish church of St Mary c1340, was rebuilt three times and destroyed in 1952. **Whitechapel High Street** is the high or principal street at the white chapel.

White Church Lane E1 (Whitechapel, T. Ham.). Originally a narrow way called Church Lane along the W side of St Mary's church and churchyard; the churchyard covered the area to present Adler Street (*see* **Whitechapel Road**).

White Conduit Street N1 (Islington). Site of a mediaeval water-conduit housed in white stone. The water supply began to be unreliable in the 17th century and it was demolished in 1833. The *White Conduit House* tavern nearby was built in the early 17th century and possessed extensive pleasure grounds on the area around the conduit called White Conduit Fields. The inn was rebuilt in 1829 and in 1849, when streets were laid out on the Fields, it was pulled down and replaced by a small public house.

White Cross Street EC1, EC2 (Cit. Lond./Islington). Street leading to a white cross which is recorded in the 13th century.

Whitefriars Street EC4 (Cit. Lond.). Land here and in nearby **Carmelite Street** was granted to Carmelite or 'White' friars (from the colour of their robes). The grant was made by Edward I (1272–1307).

Whitehall SW1 (Cit. West.). Runs past the site of Whitehall Palace of which only the Banqueting Hall, added in the early 17th century,

survives. York House, London residence of the archbishops of York, was improved and enlarged as a palace by Cardinal Wolsey, who became Archbishop of York in 1514; on his downfall in 1529 it was appropriated by Henry VIII and renamed Whitehall Palace, from its colour. All of it except the Banqueting Hall was burnt down in 1698.

White Hart Court EC2 (Cit. Lond.). Laid out c1787 on the former courtyard of the *White Hart* inn.

White Hart Street SE11 (Kennington, Lambeth). On the Duchy of Cornwall estate (*see* **Black Prince Road**). The Black Prince's son, Richard II, took the emblem of the white hart as his crest.

White Hart Yard SE1 (Southwark). The *White Hart* which stood here was demolished in 1889; the inn was thought to have been of 14th-century origin, when the sign became popular for taverns as the badge of Richard II (1377–99).

Whitehaven Street NW8 (Lisson Grove, Cit. West.). *See* **Salisbury Street**.

Whitehead's Grove SW3 (Chelsea, Ken. Chel.). Built by William Whitehead on land leased from the manor of Chelsea in 1810.

White Horse Lane E1 (Stepney, T. Ham). Recorded in 1830 as running S from the *White Horse* tavern on Mile End Road. **White Horse Road** was originally White Horse Street and continued S to Butcher Row; it was named from its junction there with a second Whitehorse Lane, an old road which ran roughly along the line of Commercial Road and was also named from an inn.

White Horse Street W1 (Mayfair, Cit.

West.). Named from the sign of an inn, now demolished.

White Horse Yard EC2 (Cit. Lond.). Approached an inn of that name recorded in 1746.

White Kennett Street E1 (Cit. Lond.). White Kennet (1660–1728) was rector of Aldgate in 1700–7. At first a loyal admirer of the Stuarts, he became a supporter of the House of Orange and a Whig in politics. He is said to have been caricatured as Judas Iscariot in an altar-piece commissioned by the pro-Stuart rector of Whitechapel. White Kennet later became Bishop of Peterborough; he was a famous controversialist in his time.

White Lion Court EC3 (Cit. Lond.). This originally led from Cornhill to the rear of the *White Lion*, a large tavern on Bishopsgate which was burnt down in 1765.

White Lion Hill EC4 (Cit. Lond.). Commemorates White Lion Wharf, which lay at the S end, W of Paul's Wharf, in the 18th century. The wharf was probably named from an inn sign.

White Lion Street N1 (Islington). Built 1770–80, opening from Islington High Street through part of the *White Lion Inn*, a large Tudor (and possibly earlier) tavern consisting of rows of buildings round a court; the N row was demolished for this street.

White Post Street SE15 (Old Kent Road, Lewisham). Remnant of an old lane marked by white boundary posts and running up the present Ilderton Street, between the parishes of St Giles, Camberwell, and St Paul, Deptford.

White's Row E1 (Spitalfields, T. Ham.). This was built as New Fashion Street by John and Nathaniel Tilly (from c1650) and Messrs Nicholas and Cooke (from c1673). (*See* **Fashion Street.**) The name White's Row first appears in 1709, and presumably comes from a resident or proprietor.

Whitethorn Street E3 (Bow Common, T. Ham.). *See* **Blackthorn Street**.

Whitfield Street W1 (Tottenham Court Road, Camden). Properly Whitefield; George Whitefield, founder of the Calvinistic Methodists, established a tabernacle here in 1756 which is now the Whitefield Memorial Church. **Whitfield Place** adjoins.

Whitgift Street SE11 (Lambeth). By association with Lambeth Palace (*see* **Lambeth Palace Road**). Archbishop Whitgift (1583–1604) bought part of the former Norfolk House, nearby, in 1590.

Whitmore Road N1 (Hoxton, Hackney). Sir George Whitmore held the manor of Balmes (*see* **Balmes Road**) from 1634. His successor William Whitmore sold it to Richard de Beauvoir in 1687.

Whittaker Street SW1 (Belgravia, Cit. West.). Built from 1836 by John Wittaker of Bourne Street, on lease from the Grosvenor estate.

Whittington Avenue EC3 (Cit. Lond.). The approach to Leadenhall Market; the market rights were acquired in 1411 by Richard Whittington.

Wicker Street E1 (Whitechapel, T. Ham.). John Wicker held the manor of Stepney from 1720, having bought it from the Wentworth family (*see* **Wentworth Mews**). The Parmiter Charity trustees obtained their Cambridge Heath wasteland from Wicker in 1722 (*see* **Parmiter Street**).

Wickham Road SE4 (Brockley, Lewisham). The surrounding manor of Brockley, of which the manor farm lay here, passed from William Boulter to his grandson Richard Wilkinson by a settlement of 1709. In 1725 it passed from Richard to his sister Mary Wickham and her husband William Wickham. The Wickham family held the manor until the 1780s (*see* **Drake Road**).

Wick Road E9 (Hackney). Leads E to Hackney Wick, part of a manor belonging to the Order of Knights Templar and leased by them to Robert de Wyke or de Wick before 1308. **Wick Lane** is nearby.

Wickwood Street SE5 (Brixton, Lambeth). Site of a wood in Lambeth Wick or Wyk, a manor first recorded in the 13th century and leased to the Fox family from 1701. The streets were built up during the 19th century. The woods had been cut down under Cromwell, Lord Protector 1648–65.

Widdenham Road N7 (Upper Holloway, Islington). *See* **Biddestone Road**.

Widegate Street E1 (Spitalfields, T. Ham.). Also called Whitegate Alley (1677). This street ran W into Bishopsgate before *c*1902, and may have had a gate which closed it at the Sandy Row end.

Widley Road W9 (Bayswater, Cit. West.). *See* **Southwick Street**.

Wigmore Street W1 (Marylebone, Cit. West.). Built on the Cavendish–Harley estate by Edward Harley, Earl of Oxford, *c*1720. The street was named from Wigmore Castle, the Harley family seat. **Wigmore Place** adjoins.

Wilcox Place SW1 (Victoria, Cit. West.). *See* **Francis Street**.

Wild Street WC2 (Covent Garden, Camden/Cit. West.). Corruption of Weld; built on land belonging to Humphrey Weld, who lived there in Weld House from 1640 until the late 1670s. **Wild Court** adjoins.

Wildwood Road NW11 (Hampstead, Barnet). Road leading to the NW part of Hampstead Heath, called the Wildwood.

Wilkes Street E1 (Spitalfields, T. Ham.). Built by Nathaniel Wilkes *c*1760 on land partly owned by his father since 1718. Nathaniel's brother John Wilkes, Lord Mayor of London 1774–5, was a radical politician and opponent of the government of Lord Bute. His journal *The North Briton* brought him to trial for 'seditious and dangerous libel' and gained him a reputation as a champion of the people; 'Wilkes and Liberty' became the battle-cry for numerous riots.

Wilkinson Street SW8 (Kennington, Lambeth). Built in the 1840s on land sold from the Cleaver Estate to John Wilkinson of Woodford in 1793 (*see* **Cleaver Street**).

Willard Street SW8 (Clapham, Lambeth). Commemorates an American author, Frances Elizabeth Willard (1839–98), a noted campaigner for temperance.

Willes Road NW5 (Kentish Town, Camden). Commemorates Lieutenant-General James Willes, commander of marines during the Crimean War (*see* **Alma Grove**).

William IV Street WC2 (Strand, Cit. West.). Laid out as part of Nash's redevelopment scheme for Charing Cross in 1831; the street was named after the reigning king William IV, who came to the throne in that year.

William Road NW1 (Regent's Park,

Camden). Built as part of John Nash's Regent's Park scheme (*see* **Regent Street**); named after the Regent's brother William, Duke of Clarence. He became king as William IV in 1831.

William Street SW1 (Knightsbridge, Cit. West./Ken. Chel.). Built on land belonging to William Lowndes (*see* **Lowndes Square**). **William Mews** adjoins.

Willoughby Road NW3 (Hampstead, Camden). The Willoughby family inherited land here which had belonged to their maternal grandfather Edward Carlile; they sold it for development in the 1870s.

Willoughby Street WC1 (Holborn, Camden). Commemorates G.P. Willoughby, mayor of the Borough of Holborn in 1904.

Willow Bridge Road N1 (Canonbury, Islington). An old name for a bridge which here crossed the New River, and self-explanatory. A short section of the river remains here as a lake (*see* **Myddelton Square**).

Willow Place SW1 (Pimlico, Cit. West.). Adjoined an old path through the marshy riverside land, called Willow Walk from the willow trees growing beside it. The Walk was improved and became Warwick Way.

Willow Street EC2 (Shoreditch, Hackney). Adjoins Great Eastern Street, part of which was built on the line of the former Willow Walk, named from the trees growing there on the former marsh land. **Willow Court** adjoins.

Wilmington Square WC1 (Clerkenwell, Islington). Built on land belonging to the Marquis of Northampton and named from his second title of Baron Wilmington.

Wilmington Street approaches (*see* **Compton Road**).

Wilshaw Street SE14 (Deptford, Lewisham). A local family name. Mrs Elizabeth Wilshaw or Willshaw, by her will of 1706, gave £120 to buy land, the profit therefrom to be given to the Deptford poor 'as are constant frequenters of their parish church'. John and Thomas Wilshaw appear as charity trustees in 1679.

Wilson Grove SE16 (Rotherhithe, Southwark). Captain Henry Wilson, of the East Indiaman *Antelope*, lived in Paradise Row (later Union Road). The *Antelope* was wrecked off the Pelew Islands in 1783 (*see* **Rupack Street**).

Wilson Road SE5 (Camberwell, Southwark). The Rev. Edward Wilson, vicar of Camberwell, founded the Wilson Grammar School, Peckham Road, in 1615. The school was dissolved and the building demolished in 1845. The second Wilson School was opened in 1883 by the charity Commissioners

Wilton Crescent SW1 (Belgravia, Cit. West.). Part of the Grosvenor estate. Robert Grosvenor, who became first Marquis of Westminster in 1831, married Eleanor Egerton, daughter of the first Earl of Wilton. **Wilton Place**, **Row** and **Terrace** adjoin. **Wilton Road** is on the Grosvenor Pimlico estate.

Wimpole Street W1 (Marylebone, Cit. West.). Built from c1730 on part of the Cavendish–Harley estate. Wimpole was the Cambridgeshire seat of the Harley family, earls of Oxford and Mortimer. **Wimpole Mews** is nearby, and **Upper Wimpole Street** approaches.

Winchester Road NW3 (Swiss Cottage, Camden). On the Eton college estate (*see* **Eton Avenue**). A

Bishop of Winchester was the first Provost of Eton College.

Winchester Walk SE1 (Southwark). Site of Winchester House, London palace of the bishops of Winchester from the 12th century until *c*1642. The bishops had parted with some of their property here in the reign of Henry VIII (for the Bishop of Rochester); their main palace extended along the S side of Clink Street and S to this street.

Winders Road SW11 (Battersea, Wandsworth). Winder Senior and Junior were builders active in S London from the 1850s.

Windlass Place SE8 (Deptford, Lewisham). *See* **Capstan Square**.

Windmill Drive SW4 (Clapham, Lambeth/Wandsworth). The manor of Clapham is recorded as possessing two windmills in the early 17th century. The exact site of this one is not known. The inn called *The Windmill* (NE end of this road) is recorded in the early 18th century and was presumably named from the mill.

Windmill Hill NW3 (Hampstead, Camden). Site of the flour mill which belonged to the manor of Hampstead and is recorded in the 14th century.

Windmill Road SW18 (Battersea, Wandsworth). William Watson put up a windmill water-pump on this part of Wandsworth Common in 1815. It was designed to provide a water supply to a pond called the Black Sea Pond.

Windmill Street W1 (Tottenham Court Road, Camden). Built up gradually (1724–62) under building leases from the Goodge family; site of a windmill which stood at the junction with Charlotte Street until *c*1750.

Windmill Walk SE1 (Lambeth). Formerly Windmill Street, site of a group of mills in an open field; the land was built up from *c*1820 when The Cut was made (*see* **Cut, The**).

Windsor Walk SE5 (Camberwell, Southwark). *See* **De Crespigny Park**. Sir William Champion de Crespigny married Lady Sarah Windsor in 1786.

Windus Road N16 (Stamford Hill, Hackney). A house here called 'Gothic Hall' was occupied in the 19th century by Thomas Windus, antiquarian and collector.

Wine Office Court EC4 (Cit. Lond.). Sometimes called Wine Licence Court; site of an office issuing licences to sell wine. The name is first recorded in 1677.

Winnett Street W1 (Soho, Cit. West.). Formerly Upper Rupert Street; renamed in 1935 after Alderman William Winnett who had a business here.

Winsland Street W2 (Paddington, Cit. West.). Named after the builders of adjacent St Mary's Hospital.

Winslow Street W6 (Fulham, Hammersmith). Dr Forbes Winslow (1810–74), doctor of mental diseases, had an asylum nearby. Winslow published work on insanity in the 1840s; he opened his Fulham asylum in 1847 and pioneered there the compassionate treatment of lunacy.

Winterton Place SW10 (Chelsea, Ken. Chel.). William Winterton built the street on land leased from the Chelsea manor estate in 1797.

Withers Place EC1 (Finsbury, Islington). From William Withers or Wythers, property owner in Whitecross Street in 1730.

Wivenhoe Road SE15 (Peckham,

Winchester Square and St Mary Overy's Wharf, Bankside

Southwark). On the Crespigny estate
(*see* **De Crespigny Park**). Wivenhoe
Hall, Essex, was the home of the
third baronet, Sir Claude William
Champion de Crespigny, in the early
19th century.

Wix's Lane SW4 (Clapham,
Wandsworth). A local builder called
Charles Wix had a house on the
corner with North Side in the early
19th century.

Woburn Place WC1 (Bloomsbury,
Camden). Part of the Bedford estate
and named from the principal seat of
the dukes of Bedford, Woburn
Abbey. **Woburn Mews**, **Square** and
Walk are nearby, and **Upper Woburn
Place** continues.

Wodeham Street E1 (Whitechapel,
T. Ham.). William Wodeham is
recorded as rector of Whitechapel in
1396.

Wolseley Street SE1 (Bermondsey,
Southwark). Named in 1890 after
Garnet Wolseley, First Viscount
Wolseley and Field Marshal (1833–
1913). He was active in the Crimea
and in Egypt and the Sudan; he is
mainly remembered for his army
reforms which carried on the work of
Cardwell (*see* **Cardwell Road**).

Wolsey Mews NW5 (Kentish Town,
Camden). Built on land belonging to
Christchurch Cathedral, Oxford (*see*
Caversham Road). Christchurch was
originally part of the college of that
name which Cardinal Wolsey
founded as Cardinal College in 1525;
it was re-endowed as Christchurch in
1546 (*see* **Wolsey Road**).

Wolsey Road N1 (Kingsland,
Islington). Commemorates Cardinal
Wolsey, omnipotent minister of
Henry VIII in 1515–30; named by
association with King Henry's Walk
nearby. Extremely able, he became
unpopular with parliament and the
people over taxation, and lost favour
with the king when he failed to
negotiate the royal divorce (from
Katharine of Aragon) with sufficient
speed. He was dismissed in disgrace,
surrendering his enormous wealth to
the king.

Woodbridge Street EC1 (Clerkenwell, Islington). Built on part of the
Sekforde estate. By his will of 1587
Thomas Sekforde (*d* 1588) left the estate for the maintenance of
almshouses in Woodbridge, Suffolk.
The Sekforde family were of Suffolk
origin.

Woodchester Square W2
(Paddington, Cit. West.). Built on
land belonging to Richard Clarke,
farmer, of Woodchester near
Cirencester. **Cirencester Street**
adjoins.

Woodchurch Road NW6 (W
Hampstead, Camden). Kentish place
name; built by the Powell-Cotton
family of Quex Park, Birchington,
Kent.

Woodfall Street SW3 (Chelsea, Ken.
Chel.). Henry Sampson Woodfall
(1739–1805), journalist and printer,
lived nearby in the last years of his
life. He took over the *Public
Advertiser* newspaper from his father
at 19, and ran it until 1793.

Woodland Road SE19 (Norwood,
Lambeth). *See* **Low Cross Wood
Lane**.

Wood Lane N6 (Hornsey, Haringey).
See **Southwood Lane**.

Wood Lane W12 (Shepherd's Bush,
Hammersmith). Leading N to the
'Worm Holt', or snake-infested
wood, which is first recorded in 1408
(*see* **Wormholt Road**).

Woodsford Square W14 (Kensington, Ken. Chel.). Built on the es-

tate surrounding Holland House, inherited in 1859 by Henry Fox-Strangways, Earl of Ilchester and Baron Woodsford Strangways.

Woodside Avenue N6, N10 (Hornsey, Haringey). *See* **Southwood Lane**.

Wood's Mews W1 (Mayfair, Cit. West.). Built by Richard Wood on land leased from the Grosvenor family in 1731.

Woodsome Road NW5 (Highgate, Camden). *See* **Dartmouth Park Hill** named from a Yorkshire property owned by the Earl of Dartmouth.

Woods Road SE15 (Peckham, Southwark). Charles Wood is recorded as the landowner c1830.

Woodstock Mews W1 (Marylebone, Cit. West.). Built on land belonging to the dukes of Portland which they acquired through the marriage of the second Duke of Portland, who was also Viscount Woodstock, with Margaret Cavendish Harley.

Woodstock Street W1 (Oxford Street, Cit. West.). Adjoins Blenheim Street; Blenheim Palace at Woodstock in Oxfordshire was built for the Duke of Marlborough (*see* **Blenheim Road** and **Marlborough Place**).

Wood Street EC2 (Cit. Lond.). Place where firewood and timber were sold as part of the mediaeval market along Cheapside.

Wood Vale N10 (Hornsey, Haringey). *See* **Southwood Lane**.

Woodwarde Road SE22 (Dulwich, Southwark). *See* **Townley Road**.

Woolmore Street E14 (Poplar, T. Ham.). John Woolmore, shipowner, was one of the founders of the East India Dock Company, of which he became deputy chairman in 1803.

Woolstone Road SE23 (Forest Hill, Lewisham). Probably a corruption of Wollastone. One Charlton Wollaston is recorded as a property owner in Perry Mount in 1857.

Worcester Place EC4 (Cit. Lond.). The earls of Worcester had a London house on the site, which they had abandoned by c1600 and let out in small tenements.

Wordsworth Road N16 (Shacklewell, Hackney). *See* **Shakespeare Walk**.

World's End Passage SW10 (Chelsea, Ken. Chel.). Formerly approached a 17th-century inn and pleasure garden called *The World's End* because of its position at the W limit of Chelsea.

Worlidge Street W6 (Hammersmith). The artist Thomas Worlidge (1700–66) spent much time at a country house attached to Kennedy and Leigh's nursery-gardens nearby, where he died. He was noted for miniature portraits, pencil drawings and dry-point etchings.

Wormholt Road W12 (Wormwood Scrubs, Hammersmith). Approached Wormholt Park; this preserves the original name for the woods of Wormwood Scrubs (*see* **Wood Lane**, Shepherd's Bush).

Wormwood Street EC2 (Cit. Lond.). *See* **Camomile Street**.

Woronzow Road NW8 (St John's Wood, Cit. West.). Simon, Count Woronzow, who lived in Marylebone, left a bequest for the poor in 1827; the money was used to build the St Marylebone Almshouses at the SW corner of this road.

Worship Street EC2 (Finsbury, Islington/Hackney). Corruption of

Worsop; John Worsop, merchant-tailor, is recorded as holding property here in a survey of 1567. He held six and a half acres of Finsbury or High Field, across which this street runs, as well as ten acres in the Moorfield. The street was so named from the Finsbury end; the Norton Folgate end was called Hog Lane.

Wren Road SE5 (Camberwell Road, Southwark). Built on the site of a house on Camberwell Green, occupied, according to tradition, by Sir Christopher Wren. The house was demolished c1850.

Wren Street WC1 (Gray's Inn Road, Camden). Commemorates the architect Sir Christopher Wren (1632–1723), architect of St Paul's Cathedral and much else in London as it was rebuilt after the Great Fire of 1666.

Wright's Lane W8 (Kensington, Ken. Chel.). Begun by Gregory Wright c1775 on the line of an old path from Kensington to Earl's Court (*see* **Kenway Road**).

Wulfstan Street W12 (Wormwood Scrubs, Hammersmith). Wulfstan was Bishop of London c952, and a second Wulfstan was Bishop 996–1003. The bishops of London later held Hammersmith manor.

Wyclif Street EC1 (Clerkenwell, Islington). Commemorates John Wyclif (*d* 1384), religious reformer and forerunner of Protestantism; named by association with the Smithfield Martyrs' Memorial Church which stood on this site.

Wylde's Close NW11 (Hampstead, Barnet). Gives on to land which used to be Wylde's Farm, now part of the NW end of Hampstead Heath.

Wymering Road W9 (Bayswater, Cit. West.). *See* **Southwick Street**.

Wyndham Place W1 (Marylebone, Cit. West.). Built on the Portman estate (*see* **Portman Square**). The street was made c1810 as an approach to Bryanston Square. Henry Portman married Anne Wyndham. **Wyndham Street** approaches.

Wyndham Road SE5 (Camberwell, Southwark). Approaches **Bowyer Place**. Edmond Bowyer (*d* 1718) left his estates in Camberwell to his niece Martha Wyndham or Windham. They remained in the Windham family until 1810 when they passed to Martha's grand-daughter and her husband Sir William Smythe or Smijth.

Wynyatt Street EC1 (Clerkenwell, Islington). Properly Wynyate Street; built in 1803 on land belonging to the Earl of Northampton and named from his family seat, Compton Wynyates (*see* **Compton Road**).

Wythburn Place W1 (Marylebone, Cit. West.). Named by association with adjacent Great Cumberland Place. Wythburn Fells lie S of Thirlmere in the former county of Cumberland.

Y

Yardley Street WC1 (Clerkenwell, Islington). Built on land belonging to the Marquis of Northampton, who was born at Yardley Hastings, Northamptonshire (*see* **Compton Road**).

Yarmouth Place W1 (Mayfair, Cit. West.). Francis Charles Seymour-Conway, Marquis of Hertford and Earl of Yarmouth, lived nearby; he died at Dorchester House, Park Lane, in 1842. His mother, Lady Hertford, had been the mistress of George IV.

Yeldham Road W6 (Hammersmith). Built on land belonging to the Yeldham family, market gardeners of Fulham from the 1820s and possibly earlier.

Yeoman Street SE8 (Rotherhithe, Southwark). Possibly built by Yeomans, builders and engineering contractors active in the 1860s.

Yeo Street E3 (Bromley, T. Ham.). Alfred Yeo represented Bromley on the Poplar District Board of Works in the 1890s. He became one of the first Poplar Borough councillors and represented Limehouse on the London County Council from 1910.

York Buildings WC2 (Strand, Cit. West.). A house was built here for the bishops of Norwich in the 14th century; under Mary I (1553–8) it was acquired by the archbishops of York and called 'York House'. The building later became a private house and passed to the Duke of Buckingham in 1617. **York Place** is nearby.

York Grove SE15 (Peckham, Southwark). Named in the 1890s in honour of the newly-created Duke of York, afterwards George V.

York House Place W8 (Kensington, Ken. Chel.). Thomas Hodges (*d* 1672), vicar of Kensington, bought land here and built two houses, rebuilt by John Gorham in 1764 and 1781. One, called 'York House', was occupied 1839–48 by Princess Sophia, daughter of George III. The house was demolished for redevelopment *c*1904.

York Place SW11 (Battersea, Wandsworth). Site of a mansion bequeathed to the archbishops of York by Lawrence Booth *c*1475; the house stood on the NE side. The estate was known as the manor of Bridge Court or Bridge, from the nearby bridge over the Falcon Brook. **York Road** approaches. York Place was sometimes known as Silk Factory Lane, from a factory set up on the SW side by Messrs Curnell, Tyell and Webster, carrying on a 17th-century Huguenot tradition. The factory closed in the 1840s.

York Place WC2 (Strand, Cit. West.). *See* **Buckingham Street**.

Yorkshire Grey Yard WC1 (Holborn, Camden). From the sign of an inn, now demolished, recorded in the 18th century. The Yorkshire Grey was a widely-used coach horse.

Yorkshire Road E14 (Stepney, T. Ham.). *See* **Flamborough Street**.

York Street W1 (Marylebone, Cit. West.). Commemorates Frederick, Duke of York and Albany, brother of George IV, who died in 1827.

York Terrace, West and East NW1
(Regent's Park, Cit. West.). Part of
John Nash's Regent's Park scheme
(*see* **Regent Street**). laid out when
George IV was still Prince Regent,
and named after his brother
Frederick (*see* **York Street**). **York
Bridge** and **Gate** adjoin.

York Way N1, N7 (King's Cross,
Camden/Islington). Runs beside
King's Cross railway station, built
1851–2 for the Great Northern
Railway Company, formerly the
London and York. The road was
originally a country way called
Maiden Lane, which continued up
the line of Brecknock Road and
Dartmouth Park Hill to Highgate.

Young Street W8 (Kensington, Ken.
Chel.). Thomas Young, builder,
bought land near the incomplete
Kensington Square (then called
King's Square after James II) in 1687
and began to build. His completed
street and square accommodated
those in attendance at Kensington
Palace after 1689 (*see* **Kensington
Palace Gardens**).

Z

Zenoria Street SE22 (E Dulwich, Southwark). From a Christian name recorded in St Giles's churchyard, Camberwell: Zenoria Sill, 'child of Major Sill who fell in the American War'.

Zetland Street E14 (Poplar, T. Ham.). *See* **Leven Road**.

Zoar Street SE1 (Southwark). Biblical name of a place of sanctuary; the street originally extended E from a Baptist chapel, Zoar Chapel, which stood beside the present Falcon Close, Sumner Street. The street was heavily bombed during World War II and rebuilt on its present, shorter line.

Bibliography

Acts of Parliament relating to the County of London
Complete Peerage (all editions)
Descriptive Catalogue of Ancient Deeds in the Public Record Office
Dictionary of National Biography
Statutes at Large
Victoria County Histories of London (from 1909); Middlesex (from 1969); Surrey (from 1902)
Who Was Who

The Builder
The Gentleman's Magazine
The Illustrated London News

Arnold, F. *History of Streatham* (1886)
Baines, F.E. *Records of Hampstead* (1890)
Barker, F. and Jackson, P. *London: 2,000 Years of a City and its People* (1974)
Bebbington, G. *London Street Names* (1972)
Beck, E.J. *History of Rotherhithe* (1907)
Beresford Chancellor, E. *Knightsbridge and Belgravia* (1902)
Birch, J.G. *Limehouse through Five Centuries* (1930)
Blanch, W.H. *Ye Parish of Camerwell* (1875)
Boase, F. (ed.) *Modern English Biography* (1892, repr. 1965)
Boger, E. *Bygone Southwark* (1895)
Boswell, J. *The Life of Samuel Johnson* (1791)
Bowers, R.W. *Sketches of Southwark Old and New* (1905)
Bumpus, T.F. *London Churches Ancient and Modern*
Burgess, J.H.M. *The Chronicles of Clapham* (1929)
Butler, D. and Freeman, J. *British Political Facts 1900–1968* (3/1969)
Clarke, E.T. *Bermondsey, its Historic Memories and Associations* (1901)
Clinch, G. *Bloomsbury and St. Giles* (1890)
          Marylebone and St. Pancras (1890) *Mayfair and Belgravia* (1892)
Cook, C. and Paxton, J. *European Political Facts: I.1789–1848; II.1848–1918; III.1918–73*
Course, E. *London Railways* (1962)
Cowper, B.H. *Milwall* (1853)
Dews, N. *The History of Deptford* (1884)
Draper, W. *Chiswick* (1923)
Duncan, L.L. *History of the Borough of Lewisham* (1908)
Dunkin, A. *History of the County of Kent: Hundred of Blackheath* (1854)
Dunstan, J. *History of the Parish of Bromley St. Leonard's* (1862)
Dyos, H.J. *Victoria Suburb* (1961)
Edwards, P.J. *History of London Street Improvements* (1898)
Ekwall, E. (ed.) *Oxford Dictionary of English Place Names: Street Names of the City of London* (1954)
Elmes, J. and Shepherd, T.H. *Metropolitan Improvements* (1827)
English Place Name Society *The Place Names of Middlesex* (1942)
          The Place Names of Surrey (1934)
Farmer, D.H. *The Oxford Dictionary of Saints* (1978)
Faulkner, T. *Historical Account of Chelsea and its Environs* (1810)
          Historical and Topographical Account of Fulham (1813)
          History and Antiquities of Kensington (1820)
          History and Antiquities of the Parish of Hammersmith (1839)
Feret, C.J. *Fulham Old and New* (1900)
Field, J. *Place Names of Greater London* (1980)
Gaunt, W. *Kensington and Chelsea* (rev.1975)
Green, G.W.C. *The Story of Wandsworth and Putney* (19XX)
Halliday, F.E. *Shakespeare* (1956)
Harben, H.A. *Dictionary of London* (1918)
Hazlitt, W.C. *The Livery Companies of the City of London* (1892)
Hendricks, L. *The London Charterhouse* (1889)
Hobhouse, H. *Thomas Cubitt, Master Builder* (1971)
Hurley, A.J. *Days that are Gone* (1947)
Lewis, S. *The History and Topography of the Parish of St. Mary, Islington* (1842)
Lillywhite, B. *London Signs* (1972)
Llewellyn Smith, H. *History of East London* (1939)
Lloyd, J.H. *The History, Topography and Antiquities of Highgate* (1888)

London and Middlesex Archaeological Society, Transactions 1872–1979
London County, Minutes of Proceedings
   Names of Streets and Places in the Administrative County of London (all editions)
London Topographical Society *Annual Record* 1900–80
Lubbock, B. *Romance of the Clipper Ships* (1948)
Mackenzie, G. *Marylebone* (1972)
Mangan, J.R. *Street Names of the London Borough of Lewisham* (1969)
Metcalfe, P. *The Park Town Estate and the Battersea Tangle*
Metropolitan Board of Works, *Minutes of Proceedings* 1856–89
Morden, W.E. *History of Tooting Graveney* (1897)
Olsen, D.J. *The Growth of Victorian London* (1976)
Osborne, H. (ed.) *The Oxford Companion to Art* (1970)
   The Oxford Companion to the Decorative Arts (1975)
Palmer, A.W. *A Dictionary of Modern History* (1962)
Palmer, S. *St. Pancras* (1870)
Papworth, J.W. and Morant, A.W. *Alphabetical Dictionary of British Armorials* (1858–74)
Pickering, D. *General Statutes* (1762)
Pinks, W.J. *History of Clerkenwell* (1865)
Pullen, D.M. *Forest Hill* (1979)
Ramsay, S. *Historic Battersea* (1913)
Rendle, W. *Old Southwark and its People* (1878)
Robinson, W. *The History and Antiquities of the Parish of Stoke Newington* (1820)
   The History and Antiquities of the Parish of Hackney (1842)
Rolt, L.T.C. *Isambard Kingdom Brunel* (1957)
Sherwood, L.S. *Camberwell Place and Street Names and their Origin* (1964)
Smallshaw, J. *Henry Rydon and the Highbury New Park Estate* (1981)
Smith, E.E.F. *Clapham* (1976)
Society of Antiquaries of London *Proceedings* 1843–1919
Steinberg, S.H. *Historical Tables* (10/1979)
Summerson, J. *The London Building World of the 1860s*
Tanswell, J. *History and Antiquities of Lambeth* (1858)
Thompson, F.M.L. *Hampstead, Building a Borough 1650–1964* (1974)
Thornbury, G.W. and Walford, E. *Old and New London* (1873)
Tomlins, T.E. *A Perambulation of Islington* (1858)
University House, *East London Papers* (1958–73)
Velvick, S.L. and Willson, E.J. *Street Names of Fulham and Hammersmith* (1977)
Walford, E. *Greater London* (1883)
Welch, C. *A Modern History of the City of London* (1896)
Wheatley, H.P. (ed.) *John Stow's Survey of London* (rev.1956)
White, H.P. *Regional History of the Railways of Great Britain* vol. 3, *Greater London* (1963)
Woodham-Smith, C. *The Reason Why* (1953)
   Queen Victoria (1972)
Yeandle, W.H. *A Corner of Finsbury* (1934)